Dubai
EXPLORER

EXPLORER

www.Explorer-Publishing.com

Passionately Publishing...

Dubai Explorer 2005/9ᵗʰ Edition

First Published 1996
Second Edition 1997
Third Edition 1998
Fourth Edition 1999
Fifth Edition 2000
Sixth Edition 2001
Seventh Edition 2003
Eighth Edition 2004
Nineth Edition 2005   ISBN 976-8182-60-1

Front Cover Photograph — Victor Romero (+971 50) 844 8564

Printed and bound by Emirates Printing Press, Dubai, United Arab Emirates.

Explorer Publishing & Distribution
PO Box 34275, Zomorrodah Bldg, Za'abeel Rd, Dubai
United Arab Emirates
Phone   (+971 4) 335 3520
Fax   (+971 4) 335 3529
Email   Info@Explorer-Publishing.com
Web   www.Explorer-Publishing.com

EXPLORER

www.Explorer-Publishing.com

Publishing
Publisher — Alistair MacKenzie
Alistair@Explorer-Publishing.com

Editorial
Editors — Claire England
Claire@Explorer-Publishing.com
Jane Roberts
Jane@Explorer-Publishing.com

Writer — David Quinn
David@Explorer-Publishing.com

Reporter — John King
Proofreader — Jo Holden-MacDonald

Research Manager — Tim Binks
Tim@Explorer-Publishing.com

Researchers — Helga Becker
Helga@Explorer-Publishing.com
Yolanda Singh
Yolanda@Explorer-Publishing.com

Design
Graphic Designers — Jayde Fernandes
Jayde@Explorer-Publishing.com
Zainudheen Madathil
Zain@Explorer-Publishing.com
Sayed Muhsin
Muhsin@Explorer-Publishing.com

Photography — Pamela Grist
Pamela@Explorer-Publishing.com

Sales & Advertising
Media Sales Manager — Alena Hykes
Alena@Explorer-Publishing.com

Media Sales Executive — Laura Zuffová
Laura@Explorer-Publishing.com

Sales/PR Administrator — Janice Menezes
Janice@Explorer-Publishing.com

Distribution
Distribution Manager — Ivan Rodrigues
Ivan@Explorer-Publishing.com

Distribution Supervisor — Abdul Gafoor
Gafoor@Explorer-Publishing.com

Distribution Executives — Mannie Lugtu
Mannie@Explorer-Publishing.com
Stephen Drilon
Stephen@Explorer-Publishing.com
Rafi Jamal
Rafi@Explorer-Publishing.com

Administration
Accounts Manager — Kamal Basha
Kamal@Explorer-Publishing.com

Accounts Assistant — Sohail Butt
Sohail@Explorer-Publishing.com

Administration Manager — Nadia D'Souza
Nadia@Explorer-Publishing.com

IT & Web Manager — Joe Nellary
Joe@Explorer-Publishing.com

Dear Dubai dudes and dudettes,

Do you like to live life to the full? Have you got the get up and go of a playboy or girl? Do you just luuurrvve hitting the town, heading for the hills or having your cake and eating it? Well of course you do or you wouldn't be holding the absolutely fabulous **Dubai Explorer 9th Edition** in your hands, now would you.

First let us congratulate you for shunning the life of the couch potato, for standing up for your right to partake and partaaay and, of course, for getting your hands on the delicious new edition of this masterful book. If we do say so ourselves. We have sweated, bled and cried our way through the administrative maze that goes hand in hand with this city that never sleeps. Which is exactly what we have done for months – kept our eyes wide open and our ears firmly attached to the ground to bring you the true insider's track to Dubai and all its idiosyncratic ways and hedonistic days!

We've shopped till we dropped, pumped our adrenaline sky high and beyond the sea, wined and dined around the clock and explored every nook and cranny of this ever-expanding city to bring you THE definitive bible to Dubai. It's a tough job we know – but gallantly we have risen to these challenges – all for you!

We trust you will find all that you need to cut red tape and paint the town red in the following pages, however, if we have missed out your stamp collecting club or left a certain tastebud unturned please, please let us know. Just email us at Info@Explorer-Publishing.com or log on to our Website (www.Explorer-Publishing.com) – because without you we're nothing.

Happy hunting...

The Explorer Team

جي دبليو ماريوت دبي

JW MARRIOTT®
DUBAI

WHERE GLOBAL
TRAVELLERS INDULGE IN
NEW DIMENSIONS OF
LUXURY

Amidst a well established business
destination, the JW Marriott
Dubai remains distinctive and
unique; with warm approachable
surroundings, gracious service
and imaginative dining. Going
above and beyond.℠

IT'S THE MARRIOTT WAY.℠

JW Marriott Dubai
P.O. Box 16590,
Hamarain Centre,
Dubai,
United Arab Emirates
Tel: +971 4 2624444
Fax: +971 4 2626264
www.marriott-middleeast.com

Alistair MacKenzie
Media Mogul

If only Alistair could take the paperless office one step further and achieve the officeless office he would be the happiest publisher alive. Remote access from a remote spot within the Hajar mountains would suit this intrepid explorer. The only problem could be staffing – unless he can persuade Midnight Cafeteria to deliver!

Claire England
Poached Ed

No longer able to freeload off the fact that she once appeared in a Robbie Williams video, Claire now puts her creative skills to better use – looking up rude words in the dictionary! A child of English nobility, Claire is quite the lady – unless she's down at Jimmy Dix.

David Quinn
Sharp Shooter

After a short stint as a children's TV presenter was robbed from David because he developed an allergy to sticky back plastic, he made his way to sandier pastures. Now that he's thinking outside the box, nothing gets past the man with the sharpest pencil in town.

Alena Hykes
Sales Supergirl

A former bond girl, Alena speaks more languages than we've had hot dinners and she's not afraid to be heard. She dresses to kill and has a sales pitch to die for with everything she touches turning to gold - must be that Goldfinger!

Pete Maloney
Graphic Guru

Image conscious he may be, but when Pete has his designs on something you can bet he's gonna get it! He's the king of chat up lines, ladies – if he ever opens a conversation with 'D'you come here often?' then brace yourself for the Maloney magic.

Zainudheen Madathil
Map Captain

Often confused with football star Zinedine Zidane because of the equally confusing name, Zain tackles design with the mouse skills of a star striker. Maps are his goal and despite getting red-penned a few times, when he shoots, he scores.

Sayed Muhsin

Design Drummer

They say it's the quiet ones that you want to watch and Mushin is no exception. Laying low behind his layouts, what many of you don't know is that he used to be the drummer for Led Zepellin. Now he drums up designs that are music to our eyes.

Yolanda Singh

Fast Talker

With an iron will and a heart of gold, Yoyo manages to bounce back from every hurdle and still finds time for a good gossip. If you want to get a memo around she's far quicker than email.

Jayde Fernandes

Pop Idol

When he isn't secretly listening to Britney Spears or writing to Blue to become their fifth member, Jayde actually manages to get a bit of designing done (but not before he has got through his well practised list of 'the dog ate my homework' excuses). He's The Man, and all because the ladies love his in-tray!

Janice Menezes

Materials Girl

How does Janice manage to whiz round the office so efficiently chasing ads and artwork and generally keeping on top of the books? Rollerskates of course! When she's not practising her toe-stops, she spreads the Explorer message to over a thousand people a day.

Jane Roberts

Word Wizard

meticulous is her middle name and after creatively shrivelling in a dingy government office, Jane thankfully found her way to the Explorer offices with her red pen in tow. She's learning by other people's mistakes and teaching the rest of us that quantity and quality can live in harmony.

Helga Becker

Fantasy Foodist

From alfresco eateries to burger joints, and cocktail bars to nightclubs, Helga has been around the Dubai block a few times (in the culinary sense of course). A walking restaurant and bar guide, Helga is the goddess of going out and makes Explorer look good enough to eat.

THE EXPLORER FAMILY

Tim Binks
Cookie Monster

After flying the Explorer nest at the beginning of the Millennium in search of sushi, Tim eventually tired of egg rolls and flew back with the promise of a more calorific career. When the cookie crumbles Tim is the man to gather the pieces — as long as it's chocolate chip of course! Thankyou please.

Louise Mellodew
The Phantom

Louise hasn't been seen at her desk for months now, and while she tells us she's on the road doing essential research, we know she's actually curled up at home, watching 'Buffy' re-runs with her cat.

Nadia D'Souza
Mother Hen

Poor Nadia has the displeasure of sitting opposite the toilet, but like the Explorer adopted mother that she is she soon takes charge of any sticky toilet situations — humorous or not. When she isn't giving the boys a telling off, Nadia can be found navigating new recruits through telephonic technology.

Mannie Lugtu
Distribution Demon

When the travelling circus rode into town their master juggler, Mannie, decided to leave the Big Top and explore Dubai instead. He may have swopped his balls for our books but his juggling skills still come in handy.

Pamela Grist
Happy Snapper

If a picture can speak a thousand words then Pam's photos say a lot about her - through her lens she manages to find the beauty in everything - even this motley crew. And when the camera never lies, thankfully Photoshop can.

Joe Nellary
Head Hacker

While we once blamed the system for all our technical hiccups we can now turn to Joe for much needed support. And if he doesn't have the answer a bit of techno jargon fools us into thinking he does.

Kamal Basha
Chief Calculator

Kamal has the best bottom line in Dubai and makes many an accountant jealous with his mean index finger. In fact, he's been the UAE calculator champion in the Mathematic Games for the last three years, and now has the world title in his sights. Go Kamal!

Ivan Rodrigues

Head Honcho

After making a mint in the clip board market, Ivan came to Explorer out of the goodness of his heart. Distributing joy across the office he is the man with the master plan – if only we could understand his spreadsheets.

Abdul Gafoor

Ace Circulator

After a successful stint on Ferrari's Formula One team Gafoor made a pitstop at our office and decided to stay. As Explorer's most cheerful employee, he's the only driver in Dubai yet to succumb to road rage.

Rafi Jamal

Soap Star

After a walk on part in The Bold and the Beautiful, Rafi swapped the Hollywood Hills for the Hajar Mountains. Although he left the glitz behind, he is frequently spotted practising his pensive to-camera pose in the office's bathroom mirror.

Without our extended family of super fab reporters this book would not be the masterpiece that it is. So a big shout out of thanks goes to the following:

Amanda · Amanda H · AML · Andrew · Christine · Clay · David J · Derrick · Di · DiveCarole · Emma & Andrew · Gerrard · Grant · JAW · Jay Kay · Jeremy · Kennon · Lena M · Miki · Mish & Mike · Nick · Pete L · Peter · Peter B · Peter St · Philip L · Rabia · Rania P · Richard · Robert · Sandra · Simon · Stephen B · Tara · Tracy

Sohail Butt

Abacus Ace

By day he may be cooking the books but by night Sohail cooks up a storm at the local Karaoke bar - while his routine includes the entire back catalogue of Abba hits, it's his heartfelt rendition of 'Money Money Money' that really brings the house down.

Stephen Drilon

Record Breaker

Not to be outdone by the Burj tower, Stephen sits alongside Nakheel in the record books for successfully stacking the highest book tower ever constructed, even if it did only stand for 0.03 seconds. He has now moved his sights on to calendar castles.

THE SPIRIT

Jeep Wrangler

Jeep Cherok

There are countless delights waiting to be seen and ex
off-road. There's only one way to get there - in a Jee
vehicle that transports you to a world of adventur
its unmatched 4X4 capability and legendary perform

TRAIL RATED 4x4

Jeep *Club*
MIDDLE EAST & NORTH AFRICA

trading enterprises

An **Al-Futtaim** group company

Showrooms: Dub
Sharjah (06) 57245
e-mail: tradingent

DVENTURE

Jeep Grand Cherokee

the head-for-the-hills driving fun of Wrangler to the
nced capability of Cherokee and the luxurious power of
d Cherokee, only a Jeep vehicle ensures you don't
a thing!

Jeep.

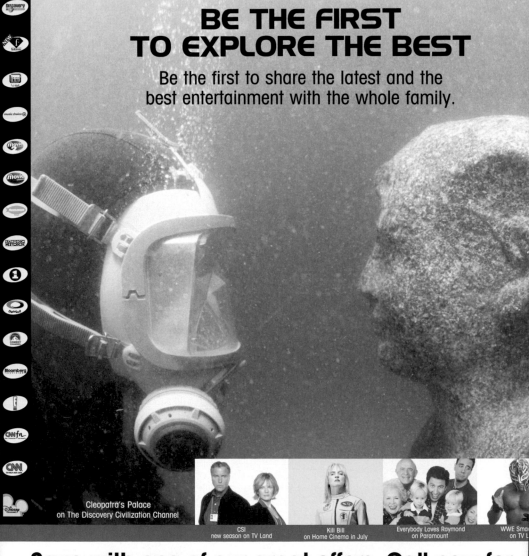

BE THE FIRST
TO EXPLORE THE BEST

Be the first to share the latest and the best entertainment with the whole family.

Cleopatra's Palace
on The Discovery Civilization Channel

CSI
new season on TV Land

Kill Bill
on Home Cinema in July

Everybody Loves Raymond
on Paramount

WWE Sma
on TV L

Save with one of our great offers. Call now for more information.

Subscribe now by calling
04 367 7777

SMS 4847 for more information and we will call you back.

Visit Showtime showrooms:
• Choithram, Safa Park • Marina Mall, Abu Dhabi • Mercato Mall, Jumeira
• Spinneys Umm Suqqeim • City Centre - Deira, Sharjah & Ajman • Al Jimi
  Shopping Center, Al Ain

OR CALL E-VISION - 800 5500

Brings you the Best in entertainm

BAB AL SHAMS
DESERT RESORT & SPA

Discover the desert. Experience the luxury.

Imagine staying in a place
where the landscape keeps changing.

Jumeirah International is pleased to present Bab Al Shams,
"The Gateway to the Sun." A desert resort and spa nestled
between the ever-changing dunes of the desert.
A resort that magically recreates the aura of a rustic Arabian
desert retreat and takes you back in time.

For further information or to make a reservation, please contact
+ 971 4 3143647 or visit www.jumeirahinternational.com

Terms and Conditions apply. Rooms subject to availability.

JUMEIRAH
INTERNATIONAL®

206 CHEFS, EVERY ONE PASSIONATE ABOUT FOOD

Tantalize your taste buds at any of our restaurants featuring Singaporean, Lebanese, American, Italian, Japanese, and Vietnamese cuisines, and we promise you will have something to be passionate about. FEEL THE HYATT TOUCH.®

For reservations call Grand Hyatt Dubai at 04 317 2222.

GRAND
HYATT
D U B A I ®

P.O. Box 7978, Dubai, United Arab Emirates. Telephone +971 4 317 1234, Facsimile +971 4 317 1235, E-mail dubai.grand@hyattintl.com, www.dubai.grand.hyatt.com

Feel better
heal better

Medical Specialities

Anesthesia • Cardiac Surgery/Cardiac Catheterization • Cardiology/Lipids • Cardiopulmonary • Diabetes/Endocrinology • Dietary Counseling • Endoscopy • ENT Surgery • Family Medicine • Gastroenterology/Hepatology • General Surgery • Internal Medicine • Medical Imaging • Nephrology/Dialysis • Neurology • Neurosurgery • Obstetrics/Gynecology • Oncology/Chemotherapy • Ophthalmology • Orthopedics • Pathology & Laboratory Medicine • Pediatrics (children) • Plastic, Cosmetic, Reconstructive and Maxillofacial Surgery • Rheumatology • Sports Medicine & Physical Therapy • Urology/Lithotripsy (Kidney Stones)

Facilities and Equipment

• 120 spacious and luxurious private rooms • 42 outpatient treatment rooms • 5 extensively equipped surgical operating rooms • 3 labor/delivery/recovery suites • 10 intensive care beds • 9 Room Outpatient GI Suite • 8 Bed Emergency Department • Pharmacy • Magnetic Resonance Imaging (MRI) • Multi-Slice Computerized Tomography (CT Scan) • Color Doppler Ultrasound • Mammography • Nuclear Medicine • ECG • EEG • Stress Echocardiogram • Sleep Studies • Pulmonary Function Testing

1

The
Number
One
Car
Rental
Company
In
The
Emirates

Car Rental

Call Toll Free 800 THRIFTY
8474389 / 800 4694

مشاريع
عبدالله احمد الموسى
A . A . ALMOOSA
ENTERPRISES

www.aaagroup.com

AHLAN!

INTERNATIONAL GLAMOUR & LOCAL STYLE EVERY WEEK

THE UAE'S BIGGEST-SELLING MAGAZINE
On sale every Thursday

An ITP Consumer Publication

DEIRA
CITY CENTRE

You'll find it all
in the
City

Dubai's most popular
shopping destination,
with over 300 outlets.

www.deiracitycentre.com

Explorer Insider's City & Country Guides

These are no ordinary guidebooks. They are your lifestyle support system, medicine for boredom, ointment for obstacles, available over the counter and prescribed by those in the know. An essential resource for residents, tourists and business people, they cover the what, the how, the why, the where and the when. All you have to do is read!

Abu Dhabi Explorer

The ultimate guide to the UAE's capital just got bigger and better. Now covering Al Ain you'll wonder how you ever managed without it.

Bahrain Explorer

The inside track on where and how to experience everything this fascinating gulf state has to offer.

Dubai Explorer

The original, and still the best by far. Now in its 9th year, this is the only guide you'll ever need for exploring this fascinating city.

Geneva Explorer

Your very own personal guide giving the low-down on everything to do and see in this European gem of a city and its surroundings.

Oman Explorer

All the insider info you'll ever need to make the most of this beautiful, beguiling country.

Explorer Photography Books

Where words fail, a picture speaks volumes. These award-winning photography books take you across landscapes and seascapes, through bold architecture, the past and the present, introducing a wonderland of diversity. They're an optical indulgence as well as stimulating additions to bookshelves and coffee tables everywhere.

Dubai: Tomorrow's City Today

A photography book showcasing the sheer splendour and architectural audacity of this stunning city.

Images of Geneva

From snow-capped mountains and azure waters to historic cobbled streets and contemporary architecture, the beauty of Geneva and its surroundings is captured in a stunning collection of photographs.

Sharjah's Architectural Splendour

Magnificent photographs show how modern-day Sharjah has remained true to its cultural heritage.

Images of Dubai & the UAE

Breathtaking images from this land of contrasts - from unspoilt desert, to the truly 21st century city of Dubai.

Images of Abu Dhabi & the UAE

Awe inspiring images of exquisite natural beauty and ancient cultures juxtaposed with the modern metropolis of Abu Dhabi.

Introduction

Explorer Products

Explorer Activity Guides

Why not visit stunning marine life and mysterious wrecks, or stand poised on the edge of a natural wadi or pool in the mountains? Get a tan and a life with our activity guidebooks.

Off-Road Explorer (UAE)

Let's go off-road! Over 20 adventurous routes covered in minute detail. Go off the beaten track and discover another side to the UAE.

Underwater Explorer

Dive dive dive! Detailed info on all the underwater action, from reefs to wrecks, all around the UAE.

Family Explorer (Dubai & Abu Dhabi)

The only family-friendly guide of its kind for the UAE – just add kids!

Trekking Guide (Oman)

A booklet and individual cards detailing amazing walks through spectacular scenery. The maps correspond to waypoints that are actually painted on the ground to aid navigation.

Street Map Explorer (Dubai)

Never get lost again. A first of its kind for Dubai, this handy map book lists every highway and byway in crystal clear detail.

Explorer Other Products

With such an incredible array of insider's guides and photography and activity books you'd think we wouldn't have the time or energy to produce anything else. Well think again! Here are some of our other products – no home should be without them.

2005 Calendar (Abu Dhabi)

Spend a whole year in the company of stunning images of the capital of the Emirates.

2005 Calendar (Dubai)

A 12-month visual feast, featuring award-winning images of Dubai's finest sights.

Starter Kit (Dubai)

Three great books - the Dubai Explorer, Zappy Explorer and Street Map - everything you need to get started and sorted!

Images Collection (UAE)

A combination of award-winning excellence, containing both the Images of Dubai and Images of Abu Dhabi photography books (Limited Edition).

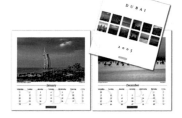

Zappy Explorer (Dubai)

Page after page of fuss-free advice on getting things done in Dubai. All the info you'll ever need to get yourself sorted.

General Information   1

New Residents   61

Continued...

Exploring — 149

Shopping 201

Activities 255

Continued...

And the fun doesn't stop there! If you're a budding food critic we want to hear from you. Check out www.EatOutSpeakOut.com and give us your take on the restaura

Four Easy Ways...

In order to make the **Dubai Explorer** the best guidebook in the history of the universe we need you to tell us what you think - whether it's good, bad or ugly!

The more we know about you and your loves, hates, gripes and wishes the better job we can do - especially as everything we do, we do it for you!

1. If you're a surfer you can fill in the Reader Response form on our website
www.Explorer-Publishing.com

2. If you're a talker you can phone us on 04 335 3520

3. If you're a scribbler you can fax 04 335 3529 or we can fax you the response form

4. If you're an Outlooker you can email
Info@Explorer-Publishing.com

& WIN!

'But what's in it for me?' you ask

Firstly you'll be helping us to help you by making the next edition even better than this one, and as a reward everyone who fills in a Reader Response form will be entered into a super prize draw!

Secondly, five lucky readers will win the complete works of Explorer Publishing – that's a copy of every Insider's Guide, activity book, photography book and calendar we make for your area. Valued at almost Dhs.1500, the prize will include the eagerly anticipated 10th anniversary issue of the **Dubai Explorer**.

and nightclubs featured in the book. Who knows - you could be enjoying a few free dinners yourself as an undercover food reporter for our next edition.

palmOne

The Smarter Smartphone

The Treo™ smartphones by palmOne™ are sma easy to use smartphones with built-in backlit QWERTY keyboards. They seamlessly combine a full-featured mobile phone and Palm OS® handheld with wireless communication applications like digital camera, picture messaging and web browsing, and it's fantastic for email, simplifying both your business and personal life.

GSM/GPRS*

Email, SMS, MMS*

Calendar

Contacts

Word, Excel

VGA Camera

Trēo

General
Information

General Information

What's new?

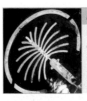

Key Dubai Projects
Page 9

Bigger, better, and taller – that's the motto of Dubai's developers. With so many key developments on the drawing board or under construction at the moment you could be forgiven for losing track. Ever more ambitious retail, residential, leisure and entertainment projects are announced on what seems like a weekly basis and with Dubai's population blossoming and tourist numbers expected to hit 15 million a year by 2010, there are no signs of the expansion slowing down just yet.

Desert Resorts
Page 41

Dubai has a plethora of five star hotels located within its city limits, and no end of desert beyond, so it was only a matter of time before someone combined the two to create luxury desert resorts. Al Maha Desert Resort and Spa resembles a typical Bedouin camp, but has certain 'non-Bedouin' features such as sumptuous suites and chilled private pools. Bab Al Shams Resort and Spa is built in the style of an Arabian fort, where guests can enjoy unrivalled hospitality amongst the dunes.

Geography

Situated on the north eastern part of the Arabian Peninsula, the United Arab Emirates (UAE) is bordered by the Kingdom of Saudi Arabia to the south and west, and the Sultanate of Oman to the east and north. The UAE shares 457 kilometres of border with Saudi Arabia and 410 kilometres with Oman. It has a coastline on both the Gulf of Oman and the Arabian Gulf, and is south of the strategically important Strait of Hormuz. The geographic co-ordinates for the UAE are 24 00 N, 54 00 E.

Maps

For in-depth information, your best bet is the Street Map Explorer (Dubai) – a street guide with detailed maps charting every nook and cranny of this city. For a one page fold out option, the Dubai Tourist Map (Dubai Municipality) gives visitors a good overview. Both are easily available from all good bookstores around Dubai.

The country is made up of seven different emirates (Abu Dhabi, Ajman, Dubai, Fujairah, Ras Al Khaimah, Sharjah and Umm Al Quwain) which were formerly all independent sheikhdoms. The total area of the country is about 83,600 square kilometres, and a major chunk of this land lies in the Abu Dhabi emirate. Dubai, with an area of 3,885 square kilometres, is the second largest emirate.

Golden beaches dot the country's 1,318 kilometres of coastline, of which 100 kilometres are on the Gulf of Oman. The Arabian Gulf coast is littered with coral reefs and over 200 islands, most of which are uninhabited. Sabkha (salt flats), stretches of gravel plain, and desert characterise much of the inland region.

Dubai and its surrounding area consists of flat desert and sabkha. However, to the east, rise the Hajar Mountains ('hajar' is Arabic for rock). Lying close to the Gulf of Oman, they form a backbone through the country, from the Mussandam Peninsula in the north, through the eastern UAE and into Oman. The highest point is Jebel Yibir at 1,527 metres.

Most of the western part of the country lies in the Abu Dhabi emirate and is made up of the infamous Rub Al Khali or Empty Quarter desert, which is common to the Kingdom of Saudi Arabia and the Sultanate of Oman. The area consists of arid, stark desert with spectacular sand dunes, broken by an occasional oasis. It is the largest sand desert in the world, covering nearly a quarter of the Arabian Peninsula with dunes rising, at times, to well over 300 metres.

Visitors to Dubai will find a land of startling contrasts, from endless stretches of desert to rugged mountains and modern towns. The city of Dubai is situated on the banks of a creek, a natural inlet from the Gulf that divides the city neatly into two. You can read more about Dubai's geography in the Exploring section [p.150].

History

Dubai's transformation from a flourishing trading port to today's modern metropolis makes for an interesting history. The south western Arabian Gulf coast (or Persian Gulf) was an important trading post as far back as the Kingdom of Sumer in 3000 BC. The region, known as Sumer, is centred round the area where the Tigris and Euphrates rivers meet and is believed to be the birthplace of modern civilisation. This great kingdom at the north of the Gulf had great influence, if not control, over trading points throughout the Gulf, and probably further. Deira/Dubai was one of these key positions, a safe haven before entering the narrow straits of Hormuz and the open sea.

Emirs or Sheikhs?

While the term emirate comes from the ruling title of 'emir', the rulers of the UAE are called 'sheikhs'.

Dubai's further existence is closely linked with the arrival and development of Islam in the greater Middle East region. Islam developed in western Saudi Arabia at the beginning of the seventh century AD with the revelations of the Koran being received by the Prophet Mohammad. Military conquests of the Middle East and North Africa enabled the Arab empire to spread the teachings of Islam from Mecca & Medina to the local Bedouin tribes, where it was widely embraced, although some local tribes reverted to paganism and had to be forcibly reconverted to Islam.

Following the Arab Empire came the Turks, the Mongols, and the Ottomans, each leaving their mark on local culture and all championing the Islamic religion. After the fall of the Muslim empires both the British and the Portuguese became interested in the area for it strategic position between India and Europe, but also to control the activities of numerous pirates based in the area, which earned it the title the 'Pirate Coast'.

General Info

UAE Overview

During a naval attack in 1820 the British defeated the pirates and the influence of the land based Bedouin tribes became established. A general treaty was agreed by the rulers of the region to denounce piracy and create the 'Trucial States'.

Nothing much changed for Dubai until the late 1800s, when the then ruler, Sheikh Maktoum bin Hasher Al Maktoum, granted tax concessions to foreign traders, encouraging many of them to switch their bases of operation (from Iran and Sharjah) to Dubai. By 1903, a British shipping line had been persuaded to use Dubai as its main port of call in the area, giving traders direct links with British India and other important trading ports in the region. Encouraged by the farsighted and liberal attitudes of the rulers, Indian and Persian traders settled in the growing town, which soon developed a reputation as the leading commercial market in the region.

Dubai's importance was further helped by Sheikh Rashid bin Saeed Al Maktoum, father of the current ruler of Dubai, who recognised the importance of Dubai's Creek and improved facilities to attract more traders. The city came to specialise in the import and re-export of goods, mainly gold to India, and trade became the foundation of this emirate's wealthy progression.

In the broader perspective, Dubai and the other emirates had accepted the protection of the British in 1892 in the culmination of a series of maritime truces. The British regarded the Gulf region as an important communication link with its empire in India, and wanted to ensure that other world powers, in particular France and Russia, didn't extend their influence in the region. In Europe, the area became known as the Trucial Coast (or Trucial States), a name it retained until the departure of the British in 1971.

In 1968, Britain announced its withdrawal from the region and tried to create a single state consisting of Bahrain, Qatar and the Trucial Coast. The ruling sheikhs, particularly of Abu Dhabi and Dubai, realised that by uniting forces they would have a stronger voice in the wider Middle East region. Negotiations collapsed when Bahrain and Qatar chose to become independent states. However, the Trucial Coast remained committed to forming an alliance and in 1971, the federation of the United Arab Emirates was born.

The new state comprised the emirates of Dubai, Abu Dhabi, Ajman, Fujairah, Sharjah, Umm Al Quwain and, in 1972, Ras Al Khaimah (each emirate is named after its main town). Under the agreement, the individual emirates each retained a certain degree of autonomy, with Abu Dhabi and Dubai providing the most input into the federation. The leaders of the new federation elected the ruler of Abu Dhabi, His Highness Sheikh Zayed bin Sultan Al

The Beloved Sheikh

Sheikh Zayed bin Sultan Al Nahyan was not only revered by his peers but also adored by his public. Over the 33 years that he ruled the UAE he was responsible for major developments to the region's economy and was the pioneer of extending privileges to expatriates, from employment opportunities to real estate purchasing power. In a world where conflicts of interest play havoc with peace, Sheikh Zayed managed to embrace change without compromising the principles of Arabic heritage and culture and as a result, when he passed away in November 2004 the entire population, from locals to expats of every nationality, mourned. A well-respected international figure, the condolences that flooded in from world leaders were testament to the standing of this inspirational leader.

Sheikh Zayed Road skyline

Nahyan, to be their president, a position he held until he passed away on 2nd November last year. His eldest son was then elected to take over the presidency and His Highness Sheikh Khalifa Bin Zayed Al Nahyan is now the ruler of the UAE.

Although the UAE government is not elected by national voting, Sheikh Zayed was always seen as a people's ruler, and would no doubt have won a democratic vote. However, despite the unification of the seven emirates the region hasn't been without its problems. Boundaries between the different emirates have been the main cause of disputes in the past. At the end of Sheikh Zayed's first term as president, in 1976, he threatened to resign if the other rulers didn't settle the demarcation of their borders. The threat proved an effective way of ensuring co-operation; although the degree of independence of the various emirates has never been fully determined. The position still isn't settled but there does seem to be more focus on the importance of the federation as a whole, led by Abu Dhabi whose wealth and sheer size makes it the most powerful of the emirates.

The formation of the UAE came after the discovery of huge oil reserves in Abu Dhabi in 1958 (Abu Dhabi has an incredible ten percent of the world's known oil reserves). This discovery dramatically transformed the emirate from one of the poorest states into the richest. In 1966, Dubai, which was already a relatively wealthy trading centre, also discovered oil. The oil revenue allowed the development of an economic and social infrastructure, which is the basis of today's modern society. Education, healthcare, roads, housing, and women's welfare were all priorities. Much of the credit for this development can be traced to the vision and dedication of the late Ruler of Dubai, His Highness Sheikh Rashid bin Saeed Al

Maktoum, who ensured that Dubai's oil revenues were deployed to maximum effect. His work has been continued by the present Ruler, His Highness Sheikh Maktoum bin Rashid Al Maktoum.

Although it seems that the story of the UAE is rather short, history is, nevertheless, being made on a daily basis.

Economy

UAE Overview

The UAE has an open economy today, with one of the world's highest per capita incomes (estimated at Dhs. 72,000 / US$20,000 in 2003) and is considered the second richest Arab country, after Qatar, on a per capita basis. The UAE's wealth, once chiefly based on the oil sector, now sees an estimated oil contribution of only 34% to the country's gross domestic product (GDP). The GDP for 2003 was approximately Dhs.293 billion, with Abu Dhabi and Dubai contributing the lion's share.

Over 90% of the UAE's oil reserves lie in Abu Dhabi, and there is enough, at the current rate of production (just over 2.5 million barrels per day), to last a further 100 years. However, although there is a heavy dependence on the oil and gas industry, trade, manufacturing, tourism and construction also play an important part in the national economy. Investment in infrastructure and development projects exceeded an estimated Dhs.250 billion in 2001. The UAE's main export partners are Saudi Arabia, Iran, Japan, India, Singapore, South Korea, and Oman. The main import partners are Japan, USA, UK, Italy, Germany and South Korea.

The situation in the UAE is radically different from that of 30 – 40 years ago, when the area consisted of small, impoverished desert states. Visitors will find a unified and forward looking state with a high standard of living and a relatively well balanced and stable economy. Current reports note that the country's economy is roughly 36 times larger than it was just a mere 34 years ago in 1971. With an annual growth rate of 6.9% in 2003, the UAE has one of the fastest real GDP growth rates in the world. The UAE's credit rating was ranked A2 (tied with Kuwait for first place in the GCC) by the leading investors services resource, Moody's, for the year 2003.

Dubai Overview

While oil has been crucial to Dubai's development since the late 1960s, contributing about US$29.5 billion in 2003, the non oil sector currently contributes some 90% of the total gross domestic product and is continuing to expand in importance. Dubai is targeting for the economy to become totally non oil driven by the year 2010 when, it is reported, the emirate's reserves may run out. Manufacturing and tourism are both growing at a steady rate, helping to create a well balanced and diverse economy. Dubai's ever expanding skyline is testimony to its strong commitment to becoming a world leader in high end tourism and a regional hub for large multinationals. This strategy is already a success, evident by the number of industries that use Dubai as a conference centre for the region. (A multitude of trade shows held here attract customers, vendors and suppliers from many industries). The effort to develop tourism has been very successful. Five to ten years ago, any detailed discussion on Dubai's economy would have made only a cursory mention of tourism. Today, it is one of the most important factors driving the economy of the city.

Trade remains the lifeblood of Dubai's business sector, as it has for generations. This long trading tradition, which earned Dubai the reputation of 'the city of merchants' in the Middle East, continues to be an important consideration for foreign companies looking at opportunities in the region today. It is reflected not just in a regulatory environment that is open and liberal, but also in the local business community's familiarity with international commercial practices and the city's cosmopolitan lifestyle. Strategically located between Europe and the Far East, Dubai attracts both multinational and private companies wishing to tap the lucrative Middle Eastern, Indian and African markets (which have a combined population of 1.4 billion people). Annual domestic imports exceed US$17 billion and Dubai is the gateway to over US$150 billion (annual) in trade.

The pace of economic growth in Dubai over the past 20 years has been incredible, trade alone has grown at more than nine percent per annum over the past ten years. Looking to the future, Dubai stands poised for further growth with the development of many multi billion dollar coastal extension projects (ie, The three Palm Islands projects, The World, Dubai Marina and more) plus new business and financial ventures. With the vision of the rulers of Dubai and the UAE, both the legislation and government institutions have been designed to minimise bureaucracy and create a business friendly environment.

Government officials take an active role in promoting investment in the emirate, and decisions are taken (and implemented) swiftly. Government departments have also, in recent years, placed increasing importance on improving customer service levels, including free zones, such as the Internet, Media and Healthcare Cities which foster a community environment for the specific industries and are very easy to set up and operate in.

However, don't be blinded by the healthy economy into believing that the average expat coming to work in Dubai will necessarily be on a huge salary. The wealth isn't spread evenly and, except for highly skilled professionals, the salaries for most types of work are dropping. This downward trend is attributed in part to the willingness of workers to accept a job at a very low wage. While the UAE GDP per capita income was estimated at approximately Dhs.72,000 in 2003, this figure includes all sections of the community and the average labourer, of which there are many, can expect to earn as little as Dhs.600 (US$165) per month.

While the unemployment level of the national population in the UAE is lower than that of many other Arab states (six percent in comparison to 17% in Oman) there are still a significant number of local nationals out of work (approximately 13,000). This is partly due to their desire to work in the public sector (where salaries and benefits are better), and partly because of qualifications, and salary expectations, not matching the skills required in the private sector. However, the government is trying to reverse this scenario and reduce unemployment in the local sector with a 'Nationalisation' or 'Emiratisation' programme (this is common to countries throughout the region). By putting the local population to work, the eventual

goal is to rely less on an expat workforce. This is being achieved by improving vocational training and by making it compulsory for certain categories of company, such as banks, to hire a determined percentage of Emiratis. In another attempt to get more Nationals attracted to the private sector, the government has a pension scheme where private companies are required to provide a pension for their national employees. However, Nationals still largely shun the private sector, preferring instead the additional benefits of the public sector (shorter working hours being a distinct advantage), and the relative lack of competition in that job market compared to the private sector. The IMF has also encouraged all GCC countries to reduce public sector wage levels to nationals to encourage them into the more competitive private sector.

Tourism Developments

Other options → Annual Events [p.54]
Key Dubai Projects [p.9]

With tourism contributing over 40% to Dubai's economy, the emirate is well ahead of other countries in the Middle East as far as the travel industry is concerned. It has successfully cornered a niche that seems near on impossible for other countries in the region to achieve. Over 5.3 million tourists visited Dubai in 2003; this figure is expected to grow to 15 million by 2010. Good infrastructure, the practically crime free environment and a luxury lifestyle, all add to the draw of the sun, the sands and the shopping. Revenue generated from the tourism sector stood at approximately Dhs.3 billion in 2001.

Really Tax Free?

Taxes. Do they exist in Dubai? Well, yes and no. You don't pay income or sales tax except when you purchase alcohol from a licensed liquor store – and then you'll be hit with a steep 30% tax. The main tax that you will come across is the municipality taxes of 5% rent tax and 10% on food, beverages and rooms in hotels. The rest are hidden taxes in the form of 'fees', such as your car registration renewal and visa/permit fees.

The hugely successful Dubai Shopping Festival attracts an ever increasing number of visitors each year (3.1 million in 2004), with shopping bargains to be found all over the city. There are also attractions such as the Global Village, where people can visit pavilions representing various countries, learn more about each culture and purchase traditional items, plus some real junk! The Dubai Shopping Festival's annual ad campaigns stretch worldwide and cost millions of dirhams. Dubai Summer Surprises, held annually during July and August, brings in large numbers of mostly GCC visitors and features numerous events that focus on children and the family. For more information see Shopping [p.202].

Almost all leading hotel chains are represented in Dubai. There are currently nearly 400 hotels in operation, and more coming on the market on what seems a daily basis. It has been said that wherever you stand in Dubai you will be able to see a crane within your 360° periphery. Construction developments are vast, both in the tourist and business sectors, and the skyline seems to change month by month. Lofty ambitions for world breaking buildings are coming to fruition on Dubai's soil giving this emirate a unique luxury appeal for tourists and international investors, without the exorbitant prices of the Caribbean or Hong Kong. This is not to say, of course, that Arab opulence comes cheap.

In addition to the construction boom, steps are continually being taken to ensure that Dubai's image remains spotless. It is now rare to find street vendors hawking Russian army binoculars or woodcarvings, and you'll no longer see newspaper vendors at the traffic lights. Car washing without permission and begging are also illegal. You are also less likely to see vendors with temporary 'stalls' set up on the pavement, selling pirated DVDs and VCDs from the Far East. The Dubai Police are making a concerted effort to stop this trade, but the vendors have just become more targeted in their marketing, taking their business underground.

While on first inspection Dubai may not seem like a backpackers paradise, due to the luxury hotels and relatively expensive shopping, many independent travellers have found that Dubai is a good gateway to South East Asia and Australia. There are six youth hostels spread over the emirates, although many backpackers opt for hotels (which are cheaper in town than they are on the beachfront). With cheap public transport, a myriad of local independent restaurants serving traditional fare for a pittance and so many free sights, Dubai can easily be explored on a budget.

Investment in tourism is truly phenomenal and upcoming projects are literally out of this world. From the three Palm Islands slowly emerging from the Arabian Gulf, and the ambitious The World island joining the horizon, to the world's first underwater hotel, the Hydropolis, and the equally record breaking Burj Tower, Dubai will stop at nothing to create the biggest and the best.

Following is a list of the key projects currently under construction or in the planning stages that will significantly change, not only the skyline of this fantastical emirate, but also the tourist appeal, putting Dubai firmly on the international map.

Key Dubai Projects

Dubai's strategic location gives this city an edge over others in reaching its aim – to be known as the hottest tourist and trade destination on the global map. The government is investing large amounts of capital in major ventures and hence, new developments are constantly popping up on the proverbial drawing board. Below are the top development projects – some completed, others currently underway...

Burj Dubai

Construction is already under way on what will become the tallest building in the world. The exact finished height is a closely guarded secret, but the estimated figure is around 700 metres, making it taller than the proposed Freedom Tower in New York – and twice the height of Dubai's current champion – the Emirates Office Tower on Sheikh Zayed Road. The tower will house a mixture of office and retail space, and some of the most exclusive apartments on the planet. The Burj Dubai will also be the centrepiece of a development featuring yet more residential and retail space, including the biggest shopping mall in the world (see Dubai Mall [p.10]).

www.burjdubai.com

Business Bay

Announced in December 2004, Business Bay is a proposed multi-billion Dirham property development that aims to create a global commercial and business centre in the heart of Dubai. It is hoped that this new free zone will encourage multi-national and regional companies to establish local headquarters here. Based around an extension to the creek that will stretch all the way to Sheikh Zayed Road, the project will cover 64 million square feet when finished.

Website: *na*

Dubai Autodrome & Business Park

Drivers with nerves of steel attempting impossible manoeuvres at break-neck speeds – no, not Sheikh Zayed Road at rush-hour, but the new home of motor racing in the region. The opening of this state-of-the-art facility proves that Motor Sport is big business in Dubai. The circuit has six different track configurations, including a 5.39km FIA-sanctioned GP circuit, and is set to host a round of the recently launched A1 Grand Prix series in late 2005. The business park will be home to various motor industry companies.

www.dubaiautodrome.com.

Dubai Festival City

Almost four kilometres of prime creek-side real estate is to be transformed into a resort style city that will be a complete housing, shopping and recreational paradise. Highlights include a marina and canals, along with a signature 18 hole golf course designed by Robert Trent Jones II. Upon its completion, the area is set to become the focal point for the annual Dubai Shopping Festival.

www.dubaifestivalcity.com

Dubai International Airport

Accommodating 100 airlines flying to over 140 destinations, Dubai International Airport is one of the fastest growing in the world, and is recognised as being the aviation hub of the Middle East. The new ultra-modern Sheikh Rashid terminal opened in April 2000, but with passenger numbers set to increase dramatically, a further US$4 billion expansion is under way. The extension includes a new terminal (Terminal 3) and two new concourses dedicated to Emirates Airline, and will eventually give Dubai the capacity to handle 70 million passengers a year. The work also includes a new Cargo mega-terminal, but to ease the burden somewhat, plans for a second Dubai airport have been brought forward. Situated near Jebel Ali, this new airport will initially cater for business jets and freight, and is scheduled to be operational by 2006.

www.dubaiairport.com

Dubai International Airport

Dubai International Financial Centre

Money talks and the Dubai International Financial Centre (DIFC), designated as a free zone, is quickly becoming established as a regional hub for corporate financing activities and share trading; both on a local and international level. Occupying a 110 acre site parallel to Sheikh Zayed Road, behind the Emirates Towers, the centre will eventually feature residential and leisure facilities alongside tailor-made office spaces.

www.difc.ae

Dubailand

Proclaiming it will be the biggest tourism, leisure and entertainment attraction on the planet, Dubailand will consist of six themed worlds such as Attractions and Experience World, and Eco-Tourism World, and aims to out-do the best that Disney and the like have to offer. As an example of its scale, Sports & Outdoor World will be home to Sports City, featuring a number of stadiums, golf courses, academies (including a Manchester United Soccer School), and facilities for almost every sport known to man.

www.dubailand.ae

Dubai Mall, The

Just what Dubai needs – another shopping mall! Situated within the same development as the world's tallest tower (the Burj Dubai – see above), it's not surprising that the Dubai Mall is also aiming to become the world's biggest. Staying with the record-breaking theme, it will also house the world's largest gold souk and the extensive leisure facilities will feature an Olympic size ice rink and an Imax cinema.

www.thedubaimall.com

Dubai Marina

Once considered something of an outpost, this end of town (near Dubai Internet and Media City) is now being developed at an astonishing rate, and the completed towers are already something of a landmark. The man-made marina has 11 km of marine frontage and will eventually be home to a wealth of housing, including apartment towers and marina facing luxury villas, as well as private yacht moorings and recreational facilities.

www.emaar.com/new/projects_dubai_marina

Dubai Metro/Railway Project

With Dubai (and its population) growing at such a rapid rate, reliance on car travel threatens to bring the city's streets grinding to a halt. Ambitious to say the least, the Dubai Metro (AKA The Urban Rail Transit System) aims to beat the jams with a fleet of over 100 driverless electric trains operating both above and below ground. The metro system is expected to cost US$4 billion. The system will be approximately 70km in length, of which 30% will be underground and the remainder on an elevated line. The trains will comprise standard class and first class sections. One line will run from the centre of Deira across to Bur Dubai and Sheikh Zayed Rd, and will be progressively extended towards Jebel Ali Port. The other line will connect the airport to the central areas of Bur Dubai and Deira. With the first trains not due to leave the station until at least 2009 however, Dubai commuters will be sweating it out in their cars for a few years to come.

http://vgn.dm.gov.ae/DMEGOV/dm-mp-metro

Hydropolis Hotel

Talk about a hotel with a sea-view! Due to open late 2006, the Hydropolis will be the world's first underwater hotel. Upon arrival at the land station (near the Dubai Marina) guests will be transported through a connecting tunnel to the hotel itself situated 20 metres below the surface of the Arabian Gulf. This five star retreat is sure to become a 'must-do' for wealthy tourists who like hotels with a difference.

www.hydropolis.com

International City

Situated on the Dubai to Hatta road, International City will be a hub for traders and retailers from around the world, as well as comprising tourist attractions and housing for 60,000 people. The Residential District will feature buildings designed to reflect the architectural styles of different countries, including Spain, Italy, England and China. The Chinese theme continues with the Dragon Mart, a huge covered mall built in the shape of a dragon, which will be home to 3,000 Chinese trading and retail companies. The site will also feature a replica of China's ancient Forbidden City.

www.internationalcity.ae

Jumeirah Beach Residence

This project is squeezing 36 residential towers and four hotels towers into the last stretch of Dubai beachfront real estate available to developers (for the time being at least). Currently resembling the world's largest building site, JBR will eventually be a self-contained community with its own shopping centres, restaurants, cinema, beach club and health facilities.

www.jbr.ae

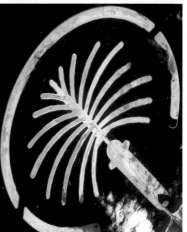

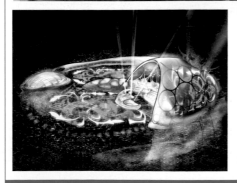

Some of Dubai's key developments

Dubai Key Projects

❶	Burj Dubai	E-3
❷	Business Bay	E-3
❸	Dubai Autodrome and Business Park	C-4
❹	Dubai Festival City	E-3
❺	Dubai Healthcare City	E-3
❻	Dubai Humanitarian City	E-3
❼	Dubai International Airport	F-3
❽	Dubai International Financial Centre	E-3
❾	Dubai Investment Park	B-4
❿	Dubai Mall	E-3
⓫	Dubai Marina	C-3
⓬	Dubai Maritime City	E-2

Dubai Key Projects Overview Map

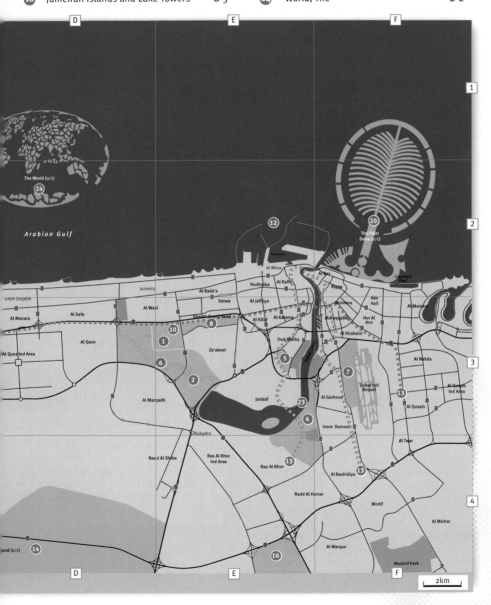

Jumeirah Islands and Lake Towers

Located in Emirates Hills (1), the Jumeirah Islands project will bring lakeside living to its lucky residents. The development features 46 'clusters' or islands, each with 16 waterfront villas, all surrounded by a system of lagoons, waterfalls and canals. Jumeirah Lake Towers will be rising from the sand nearby, comprising 26 sets of three towers designed for residential, retail and office use.

www.jumeirahislands.ae
www.jumeirahlaketowers.ae/

Lost City

A tomb-raider's dream is the The Lost City development which will comprise a 560 hectare site boasting ancient architecture influenced by South America, Persia and the Arab world, in a series of lost cities. The area will also benefit from fresh-water streams, cycle paths, and an 18 hole golf course designed by Greg Norman. Neighbouring the new Ibn Battuta shopping mall, the city and golf course are scheduled for completion by the end of 2007.

www.nakheel.ae/nakheelweb/

Mall of the Emirates

Situated in the quiet area of Al Barsha, this mall was all set to become the biggest in the world until the even bigger Dubai Mall was announced. Still, it will house the first ski and snow resort in the region, two hotels, and a 14 screen multiplex cinema. All the big name retailers will also have a presence, including new outlets for Carrefour, Debenhams, and the ultra-chic Knightsbridge department store Harvey Nichols. Completion date – late 2005.

www.majidalfuttaim.com

Palm Islands, The

First Jumeirah, then Jebel Ali, and now Deira – at this rate there'll be more Palm Islands than shopping malls in Dubai! Visible from space with the naked eye, these palm tree shaped islands will be home to luxury villas, apartments and hotels, as well as leisure and entertainment facilities. Construction of The Palm Jumeirah was well under way when it was announced that a second, bigger, palm island would be built further along the coast at Jebel Ali. In addition to the homes built on the trunk and the fronds, this palm will feature over a thousand 'water homes' on stilts, which, when viewed from above, will collectively spell out an Arabic poem written by HH Shk. Mohammed bin Rashid Al Maktoum. In late 2004 a third, even bigger, palm was announced, which is to be built

off the coast at Deira. This latest project will be a staggering 14.3km in length, and will add an extra 400km to Dubai's shoreline. The Palm Jumeirah is scheduled for completion in late 2005/early 2006, Jebel Ali towards the end of 2007, and Deira about two years later. If that wasn't enough, 'The Pinnacle'; a tower, planned for the trunk of the Palm Jumeirah, promises to rob the Burj Dubai of the title of 'world's tallest building.'

Third Bridge over the Creek

Part of the much needed Dhs.400 million project to combat Dubai's traffic congestion problem. This 12-lane bridge will ease the pressure off Al Garhoud Bridge, Maktoum Bridge and the Shindagha tunnel, and will be part of a new road network eventually linking Shk. Zayed Road to the airport. The bridge is scheduled to be finished by the end of 2006.

www.dm.gov.ae

World, The

Nakheel is heading this US$1.8 billion project to create 300 islands, which will resemble the shape of the world. Built four kilometres offshore, each island will be sold to developers to turn into a private water retreat. Estimated completion is 2008.

www.theworld.ae

International Relations

The UAE is committed to the support of Arab unity but also remains open in its foreign relations. The country became a member of the United Nations and the Arab League in 1971. It is a member of the International Monetary Fund (IMF), the Organisation of Petroleum Exporting Countries (OPEC), the World Trade Organisation (WTO) and other international and Arab organisations. It is also a member of the Arab Gulf Co-operation Council (AGCC, also known as the GCC), whose other members are Bahrain, Kuwait, Oman, Qatar and Saudi Arabia. Pioneered by the late Sheikh Zayed bin Sultan Al Nahyan, the UAE had a leading role in the formation of the AGCC in 1981 and the country is the third largest member in terms of geographical size, after Saudi Arabia and Oman. All major embassies and consulates are represented either in Dubai or in Abu Dhabi, or both.

Government & Ruling Family

The Supreme Council of Rulers is the highest authority in the UAE, comprising the hereditary rulers of the seven emirates. Since the country is governed by hereditary rule, there is little distinction between the royal families and the government. The Supreme Council is responsible for general policy matters involving education, defence, foreign affairs, communications and development, and for ratifying federal laws. The Council meets four times a year and the Abu Dhabi and Dubai rulers have effective power of veto over decisions. Whilst this system is non-democratic, there is little indication that UAE nationals wish for any change.

The seven members of the Supreme Council elect the chief of state (the President) from among its members. The former President of the UAE, HH Sheikh Zayed bin Sultan Al Nahyan was also Ruler of Abu Dhabi, as is his son and current President HH Sheikh Khalifa bin Zayed Al Nahyan. Sheikh Zayed was President since UAE independence was granted on December 6, 1971, and ruler of Abu Dhabi since August 6, 1966 before his demise on 2nd November 2004. The Supreme Council also elects the Vice President, who is HH Sheikh Maktoum bin Rashid Al Maktoum, Ruler of Dubai. The President and Vice President are elected and appointed for five year terms, although, as was the case with Sheikh Zayed, are often re-elected time after time. The President appoints the Prime Minister (currently HH Sheikh Maktoum bin Rashid Al Maktoum) and the Deputy Prime Minister. Dubai is currently governed by Sheikh Maktoum bin Rashid Al Maktoum and his two brothers Sheikh Mohammed bin Rashid Al Maktoum, the Crown Prince and Minister of Defence who is considered the driving force behind Dubai's exponential growth, and Sheikh Hamdan bin Rashid Al Maktoum, the Minister of Finance.

The Government is split into various departments that closely resemble those of other developed nations, such as the Ministries of Health, Education and Finance etc. In a boost to women's rights in the region the UAE Government appointed its first female minister in November 2004. Sheikha Lubna al-Qasimi (a member of the Sharjah royal family) was named as Minister for Economy and Planning.

The Federal Council of Ministers is responsible to the Supreme Council. It has executive authority to initiate and implement laws and is a consultative assembly of 40 representatives who are appointed for two years by the individual emirates. The council monitors and debates government policies, but has no power of veto.

The individual emirates still have a degree of autonomy, and laws that affect everyday life vary between the emirates. For instance, if you buy a car in one emirate and need to register it in a different emirate, you will first have to export and then re-import it. All emirates have a separate police force, with different uniforms and cars, and while it is possible to buy alcohol in Dubai, it is not in Sharjah. However, while there are differences between the emirates, the current move is towards greater interdependence and the increasing power of the Federation.

Facts & Figures

Population

Figures from the Ministry of Planning, show that the population of the UAE reached 4,041,000 by

General Info

Facts & Figures

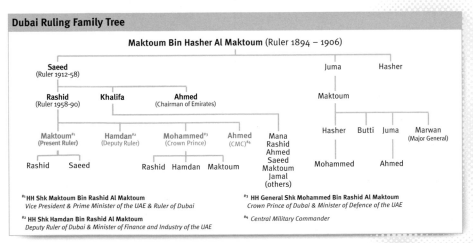

Dubai Ruling Family Tree

Maktoum Bin Hasher Al Maktoum (Ruler 1894 – 1906)

- **Saeed** (Ruler 1912-58)
  - **Rashid** (Ruler 1958-90)
    - **Maktoum**[*1] (Present Ruler)
      - Rashid
      - Saeed
    - **Hamdan**[*2] (Deputy Ruler)
    - **Mohammed**[*3] (Crown Prince)
      - Rashid
      - Hamdan
      - Maktoum
    - Ahmed (CMC)[*4]
    - Mana
      Rashid
      Ahmed
      Saeed
      Maktoum
      Jamal
      (others)
  - **Khalifa**
  - **Ahmed** (Chairman of Emirates)
- Juma
- Hasher
  - Maktoum
    - Hasher
    - Butti
    - Juma
      - Mohammed
      - Ahmed
    - Marwan (Major General)

[*1] **HH Shk Maktoum Bin Rashid Al Maktoum**
Vice President & Prime Minister of the UAE & Ruler of Dubai

[*2] **HH Shk Hamdan Bin Rashid Al Maktoum**
Deputy Ruler of Dubai & Minister of Finance and Industry of the UAE

[*3] **HH General Shk Mohammed Bin Rashid Al Maktoum**
Crown Prince of Dubai & Minister of Defence of the UAE

[*4] *Central Military Commander*

the end of 2003 compared to 2,377,453 in 1995. Dubai's population by the end of 2003 had risen to 1,204,00 compared to 674,101 in 1995 and 276,301 in 1980. By 2017 it is estimated that the population of Dubai will have reached three million. These figures include both Nationals and expat residents. The annual growth rate for Dubai in 2003 was 8.2% and 7.6% for the UAE, and there are 2.4 men to every woman in Dubai. A recent Dubai Municipality statistical survey revealed that the average size of a UAE National household is 7.6 members, while that of the expat is 3.7.

According to the United Nations Development Program (UNDP), the UAE has the highest life expectancy in the Arab world at 72.2 years for males and 75.6 years for females.

Source: www.uae.gov.ae/mop

National Flag

In a nation continually striving for world records, when 30 year anniversary celebrations were marked on National Day 2001, the world's tallest flagpole (at the time) was erected in Abu Dhabi and the world's largest UAE flag was raised at the Union House in Jumeira, Dubai. The UAE flag comprises three equal horizontal bands: green at the top, white in the middle and black at the bottom. A thicker vertical band of red runs down the hoist side. The colours on the flag are common to many of the Arab nations and they symbolise Arab unity and independence. The UAE flag is thought to be based on the Arab Revolt Flag, created in 1916 by Arab nationals during their liberation battle against the then Ottoman (Turkish) rule.

Local Time

The UAE is four hours ahead of UCT (Universal Co-ordinated Time – formerly known as GMT). There is no summer time saving when clocks are altered. Hence, when it is 12:00 midday in Dubai, it is 03:00 in New York, 08:00 in London, 13:30 in Delhi, and 17:00 in Tokyo (not allowing for any daylight saving in those countries).

Social & Business Hours

Other options ➜ Business [p.78]

Social hours are very Mediterranean in style, especially for the national population, although as the region attracts more international

Population by Emirate

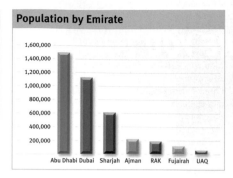

Population Age Breakdown

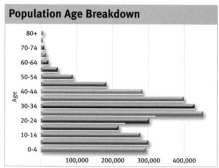

Education Levels

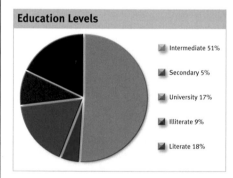

Intermediate 51%

Secondary 5%

University 17%

Illiterate 9%

Literate 18%

Gross Domestic Profit Trends

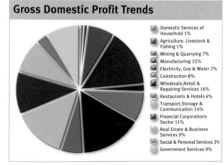

Domestic Services of Household 1%
Agriculture. Livestock & Fishing 1%
Mining & Quarrying 7%
Manufacturing 15%
Electricity, Gas & Water 2%
Construction 8%
Wholesale,Retail & Repairing Services 16%
Restaurants & Hotels 6%
Transport,Storage & Communication 14%
Financial Corporations Sector 11%
Real Estate & Business Services 9%
Social & Personal Services 3%
Government Services 9%

Source: Ministry of Planning

investment afternoon siestas are reserved for government offices and some local retail/restaurant outlets.

While Friday has always been the holy day there is no strict two day weekend akin to many other countries around the world. In the modern UAE, the weekend has established itself on different days, generally according to the company. Until recently, government offices had Thursday afternoon and Friday off, but a 1998 ruling established a five day week for government offices and schools, which are now closed all day Thursday and Friday. Some private companies still take half of Thursday and all day Friday off, while others take all day Friday and Saturday as their weekend. Understandably, these differences cause difficulties, since companies may now be out of touch with international business for up to four days, plus families do not necessarily share weekends. A six day working week is not uncommon either.

Government offices are open from 07:30 – 13:30, Saturday to Wednesday. Private sector office hours vary between split shift days, which are generally 08:00 – 13:00, re-opening at either 15:00 or 16:00 and closing at 18:00 or 19:00; or straight shifts, usually 09:00 – 18:00, with an hour for lunch.

Shop opening times are usually based on split shift hours, although outlets in many of the big shopping malls now remain open all day. Closing times are usually 22:00 or 24:00, while some food shops and petrol stations are open 24 hours a day. On Fridays, many places are open all day, apart from prayer time (11:30 - 13:30), while larger shops in the shopping malls only open in the afternoon from either 12:00 or 14:00.

Embassies and consulates open from 08:45 - 13:30. They are closed on Fridays and in most cases on Saturdays, but generally leave an emergency contact number on their answering machines.

During Ramadan, work hours in most public and some private organisations are reduced by two to three hours per day, and business definitely slows down during this period. Many offices start work an hour or so later and shops are open till late into the night. The more popular shopping malls are crowded at midnight and, believe it or not, parking at that time is tough to find.

Public Holidays

Other options → Annual Events [p.54]

The Islamic calendar starts from the year 622 AD, the year of Prophet Mohammed's (Peace Be Upon Him) migration (Hijra) from Mecca to Al Madinah. Hence the Islamic year is called the Hijri year and dates are followed by AH (After Hijra).

The Hijri calendar is based on lunar months; there are 354 or 355 days in the Hijri year, which is divided into 12 lunar months, and is thus 11 days shorter than the Gregorian year.

As some holidays are based on the sighting of the moon and do not have fixed dates on the Hijri calendar, the dates of Islamic holidays are notoriously imprecise, with holidays frequently being confirmed less than 24 hours in advance. Some non religious holidays are fixed according to the Gregorian calendar.

Public Holidays – 2005	
New Year's Day (1)	Jan 1 Fixed
Eid Al Adha (4)	Jan 21 Moon
Islamic New Year's Day (1)	Feb 10 Moon
Prophet Mohammed's Birthday (1)	Apr 21 Moon
Accession of H.H Sheikh Zayed (1)	Aug 6 Fixed
Lailat Al Mi'Raj (1)	Sept 1 Moon
Eid Al Fitr (3)	Nov 3 Moon
UAE National Day (2)	Dec 2 Fixed

The different emirates also have their own different fixed holidays. The number of days a holiday lasts is in brackets in the table shown above. However, this applies to the public sector only since not all the listed holidays are observed by the private sector and often, the public sector gets a day or two more.

The main festivals celebrated by Muslims are most notably Ramadan, which is the Muslim holy month (see below), Al Eid, or Eid al Fitr, which marks the end of Ramadan and the breaking of the fast; most Muslims also make a Zakah, which is a charitable donation to ensure everyone can celebrate on this day. Eid al Adha is part of the four day hajj celebrations. It commemorates Abraham's willingness to sacrifice his son at God's request. Near Mecca animal sacrifices are still made to commemorate the event. Mawlid al Nabee celebrates the Prophet's birthday, and Lailat Al Mi'raj celebrates the Prophet's Ascension into heaven.

Electricity & Water

Other options → Electricity & Water [p.110]

Electricity and water services in Dubai are excellent and power cuts or water shortages are almost unheard of. Both of these utilities are provided by Dubai Electricity & Water Authority (known as DEWA).

Modern Renaissance School

مدرسة النهضة الحديثة
Modern Renaissance School

a
nurturing
concept
in
primary
education

ritish Curriculum Grades & Montessori Kindergarten

e Modern Renaissance School is an international institution dedicated to the unique requirements and needs of KG
d elementary students. The school's overall approach is predicated on the fact that younger children require their
/n special place to begin their education and the process of socialization outside the home. At Modern Renaissance,
ildren are welcomed into a caring environment where seasoned early childhood and elementary education profes-
nals ensure a meaningful learning experience. Modern Renaissance teaches the National Curriculum of England.

P. O. Box: 1522, Dubai, U.A.E. Tel: +971- 4 - 2641818, Fax: +971- 4 - 2641919
E-mail: info@modernrensch.com • Website: www.modernrensch.com

The electricity supply is 220/240 volts and 50 cycles; the socket type is the same as the three pin British system; most hotels and homes have adapters for electrical appliances.

The tap water is heavily purified and safe to drink, but most people prefer to drink the locally bottled mineral waters, of which there are several different brands available. Bottled water is usually served in hotels and restaurants.

Photography

Normal tourist photography is acceptable but, like anywhere in the world, it is courteous to ask permission before photographing people, particularly women. In general, photographs of government buildings, military installations, ports and airports should not be taken. See Camera Equipment in Shopping [p.210].

Environment

Climate

Dubai has a sub tropical and arid climate. Sunny blue skies and high temperatures can be expected most of the year, and rainfall is infrequent and irregular, falling mainly in winter (November to March), and you rarely see more than a few random days of rain a year. However in the Hajar mountains the amount of rainfall does increase causing occassional flash floods through the various wadis, so take care when visiting this area.

Temperatures range from a low of around 10°C (50°F) in winter, to a high of 48°C (118°F) in summer. The mean daily maximum is 24°C (75°F) in January, rising to 41°C (106°F) in August.

During winter there are occasional sandstorms when the sand is whipped up off the desert (the wind is known as the shamal). More surprisingly, winter mornings can be foggy, but by mid morning, the sun invariably burns the cloud away. The summer humidity can be a killer (approaching 100%), so be prepared to sweat! The most pleasant time to visit Dubai is in the cooler winter months.

For up to date weather reports, log on to www.bbc.co.uk/weather and choose your destination or check out

www.dubaitourism.co.ae/www/main/weather.

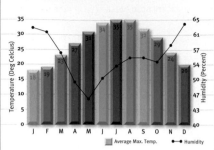

Dubai Temperature & Humidity

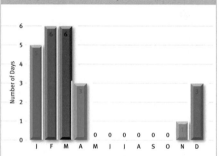

Average Number of Days With Rain

Flora & Fauna

Other options → Arabian Wildlife [p.176]

As you would expect in a country with such an arid climate, the variety of flora and fauna is not as extensive as in other parts of the world. Still, a variety of creatures and plant forms have managed to adapt to a life of high temperatures and low rainfall.

Despite its sandy nature the UAE is adorned with many parks and green belts and Dubai is no exception. The Municipality has an extensive 'greening' programme and areas along the roads are incredibly colourful for a desert environment, with grass, palm trees and flowers being constantly maintained by an army of workers and round the clock watering. The city boasts a large number of well kept parks (see Parks [p.178]).

The region has about 3,500 endemic plants – amazing considering the high salinity of the soil and the harsh environment. The date palm is the most flourishing of the indigenous flora and provides wonderful seas of green, especially in the oases. Heading towards the mountains, flat topped Acacia trees and wild grasses give a feel of an African savannah. The deserts are often surprisingly green in places, even during the dry summer months, but it takes an experienced botanist to get the most out of the area.

Indigenous fauna includes the Arabian Leopard and the Ibex, but sightings of them are extremely rare. Realistically, the only large animals you will see are camels and goats (often roaming dangerously close to roads). Other desert life includes the Sand Cat, Sand Fox and Desert Hare, plus gerbils, hedgehogs, snakes and geckos.

Starter Kit Explorer

Reside in peace. By pairing up the Dubai Explorer with the Zappy Explorer, you now have the ultimate culture shock antidote that shows you where to eat, sleep, shop and socialise, and simplifies your life with step by step procedures on opening a bank account, buying a car or even renting a home.

Birdlife in the city is a little limited – this isn't a place for hearing a dawn chorus, unless you're lucky with where you live. However, recent studies have shown that the number of species of birds is rising each year, due in part to the increasing lushness of the area. This is most apparent in the parks, especially in spring and autumn, as the country lies on the route for birds migrating between Central Asia and East Africa. You can also see flamingos at the Khor Dubai Wildlife Sanctuary at the southern end of Dubai Creek.

Off the coast the seas contain a rich abundance of marine life, including tropical fish, jellyfish, coral, the dugong ('sea cow') and sharks. Eight species of whale and seven species of dolphin have been recorded in UAE waters. Various breeds of turtle are also indigenous to the region. These include the loggerhead, green and hawksbill turtles, all of which are under threat from man. These may be seen by divers off both coasts and if you are blessed, near the East Coast at Kalba (see Khor Kalba [p.195]). The most popular local fish is hammour, which is a type of grouper and makes for a delicious dish on most restaurant menus.

Protection

The UAE's, and specifically the ruling families', commitment to the environment is internationally recognised. At the Environment 2001 Conference and Exhibition in Abu Dhabi, a statement was made that the UAE would invest US$46 billion on projects related to the environment over the next ten years. The late Sheikh Zayed set up the Zayed International Prize for the Environment and he was awarded the WWF's (World Wide Fund for Nature) Gold Panda Award in 1997.

Various organisations have been formed to protect the environment, as well as to educate the population on the importance of environmental issues. The Environmental Research and Wildlife Development Agency (ERWDA 02 681 7171) was established in 1996 to assist the Abu Dhabi government in the conservation and management of the emirate's natural environment, resources, wildlife and biological diversity. Sir Bani Yas Island off Abu Dhabi is home to an internationally acclaimed breeding programme for endangered wildlife. There is also an active branch of the WWF in Dubai (353 7761). In addition, The Arabian Wildlife Centre in Sharjah has a successful breeding programme for endangered wildlife, particularly the Arabian Leopard.

The UAE is party to international agreements on biodiversity, climate change, desertification, endangered species, hazardous wastes, marine dumping and ozone layer protection. In addition to emirate wide environmental controls, Dubai has strictly enforced laws governing the use of chemical insecticides. In 2001, the Dubai government banned any further development along the coast without prior government permission.

Despite all the efforts being made, there are still some serious environmental issues facing the UAE. With no rainfall to speak of for the past few years, the water table is at record low levels. A complex of desalination plants (the biggest in the world) was recently set up in Jebel Ali to boost production, but considering the projected growth of Dubai, both businesses and residents need educating to help reduce the amount of water that is wasted. Desertification and beach pollution from oil spills are other areas of worry; one large spill off the coast in 2001 had hundreds of municipality employees and volunteers cleaning up Gulf beaches for weeks afterwards. Another concern is the impact that the Palm Island and World developments are having on the local ecosystem. Conservationists have suggested that the massive construction projects could be damaging breeding grounds for the endangered Hawksbill turtle, as well as destroying coral reefs and fish stocks. The developers, however, argue that the sites will attract sealife, and point to the recent increase in fish and marine life witnessed around the crescent on the Palm Jumeirah.

See also: Environmental Groups [p.308]

Culture & Lifestyle

Culture

Other options ➔ Business Culture [p.82]

Dubai's culture is firmly rooted in the Islamic traditions of Arabia. Islam is more than just a religion; it is a way of life that governs even the mundane of everyday events, from what to wear to what to eat and drink. Thus, the culture and heritage of the UAE is tied to its religion. In parts of the world, Islamic fundamentalism has given the 'outside' world a very extreme, blanket view of the religion. However, in contrast to this image, the UAE is very tolerant and welcoming; foreigners are free to practice their own religion, alcohol is served in hotels and the dress code is liberal. Women face little discrimination and, contrary to the policies of Saudi Arabia and Iran, are able to drive and walk around unescorted. Among the most highly prized virtues are courtesy and hospitality, and visitors are sure to be charmed by the genuine warmth and friendliness of the people here.

The rapid economic development over the last 30 plus years has changed life in the Emirates beyond recognition. However, the country's rulers are committed to safeguarding their heritage against erosion caused by the speed of development and increased access to outside cultures and material goods. They are therefore keen to promote cultural and sporting events that are representative of their traditions, such as falconry, camel racing and traditional dhow sailing. Arabic culture in poetry, dancing, songs and traditional art is encouraged, and weddings and celebrations are still colourful occasions of feasting and music.

In an attempt to give visitors a clearer appreciation of the Emirati way of life, the Sheikh Mohammed Centre for Cultural Understanding has been established to help bridge the gap between cultures.
See also: Sheikh Mohammed Centre for Cultural Understanding [p.176].

Language

Other options ➔ Learning Arabic [p.136]

The official language of the country is Arabic, although English, Urdu and Hindi are spoken and, with some perseverance, understood. Arabic is the official business language, but English is widely used and most road and shop signs, restaurant menus etc, are in both languages. The further out of town you get, the more Arabic you will find, both spoken and on street and shop signs. Refer to [p.23] for a quick list of useful Arabic phrases to get you around town.

Arabic isn't the easiest language to pick up... or to pronounce! But if you can throw in a couple of words of Arabic here and there, you're more likely to receive a warmer welcome or at least a smile. Most people are happy you're putting in the effort and will help you out with your pronunciation. Just give it a shot – it certainly won't hurt to try and it definitely helps when dealing with officials of any sort.

Poetry

Poetry is an integral and important part of Arabic culture. The ancient form of poetry is called Nabati, and is also known as Bedouin poetry. It is a rich form of literature slightly removed from classical Arabic. At its simplest it is storytelling detailing historical events and culture. The style of the poetry is simple and spontaneous, yet contains many interpretations, and the subject of the poem may remain elusive on first reading. Subject matter includes; chivalry, adulation, advice, proverbs and sometimes a riddle. Sheikh Mohammed bin Rashid al Maktoum is a renowned poet, and is a patron of poetry competitions.

Religion

Other options ➔ Annual Events [p.54]

Islam is the official religion of the UAE, and is widely practised. The basis of Islam is the belief that there is only one God and that Prophet Mohammed (Peace Be Upon Him) is his messenger. There are five pillars of the faith, which all Muslims must follow: the Profession of Faith, Prayer, Charity, Fasting and Pilgrimage. Every Muslim is expected, at least once in his/her lifetime, to make the pilgrimage or 'Hajj' to the holy city of Mecca (also spelt Makkah) in Saudi Arabia.

Additionally, a Muslim is required to pray (facing Mecca) five times a day. The times vary according to the position of the sun. Most people pray at a mosque, although it's not unusual to see people kneeling by the side of the road if they are not near a mosque. It is considered impolite to stare at people praying or to walk over prayer mats.

The modern day call to prayer, through loudspeakers on the minarets of each mosque, ensures that everyone knows it's time to pray. In Dubai, the plan is to build enough mosques so that people don't have to walk more than 500 metres to pray. Friday is the holy day.

Basic Arabic

General

Yes	na'am
No	la
Please	min fadlak (m) / min fadliki (f)
Thank you	shukran
Please (in offering)	tafaddal (m) / tafaddali (f)
Praise be to God	al-hamdu l-illah
God willing	in shaa'a l-laah

Greetings

Greeting	
(peace be upon you)	as-salaamu alaykom
Greeting (in reply)	wa alaykom is salaam
Good morning	sabah il-khayr
Good morning (in reply)	sabah in-nuwr
Good evening	masa il-khayr
Good evening (in reply)	masa in-nuwr
Hello	marhaba
Hello (in reply)	marhabtayn
How are you?	kayf haalak (m) / kayf haalik (f)
Fine, thank you	zayn, shukran (m) / zayna, shukran (f)
Welcome	ahlan wa sahlan
Welcome (in reply)	ahlan fiyk (m) / ahlan fiyki (f)
Goodbye	ma is-salaama

Introduction

My name is	ismiy ...
What is your name?	shuw ismak (m) / shuw ismik (f)
Where are you from?	min wayn inta (m) / min wayn inti (f)
I am from ...	anaa min
America	ameriki
Britain	braitani
Europe	oropi
India	al hindi

Questions

How many / much?	kam?
Where?	wayn?
When?	mata?
Which?	ayy?
How?	kayf?
What?	shuw?
Why?	laysh?
Who?	miyn?
To/ for	ila
In/ at	fee
From	min
And	wa
Also	kamaan
There isn't	maa fee

Taxi / Car Related

Is this the road to ...	hadaa al tariyq ila
Stop	kuf
Right	yamiyn
Left	yassar
Straight ahead	siydaa
North	shamaal
South	januwb
East	sharq
West	garb
Turning	mafraq
First	awwal
Second	thaaniy
Road	tariyq
Street	shaaria
Roundabout	duwwaar
Signals	ishaara
Close to	qarib min
Petrol station	mahattat betrol
Sea/ beach	il bahar
Mountain/s	jabal / jibaal
Desert	al sahraa
Airport	mataar
Hotel	funduq
Restaurant	mata'am
Slow Down	schway schway

Accidents

Police	al shurtaa
Permit/ licence	rukhsaa
Accident	Haadith
Papers	waraq
Insurance	ta'miyn
Sorry	aasif (m) / aasifa (f)

Numbers

Zero	sifr
One	waahad
Two	ithnayn
Three	thalatha
Four	araba'a
Five	khamsa
Six	sitta
Seven	saba'a
Eight	thamaanya
Nine	tiss'a
Ten	ashara
Hundred	miya
Thousand	alf

Islam shares a common ancestry with Christianity and many of the prophets sent before Mohammed can be found in Christian as well as Muslim writings.

While the predominant religion is Islam, Dubai is tolerant of many other denominations, and has a variety of Christian churches: the Evangelical Community Church, Holy Trinity, International Christian Church, St Mary's (Roman Catholic) and St. Thomas Orthodox Church. There is also a Hindu temple in Bur Dubai.

Ramadan

Ramadan is the holy month in which Muslims commemorate the revelation of the Holy Koran (the holy book of Islam, also spelt Quran). It is a time of fasting and Muslims abstain from all food, drinks, cigarettes and unclean thoughts (or activities) between dawn and dusk. In the evening, the fast is broken with the Iftar feast. Iftar timings are found in all the daily newspapers

Arabic Family Names

Arabic names have a formal structure that traditionally indicates the person's family and tribe. Names are usually taken from an important person in the Koran or someone from the tribe. This is followed by the word bin (son of) for a boy or bint (daughter of) for a girl, and then the name of the child's father. The last name indicates the person's tribe or family. For prominent families, this has Al, the Arabic word for 'the', immediately before it. For instance, the President of the UAE is His Highness Sheikh Khalifa Bin Zayed Al Nahyan. When women get married, they do not change their name. Family names are very important here and extremely helpful when it comes to differentiating between the thousands of Mohammeds, Ibrahims and Fatimas!

All over the city, festive Ramadan tents are filled to the brim each evening with people of all nationalities and religions enjoying shisha and traditional Arabic meze and sweets. In addition to the standard favourite shisha cafés and restaurants around town, the five star hotels erect special Ramadan tents for the month.

The timing of Ramadan is not fixed in terms of the western calendar, but each year it occurs around 11 days earlier than the previous year, with the start date depending on the sighting of the moon (see Public Holidays [p.17]). In 2005, Ramadan should commence around October 4th. Non Muslims are also required to refrain from eating, drinking or smoking in public places during daylight hours as a sign of respect. The sale of alcohol is restricted to after dusk, and office hours are cut, while shops and parks usually open and close later. In addition, entertainment such as live music is stopped and cinemas limit daytime screenings of films.

Ramadan ends with a three day celebration and holiday called Eid Al Fitr, or 'Feast of the Breaking of the Fast'. For Muslims, Eid has similar connotations as Diwali for Hindus and Christmas for Christians.

National Dress

On the whole, the national population always wear their traditional dress in public. For men this is the dishdash(a) or khandura – a white full length shirt dress, which is worn with a white or red checked headdress, known as a gutra. This is secured with a black cord (agal). Sheikhs and important businessmen may also wear a thin black or gold robe or mishlah, over their dishdasha at important events, which is equivalent to the dinner jacket in Western culture.

Indecent Proposal!

Sharjah has a Decency Law that penalises those who do not abide by a certain dress code and moral behaviour. 'Indecent dress' includes anything that exposes the stomach, back or legs above the knees. Tight fitting, transparent clothing is also not permitted, nor are acts of vulgarity, indecent noises or harassment. If you have offended the law, you will initially be given advice by the police on what decency is, and then warned to abide by the law in future. If the police find you breaking the law again, a more severe penalty will be imposed.

Local men and women in national dress

In public, women wear the black abaya – a long, loose black robe that covers their normal clothes – plus a headscarf called the sheyla. The abaya is often of very sheer, flowing fabric and may be open at the front. Some women also wear a thin black veil hiding their face and/or gloves, and older women sometimes still wear a leather mask, known as a burkha, which covers the nose, brow and cheekbones. Underneath the abaya, women traditionally wear a long tunic over loose, flowing trousers (sirwall), which are often heavily embroidered and fitted at the wrists and ankles. However, these are used more by the older generation and modern women will often wear the latest fashions from international stores underneath.

National Weddings

Weddings in the UAE are a serious and very large affair. Homes are lit from top to bottom with strings of white lights and the festivities last up to two weeks. Men and women celebrate separately, normally in a hotel ballroom or convention centre, depending on the number of guests. High dowries and extravagant weddings may be a thing of the past though, as the government has placed a ceiling of Dhs.50,000 on dowries, and lavish weddings can result in a prison sentence or Dhs.500,000 fine!

The government sponsored Marriage Fund, based in Abu Dhabi, assists Nationals in everything to do with marriage – from counselling and financial assistance (long term loans up to Dhs.70,000 for a UAE National man marrying a UAE National woman) to organising group weddings to keep costs down. While marriage between a National man and a non National woman is legally permissible (but frowned upon), National women are not allowed to marry non National men. One of the marriage fund's main aims is to promote a reduction in the rate of foreign marriages by UAE Nationals although with so many expatriate Muslims in Dubai this could be quite difficult.

Food & Drink

Other options → Eating Out [p.321]

Dubai offers pretty much every type of international cuisine imaginable. There is a full European selection, a huge choice of Indian restaurants, and all the flavours of the orient. Dubai is also home to virtually every international Fast Food joint known to mankind. While most restaurants are located in hotels and are thus able to offer alcohol, some of the best places to eat are the small street side stands around town. A good option for a night out is one of the 'All you can eat and drink' deals which are dotted around Dubai. These usually comprise huge international buffets, live cooking stations and house beverages for a set price. Ideal for larger groups as most tastes are catered for, and good value too. Refer to the Going Out section [p.321] for details on anything and everything available to quench both hunger and thirst.

Arabic Cuisine

With the mass of nationalities represented in Dubai there is an astounding array of cuisine on offer from Afghani to Moroccan, Persian to Turkish. However, while you're in the region you will also discover a wide variety of Middle Eastern dishes from the traditional to the modern. Sidewalk stands or local restaurants selling shawarma (lamb or chicken sliced from a spit and served in pita bread) and falafel (mashed chickpeas and sesame seeds, rolled into balls and deep fried), are worth a visit at least once. Fresh juices, especially the mixed fruit cocktails, are another highlight not to be missed. Local specialties include hummus (a dip made from chickpeas and sesame seeds), tabbouleh (chopped parsley, mint and crushed wheat), koussa mahshi (stuffed courgettes), or if attending a more elaborate occasion Ghuzi, which is a whole roast Lamb on a bed of rice and mixed nuts. There are also opportunities to sample the local Emirati food. The legacy of the UAE's trading past means that local cuisine uses a blend of ingredients imported from around Asia and the Middle East. Spices such as cinnamon, saffron and turmeric along with nuts (almonds or pistachios), limes and dried fruit add interesting flavours to Emirati dishes. Dried limes are a common ingredient in Arabic cuisine, reflecting a Persian influence. They are dried in the sun and are used to flavour dishes either whole or ground in a spice mill. They impart a distinctive musty, tangy, sour flavour to soups and stews. Interestingly dried limes are also used to make Henna, the local form of body adornment.

Eating Arabic Style

Culturally speaking, eating in the Middle East is traditionally a social affair. Whether eating at home with extended families, or out with large groups, the custom is for everybody to share a veritable feast of various dishes, served in communal bowls. Starters are generally enjoyed with flat Arabic style bread, and main courses are often eaten with the fingers.

Arabic Coffee

While in other regions coffee may just be a pleasant way to end a meal, in the Middle East it is an important ritual of hospitality. The traditional coffee or 'gahwa' of the Emirates is mild with a distinctive taste of cardamom and saffron. It is served black and never with sugar, although dates are offered to sweeten the palate between sips. It is normally polite to drink about three of the small cups (preferably an odd number) – to refuse the coffee is seen a refusal of the hosts generosity.

Pork

Pork is not included on the Arabic menu. Do not underestimate how taboo this meat is to a Muslim. It is not just in eating the meat, but also in the preparation and service of it. Thus to serve pork, restaurants need a separate fridge, equipment, preparation, cooking areas, etc. Supermarkets too, need a separate pork area in the shop and separate storage facilities. Images of pigs can also cause offence.

Additionally, in Islam it is forbidden to consume the blood or meat of any animal that has not been slaughtered in the correct manner. The meat of animals killed in accordance with the Islamic code is known as halaal.

Alcohol

Alcohol is only served in licensed outlets that are associated with hotels (ie, restaurants and bars), plus a few clubs (such as Dubai Creek Golf and Yacht Club or the Aviation Club) and associations. Restaurants outside of hotels that are not part of a club or association are not permitted to serve alcohol.

Nevertheless, permanent residents who are non Muslims can obtain alcohol for consumption at home without any difficulty. All they have to do is get a licence.

See also: *Liquor Licence [p.74]; Purchasing Alcohol [p.206]*

Shisha

Smoking the traditional shisha (water pipe) is a popular and relaxing pastime enjoyed throughout the Middle East. It is usually savoured in a local café while chatting with friends. They are also known as hookah pipes or hubbly bubbly, but the proper name is nargile. Shisha pipes can be smoked with a variety of aromatic flavours, such as strawberry, grape or apple, and the experience is unlike normal cigarette or cigar smoking. The smoke is 'smoothed' by the water, creating a much more soothing effect. This is one of those things in life that should be tried at least once, and more so during Ramadan, when

festive tents are erected throughout the city and filled with people of all nationalities and the fragrant smell of shisha tobacco.

See also: *Shisha Cafes [p.409]*

Entering Dubai

Visas

Other options → Residence Visa [p.66]
Entry Visa [p.64]

Visa requirements for entering Dubai vary greatly between different nationalities, and regulations should always be checked before travelling, since details can change with little or no warning.

All visitors, except Arab Gulf Co-operation Council nationals (Bahrain, Kuwait, Qatar, Oman and Saudi Arabia), require a visa. However, citizens of the countries listed below automatically get a visit visa stamp in their passport upon arrival. In most cases this will be valid for 60 days. If you plan to extend your stay you will either need to renew this visit visa, or get a new one by leaving and re-entering the country. (see Visa Renewals below)

> ### Visa on Arrival
> Citizens of Andorra, Australia, Austria, Belgium, Brunei, Canada, Cyprus, Denmark, Finland, France, Germany, Greece, Hong Kong, Iceland, Ireland, Italy, Japan, Liechtenstein, Luxembourg, Malaysia, Malta, Monaco, The Netherlands, New Zealand, Norway, Portugal, San Marino, Singapore, Spain, Sweden, Switzerland, United Kingdom, United States of America and Vatican City now receive an automatic, visit visa on arrival in Dubai.

Expat residents of the AGCC who meet certain criteria may obtain a non-renewable 30-day visa on arrival. Oman visitors of certain nationalities may enter Dubai on a free of charge entry permit. The same criteria and facilities apply to Dubai visitors entering Oman (although if you have Dubai residency you will face a small charge).

Tourist nationalities (such as Eastern European, Chinese, South African and members of the former Soviet Union) may obtain a 30 day, non-renewable tourist visa sponsored by a local entity, such as a hotel or tour operator, before entry into the UAE. The fee is Dhs.100 for the visa and an additional Dhs.20 for delivery.

Other visitors may apply for an entry service permit (for 14 days exclusive of arrival/departure days), valid for use within 14 days of the date of issue and non renewable. Once this visa expires the visitor must remain out of the country for 30 days before re-entering on a new visit visa. The application fee for this visa is Dhs.120, plus an additional Dhs.20 delivery charge.

For those travelling onwards to a destination other than that of original departure, a special transit visa (up to 96 hours) may be obtained free of charge through any airline operating in the UAE.

A multiple entry visa is available for business visitors who have a relationship with a local business. It is valid for visits of a maximum 30 days each time, for 2 years from date of issue. It costs Dhs.1,000 and should be applied for after entering the UAE on a visit visa. A fee of Dhs.200 per visit applies to the multiple entry visa. For an additional Dhs.150, a multiple entry visa holder is eligible for the e-Gate service (see [p.28]). Airlines may require confirmation (a photocopy is acceptable) that you have a UAE visa before check in at the airport. If you have sponsorship from a UAE entity, ensure that they fax you a copy of the visa before the flight. The original is held at Dubai International Airport for collection before passport control. Your passport should have a minimum of three months validity left. Israeli nationals will not be issued visas.

Costs: *Companies may levy a maximum of Dhs.50 extra in processing charges for arranging visas. The DNATA (Dubai National Airline Travel Agency) visa delivery service costs an extra Dhs.20.*

Note: *Visit visas are valid for 30 or 60 days, not one or two calendar months, and as the arrival and departure dates are counted in this number it is safer to consider the length as 28 or 58 days. If you overstay, there is a Dhs.100 fine for each day overstayed, plus a Dhs.100 fee. If you overstay a significantly long time, the matter may go to court where a judge will decide the penalty.*

Visa Renewals

Visit visas valid for renewal may be extended for a further 30 days at the Department of Immigration and Naturalisation (398 1010), Al Karama, near the Dubai World Trade Centre roundabout (Map Ref 10-B1). The fee is Dhs.500. At the end of this period, you must either leave the country and arrange for a new visit visa from overseas or, for certain nationalities, leave and re-enter the country on a 'visa run' (see [p.27]).

Whilst the current rules generally grant a 60-day visa free of charge to the 34 nationalities listed above, discrepancies do sometimes occur, and there have been suggestions that the UAE Naturalisation and Residency Department plans to tighten the visit visa rules. Proposals include charging a fee, and limiting some nationalities to a non-renewable 30-day visit visa. A further proposition is the introduction of a

'ban' after the expiry of all visit visas (very much like the current rules for tourist visas and entry service permits). This would force the visitor to leave the UAE and remain out of the country for a period of one month or more before re-entering on a new visa. Rules and regulations do have a habit of changing without notice, sometimes overnight, so you'd be best advised to check with the UAE consulate or embassy in your home country, or at least ask the official stamping your passport how long you're allowed to stay.

The Airport

If you're lucky enough to have friends or family to collect you from the airport, you'll avoid the hassles of fighting for a taxi with all the other passengers who have just arrived in Dubai. If not, find the curb and shove your way into the first available cab. You'll face a stiff pick up charge (usually Dhs.20) but there's nothing you can do about it (unless you don't mind hiking out of the airport with all your bags to hail a non airport licensed taxi).

If you're concerned about finding your friends or relatives when you arrive, have no fear. They have a bird's eye view of you as you stand in line waiting to go through Immigration (look up!), and there's only one narrow exit from the airport once you clear customs.

You'll have a bit of a trek before then, however, as the new terminal is huge. Apparently, it takes six escalators, two moving sidewalks and 3,446 steps to get from the aircraft door to a taxi at the main entrance... and no baggage trolleys are provided till the end! And even when you get to the end, the construction work on terminal 3 is interfering with the exterior of the main terminal, which gives the traveller a confusing impression when exiting the airport to be greeted with construction hoarding. But rest assured this work is only temporary, and has little impact on actual airport operations.

Need cash? There are ATM machines dotted around the airport in both the arrivals and departures areas. Currency exchanges are all over the departures area and outside the customs area in arrivals.

Visa Run

The 'visa run' (or 'visa change') basically involves exiting and re-entering the country to gain an exit stamp and new entry stamp in your passport. You can simply fly to a neighbouring country and back into Dubai. Driving over the border into Oman is also an option as you can get your passport stamped at the UAE border control post in Hatta. However you must make sure that your car insurance covers Oman and you must take the form to prove so at the border.

Visa run flights are usually to Doha or Muscat and return an hour or two later. Passengers remain in transit and hence do not need a visa for the country they fly to. There are several flights daily and the cost is about Dhs.400 for a return flight, depending on the season. The low price is only offered for the visa flight and does not apply if you wish to spend any time in the country to which you are flying. Flights are offered by Emirates (214 4444), Gulf Air (271 3222), Qatar Airways (229 2229) and Air Arabia flying from Sharjah. (06 558 0000). If you do fly from Sharjah to Oman you will be charged Dhs.60 for your visa whereas visitors from Dubai get their visa for free. See also Travel Agencies [p.195].

Previously, expatriates who had entered the UAE on visit visas but wished to change their status to employment or residence visas also had to do a visa run. However, in February 2004 the regulations changed and it is now not necessary to leave the country. Some companies though still prefer to send employees out of the country, as the alternative is more expensive.

The visa run is also an opportunity to stock up on good value duty free, and there are sales outlets in both the departure and arrival halls of Dubai Airport. Holders of passports that are allowed a visit visa on arrival at the airport currently have the option of making a visa run indefinitely, although it is illegal to be working in Dubai if you only hold a visit visa.

Until 2000, the visa run was an option for all nationalities that had a Dubai sponsor willing to arrange for a new visit visa. Now, unless the situation reverts, a visa run is only possible for nationalities who can gain a visa stamp on arrival at Dubai International Airport. This was implemented in a crackdown on people working in the country illegally without sponsorship or residency.

E-Gate Service

In 2002, a new rapid passenger clearing service was unveiled by the Dubai Naturalisation and Residency Department and the Department of Civil Aviation. The 'e-Gate Service' allows UAE & GCC nationals, residents and nationals of the 33 countries who qualify for visas on arrival (see [p.26]) to pass through both the departures and arrivals halls of Dubai International Airport without a passport. Swipe your smart card through an electronic gate and through you go, saving a great deal of time otherwise spent in long queues. Applications for a smart card are processed within minutes at Dubai International Airport, near the food court; you'll need your passport, and will be fingerprinted and photographed. The smart card costs Dhs.150 and is

valid for two years. Payment can be made by cash or credit card. For further information, please contact the e-Gate smart card centre on 316 6966

Meet & Greet

Two reception services are available at the airport to help people with airport formalities. The Marhaba Service (224 5780) – ideal for children, the disabled and the elderly – is run by DNATA and operates mainly at Terminal 1 (plus with a few airlines at Terminal 2), while Ahlan Dubai (216 5030) is run by the Civil Aviation Authority and is at Terminal 2 (both 'marhaba' and 'ahlan' are Arabic for 'welcome').

Ahlan is mainly a customer service and information department, assisting with visa delivery and customer queries. Marhaba staff however, greet new arrivals and guide them through Immigration and baggage collection. Through this service, you can also get general information and help with visas. To use Marhaba, a booking has to be made at least 24 hours in advance and passengers are usually met in the arrivals hall before passport control. You can also request some languages if new arrivals don't speak English or Arabic

Cost: Marhaba cost varies according to the service required, but is usually Dhs.75 for one passenger from immigration, or Dhs.150 per person from the aircraft door. A family package of Dhs.185 for up to 4 passengers is also available and the party will be met at the Arrival Gate.

Customs

No customs duty is levied on personal effects entering Dubai. It is forbidden to import drugs and pornographic items.

At Dubai International Airport, once you've collected your baggage it is X-rayed before you leave the arrivals hall. It is here that videos, DVDs, CDs books and magazines are sometimes checked and suspect items, usually movies, may be temporarily confiscated for the material to be approved. Unless it is offensive, it can be collected at a later date. The airport duty free has a small sales outlet in the Arrivals hall.

There has been talk of restrictions on the import and export of large amounts of any currency since the events of 11 September 2001. We recommend that you check this out before carry wads of cash. Additionally, a new anti money laundering law will also, eventually, come into effect, which not only penalises individuals who violate the law, but also

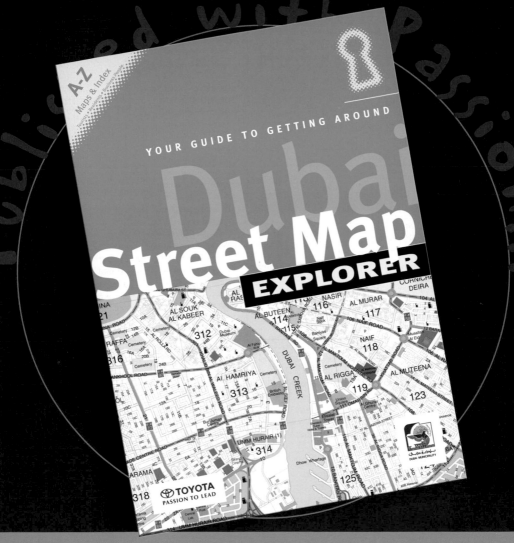

Need a Little Direction?

Street Map Explorers grace the most discerning of glove boxes. This is Dubai's first ever detailed and concise atlas, cross referenced with an A-Z index of businesses, tourist attractions, public facilities and popular locations. In this fast developing city, this expansive and handy guidebook will soon become your favourite travel mate, and a standard tool for navigating this ever growing metropolis. Now, you'll never be lost again!

Passionately Publishing...

Phone (971 4) 335 3520 • **Fax** (971 4) 335 3529 • **Email** Info@Explorer-Publishing.com

Insiders' City Guides • Photography Books • Activity Guidebooks • Commissioned Publications • Distribution

EXPLORER
www.Explorer-Publishing.com

financial institutions. The penalty for money laundering will be a prison sentence of up to seven years or a maximum fine of Dhs.300,000. The limit for undeclared cash that can be brought into the country is Dhs.40,000.

Duty Free allowances:

- Cigarettes – 2,000
- Cigars – 400
- Tobacco – 2 kg
- Alcohol (non Muslim adults only) – two litres of spirits and two litres of wine

Travellers' Info

Health Requirements

No health certificates are required for entry to the Emirates, except for visitors who have been in a cholera or yellow fever infected area in the previous 14 days. However, it is always wise to check health requirements before departure as restrictions may vary depending upon the situation at the time.

Malarial mosquitoes are not really a problem in the cities but they do exist, mainly around the wadis and the mountain pool areas where it's damp. Very few, if any, long term residents take malaria tablets, but short term visitors who plan to visit the countryside during mosquito season may be advised to take them. Check out the requirements on www.who.com (World Health Organisation) a month or so before leaving your home country.

Health Care

Other Options → General Medical Care [p.116]

There is a good standard of healthcare in the Emirates and visitors should have little trouble in obtaining appropriate treatment if they need it, whether privately or from the government run hospitals in case of an emergency. Tourists and non residents are strongly recommended to arrange private medical insurance before travelling since private medical care can become very expensive.

There are no specific health risks facing visitors, although the climate can be harsh, especially during the summer months. It is advisable to drink plenty of water, at least a litre a day. Cover up when out in the sun and use the appropriate factor sunscreen – sunburn, heat stroke and heat exhaustion can be very unpleasant.

Embassies/Consulates	
Australian Consulate	321 2444
Bahrain Consulate	665 7500
Canadian Consulate	314 5555
Chinese Consulate	398 4357
Danish Consulate, Royal	222 7699
Egyptian Consulate	397 1122
French Consulate	332 9040
German Consulate	397 2333
Indian Consulate	397 1222
Iranian Consulate	344 4717
Italian Consulate	331 4167
Japanese Consulate	331 9191
Jordanian Consulate	397 0500
Kuwaiti Consulate	397 8000
Lebanese Consulate	397 7450
Malaysian Consulate	335 5528
Netherlands Consulate	352 8700
Norway, Consulate of	353 3833
Omani Consulate	397 1000
Pakistani Consulate	397 0412
Qatar Consulate	398 2888
Saudi Arabian Consulate	397 9777
South African Consulate	397 5222
Sri Lankan Consulate	398 6535
Switzerland, Consulate of	329 0999
Thai Consulate	349 2863
UK Consulate	397 1070
USA Consulate General	311 6000

Travel Insurance

All visitors to the Emirates should have travel insurance – just in case. Choose a reputable insurer with a plan that suits your needs and the activities you plan to do while in Dubai, especially if they are extreme sports such as quad biking or diving.

Female Visitors

Women should face few, if any, problems while travelling in the UAE. Thanks to a directive by Sheikh Mohammed, men who are caught harassing women have their photo published in the local newspaper. Single female travellers who don't want extra attention should avoid wearing tight fitting clothing and should steer clear of lower end hotels in Deira and Bur Dubai. No matter what, most females receive some unwanted stares at some time or another, particularly on the public beaches. If you can ignore it, you'll save yourself some aggravation. The Dubai Police are very helpful and respectful – call them if you face any unwanted attention or hassles.

If you want worry-free vacation
Call 800 2924 for the AXA advantage
TRAVEL SMART INSURANCE
AXA covers you while you discover the world
No matter where you choose to go on holidays, AXA Travel Smart Insurance is there for you with the coverage you need - when and where you need it
Our dedicated Call Centre is your single point of contact for all your insurance needs - Automobile, Renter's, Travel and healthcare
www.axa-gulfregion.com
AXA
INSURANCE, HEALTHCARE AND INVESTMENTS
Be Life Confident

Travelling with Children

Dubai offers a lot to keep children amused. The city is dotted with numerous parks, and the beach parks (see [p.177]) are well equipped with sport and amusement facilities. Water based activities, horse riding, sports clubs and other adventure sports are all catered for and there are also a wide variety of amusement centres and theme parks, see the Activities section [p.258] for more details. Annual festivals such as the Dubai Shopping Festival and Dubai Summer Surprises offer all sorts of fun filled activities for the whole family. For a dedicated guide to family life in the UAE check out the *Family Explorer*. Hotels and shopping malls are well geared up for children, offering everything from babysitting services to kids' activities. Restaurants, on the other hand, have children's menus but tend not to have many high chairs; it's best to ask when making reservations. Discounted rates for children are common – just ask.

Disabled Visitors

Most of Dubai's five star hotels have wheelchair facilities but, in general, facilities for the disabled are very limited, particularly at tourist attractions. Wheelchair ramps are often really nothing more than delivery ramps, hence the steep angles. When asking if a location has wheelchair access, make sure it really does – an escalator is considered 'wheelchair access' to some. The Dubai International Airport is equipped for disabled travellers (see also: Meet & Greet [p.28]) and Dubai Transport has a few specially modified taxis. Handicapped parking spaces do exist, but are often taken up by ignorant drivers who don't need the facility. The Special Needs People Tourism Working Committee, formed by the Dubai Department of Tourism and Commerce Marketing (DTCM) continues to improve and plan greater access around the city for the physically challenged as well as improve heritage sites for the elderly and hearing impaired.

Hotels with specially adapted rooms for the disabled include: the Burj Al Arab, City Centre Hotel, Crowne Plaza, Emirates Towers Hotel, Grand Hyatt Dubai, Hilton Dubai Creek, Hilton Dubai Jumeirah, Hyatt Regency, Jebel Ali Hotel, Jumeirah Beach Hotel, JW Marriott, Oasis Beach Hotel, The Ritz-Carlton, Dubai, Renaissance Hotel, One&Only Royal Mirage, Shangri-La, Sheraton Jumeirah, Al Qasr and Mina A'Salam.

Dress Code

With its liberal attitude there isn't much that visitors to Dubai can't wear. However, as in all countries, a healthy amount of respect for the local customs and sensibilities doesn't go amiss – particularly during Ramadan. Short or tight clothing can be worn but it will attract attention – most of it unwelcome. Like anywhere in the world, attitudes in the rural areas are more conservative than in the cities.

Lightweight summer clothing is suitable for most of the year, but something slightly warmer may be needed in the evening during the winter months. In winter and summer, be sure to take a light jacket or sweater when visiting hotels, restaurants and shopping centres or the cinema, as the air conditioning can be pretty fierce. As a general rule the dress code in restaurants tends to be smart casual, so ring ahead if intending to wear sports gear or shorts. During the day, good quality sunglasses, hats and buckets of sunscreen are needed to avoid the lobster look!

Dos and Don'ts

Do make the most of your stay in Dubai and, while it might sound obvious, don't break the law. It's a simple and easy rule, and common sense should keep you out of trouble. In the UAE, drugs are illegal and carry a lengthy jail sentence. If you are caught bringing drugs into the country, you will be charged with trafficking, which can result in a life sentence. Pornography of any sort is also illegal and will be confiscated immediately. Never drink and drive as there is a zero tolerance law and strict penalties apply [p.44]. In general caution is advised when alcohol has been consumed, being argumentative or abusive is not permitted or advisable, nor is public drunkenness. When travelling around Dubai, as anywhere, it is advisable to carry a form of identification with you at all times, such as a passport copy or drivers licence . The best rule of thumb is to respect the local laws, culture and Muslim sensibilities of the UAE. Remember, you are a visitor here. Treat the local population with the same respect you'd expect back home.

Safety

While the crime rate in Dubai is very low, a healthy degree of caution should still be exercised. Keep your valuables and travel documents locked in your hotel room or in the hotel safe. When in crowds, be discreet with your money and wallet; don't carry large amounts of cash on you and don't trust strangers. Money and gem related scams run by con men who pray on the naive are on the increase.

With the multitude of driving styles converging on Dubai's roads, navigating the streets either on foot or in a vehicle can be a challenge. If you feel your taxi driver is driving too aggressively, tell him to slow down. Cross roads only at designated pedestrian crossings, and make sure all cars have actually stopped for you before crossing. Learn the rules of the road before getting behind the wheel, and pay extra attention to your mirrors, exerting caution at all times as traffic accidents are an all to common occurrence on Dubai's complex roads. Never drive without the correct documentation and insurance.

Tourist Police

In an effort to better serve Dubai's visitors, the Dubai Police have launched the Department for Tourist Security. The role of this department is twofold: to advise visitors by educating them on safety in Dubai, and to offer quick assistance if visitors face problems of any sort. They act as a liaison between you and the Dubai Police although in general Dubai police officers are extremely helpful. They are calm and understanding, and speak a multitude of languages. Their Website (www.dubaipolice.gov.ae) is easy to navigate, helpful, and even lists Dubai's top ten most wanted criminals!

Contact: Call their toll free number (800 4438) for assistance.

Lost/Stolen Property

To avoid a great deal of hassle if your personal documents go missing, make sure you keep one photocopy with friends or family back home and one copy in a secure place, such as your hotel room safe.

If your valuables do go missing, first check with your hotel, or if you've lost something in a taxi, call the taxi company lost and found department. There are a lot of honest people in Dubai who will return found items. If you've had no luck, then try the Dubai Police or the Department for Tourist Security (see above) to report the loss or theft; you'll be advised on the next course of action. If you have lost your passport, your next stop will be your embassy or consulate. Refer to [p.30] for a list of all embassies and consulates in Dubai.

Dubai Tourist Info Abroad

The Dubai Department of Tourism and Commerce Marketing (223 0000) operates 15 offices overseas, which promote Dubai to both travellers and businesses.

National Bank of Dubai's signature building

DTCM Overseas Offices

Australia & NZ	Sydney	+61 2 995 6620
Far East	Hong Kong	+85 2 2827 5221
France	Paris	+33 1 4495 8500
Germany	Frankfurt	+49 69 7100 020
India	Mumbai	+91 22 2283 3497
Italy	Milan	+39 02 5740 3036
Japan	Tokyo	+81 3 53 67 5450
Nordic Countries	Stockholm	+46 8 411 1135
North America	Philadelphia	+1 215 751 9750
Russia, CIS & Baltic States	Moscow	+70 95 933 6717
South Africa & East Africa	Johannesburg	+27 11 785 4600
Switzerland & Austria	Zurich	+41 43 255 4444
UK & Ireland	London	+44 207 839 0580
USA	New York	+1 212 719 5750

Places to Stay

Visitors to Dubai will find an extensive choice of places to stay, from hotels to hotel apartments, youth hostels, and even an eco tourist hotel (the Al Maha resort located amongst the dunes on the road to Al Ain).

The growth in hotels and hotel apartments over the last few years has been phenomenal. In the past nine years, the number of hotels and hotel apartments has risen from 70 to nearly 400, with many more planned. With so many rooms (approaching 25,000) needing to be filled, it's not surprising that visitors can expect excellent service and facilities - at least at the higher end of the market.

One service that the larger hotels and hotel apartments offer is to act as a sponsor for those nationalities a visit visa. This service should cost about Dhs.180 (including mark up) for a regular, and Dhs.280 for an urgent visa. The visa is deposited at the airport for collection on arrival; however, the visitor is expected to stay at the accommodation for at least a few nights.

Hotels

Other options → Weekend Breaks [p.195]

Hotels range from those costing under Dhs.100 a night to those with a published price, or rack rate, in the region of Dhs.11,000 for a night in a standard suite at the Burj Al Arab. While the hotels at the higher end of the market offer superb surroundings and facilities, those at the cheaper end vary – you pay for what you get. Refer to the Index for a list of outlets (including restaurants and bars) that can be found at each hotel.

Hotels in Dubai can be split into 'beach hotels' (grouped along the coast to the south of the Creek entrance) and 'city hotels'. Most are located within a maximum 30 minute journey from Dubai International Airport. The larger hotels all offer an airport shuttle service as well as a minibus service to the main tourist spots around the city. A taxi ride from the airport to most hotels will cost around Dhs.40 – 70. Road transport in Dubai is usually quite fast and the majority of journeys will only take 15 – 20 minutes duration, costing about Dhs.20 – 25. With so many luxury hotels and resorts in Dubai there is no reason why you can't combine a stay in a central Dubai hotel with a few nights at a desert resort, refer to Bab Al Shams and Al Maha.

The Dubai Department of Tourism and Commerce Marketing (DTCM) oversees a hotel classification system which gives an internationally recognised star rating to hotels and hotel apartments so that visitors can judge more easily the standard of accommodation they will receive.

The DTCM also operates an Internet reservation system for Dubai's hotels on their Website (www.dubaitourism.co.ae). This enables guests to reserve rooms online and allows them a virtual tour of the hotel before they book. Alternatively, the DTCM Welcome Bureau at the airport offers instant hotel reservations, often at a greatly discounted rate.

Refer to the Club Facilities table [p.302] for the list of facilities offered at each hotel. Remember that, as in anywhere else in the world, you can usually manage to get a discount on the rack rate or published price.

Hilton Dubai Jumeirah

Hotel Apartments

A cheaper alternative to staying in a hotel is to rent furnished accommodation. This can be done on a daily/weekly/monthly or yearly basis and there are a number of agencies offering this service. One advantage is that the place can feel far more like home than a hotel room, particularly on longer stays. Usually the apartments come fully furnished, from bed linen to cutlery, plus maid service. Additionally, there may be sports facilities, such as a gym and a swimming pool, in the building.

Hotels

Five Star

Five Star	Beach Access	Phone	Map	Dhs	Email
Al Bustan Rotana Hotel P.397		282 0000	14-E3	1,080	albustan.hotel@rotana.com
Al Maha Resort		832 9900	5-C4	5,880	almaha@emirates.com
Al Qasr Hotel P.243	✔	366 8888	4-A2	3,328	reservations@madinatjumeirah.com
Bab Al Shams Desert Resort & Spa P.xiii		832 6699	UAE-C2	2,040	info@babalshams.com
Burj Al Arab	✔	301 7777	4-A1	6,000	info@burj-al-arab.com
Crowne Plaza		331 1111	9-D2	1,440	cpdxb@cpdxb.co.ae
Dubai Marine Beach Resort & Spa	✔	346 1111	6-D2	1,200	reservations@dxbmarine.com
Dusit Dubai P.373		343 3333	9-A2	1,440	info@dusitdubai.com
Emirates Towers Hotel P.351		330 0000	9-C2	1,740	eth@emirates-towers-hotel.com
Fairmont Hotel		332 5555	9-E1	1,799	dubai.reservations@fairmont.com
Grand Hyatt Dubai P.xiv		317 1234	13-E3	1,460	reservations.grandhyattdubai@hyattintl.com
Hilton Dubai Creek		227 1111	11-C2	1,260	reservations.jumeirah@hilton.com
Hilton Dubai Jumeirah P.355	✔	399 1111	2-D2	1,155	reservations.jumeirah@hilton.com
Hotel Inter-Continental Dubai		222 7171	8-C4	1,416	reservations@ihcdubai.co.ae
Hyatt Regency Hotel P.339		209 1234	8-D2	930	reservations.hyattregencydubai@hyattintl.com
Jebel Ali Golf Resort & Spa	✔	883 6000	1-A1	1,890	jagrs@jaihotels.com
Jumeirah Beach Club, The	✔	344 5333	5-D1	3,660	info@jumeirahbeachclub.com
Jumeirah Beach Hotel, The P.333	✔	348 0000	4-B2	2,760	info@thejumeirahbeachhotel.com
JW Marriott Hotel P.v		262 4444	12-A3	1,500	marriott@emirates.net.ae
Le Meridien Dubai P.369		282 4040	14-E3	630	reservations@le-meridien-dubai.com
Le Meridien Mina Seyahi Beach Resort	✔	399 3333	3-A2	1,680	reservations@lemeridien-minaseyahi.com
Le Royal Meridien Beach Resort & Spa	✔	399 5555	2-E2	1,920	reservations@leroyalmeridien-dubai.com
Malakiya Villas (2 Bedroom)	✔	366 8888	4-A2	24,000	reservations@madinatjumeirah.com
Metropolitan Palace Hotel		227 0000	11-D2	1,530	reservation@metpalace-dubai.com
Mina A'Salam P.243	✔	366 8888	4-A2	3,060	reservations@madinatjumeirah.com
Mövenpick Hotel Bur Dubai P.435		336 6000	10-D4	1,140	hotel.burdubai@moevenpick-hotels.com
Palace at One&Only Royal Mirage, The P.385	✔	399 9999	3-A2	2,130	royalmirage@oneandonlyroyalmirage.ae
Renaissance Hotel		262 5555	12-A3	840	rendubai@emirates.net.ae
Ritz-Carlton Dubai	✔	399 4000	2-E2	2,150	reservation.dubai@ritzcarlton.com
Shangri-La Hotel		343 8888	9-A2	1,650	sldb.reservations@shangri-la.com
Sheraton Deira		268 8888	12-A3	1,140	sheratondeira@sheraton.com
Sheraton Dubai Creek Hotel & Towers		228 1111	11-C1	1,380	reservationsdubaiuae@sheraton.com
Sheraton Jumeira Beach Resort	✔	399 5533	2-D2	1,440	jumeira.reservations@sheraton.com
Sofitel City Centre Hotel P.381		295 5522	14-D1	1,500	reservation@sofitel.ae
Taj Palace Hotel		223 2222	11-D2	1,200	reservations@tajpalacedubai.ae

Four Star

Four Star	Beach Access	Phone	Map	Dhs	Email
Al Khaleej Palace Hotel		223 1000	11-D1	1,056	kpalace@emirates.net.ae
Ascot Hotel		352 0900	7-E3	500	info@ascothoteldubai.com
Avari Dubai International		295 6666	11-D3	1,200	reservations@avari-dubai.co.ae
Capitol Hotel		346 0111	7-A2	907	reservation@capitol-hotel.com
Carlton Tower, The		222 7111	8-C4	800	carltonvida@yahoo.com
Dubai Grand Hotel		263 2555	15-C3	900	dxbgrand@emirates.net.ae
Four Points Sheraton		397 7444	8-A4	960	fpshrdxb@emirates.net.ae
Golden Tulip Aeroplane Hotel		272 2999	8-E3	660	res@goldentulipaeroplane.com
Holiday Inn Downtown		228 8889	11-E2	960	rsvn@hidubdt.com
Ibis World Trade Centre		332 4444	9-E3	275	novotel.ibis@accorwtc.ae
Jumeira Rotana Hotel	✔	345 5888	6-E3	960	res.jumeira@rotana.com
Marco Polo Hotel		272 0000	8-E4	1,020	marcohot@emirates.net.ae
Metropolitan Deira	✔	295 9171	11-D3	990	reservation@metdeira-dubai.com
Metropolitan Hotel	✔	343 0000	5-C4	840	reservation@methotel-dubai.com
Metropolitan Resort & Beach Club Htl	✔	399 5000	2-E2	1,350	reservation@metbeach-dubai.com
Millennium Airport Hotel		282 3464	14-D3	660	sales.airdxb@mill-cop.com
Novotel World Trade Centre		332 0000	9-E3	550	reservation@accorwtc.ae
Oasis Beach Hotel	✔	399 4444	2-D2	1,740	obh@jaihotels.com

Hotels

Four Star	Beach Access	Phone	Map	Double	Email
Ramada Continental Hotel		266 2666	12-B4	1,080	ramadadb@emirates.net.ae
Ramada Hotel		351 9999	7-E3	1,080	rhdres@emirates.net.ae
Regent Palace Hotel		396 3888	11-A1	500	reservations@ramee-group.net.ae
Riviera Hotel		222 2131	8-C3	520	riviera@emirates.net.ae
Rydges Plaza Hotel		398 2222	7-A4	480	rydges@emirates.net.ae
Sea View Hotel		355 8080	7-2E	1,080	seaviewh@emirates.net.ae
Towers Rotana Hotel		343 8000	9-B2	750	res.towers@rotana.com

Three Star	Beach Access	Phone	Map	Double	Email
Admiral Plaza, The		393 5333	7-E2	390	admplaza@emirates.net.ae
Al Khaleej Holiday Hotel		227 6565	11-D2	650	kholiday@emirates.net.ae
Ambassador Hotel		393 9444	8-A2	456	ambhotel@emirates.net.ae
Astoria Hotel		353 4300	8-A2	600	astoria@astamb.com
Claridge Hotel		271 6666	8-E4	350	claridge@emirates.net.ae
Comfort Inn		222 7393	11-D2	450	comftinn@emirates.net.ae
Dubai Palm Hotel		271 0021	8-E4	500	reservations@dubaipalmhotel.com
Gulf Inn Hotel		224 3433	11-D2	600	gulfinn@emirates.net.ae
Imperial Suites Hotel		351 5100	7-E3	800	imhotels@emirates.net.ae
Kings Park Hotel		228 9999	11-E2	450	na
Lords Hotel		228 9977	11-D2	300	lords@emirates.net.ae
Lotus Hotel		227 8888	11-D1	600	lotusdbx@emirates.net.ae
Nihal Hotel		295 7666	11-D2	450	nihalhtl@emirates.net.ae
Palm Beach Rotana Inn		393 1999	7-E2	300	palmbhtl@emirates.net.ae
Palm Hotel Dubai, The		399 2222	3-A3	828	iqbal.reservation@dubaiparkhotel.com
Princess Hotel		263 5500	15-C3	400	princhtl@emirates.net.ae
Quality Inn Horizon		227 1919	11-D2	350	qualiti@hotmail.com
Sea Shell Inn		393 4777	7-E2	500	reservation@seashellinnhotel.com
Vendome Plaza Hotel		222 2333	11-D2	450	na

Two Star	Beach Access	Phone	Map	Double	Email
Deira Park Hotel		223 9922	8-C3	220	deirapak@emirates.net.ae
New Peninsula Hotel		393 9111	8-A2	550	pennin@emirates.net.ae
Phoenicia Hotel		222 7191	8-C3	340	hotphone@emirates.net.ae
President Hotel		334 6565	10-D1	300	presiden@emirates.net.ae
Ramee International Hotel		224 0222	8-D4	350	rameeint@ramee-group.com
San Marco		272 2333	8-D3	250	smhtldxb@emirates.net.ae

One Star	Beach Access	Phone	Map	Double	Email
Dallas Hotel		351 1223	6-E2	250	na
Middle East Hotel		222 6688	8-D3	180	mehgroup@emirates.net.ae
Vasantam Hotel		393 8006	8-A2	220	vhdubai@yahoo.co.in

Note

The above prices are the hotels' peak season published rack rates. Many hotels offer a discount off the rack rate if asked. Peak or high season is from October – April (except during Ramadan, refer to Ramadan & Public Holidays [p.17], for further details). For more one star hotels, contact the One Stop Information Centre (223 0000), Department of Tourism & Commerce Marketing, www.dubaitourism.com. For more hotels outside Dubai, refer to the Weekend Break table [p.198].

Classification is based on the DTCM hotel rating in accordance with bylaw No. (1) of 1998 concerning Licensing and Classification of Hotels, Guesthouses and Hotel Apartments in Dubai.

Hotel Apartments

Deluxe	Phone	Area	One B/room Apts (Weekly)	Two B/room Apts (Weekly)	Email
Al Faris Hotel Apts	336 6566	Oud Metha	3,300	-	afarisre@emirates.net.ae
Al Bustan Residence Hotel	263 0000	Al Qusais	4,620	6,300	reservations@albustan.com
City Centre Residence	294 1333	Al Garhoud	5,700	10,000	cityhotl@emirates.net.ae
Golden Sands X	359 9000	Al Karama	-	4,410	gldnsnds@emirates.net.ae
Imperial Residence Hotel	355 3555	Bur Dubai	5,250	6,650	impres@emirates.net.ae
Marriott Executive Apts	213 1000	Deira	-	-	dubaimea@emirates.net.ae
Oasis Court Hotel Apts	397 6666	Bur Dubai	2,380	3,080	oasis@gtfs-gulf.com
Pearl Residence	355 8111	Bur Dubai	3,500	-	pearlres@emirates.net.ae
Rihab Rotana Suites	294 0300	Al Garhoud	-	-	rihab@emirates.net.ae
Rolla Residence	359 2000	Bur Dubai	5,400	6,600	rollabus@emirates.net.ae
Rayan Residence	224 0888	Deira	3,850	4,200	-
Wafi Residence	324 7222	Oud Metha	-	-	mkm@waficity.com

Standard

Standard	Phone	Area	One B/room Apts (Weekly)	Two B/room Apts (Weekly)	Email
Al Awael Hotel Apts	271 1211	Dubai	1,050	1,260	alawael@emirates.net.ae
Al Deyafa Hotel Apts	228 2555	Deira 0	2,250		defuap55@emirates.net.ae
Al Faris Hotel Apartment 2	393 5847	Bur Dubai	1,750	2,350	afarisre@emirates.net.ae
Al Faris Hotel Apartments 1	393 3843	Bur Dubai			afarisre@emirates.net.ae
Al Muraqabat Plaza	269 0550	Deira	1,400	2,800	muraqabt@emirates.net.ae
Al Nakheel Hotel Apts	224 1555	Deira	2,100	3,500	alnakhel@emirates.net.ae
Al Hina Hotel Apartments	355 5510	Bur Dubai	1,750		hinarest@emirates.net.ae
Al Mas Hotel Apartments	355 7899	Bur Dubai	1,925	3,500	almasfur@emirates.net.ae
Atrium Suites	266 8666	Abu Hail	-	-	-
Baisan Residence	221 9966	Deira	1,750	3,150	-
Blanco	227 3400	Deira	1,260	1,750	sacham@emirates.net.ae
Embassy Suites	269 8070	Deira	1,225	1,750	suite@emirates.net.ae
Galleria Apartments	209 6788	Deira	4,650	5,500	dubai.regency@hyattintl.com
Golden Sands III	355 5551	Bur Dubai	3,045	-	goldensands@emirates.net.ae
Harmoody Hotel Apts	273 5222	Al Baraha	1,450		mohraah@emirates.net.ae
Premiere Hotel Apts	359 9545	Bur Dubai	5,000	6,545	preapts@emirates.net.ae
Richmond Hotel Apts	398 8456	Bur Dubai	2,450	2,800	rchmdhtl@emirates.net.ae
Rimal Rotana Suites	268 8000	Deira	5,800	-	rimal.suites@rotana.com
Savoy Hotel Apartments	355 3000	Bur Dubai	2,800	-	savoy@emirates.net.ae
Tower No. One	343 4666	Trade Centre 1&2	1,995	3,000	sales@numberonetower.com
Winchester Grand	355 0222	Bur Dubai	4,900	6,300	wingrand@emirates.net.ae
Winchester Hotel Apts	355 0111	Bur Dubai	3,850	-	winchest@emirates.net.ae

Listed

Listed	Phone	Area	One B/room Apts (Weekly)	Two B/room Apts (Weekly)	Email
Al Shams Plaza	355 1200	Bur Dubai	1,547	2,310	anbmr@emirates.net.ae
London Crown II	351 8888	Bur Dubai	1,750	-	info@londoncrown.com
Sky Hotel Apartments	273 3344	Deira	1,260	-	skydubai@hotmail.com

Note

The above prices are the hotel apartments' peak season published rack rates and are inclusive of tax and service charge. Many hotel apartments offer a discount off the rack rate if asked. Peak or high season is from October – April (except during Ramadan, refer to Ramadan & Public Holidays, General Information, for further details).

For more listed hotel apartments, contact the One Stop Information Centre (223 0000), Department of Tourism & Commerce Marketing, www.dubaitourism.com.

General Info

Places to Stay

Dubai Five Star Hotels

Al Bustan Rotana Hotel
Map Ref → 14-D3

The Al Bustan Rotana Hotel has a unique blend of traditional Arabian hospitality and modern luxury. One of 'The Leading Hotels of the World' and ideally located near the International Airport and business district, the hotel has 300 elegant rooms and offers a variety of restaurants designed to tantalise all tastes.

Burj Al Arab
Map Ref → 4-A2

This majestic landmark is the world's tallest hotel and, sitting on its own man-made island, it is also very exclusive. Architecturally unique, resembling a billowing sail, it is both dramatic and lavish. It stands at 321 metres high, and houses five restaurants and 202 duplex suites with a host of butlers to look after your every need.

Coral Deira Hotel
Map Ref → 11-E2

This hotel is located in the heart of Deira's business district, within easy reach of the airport. The contemporary interior, designed by Italian designer Saporiti, holds 126 rooms and 14 suites, a swimming pool, business centre and meeting rooms, two restaurants and a 24 hour coffee shop.

Crowne Plaza
Map Ref → 9-D2

Another of Dubai's entertainment focused hotels, the well-established 560 room Crowne Plaza places a good deal of emphasis on its food and beverage outlets – all seven of them. Convenience is key here – not only is it located on Sheikh Zayed Road, but there is a shopping mall beneath this hotel/serviced apartment complex.

Dubai Marine Beach Resort & Spa
Map Ref → 6-D2

Better known as 'Dubai Marine', this independent hotel is famed for its wide variety of restaurants and bars packed into its compact area. The property also includes a small private beach, three swimming pools, a spa and a well equipped health club. The 195 villa style rooms are nestled in gardens located off the central area.

Dusit Dubai
Map Ref → 9-A2

This architecturally inspiring, modern building on Sheikh Zayed Road comprises four restaurants, including the popular Benjarong Thai restaurant, and 174 guestrooms and serviced apartments. With a Far East flavour, much of the emphasis is on luxury combined with Thai hospitality to meet the needs of business travellers.

Emirates Towers Hotel
Map Ref → 9-C2

At 305 metres high and housing 400 rooms, this is the third tallest hotel in the world. Sophisticated and elegant, with a shopping arcade and excellent restaurants on the ground level, this hotel on the Sheikh Zayed Road is twinned with an office block. The entrance lobby is impressive and a ride in the glass fronted lifts is recommended.

Fairmont Dubai, The
Map Ref → 9-E1

At night this grand hotel, opposite the Dubai World Trade Centre, is hard to miss thanks to the four glowing pyramids that systematically change colour. The interior is even more inspirational than the exterior, and besides 394 rooms and serviced apartments, the Fairmont houses some of the trendiest restaurants in town.

Grand Hyatt, Dubai
Map Ref → 13-E2

With 674 fabulously spacious and high tech rooms and 37 acres of landscaped grounds, Grand Hyatt Dubai introduces a new concept in business/leisure travel, offering top level conference facilities in a resort environment. It also houses ten restaurants, a luxury spa and the ever popular club, MIX.

Hilton Dubai Creek
Map Ref → 11-C2

With very flash yet understated elegance, this ultra minimalist, centrally located hotel was designed by Carlos Ott and features interiors of wood, glass and chrome. There are 154 guestrooms plus the Gordon Ramsay restaurant, Verre. The hotel overlooks the Creek and has splendid views of the Arabian dhow trading posts.

General Info

Places to Stay

Hilton Dubai Jumeirah
Map Ref → 2-D2

This beachfront hotel has 330 guestrooms and 57 luxury suites, most with sea views. Home to a number of first class restaurants, particularly the world-renowned Italian, Bice, each outlet features stunning views. Located on the 'Golden Mile' Jumeira beach strip, the hotel is family friendly.

Hotel InterContinental Dubai
Map Ref → 8-C4

This somewhat dated hotel is best loved for its favoured restaurants ranging from seafood to Italian to Japanese and also houses Mystizo, a hotspot for the young and trendy. Facing the Creek in Deira, traffic and parking can be a hindrance in reaching the hotel, but the food's worth the hassle of getting there.

Hyatt Regency Dubai
Map Ref → 8-D2

One of Dubai's older hotels, the recently refurbished Hyatt Regency features 400 guest rooms and serviced suites, each with a sea view and some of Dubai's, longstanding popular restaurants. While there's no beach nearby, it's within walking distance of the gold, fish and vegetable souks.

Jebel Ali Hotel & Golf Resort
Map Ref → 1-A1

This resort, open since 1981, has enough activities and facilities to keep guests busy for their entire stay. The 406 room hotel is situated amongst acres of secluded beach, landscaped gardens, and one of the region's original golf courses. Guests can also enjoy horse riding and a variety of watersports.

Jumeirah Beach Club, The
Map Ref → 5-D1

Hidden behind high walls and excessive foliage The Jumeirah Beach Club screams exclusivity. There are 48 secluded suites (each with their own balcony or garden) and two luxury villas nestled among the club's manicured gardens and private beach, along with a full range of facilities.

Jumeirah Beach Hotel, The
Map Ref → 4-B2

Part of the Jumeirah Beach Resort, along with the Burj Al Arab and the Wild Wadi Water Park, this exclusive hotel is one of Dubai's landmarks. The main building, built in the shape of an ocean wave with a colourfully dynamic interior, features 618 sea view rooms and 25 restaurants as well as cafés, bars and shopping outlets.

JW Marriott Hotel
Map Ref → 12-A3

Located on the edge of bustling Deira and conveniently close to the airport, the Marriott boasts 305 rooms, 39 suites, and 13 bars and restaurants. A grand staircase, detailed marble floors and natural lighting provided by 'the Middle East's largest skylight' are all impressive, as is the landscaped indoor town square.

Le Meridien Dubai
Map Ref → 14-E3

Le Meridien has an ultra convenient location, just across from the Dubai airport and a stone's throw from the Aviation Club, and an attractive array of restaurants, including the Meridien Village. One of Dubai's first five star hotels, the 383 rooms don't have an exquisite view, but feature luxury standards and service.

Le Meridien Mina Seyahi
Map Ref → 3-A2

Not to be confused with the nearby Le Royal Meridien, this hotel focuses on water bound fun, from Hobie cats to fishing charters. There are 211 rooms some with views of the sea and the landscaped grounds. The clincher for families is the 'Penguin Club', which allows parents to chill while the kids are entertained with supervised activities.

Le Royal Meridien
Map Ref → 2-C2

A bit further out in the Marsa Dubai area is Le Royal Meridien. The 500 room hotel has 13 bars/restaurants all of an equally high standard and providing guests and visitors plenty to choose from. The beach and pool facilities are also impressive. One of the highlights is the Caracalla Spa, which is pure indulgence.

Dubai Five Star Hotels

Metropolitan Palace Hotel
Map Ref → 11-D2

An elegant lobby, 212 tasteful rooms and a rooftop swimming pool are the main selling points for this hotel, as well as the affordable room rate. Additionally, the convenient location, a block from the Creek in bustling Deira, merits a thumbs up. The gem in this hotel's crown is Tahiti, a Polynesian restaurant great for lively nights out.

Madinat Jumeirah
Map Ref → 4-A2

This extravagant resort has two hotels, Al Qasr and Mina A'Salam, with 940 luxurious rooms and suites, and exclusive summer houses, all linked by waterways with abras. Nestled between the two hotels is the Souk Madinat with over 20 bars, restaurants and cafés. There is also an amphitheatre, indoor theatre and spa.

Mövenpick Hotel Bur Dubai
Map Ref → 10-D4

Located near Lamcy Plaza and Wafi City, this hotel isn't quite as 'five star' as the others. With 230 rooms, the main reason Dubai residents will visit this quiet venue is to dine at Fakhreldine, one of Dubai's best Lebanese restaurants, or party the night away at Jimmy Dix, downstairs.

One&Only Royal Mirage
Map Ref → 3-A2

Quieter than the Madinat Jumeirah and blessed with an intimate atmosphere, this is one of the most tranquil hotels in Dubai. Traditional Arabian architecture and unparalleled dining and service, at the very least, a night tour of the grounds and a trip to Tagine or the fabulous Kasbar are highly recommended.

Renaissance Hotel
Map Ref → 12-A3

A little bit off the beaten track in the northern side of Deira (Hor Al Anz), this hotel features the 'all you can eat and drink' favourite, Spice Island. Though not as central as some of the other five star establishments in Dubai, the Renaissance is one of the better value hotels.

The Ritz-Carlton, Dubai
Map Ref → 2-C2

With stunning Mediterranean architecture and 138 guest rooms all enjoying a view of the Gulf and their own private balcony or patio, you'll be spending a lot of time just taking in the scenery. Match that with the hotel's exacting international standards, and you are virtually guaranteed plenty of quality for the money you are sure to spend here.

Shangri-La Hotel, Dubai
Map Ref → 9-A2

This 200 metre high structure is located on Sheikh Zayed Road just minutes away from the World Trade Centre Complex. With fantastic views of the coast and the city, 301 guest rooms and suites, 126 serviced apartments, two health clubs, restaurants/bar outlets and a ballroom are a few of the many facilities available.

Sheraton Deira
Map Ref → 12-A3

This hotel is more attractive to the business traveller or heavy duty shopper because of its location (close to the airport and the souks). With 230 rooms, a host of respectable dining outlets and relatively reasonable rates, it is probably one of Dubai's better five star deals.

Sheraton Dubai Creek Hotel
Map Ref → 11-C1

Located right on Dubai's creek, this 255 room hotel has undergone massive renovations. One of Dubai's best Japanese restaurants (Creekside) is housed here. The views from this restaurant are beautiful, the location prime, and the interior, now stunning.

Sheraton Jumeira Beach Resort
Map Ref → 2-C2

The 255 delightfully decorated rooms at this hotel are airy and bright. The hotel offers a full range of sporting facilities and is very close to the Emirates Golf Club. With 12 quality restaurants, a stunning beachfront location and a children's club, this is another good choice for families.

Dubai Five Star Hotels

Sofitel City Centre Hotel
Map Ref → 14-D1

Adjoining the Middle East's largest shopping centre – Deira City Centre, this hotel is great if you're in town for a shopping holiday. Some of the 327 rooms have a stunning view over the Dubai Creek Golf & Yacht Club. The hotel also features good conference facilities, serviced apartments, four restaurants and an English pub.

Taj Palace Hotel
Map Ref → 11-D2

Centrally located in the heart of Deira, this exquisite hotel pulls out all the stops. Boasting the largest rooms in the city, extraordinary service and magnificent interiors, the Taj Palace has created a niche for itself as the only five star hotel in Dubai to adopt a 'no alcohol' policy in respect of Islamic traditions.

Desert Resorts

Al Maha Desert Resort & Spa

Set within a 225-square-kilometre conservation reserve, this luxury getaway describes itself as 'The World's first Arabian eco-tourism resort. Al Maha resembles a typical Bedouin camp, but conditions are anything but basic. Each suite has its own private pool, and guests can dine on their own veranda. Activities include horse riding, camel trekking, and falconry.

Bab Al Shams Desert Resort & Spa

Bab Al Shams, which translates as 'The Gateway to the Sun', is an elegant desert resort in a traditional Arabic Fort setting and is home to the region's first authentic open air Arabic desert restaurant. There's a kids' club, health and leisure facilities including the luxurious Satori Spa, and a desert-side swimming pool and bar with breathtaking views over the dunes.

The Jumeirah Beach Hotel and Burj Al Arab

Youth Hostels

The Dubai Youth Hostel (298 8161), located on Qusais Road, near the Al Mulla Plaza, provides the cheapest accommodation in town. A four star wing was added to the hostel in 2002, almost tripling the number of rooms. In the old wing, there are 53 beds, available for Dhs.45 per night (YHA members) or Dhs.60 (nonmembers) in one of 20 very clean two bed dormitory rooms, including breakfast. Beds in the new wing are Dhs.65 for members and Dhs.80 for nonmembers, including breakfast. Check in is always open.

Accommodation is available for men, women and families. Annual membership costs Dhs.100; family membership is Dhs.300 and for groups of more than 25, the yearly charge is Dhs.1,000. Women travelling alone should check availability, since the management reserves the right to refuse bookings from single women when the hostel is busy with men. The hostel is well served by a cheap, regular bus service into the centre of Dubai and reasonably priced taxis are plentiful. By car, the hostel is about 15 minutes from airport Terminal 1.

Hostels are also located in some of the other emirates, including Sharjah (06 5225070) and Fujairah (09 222 2437). Additional information on other hostels and rates can be found at www.uaeinteract.com.

Camping

Other options ➔ Camping [p.263]

There are no official campsites in the UAE, but there are plenty of places to camp. For sites near Dubai, the desert dunes on the way to Hatta are a good option. So is the Jebel Ali beach, where, if you get there early enough in the cooler months, you can have your own shelter and shower right on the beach. However, camping on the beaches in Dubai has caused a littering problem in the past and you now must apply for a permit from the Municipality (221 5555), free of charge. Although checking of permits is sporadic, fines are given to people found camping without one.

For the best camping options in the UAE, pick up a copy of the *Off-Road Explorer (UAE)*. This guidebook advises you of the best camping spots and how to get there, ideas on what to take and how to prepare as well as where to buy what you'll need for your trip.

Getting Around

Other options ➔ Exploring [p.156]

Cars are the most popular method of getting around Dubai and the Emirates, either by private vehicle or by taxi, probably because public transport is somewhat limited in the region. There is a reasonable public bus service, and walking and cycling are possible but soaring heat and multiple lane roads put most people off. There are a few motorcyclists on the roads, but most of them are couriers or restaurant delivery drivers as Dubai's aggressive driving reputation makes it an unsafe place for two wheelers. There are no trains and trams, but the metro transit system, with initial segments due to be operational by 2009, will see Dubai's first metro running both under and above ground, refer to Key Projects [p.9].

Sheikh Zayed Road

The city's road network is excellent, if not a little complicated, and the majority of roads are two, three or four lanes. They are all well signposted and, in this respect, Dubai is probably the best emirate. Blue or green signs indicate the main areas or locations out of the city and brown signs show heritage sites, places of interest, hospitals etc.

Dubai is a relatively easy city to negotiate. The Creek divides Bur Dubai (to the south) from Deira (to the north). These are further sub-divided into several different areas, such as Satwa in Bur Dubai and Al Hamriya in Deira. The Creek currently three main crossing points – Al Shindagha Tunnel, Maktoum Bridge and

Garhoud Bridge (a third bridge is due for completion in 2006). The Creek can also be crossed by a pedestrian foot tunnel near Shindagha, or by boat (these water taxis are known locally as abras).

To ease the pressure on inner city roads, a ring road or bypass, called the Emirates Road 311, was built at a cost of Dhs.150 million. This connects Abu Dhabi directly to Sharjah and the Northern Emirates. In 2004 Al Khail Rd was opened with the hope of further relieving the congestion on Sheikh Zayed Road. There is also a ban on all trucks on main routes between 06:00 and 22:00. Although never ending roadworks will eventually provide extra lanes and interchanges, they create further road blocks in the meantime.

Lane Discipline?

As so many different nationalities converge on Dubai's roads, there are bound to be some major differences in driving styles, and lane discipline seems to have been thrown out the car window! There is little etiquette for overtaking and cars tend to swerve from the far right to far left lanes in a bid to avoid the slow-paced Nissan trundling along in the middle lane. Aggressive driving is a real problem and you can expect to get incessantly flashed from a speed demon behind you despite there being a truck to your right meaning you have nowhere to go.

Roads are named with white road signs although for many streets these are rarely referred to. People generally rely on landmarks such as shops, hotels, petrol stations or notable buildings to give directions or to get their bearings. Similarly, while there is a numbered address system, few people actually use it. Thus an accommodation 'address' may read something like 'Al Hamriya area, behind Abu Hail Centre, near Happyland supermarket in the pink building', rather than Building 10, Road 63c, Al Hamriya.

To confuse matters further, places may not be referred to by their 'official' name. For instance, Al Jumeira Road is often known as the Beach Road and Interchange One, on Sheikh Zayed Road, is invariably called the Defence roundabout.

Recently, Sheikh Hamdan bin Rashid Al Maktoum ordered certain streets around Dubai to be given the names of prominent Arab cities, such as 'Amman Road', 'Cairo Road', 'Marrakech Road' etc, to demonstrate the strong ties that exist between the UAE and other Arab nations.

You can avoid all this confusion, however, by simply getting a copy of the *Street Map Explorer (Dubai)*. This detailed street guide is a concise and comprehensive compendium of street names cross referenced with an A to Z index of businesses and tourist attractions. In this fast developing city, this handy guidebook is the best tool for navigating this ever growing metropolis.

Car

Other options → Transportation [p.136]

Over the past two decades Dubai has built, and is still building, an impressive network of roads. The Municipality estimates that, in the last ten years, the number of roads in Dubai has literally doubled, although congestion has still become a definite problem, mainly due to the fact that the Creek crossings are limited. There are two bridges and a road tunnel linking the two main districts on either side of the Creek, with another bridge under way (see Key Projects [p.9]). The roads to all major areas are excellent and an eight lane highway heads south from the city to Abu Dhabi, which takes about one to one and a half hours to reach. As the population grows at such an exponential rate only time will tell whether the increasing numbers of cars on the road will result in horrendous traffic jams. Rush hour on Sheikh Zayed Road or on either of the bridges is pretty close to total gridlock now.

e-Service

For traffic updates on Bur Dubai and Deira, log on to www.dm.gov.ae. This e-Service provides a direct traffic broadcast through cameras installed on all important roads and junctions, snapshots of which are uploaded on the Website every 30 seconds. Maps of the areas help you click on to your choice of road (and camera).

Driving Habits & Regulations

Whilst the infrastructure is superb, the general standard of driving is not. The UAE has one of the world's highest death rates per capita due to traffic accidents. According to the Dubai Police, one person is killed in a traffic related accident every 48 hours, and there is one injury every four hours – not the most positive statistics. Drivers often seem completely unaware of other cars on the road and fast, aggressive driving, swerving, pulling out suddenly, lane hopping, tail-gating or drifting, happen far too regularly.

One move to help the situation on the roads was a ban placed on using handheld mobile phones whilst driving. Predictably the sales of hands free systems rocketed before people went back to their old bad habits.

In Dubai, you drive on the right hand side of the road, and it is mandatory to wear seatbelts in the front seats. Children under ten years of age are no longer allowed to sit in the front of a car. This ban is now countrywide, though you'll still see people driving with their child on their lap.

Details of fines for any traffic violations are found on the Dubai Police Website www.dubaipolice.gov.ae. Speeding fines are Dhs.200 and parking fines start at Dhs.100. You are also issued a certain number of black points against your licence according to the particular violation. Most fines are paid when you renew your annual car registration. However, parking tickets appear on your windscreen and you have a week or two to pay – the amount increases if you don't pay within the time allotted on the back of the ticket.

ZERO Tolerance!

The Dubai Police exercise a strict zero tolerance policy on drinking and driving. This means that if you have had ANYTHING to drink, you are much better off taking a taxi home or having a friend who has consumed nothing drive you home. If you get into an accident, whether it is your fault or not, and you fail a blood-alcohol test you could find yourself spending a night in a police cell before a trial in Dubai Courts, after which short jail sentences may be applied. In addition your insurance is automatically void. Police have also increased the number of random drink-driving checks. Penalties are severe, so the simple message is to be safe: if you're going to drink, don't even think of driving.

Try to keep a reasonable stopping distance between yourself and the car in front; you also need to be more aware of the other cars on the road and check your mirrors frequently. You may consider yourself the safest of drivers but with so many bad drivers on the road it pays to be extra cautious.

If you wish to report a traffic violation, call the Traffic Police's toll free hotline (800 4353). The Dubai Police Website (www.dubaipolice.gov.ae) offers all information relevant to driving, such as traffic violations, road maps, contact numbers, etc. For complete information on Highway Codes, safety and Dubai's road rules, check out the *Safe Driving Handbook* available from the Emirates Motor Sports Federation (282 7111).

Speed Limits

Speed limits are usually 60 – 80 km around town, while roads to other parts of the Emirates are 100 – 120 km. The speed limit is clearly indicated on road signs and there is no leeway for breaking the limit. Both fixed and movable radar traps, and the Dubai Traffic Police, are there to catch the unwary violator. In 2001, 361,500 fines were given for speeding – that number amounted to 64% of all traffic violations. On the spot traffic fines for certain offences have been introduced, but in most cases, you won't know you've received a fine until you check on the Website or renew your vehicle registration.

Traffic Jam Session

Be smart. Avoid a traffic jam by tuning in to any of the following radio channels – Al Arabiya 98.9 FM, Al Khallejiya 100.9 FM, Dubai 92, Channel 4 FM (104.8 FM), and Emirates 1 FM (99.3FM, 100.5 FM). Regular updates about the traffic situation on main roads are provided throughout the day, forewarning you if a certain road is blocked, so you can take an alternative route.

Driving Licence

Visitors to Dubai have two options for driving. You can drive a rental vehicle with either an international driving licence or a licence from your country of origin. The latter is applicable only if you are from one of the countries listed on the transfer list (see [p.26]).

If you wish to drive a private vehicle, you must first go to the Traffic Police to obtain a temporary licence. Please note that unless you have a Dubai driving licence, either permanent or temporary, you are not insured to drive a private vehicle. For permanent licences see Driving Licence, New Residents [p.72].

For more information see the *Zappy Explorer*.

Accidents

If you are involved in a traffic accident, however minor, you must remain with your car at the accident scene and report the incident to the Traffic Police, then wait for them to arrive. Unfortunately when you have an accident, you become the star attraction as the passing traffic slows to a crawl thanks to rubberneckers. Stationery vehicles that block the road after an accident as they wait for the police can cause serious tail backs. While you are now allowed to move your vehicle out of traffic while you wait for the police, you should only do so if no-one is injured and you and the other driver agree on the fault. When the police arrive you will have to explain how the accident happened. If the vehicles have been moved and there is a discrepancy between your version and the other driver's it could be harder to fight your case.

Stray animals (mostly camels) are something else to avoid on some of the desert through roads in the UAE. If the animal hits your vehicle and causes damage or injury, the animal's owner should pay compensation, but if you are found to have been speeding or driving recklessly, you must compensate the owner of the animal – this can be expensive.

See also: Traffic Accidents [p.144].

Non Drivers

In addition to dealing with bad drivers, you will find that many pedestrians and cyclists also seem to have a death wish! The few cyclists who do brave the roads will often be cycling towards you on the wrong side of the road, invariably without lights if it's at night. Pedestrians often step out dangerously close to oncoming traffic and a lack of convenient, safe crossings makes life for those on foot especially difficult. However, the numbers of pedestrian footbridges and pedestrian operated traffic lights are gradually increasing – but unfortunately at a very slow pace.

Parking

In most areas of Dubai, parking is readily available and people rarely have to walk too far in the heat. Increasing numbers of pay and display parking meters are appearing around the busier parts of the city. The areas are clearly marked and the charge ranges from Dhs.1 – 2 for an hour. Try to have loose change with you since there are no automatic change machines available. Meters operate between 08:00 – 13:00 and 16:00 – 21:00 Saturday to Thursday. If you haven't purchased a ticket, you may be unlucky enough to receive one from the police for the bargain price of Dhs.100.

Petrol/Gas Stations

Petrol stations in the Emirates are numerous and run by Emarat, EPPCO and ENOC (Adnoc in Abu Dhabi). Most offer extra services, such as a car wash or a shop selling all those necessities of life that you forgot to buy at the supermarket.

The majority of visitors will find petrol far cheaper than in their home countries – prices range from Dhs.4.50 per gallon for Special (95 octane) to Dhs.5.50 for Super (98 octane).

At present the pump price is capped by the government, and the sharp rises in oil prices at the end of 2004 led to complaints by the petrol station companies that they were actually selling petrol at a loss. It's possible that this could lead to a price rise in the future. Interestingly, the UAE must be one of the few countries in the world where diesel fuel actually costs more than other fuels.

Blood Money

If you are driving and cause someone's death, you may be liable to pay a sum of money, known as 'blood money', to the deceased's family. The limit for this has been set at Dhs.200,000 per victim and your car insurance will cover this cost (hence the higher premiums). However, insurance companies will only pay if they cannot find a way of claiming that the insurance is invalid (i.e., if the driver was driving without a licence or, for example, under the influence of alcohol). The deceased's family can, however, waive the right to blood money if they feel merciful.

Car Hire

All the main car rental companies, plus a few extra, are in Dubai and it is best to shop around as the rates vary considerably. The larger more reputable firms generally have more reliable vehicles and a greater capacity to help in an emergency (an important factor when handling the trying times following an accident). Depending on the agent, cars can be hired with or without a driver, and the minimum hire period is usually 24 hours. Prices range from Dhs.70 a day for smaller cars to Dhs.1,000 for limousines. Comprehensive insurance is essential (and make sure that it includes personal accident coverage).

The rental company will also arrange temporary local driving licences for visitors. To rent a car, you are usually required to produce a copy of your passport, a valid international or national driving licence and two photographs. Your licence needs to be from any of the following countries: Austria, Belgium, Canada, Denmark, Finland, France, Germany, Greece, Holland, Ireland, Italy, Japan, Norway, Singapore, Spain, Sweden, Switzerland, Turkey, UK and the USA.

See also: Vehicle Leasing [p.136].

Car Rental Agencies

Autolease	282 6565
Avis Rent a Car	224 5219
Budget	282 3030
Diamond Lease Rent a Car P.139	331 3172
Hertz Rent a Car	282 4422
Thrifty Car Rental P.xvii	224 5404
United Car Rentals	266 6286

Taxi

If you don't have a car, taxis are the most common way of getting around. Currently, visitors have the choice of metered taxis operated under franchise from Dubai Transport Corporation (DTC).

In 2000, the DTC cleverly decided to take over the entire taxi business in Dubai and private taxis were phased out by the end of the year. There are four taxi companies operating a fixed fare structure – Dubai Transport Corporation (sand/camel coloured cars), Cars Taxis (white with blue and red stripes), Metro Taxis (sand coloured) and National Taxis (silver).

Pickup fare is either Dhs.3 or Dhs.3.50, depending on time of day or taxi company. But the starting fare inside the airport area is an extortionate Dhs.20. It is also possible to hire a taxi for 12 or 24 hour periods.

No Passport Required

Although rental companies may ask for one, your original passport must never be handed over. When renting a car, your passport details are added into the system, which has an electronic link with the Dubai Traffic Police Department. Hence, passports need not be surrendered for security anymore. If you are asked to hand over your passport, don't... and report the matter to the police.

Towards the end of 2002, three non metered taxi companies were once again permitted to work on Dubai's roads. Under Dubai Transport franchise as well, non metered cabs, such as Dubai Taxi, Khaibar Taxi and Palestine Taxi, allow customers the option of bargaining the fare down. A word of warning: determine the fare before the ride and try to find out what the normal cab fare should be first.

Cabs can be flagged down by the side of the road or you can make a Dubai Transport taxi booking by calling 208 0808. If you make a booking, you will pay a Dhs.4.50 starting fare. Alternatively, if you drop Dhs.1 into one of the 15 electronic booking machines dotted around town, a taxi is immediately despatched to the machine's location.

To make life a little more confusing, taxi drivers in Dubai occasionally lack any knowledge of the city and passengers may have to direct them. Start with the area of destination and then choose a major landmark, such as a hotel, roundabout or shopping centre. Then narrow it down as you get closer. If you are going to a new place, try to phone for instructions first – you will often be given a distinctive landmark as a starting point. It's also helpful to take the phone number of your destination with you, in case you're going around in circles trying to find it. If your taxi driver is well and truly lost, ask him to radio his control point for instructions. For residents, once you have provided instructions to Dubai Transport when you telephone their automated service on the above number you can order a taxi by the push of one button without having to explain your location time and time again.

Illegal Pickups

There is also an illegal taxi system, where unlicensed drivers in unmarked cars tout for passengers at the roadside. These cars are unregulated and are not insured to carry passengers. This practice is not looked upon favourably by Dubai Police and hefty fines are levied on convicted drivers.

Taxi Companies

Cars Taxis	269 3344
Dubai Transport	208 0808
Gulf Radio Taxi	223 6666
Metro Taxis	267 3222
National Taxis	339 0002
Sharjah: Delta Taxis	06 559 8598

Airport Bus

The Dubai Municipality, in conjunction with the Dubai Department of Civil Aviation, operates airport buses departing from and arriving at Dubai International Airport every 30 minutes, 24 hours a day. Currently, there are two loop routes: Route 401 services Deira, while Route 402 services Bur Dubai. The fare is Dhs.3 and is paid when boarding the bus. Airport bus route maps are available at Dubai International Airport.

Route 401: Terminal 1 – DNATA – Al Maktoum Rd – Deira Taxi Station – Al Sabkha Bus Station

Route 402: Terminal 1 – Deira City Centre – Al Karama – Golden Sands – Al Mankhool – Al Ghubaiba Bus Station

Dubai Municipality Bus Information (800 4848)

Bus

Dubai Municipality's Transport Section operates around 59 bus routes for the emirate serving the main residential and commercial areas, from Al Qusais in the north east to Jebel Ali in the southwest and some destinations out of the city. Around 150,000 passengers are transported daily. However, the service is gradually being extended, with more buses covering more routes. Efforts are also being made to display better timetables and route plans at bus stations to encourage people to use this inexpensive method of transport. While the buses are air-conditioned and modern they do tend to be rather crowded.

In Deira, the main bus station is near the Gold Souk and in Bur Dubai, on Al Ghubaiba Road near the Plaza Cinema. Buses run at regular intervals from 06:00 to around 23:00, and fares are cheap at Dhs.1 – 3 per journey. Fares are paid to the driver when you board, so try to have the exact change ready. Also available are monthly discount tickets and e-Go cards (see below). Buses also go from Dubai to Al Khawaneej, Al Awir and Hatta for very reasonable prices; a one way ticket to Hatta, which is 100 km away, is Dhs.7. Dubai Transport also operates a service to and from Al Arouba Rd and Al Wahda in Sharjah to both Bur Dubai and Deira. This service operates every ten minutes.

Dubai Transport Corporation offers a minibus service in addition to their taxis. These buses run to Ajman, Umm Al Quwain, Ras Al Khaimah, Fujairah, Al Ain and Abu Dhabi. The minibuses are modern, air conditioned and offer a good value service to the cities of the UAE. Unfortunately, at present, these services only carry passengers on the outward journeys. Anyone wishing to return to Dubai by public transport must make alternative arrangements.

- Dubai Transport – Northern Emirates (286 1616 or 227 3840)
- Dubai Municipality – Bus information (800 4848) and lost & found (285 0700)

e-Go Card

This electronic smart card helps bus passengers save time and avoids the hassle of small change. Available for Dhs.5, the e-Go card can be filled with credits (Dhs.20 for the first time and multiples of Dhs.10 after). When placed on the ticket machine in the bus, the ticket amount is automatically deducted, and the balance is adjusted and stored. The monthly pass (Dhs.90) gives multiple ride options to bus users as well as offering various shopping discounts.

Train

Currently, there are no trains or trams, but plans for a metro transit system are underway with an expected completion date of 2009. See Key Projects [p.9] for more information.

Air

Other options → Meet & Greet [p.28]

Dubai's location at the crossroads of Europe, Asia and Africa makes it an easily accessible city. London is seven hours away, Frankfurt six, Hong Kong eight, and Nairobi four. Most major cities have direct flights to Dubai, many with a choice of operator. There are also now direct flights to North America and Australia.

Airlines

Air Arabia	06 508 8888
Air France `P.7`	294 5899
Air India	227 6787
Alitalia	224 2256
Austrian Airlines	294 5675
British Airways	307 5777
Cathay Pacific Airways	295 0400
CSA Czech Airlines	295 9502
Cyprus Airways	221 5325
Emirates	214 4444
Etihad	02 505 8000
Gulf Air	271 3111
KLM Royal Dutch Airlines	335 5777
Kuwait Airways	228 1106
Lufthansa	343 2121
Malaysia Airlines	397 0250
Olympic Airways	221 4761
Oman Air	351 8080
PIA	222 2154
Qatar Airways	229 2229
Royal Brunei Airlines	351 4111
Royal Jet	02 575 7000
Royal Jordanian	266 8667
Royal Nepal Airlines	295 5444
Saudi Arabian Airlines	295 7747
Singapore Airlines	223 2300
South African Airways	397 0766
Sri Lankan Airlines	294 9119
Swiss	294 5051
United Airlines	316 6942

Dubai International Airport is a world renowned airport, handling almost 14 million passengers in 2003. An ambitious US $540 million expansion programme has transformed the already excellent airport into a state of the art facility, ready to meet the needs of passengers for the next 30 years. Work has already started on an even larger third terminal due to service all Emirates flights. See Key Projects [p.9] for more information.

General Info

Getting Around

Currently, more than 90 airlines take advantage of Dubai's open skies policy, operating to and from over 120 destinations. Dubai's award winning airline, Emirates, is based here and operates scheduled services to over 70 destinations.

There are currently two terminals, which are located on different sides of the airport (a 15 – 30 minute taxi ride, depending on the traffic). Both terminals offer car rental, hotel reservations and bureau de change services. Most of the better known airlines use Terminal 1, but a selection of over 20 airlines operates from Terminal 2. Primarily focused on the former Soviet countries, the airlines include Chelyabinsk Airlines, Nizhegorodsky and Zitotrans (yes, they do exist!).

Duty Free shops are located in both the arrival and departure halls, although the arrivals hall outlet is limited. All travellers have the opportunity to enter the prestigious raffle to win a luxury car, which can be shipped anywhere in the world (tickets Dhs.500 each).

Dubai National Airline Travel Agency (DNATA) (316 6666), is home to most of the main airline offices in Dubai. Here, you can make enquiries, collect tickets etc. DNATA is located in the Airline Centre building on Sheikh Zayed Road (Map Ref 5-C4).

Flight Info: 216 6666

Launched in October 2003, Etihad Airways, the national airline of the UAE (based in Abu Dhabi), has ambitious plans to grow exponentially (eight carriers and 16 destinations by end 2004). Another newcomer is the budget airline, Air Arabia (based in Sharjah). The attractions of this airline are reduced costs and ticketless travel. While neither fly directly to Dubai, they do provide an alternative to visitors coming to the UAE, often at more affordable rates and are not a million miles away by taxi from Dubai (Abu Dhabi is approximately a 90 minute drive and Sharjah 45 minutes).

Boat

Opportunities for getting around by boat in the Emirates are limited... unless you wish to travel by dhow, and then your opportunities are limitless. Crossing the Creek in low wooden boats (known locally as abras) is a very common method of transport for many people in Dubai. See Exploring [p.150]. There is a cruise ship terminal at Port Rashid, currently the only dedicated complex in the region. It comprises a 335 metre quay with simultaneous berthing capacity for two ships, and a 3,300 square metre terminal.

It is also possible to travel from Dubai and Sharjah to several ports in Iran by boat, including a hydrofoil and traditional Dhow option. Prices vary between Dhs.130 – 250, and journey time can be up to 12 hours depending on the travel option chosen. For more information, contact the Oasis Freight Co. (06 559 6325).

Abras on Dubai Creek

Walking & Biking

Other options → Cycling [p.266]

Cities in the Emirates are generally very car orientated and not designed to encourage either walking or cycling. Additionally, summer temperatures of 45° C are not conducive to fast pedalling!

In the winter months, temperatures are perfect for outdoor activities. At this time of year, walking is a popular evening pastime, especially in the parks, along the seafront in Deira and Jumeira, or on the pedestrian paths along both sides of the Creek.

Cycling can be an enjoyable way to explore the city – you can cover more ground than on foot and see more than from a car. However, a lot of care is needed when cycling in traffic, since drivers in speeding cars pay little attention to anything with less than four wheels!.

In the quieter areas, many of the roads are wide enough to accommodate cyclists as well as cars, and where there are footpaths, they are often broad and in good repair. There are no dedicated bike lanes, apart from a 1.2 km cycling track along Al Mamzar Corniche (which should take all of 6 minutes to cover!).

Cash is still the preferred method of payment in the Emirates, although credit cards are now widely accepted. Foreign currencies and travellers' cheques can be exchanged in licensed exchange offices, banks and hotels – as usual, a passport is required for exchanging travellers' cheques.

There is more confidence in cheques these days; strict enforcement of laws concerning passing bad cheques has helped and it's a criminal offence to bounce a cheque.

Exchange Rates

Foreign Currency (FC)	1 Unit FC = x Dhs	Dhs.1 = x FC
Australia	2.78	0.35
Bahrain	9.74	0.1
Bangladesh	0.06	15.82
Canada	2.99	0.33
Cyprus	8.55	0.11
Denmark	0.65	1.51
Euro	4.88	0.2
Hong Kong	0.47	2.11
India	0.08	12.01
Japan	0.03	28.54
Jordan	5.21	0.19
Kuwait	12.52	0.07
Malaysia	0.96	1.03
New Zealand	2.6	0.38
Oman	9.56	0.1
Pakistan	0.06	16.19
Philippines	0.06	15.31
Qatar	1	0.99
Saudi Arabia	0.97	1.02
Singapore	2.23	0.44
South Africa	0.64	1.55
Sri Lanka	0.03	28.61
Sweden	0.54	1.83
Switzerland	3.18	0.31
Thailand	0.09	10.73
UK	7.07	0.14
USA	3.67	0.27

Rates updated — December 2004

Local Currency

The monetary unit is the 'Dirham' (Dhs.), which is divided into 100 'fils'. The currency is also referred to as AED (Arab Emirate Dirham). Notes come in denominations of Dhs.5, Dhs.10, Dhs.20, Dhs.50, Dhs.100, Dhs.200, Dhs.500 and Dhs.1,000. Coin denominations are Dhs.1, 50 fils and 25 fils, but be warned, there are two versions of each coin and

they can look very similar. Because 5 and 10 fil coins are rarely available, you will often not receive the exact change.

The Dirham has been pegged to the US dollar since the end of 1980, at a mid rate of US$1 ~ Dhs.3.6725. Exchange rates of all major currencies are published daily in the local newspapers.

Banks

The well structured and ever growing network of local and international banks, strictly controlled by the UAE Central Bank, offers a full range of commercial and personal banking services. Transfers can be made without difficulty as there is no exchange control and the dirham is freely convertible. Many banks have also introduced an on-line service.

For further information on opening a bank account in the UAE, refer to the *Zappy Explorer (Dubai)*.

Normal banking hours are Saturday to Wednesday 08:00 – 13:00 (some are also open 16:30 – 18:30). Thursday 08:00 – 12:00.

Main Banks

ABN AMRO Bank	351 2200
Abu Dhabi Commercial Bank	295 8888
Abu Dhabi National Bank	222 6141
Bank of Sharjah	282 7278
Barclays Bank Plc	335 1555
Citibank	324 5000
Dubai Islamic Bank	295 9999
Emirates Bank International	225 6256
HSBC Bank Middle East I.F.C.▶	353 5000
Lloyds TSB Bank Plc P.85▶	342 2000
Mashreq Bank	222 3333
National Bank of Dubai P.87▶	222 2111
RAK Bank	224 8000
Standard Chartered	800 4949
Union National Bank	800 2600

ATMs

Most banks operate ATMs (Automatic Teller Machines, also known as cash points or service tills) which accept a wide range of cards although the number of ATMs around Dubai is somewhat limited and you may find you have to go out of your way to get cash. Most shopping centres have at least one ATM and a few hotels have an ATM in their lobby but if you're on a night out and want cash you will probably have to make a stop on your way. If you are lucky you may find one at a petrol station. For non UAE based cards, the exchange rates used in the transaction are normally extremely competitive and the process is faster and much less hassle than traditional travellers' cheques.

Common systems accepted around Dubai: American Express, Cirrus, Global Access, MasterCard, Plus System and Visa.

Money Exchanges

Money exchanges are available all over Dubai, offering good service and reasonable exchange rates, often better than the banks. Additionally, hotels will usually exchange money and travellers' cheques at the standard (and not very good) hotel rate.

Exchange house hours: 08:30 – 13:00 and 16:30 – 20:30

Exchange Centres	
Al Ansari Exchange	335 3599
Al Fardan Exchange P.51	228 0004
Al Ghurair Exchange	295 3530
First Gulf Exchange	351 5777
Orient Exchange Company	226 7154
Thomas Cook Al Rostamani	295 6777
Wall Street Exchange Centre	800 4871
World Link Exchange Co. (LLC)	225 2666

Credit Cards

Most shops, hotels and restaurants accept the major credit cards (American Express, Diners Club, MasterCard and Visa). Smaller retailers are sometimes less keen to accept credit cards and you may have to pay an extra five percent for processing (and it's no use telling them that it's a contravention of the card company rules – you have to take it or leave it!). You can, however, call your local credit card company to lodge a complaint if you are charged this five percent 'fee'. Conversely, if you are paying in cash, you may sometimes be allowed a discount – it's certainly worth enquiring.

Tipping

Tipping practices are similar to most parts of the world. An increasing number of restaurants include a service charge, although it is unlikely to end up with your waiter. Otherwise, ten per cent is the usual. See Going Out for more information [p.322].

Media & Communications

Newspapers/Magazines

The Gulf News, Khaleej Times and The Gulf Today (all Dhs.2 and Dhs.3 on Fridays) are the daily English language newspapers in the UAE. Arabic newspapers include Al Bayan, Al-Ittihad and Al-Khaleej. There is also the free daily paper, 7 Days, that is circulated early morning to residential buildings.

Foreign newspapers, most prominently French, German, British and Asian, are readily available in supermarkets and hotel book shops, although they are more expensive than at home (about Dhs.8 – 12) and slightly out of date. Also available are good hobby magazines, such as computing, photography, sports, and women's magazines (expect to find censored portions or occasionally, even whole pages or sections missing). These are expensive, usually costing two or three times more than at home (between Dhs.30 – 50). However, there are a number of locally produced magazines worth a flick over a coffee – for celebrity gossip there's Ahlan! and for fashion and lifestyle try Viva or Emirates Woman.

Further Reading

Visitors will find a variety of books and magazines available on the Emirates, from numerous coffee table books (such as *Images of Dubai & the UAE* or *Dubai: Tomorrow's City Today*) to magazines with details of aerobics classes. Monthly publications range from the free Connector or Aquarius (both focusing on health and beauty) to the event focused Time Out and What's On.

Guides to the region include the Lonely Planet series, as well as Explorer Publishing's *Abu Dhabi Explorer* and *Oman Explorer* (formerly *Muscat Explorer*). *Sharjah The Guide* and the *Spectrum Guide to the United Arab Emirates* also offer more information on the region.

For the finer points on life in Dubai, books to refer to include: the *Family Explorer (Dubai & Abu Dhabi)*, a family guide to life in the UAE; the *Zappy Explorer (Dubai)*, a step by step guide to the administrative procedures and red tape in Dubai; the *Off-Road Explorer (UAE)*, the ultimate outdoor guide to the region; and the *Underwater Explorer (UAE)*, a detailed guide to scuba diving in the area. These can be found in all good book shops around town.

Easy... Fast... Global Transactions...

When time is money and the need of the hour are speed, security and reliability, trust Al Fardan to take better care of you!
Be it sending money, exchanging currency or business transactions, our long years of experience
is all the reassurance you need with your hard earned savings.

Services:

Demand Draft | Courier Draft | Electronic Transfer | Mail Transfer | Telex Transfer | Travellers Cheques | Foreign Currency sale
and purchase | Cash against credit cards | Al Ahli Filahza | Instant cash | MoneyGram | Cash Passport | Cash Switch.

AL FARDAN EXCHANGE

It's about service

Call our toll free number 800 5440

AD OFFICE : Liwa St. Amin Tower, Abu Dhabi, Tel: 02-6223222, **BRANCH OFFICES: ABU DHABI:**, Tourist Club, Opp. Abu Dhabi Mall,
Tel: 02-6454111, **DEIRA:** Al Maktoum Street Deira, Tel: 04-2280004, **BUR DUBAI:** Tel: 04-3513535, **JEBEL ALI:** Tel: 04 - 8814455,
SHARJAH:, Tel: 06-5635581, 5635371 **SHARJAH:**, Al Fardan Center Tel: 06-5561955, **AL AIN:**, Al Takhtit Street:Tel: 03-7554325,
7555934, Souk Branch Al Ain, Tel: 03-7661010, **RUWAIS:** Tel: 02-8774877.

Introducing...

Visit us www.alfardanexchange.com, Email: exchange@alfardangroup.com

Post & Courier Services

Other options ➔ Postal Services [p.114]

Empost is the sole provider of postal services in the UAE. Plenty of courier companies operate both locally and internationally, such as Aramex, DHL, Federal Express, etc. Empost also operates an express mail service, Mumtaz Express.

Post within the UAE takes two to three days to be delivered. Mail sent to USA, Europe, Australia and India is usually delivered within ten days. Airmail letters cost Dhs.3 – 6 to send, depending on weight, and postcards cost Dhs.1 – 2. Aerogrammes can be bought for Dhs.2 each from post offices and save the bother of buying a stamp before posting.

Stamps can be bought from post offices and certain shops – card shops often sell a limited range of stamps. Deira City Centre and Lamcy Plaza shopping malls both have full postal facilities, and some Emarat petrol stations now have them too. Red post boxes for outbound mail are located at post offices and near shopping centres. Hotels will also handle your mail if you are a guest.

There's no house address based postal service; all incoming mail is delivered to a PO Box at a central location and has to be collected from there.

Courier Companies

Aramex	286 5000
DHL P.53	800 4004
Emirates Post	800 5858
Federal Express	800 4050
Immex – Immediate Courier Express LLC	282 4444
Memo Express	211 8111
TNT	285 3939
UPS	800 4774

Radio

The UAE has a number of commercial radio stations broadcasting in a range of languages, from Arabic and English to French, Hindi, Malayalam and Urdu. Daily schedules can be found in the local newspapers.

Operating 24 hours a day, everyday, there are four main English language stations. Dubai 92, Channel 4 FM (104.8 FM), and Emirates 1 FM (99.3FM, 100.5 FM) all play modern music for a 'younger' audience, while Emirates 2 FM (90.5FM, 98.5 FM) broadcasts a mixture of news, talk shows and modern music. Abu Dhabi Capital Radio (100.5 FM) can also be picked up in Dubai playing popular music. QBS

Dubai (97.5FM, 102.6FM) focuses on radio plays and jazz music. Dubai Eye (103.8) plays less music and concentrates more on talk radio, and topics relevant to Dubai residents and tourists.

Umm Al Quwain's Hum FM (106.2 FM) broadcasts mainly in Hindi with a bit of English, and if you want to hear Arabic music, tune in to 93.9 FM. With the right equipment, the BBC World Service can also be picked up.

Television/Satellite TV

Other options ➔ Television [p.114]
Satellite TV & Radio [p.116]

Local television offers four channels: Dubai 2, 10 and 41 show Arabic programmes, while Dubai 33 broadcasts mainly in English. Emirates Dubai Television broadcasts by satellite throughout the world in Arabic and English.

There are also a great variety of services available via satellite. Most hotels and hotel apartments have satellite television available for residents and many apartment blocks have dishes installed, ready for residents to acquire a decoder. Satellite programmes that can be received range from news programmes, international entertainment or films to sports, cartoons and current events. News channels from the US and the UK are readily available, as are sitcoms like *Friends* (First Net and Showtime) and soaps like *Eastenders* (Orbit). Sports channels, movie channels, nature channels such as National Geographic and music shows are all available. Digital television with similar channels to satellite is also on the increase.

Telephones

Other options ➔ Telephone [p.112]

Telecommunications are very good, both within the UAE and internationally. While all communication was once only provided by the monopoly organisation, Emirates Telecommunications Corporation, known as Etisalat there are now other companies in the market such as Sahm, who service the telecommunication needs of Emaar properties. Plans are in place for the introduction of a two new mobile licences, but as yet neither have been awarded. Calls from a landline to another landline within Dubai are free of charge and direct dialling is possible to over 170 countries. GPRS, WAP and Hot Spot services are also available in the UAE.

Public payphones are all over the city. A few accept coins, but the majority require phone cards, which

Ten kilos or ten tons, DHL moves the Middle East.

With DHL's Road Express, you can now transport all your light or heavy goods across the region with total peace of mind and reliability from the world's leading provider of customised logistics solutions. Call us now toll free on 800 4004.

WE MOVE THE WORLD **=DHL=**

are available at most shops and supermarkets. They come in a variety of values, but for international calls, beware – the units vanish at a truly amazing rate. Etisalat has a new generation of prepaid phone cards called 'Smart Cards', which are available for Dhs.30.

Etisalat

Area Codes & Useful Numbers

UAE Country Code	+971	Directory Enquiries	181
Abu Dhabi	02	Operator	100
Ajman	06	Etisalat Information	144
Al Ain	03	Fault Reports	171
Dubai	04	Billing Information	142
Fujairah	09	Etisalat Contact Centre	101
Hatta	04	Speaking Clock	140
Jebel Ali	04	Recharge Al Wasel	122
Ras al Khaimah	07	Al Wasel Credit Balance	121
Sharjah	06	To dial a typical Dubai	
Umm Al Quwain	06	number from overseas, it	
Mobile Telephones	050	is 00 **971 4** 335 3520	

Internet

Other options → Internet Cafés [p.410]
The Internet [p.113]

The UAE has embraced the Internet revolution. Internet or cyber cafés around town provide easy and relatively cheap access. Internet cafés charge between Dhs.5 and Dhs.10 per hour. Using a prepaid calling card, it is approx. Dhs.7 per hour. Subscriber rates are significantly less, and can be as low as Dhs.1 off-peak.

Etisalat is the main provider of Internet services within the UAE and in order to maintain the country's moral and cultural values, all sites are provided via Etisalat's proxy server. This occasionally results in frustrated users being unable to access perfectly reasonable sites. If you come across such a site, you can report it to Etisalat. Please see [p.55] for helpful Websites and numbers.

You can also surf the Internet without being a subscriber. All that's needed is a computer with a modem and a regular phone line. To dial 'n' surf, simply call 500 5555. For information on charges, see Dial 'n' Surf on [p.114].

Websites

There are numerous Websites on Dubai and the Emirates in general, and new ones are being uploaded all the time. Some are more interesting, successful and relevant than others. The table on [p.55] lists those that the Explorer team has found to be the most useful – if you have any suggestions for other relevant and helpful Websites let us know so we can include them in the next edition.

UAE Annual Events

Throughout the year, Dubai hosts a number of well established annual events, some of which have been running for years. The events described below are the most popular and regular fixtures on Dubai's social calendar.

Camel Racing

A traditional sport, the sight of these ungainly animals, ridden by young boys, is an extraordinary spectacle. Racing camels can change hands for as much as Dhs.10 million! Morning races take place throughout the year at the Nad Al Sheba club and start very early, you need to be there by 07:00 as the races are over by 08:30. Admission is free.

Desert Rallies   www.emsf.ae

The highest profile event is the Desert Challenge [p.57], which is the climax of the World Cup in Cross Country Rallying. It attracts top rally drivers from all over the world and is held in October or November, depending on other events. There are numerous other events throughout the year, for information contact EMSF (282 7111).

See also: *Emirates Motor Sports Federation – Rally Driving [p.284] and UAE Desert Challenge [p.57]*

Websites

Dubai Information

www.arabicnews.com	News of the Arab world
www.crazyspin.com	Lists current and upcoming events
www.diningindubai.com	Make reservations online after consulting the Dubai Explorer
www.doctorelite.com	24 hour doctor/pharmacy/medical service
www.dubai.com	Online newspaper type site – Dubai and international news
www.dubaicityguide.com	Updated daily, lists upcoming and current events
www.dubailocator.com	A superb interactive map site for Dubai
www.dubailook.com	Lists current and upcoming events
www.dubaishoppingmalls.com	List of major shopping centres around Dubai
www.expatsite.com	Find out what's going on back home
www.explorer-publishing.com	Our site!
www.godubai.com	Covers all the events and news of Dubai
www.gulf-news.com	Local newspaper
www.khaleejtimes.com	Local newspaper
www.roomservice-uae.com	Deliveries from your favourite restaurants
www.sheikhmohammed.co.ae	His Highness Sheikh Mohammed Bin Rashid Al Maktoum's site
www.sheikhzayed.com	A site dedicated to the life of the late UAE President
www.uaemall.com	Shop online in the UAE
www.weather.com	Weather in the UAE

Business/Industry

www.dcci.org	Dubai Chamber of Commerce & Industry
www.djd.gov.ae	Dubai Courts (Department of Justice – Dubai)
www.dubaidutyfree.com	Dubai Duty Free
www.dewa.gov.ae	Dubai Electricity & Water Authority
www.dm.gov.ae	Dubai Municipality
www.dubai2003.ae	Dubai 2003 IMF site
www.dubaiairport.com	Dubai International Airport
www.dubaipolice.gov.ae	Dubai Police Headquarters
www.dubaitourism.co.ae	Department of Tourism & Commerce Marketing (DTCM)
www.dwtc.com	Dubai World Trade Centre
www.dxbtraffic.gov.ae	Dubai Traffic Police – great for viewing traffic fines
www.emirates.net.ae	Emirates Internet – Dubai's Internet service provider
www.etisalat.co.ae	Etisalat – Dubai's telephone service provider

Embassies

www.dwtc.com/directory/governme.htm	Embassies in Dubai
www.embassyworld.com	Embassies abroad

Hotels/Sports

Hotel details listed in General Information [p.36],
and sporting organisations in Activities

Wheels

www.4x4motors.com	A little more sand than tar
www.diamondlease.com	Car leasing/rental
www.motorhighway.com	Buy a vehicle online
www.valuewheels.com	Buy a vehicle online

Dhow Racing
www.dimc-uae.com

This traditional Arabic sport is great to watch as there is something very enigmatic about wooden dhows, especially when they race. The vessels are usually 40 – 60 ft in length and are either powered by men (up to 100 oarsmen per dhow) or by the wind. Fixed races are held throughout the year as well as on special occasions, such as National Day. Most events are held at Dubai International Marine Club.

See also: Dhow Charters [p.266]

Dog Show, The

Held at Nad Al Sheba, The Dog Show is a popular family outing and the only show of its kind in the Middle East. You are guaranteed to see both pedigree and crossbreed dogs of every shape, size and colour imaginable. One of the most popular events is the 'Dog Most Like its Owner' competition – the likenesses are uncanny!

Dubai Desert Classic
www.dubaidesertclassic.com

Incorporated into the European PGA Tour in 1989, this popular golfing tournament attracts growing numbers of world class players.

Dubai Int'l Film Festival
www.dubaimediacity.com

Having debuted in December 2004, this promises to be an annual event and marks an achievement for the film industry in Dubai. Last year it was hosted at Madinat Jumeirah. The festival brings together a collection of international films, including those from the Arab world.

Dubai Int'l Jazz Festival
www.chilloutproductions.com

If you are looking for three nights of chilled moods, then this is the place to be. Established as annual event over the last few years, this festival attracts a strong line up of top artists from all around the world, and is growing from strength to strength each year. Part of the Dubai Shopping Festival calendar, it will be held in Dubai Media City in February 2005.

Dubai Marathon
www.dubaimarathon.org

Normally held in January (so good for working off that festive tummy!), the Dubai Marathon now offers a full marathon as well as a 10 km and 3 km fun run. Attracting all types of runners, the emphasis here is more on fun and participation than competition.

Dubai Raft Race
www.dimc-uae.com

On the weekend of the Raft Race, the marina comes alive with a carnival atmosphere as teams battle against each other on their coloured rafts. Landlubbers can enjoy the spectacle, as well as land activities such as beach games and music by live bands.

Dubai Rugby Sevens
www.dubairugby7s.com

This three day event is a very popular sporting and spectator fixture. With alcohol on sale at the stadium, the party atmosphere carries on until the small hours! Top international teams compete for the coveted 7s trophy while local teams from all over the Gulf to try their luck in the various competitions, including women's rugby. This has become one of the biggest sporting and partying weekends of the year in Dubai and attracted a 25,000 strong crowd in 2004.

Dubai Shopping Festival
www.mydsf.com

A combination of a festival and a shopping extravaganza, DSF, as it is popularly known, is hard to miss as buildings and roads are decorated with coloured lights and there are bargains galore in the participating outlets. Highlights include spectacular fireworks each evening, the international wonders of Global Village and the numerous raffles.

Dubai Summer Surprises
www.mydsf.com

Similar to DSF but smaller, Dubai Summer Surprises is held to attract visitors during the hot and humid summer months. Aimed at families, DSS offers fun packed activities, which are generally held in climate controlled facilities, such as shopping malls, specially constructed areas and hotels. Events are often based on food, heritage, technology, family values, schools etc.

Dubai Tennis Open
www.dubaitennischampionships.com

Usually held in the middle of February, the US$1,000,000 Dubai Duty Free Tennis Open is a popular and well supported event. It is firmly established on the international tennis circuit and offers the chance for fans to see top seeds, both male and female, in an intimate setting, battling it out. Held at the tennis stadium at the Aviation Club, in between matches you can nip to the Irish Village for a pint!

Dubai World Cup
www.dubaiworldcup.com

The Dubai World Cup is billed as the richest horse race in the world – last year's total prize money was over US$15,000,000. The prize for the Group 1 Dubai World Cup race alone was a staggering

US$6,000,000. It is held on a Saturday to ensure maximum media coverage in the West, and with a buzzing, vibrant atmosphere, is a great opportunity to dress up and bring out your best hat.

Exhibitions
www.dubaitourism.com

With the increasing importance of MICE (Meetings, Incentives, Conferences, Exhibitions) tourism to Dubai, there are currently two large state of the art exhibition spaces showcasing a variety of exhibitions each year. These are the Airport Expo (Map Ref 15-A4) and the exhibition halls at the Dubai World Trade Centre (Map Ref 10-A2). For details of exhibitions in Dubai, contact Dubai Tourism and Commerce Marketing (223 0000). See [p.58] for a monthly listing of annual events and exhibitions.

Fun Drive
www.gulf-news.co.ae

If your idea of fun is venturing through the wilderness of the UAE with 750 other four wheel drives, then this event if for you. Spread over two days, the Fun Drive is a popular and very sociable, guided off-road trip. Early booking is advised. Contact the Gulf News Promotions Department for more information.

GITEX
www.gitex.com

One of the largest and most successful international exhibitions for computing, communications systems and applications in the Information Technology industry, Gitex had 114,000 visitors in 2004 (63,000 from overseas) over the five day event. The exhibition has been running for over twenty years and is renowned for its Gitex Computer Shopper where deals can be had.

Great British Day
www.britbiz-uae.com

With a village fête atmosphere, cream teas and fish and chips, Great British Day guarantees a good family day out. It is organised by the British Business Group and usually held on a Friday. Thousands of people of all nationalities attend the event and enjoy competitions, bouncy castles, live music, handicraft stalls etc, and a terrific fireworks display as the grand finale.

Horse Racing
www.nadalshebaclub.com

Nad Al Sheba racecourse is one of the world's leading racing facilities and home to the Dubai World Cup race. Racing takes place at night under floodlights, and usually begins at 19:00 (except during Ramadan when it is 21:00). General

admission and parking are free, and the public has access to most areas with a reserved area for badge holders and members.

The clubhouse charges day membership on race nights at Dhs.60. Everyone can take part in free competitions to select the winning horses, with the ultimate aim of taking home prizes or cash.

Islamic New Year's Day

Islamic New Year's Day marks the start of the Islamic Hijri calendar. It is based on the lunar calendar and should fall on February 14 this year.
See also: Public Holidays [p.18].

Powerboat Racing
www.dimc-uae.com

The Emirates is well established on the world championship powerboat racing circuit – in Abu Dhabi with Formula I (Inshore) and in Dubai and Fujairah with Class I (Offshore). These events make a great spectacle, ideal for the armchair sports fan.

Events in Dubai are held at the Dubai International Marine Club (DIMC), (399 4111).

Sharjah World Book Fair
www.swbf.gov.ae

This annual event takes place at the Sharjah Expo Centre and boasts participation from 35 countries. One of the oldest and largest book fairs in the Arab World, thousands of titles in Arabic, English and many other languages are displayed by private book publishers, governments and universities.

Terry Fox Run
www.terryfoxrun.org

Last year, thousands of individuals ran, jogged, walked, cycled, wheeled and even roller bladed their way around an 8.5 km course for charity. The proceeds go to cancer research programmes at approved institutions around the world. Check the local media for contact details nearer the time.

UAE Desert Challenge
www.uaedesertchallenge.com

This is the highest profile motor sport event in the country, and is often the culmination of the World Cup in cross country rallying. Following prestigious events, such as the Paris – Dakar race, this event attracts some of the world's top rally drivers and bike riders who compete in the car, truck and moto-cross categories. The race is held on consecutive days over four stages, usually starting in Abu Dhabi and travelling across the harsh and challenging terrain of the deserts and sabkha to finish in Dubai. For more details call 282 3441.

Main Annual Events – 2005

January

1	New Year's Day (Fixed)
7	Dubai Marathon
7	Dubai Jet-Ski Race (Heat 5)
12	Dubai Shopping Festival begins
20	Dubai International Racing Carnival begins
23 - 30	Dubai International Junior Sailing Regatta
23	Eid Al Adha (Moon) (4)

February

1 - 4	Dubai International Jazz Festival
3 - 4	Maktoum Offshore Sailing Trophy
11	Dubai Wooden Powerboat Race (Heat 3 – UAE)
12	Dubai Shopping Festival ends
14	Islamic New Year's Day (Moon)
18	Dubai Traditional Rowing Race (Heat 2)
18 & 25	Dubai Traditional Dhow Sailing Race 22ft
21	Dubai Tennis Open Begins
tbc	Dog Show (mid Feb)
tbc	Terry Fox Run

March

1	PhotoWorld
3 - 6	Dubai Desert Classic 2005
3 - 7	Dubai - Muscat Offshore Sailing Race
4	Dubai Traditional Rowing Race (Heat 3)
5	Dubai Tennis Open ends
11	Dubai Traditional Dhow Sailing Race 22ft (Heat 7)
12 - 14	International Fashion, Jewellery & Acc. Show
15 - 17	Automotive Aftermarket Middle East (AAME)
15 - 19	Dubai International Boat Show
26	Dubai World Cup
26	Dubai International Racing Carnival ends
26 - 28	The International Art & Craft Expo
27 - 30	International Arabian Horse Championship
31	UAE National Sailing Championship begins

April

1	Dubai Jet Ski Race (Heat 6 – UAE)
1	UAE National Sailing Championship ends
1	Camel Racing begins (Nad Al Sheba Racecourse)
3 - 8	International Spring Trade Fair
4 - 6	International Silver Show
5 - 8	Gulf Education & Training 2005
7	'Jumeirah' Traditional Dhow Sailing Race 43ft
12 - 15	Bride 2005
15	Dubai Wooden Powerboat Race (5th & Final Heat)
18 - 21	ME Flower & Garden Show (GARDENEX)
22	"Maktoum Cup" Traditional Rowing Race – 30ft
23	Prophet Mohammed's Birthday (Moon)
24 - 26	Theme Parks & Fun Centres Show 2005
30	Camel Racing ends (Nad AL Sheba Racecourse)

May

2 - 4	Gulf Beauty
3 - 6	Arabian Travel Market
9 - 11	Career Fair 2005
13	Dubai Traditional Dhow Sailing Race 22ft (Heat 8)
15 - 17	Gardening Landscaping & Outdoor Living
15 - 17	Kitchen & Bathroom Exhibition
15 - 17	Hardware & DIY Exhibition
22 - 24	The Hotel Show
22 - 24	The ME Office Interiors & Facilities Man. Exhibition
26	Sir Bu Naa'ir Traditional Dhow Sailing – 60ft
28 - 30	Housewares & Homestyle Middle East
28 - 30	Middle East Toy Fair

June

29	UAE National Sailing Championship (6th & Final) begins
tbc	Dubai Summer Surprises begins

July

1	UAE National Sailing Championship (6th & Final) ends

August

6	Accession Day of His Highness Sheikh Zayed
tbc	Dubai Summer Surprises ends

September

3	Lailat Al Mi'Raj (Moon)
12 - 14	Sportex Middles East/Gulf Stadia 2005
25 - 29	GITEX 2005
26 - 29	Arabian Adventure Show

October

6	Ramadan begins (Moon)
tbc	UAE Desert Challenge

November

5	Eid Al Fitr (Moon) (3)
6 - 9	International Autumn Trade Fair (IATF)
16 - 20	Big 5 Show
20 - 24	Dubai Airshow 2005
28	INDEX 2005 begins

December

2	UAE National Day (Fixed)
2	INDEX 2005 ends
6 - 12	International Jewellery Dubai 2005
9 - 11	Mother, Baby & Child Show
6 - 15	Sharjah World Book Fair
12 - 16	The ME International Motorshow
tbc	Dubai International Film Festival
tbc	Dubai Rugby Sevens

tbc – to be confirmed

Denotes public holidays

For more information on these events, see [p.54].

The treasure hunt for talent is on...

UAE · Bahrain · Kuwait · Qatar · Oman

We are on the trail for talented treasures in the above countries to join our merry band of geniuses. So if you are a bright and sparkly gem of the literary world, twiddling your talented ballpoint aimlessly, or a diamond in the rough awaiting discovery and polish... **WE NEED YOU!**

Eloquent **editors** with the ability to apply as well as spell 'punctuation'

Stupendous **sales people** who could sell snow to eskimos

Resourceful **researchers** with an obsession for accuracy

Remarkable **writers** with a talent for pleasing prose

If you are also charming, entertaining, flexible, clever, dedicated, impervious to criticism, hold an unhealthy passion for detail and look great in swimwear, email us NOW.

Still twiddling those ballpoints? Full time, part time, anytime – what are you waiting for?

You could be the next gem in our treasure trove!

Info@Explorer-Publishing.com

Passionately Publishing...

Insiders' City Guides · Photography Books · Activity Guidebooks · Commissioned Publications · Distribution

Moving back to
Boston with husband,
daughter, three dogs
and two containers
of treasured
possessions.
When?
Tomorrow.

Simplify your life

Relocating can be a trying experience with so much to plan, organize and accomplish. There is also less time to spend on things that really matter like friendships or special places you've enjoyed. This is why Writer Relocations provides unparalleled move support so that you can continue to enjoy life right until the time you leave.

Writer Relocations
P.O. Box 34892, Dubai UAE
Phone: 04 340 8814 Fax: 04 340 8815
writerdubai@writercorporation.com
www.writercorporation.com

WRITER
RELOCATIONS

New
Residents

What's new?

Who's left holding the baby?

The new Setting up Home section of this book will help you settle into your new home with hints and tips on everything from furnishing, insuring and cleaning your new home, to finding a babysitter and getting your pet through passport control! For more information on childcare and babysitting, get your hands on the Family Explorer - the definitive guide to family life in the UAE.

Overview

Dubai has come a long way from the 'diamond in the rough' that it was a mere 30 years ago. However, don't be fooled into thinking that settling down in this city will be a simple, hassle free task. You should be prepared for the paperwork, the heat, and the constantly changing policies that come hand in hand with a city that is continuing to grow every day. Despite the red tape, and sometimes frustrating bureaucracy, when your paperwork is in order you can reap the benefits of this land of opportunity... and glorious sunshine, of course!

As government departments are encouraged to be more efficient, processes are now becoming more streamlined. The Internet is used far more liberally for the issue of documents like trade licences, health cards and visit visas. However, this government directive is taking its time to translate into improved practices and until the simplification process makes its way through all the individual departments, you can still expect to be sent from counter to counter with your documents. This can be confusing and frustrating, but remember, wherever you go, people are invariably friendly and ready to point you in the right direction.

The following information is meant only as a guide to what you will have to go through to become a car owning, phone owning, Internet connected, working resident. For step by step instructions and details on all the procedures and formalities related to living in Dubai, pick up the *Zappy Explorer* (Dubai). Note that requirements and laws change regularly, often in quite major ways. Changes are generally announced in the newspapers and can be implemented literally overnight – so be prepared for the unexpected!

The following information applies only to Dubai. While Sharjah and Dubai are close geographically and share many rules and regulations, there are also many differences between the two emirates. If you're planning to live in Sharjah you should check out Sharjah's specific regulations.

In The Beginning...

To become a resident in Dubai you need someone to legally vouch for you. This is usually your employer, who will also be your legal sponsor. Once you have residency, you may then be in a position to sponsor your spouse, parents or children, should you wish to do so.

The first step to acquiring residency is to enter the country on a valid entry visa (see Documents [p.64]). The *Zappy Explorer* (Dubai) will also guide you step by step through the visa application process. Your employer in Dubai will usually provide your visa. If you do not already have a job secured, you may obtain a visit visa to enter the UAE for a short time (see Visas – Entering Dubai [p.26]). If you are already in Dubai and are applying for a family member or friend, the application form may be collected from the Immigration Department near Trade Centre roundabout (Map Ref 10-B1).

If you have been recruited from your home country then your new employer should have the original entry visa documentation waiting for you to collect at the visa desk before you reach Immigration at the airport. You will then present the form with your passport at Immigration. Once you have entered the country on the correct visa the next step is to apply for a health card, which includes a medical test. After this, you can apply for residency. This should be done within 60 days of entering the country or a fine will be incurred. To legally work, you also require a labour card. Your employer will usually take care of processing all required documentation for you, and sometimes for your family as well.

Labour cards and residence visas are valid for three years and can be renewed (this does not apply to elderly parents or maids – see Residence Visa [p.66] and Domestic Help [p.104]). Health cards are valid for one year. If you are a qualified professional with a university degree or have an established employment history, there should be few difficulties in obtaining the necessary paperwork to become a resident.

A new way of looking at things...

Useful Advice

When applying for a residence visa, labour card, driving licence etc, you will always need a handful of essential documents (see below) and you will need to complete countless application forms – invariably typed in Arabic. Don't despair – most government offices, such as the Immigration Department, Labour Office, Traffic Police, Ministry of Health, government hospitals etc, have small cabins full of typists offering their services in English and Arabic for Dhs.10 - 15. Most also offer photocopying services and some even take instant passport sized photos. If you want to speed up the visa application process you may pay an additional Dhs.100 ('urgent visa' fee) when you apply for the visa at the Immigration Department.

Essential Documents

For your ease, and to avoid repetition throughout this section, a list of essential documents has been compiled here. These are standard items that you will most likely need to produce when processing documentation. Additional documents will be referred to in the appropriate paragraph.

• Original passport (for inspection only)

• Passport photocopies (personal details)

• Passport photocopies (visa/visit visa details)

• Passport sized photographs

You will need countless photographs over the next few months. Usually two passport photocopies and two photographs will be required each time you file for something, apply for a job, or join a gym. To save time and money ask for the original negative when you order your first set of photos. Duplicate photos can then be made easily. There are many small photo shops that offer this service; look in your local area.

Often when renting a house or opening a bank account you may have to produce a salary certificate from your employer to confirm that you are employed and earn the minimum salary requirement. In the past you may have also been asked for an NOC (no objection certificate) from your employer when renting a property, buying a car, opening a bank account or applying for your driving licence although it is rarely a requirement nowadays. Either way, any paperwork to be provided by your employer should be on company letterhead paper, signed and stamped with the company stamp to make it undeniably 'official'. Remember to take a photocopy of this document for future use.

Documents

Entry Visa

Other options → **Visas [p.26]**

In order to initiate your residence visa application process, make sure you enter Dubai on the correct entry visa. This is either a residence or an employment visa. The other two kinds of visa (visit and transit) only allow you to remain here temporarily, as the names imply, and their rules vary depending on your nationality. For a list of countries that are granted a visa on arrival, refer to Entering Dubai in General Information [p.26]

If you manage to secure work while on a visit visa you will have to transfer to an employment visa in order to apply for your residence visa and labour card. You can transfer your visa status through the Immigration Department. You will need the relevant application form (obtainable from the Immigration Department) typed in Arabic, Essential Documents (see [p.64]), a copy of your original labour contract from your new employer and a copy of your sponsor's original passport, plus Dhs.500. However, in most cases your employer should take care of this process, both the paperwork and any fees incurred.

Health Card

Once you have the correct visa status (see above), the next step to becoming a resident is to apply for a health card, this needs to be renewed each year. Larger companies and multinationals will usually process this for you through their HR department. The card entitles residents to low cost medical treatment at public hospitals and clinics. However, the consultation charges of Dhs.50 do not include x-rays and other necessary care. Some employers provide additional private medical insurance and, as in most countries, this is regarded as preferable to state care.

To apply for a health card, start off with the application form – available at any public hospital, like Iranian, Al Baraha (Kuwait Hospital), Maktoum or Rashid Hospitals, the Ministry of Health, or any First Health Care Centre. Submit the application form (typed in Arabic) along with the essential documents (see [p.64]), employment verification letter and Dhs.300. If you are not employed and are a dependant you will be required to produce your tenancy contract, electricity and phone bills

Only after 360 full moons, 5 eclipses,
2 comets and 1 meteor shower are
we finally prepared to say we've created
the perfect headlight for driving at night.

The new Golf. Welcome to the family.

Many a long night has been spent at our Wolfsburg factory developing
the intelligent headlights for the new Golf. Headlights that can, in
essence, see around corners. When you turn the wheel the headlights
adjust themselves to perfectly light the way around a bend. And because
they're light sensitive, they also self-activate when it gets dark or when
weather conditions deteriorate. They can even be set to stay on for up to
140 seconds after you leave your car. Ensuring the way to your front door
is safe and well-lit, even on moonless and starless nights.

For the love of automobiles

(original and photocopy of all documents) instead of your employment letter. In return, they will issue you with a temporary health card and a receipt for Dhs.300.

You can then go for your medical test, check with your employer which hospital to go to but it will most likely be the Al Baraha Hospital, which despite appearances is relatively efficient. You will need your temporary health card, a copy of the receipt for Dhs.300, and two passport photos. The test fee is Dhs.205; this includes Dhs.5 for typing the application form in Arabic (done by the hospital). The medical test includes a medical examination, a chest X-ray, and a blood test for HIV, Hepatitis and other infectious diseases. If you are processing a health card for a maid, you will need to pay an additional Dhs.100 to have him or her vaccinated against Hepatitis, and an additional Dhs.10 for typing out the form (refer to Domestic Help [p.104]).

Your temporary health card will be returned to you and after one to two working days you can collect your medical certificate. The temporary health card will have a date on it stating when to collect your permanent health card. This can take anywhere from a week to a few months; in the meantime, the temporary health card can be used at hospitals should you require treatment.

Office locations:

- Al Baraha (Kuwait) Hospital, near Hyatt Regency Dubai hotel, Deira (Map Ref 12-A2)
- Iranian Hospital, Al Wasl Road, Jumeira (Map Ref 6-D3)
- Maktoum Hospital, near Al Ghurair City, Deira (Map Ref 8-D4)
- Rashid Hospital, near Al Maktoum Bridge, Bur Dubai (Map Ref 11-A4)

Children under 18 do not need to have a medical test; all you need do is apply for a health card and you can then directly submit their residence visa application.

Residence Visa

Other options ➜ **Visas [p.26]**

There are two types of residence visas, one for when you are sponsored for employment, and the other for residence only (when sponsored by a family member who is already sponsored by an employer). Once a resident, you must not leave the UAE for more than six months without revisiting, otherwise your residency will lapse. This is not relevant to children studying abroad who are on their parent's

sponsorship here, as long as proof of enrolment with the educational institution overseas is provided. Once you have your health card you can go to the Immigration Department to process your visa.

Office location:

- Immigration Department, near Trade Centre roundabout (Map Ref 10-B1)

Sponsorship by Employer

Your employer should handle all the paperwork and often will have a staff member (who is thoroughly familiar with the ins and outs of the bureaucracy) dedicated for this task alone. After arranging for your residency, they should then apply directly for your labour card (see below). The Ministry of Labour Website (www.mol.gov.ae) has been expanded to include a feedback section as well as a facility for companies to process their applications and transactions over the Internet.

You will need to supply the essential documents and education or degree certificates. You may have to have your certificates attested by a solicitor or public notary in your home country and then by your foreign office to verify the solicitor as bona fide. The UAE embassy in your home country must also sign the documents. Of course, it makes life much simpler if you can do all of this before you come to Dubai. Check with your employer before you embark on the process. If you are entering the country on a visit visa and then secure employment you may be required to then get your education certificates attested. However, this is not always the case, especially if you are working within one of the free zones [p.70], so while planning ahead is always beneficial this is one bridge you can cross when you come to it.

Sheikh Zayed Road

New Residents

Documents

Family Sponsorship

If you are sponsored and are arranging sponsorship for family members, as your employer will not do so, you will have a somewhat lengthy and tedious process ahead (see below). To sponsor your wife or children you will need a minimum monthly salary of Dhs.3,000 plus accommodation, or a minimum all inclusive salary of Dhs.4,000. Only what is printed on your labour contract will be accepted as proof of your earnings.

For parents sponsoring children, difficulties arise when sons (not daughters) become 18 years old. Unless they are enrolled in full time education in the UAE they must transfer their visa to an independent sponsor or, the parents can pay a Dhs.5,000 security deposit (once only) and apply for an annual, renewable visa. If they are still in education they may remain under parental sponsorship, but again, only on an annual basis.

Babies born abroad to expatriate mums holding a UAE residency are required to have a residence visa or a visit visa before entering the UAE. The application should be filed by the father or family provider, along with the essential documents, a salary certificate and a birth certificate. The residence visa for newborns does not require a security check, so the process promises to be faster than most.

It is very difficult for a woman to sponsor her family but there are some exceptions to this rule. Those women employed as doctors, lawyers, teachers etc, earning a minimum stipulated salary, may be permitted to sponsor family members. In most cases though, the husband/father will be the sponsor. When sponsoring parents there are certain constraints depending on your visa status, i.e. you should be in a certain category of employment, such as a manager, and earning over Dhs.6,000 per month. In addition, a special committee meets to review each case individually – usually to consider the age of parents to be sponsored, health requirements etc. Even when a visa is granted it is only valid for one year and is reviewed for renewal on an annual basis.

If you are resident under family sponsorship and then decide to work you will need to apply for a labour card. You will also need a second medical test – your employer should pay for this.

The Process

To become a resident, collect a residency application form from the Immigration Department and have it typed in Arabic. Then submit the application along with the essential documents, medical certificate and Dhs.100.

Once the application is approved (this may take up to a month), you will be issued with a permit of entry for Dubai. You must then either exit and re-enter the country, submitting the entry permit on re-entry to Immigration (i.e. passport control) who will then stamp your passport or pay a Dhs.500 fee to get the stamp without leaving the country. You should then submit your original passport, to the Immigration Department, the original passport of your nominated sponsor, along with your medical certificate, four passport photos and Dhs.300 in order to get your permanent residency stamp. This can take anywhere from ten days to one to two months or longer. Fees that are paid at the Immigration Department are not accepted in cash but instead you must use e-dirhams which come in cards of varying denominations and are available from most banks and are refundable with the receipt.

Once you have your residency stamp, your sponsor or employer may insist that they need to keep your passport. This seems to be the accepted practice amongst many local sponsors. However, unless you work in Jebel Ali, there are currently no legal requirements under UAE law for you to hand over your passport. If you aren't comfortable with them keeping it, don't let them! Additionally, you may need it when visiting your consulate, setting up a bank account etc. Other sponsors will keep your labour card in return for you keeping your passport.

As a fully fledged resident you are now welcome to take out a bank loan, buy a car, rent an apartment in your own name, get a liquor licence etc.

See also: Visa Run – Entering Dubai [p.26]; refer to the Zappy Explorer (Dubai)

Labour Card

To work in the UAE you are legally required to have a valid labour card. This card is very important – if an officer asks to see your card, and you are unable to produce one, you can be fined Dhs.1,200 and sent to jail. The labour card can only be applied for once you have residency. Additionally, expatriate workers who do not renew their labour card will face a penalty: a Dhs.500 fine will be imposed for a card expired six months, Dhs.1,000 for a card expired one year, and Dhs.2,000 for cards expired longer than one year.

If your employer is arranging your residency you will need to sign your labour contract before the

Every good move deserves a toast!

Not many movers understand the emotional stress that you go through during relocation and the sentiments attached to your possessions. What you need is someone who understands your anxiety and can put your mind at rest.

Using **state-of-the-art relocation procedures, precise timing and co-ordination, and the resources of a global network,** Interem's team of professionals takes complete control of every little detail right from **packing, documentation, customs formalities, shipping, finding you a new home in a new country to unpacking and setting up your home**. We will make sure your relocation process is an **absolutely stress-free** experience assuring you complete peace of mind.

Call us and together we'll toast to your new begining!

International Removals Division of Freight Systems Co. Ltd. (L.L.C.)

Tel: +971 4 3141201 / 3355455. Dubai. UAE. E-mail: albert@freightsystems.com Website: www.freightsystems.com

INTERNATIONAL PACKAGING SERVICES • OFFICE & RESIDENTIAL RELOCATIONS • HOME SEARCH
SHORT & LONG TERM STORAGE FACILITIES • COMPREHENSIVE INSURANCE COVER

labour card is issued. This contract is printed in both Arabic and English. It's a standard form issued by the labour authorities and completed with your details. Unless you read Arabic it may be advisable to have a translation made of your details, since the Arabic is taken as the legal default if there is any dispute (see Employment Contracts [p.82]).

If you are on a family residency and decide to work, your employer, not your visa sponsor, will need to apply for a labour card. Your spouse or sponsor will need to supply a letter of no objection (NOC) before you can sign a contract with your new employer. Documents to supply include: the essential documents (see [p.64]), NOC, education certificate/s (if appropriate), and usually a photocopy of your sponsor's passport – they may also require the sponsor's original passport.

Expat students on their parent's visa who wish to work in Dubai during the summer vacation should apply to the Department of Naturalisation & Residency for a permit allowing them to work legally.

Location: Ministry of Labour, near Galadari roundabout, (269 1666, Map Ref 12-B4)

Free Zones

Employees of companies in free zones have different sponsorship options depending on the free zone. For example, in Jebel Ali you can either be sponsored by an individual company or by the free zone authority itself. Whether the Jebel Ali Free Zone, Dubai Internet City, Media City, Knowledge Village, Healthcare City or the Dubai Airport Free Zone, the respective authority will process your visa through the Immigration Department. They are usually able to get this done very quickly. Once Immigration has stamped your residence visa in your passport, the free zone will issue your labour card – this also acts as your security pass for entry to the free zone (your passport will be retained in Jebel Ali but not in the other free zones). Your visa is valid for three years and the labour card either one or three years, depending on the free zone.

Dubai Technology and Media Free Zone

Located in Al Sufouh, this free zone comprises three separate areas:

Dubai Media City (DMC) has quickly established itself as a global hub for broadcasting and media production. As well as the ownership and taxation benefits associated with free zones, Media City partners enjoy greater freedom of expression, meaning that their output is less prone to scrutiny by government ministries. DMC is home to over 850 companies including big recognisable names such as CNN, Associated Press, Reuters and MBC.

Dubai Internet City (DIC) prides itself as the world's first free trade zone for Information Technology and e-Business. Companies here take advantage of Dubai's strategic location as a gateway between Europe and the West, and the emerging technology markets of the Middle East, Africa, and the Indian Subcontinent. The company names visible from Sheikh Zayed Road, include Microsoft, Dell, Siemens and IBM, and are testament to DIC's importance to the global IT players.

> ### Free Zones
> *Free Zones are designed to encourage investment from overseas, they allow 100% foreign ownership and offer exemption from taxes and customs duties. An added attraction is the promise of much less bureaucracy and red tape.*

Knowledge Village is the latest addition to the free zone and aims to create a community of both local and international educational establishments. As well as attracting institutions and students from overseas, the development is intended to provide education and training to UAE locals in an effort to bridge the so-called talent gap in the region. Australia's University of Southern Queensland and University of Wollongong, and the UK's Middlesex University are just three of the academic institutions to have set up campuses here so far.

Dubai Media City

Jebel Ali Free Zone (JAFZA)

Built around the largest man-made port in the world and opened in 1985, the Jebel Ali Free Zone now covers over 100 square kilometres. Modern factories, warehouses, offices, and the huge container port, coupled with Dubai's location within easy reach of Europe, Asia and India, have guaranteed JAFZ's importance in regional and global manufacturing and distribution.

Dubai Healthcare City (DHCC)

Currently under construction in Umm Hurair (2), the Healthcare City initiative is hoping to become a regional and global centre of excellence for both healthcare provision and medical education. International institutions have been invited to participate, and all will be able to take advantage of the usual legal and financial free zone benefits.

Certificates & Licences

Driving Licence

Other options ➔ **Transportation [p.136]**

Until you acquire full residency you can drive a hire car, provided you have a valid driving licence from your country of origin or an international licence (this only applies to those countries on the transfer list below). To drive private vehicles you must first apply for a temporary Dubai licence with the Traffic Police. You will need to fill out the application form, take the essential documents and Dhs.10 to obtain a temporary licence that is valid for one month (temporary licences for longer periods are also available).

Once you have your residence visa you must apply for a permanent UAE licence. Nationals of certain countries can automatically transfer their driving licence, providing the original licence is valid.

Some of the above licences will need an Arabic translation by your consulate – check with the Traffic Police. You may also be required to sit a short written test on road rules before the transfer will take place. You will need to take your existing foreign licence and your passport to the registration office, near the Dubai Police College or one of the other locations listed below. For a Dhs.100 processing fee they will take your picture and give you your temporary driving licence. When applying for your permanent licence you will need to have an eye test. It costs around Dhs.25 and you'll need to take along two passport photos to the opticians. In return you'll get the certificate needed for when you apply for a licence.

If you aren't from one of the countries listed [p.72] you will need to sit a UAE driving test. To apply for a permanent driving licence, submit the following documents below to the Traffic Police, plus your valid Dubai residence visa and Dhs.100. Always carry your Dubai driving licence when driving. If you fail to produce it during a police spot check you will be fined. Driving licences can be renewed at the Traffic Police as well as other sites around Dubai including Al Safa Union Co-operative (394 5007, Map Ref 5-B2), Al Tawar Union Co-operative (263 4857, Map Ref 15-C2) and Jumeirah Plaza (342 0737 Map Ref 6-C2). The licence is valid for ten years and if you manage to drive on the UAE roads for this long without going crazy, you deserve a medal!

> **Automatic Licence Transfer**
>
> Australia, Austria, Belgium, Canada, Cyprus, Czech Republic, Denmark, Finland, France, GCC member countries, Germany, Greece, Iceland, Ireland, Italy, Japan, Luxembourg, Netherlands, New Zealand, Norway, Poland, Portugal, Singapore, Slovakia, South Africa, South Korea, Spain, Sweden, Switzerland, Turkey, United Kingdom, United States.

Driving Licence Documents

- The relevant application form from the Traffic Police typed in Arabic

Plus these essential documents:

- A copy of your sponsor's passport or a copy of the company's trade licence
- An NOC from your sponsor/company in Arabic (although this is not always required)
- Your original driving licence along with a photocopy (and translation, if requested by the Traffic Police)
- Sometimes your sponsor's original passport is requested as well as a copy. However, it seems to depend on a whim rather than anything concrete.

Office locations:

- Traffic Police HQ – near Galadari roundabout, Dubai-Sharjah Road (269 2222, Map Ref 15-B1)
- Bur Dubai Police Station – Sheikh Zayed Road, Junction 4 (398 1111 Map Ref 10-A1)

Driving Test

If your nationality is not on the automatic transfer list you will need to sit a UAE driving test to be eligible to drive in Dubai, regardless of whether you hold a valid driving licence from your country or not.

DUBAI COUNTRY CLUB

P.O. Box 5103
DUBAI
TEL.: 04 3331155, FAX: 04 3331155
Email: dcc@emirates.net.ae
Website: www.dubaicountryclub.com

ubai Country Club is an idyllic oasis in the heart of a modern, ever
owing city, offering a superb range of facilities for both families and
dividuals who just need to relax for a while, or enjoy their social and
orting life with like-minded people.

he site covers 200 acres of land, which was kindly donated by the
te His Highness Sheikh Rashid Bin Saeed Al Maktoum in 1970,
d as the city has expanded over the years, so too has Dubai Country
lub, to the extent whereby we are considered one of the foremost
mily leisure venues in the country.

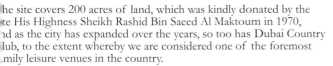

here else can you indulge in golf, tennis, squash and keeping fit while
so being able to simply switch off by the pool, relax in the library or
joy a great meal, all the time being looked after by experienced
rofessionals who all maintain a commitment to traditional hospitality?

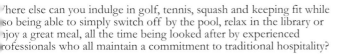

ith a variety of restaurants, bars and sports facilities geared
all tastes and ages, there is literally something for everyone - and it is
incredible value for money.

ubai Country Club also plays host to a vast array of special
ents throughout the year: from international sporting clashes to live
oncerts featuring top entertainment from around the world.

ubai Country Club has a warm welcoming atmosphere and is a place
here you and your family can enjoy a relaxing day out - at a pace that
its you.

The first step is to obtain a learning permit – start by picking up an application form from the Traffic Police. You will need the essential documents (see above), the driving licence documents and Dhs.40. You will be given an eye test at the Traffic Police. Then find a reputable driving school – check the Yellow Pages or try one of the ones listed in the table opposite.

Some driving institutions insist that you pay for a set of pre-booked lessons. In some cases, the package extends to 52 lessons and can cost up to Dhs.3,000. The lessons must be taken on consecutive days and usually last 30 - 45 minutes. Other companies offer lessons on an hourly basis, as and when you like, for Dhs.35 per hour. Women are required to take lessons with a female instructor, at a cost of Dhs.65 per hour. If a woman wants to take lessons with a male instructor she must first obtain NOC's from her husband/sponsor and the Traffic Police.

No UAE Licence?

You cannot drive a privately registered vehicle on an international or foreign driving licence, as the vehicle is only insured for drivers holding a UAE driving licence.

When your instructor feels that you are ready to take your test you will be issued with a letter to that effect and can apply for a test date. You'll need to fill out an application form at the Traffic Police, hand over your essential documents, as well as driving licence documents and Dhs.35. You must also take another eye test elsewhere and bring the certificate the optician supplies you. The time between submitting your application and the test date can be as long as two to three months.

Al Futtaim Automall

You will be given three different tests on different dates. One is a Highway Code test, another an 'internal' test which includes garage parking etc, and the third is a road test. Once you pass all three tests you will be issued with a certificate (after about five days), which you should take to the Traffic Police to apply for your permanent driving licence. Before you are issued with your permanent driving licence you will have to attend two compulsory hour long road safety lectures, the cost of which is incorporated into the price of your lessons. For detailed, step by step information on licence procedures, refer to the *Zappy Explorer* (Dubai).

Driving Schools	
Al Hamriya Driving School	269 9259
Belhasa	344 0277
Dubai Driving School	271 7654
Emirates Driving Institute	263 1100

Liquor Licence

Other options → Alcohol [p.206]

Dubai has the most liberal attitude towards alcohol of all the emirates. To buy alcohol for home you will need a special liquor licence so you can purchase from a liquor shop (alcohol is not available at the local supermarket). In public, only four and five star hotels are licensed to serve alcoholic drinks in their bars and restaurants, as are some private sports clubs. You don't need a liquor licence to drink at a hotel or a club, but you will require a valid ID to prove you are 21 or older.

The licence allows you to spend a limited amount on alcohol per month – this amount is based on your monthly salary. Only non-Muslims with a residence visa may obtain a licence, and for married couples, only the husband may apply. To apply, collect an application form from any MMI (321 1223) or A&E (222 2666) branches in Dubai – these are the two licensed liquor store chains. Your employer must sign and stamp the form, then you should submit it (in both Arabic and English) at an MMI or A&E branch along with your essential documents (p.74), a photocopy of your employment contract, a photocopy of your tenancy contract, and Dhs.150. If you work in Jebel Ali or Media City, a salary letter is also required. Your liquor licence should be processed in less than two weeks and you will be provided with an electronic card which records how much you purchase each time you shop. Note that the Dubai Police no longer process liquor licence applications directly.

Turn up at any MMI outlet to get your liquor licence

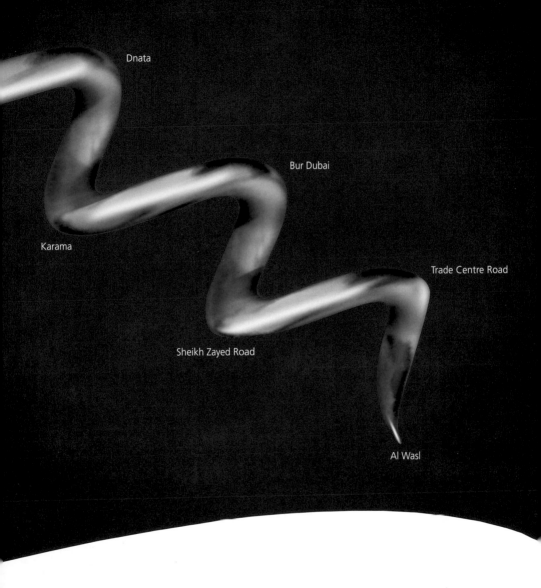

Dnata

Bur Dubai

Karama

Trade Centre Road

Sheikh Zayed Road

Al Wasl

We've made getting a liquor licence easy; no queues, no hassle, fast processing. And with 6 convenient locations throughout Dubai you're never far from an MMI outlet. Al Wasl Store open Saturday to Thursday 10am - 9pm, all other stores open Thursday and Saturday 10am - 9pm, Monday to Wednesday 10am - 2pm and 5pm - 9pm, (Dnata Wednesday 10am - 9pm).

AL WASL
next to Spinney's
Al Wasl Road
Tel: 04 394 0351

TRADE CENTRE RD
Behind Spinney's
Trade Centre Road
Tel: 04 352 3091

DNATA
Emirates Group Head Quarters
(Old Dnata Bldg), Deira
Tel: 04 294 0390

BUR DUBAI
Khalid Bin Waleed Road
Opposite Sea Shell Inn Hotel
Tel: 04 393 5738

KARAMA
Al Maskan Blg.
near Karama Fish market
Tel: 04 335 1722

SHEIKH ZAYED ROAD
Saeed Tower 2
Next to Pizza Hut
Tel: 04 321 1223

mmi
bringing more to life

Buying alcohol from liquor shops can be expensive, as you have to pay an additional tax of 30% on all items. However, the range is excellent. There are cheaper alternatives for buying alcohol where a licence is not required, such as Ajman's 'Hole in the Wall', near the Ajman Kempinski. Umm al Quwain also has outlets by the Barracuda Resort, next to the Dreamland Aqua Park, and next to the Umm al Quwain Beach Hotel. However, be aware that it is illegal to transport alcohol around the Emirates without a liquor licence. This law is particularly enforced in Sharjah. Drinking on the beach, in public parks or even out in the Dubai 'outback' is not tolerated, whether you have a licence or not.

Office hours: MMI and A&E both open from 10:00 - 21:00 Thur & Sat; 10:00 - 14:00 & 17:00 - 21:00 Sun to Wed, Closed Fri

Birth Certificates & Registration

Every expat child born in the UAE must be registered with a residence visa within 40 days of birth. Without the correct documentation you may not be able to take your baby out of the country.

The hospital that the baby is delivered at will prepare the official 'notification of birth' certificate in English or Arabic upon receipt of hospital records, photocopies of both parents' passports and marriage certificate, and a fee of Dhs.50. Take the birth certificate for translation into English to Dubai Hospital's Preventative Medicine Department (behind Al Baraha Hospital) where you will be issued with an application form, which must

'I already have my very own passport!'

then be typed in English (Dhs.50 fee). You should also take the certificate to be attested at the Ministry of Health (Dhs.10 fee) and the Ministry of Foreign Affairs (Dhs.50 fee).

Once this is done ensure you register your child's birth at your embassy or consulate. To do this you will require the local notification of birth certificate, both parents' birth certificates, passports and marriage certificate. In addition, you must arrange a passport for your baby. Then, you have to apply for a residence visa through the normal UAE channels.

Before the birth it is worth checking the regulations of your country of origin for citizens born overseas, especially if you yourself were also born outside of your parents' country of origin. See [p.30] for a list of embassies and consulates in Dubai.

Marriage Certificates & Registration

While many people return to their country of origin to get married there are plenty of options here if you want to tie the knot in the sun!

Muslims

As a Muslim marrying another Muslim, apply at the marriage section of the Sharia Court (Dubai Court), next to Al Maktoum Bridge. You will need two male witnesses and the bride should ensure that either her father or brother attends as a witness. You will require your passports with copies, proof that the groom is Muslim and Dhs.50. You can marry there and then.

For a Muslim woman marrying a non-Muslim man, the situation is little more complicated, but possible if the man first converts to Islam. For further information, the Dubai Court (334 7777) or the Dubai Court Marriage Section (303 0406) can advise.

Opening hours: 07:30 - 14:30 (General) & 17:30 - 20:00 (Notary Public only)

Christians, Catholics and Anglicans

Christians can choose to have either a formal church ceremony with a congregation, or a small church ceremony and a blessing afterwards at a different location, such as a hotel.

At the official church ceremony you will need two witnesses to sign the marriage register – the church then issues a marriage certificate. Take this, along with your essential documents to your embassy in order to attest the document.

Catholics must also undertake a Marriage Encounter course, this usually takes place at St

New Residents

Certificates & Licences

Mary's Church (337 0087) on a Friday. You will need to fill out a standard form and at the end of the course, you are presented with a certificate. You should then arrange with the priest to undertake a pre-nuptial ceremony and again, you are asked to fill out a form. You will need to take your birth certificate, baptism certificate, passport and passport copies, an NOC from your parish priest in your home country and a Dhs.300 donation. If you are a non Catholic marrying a Catholic you will need an NOC from your embassy/consulate stating that you are legally free to marry. A declaration of your intent to marry is posted on the public noticeboard at the church for three weeks, after which time, if there are no objections, you can set a date for the ceremony.

Anglicans should contact the Chaplain at Holy Trinity Church (337 0247) for an appointment. You will need to fill out a number of forms, basically stating your intention to marry, that you aren't a Muslim and confirming that you are legally free to do so. Take the essential documents (p.64). If you have previously been married you will need to produce either your divorce certificate or the death certificate of your previous partner. Fees differ depending on your nationality and circumstances. If you wish to hold the ceremony outside the church an additional Dhs.500 will be charged. If you're not overly concerned about sticking to a particular doctrine, but want a church wedding, the Anglican ceremony is far simpler to arrange and much less time consuming than the Catholic one.

These marriages are recognised by the Government of the UAE but must be formalised. To make your marriage 'official', get an Arabic translation of the marriage certificate and take it to the Dubai Court after the ceremony. Filipino citizens are required to contact their embassy in Abu Dhabi before the Dubai Court will authenticate their marriage certificate.

Zappy Explorer (Dubai)

Aptly dubbed 'the ultimate culture shock antidote', this guide is Explorer's solution to the complexities and perplexities of Dubai's administrative maze. A clear, straightforward set of procedures assists residents through the basics of life, from opening a bank account to connecting your phone and marrying your true love. Including detailed information on ministry and government department requirements, what to bring lists, reference maps and much more, this is your best chance of getting things done next to bribery or force!

Hindus

Hindus can be married through the Hindu Temple and the Indian Embassy (397 1222). The Embassy publishes a booklet with guidelines on how to get married and you will have to fill out an application form on the premises. Formalities take a minimum of 45 days.

Civil Weddings

If you don't want a religious wedding you should contact your local embassy or consulate as they may have regulations and referrals to arrange for a local civil marriage which can then be registered at their embassy.

Death Certificates & Registration

In the unhappy event of a death of a friend or relative, the first thing to do is to notify the police of your district. On arrival the police will make a report and the body will be taken to hospital where a doctor will determine the cause of death. The authorities will need to see the deceased's passport and visa details. The hospital will issue a death certificate declaration on receipt of the doctor's report for a fee of Dhs.50. Contact the deceased's embassy or consulate for guidance.

Then take the declaration of death and original passport to the police who will issue a letter addressed to Al Baraha (Kuwait) Hospital. This letter, plus death declaration, original passport and copies should be taken to Al Baraha Hospital, Department of Preventative Medicine, where an actual death certificate will be issued. If you are sending the deceased home you should also request a death certificate in English (an additional Dhs.100) or appropriate language – check this with the embassy.

Take the certificate to the Ministry of Health and the Ministry of Foreign Affairs for registration. Notify the relevant embassy for the death to be registered in the deceased's country of origin. They will also issue their own death certificate. Take the original passport and death certificate for the passport to be cancelled. The deceased's visa must also be cancelled by the Immigration Department – take the local death certificate, original cancelled passport and embassy-issued death certificate.

To return the deceased to their country of origin you will need to book a flight through DNATA and get police clearance from airport security to ship the body out of the country, as well as an NOC

New Residents

Certificates & Licences

from the embassy. The body needs to be embalmed and you must obtain a letter to this intent from the police. Embalming can be arranged through Al Maktoum Hospital for Dhs.1,000, which includes the embalming certificate. The body must be identified before and after embalming, after which it should be transferred to Cargo Village for shipping.

The following documents should accompany the deceased: local death certificate, translation of death certificate, embalming certificate, NOC from the police, embassy/consulate death certificate and NOC, and cancelled passport.

A local burial can be arranged at the Muslim or Christian cemeteries in Dubai. The cost of a burial is Dhs.1,100 for an adult and Dhs.350 for a child. You will need to arrange for a coffin to be made, as well as transport to the burial site. Cremation is also possible, but only in the Hindu manner and with the prior permission of the next of kin and the CID. For more information see the *Zappy Explorer* (Dubai).

See also: *Support Groups [p.128].*

Work

Working in Dubai

Expat workers come to Dubai for a number of reasons – to advance their career, for a higher standard of living, to take advantage of new career opportunities or to simply experience living and working in a new culture. Whatever the reason there are various advantages to working here. Most obviously this is the tax free salaries – although this benefit has been somewhat

Parking's at a premium in Bur Dubai

outweighed by the fact that the Dirham is tied to the dollar and hence has lost its strength against the UK pound and the Euro which has resulted in salary packages seeming less lucrative than they were four or five years ago for many expats. Many people are seconded by companies based in their home country, others are recruited from their country of origin and then there are those partners or spouses, or career hopefuls, who arrive to look for new work opportunities. There is a strong work ethic in Dubai and many people are a little taken aback at the commitment, dedication and sheer man-hours that are expected of them or find themselves caught up in the ambiguous labour laws. However, while it may not be all sunshine and living it up, working in Dubai has its distinct advantages – skilled professionals will find that they may be able to climb the corporate ladder a lot quicker than they could in their home country. Opportunities also exist for professionals to transfer industries, and skill sets are less pigeonholed meaning you may be able to get into the career you always dreamed of!

Working Hours

Working hours vary quite dramatically within the emirate and are based on straight shift and split shift timings. Split shift timings allow for an afternoon siesta and are generally 08:00 - 13:00 and 16:00 - 19:00. Straight shift timings vary from government organisations (07:00 - 14:00) to private companies (09:00 - 18:00). Some companies work five and a half days, with the weekend on Thursday afternoon and Friday. However, more companies are adopting a five day working week with government departments and some private sector companies observing a Thursday/Friday weekend and other private sector companies observing a Friday/Saturday weekend.

Public holidays are set by the government and religious holidays are governed by the moon. During Ramadan private organisations are meant to reduce working hours for Muslims, and all employers in the public sector work a six hour day. (For further details on holidays, refer to Public Holidays [p.17].)

Finding Work

If you do not have employment on arrival to Dubai, the best way to find a job is to register with the recruitment agencies and to check the small ads and employment pages in the main newspapers. An employment supplement is published in the Gulf

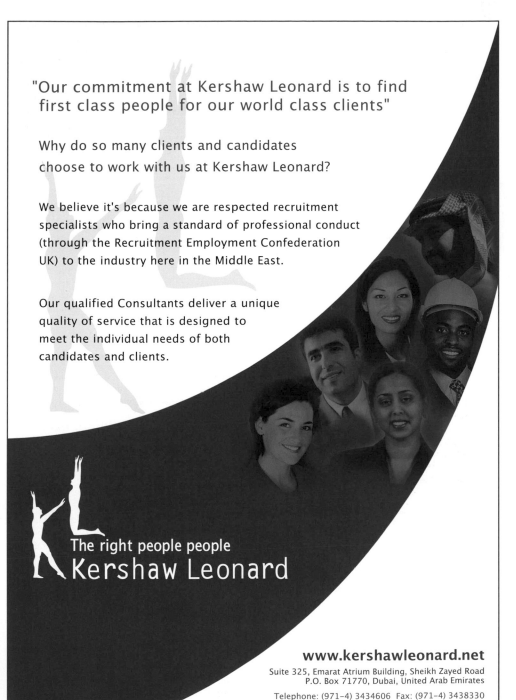

News on Sunday to Thursday, and in the Khaleej Times on Sunday, Monday and Wednesday.

Be aware that use of the words 'UK/US educated' indicates a preference for Anglo candidates, and the caption 'Ability to speak Arabic is an advantage' indicates a preference for Arab nationals or expats. Most government departments are moving towards 'Emiratisation' which is a positive discrimination programme aimed at increasing the number of UAE Nationals in management roles. Private organisations and multinationals are less obliged to comply with this programme but often have a 'National Development' programme in place to appease local partners and Government agencies.

Moving between jobs or finding work after your employment contract has expired is also possible although it is not as simple as you might think and depends upon the flexibility of your previous employer. See Banning [p.83].

Recruitment Agencies

There are a lot of recruitment/employment agencies in Dubai. To register, check with the agency to find out if they take walk ins. Most only accept CVs via email these days and will then contact you for an interview. For the interview you will need both your CV and passport photographs. Invariably you will also have to fill out an agency form summarising your CV. The agency takes its fee from the registered company once the position has been filled. It is illegal for a recruitment company to levy fees on candidates for this service, although some of the smaller, more unscrupulous agencies still try this.

The Rumour Mill

Although Dubai is growing exponentially it is still a small place and fast tongues means gossip travels pretty quickly so be careful what you say and who you say it to! You will find out pretty quickly that your neighbour's work colleague's wife's brother is your new manager so don't bad mouth anyone unless you're willing to face the consequences of Chinese whispers!

Don't rely too heavily on the agency finding a job for you; more often than not, they depend on you spotting a vacancy that they have advertised in the paper and telephoning them to submit your interest. Should you be suitable for the job the agency will mediate between you and the employer and arrange all interviews.

Below is a list of recruitment agencies operating out of the UAE. Some of these agencies are specialised for certain industries so do your

Emirates Towers

research and register accordingly. You may find that two or three separate agencies try and send you on interviews for the same job, so when you find an agency you like then give them the head's up. That way they will be more proactive in negotiating the job and salary package for you.

Recruitment Agencies	
BAC	336 0350
Bayt	391 1900
Clarendon Parker P.81	391 0460
IQ Selection	324 2878
Job Scan	355 9113
Job Track	397 7751
Kershaw Leonard P.79	343 4606
Nadia	331 3401
Search	268 6100
Seekers	351 2666
SOS	396 5600
Talent	335 0999

Business Groups & Contacts

In addition to the various government departments specifically responsible for providing commercial assistance to enterprises in Dubai, there are various chambers of commerce and other business groups that help facilitate investments and provide opportunities for networking with others in the community. Some business groups and councils provide information on trade with their respective country, as well as on business opportunities both in Dubai and internationally. Most also arrange social and networking events on a regular basis.

Work · New Residents

It's worth contacting the Dubai Chamber of Commerce (228 0000 Map Ref 11-C2) and the Economic Department (222 9922 Map Ref 11-C1), both located along the Corniche in Deira. Embassies or consulates can also be a good business resource and may be able to offer contact lists for the UAE and the country of representation. For information and details, refer to the Dubai Commercial Directory, Hawk Business Pages and the *Zappy Explorer* (Dubai)

Business Culture

Despite its cosmopolitan outward appearance, Dubai is still an Arab city in a Muslim country and people doing business in Dubai must remember this fact. Even if your counterpart in another company is an expatriate, the head decision maker may be a UAE National who could quite possibly take a different approach to business matters. Your best bet when doing business in Dubai for the first time is to observe closely, have lots of patience and make a concerted effort to understand the culture and respect the customs. Once you get a hang of the customs you will find doing business makes for a refreshing change and, if nothing else, adds another string to your work communications skills and ultimately your CV.

Remember, as in any community, networking is critical even across industries. Dubai is a very small community within the setting of a large urban city. Business acumen here can, at times, be more important than specific industry knowledge. Keep your finger on the pulse of activity by attending business events and trade shows. Make friends in government departments where your business has direct interfaces, and this will often land you in the front line of opportunities. Likewise, bad news is rarely made public here, so staying in tune with the grapevine can help prevent wrong decisions.

Business Councils & Groups	
American Business Council	331 4735
Australian Business in the Gulf	395 4423
British Business Group	397 0303
Canadian Business Council	335 8975
Denmark Business Council	222 7699
French Business Council	335 2362
German Business Council	359 9930
Iranian Business Council	344 4717
Pakistan Business Council	337 2875
South African Business Group	397 5222
Swedish Business Council	337 1410
Swiss Business Council	321 1438

Business Etiquette

Tea and coffee are a very important part of Arabic life and it may be considered rude to refuse this offer of hospitality during a meeting. Tilting the small Arabic coffee cup back and forth several times with your fingers will signal that you do not want another refill.

Although proper dress is important for all business dealings, the local climate has dictated that a shirt and tie (for men) is sufficient for all but the most important of business encounters; women usually choose a suit or a skirt and a blouse that are not revealing.

In Arabic society a verbal commitment (once clearly made) is ethically if not legally binding; reasonable bargaining is an important part of reaching any such agreement. Finally, it is important to remember that Dubai, despite significant and ongoing growth and international exposure, is still a relatively small business community, so confidentiality and discretion are of the utmost importance in all business dealings.

Meetings

A strong handshake should not only start each meeting but also end the encounter – a longer handshake at the end is an indication that the meeting has gone well. It is always preferable to start a meeting with a non business discussion but avoid enquiring about somebody's wife, even if you know the wife – general enquiries about the family are more appropriate.

Don't be surprised if other people walk in and out during the meeting to discuss unrelated matters, and be prepared for the meeting to run longer than expected.

It is also a good idea not to jump to conclusions at the end of a good meeting. Try to do background work on the people you have met to understand how much influence they wield in the decision making process. You will rarely have someone admit (due to cultural norms) how little or how great their influence is on a business decision!

Employment Contracts

Never accept an initial offer and never sign a contract on the spot. It is common practice here to negotiate the initial offer and contract (particularly if you are a professional), although many employers don't take kindly to inflexibility or brash tactics by prospective employees, so be diplomatic in your negotiations. Contracts are legal and binding so before you leap in check all clauses thoroughly. Pay special attention to things like probation periods, accommodation allowances, annual leave and travel entitlements, medical and dental cover, notice periods, and repatriation entitlements. Also check if there are restrictions related to anti-competitive behaviour once employment has been terminated, such as setting up your own business, working for a competitor etc. If you're not happy, discuss your grievances with your recruitment agent as they have the skills to negotiate for you. You can even opt to put an initial three month introductory (probation) period into your contract before processing your visa under the company.

Once you have accepted a job offer you may be asked to sign a copy of your contract in Arabic as well as in English. Be sure to check the Arabic translation before you sign as this is taken as the legal default if there is a dispute. There have been instances of the Arabic reading differently from the English. You should also refer to a copy of the UAE Labour Law (see below) for details of other benefits and entitlements.

Labour Law

The Labour Law outlines everything from employee entitlements (end of service gratuity, workers' compensation, holidays etc) to employment contracts and disciplinary rules. The law tends to favour employers but it also clearly outlines employee rights which do exist in the UAE.

Labour unions are, at present illegal, as are strikes. Recent moves have been made by the Ministry of Labour to assist workers (particularly labourers) in labour disputes against their employers. Non payment of salaries is the most common problem, and if you are in this situation you do have recourse. You can file a case with the UAE Labour Department who will follow up with your employer and pressure them to pay you your dues. This approach usually works but takes time.

You may also opt to get a lawyer to deal with the claim on your behalf, see the table [p.88] for recommended law firms. This can add significant leverage and, although lawyers are expensive here, the employer will have to bear this cost if the case is reconciled in your favour. For recommendations, referrals and consultation, call your embassy.

A copy of the UAE Labour Law may be available from your employer or it can be obtained through the Ministry of Labour & Social Affairs (269 1666). The UAE Labour Guide, published by the Ministry in 2002, also outlines workers' rights.

'Banning'

This is one area of the law that seems to change frequently so it's always best to check with the Labour Department, a Labour lawyer or someone who's in the know for the latest version.

The government's aim is to stop people from job hopping and thanks to rumours and scare mongering many expats live in fear of being banned if they change employer. While there is the possibility of receiving a six month ban if you resign from your job, for many people this doesn't mean you can't work during that time or have to leave the country.

With an NOC (No Objection Certificate) from your previous employer it is likely that your visa can be transferred (although this is somewhat of a grey area and in some cases people have still been banned despite having an NOC). If you want to move employers and work in a free zone or have managerial status the transition will be a lot smoother. The labour laws that apply to the free zones are different to the rest of Dubai and those with a residence visa from a free zone should not receive a ban when changing employment. As far as managerial positions go it is much harder for companies to ban you, however if your previous employer is vindictive and has friends in the right places anything can happen.

If you do resign from your job and have a passport from one of the countries listed in the Visas section in General Information [p.26] then regardless of whether you get a ban you can always work on a visit visa as a 'consultant' and do visa runs for the interim, See Visa Runs, General Information [p.27]. If however you are not a passport holder from one of those countries things can be more difficult. In addition, while a work permit ban means that in most cases your residence visa is cancelled, in the case of family sponsorship or residence visas tied to property ownership your previous employer can cancel your labour card but they cannot cancel your residence visa

Whenever you change jobs, there's always some red tape and visa transferring hassles, so find out what you're in for before making a move. If you do have an NOC and if the Ministry of Labour approves the move the transition should be pretty hassle free – although never say never! If you do want to move to a new job and you know that your present employer is likely to try and ban you then maybe the best thing to do is leave the job under the pretence that you are returning to your country of origin. They will then cancel your visa and will have no reason to seek a ban, you can then start the residence visa process again with your new employer.

Company Closure

Some dubious people and companies see Dubai as a place to make money and run. Employees who face the unlucky situation of company bankruptcy or company closure are entitled under UAE Labour law to receive their due gratuity payments, holidays etc, but you will need to speak to the labour department for the proper process. Additionally, no employee of a firm that has been closed is allowed to transfer sponsorship to their new employer unless an attested certificate of closure by their previous employer is issued by the court and submitted to the Ministry of Labour and Social Affairs. If you are unfortunate enough to have to deal with this, consult the appropriate government offices to get your paperwork right, or you may have to invest in the services of a lawyer.

Financial & Legal Affairs

Bank Accounts

Dubai is full of internationally recognised banks that offer current, deposit and savings accounts, credit cards, and loans. Most of them also offer the convenience of online banking, so you can check balances, transfer money, and pay bills with just a few clicks of the mouse. There are plenty of ATM machines around Dubai and most cards are compatible with other Dubai based banks (some also offer global access links).

To open a bank account in most banks in Dubai you need to have a residence visa or to have your residency application underway. You will need to present the banking advisor with your original passport, copies of your passport (personal details and visa) and an NOC from your sponsor. Some banks set a minimum account limit – this can be around Dhs.2,000 for a

deposit account and as much as Dhs.10,000 for a current account. This means that at some point in each month your account balance must be above the minimum limit. Without a residence visa, Middle East bank, known as ME bank, will open an account for you and provide an ATM card, but not a chequebook. ME bank also allows you to apply online for a bank account at www.me.ae/mebank. General bank opening hours are Saturday - Wednesday 08:00 - 13:00; Thursday 08:00 - 12:00. Although some banks open later or again in the evening.

Financial Planning

Planning for the financial future (unless you take the head in the sand approach) is an important aspect of modern day life and especially necessary for expats. Before you do anything you should contact the tax authorities in your home country to ensure that you are complying with the financial laws there. Most countries will consider you not liable for income tax once you prove your UAE residence or your non residence in your home country (a contract of employment is normally a good starting point for proving non residence). As a non resident however, you may still have to fulfil certain criteria (such as only visiting your home country for a limited number of days each year).

Generally, one of the main benefits when accepting an expat posting is the ability to improve your financial situation. It is recommended not to undertake any non cash investments until you know your monthly savings capacity, even though this may take up to six months to ascertain. If you have a short term contract, stay away from long term investment contracts. Once you have decided that expat life is for you and that you are ready to plan for the future, you might want to establish the following: emergency cash buffer (3 - 6 months salary), retirement home, retirement income, personal and family protection (life insurance, health coverage) etc.

When selecting a financial planner, use either a reputable name or at least an institution regulated by the UAE Central Bank. If another authority is 'regulating' your advisor, you cannot expect the principal UAE authority to be of assistance to you, and your chances of recourse in the event of a problem may be severely hampered. For financial planners, try any of the major international companies or word of mouth.

We make Mr Johnson's money work hard, so he doesn't have to

Lloyds TSB Dubai has a full range of services to meet all your personal, business and offshore banking needs

Personal Banking
- Current & Savings Accounts
- Auto Loan Accounts
- Home Loans
- Visa Credit and Debit Cards
- Telephone Banking

Business Banking
- Multi-currency Accounts
- Treasury Services
- Trade Finance Services
- Electronic Banking

Call: +9714 342 2000

OVERSEAS *Club*

- Choice of Dollar, Sterling or Euro Denominated Accounts
- Free Money Transfers from Dubai
- Credit & Debit Cards
- Internet Banking
- Telephone Banking
- Personal Club Manager & Team
- Independent Investment Advice

www.lloydstsb.ae

BANKING WORTH TALKING ABOUT

 Lloyds TSB

OPEN from 8am - 6pm, Saturday to Thursday. For more information, please contact us at: Lloyds TSB Bank plc, PO Box 3766, Dubai, United Arab Emirates 714 342 2000 Fax: +9714 342 2660 e-mail: ltsbbank@emirates.net.ae. The opening of an account and all credit is subject to status. Lloyds TSB Bank plc ns apply. Lloyds TSB Bank plc. Registered Office: 25 Gresham Street, London EC 2V 7HN. Registered in England and Wales No. 2065

Cost of Living

Drinks

Beer (pint/bottle)	Dhs.20
Fresh fruit cocktail	Dhs.10
House wine (glass)	Dhs.22
House wine (bottle)	Dhs.90 - 130
Milk (1 litre)	Dhs.5
Water	
1.5 litres (supermarket)	Dhs.1.50
1.5 litres (hotel)	Dhs.10 - 18

Food

Big Mac	Dhs.10
Bread (large)	Dhs.4 - 8
Cappuccino	Dhs.10 - 15
Chocolate bar	Dhs.2
Eggs (dozen)	Dhs.6
Falafel	Dhs.3
Fresh meat	Dhs.15-40/kg.
Imported Fresh fruit	Dhs.5-20/kg.
Shawarma	Dhs.3
Sugar	Dhs.3.5/kg.
Tin of tuna	Dhs.4

Miscellaneous

Cigarettes (per packet)	Dhs.6
Film	Dhs.8
Film processing (colour, 36 exposures)	Dhs.35 - 45
Hair cut (female)	Dhs.70+
Hair cut (male)	Dhs.25-60
Postcard	Dhs.2

Getting Around

Abra Creek crossing	50 fils
Car rental (compact)	Dhs.100/day
Private Abra Creek tour (30 mins)	Dhs.40
Taxi (airport to city)	Dhs.40 - 50
Taxi (airport to beach)	Dhs.70 - 80
Taxi (+ Dhs.1.25 every km)	Dhs.3 pick up charge
City tour (half day)	Dhs.110
Bus from airport to downtown	Dhs.3
Desert safari (half day)	Dhs.200-280

Entrance Fees

Beach club (may include lunch)	Dhs.60 - 200
Cinema	Dhs.30
Museum	Dhs.2 - 10
Park	Dhs.3 - 5

Sports

Fishing (two hours)	Dhs.100
Fishing (2 hours)	Dhs.100
Go Karting (15 mins)	Dhs.75
Golf (18 holes)	Dhs.80 - 375
Jet ski hire (30 mins)	Dhs.100
Parasailing (1 ride)	Dhs.200

Taxation

The UAE levies no personal income taxes or withholding taxes of any sort. The only noticeable taxes you are obliged to pay as an expat are a five percent municipality tax on rental accommodation and a 30% tax on alcohol bought at liquor stores. Also, there is a ten percent municipality tax and a 15 - 16% service tax at hotel food and beverage outlets, but these are usually built into the displayed price.

Legal Issues

The UAE is governed by Sharia law – this is Islamic canonical law that is based on the traditions of Prophet Mohammed (PBUH) and the teachings of the Koran – and only a graduate of a Sharia college can practice in court here. All court proceedings are conducted in Arabic, so you will find it important to hire legal representation that you trust.

The most common situation for expatriates to find themselves on the wrong side of the law is in cases of drunk driving (see [p.43]). If you are involved in an accident or are spot checked by the police and found to have consumed alcohol the likelihood is that you will spend some time behind bars and could end up losing your job. So the smart move is - don't do it – but if you do end up in mitigating circumstances with the law then, if the situation is serious, you may need to contact your embassy or consulate as soon as possible and follow their advice, plus find yourself a good lawyer. For most people, any sort of brush with the 'wrong' side of

Foreign and local banks, side by side

Tomorrow is shaped by capable hands.

بنك دبي الوطني
National Bank of Dubai

the law can be a worrying experience, but in a foreign country and with an alien language this can be particularly unnerving.

Neighbourhood Watch

In their efforts to maintain and promote a safe community the Dubai Police recently launched Al Ameen, with a confidential toll free telephone service where you can report anything suspicious. For example if you have seen someone hanging around your property or loitering at cash points you can pass the information on anonymously to the police via Al Ameen on 800 4888. You can also email information to alameen@emirates.net.ae.

In addition, do not be fooled into thinking that Dubai has a liberal attitude when it comes to the law and the best advice is NEVER get involved with drugs - even the smallest amounts of marijuana or hashish possession can land you in prison for four years or more.

Aside from criminal proceedings, other areas where you may find you need the services of a lawyer may be in labour disputes (see Labour Law and Banning [p.83]), for real estate purchasing (see Real Estate Law [p.99]) or for divorce cases.

Divorce Law

Recent statistics show that the UAE has one of the highest divorce rates in the Arab world. In a bid to counter this bodies such as the State Marriage Fund have launched schemes offering education and counselling services to National couples.

Under Islamic Sharia law a Muslim man can divorce his wife by a stating 'I divorce thee' three times. If he makes the statement only twice the husband can change his decision within three months.

Non Nationals can apply for divorce in Dubai, and in some cases the procedure can be relatively straightforward. However, expatriate couples wishing to divorce here are governed by the laws of their home country (if the couple has mixed nationalities the home country of the husband applies), so it is advisable to seek legal advice. It is worth remembering that a husband who sponsors his wife has the right to have her residence visa cancelled in the event of a divorce.

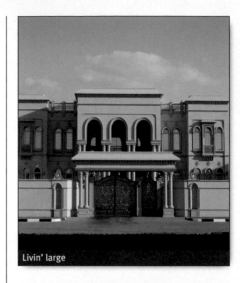

Livin' large

Housing

Renting in Dubai

Although non Nationals now have the opportunity to purchase a home in Dubai, many of the developments have only just been completed or have another year or so until they are ready for occupancy. Therefore, for now, rental is still the main option. Many new residents arriving in Dubai on a full expat package may have accommodation included in their employment contract. This is either by way of a monetary value (which many people top up because they wish to live in a more expensive area or accommodation type) or by housing being provided (which is often the case for many teachers and airline staff). If your employment contract has specific accommodation provided for you and you would rather take the cash equivalent in your salary and live somewhere else most employers are willing to be flexible so it's worth asking – politely of course!

Law Firms	Tel	Fax	Web/Email
Afridi & Angell	330 3900	330 3800	www.afridi-angell.com
Al Sharif Advocates & Legal Consultants	262 8222	262 8111	www.dubailaw.com
Hadef Al Dhahiri & Associates P.89	332 3222	332 3300	www.hadalaw.com
Tal Al Tamimi Advocates & Legal Consultants	295 3366	295 3399	ibrahimalnahel@yahoo.com
Trench & Associates	355 3146	355 3106	www.trenchlaw.com

Rents over the past few years have consistently risen and, in general, are very high. Accommodation at the higher end of the market (over Dhs.65,000 for apartments and Dhs.100,000 for villas per annum) may drop eventually if supply exceeds demand, and more freehold property is released. However, this is far from certain, with many pundits predicting a lack of supply driven by huge population growth, in which case prices will continue to increase. Prices at the lower/middle end will remain firm due to heavy demand.

Rents are always quoted for the year, unless otherwise stated, and tenants will usually pay via a number of post-dated cheques – typically two or three, although it is not uncommon for landlords to request the entire annual rent in one cheque (this can be a good bargaining tool in negotiating rent prices). Paying monthly in Dubai is practically unheard of, unless you are staying in a hotel apartment [p.37]. If you are able to pay more money up front it's worth asking the landlord if he would consider a discount on the yearly rent. After all, he'll have more of your money earning interest in his bank account. Also, when renting a property try to negotiate a fixed rate for two, three, or more years – that way you won't get any nasty shocks after your first year. As a rule, the maximum rent increase allowed is 20%, and then only after two years of occupation, although it seems that the rules are made up to suit the landlord. Not long ago the unofficial rules was that only a five percent increased could be applied, although in reality landlords often decrease the rent in the second or third year in order to retain tenants. This has changed due to increased demand and it is likely that your landlord will try to increase your rent – but that doesn't mean you can't try to fight it. The landlord must give written notice of any increase, at least one month in advance. If your landlord does try to increase the rent unfairly then there are government channels to dispute rent matters. See Rent Disputes, [p.90].

Renting the Smart Way

Like anywhere else in the world, Dubai too has its fair share of cons. To avoid falling into a landlord trap, the Rent Committee advises that both parties produce a written agreement. This contract reduces the risk of either party falling out on the rental terms discussed.

Do remember to ask for a copy of the estate agent's identification card and make sure you save copies of all receipts, contracts and other documents.

Search Tips

Location, location, location
Check proximity of potential homes to church bells, mosques, rubbish bins, schools, and the airport flight path.

New Buildings
Look out for buildings under construction – it's often a good way to find a place you like and be one of the first on the waiting list. The guys on site should be able to give you the name of the real estate agent or landlord.

Noise Control
In the less built up areas, beware that the area around your new home could be ripe for development – few people really appreciate a noisy building site just a few metres from their bedroom window! Construction work, in theory, starts at about 06:00 and finishes by 21:00 or 22:00, with the odd 01:00 concrete pour, often seven days a week. However with the current construction boom you may find that many sites operate 24 hours a day and complaints seem to fall on deaf ears.

Rent Disputes

The Rent Committee of the Dubai Municipality (206 3833) assists both tenants and landlords in rent disputes. Amongst recent cases the majority of disputes were raised by landlords rather than by tenants. To help improve the system it's important that you use these services if trouble ever arises.

Government Apartments and Villas

The Dubai Government owns and manages more than 18,000 residential and commercial properties around Dubai with rents suitable for all levels of income. Because these properties tend to be very good value for money, many have long waiting lists. To find out more or to put your name on a wait list, contact the Dubai Real Estate Department (398 6666) or log on to www.realestate-dubai.gov.ae.

Dubai Property Group

In 2002 a group of professional real estate companies banded together to work towards ensuring proper conduct in real estate dealings in Dubai. Examining current real estate industry practices, they make proposals for change that will benefit all concerned. Their goal is to try to make a difference for the residents of Dubai, working closely with the Rent Committee and the Government of Dubai (through the Dubai Development Board). For more information log on to www.dubaipropertygroup.com.

WHAT'S IN A NAME?
EVERYTHING

You don't get respect and an excellent reputation easily in the UAE. 18 years experience and a dedication to service has earned Better Homes its place as one of the largest and most successful real estate companies in Dubai.

Sales   **Leasing**   **Property Management**
Head office +971 4 344 7714 or visit www.bhomes.com

Real Estate Glossary

It is generally best to rent from a real estate agent as they will handle all the paperwork for you. Single women occasionally have difficulty renting apartments and they may need to put their employer's name on the lease – but this is very rare. Several good agents exist and all are helpful and interested in getting you settled in your new home (see [p.98]).

Housing Abbreviations	
BR	Bedroom
Ensuite	Bedroom has private bathroom
Fully fitted	Includes appliances (oven, refrigerator, washing machine)
L/D	Living/dining room area
W/robes	Built in wardrobes (closets)
Hall flat	Apartment has an entrance hall (ie, entrance doesn't open directly onto living room)
D/S	Double storey villa
S/S	Single storey villa
C.A/C	Central air conditioning (usually included in the rent)
W.A/C	Window air conditioning (often indicates an older building)
S/Q	Servant quarters
Ext S/Q	Servant quarters located outside the villa
Pvt garden	Private garden
Shared pool	Pool is shared with other villas in compound

The Lease

To take out a lease personally, you need to be a resident. The real estate agent will need a copy of your passport and visa, a no objection letter (NOC) from your company, a copy of your salary certificate and an initial signed rent cheque (plus up to three post dated cheques covering the remaining period of the lease). Unlike elsewhere in the world, rent cheques have to be paid to the landlord up front and not on a monthly basis. This can cause problems as many new residents do not have the cash available to pay this sort of lump sum in advance. Needless to say banks are quick to offer loans! To rent through your company you require a copy of the company trade licence, a passport copy of whoever is signing the rent cheque and, of course, the rent cheque/s.

Main Accommodation Options

Apartment/Villa Sharing

For those on a budget the solution may be to share an apartment or a villa with colleagues or friends. Check the notice boards in supermarkets such as Choithrams, Park n Shop or Spinneys, or even sports clubs, for people advertising shared accommodation. The classified sections of local newspapers also advertise accommodation.

Standard Apartment

There are generally two types of apartments available for rent – those with central air conditioning (A/C) and those with the noisier window A/Cs where the unit is in the apartment wall. Central A/C accommodation is always more expensive, although in some buildings the charge for A/C is absorbed into the rent. Top of the range, central A/C apartments often come semi-furnished (with a cooker, fridge and washing machine), boast 24 hour security, satellite TV, covered parking, gym, pool etc. Normally, the more facilities that come with the apartment, the more expensive the rent.

Villa

The same procedure for leasing apartments applies to leasing villas. Value for money villas are very hard to find and, where you used to be able to find older, cheaper villas in some parts of Jumeira, many are being demolished for redevelopment. As with apartments, villas differ greatly in quality and facilities, such as in a compound, shared pool, security, etc.

Hotel Apartment

An alternative option is to rent a hotel apartment – ideal if you require temporary, furnished accommodation, although they are expensive. Most hotel apartments are in Bur Dubai near the BurJuman shopping mall. Apartments can be rented on a daily/weekly/monthly or yearly basis. They come fully furnished (from sofas to knives and forks) and serviced (maid service) with satellite TV, and usually have sports facilities (pool and gym etc). Water and electricity are also included in the rent. If you can, call around first for rates, as they

have high and low seasons based on the heat and the tourism in Dubai. See the Hotel Apartments table in General Information, [p.37].

Residential Areas

Other options ➜ Exploring [p.148]

As in all cities, some residential areas in Dubai are more desirable than others. The more upmarket areas for villas are Jumeira and Umm Suqeim, with some cheaper options in Satwa, Al Garhoud, Mirdif and Rashidiya, but with so many new developments being built, new residents now have a greater choice than ever. The most popular area for apartments tends to be Bur Dubai behind the BurJuman shopping mall, and along Sheikh Zayed Road, which is lined with modern glass skyscrapers. Cheaper options are in Deira, Al Qusais, Satwa, and Karama. However, the odd top of the range building can be found in these cheaper areas and likewise the odd bargain can still be found in the more upmarket districts.

> ### Renter's Nightmare
>
> *The majority of leases in Dubai are fixed for one year. If you choose to leave before the year is up, you might not get your deposit back and you will likely have to pay at least one month's penalty. You may even forfeit the entire year's rent! So, be careful when you sign your lease. You will have to pay your entire year's rent in one to three cheques, so make sure the apartment or villa you've just found is really the one you'd like to make your home for the next year!*

Villas are also available towards Jebel Ali in the new Meadows, Lakes, and Springs developments, and apartments at the Greens. A cheaper option is to live in The Gardens near Jebel Ali, or in the nearby emirates of Sharjah or Ajman. Here prices for apartments are generally lower by at least Dhs.10,000 - 20,000 per year, and villas are cheaper still. However, while there are great savings to be made by living in either of these emirates, beware the Sharjah Decency Law. Also, beware the Sharjah-Dubai highway – renowned for mammoth delays around rush hour. If your work or social life is based in Dubai you could find that living outside the city and facing daily delays may not be worth the savings.

A glance through the property pages in the newspapers will give you an idea of what is available where and for how much. You can also check online in the classifieds of Gulf News and Khaleej Times. The following section gives an overview of each area and how much you can expect to pay to live there. Obviously there will be properties that cost less, and some a lot more, as so much depends on the age and condition of the building, the facilities on offer, and the particular location. Use the suggested prices as a starting point and then shop around.

Al Barsha   Map Ref ➜ 3-D3

This is certainly an up and coming area and the increasing rental prices reflect this. Its location makes it especially attractive to those working in Media and Internet cities, but with Shk. Zayed Road and the E44 and E311 highways also easily accessible, it's also handy for those working further into Dubai. Apart from having a lot of schools it is a bit short of facilities at present, but with the new Mall of the Emirates arriving on the doorstep things are improving. Barsha has a mix of old and new villas and apartments. Expect to pay around Dhs.60,000 for a two bedroom apartment and Dhs.130,000 for a four bedroom villa.

Al Garhoud   Map Ref ➜ 14-D4

A great location for airline staff, Garhoud has some great villas and a few new developments near the back of Cambridge High School. It's handy for central Dubai too, but the traffic can be a problem once you get outside the central residential area. There's been very little new building so finding available accommodation here isn't always easy. Being so close to the airport there is a chance of aircraft noise depending on the wind direction. Rents are slightly lower than some other central areas, with a four bedroom villa likely to start at Dhs.100,000.

Al Qusais   Map Ref ➜ 15-D2

The biggest draw here is the low rent, with prices much less than some other areas of Dubai. It's not far from the border with Sharjah so if you're planning on commuting in and out of Dubai be prepared for a lot of traffic. Shopping and leisure facilities are limited. The area consists mainly of apartments and you can expect to pay Dhs.30,000 for two bedrooms.

Arabian Ranches   Map Ref ➜ UAE-C2

A prestigious new Emaar development taking shape away from the centre of town, on the E311 Emirates Road near Dubai Autodrome. Arabian Ranches is an all-villa project, set amongst lush greenery and featuring lakes and a golf course. It will be especially attractive to horse-lovers as the site has stabling, polo lawns, and a network of bridle paths. The properties have been sold on a freehold basis so it's too early to give an indication of the average rental prices.

Bur Dubai – Creek   Map Ref ➜ 8-A2

A good central location, ideal for the Creek, downtown Dubai and the BurJuman centre. The area has low rents and plenty of character. The further towards the heart of Bur Dubai you go, the cheaper the accommodation, but be prepared for lots of hustle and bustle and limited parking. There's a real mixture of old and new, so rents do vary considerably. For a two bedroom apartment you could pay between Dhs.40,000 and Dhs.60,000 depending on the age of the building etc.

Bur Dubai – Al Mankhool   Map Ref ➜ 7-E4

Not too many years ago this was one of the most popular destinations for new residents in Dubai, but these days new arrivals have a much wider choice. Made up of old and new apartment blocks, it is something of a concrete jungle with no green spaces, and traffic congestion can be a problem. Despite this, rents are not cheap and many still prefer this area for its convenient central location. A two bedroom apartment in a new building could set you back around Dhs.65,000, but for that you should expect excellent facilities.

Deira – Creekside   Map Ref ➜ 8-E2

Lots of new buildings here offering modern upmarket apartments, many with a view of the Creek. Convenient access to main roads and the two bridges, and close proximity to a variety of entertainment facilities makes this area a popular choice for young professionals. Rents in the region of Dhs.65,000 for a two bedroom apartment.

Deira – Old District   Map Ref ➜ 8-E2

A heavily built-up area with lots of old apartment blocks and hardly any greenery, but a perfect location for exploring the souks. Rents are relatively low but the area does suffer from traffic problems, especially at rush hour. A studio flat will cost around Dhs.25,000.

Emirates Hills   Map Ref ➜ 2-E4

With The Greens, The Lakes, The Meadows and The Springs adding thousands of new homes to the Dubai landscape, Emirates Hills has become THE hot new property area. Perfect for those who want to escape the chaos of city life and enjoy green open spaces, it's out of town location is convenient for Media and Internet Cities and Jebel Ali Free Zone. On the downside it is quite a commute into central Dubai. Rents are not cheap – a one bedroom apartment in The Greens will average Dhs.50,000, whilst a four bedroom villa in The Meadows will cost from Dhs.130,000.

Green Community   Map Ref ➜ UAE-C2

The Green Community is a self-contained development of villas, apartments, and leisure and shopping facilities, situated within the Dubai Investment Park near Jebel Ali. As the name suggests, the homes are set within acres of landscaped greenery with pedestrian walkways, cycle lanes and a large lake. The developers have also attempted to reduce the environmental impact of the project, for instance, by providing ample recycling facilities. If, and when, a property does become available you can expect to pay around Dhs.90,000 for a three bedroom villa.

Jebel Ali   Map Ref ➜ 2-A3

Convenient for people working at this end of town, Jebel Ali village features a mixture of different sized villas, and rents vary from reasonable to expensive. The Gardens is a new community of 3,800 apartments and 200 villas with the main attraction being the comprehensive leisure facilities and low rents. There isn't too much in the way of entertainment, but The Gardens mall is a welcome addition for shoppers. A two bed Gardens apartment should cost around Dhs.32,000.

Jumeira   Map Ref ➜ 5-D2

One of the most desirable addresses in Dubai, so it figures that prices are some of the highest around. The housing is mostly made up of large, walled villas with gardens, giving Jumeira quite a suburban feel. The area is ideally located for schools, beach clubs and lots of shopping. One of the only drawbacks is the traffic on Al Jumeira Road (Beach Road) which can be a problem at rush hour. Average price for a four bedroom villa is Dhs.150,000.

Al Karama   Map Ref ➜ 10-D2

A convenient central location near the heart of downtown Dubai, but as you'd expect it is another concrete jungle with little green space. Accommodation is predominantly made up of four-storey apartment blocks. With its wealth of low-cost cafés and restaurants, the souk selling nearly everything imaginable, and rents cheaper than Bur Dubai, Karama is a good choice for Dubai residents on a budget, although many new apartment blocks are adopting Bur Dubai prices. Too many cars and too few parking spaces mean traffic can be a real headache and don't expect much peace and quiet as Karama is a lively place. One bedroom apartments average Dhs.30,000.

Marsa Dubai   Map Ref → 2-D2

Another prime location with sky-high rents to match, the area around the marina has lots of brand new waterfront buildings, mainly towers with luxury apartments but a few villas too. Be prepared for ongoing construction for a few years to come and, as more buildings are completed, expect more and more traffic. A two bedroom apartment with a balcony and sea view, and access to first-class facilities, will set you back around Dhs.125,000.

Mirdif   Map Ref → 16-B4

Previously a sleepy backwater located away from town, Mirdif is under extensive development. While it was once a much more inexpensive option for renting villas rent increases have been quite drastic over the last year. It has a pleasant suburban feel and is great for families, but facilities are limited. However, that is set to change with the new 'UP Town Mirdiff' development featuring retail outlets, a cinema, swimming pool and gym, as well as apartments and villas. The Spinneys supermarket there is set to open early 2005. Not far from Dubai International Airport, aircraft noise is an issue depending on whereabouts in Mirdif you are, so listen for planes when house hunting. A three bedroom villa will cost in the region of Dhs.70,000.

Oud Metha   Map Ref → 13-E1

A good central location within easy reach of the highways, plenty of restaurants, and the Wafi shopping mall. With no villas to speak of, the accommodation is mainly four-storey apartment blocks, but Oud Metha is not as densely populated as other areas. There is a fair amount of construction going on but at present apartments are not easy to find. For two bedrooms in a modern building you'll pay around Dhs.65,000.

Satwa   Map Ref → 6-D3

Satwa is an area of real contrasts. At one end you've got the hustle and bustle of Al Dhiyafah Street and the crowded shopping area around the one-way system, but head south towards Al Wasl and you'll find villas old and new, and plenty of greenery. Centrally located, with schools, shopping, and the beach all close at hand, this is a popular destination and properties are hard to come by. With such a variety of housing, rents vary enormously, from Dhs.25,000 for a one bed apartment, to Dhs.150,000 for a four bedroom villa.

Sharjah   Map Ref → 6-D3

Still a popular choice for many people working in Dubai, most of whom are lured by the much lower rents. The biggest drawback is the infamous E11 Sharjah to Dubai highway – if you're commuting into Dubai in the morning rush hour be prepared for journey times of an hour or more, and the same when you return in the evening. You will be smiling though when rent day comes around – a one bed apartment could cost as little as Dhs.15,000 and three bedroom villas can be found for Dhs.45,000.

Trade Centre 1 & 2   Map Ref → 9-C2

Located on the strip between the Trade Centre and interchange one, the high-rises on either side of Sheikh Zayed Road house thousands of apartments. With easy access to the road network and nearby offices, this is a favourite location for young professionals. A big advantage is the number of bars, restaurants, and hotels within easy walking distance. The higher you go the better the view, but apartments facing the road could suffer from noise problems depending on the quality of the double glazing. Parking can be an issue too, as new building sites swallow more and more car parks. Prices are not cheap, but not astronomical either, with an average two bedroom apartment costing around Dhs.65,000.

Umm Suqeim   Map Ref → 4-C2

A pleasant suburban area, Umm Suqeim has a good mix of new luxury villas, and older ones that are snapped up as soon as they are advertised. Prices are slightly lower than Jumeira, but not significantly, as the same facilities are only a short drive away. Prices vary depending on the age and size of villa, and rents in Umm Suqeim 3 will be a little lower than Umm Suqeim 1, but a four bedroom villa will average Dhs.140,000.

Dubai housing options

Other Rental Costs

Extra costs to be considered are:

- Water and electricity deposit (Dhs.2,000 for villas, Dhs.1,000 for apartments) paid directly to Dubai Electricity & Water Authority (DEWA) and fully refundable on cancellation of lease
- Real estate commission – five percent of annual rent (one off payment)
- Maintenance charge – five percent of annual rent (may be included)
- Municipality tax – five percent of annual rent
- Fully refundable security deposit and/or deposit against damage - Dhs.1,500 - 5,000

If you are renting a villa don't forget that you may have to maintain a garden and pay for extra water etc. To avoid massive water bills at the end of every month many people prefer to have a well dug in their backyard for all that necessary plant and grass watering. Expect to pay around Dhs.1,500 - 3,000 to have a well dug and a pump installed.

Some of the older villas may also need additional maintenance which the landlord may not cover. Often the more popular accommodation has waiting lists that are years long. To secure an immediate tenancy many people offer the landlord 'key money', a down payment of several thousand dirhams to secure the accommodation.

Purchasing a Home

Until relatively recently only UAE and GCC Nationals could own residential property in Dubai. However, in 2002 H.H. General Sheikh Mohammed bin Rashid Al Maktoum, Crown Prince of Dubai and

Main Developers	
Al Nakheel Properties	390 3388
Damac Properties Co. LLC	399 9500
Emaar Properties	800 4990
Estithmaar Realty FZ - LLC	391 1114

UAE Defence Minister, announced that foreign nationals would be able to purchase certain Dubai properties on a freehold basis, sparking the current real estate boom. The big developments such as the Palms [p.14], Dubai Marina [p.10], Arabian Ranches [p.94] and Burj Dubai [p.9] offer residential units for sale, with many also promising residency visas for owners, renewable every three years. Emirates Hills [p.95] is one of Dubai's most exclusive addresses, while Jumeirah Beach Residence [p.10] boasts beach front living. The Greens [p.95] is a popular area for buyers looking for more affordable options than the aforementioned. The table below gives contact details for some of the biggest property developers. With regard to the term 'freehold', it should be noted that at present the laws have not been passed confirming a foreigner's right to legally own the freehold title to a Dubai property, although it is expected that they will be shortly, see Real Estate Law, [p.99]. As with buying any property, legal assistance is recommended and many legal firms in Dubai now have departments that deal specifically in real estate law.

Mortgages

Soon after the government announced the granting of freehold status of residential property to foreign nationals, mortgage plans were introduced for those wishing to purchase.

Real Estate Agents	Tel	Email	Web
Al Futtaim Real Estate	211 9111	realestate@alfuttaim.ae	www.al-futtaim.com
Alpha Properties	228 8588	info@alphaproperties.com	www.alphaproperties.com
Arenco Group	337 0550	arencoar@emirates.net.ae	www.arencore.com
Asteco Property	269 3155	asteco@astecoproperty.com	www.astecoproperty.com
Better Homes P.91	344 7714	bhomes@emirates.net.ae	www.bhomes.com
Cluttons	334 8585	cluttons@emirates.net.ae	www.cluttonsuae.com
Dubai Government Real Estate	398 6666	na	www.realestate-dubai.gov.ae
Dubai Luxury Homes	355 1484	info@dubailuxuryhomes.com	www.dubailuxuryhomes.com
Dubai Property Group	262 9888	dubaipg@hotmail.com	www.dubaipropertygroup.com
Landmark Properties	331 6161	info@landmark-dubai.com	www.landmark-dubai.com
Property Shop, The	345 5711	propshop@emirates.net.ae	www.propertyshopdubai.com
Real Estate Specialists, The P.93	331 2662	Restate@emirates.net.ae	www.dubaiuae.com
Rocky Real Estate	353 2000	rocky53@emirates.net.ae	www.rocki.com
Sherwoods	343 8002	shwoods@emirates.net.ae	www.sherwoodsproperty.com
Union Properties	294 9490	up@unionproperties.com	www.unionproperties.com

This was another first in the region and a further indication of Dubai's seriousness in encouraging foreign investment in real estate. The maximum mortgage granted is Dhs.5 million and financing companies offer up to 90% of the purchase price or valuation to UAE Nationals, and up to 80% to GCC and foreign nationals. Mortgages must be paid back in monthly instalments within a maximum of 25 years, and rates are comparable to international norms. The mortgage amount depends on the chosen mortgage plan and is limited to an amount no greater than 60 times the monthly household (both husband and wife's) income. Currently not all banks offer mortgages and some of those that do only do so for specific developments, refer to the table below.

Mortgage Providers

Amlak	800 4337
Tamweel	295 2259
HSBC Bank IFC	394 8252
RAK Bank	224 8000
Lloyds TSB P.85	342 2000
Dubai Islamic Bank	295 3000
Dubai Bank	332 8989
Mashreqbank	222 3333

Other Purchasing Costs

As well as the usual costs associated with buying a property, such as a mortgage and insurance, there are other charges you should take into account when buying in Dubai. Most owners will be liable for a maintenance charge to cover the upkeep of the building, gardens and pool etc, and for services such as refuse collection. In certain Emaar properties this price is fixed (currently Dhs.600 per month) regardless of size, but other developers charge between Dhs.4 and Dhs.15 per square foot per year. In a big villa this could add up to quite a substantial amount. Another consideration is the transfer fee. If you're purchasing directly from the developer this won't apply, but buy 'second-hand' and the developer will require a percentage of the sale price. This is usually around one or two percent but can be as high as seven. The buyer is responsible for this fee, but it may be possible to negotiate with the seller to share the cost. Finally, the buyer and seller will also owe a fee to the real estate agent, and this is likely to be around one percent of the selling price.

Real Estate Law

The new law to open up the real estate arena to non Nationals is still in its infancy and therefore there are a number of ambiguous issues when it comes to the status of ownership. While there is now no law in the UAE which specifically prohibits expatriates from owning property, when it comes to registering title deeds with the Dubai Land Registry difficulties may arise for some developments unless you are a UAE or GCC national. Expatriate property owners in the UAE are therefore not the registered owners in the same legal sense as they may be in other countries, but are rather the beneficial owners, with the developers being the legal owners holding the property on behalf of the expatriate. With this ambiguity existing in current legislation it is important that you seek legal advice from a law firm specialising in real estate law before you sign on the dotted line. Sale and purchase contracts should be reviewed thoroughly by your lawyer. Hadef Al Dhahiri & Associates (www.hadalaw.com) has a dedicated Real Estate department while Trench & Associates have a good FAQ section on their Website, www.trenchlaw.com.

Therefore if a property is referred to as 'freehold' do not assume that this means the same as it would in your country of origin. Not only because of the issues involved with legal ownership but also with restrictions on the property. For example, it may not be as straightforward as you think to sell the property on to a third party or to make structural changes to it. Additionally, most developments require payments of annual service charges and significant transfer fees when selling the property to a third party. Problems may also arise in the event of the owner's death, since under Sharia law (which applies in the UAE from a family law perspective) it may not necessarily be transferred to the spouse. In order to ensure that the property is passed on to those you wish, your lawyer may be able to establish an offshore company which may avoid application of Sharia requirements.

With the process of expatriate purchasing in Dubai at such an early stage the law is yet to be as developed as it may be in your country of origin so risks could be potentially higher, especially as many purchases are conducted in a less formal manner. While there are risks, buying property in Dubai also has its advantages – with property developments that you will not find anywhere else in the world. The best advice when purchasing in Dubai is – get a lawyer!

New Residents

Housing

Setting up Home

Moving Services

Two main options exist when moving your furniture and personal effects either to or from Dubai: air freight and sea freight. Air freight is a better option when moving smaller amounts but if you have a larger consignment sea freight may be financially beneficial. Either way, ensure your goods are packed by professionals.

A removal company with a wide international network is usually the best and safest option, but more importantly, you must trust the people you are dealing with. Ensure they are competent in the country of origin and have reliable agents in the country to which you are shipping your personal belongings. Most removal companies offer free consultations, plus advice and samples of packing materials – call around.

When your belongings arrive in Dubai they will need to be custom checked to make sure they contain nothing inappropriate or illegal. This will happen at Cargo Village and you will need to be

Moving Tips

- Book moving dates well in advance
- Don't forget insurance and purchase additional insurance for irreplaceable items
- Make an inventory of the items you want moved (keep your own copy!)
- Ensure everything is packed extremely well and in a way that can be checked by customs and repacked with the least possible damage; check and sign the packing list
- Keep a camera and film handy to take pictures at each stage of the move (valuable in case of a dispute)
- Do not pack customs restricted goods of any kind
- If moving to Dubai, ensure videos, DVD's and books are not offensive to Muslim sensibilities

Removal Companies

ADSA International Movers	282 6999
Allied Pickfords P.101	338 3600
Blue Line	06 562 5111
Crown Worldwide Movers P.67	289 5152
Gulf Agency Company (GAC) P.103	345 7555
Interem (Freight Systems Co. Ltd) P.69	314 1201
Mover's Packaging	267 0699

present. After this, depending on the agreement you have with the removal company, either their representative in Dubai will help you transport the boxes to your new home, or you can make the arrangements locally.

Orientation/Relocation Experts

Once your household goods have arrived you may wish to enlist the help of an orientation or relocation expert. They offer services designed to help you settle into your new life in Dubai as quickly as possible. Practical help ranges from finding accommodation or schools for your children to connecting a telephone or information on medical care. In addition, some offer advice on the way of life in the city, putting people in touch with social and business networks to help them establish a new life. For example, The Specialists (see table) have a 'first friend' support programme, and also offer cultural training.

Relocation Companies

Global Relocations	352 3300
In Touch Relocations	332 8807
Interem (Freight Systems Co. Ltd) P.69	314 1201
Simply Settled	394 2166
Real Estate Specialists P.93	331 2662
The Specialists	332 4111
Writer Relocations P.60	340 8816

Furnishing Accommodation

Other options → Home Furnishing
& Accessories [p.220]
Second-Hand Items [p.230]

One of the great things about Dubai is that if you can't buy it (or don't want to) virtually anything can be made for you, be it tailoring or furniture making. You can easily pick out the latest Italian furniture from photos and, after a bit of research and bargaining, have it custom made for you. Furniture shops along the Naif Road, and most of the large furniture showrooms in Sharjah offer this service.

Ready made, good quality furniture and household items can be found at reasonable prices. The most popular furniture outlets in Dubai are IKEA, THE One, Home Centre and Pan Emirates Furniture (located in Dubai and Sharjah). ID Design, and AATI offer funky designer furniture at premium prices. Other favourites for Indian teak and wrought iron are Marina Gulf Trading, Khans (06 562 1621), Pinkies and Luckys (06 534 1937) in Sharjah, and Indian Village in Dubai.

Cheap, and second-hand furniture is widely available in Karama, with plenty of shops selling inexpensive, basic furniture, pots, pans and almost every household item.

Home furnishings

Garage Sales

One man's trash is another man's treasure and with so many people moving in and out of Dubai, you can find a lot of decent household items at garage sales. Check out the noticeboards at Spinneys, Park 'n' Shop, Choithrams or Safestway for the latest happenings in garage sales. Also read the classifieds section of newspapers for advertised garage sales.

Similarly, if you're leaving the Emirates and have some items that you don't want to ship back home you can hold your own garage sale. It's a great way to earn some cash while getting rid of all the junk that you couldn't fob off on friends! Ask your neighbours if they have some unwanted treasures to dispose of and then advertise the sale on local supermarket noticeboards and place ads in the classifieds of daily newspapers. If permitted, post some easy to follow direction signs with arrows in prominent locations. Clearly mark the goods with prices but be prepared for shoppers that love to haggle!

Household Appliances

Carrefour, Jashanmal, Jumbo Electronics and Plug Ins have a decent selection of heavy household appliances. Make sure that your purchases come with a warranty! All the main brands are found in the UAE but most are for European fittings.

Prices are quite reasonable for new appliances but if you would prefer to buy second-hand have a look around Karama, or at the noticeboards at the various supermarkets around town. Of course, there is no guarantee with second-hand goods, and if the bargain fridge you got goes on the blink then there is not a lot you can do apart from try and get it repaired and bare the financial consequences.

> #### On the Move
>
> *When moving from once place to another in Dubai, you can opt for a moving company or hire a few guys with their own truck from downtown Bur Dubai. The latter is a much cheaper option but be prepared to supervise strictly so that the scratches are at a minimum. Just choose a vehicle from the many standing at 'truck roundabout' (near the furniture section of Naif road or on the corner of Mankhool and Kuwait Roads in Bur Dubai) and request the driver's help in moving your stuff. Make sure you agree a price up front to avoid any conflict later on – work on around Dhs.50-70 per hour including two men.*

Household Insurance

No matter how crime free Dubai may seem it's still wise to insure the contents of your home as burglaries do occur and no matter how slim the chance may be nature's wrath can be unpredictable. There are many internationally recognised insurance companies operating in Dubai – check the Yellow Pages, or Hawk Business Pages for details.

When forming your policy the general information insurance companies need is your home address in Dubai, a household contents list and valuation, and invoices for items over Dhs.2,500. Cover usually extends to theft, storm damage, fire etc. For an additional fee, you can insure personal items outside the home, such as jewellery, cameras etc.

Most companies allow you to pick and choose the home owner's or renter's insurance best suited to you. A good coverage gives you flexibility, so you

Household Insurance	
AXA Insurance P.143 ▶	343 6161
BUPA	331 8688
Millennium Insurance	335 6552
National General Insurance	222 2772
Norwich Union Insurance	324 3434

can rest easy when you go on that long vacation or business trip. Coverage generally includes buildings, home contents, decorations, personal belongings and more, for you and family members residing with you. Call around for the best rates and options.

Laundry Services

Whilst there are no self service launderettes in Dubai there are hundreds of small outlets plus larger ones in supermarkets offering laundry and dry cleaning services at very cheap rates and with next day delivery (Champion Cleaners, 800 4556). Most also offer ironing and will service special cleaning requests for delicate items. Hotel services, however, are much more expensive.

Quick, easy and inexpensive

Domestic Help

Other options → Entry Visa [p.64]

Domestic help is commonplace in Dubai, whether a full time live in who cooks, cleans and looks after children and pets or part time help to do cleaning and ironing. To employ the services of a full time live in domestic helper or housemaid, you must have a minimum monthly salary of Dhs.6,000. As the employer you must sponsor the person and deal with all residency papers, including the medical test etc. Singles and families in which the wife isn't working may face difficulties sponsoring a helper. Finding the suitable candidate can also

be a challenge unless you are lucky enough to have a referral from someone who is leaving the country and has domestic help looking for new employment. It's normally best to find someone through an agency dedicated to hiring domestic helpers. You will be asked to sign a contract stating that you will pay your employee a minimum salary of about Dhs.750 each month with an airfare home once a year.

The residence visa for a housemaid will cost around Dhs.5,000. Residency is only valid for one year. You can obtain a residence visa through the normal channels, after which some embassies (e.g. the Philippines) require to see the labour contract of your newly appointed housemaid. This is to ensure that all paperwork is in order and that the maid is receiving fair treatment.

It is illegal to share a maid with another household and this could result in a Dhs.50,000 fine and a ban on sponsoring a housemaid in the future. The housemaid will also be deported and banned from entering the UAE for a period of one year. However this law is rarely prosecuted and many live in housemaids take on extra babysitting or cleaning jobs from other families.

If, for any reason, the domestic worker leaves their employer before their contractual agreement ends, they are banned from working in the UAE for six months and they will have to re-enter the country with a new visa. This applies even if they receive a no objection letter (NOC) from their employer. Those who change housemaids frequently or have complaints filed against them for mistreatment will be unable to sponsor housemaids in the future.

An alternative and cheaper option is to have part time home help and there are a number of agencies that offer domestic help on an hourly basis. The standard rate is about Dhs.20 - 25 per hour, with a minimum of two hours per visit. Try to get recommendations from friends who employ maids on a part time basis. The service includes general cleaning, washing, ironing and sometimes babysitting, but your mess level will determine the hours they spend cleaning.

Domestic Help Agencies	
Dialamaid	398 0850
Home Help	355 5100
Molly Maid	398 8877
Ready Maids	339 5722
Sky Maid Services	332 4600

HAMPION LEANERS
The Professional Choice!

with you everywhere

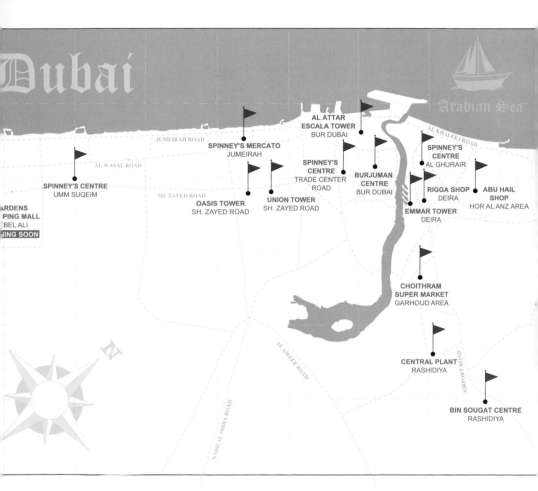

Dubai

Arabian Sea

JUMEIRAH ROAD

AL WASAL ROAD

AL KHALEEJ ROAD

AL ATTAR ESCALA TOWER
BUR DUBAI

SPINNEY'S MERCATO
JUMEIRAH

SPINNEY'S CENTRE
AL GHURAIR

SPINNEY'S CENTRE
TRADE CENTER ROAD

BURJUMAN CENTRE
BUR DUBAI

RIGGA SHOP
DEIRA

ABU HAIL SHOP
HOR AL ANZ AREA

SPINNEY'S CENTRE
UMM SUQEIM

SH. ZAYED ROAD

OASIS TOWER
SH. ZAYED ROAD

UNION TOWER
SH. ZAYED ROAD

EMMAR TOWER
DEIRA

RDENS
PING MALL
BEL ALI
ING SOON

CHOITHRAM SUPER MARKET
GARHOUD AREA

AL AWEER ROAD

NADD AL SHIBA ROAD

CENTRAL PLANT
RASHIDIYA

AIRPORT ROAD

BIN SOUGAT CENTRE
RASHIDIYA

Full Dry Cleaning & Laundry Services

4 winning locations :

pinneys (Al Ghurair),	04 - 2246403	Union Tower (Sh. Zayed Rd.),	04 - 3437805
pinneys (Mercato Mall),	04 - 3449727	Burjuman Centre (Bur Dubai),	04 - 3597170
pinneys Jumeirah,	04 - 3940986	Choithram (Garhoud),	04 - 2828297
pinneys (Trade Centre Rd.),	04 - 3512998	Bin Sougat Centre (Rashidiya),	04 - 2852822
l Rigga Rd.,	04 - 2957197	Abu Hail,	04 - 2654981
asis Tower (Sh. Zayed Rd.),	04 - 3211216	Central Plant,	04 - 2858581
maar Tower,	04 - 2287447	Al Attar Escala,	04 - 3986766

Another great location is opening soon - Gardens Shopping Mall, Jebel Ali

For Free Pick-up & Delivery Call Toll Free **8004556**.

AIR MILES
Shopping Rewards

Babysitting & Childcare

There are a growing number of nurseries in Dubai with varying degrees of flexibility when it comes to times and fees. Some nurseries will allow you to pick and choose how often you want your child to be at nursery and will charge accordingly. However others have stipulated term dates and fees and therefore appeal more to working mothers. The latter do have the bonus of a curriculum and tend to have organised classes while many of the other more flexible nurseries may be more like a 'drop off' service, where your child is 'minded' rather than 'taught'.

As for evening babysitting services, many people have live in housemaids and therefore have a 24 hour babysitter. For those who don't most of the Domestic Help Agencies offer babysitting services for Dhs. 20-25 per hour. Home Help, Ready Maids and Sky Main Services (all listed in the table above) offer babysitting services. The best thing to do is employ a maid from an agency to clean for you whilst you are in the house with your child and after you feel comfortable with the maid you can request they babysit too. Agencies allow you to book the same maid each time, and you may even be able to come up with a regular arrangement so that you will not miss out if you haven't booked her in time. Alternatively many people use the housemaids of friends as they automatically come with a recommendation. In addition many of the hotels offer babysitting for guests, which tends to be a monitor in the room or a member of the hotel staff sitting in your room while your baby sleeps. Either way when your child wakes up the hotel staff will contact you in the hotel restaurant you are dining in.

Fun in Dubai's sun

Domestic Services

Need a plumber? Or would you rather continue pretending you can fix that leak on your own? If you've done your best but the overflowing sink still threatens to flood the entire apartment, call a professional. Most buildings provide maintenance services, however if you do need help then have a look in the local papers in the classifieds section.

Pets

Bringing Your Pet to Dubai

While many people bring their pets to Dubai, it does involve paperwork and time. The following steps need to be taken to import pets into Dubai:

- Have the pet vaccinated and its booklet updated (in English) by the veterinarian in your country of origin

- Get an export certificate from the Ministry of agriculture and fisheries of the country from where the animal is being exported, certified by the vet there

- Book a space for your pet with your airline and beware, not all airlines allow them!

Dubai Kennels & Cattery (285 1646), The Doghouse (347 1807) or the Al Zubair Animal Care centre in Sharjah (06 7435988/050 727 8827) (Formerly the Ajman Pet Resort) can help you obtain an import permit, customs clearance and collection from the airport, delivery and/or boarding of your pet, if required. If you choose not to use their services, either your local vet or the originating country's local embassy will be able to advise you of the necessary requirements. There is no quarantine requirement for pets brought into the UAE.

Taking Your Pet Home

If you import your pet when you move to Dubai chances are that when you leave you will take them with you again. However, if you purchase or adopt a pet (see K9 and Feline Friends, [p.108]) you should still feel obliged to take them home again – too many dogs and cats are abandoned because their owners have left the country. You will be able to get an export permit from the Ministry of Agriculture and Fisheries (295 8161). The process may take a few weeks. Remember to check with your airline to see if you can take your pet as cargo or carry on, which is generally preferred by owners of small pets. The regulations for 'exporting' your pet depend on the laws of the country to which you

Commonly Regarded As The Most Perfect Design

Until now...

are moving and your local vet, kennels or the airline that you are using can inform you of the specific destination requirements, such as the country's quarantine rules etc.

Basic requirements are:

- A valid vaccination card not older than one year but not less than 30 days
- A health certificate issued by the Municipality or the Ministry of Agriculture and Fisheries, normally issued one week before departure
- A travel box, normally wooden or fibreglass that meets airline regulations.

Getting a UAE Pet Health Certificate

To obtain a UAE pet health certificate, you need to go to the Ministry of Agriculture and Fisheries (Clocktower R/A – look out for building which has the 'Omega' sign on the roof) and do the following:

1. Get an export application form from the Ministry of Agriculture

2. Submit a copy of the pet owner's passport, including the residence visa page

3. Submit a copy of the pet's vaccination booklet, along with Dhs.200 (processing fee).

Cats & Dogs

In the Middle East, animals are generally treated with a lot less sympathy than you may be used to. It is best to keep your pets indoors to protect them from the heat, traffic and attitude of some people here towards animals. You are also prohibited from taking your dog running with you along the beach or at public parks. Although many people do it, they can be fined. As usual, your pet must be vaccinated regularly and wear the Municipality ID disc (supplied on vaccination) on its collar at all times. The Municipality controls Dubai's huge stray population by trapping and either passing them on to a rescue home, or in most cases putting the animal to sleep. If your pet is trapped without an ID disc, it will be treated as a stray.

All pets should also be sterilised and kept safely on your premises. Once sterilised, they will wander less and will therefore be less exposed to danger. If you feed stray animals around your home they may come to rely on you, creating a problem for yourself and your neighbours.

Pet Services

Al Zubair Animal Care	06 7435988
Doghouse	347 1807
Dubai Kennels & Cattery	285 1646
Pets At Home	331 2186

Best friends

Animal Rescue

For the sick, stray and abandoned dogs and cats in Dubai, help is at hand in the shape of K9 Friends and Feline Friends. K9 Friends (347 4611) has been caring for and re-homing unwanted dogs since 1989, and to date has found new homes for over 1000 dogs. Staffed entirely by volunteers they rely on donations from the public and sponsors, organising frequent charity functions and sponsored dog walks. If you want to adopt, foster, or sponsor a dog, or simply make a donation, contact the above number or log on to www.k9friends.com for more information.

Feline Friends operates very much along the same lines, helping to rescue and re-home stray cats, and pursuing a sterilisation and re-release programme to control the street population. Again, they rely on volunteers, and always welcome donations and the offer of a foster home. If you do spot a cat in distress and you think it needs help you can reach a Dubai volunteer on 050 451 0058. Their Website is www.felinefriendsuae.com

Veterinary Clinics

Dr Matt's Veterinary Clinic	349 9549
European Veterinary Clinic	343 9591
Jumeirah Veterinary Clinic	394 2276
Modern Veterinary Clinic	395 3131
Veterinary Hospital	344 2498

Pet Shops

Though regulations governing the sale of animals in pet shops exist, they are rarely actively enforced. Animals are often underage (although their papers

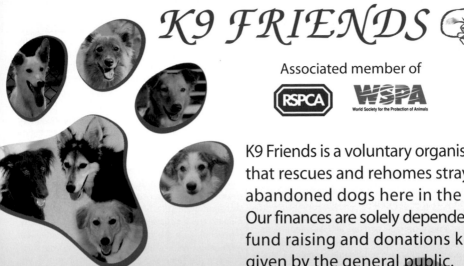

K9 FRIENDS

Associated member of

K9 Friends is a voluntary organisation that rescues and rehomes stray and abandoned dogs here in the UAE. Our finances are solely dependent on fund raising and donations kindly given by the general public.

If you can:-
* Give a dog a home
* Foster a dog until a permanent home can be found for it.
* Help with fund raising and marketing or organising events.
* Give some of your time to help with our rescue dogs.
* Sponsor a kennel or a dog on an annual basis to help pay expenses.

Please give us a call on **04 347 4611**
email us at **k9@emirates.net.ae**
www.K9friends.com

Your help would be greatly appreciated

 Proud Supporters of K9 Friends

state differently), sometimes sick or even pregnant, and are kept in poor conditions. Rather than encouraging this trade you would do better to give a home to one of the many stray animals in Dubai. Contact Feline Friends or K9 Friends to see who needs a home. Also check in the classifieds section of the newspapers for lost and found animals and animals that need homes.

Animal Souks

The CITES protected list is disregarded in these souks and wild animals are still captured abroad, smuggled, and sold here. This is an illegal and inhumane blot on Dubai's copybook, and you would do well to avoid purchasing a wild creature from one of these souks. It is unlikely that you will have enough space that an animal needs to be healthy and normal, and vaccinations are very expensive and almost impossible to come by. Most of these sad creatures are destined for insanity and death. If you love animals, donate to WWF and just opt for a dog from K9 Friends.

Utilities & Services

Electricity & Water

These utilities, along with sewerage, are provided by Dubai Electricity & Water Authority (commonly known as DEWA). The authority provides an excellent service, and electricity or water shortages/stoppages are practically unheard of.

When you sign up you will have to pay a water and electricity deposit (Dhs.2,000 for villas; Dhs.1,000 for apartments) directly to DEWA. This is fully refundable on cancellation of your lease. Monthly bills can be paid at any DEWA office, through various banks or on the Internet. Those banks offering this service are listed on the reverse of the bill. Bills are assessed one month and the meter read the next month.

Main office: next to Wafi Shopping Mall, Bur Dubai (324 4444, Map Ref 13-D2)

Opening hours: Saturday - Wednesday 07:30 - 21:00 bill payments and 07:30 - 14:30 enquiries. Thursday 07:30 - 21:00 bill payments only, and telephone enquiries 08:30 - 14:00

Electricity

There's plenty of it! The electricity supply in Dubai is 220/240 volts and 50 cycles. Socket type is identical to the three point British system. Adaptors can be purchased at any grocery or hardware store.

Water

Tap water is safe to drink but not always pleasant, and visitors generally prefer the locally bottled mineral water, which is widely available. Bottled water, both local and imported is served in hotels and restaurants.

Buying 20 litre water bottles rather than small one and a half litre bottles is more environmentally friendly and can make a considerable cost saving for drinking water. The bottle deposit is usually Dhs.25 - 35 and refills Dhs.5 - 7. These large bottles can be used with a variety of methods for decanting the water. Choices include a hand pump available from supermarkets and costing about Dhs.3, a fixed pump costing about Dhs.60, or a variety of refrigeration units are also available. Prices for these vary, depending on the model, but on average are about Dhs.400. Water suppliers will deliver to your door, saving you some backache.

Sharing secrets at the water cooler

Water Suppliers	
Culligan	800 4945
Desert Springs	800 6650
Nestle Pure Life P.111	800 4404
Oasis Drinking Water	884 5656

Gas

Gas mains don't exist in Dubai, despite most cookers using gas. Therefore individual gas canisters need to be purchased and connected to a gas oven via an outside tap. Canisters generally cost about Dhs.280 initially and then between

Dhs.40-50, depending on the size of the canister, each time you need a new one. There are numerous companies around town supplying gas canisters, who will deliver and connect them for you at no extra charge. These vans that drive around the residential areas are super efficient. Chances are that if you run out of gas in the middle of cooking your oven chips (regardless of what time of day it is), one call and the gas man can be with you in less than 20 minutes – just make sure you keep the telephone number at hand!

Gas Suppliers

New City Gas Distributors	351 8282
Oasis Gas Suppliers	396 1812
Salam Gas	344 8823
Union Gas Company	266 1479

Telephone

The groovy glass building with the big ball on top near the Creek in Deira is home to the Emirates Telecommunications Corporation (known as Etisalat, meaning communications). Etisalat is currently the main telecommunications provider in the Emirates, although planned deregulation of the industry will introduce more choice. (Indeed, TV, telephone, and internet services in all new Emaar properties are provided by Sahm Technologies [p.114]). Etisalat are generally an efficient and innovative company, continuously introducing new services and even cutting charges from time to time. You should have few problems in processing paperwork, receiving services or rectifying problems. You need a residence visa to get a landline, but you can get a SIM card for a mobile phone and corresponding telephone number without residency.

Opening hours: Saturday - Wednesday 07:00 - 13:00, and 15:00 - 17:00 (bill payments only); Thursday 08:00 - 13:00 (bill payments only). The main office in Deira, opposite the Sheraton Hotel & Towers, is open 24 hours for bill payments and pre-paid SIM cards. Jebel Ali Free Zone office: Saturday - Thursday 09:00 - 17:00

Landline Phones

To install a regular landline phone connection in your home you need to apply directly to Etisalat with the following: Etisalat application form in English (handwritten is acceptable), copy of passport and residence visa, Dhs.250 and a copy of your tenancy agreement.

Once you have submitted the application your connection is installed within 24 hours. Even if you have your own phone handset Etisalat will provide one. If you require additional phone sockets, order them at the same time and pay a further Dhs.50 for the first socket and then Dhs.15 per socket thereafter. The procedure is usually extremely efficient and streamlined.

Etisalat offers many additional services, such as call waiting, call forwarding and a 'follow me' service – for more information contact you nearest Etisalat branch, check the Etisalat home page (www.etisalat.ae) or have a look at the Zappy Explorer (Dubai).

Quarterly rental: standard landline (for all sockets) – Dhs.60. All calls made locally within Dubai on and to a landline are free. For international and mobile rates, check the phone book. Discount long distance rates are all day Friday and government declared national public holidays. Also weekdays (outside GCC): 21:00 - 07:00; weekdays (GCC only): 19:00 - 07:00

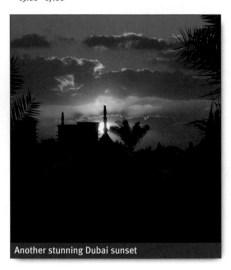

Another stunning Dubai sunset

Mobile Phones

It's really easy to have a GSM connection in Dubai. You can even register for your new number online and get it delivered straight to your door the same day! Check out the Etisalat 4 Me service at www.e4me.co.ae or call 800 888 3463. Mobiles can be purchased from Etisalat, telecommunications shops, most electronics shops and large supermarkets, such as Carrefour, see Shopping [p.227]. Etisalat GSM assistance telephone service: dial 101 for enquiries.

New Residents

Utilities & Services

Simple, Effective, Appealing – three qualities essential to great design.

The **Explorer Designlab** team approaches every project with this in mind, creating perfect solutions to everyday design problems while challenging trends and exploring the boundaries of creative design.

Design is central to your company's image, and has a direct effect on how you are perceived by your customers. Contact us to learn how you can benefit from our services.

CORPORATE IDENTITY • BROCHURES & REPORTS • PACKAGING • ADVERTISING • PRINT • WEB

PO Box 34275 Dubai, UAE
Phone (+971 4) 335 3520 **Fax** (+971 4) 335 3529
Email Info@Explorer-Publishing.com

www.Explorer-Publishing.com

Non Resident

If your visa is not fully processed, or if you're visiting the country and want to use your mobile, your only option currently, is Wasel GSM service. The subscription is for one year and payment for outgoing calls needs to be made in advance. The first year's subscription is Dhs.165 and you can apply at any branch office or Carrefour supermarket. Many mobile phone retailers can also sell you Wasel. To apply, fill out the application form and submit it along with your essential documents. The service includes connection, one year's rental, SIM card and Dhs.10 free credit. You may 'recharge' your card for outgoing calls in Dhs.30 units, and cards can be purchased at any gas station or grocery store. Annual renewal is Dhs.100.

Sahm Technologies

Sahm Technologies is a subsidiary of Emaar Properties and provides all the telecommunication facilities for the company's new residential developments (such as Dubai Marina, Arabian Ranches, Emirates Hills, The Greens/Springs/Lakes etc.). All villas and apartments are equipped with multiple sockets, through which the telephone, internet, and TV signals are routed, eliminating the need for further cables or dishes.

Missing Mobile?

Lost your mobile? Call 101 to temporarily disconnect your number (you will need to know your passport number for security). Your SIM card can be replaced, but sadly, all the numbers you had saved in your phone's memory will be gone. To replace the SIM you will need to go to a branch of Etisalat with your essential documents in hand and Dhs.50. If you need to cancel your mobile number permanently go to Etisalat and fill in the cancellation forms.

To apply for any of their services you'll need a copy of your passport and tenancy agreement and a letter of no objection from your employer. A basic telephone line will cost Dhs.15 per month plus a one-off installation charge of Dhs.200, and you then pay for added features such as additional sockets, call waiting and caller ID etc. Call charges are in line with those charged by Etisalat.

Sahm offers a number of internet packages, with a 64kbps connection costing from Dhs.75 per month. Faster speeds (up to 2mbps) are available but monthly rental is obviously more. Regardless of the speed you choose the connection is 'always on' so you don't pay for the amount of time online, just the monthly fee. Also, because the internet is on a separate system it won't tie up your phone line. The internet connection isn't via a dial-up so your computer won't need a modem, but it will require an Ethernet (network) card. Most computers already have this card built in.

The television service varies in price depending on what you choose. The same sockets that carry the phone and internet signals also carry the TV signal, which is decoded by a Set Top Box connected to your TV. The box is provided free of charge when you subscribe to certain packages, otherwise you can buy or rent from Sahm. As with most pay-TV packages, you are required to subscribe for an initial period of at least 12 months.

The Sahm Technologies office is located within Emaar's Dubai Marina sales centre. You can call customer services on 390 5555 or visit www.sahm.ae.

Other options → Internet Cafés [p.410]
Websites [p.55]

Internet

For connection to cyberspace, Etisalat's sister company, Emirates Internet & Multimedia (EIM) is the sole provider of Internet services through its UAE proxy server (unless you live in a new Emaar property – see Sahm Technologies [p.114]). Access to some sites is restricted. You can access Emirates Internet from any standard telephone line using a 56k modem. If you require higher speed access you can apply for an ISDN line (128 Kbps) or an ADSL line (256 - 512 Kbps); for more information contact Etisalat (800 6100). Check out the Website listing on [p.55] for sites on the UAE.

To get yourself connected you will require a landline in your name or your company's name, a copy of your passport and residence visa, and the Internet application form from Etisalat.

Registration and installation charge: Dhs.100 for dialup; ISDN costs Dhs.200 plus Dhs.415 for modem; ADSL Dhs.200 plus Dhs.275 for modem.

Rental: Standard Internet connection – Dhs.20 per month; ISDN line – Dhs.100 quarterly; ADSL line Dhs.190-250 per month, depending on speed.

User charge: For the standard connection, there is an additional user charge: peak rate – Dhs.1.80 per hour (06:00 - 01:00); off-peak rate – Dhs.1 per hour. ISDN charges are Dhs.3.60 peak and Dhs.2 off peak. With an ADSL line, you are logged on 24 hours a day and pay no further charges.

قرية دبي الطبية
Dubai **M**edical **V**illage

NOW in DUBAI

Laser
& Radiofrequency
Surgeries

DMV gives you the best of what modern medicine has to offer!
• **Same-day surgeries under local anesthesia*** • **Time & money saving** •
• **NO hospitalization *** • **Fast recovery** •

• **Skin & Nail Surgery** (Biopsy, Moles, Lipoma, Bumps, Ingrown nails,...) • **Hemorrhoids** (Piles) •
• **Hernia** • **Anal Fissure** • **Circumcision** • **Hydrocele** • **Drainage of Abscesses** • **Breast Biopsy** •
• **Pilonidal Sinus** (hairy cyst mostly at lower back)... •
• **FDA Approved Laser Hair Removal** •

DR. HAMID TAGHADDOS
General Surgeon
Laser Specialist - HARVARD MEDICAL SCHOOL

AD Approved by The Department of Health & Medical Services DOH # 03/5088

*Depending on each medical case

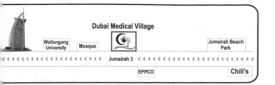

Dubai Medical Village

Wollongong University	Mosque		Jumeirah Beach Park
Jumeirah 3			
		EPPCO	Chili's

قرية دبي الطبية
Dubai **M**edical **V**illage

Jumeira 3, Villa no. 510, P.O. Box 73130 Dubai, UAE
Tel. +971 4 395 6200 • Mob +971 50 559 6621
Fax +971 4 395 5117 • E-mail dmv@emirates.net.ae

Dial 'n' Surf

This facility allows you to surf without subscribing to the Internet service. All that's needed is a computer with a modem and a regular phone (or ISDN) line – no account number or password is required. In theory, you then simply dial 500 5555 to gain access. However, in practice it may not be quite so straightforward, since there are different set ups depending on your software. If you have difficulties, contact the helpdesk (800 5244).

Charges: A charge of 15 fils per minute is made for the connection and billed to the telephone line from which the call is made.

Internet Cafés

A cheaper option would be to step out and use the Internet café in the mall or the restaurant below your apartment. Lots and lots of Internet cafés exist, from the chic and sleek to the down and dirty. Rates vary dramatically, from Dhs.5 - 15 per hour. If they serve food and you order a meal they may let you cruise the Internet for free. Some however stipulate that you must order from the menu in order to use the Internet station and they then charge you an hourly rate to boot!

Internet Help

www.eim.ae
Etisalat homepage & Emirates Internet & Multimedia products and services

help@eim.ae
General enquiries

abuse@emirates.net.ae
Report hacking, illegal use of the Internet, spamming etc

www.eim.ae/feedback
Subscribers queries, comments, complaints and suggestions

800 6100
Internet Help Desk

Bill Payment

Bills are mailed monthly and are itemised for international and mobile calls, SMS (short message service) and service charges. All bill payments can be paid on the Internet, with telephone banking if your account has such facilities or at Etisalat branch offices, as well as at certain banks. Etisalat also has cash payment machines at several sites around Dubai, such as supermarkets, saving you the hassle of queuing at Etisalat or the bank. You can also recharge your Wasel service using these machines. Contact Etisalat for more details about bill payment options.

If you don't pay your landline telephone bill within the first ten days of the month, or your GSM bill within 45 days, your outgoing calls will be cut off and you will only receive incoming calls for up to 15 days before complete disconnection. However, your bill needs to be over Dhs.200 for this to happen. Etisalat very kindly automatically calls landlines and sends SMS reminders to people to pay up.

Bill Enquiry Service

Etisalat provides a useful bill enquiry service, enabling customers to obtain the current amount payable on their phone/s up to the end of the last month. The aim is to help customers budget their calls and to facilitate prompt settlement of bills, leading to fewer disconnections.

The information is only available for the phone that the call is made from (in theory) and the cost of the call inquiry is charged at the normal rate. To use the service, dial 142 (English) or 143 (Arabic). You may also use Etisalat cash payment machines for this service, and Etisalat's 'online billing service' to pay Internet bills.

Postal Services

Other options → **Post & Courier Services [p.52]**

There is no house address based mailing system in the UAE. All mail is delivered to the Central Post Office and then distributed to centrally located post office boxes (many apartment blocks have PO boxes which is a close as you'll get to a home address). While many residents direct mail to a company mailbox it's also possible to rent a personal PO Box. To apply you require an application form from the Central Post Office and between Dhs.80 and Dhs.230 depending on how long you initially want the box for (4-16 months). You can then select a PO Box at a convenient location near to your home (if one is available).

Emirates Postal Service (Empost) will send you notification by email when you receive registered mail or parcels in your PO Box. For an extra Dhs.9 you can have the item delivered to your door. However, you may be required to pay Customs charges on international packages, which are about Dhs.15.

Location: Central Post Office (337 1500), Zabeel Road, Karama (Map Ref 10-E2).

Opening hours: Saturday -Thursday 08:00 - 20:00; Friday 1700 - 2100.

Television

While the local television channels in Dubai leave a little to be desired (see Television in General Information, [p.52]), there is a good selection of

All the Western Entertainment you want and more!

satellite channels to choose from, or video/DVD rentals (rental stores are plentiful in Dubai – especially handy are the ones at Spinneys). Emaar properties television services are provided through Sahm Technologies [p.114].

The UAE's cable TV network, Emirates Cable TV & Multimedia (E-Vision), is a subsidiary of Etisalat. Subscription currently includes approximately 70 or more Arabic, Asian and Western channels, though this will rise to 100 channels in the future. The basic subscription fee is Dhs.55 and for an extra charge you can add pay satellite channels. For further information, call 800 5500 or log on to www.evision.ae.

Satellite TV & Radio

The most popular satellite networks are Firstnet, Showtime and Orbit which show a variety of American and British programmes, international channels, movies, sports, documentaries and radio channels. Showtime is generally favoured for its movies and sitcoms, Firstnet for its sport coverage and Orbit for BBC Prime (particularly *Eastenders*!). Make sure you compare the packages, prices, payment options and channel selections of each network before purchasing. Generally when you sign with a network they will provide a dish if necessary (some apartment blocks and villas already have the dish installed) and the decoder. Couch potatoes first have to decide what types of programmes they want to watch and then what they are willing to pay for them.

The various channels available can be split into two types:

1. Pay TV Satellite Channels

These are channels that require payment for installation and equipment, such as the decoder, dish etc, followed by a viewing subscription for the channels you choose to watch. Generally, subscriptions can be paid monthly, quarterly or annually. Take your time making the right choice because the Middle East has a competitive pay TV market with four pay TV networks all offering a range of channels.

2. Free to Air Satellite Channels

These are channels that require payment for the installation and reception equipment, but there is no viewing subscription. There are more than 200 of these types of channels.

Satellite/Cable Providers

Arabtec SIS	286 8002
Bond Communications	343 4499
E-Vision	www.evision.ae
	800 5500
Eurostar	808 7777
Firstnet	www.adduniverse.com
Global Direct Television	339 5585
Orbit Direct P.117	www.orbit.net
	800 4442
Showtime P.xii	www.showtimearabia.com
	367 7777

Equipment

Equipment can be bought from various locations: directly from the main dealers, electrical shops, second-hand shops or classified ads. The majority of dealers offer installation. For apartment blocks or buildings with a large number of viewing points a central system is recommended, making it economical as well as offering more choice. Persuade your landlord to install the system if the block does not already come with satellite receiving equipment.

Health

General Medical Care

The general standard of healthcare in the UAE is high, both in the public and private sectors, although private hospitals do have some distinct advantages (predominantly English speaking, less waiting time, less cultural restrictions and more comfortable in-patient facilities). While public healthcare is available for UAE Nationals and expatriate residents for a minimal cost at the government hospitals and clinics, some specialised care may not be available

Hospitals

Al Amal Hospital	344 4010
Al Baraha Hospital	271 0000
Al Maktoum Hospital	222 1211
Al Wasl Hospital	324 1111
Al Zahra Hospital P.123	06 561 9999
American Hospital P.xvi	336 7777
Belhoul European Hospital	345 4000
Dubai Hospital	271 4444
Emirates Hospital	349 6666
International Private Hospital	221 2484
Iranian Hospital	344 0250
Rashid Hospital	337 4000
Welcare Hospital	282 7788

Private Centres/Clinics

Al Borj Medical Centre	321 2220
Al Zahra Private Medical Centre P.123	331 5000
Allied Diagnostic Centre	332 8111
Belhoul European Hospital	345 4000
Dr Akel's General Medical Clinic	344 2773
Dubai London Clinic	344 6663
Dubai Medical Village P.121	395 6200
Dubai Physiotherapy Clinic	349 6333
General Medical Centre	349 5959
Health Care Medical Center	344 5550
Jebel Ali Medical Centre	881 4000
Manchester Clinic	344 0300
New Medical Centre	268 3131

Diagnostics

Al Zahra Private Medical Centre P.123	331 5000
Allied Diagnostic Centre	332 8111
American Hospital P.xvi	336 7777
Dr. Leila Soudah Clinic	395 5591
Medic Polyclinic	355 4111
Medical Imaging Department	309 6642
Welcare Hospital	282 7788

Dermatologists

Al Zahra Private Medical Centre P.123	331 5000)
Belhoul European Hospital	345 4000
Dr. Simin Medical Clinic	344 4117

so it is always worth taking out health insurance. (You may find that your employer provides healthcare as part of your contract but check what the policy covers before solely relying on it.). In Dubai, the Department of Health and Medical Services runs New Dubai, Rashid, Al Baraha, Maktoum and Al Wasl hospitals. Dubai Hospital is one of the best medical centres in the Middle East with specialised clinics, while Al Wasl is a specialised maternity and gynaecology hospital. The department also operates a number of outpatient clinics. Additionally, there are government initiatives to build Dubai Healthcare City to serve as a hub for treatment, prevention, education and research on healthcare in the region, see Free Zones [p.70] for more information.

Currently expatriates can go to any hospital as long as they have a valid health card. However, in the future this may change and some government sectors are pushing to make it mandatory that all expatriates have private insurance coverage. There are various private hospitals and clinics that offer thorough services, such as the American Hospital. Additionally, each emirate must have at least one pharmacy open 24 hours a day. The location and

telephone numbers are listed in the daily newspapers and on the Dubai Police Website (www.dubaipolice.gov.ae). The Municipality has emergency numbers (223 2323 or 266 3188), which also give you the name and location of open pharmacies. Pharmacies are open Saturday - Thursday from 08:30 - 13:30 and 16:30 - 22:30, and on Fridays 16:30 - 22:30, although some pharmacies may open on Friday mornings, 09:00 - 13:00 and quite are few are open 24hours.

Dubai Medical Village

Maternity

Other options → Maternity Clothes [p.227]

Every expatriate child born in the UAE must be registered at the Ministry of Health within two weeks and hold a residence visa within four months of birth, otherwise you may not be able to take the child of the country. See Birth Certificates & Registration [p.76] for the process.

There are various considerations when deciding where to give birth and many expatriates return to their home country to do so. If you decide that you would rather have the baby in your home country, keep in mind that airlines do have restrictions on taking heavily pregnant passengers, so check when their cut off date is. If you have your heart set on a water or home birth you may want to consider going home, since those options are not available

FDA* Approved Laser
For Unwanted Hair Removal

- First Lightsheer Diode Laser in the U.A.E

- Thousands of Cases SIDE-EFFECT FREE

- No Age Limits

- 100% Safe for Everyone, even for Pregnant Women

- Very Effective for Men (Neck, Cheek, Ear, Shoulder...)

- Best solution for ingrowing hair

- Lady Laser Technicians Licensed by Department of Health

DR. HAMID TAGHADDOS
General Surgeon
Laser Specialist - HARVARD MEDICAL SHCOOL

* **FDA** is the legal board controlling medical health products in the USA

AD Approved by The Department of Health & Medical Services DOH # 03/5087

in the UAE. However, if you do decide to have your baby here you will find the level of care is excellent. The Al Wasl government hospital may lack some of the frills of private hospitals but has an excellent reputation for maternity care and paediatrics. Before you decide on a government hospital check their policy regarding husbands and family members in the labour ward. Certain hospitals may not allow your husband to be with you in the labour ward (although he can be present at delivery). All government hospitals now charge expatriates for maternity services and delivery, and costs vary depending on the package you choose (e.g. pre-natal and delivery; just delivery, etc.). Private hospitals will be more expensive, although if you shop around you may be surprised to find that in some cases the difference between government and private is not as great as you might think. No matter which you choose if you have medical insurance check that it covers maternity costs – some have a limitation clause and some may not cover any costs at all. Private hospitals offer maternity packages that include prenatal care, delivery and postnatal care for you and the baby. But remember that the price you are quoted by the hospital is for the basic, 'best-case-scenario' delivery, and if you have additional requirements, such as an epidural (when the anaesthetist must be present) or an assisted delivery (when the paediatrician must be present), you will be charged extra. If you give birth by Caesarean Section, the cost is usually significantly higher and the hospital stay is longer (five days, compared to two days for standard delivery).

Al Zahra Private Medical Centre

Maternity leave in the UAE is short compared to some other countries. Although a new mother is entitled to 45 days leave on full pay (whether this is calendar days or working days depends on your employer), a lot of employers here are not that flexible about giving further leave on an unpaid basis. New dads are not entitled to any paternity leave, so will have to take annual leave if they want to help with sleepless nights and nappy changing!

Ante and Post Natal Care

Ante	Al Zahra Private Medical Centre P.123	331 5000
Ante	Ballet Centre, The	344 9776
Ante	Dubai London Clinic	344 6663
Post	Essensuals Aromatherapy Centre	344 8776
Both	American Hospital P.xvi	336 7777
Both	Belhoul European Hospital	345 4000
Both	Dr. Leila Soudah Clinic	395 5591
Both	Fakih Gynecology & Obstetrics Center	349 2100
Both	General Medical Centre	349 5959
Both	Medlink Clinic	344 7711
Both	Royal Medical Centre	345 6780
Both	Welcare Hospital	282 7788

Paediatrics

Most public and private hospitals have full time paediatricians on staff. However, only Al Wasl (Government) and the American Hospital (Private) have devoted paediatric departments. The American Hospital has a team of general paediatric doctors, while Al Wasl has dedicated paediatric

Al Wasl Hospital

Where HOPE becomes ...
A REALITY

...e're recognised for our medical care in the UAE with good reason. For over two decades, we've ...ought healing and hope to our patients with the latest techniques and specialist expertise in:

- Anaesthesiology
- Cardiology
- Cosmetic, Reconstructive & Hand Surgery
- Dietetics
- Dentistry, Periodontics, Orthodontics & Oral Implantology
- Dermatology and Laser Skin Surgery
- E.N.T., Audiology and Speech Therapy
- Endocrinology and Diabetology

- Family Medicine
- Gastroenterology
- General Practice
- General and Laparoscopic Surgery
- Internal Medicine
- Neurology
- Neurophysiology
- Neurosurgery
- Nuclear Medicine
- Obstetrics & Gynaecology

- Ophthalmology & Excimer Laser Surgery
- Orthopaedics & Physiotherapy
- Paediatrics & Neonatology
- Pathology
- Psychiatry
- Psychology
- Radiology & Imaging & Interventional Radiology
- Urology

surgeons and neurodevelopment therapists that care for children with special needs and learning difficulties. The Dubai Community Health Centre (395 3939) also provides professional services such as speech therapy and social skills training for children with special needs.

Gynaecology & Obstetrics

Al Wasl Hospital	324 1111
Al Zahra Private Medical Centre P.123	331 5000
American Hospital P.xvi	336 7777
Belhoul European Hospital	345 4000
Dr. Leila Soudah Clinic	395 5591
Dr. Taher H Khalil Clinic	268 7655
Dubai London Clinic	344 6663
Fakih Gynecology & Obstetrics Center	349 2100
General Medical Centre	349 5959
International Private Hospital	221 2484
Manchester Clinic	344 0300
Medlink Clinic	344 7711
Royal Medical Centre	345 6780
Welcare Hospital	282 7788

Dentists/Orthodontists

Dentistry in Dubai is, like most other medical services, of a high standard and various practitioners offer dental surgery, cosmetic cleaning and general checks. Prices, however match the level of service, and most health insurance packages do not cover dentistry, unless it's an emergency treatment brought about by an accident.

Views of Dubai

If you have a health card you are entitled to dentistry by your assigned hospital, and if they do not have a dental section, they will give you a reference to another public hospital that does, such as Rashid Hospital. You will be charged Dhs.50 for the visit plus any other services that are performed, such as cleaning, filling etc. Services are generally professional and accurate, but the rates may not be any lower than going to a private dental clinic.

Private Dentists/Orthodontists

Anglo American Dental Clinic	228 3948
Al Zahra Private Medical Centre P.123	331 5000
American Dental Clinic P.125	344 0668
British Dental Clinic	342 1318
Clinic for Orthodontics & Aesthetic Dentistry	330 0220
Dr M.S. Ahmadi	344 5550
Dr Michael's Dental Clinic	349 5900
Dr. Nicolas & Asp Dental Centre P.127	345 4443
24 hour emergency hotline	050 551 7177
Dubai London Clinic	344 6663
Jumeirah Beach Dental Centre	349 9433
Swedish Dental Clinic	223 1297
Talass Orthodontic & Dental Centre P.119	349 2220

Opticians

You're never far from an optician in Dubai, with most of the malls having at least one outlet selling a range of sunglasses and providing eye tests and prescription lenses. The bigger branches such as Al Jaber Optical in Deira City Centre (295 4400) and Yateem in the BurJuman Centre will also carry out the eye test required for a driving licence. See Driving Licence, New Residents [p.72].

For eye problems requiring specialist treatment many hospitals and clinics offer consultation and are able to carry out appropriate treatment, especially the American Hospital Dubai (336 7777) and the Welcare Hospital (282 7788) which both have well-equipped Ophthalmology departments. See Eyewear, [p.217], for a list of opticians.

Cosmetic Surgery & Treatments

In a city where appearance is everything, there are a number of clinics that specialise in reducing, reshaping, removing and enlarging various parts of your anatomy to help you look and feel good. Many are located in Jumeira, especially along the Beach Road, including Dubai Medical Village (395

AMERICAN DENTAL CLINIC
&
ADVANCED DENTAL CLINIC

BRITE SMILE

Smile experts at work...

Specialized in the Following:

General Dentistry   Orthodontics (Braces)   Root Canal Therapy   Children Dentistry
Cosmetic Dentistry   White Fillings   Oral Surgery   Crown/Bridges/Dentures
Joint/Muscle problems (TMJ)   Dental Hygiene   Teeth Whitening (Brite Smile)
Smile Analysis   Digital X- rays with 90% less radiation   In house Porcelain Laboratory

American Dental Clinic- Dubai
Jumeirah Beach Road Villa# 54
P.O.Box 74400 Dubai U.A.E
Office: + 971 4 344 0668
Fax: + 971 4 342 9166
E-mail: amerdent@emirates.net.ae
Website: www.american-dental-clinic.com

Advanced Dental Clinic- Abu Dhabi
Apt 309, New Spinneys Bldg. Khalidiya
P.O.Box 41269 Abu Dhabi U.A.E
Office: + 971 2 6812921
Fax: + 971 2 6811998
E-mail: advdent@emirates.net.ae
Website: www.advanced-dental-clinic.com

6200) whose dedicated team of surgeons offer a range of surgical procedures, eye care, and laser treatment including hair removal.

Cosmetic Treatment & Surgery	
Al Rustom's Skin & Laser Clinic	349 8800
Belhoul European Hospital	345 4000
CosmeSurge	344 5915
Euro Gulf Medical Centre	331 7544

Hairdressers

Dubai has a wide range of options for getting a cut, colour or re-style. At one end you have the small barber shops where gents can get a hair cut (and relaxing head massage) for as little as Dhs.10, with the option of a shave with a cut-throat razor for a few extra dirhams. Ladies should be able to find salons where a basic haircut starts at around Dhs.40. At the other end of the scale you have upmarket boutiques and salons offering the latest styles and treatments to men and women, where you could pay Dhs.300 or more for a cut and blow dry. Many of the shopping malls have hairdressers, as do some of the bigger hotels.

Hairdressers	
Carla K.Styling Centre	343 8544
Hair@Pyramids	324 1490
Hair Corridor, The	394 622
Lotus Salon	349 6760
Pretty Lady	398 5255
Toni & Guy	330 3345

Alternative Therapies

Given the vast number of Dubai's residents that come from countries practising traditional, herbal and alternative therapies, Dubai offers a well balanced choice of Western and holistic therapies.

Additionally, the Dubai Herbal & Treatment Centre (335 1200) offers a full range of Chinese, Indian and Arabic herbal medicines. The facility, which is unique in the GCC region, offers out-patient services and there are plans to expand the facility to offer in-patient services.

Natural medicine can be very specialised, so ask questions and explain your needs and expectations to ensure practitioners can help with your situation. Prices vary and can run comparable to Western medicine, and most insurance will not cover the costs. As always, word of mouth is the best way of establishing who might offer the most appropriate treatment. There are also a range of new clinics opening up offering 'well-being' services such as the 'u concept' Centre, in the Village Mall, Jumeira (344 9060). A new venture in the health and fitness industry offering services in nutrition, weight loss, pregnancy and breast feeding and holistic approaches to general health.

The UAE office of Complementary & Alternative Medicine is governed by the Ministry of Health, and grants licences to qualified practitioners of alternative medicine. This legal process helps weed out the quacks.

The following are some of the services offered and the main practitioners in Dubai.

Acupressure/Acupuncture

Among the oldest healing methods in the world, acupressure involves the systematic placement of pressure with fingertips on established meridian points on the body. This therapy can be used to relieve pain, soothe the nerves and stimulate the body, as determined necessary by the therapist. Acupuncture is an ancient Chinese technique that uses needles to access the body's meridian points. The technique is surprisingly painless and is quickly becoming an alternative or complement to Western medicine as it aids ailments such as asthma, rheumatism, and even more serious diseases.

Acupressure/Acupuncture	
Dubai Herbal & Treatment Centre	335 1200
Dubai Physiotherapy Clinic	349 6333
Gulf American Clinic	349 8556
House of Chi & House of Healing	397 4446
Jebel Ali Medical Centre	881 4000

Homeopathy

Homeopathy strengthens the body's defence system. Natural ingredients are used to address physical and emotional problems. The discipline extracts elements from traditional medicines of various origins but was recently organised into a healthcare system in Europe. Practitioners undergo disciplined training and some are also Western medical doctors.

• Holistic Healing Medical Centre 228 3234

Reflexology & Massage Therapy

Other options → Massage [p.298]

Reflexology is a detailed scientific system, with Asian origins, which outlines points in the hands and feet that impact other parts and systems of the

INTRODUCING FOR THE FIRST TIME

HEALOZONE™

...RIES REVERSAL TECHNOLOGY WITH NO DRILLING OR PAIN

BRITE✳SMILE

1 HOUR TEETH WHITENING PROCEDURE

Drs. Nicolas & Asp

SPECIALISED DENTAL CARE FOR ALL THE FAMILY

GENERAL DENTISTRY

- **DR. E NICOLAS**
  General Dentistry & Dental Implant Specialist, USA
- **DR. SVEN ASP**
  General Dentistry, Sweden
- **DR. JOAN ASP**
  General Dentistry, Sweden
- **DR. TOMAS VON POST**
  General Dentistry, Sweden
- **DR. TIINA NYBERG**
  General Dentistry, Sweden

ORTHODONTICS (BRACES)

- **DR. (MS) SALAM AL-KHAYYAT**
  Orthodontic & Cleft Palate Specialist, Turkey
- **DR. AGNETA MARCUSSON**
  Orthodontic & Cleft Palate Specialist, Sweden
- **DR. BRITTANY NICOL**
  Orthodontist, Australia

SURGERY & IMPLANTS

- **DR. DAVID ROZE**
  Oral Surgeon & Implant Specialist, France
- **DR. MICHAEL GAHLERT**
  Oral Surgeon & Implantologist, Germany
- **DR. HEINZ KNIHA**
  Maxillofacial Surgeon & Implantologist, Germany
- **DR. DIRK NOLTE**
  Specialist in Oral & Maxillofacial Surgery,
  Regional Plastic Surgery, Germany

ENDODONTICS

- **DR. DAVID ROZE**
  Endodontic Specialist, France

PAEDIATRIC DENTISTRY

- **DR. AGNES ROZE**
  Specialist Paediatric Dentist, France

CLEFT LIP & PALATE

- **DR. ANDERS BERGGREN**
  Specialist in Plastic Surgery,
  Cleft Lip & Palate Specialist, Sweden

LASER & AESTHETIC DENTISTRY

DENTAL HYGIENIST

- **KATE PASZKOWSKA**
  Dental Hygienist, Poland

DOH: 7174/204

DRS. NICOLAS & ASP
DENTAL CENTRE

مركز دكتور نيقولا
و آسب لطب الاسنان

Phone: (04) 345 4443
www.nicolasandasp.com

24 - Hours Emergency Mobile 050-5517177

Health

body. In addition to stress reduction and improved health, the pressure applied to these points directly addresses issues in those specific corresponding parts of the body. While many spas and salons offer massage and reflexology, the following centres have a more focused approach to the holistic healing qualities of reflexology and massage. For a listing of spas that offer massage for relaxation and beauty, see Activities [p.254].

Reflexology/Massage Therapy	
Essensuals Aromatherapy Centre	344 8776
Herbalpan Ayurvedic Centre	321 2553
House of Chi & House of Healing	397 4446
Thai Relaxation Therapy Centre	321 2345
The Haven	345 6770

Aromatherapy

Essential oils derived from plants and flowers can be used in a myriad of ways to add balance to your health. Specialists use such oils when delivering massages as well as a number of other methods to address your needs. While no certification is required to practice aromatherapy, it's a healthy decision to make sure your practitioner has studied plants and can make the best choices for you. Additionally, for cosmetic and relaxing purposes alone, it is nice to have an aromatherapy facial or massage, which many spas and salons offer. While these are intended to be for pleasure rather than health related, they can work wonders on your soul!

• Essensuals Aromatherapy Centre 344 8776

Healing Meditation

Meditation can offer inner peace as well as a disease free mind and body. With quiet settings and various breathing techniques, movements and mantras, group and individual meditation sessions can be a powerful tool in healing and stress relief. More and more of Dubai's residents are trying out meditation as a means to unwind.

Healing Meditation	
Art of Living	344 9660
SSY (Siddha Samadhi Yoga)	344 6618
World Pranic Healing Foundation	336 0885

Back Treatment

Back problems plague many people, whether they are young and fit sports fanatics or sedentary people in their later life. Luckily, treatment is widely available in Dubai with excellent specialists from all around the world practising here.

Chiropractic and osteopathy treatments concentrate on manipulating the skeleton in a non intrusive manner to improve the functioning of the nervous system or blood supply to the body. Chiropractic is based on the manipulative treatment of misalignments in the joints, especially those of the spinal column, while osteopathy involves the manipulation and massage of the skeleton and musculature.

Craniosacral therapy aims to relieve pain and tension by gentle manipulations of the skull to balance the craniosacral rhythm. Pilates is said to be the safest form of neuromuscular reconditioning and back strengthening available. It is also a form of exercise that's gaining popularity. Check with your gym to see if they offer any classes.

Back Treatment	
Canadian Chiropractic & Natural Health Centre	342 0900
Clark Chiropractic Clinic	344 4316
General Medical Centre	349 5959
Gulf American Clinic	349 8556
House of Chi & House of Healing	397 4446
Neuro Spinal Hospital	342 0000
OrthoSports Medical Center P.129➤	345 0601
Osteopathic Health Centre	344 9792
Pilates Studio, The	343 8252
Specialist Orthopaedic & Rehab Centre	349 5528

Rehabilitation & Physiotherapy

Many Dubai residents lead an active lifestyle, working hard and then playing hard. But accidents and injuries do happen, so whether you got roughed up playing rugby, pulled something in the gym or simply tripped over the cat you'll be pleased to hear that the city has some excellent facilities to help you on the road to recovery. The Orthosports Medical Centre (345 0601) in Jumeira specialises in orthopaedic and sports medicine, offering physiotherapy, hydrotherapy and orthopaedic surgery to international standards.

Mental Health

Even the most resilient of personalities can be affected by expat culture shock or homesickness. Whatever the origin of the stress, a new environment takes some getting used to, and can

Bounce back with confidence...

Orthosports Medical Center is dedicated to the treatment and rehabilitation of orthopedic and sports related conditions and to their prevention.

In a caring and friendly environment, we deliver the highest standards of international orthopedic and sports medicine management, always aiming to exceed our client´s expectations.

Located on Jumeira Beach Road, in Dubai, the Center is easily accessible from all locations and extensive parking facilities are available.

The clinic is under direction of Dr. Moosa Kazim, FRCS (C), FACS, Orthopedic Specialist.

Al Jasar

PECIALISTS IN ORTHOPEDICS AND REHABILITATION

Orthopedic surgery • Osteopathy • Physiotherapy • Hydrotherapy • Sports Medicine

ORTHOSPORTS
MEDICAL CENTER
THE SPORTS MEDICINE SPECIALISTS

BEACH ROAD JUMEIRA
TEL: 04-345 0601 FAX: 04-345 0028

be demanding on your nerves. The good news is there are a number of support groups [p.128] where problems can be shared (and halved) and much needed ears bent. In addition there are various psychologists and therapists who can help with matters of stress, neurosis, child psychology and various emotional disorders.

The Dubai Community Health Centre is a non-profit organisation that offers workshops and other psychiatric services at competitive rates. The Centre is the GCC region's first dedicated mental health centre, and also specialises in educational psychology for children and adults, marriage and family counselling, as well as Yoga and Reiki programmes.

Counselling & Psychology

Dubai has a number of well-qualified counsellors and psychologists able to provide help and advice to people with emotional problems. Some clinics also have specialists to help children with behavioural issues.

Counsellers/Psychologists	
Comprehensive Medical Centre	331 4777
Dr. Roghy McCarthy Psychology Clinic	394 6122
Dr. Samy Ayad	262 4774
Dubai Community Health Centre	395 3939

Psychiatry

Psychiatry is the diagnosis and treatment of mental illness. If you think you may be affected by mental illness, or you just want some expert advice, the clinics listed in the table below are a good place to start.

Psychiatrists	
Dr Akel's General Medical Clinic	344 2773
Dubai Community Health Centre	395 3939
Welcare Hospital	282 7788

Support Groups

Dubai can be a challenging place to live and with many residents originating from overseas, there is often a lack of the family support that many people are used to. Making the first step of reaching out for help can be tough; however, there are groups out there offering a hand through the difficult patches.

- Adoption Support Group (394 6643). Meetings held once a month at different locations.
- Alcoholics Anonymous (AA) (344 1542) - 24 hour hotline. Information on weekly meetings can be found on www.aainarabia.com
- Diabetic Support Group (309 6876). Meets every three months on a Wednesday evening at 17:30. Based at the American Hospital Dubai. Contact Nibal.
- Fertility Support Group. Contact Ram Kumar/ Lalitah/Tricia. (050 646 5148/050 632 4365/ 050 456 4109). Online chat at http://groups.yahoo.com/group/fertilitysupport group, or email fertilitysupportgroup @yahoogroups.com
- Mother 2 Mother (050 452 7674 or 348 3754). Support, friendship, fun and advice for all mothers, from those who are expecting to those who have already delivered.
- Special Families Support (393 1985). Monthly meetings. For the families of special needs children. Contact Ayesha Saeed.
- Twins, Triplets or More! (288 6816) Baby Circle (for pregnant mothers and mothers with multiples up to one year) meets every Monday. Double Trouble (for those with multiples aged one year and up) meets every other Tuesday. (www.twinsormore.2om.com). Contact Paula.

The Dubai Community Health Centre (395 3939) offers a pleasant, healing space for support group meetings for no charge, so if your group isn't already in existence in Dubai – be a pioneer and start it!

Support Groups	
Adoption Support Group	394 6643
Alcoholics Anonymous	344 1542
Breastfeeding Telephone Support Group	050 453 4670
Diabetic Support Group	309 6876
Fertility Support Group	050 646 5148
Mother to Mother	050 452 7674
Special Families Support	393 1985
Still Birth & Neo Natal Death Society	348 2801
Twins, Triplets or More!	288 6816

Leadership starts with the right perspective.

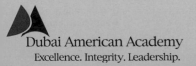

The following groups do not charge to attend their meetings:

SANDS Support Group: A UK based charity for those families experiencing pregnancy loss either through still birth, neonatal death, late miscarriage etc. Meetings held every 2 months. Contact Angela 348 2801, Anita 394 0384, or June 884 6309. SANDS also offer hospital and home visits.

Dubai Down Syndrome Association: Meets on the first Saturday of each month at 20:00. Also a drop in morning for parents and children each Wednesday at 10:00 at a villa on Al Wasl Rd. Call 050 880 9228, or email clubdownsyndrome@yahoo.co.uk

Multiple Sclerosis Support Group: For sufferers and their families. Meets on the first Monday of every month at 20:00. Contact Ms. Coreen Dolan on 03 761 5668

A.D.H.D (Attention Deficit Hyperactive Disorder). Meetings every second Sunday (344 6700).

Check out the list above, or any of the monthly health focused magazines that are usually available in surgeries, nutrition stores etc, for updates of support groups. If possible, get personal recommendations first, as standards can vary enormously, especially if a group or workshop is linked to a business. Be wise and use your discretion.

Education

Due to Dubai's diverse expat culture, the education system is varied and there are many international schools from which to choose. There is no government-funded education for expatriate children, so all these schools charge fees. Seek the advice of friends and colleagues to get an idea of which schools are suitable for your child and then visit a few schools before you make your decision. Most of the top schools operate waiting lists and you may not be able to get your child into your first choice. It is important to check that the school you choose is accredited by the Ministry of Education; a full list of approved schools can be found on www.uae.gov.ae/mohe. For more information on the ins and outs of the education system, refer to the *Family Explorer (Dubai & Abu Dhabi)*.

Knowledge Village

Knowledge Village is a key part of Dubai's committment to improving educational services and attracting more international students to the country as well as providing opportunities for local students to study here rather than abroad. See [p.70]

School terms: autumn (mid September - mid December); spring (early January - early April); summer (mid April - early July).

Generally, to enrol your child at a school, the following documents are needed:

- School application form
- Copies of student and parents' passports – both information page/s and residence visa stamp
- Passport photographs (usually eight)
- Copies of student's birth certificate
- School records for the past two years
- Current immunisation records and medical history
- Official transfer certificate from the student's previous school detailing his/her education.

Original transfer certificates must contain the following details:

- Date of enrolment
- Year of placement
- Date the child left the school
- School stamp
- Official signature

The Ministry of Education also requires the following documentation for any student enrolling at any school in Dubai:

- Original transfer certificate (to be completed by the student's current school)
- Most recently issued original report card

If the student was attending a school anywhere other than the UAE, Australia, Canada, Europe or USA, the transfer certificate and the most recently issued original report card must be attested by the Ministry of Education, Ministry of Foreign Affairs and the UAE embassy in that country.

Nursery & Pre-School

(Age: Babies - 4 1/2 years)

Some nurseries accept babies from as young as three months, although most prefer to accept children who are at walking age (around 12 months). Fees vary dramatically and so do timings so it's best to call around and visit a few nurseries to get an idea of what's available. As a general rule of thumb, most nurseries are open for four or five hours in the morning and charge anything from Dhs.3,000 to Dhs.12,000 per year. The more popular nurseries have long waiting lists so you should enrol your child before it's even born! The

following table lists some of the more popular nurseries in Dubai, but for a more complete list, refer to the *Family Explorer*.

Nurseries & Pre Schools

Jumeirah International Nurseries	349 9065
Kids Cottage Nursery School P.133	394 2145
Kid's Island Nursery	394 2579
Kid's Village	348 5991
Ladybird Nursery	344 1011
Modern Renaissance School	264 1818
Palms	394 7017
Safa Kindergarten Nursery School	344 3878
Small World Nursery	345 7774
Yellow Brick Road Nursery	282 8290

Primary & Secondary School

(Age: 4 1/2 - 11 years) (Age: 11 - 18 years)

In addition to the documents listed above, your child may also be required to take a short entrance exam and there may even be a physical examination and a family interview. Translated school certificates must have the student's name spelled exactly as it is found on the student's school record and passport. Depending on your nationality and educational requirements, most national curriculum syllabuses can be found in Dubai schools, covering GCSEs, A levels, French and International Baccalaureate and CNEC as well as the American and Indian equivalent.

Standards of teaching are usually high and schools have excellent facilities with extracurricular

Where young minds are nurtured

activities offered. The Ministry of Education regularly inspects schools to ensure rules and regulations are being upheld, and most schools insist on a school uniform. Some school fees include books and transport to school by bus but mostly fees only cover the basic education.

Hours: Most schools are open from 08:00 to 13:00 or 15:00, from Saturday to Wednesday.

Fees: Primary school fees can range from Dhs.10,000 to Dhs.20,000 per year, while secondary school fees are approximately Dhs.15,000 to Dhs.45,000 per year. Other costs may include a deposit or registration, medical fees, excursion fees and arts/activity fees.

Primary & Secondary Schools

Al Mawakeb School	347 8288
American School of Dubai	344 0824
Cambridge High School, The	282 4646
Dubai American Academy P.131	347 9222
Dubai College	399 9111
Dubai English Speaking School	337 1457
Dubai Infants School	337 0913
Emirates International School	348 9804
English College, Dubai	394 3465
Horizon English School	394 7879
International School of Choueifat	399 9444
Jebel Ali Primary School	884 6485
Jumeirah College P.135	395 4950
Jumeirah English Speaking School, The	394 5515
Jumeirah Primary School P.137	394 3500
Kings' Dubai	348 3939
Modern Renaissance School	264 1818
Regent School	344 2409
School of Research Science	298 8776
St. Mary's Catholic High School	337 0252

University & Higher Education

A number of universities and colleges around the UAE, with American, Australian and European affiliates, offer degree and diploma courses in Arts, Sciences, Business & Management, and Engineering & Technology. Many commercial organisations also offer higher education courses for school leavers, mature students and adults alike. Details of these establishments can be found in the Hawk Business Pages or Yellow Pages. Several tertiary establishments can be found in Knowledge Village, an education free zone that opened in 2004. The University of Wollongong is now based at Knowledge Village, but for a complete list of establishments, visit the Knowledge Village Website at www.kv.ae. Both the American

Life gives you one chance to make a point.

JUMEIRAH COLLEGE

Jumeirah College has achieved results that consistently place it amongst the top five percent of schools in the world following the National Curriculum for England. Emphasising individual attention, high service standards and a strong partnership with parents, Jumeirah College matches the aspirations of global achievers of tomorrow with the knowledge and guidance to successfully get them there.

JUMEIRAH COLLEGE

Please contact:
Jumeirah College,
PO Box 74856, Dubai
United Arab Emirates
Tel: 04-395 4950, Fax: 04-395 4586
Email: jumcoll@emirates.net.ae
Website: www.jc-dxb.sch.ae

GEMS
— EDUCATION —

Educating for Brilliant Futures

University of Dubai and the University of Wollongong are accredited, and offer undergraduate and graduate degrees. The American College of Dubai offers degrees in business, IT and liberal arts; and their transfer programme is very popular with expats as it allows them to complete part of their university degree here and then transfer to leading universities in USA, Canada, UK or elsewhere for completion.

Universities

American College of Dubai	282 9992
American University of Dubai	399 9000
American University of Sharjah	06 558 5555
University of Wollongong (Australia)	367 2400

Special Needs Education

If your child has physical or learning difficulties, there are several organisations you can contact in order to find out what activities or facilities are available to suit the special needs of your child. Some mainstream schools will try to accommodate children suffering from dyslexia, ADHD and other more manageable challenges. Special needs schools operate without government assistance, and therefore rely on donations, sponsorship, grants and help from volunteer workers. All charge tuition fees.

- The Al Noor Centre for Children with Special Needs (394 6088) provides therapeutic support and comprehensive training to special needs children of all ages. The centre also equips its 220 students with work related skills, assisting them to functionally integrate into society as young adults. www.alnooruae.org

- The Dubai Centre for Special Needs (344 0966) currently has 130 students, all of whom have an individual programme, including physiotherapy, speech therapy and/or occupational therapy. A pre-vocational programme is offered for older students, which includes arranging work placements.

- Rashid Paediatric Therapy Centre (340 0005) includes physical, occupational and speech therapy. In the afternoons, therapists see children on an outpatient basis, also working on early intervention and assisting school children with motor, learning, speech and communication difficulties.

- There is a therapeutic horse riding programme for children with special needs - Riding for the Disabled (rdaddubai@hotmail.com).

- Dubai Autism Centre provides a support network for parents and teacher training for teaching autistic children (398 6862).

- A Dyslexia Support Group is run by volunteer mums, and offers advice and support to families. Call 344 6657 or 344 0738 for more information.

In general the UAE has some catching up to do before it meets Western standards of catering to those with special needs. If you are considering employment in the Emirates, check with your prospective employer about issues like access and healthcare for people with special needs. See also Disabled Visitors [p.32].

Learning Arabic

Other options → Language Schools [p.309]

Learning a foreign language is by no means easy, and many people have good intentions when they

Knowledge Village

Education isn't child's play. Or is it?

With specialised expertise and world class resources, Jumeirah Primary School offers a unique holistic education. We understand that each child is different, with unique interests and skills, and we structure our high standards of teaching and learning to develop their individual potential. Teaching The National Curriculum for England, Jumeirah Primary School provides an exceptionally high quality education and world class facilities to students from Nursery to Year 4.

JUMEIRAH PRIMARY SCHOOL

Please contact:
Jumeirah Primary School
PO Box 29093, Dubai
United Arab Emirates
Tel: 04-394 3500, Fax: 04-394 3960
Email: office@jpsdubai sch.ae
*Website: **www.jpsdubai.com***

GEMS
— EDUCATION —

Educating for Brilliant Futures

arrive in Dubai but don't always follow through. It's certainly worth making the effort though, and whether it's for business or just to be able to exchange the odd word there are many schools here offering classes in Arabic, English, and other languages.

Transportation

With few other alternatives (although the bus system is adequate, in such a hot country not many people relish standing in the sun waiting for a bus which will in variably be overcrowded) most people tend to travel by car – be it owned or hired. Also many couples or families tend to have two cars. To buy a car you must be a resident and you need a UAE driving licence in order to legally drive it. If you are on a visit visa and wish to drive a car you have to either apply for a temporary licence (valid for one month) or lease a hire car. If you have family or friends in town and you are happy for them to drive your vehicle make sure you get a temporary licence for them from the Traffic Police, see Certificates & Licences [p.72]. There are numerous rental companies for short or long term leasing and you will need your international driving licence.

The following section covers leasing, buying (new or used vehicles), registration, fines, insurance and traffic accidents.

The Dubai Traffic Police interactive voice response system (268 5555) or Website (www.dxbtraffic.gov.ae) (Arabic and English) tells you all you ever wanted to know about fines, speeding tickets, registering vehicles, applying for driving licences, emergency numbers, suggestions etc.

Office locations:

Traffic Police HQ – near Galadari roundabout, Dubai-Sharjah Road (269 2222, Map Ref 15-C1)

Bur Dubai Police Station – Sheikh Zayed Road, Junction 4 (398 1111, Map Ref 10-A1)

Vehicle Leasing

Many people find that they have no other option (due to visa requirements) than to lease a vehicle, and while it may be advantageous in the short term as you have fewer hassles when it comes to breakdowns, re-registration etc, long term leasing can be expensive.

All services are provided inclusive of registration, maintenance, replacement, 24 hour assistance and insurance (comprehensive with personal accident is advisable). You may find that your employer has connections with a car hire company and can negotiate better rates for long term hire than you can on an individual basis.

Leasing is generally weekly, monthly or yearly. Cars typically range from Mitsubishi Lancers or Toyota Corollas to Mitsubishi Pajero 4 wheel drive vehicles. Monthly lease prices range from Dhs.1,500 for a small vehicle to Dhs.1,900 for larger cars and Dhs.3,500 for a four wheel drive. As the lease period increases, the price decreases.

For short term rental there are many companies offering daily services – check the Hawk Business Pages for the most competitive rates. To hire any vehicle you will need to provide a passport copy, credit card and a valid driving licence from your home country, or a valid international driving licence.

Vehicle Leasing Agents	
Autolease Rent-a-Car	282 6565
Diamond Lease P.139	331 3172
FAST Rent-a-car	332 8988
United Car Rentals	285 7777

Bright lights, busy nights

Buying a Vehicle

You must have a residence visa in order to own a car, although anyone can then drive it (i.e. your spouse or family members) as long as they have a temporary or permanent UAE driving licence, see Certificates & Licences [p.72]. Choosing a car here can be a tough decision as the market is huge. Most people will find that cars are far cheaper here than in their home countries and that, with the low cost of petrol and maintenance, they can afford something a little more extravagant than they would otherwise think of buying.

New Vehicles

If you are going to invest in a brand new vehicle you will find most models available on the market through the main dealers.

Used Vehicles

Due to the relatively low price of cars and the turnover of expats in the Emirates, there is a thriving second-hand market. Dealers are scattered around town but areas to start with include Sheikh Zayed Road and Garhoud. Expect to pay a premium of about Dhs.5,000 for buying through a dealer, since they also offer a limited warranty, insurance, finance and registration, unlike private sales. Sometimes the main dealers will offer good deals on demonstration cars which are basically new but have been used by the showroom for test drives.

Chasing the sunset

New Car Dealers

Alpha Romeo	Gargash Motors	266 4669
Aston Martin	Al Habtoor Motors	269 1110
Audi	Al Nabooda Automobiles	347 5111
Bentley	Al Habtoor Motors	269 1110
BMW	AGMC	339 1555
Cadillac	Liberty Automobiles	282 4440
Chevrolet	Al Yousuf Motors	339 5555
Chrysler	Trading Enterprises	295 4246
Dodge	Trading Enterprises	295 4246
Ferrari	Al Tayer Motors	266 6489
Fiat	Al Ghandi Auto	266 6511
Ford	Al Tayer Motors	201 1001
GMC	National Auto	266 4848
Honda	Trading Enterprises	295 4246
Hyundai	Juma Al Majid	269 0893
Isuzu	GENAVCO	396 1000
Jaguar	Al Tayer Group	266 6489
Jeep	Trading Enterprises	295 4246
Kia	Al Majed Motors	269 5600
Land Rover	Al Tayer Group	201 1001
Lexus	Al Futtaim Motors	228 2261
Mazda	Galadari Automobiles	299 4848
Maserati	Al Tayer Motors	266 6489
Mercedes	Gargash Enterprises	269 9777
Mini	AGMC	339 1555
Mitsubishi	Al Habtoor Motors	269 1110
Nissan	Arabian Automobiles	295 1234
Opel	Liberty Automobiles	282 4440
Peugeot	Swaidan Trading	266 7111
Porsche	Al Nabooda Automobiles	338 6999
Renault	Al Majed Motors	269 5600
Rolls Royce	AGMC	339 1555
Saab	Gargash Motors	266 4669
Skoda	Autostar Trading	269 7100
Suzuki	Al Rostamani Trading	347 0008
Toyota	Al Futtaim Motors	228 2261
Volkswagen	Al Nabooda Automobiles	338 6999
Volvo	Trading Enterprises	295 4246

Used Car Dealers

4 x 4 Motors	Opp Al Bustan Rotana	282 3050
Al Futtaim Automall	Al Quoz P.147	347 2212
Autoplus	Sheikh Zayed Road	339 5400
Boston Cars	Al Awir	333 1010
House of Cars	Sheikh Zayed Road	343 5060
Motor World	Nr Ports & Customs	333 2206
Off Road Motors	Jct 3, Sheikh Zayed Rd	338 4866
Quality Cars	Trading Enterprises	295 4246

Alternatively, visit Dubai Municipality's Used Car Complex at Al Awir/Ras Al Khor. Even here you need to be careful – many cars have been wrecked and rebuilt, so make sure you use the on-site Tasjeel checking service – a small price to pay for peace of mind. If you're online, have a look at www.valuewheels.com.

For other second-hand deals check the classifieds section in the newspapers and supermarket noticeboards (mainly Spinneys or Park n Shop).

Before buying a second-hand car, have it checked by a reputable garage, especially four wheel drives as you may not be aware how vigorously they have been driven off road. 4X4 Motors on Sheikh Zayed Road, and AAA or Max Garage (285 9500) in Rashidiya offer an excellent checking service. Expect to pay around Dhs.200-300.

All transactions for vehicles must be directed through the Traffic Police. A Dhs.3,000 fine is imposed on both buyer and seller for cars sold unofficially.

Ownership Transfer

To register a second-hand car in your name you must transfer vehicle ownership. You will need to submit an application form, the valid registration card, the insurance certificate, the original licence plates and Dhs.20 to the Traffic Police, plus an NOC from the finance company, if applicable. The previous owner must also be present to sign the form.

Vehicle Import

A requirement for cars imported by individuals or private car showrooms that were manufactured after 1997/98, is an NOC from the official agent in the UAE or from the Ministry of Finance and Industry (if no official agent exists). This is to ensure that the car complies with GCC specifications (or rather that the local dealers are not outdone by the neighbouring competition!).

Additionally, believe it or not, if you are buying a vehicle from another part of the Emirates you have to export and import it into Dubai first! This means lots of paperwork and lots of hassle. You will need to take your essential documents, the sale agreement, current registration and Dhs.60. You will then be issued with a set of temporary licence plates, which are valid for three days – enough time to submit a new registration application in Dubai.

Cars toting export plates may not drive on Dubai roads. This ban came about because cars have been illegally sold under the guise of a foreign registration – export plates were used to avoid registration in Dubai.

Vehicle Insurance

Before you can register your car you must have adequate insurance and many companies offer this service. The insurers will need to know the year of manufacture and may need to inspect the vehicle. Take along copies of your UAE driving licence, passport and the existing vehicle registration card.

Annual insurance policies are for a 13 month period (this is to cover the one month grace period that you are allowed when your registration expires). Rates depend on the age and model of your car and your previous insurance history. The rates are generally 4 - 7% of the vehicle value or 5% for cars over five years old. Fully comprehensive with personal accident insurance is highly advisable. For more adventurous drivers, insurance for off-roading accidents is also recommended for people with 4X4 vehicles. Norwich Winterthur is one of the few insurers who will cover off-road accidents. For details on all insurance companies, look in the Yellow Pages or Hawk Business Pages.

> ### To Oman and back!
>
> *It is wise to check whether your insurance covers you for the Sultanate of Oman as, within the Emirates, you may find yourself driving through small Omani enclaves (especially if you are off-road eg, near Hatta, through Wadi Bih and on the East Coast in Dibba, see Exploring [p.197]). Insurance for a visit to Oman can be arranged on a short term basis, usually for no extra cost.*

Registering a Vehicle

All cars must be registered annually with the Traffic Police. There is a one month grace period after your registration has expired in which to have your car re-registered (hence the 13 month insurance period). Please beware that some second-hand dealers may sell you a car that under normal circumstances would not pass the annual vehicle testing. However, with 'friends' at the test centre, they are

Registration Service	
AAA Service Center	285 8989
Al Sayara Tasjeel	800 4258
Midland Cars	396 7521
Protectol	285 7182

able to get the car 'passed', leaving you stuck when you come to do it yourself the following year.

The Process

In order to obtain licence plates for the vehicle, the car must first be tested, then registered with the Dubai Traffic Police. If you have purchased a new

Seize the moment

Call 800 2924 for the AXA advantage

AUTOMOBILE INSURANCE
With AXA, you have every reason to feel optimistic

AXA comprehensive motor package gives you better protection and exclusive advantages at the best possible price. Our dedicated Call Centre is your single point of contact for all your insurance needs – Automobile, Renter's, Travel and Healthcare. Our job is to give our client confidence.

www.axa-gulfregion.com

INSURANCE, HEALTHCARE
AND INVESTMENTS

Be Life Confident

AXA INSURANCE B.S.C. Dubai: Al Attar Tower, 3rd Floor, 305, Sheikh Zayed Road, Dubai - Abu Dhabi tel:02 644 2332

vehicle from a dealer, the dealer will register the car for you. You do not need to test a new vehicle for the first two years though you must re-register it after one year. There are several ways to test your car. Ras Al Khor boasts a five lane testing centre (Al Ghandi) that is run in conjunction with the Traffic Police. The centre is paperless and this saves you time in necessary procedures. Following this centre's success, EPPCO and Emarat are making life easier for motorists. They offer a full registration service for a fee, which includes collecting your car, testing and registering it, and delivering it back to you all in the same day. EPPCO Tasjeel (267 3940) offers a service called Al Sayara, which costs Dhs.200, plus the testing and registration fees. Emarat (343 4444) also has five full registration and vehicle testing service centres called Shamil, where they will test and register your car with the police. You can also pay any traffic fines here.

Remember to take all your essential documents, insurance valid for 13 months existing registration card, plus the proof of purchase agreement and vehicle transfer or customs certificate (if applicable) and Dhs.360. Before the registration procedure can be completed, all traffic offences and fines against your car registration number must be settled – a potentially expensive business! The following charge a fee for undertaking registration, in addition to normal registration costs.

Traffic Fines & Offences

If you are caught driving or parking illegally, you will be fined (unless the offence is more serious). You can also be fined Dhs.50 on the spot for being caught driving without your licence. If you are involved in an accident and don't have your licence with you, you will be given a 24 hour grace period in which to present your licence to the police station. If you don't you risk having your car impounded and may have to go to court.

There are a number of police controlled speed traps, fixed cameras and mobile radars around Dubai. There is no leeway for breaking the speed limit – although for some speed demons this seems of little consequence. The fines have been restructured because of the high number of traffic accidents, many of which could be avoided with better care and judgement. The fines for speeding start at Dhs.200, parking tickets are Dhs.150. Cars without exhaust control are fined Dhs.150 - 300, and overloaded cars Dhs.150. In addition, a black point penalty system operates for certain offences (see [p.146]).

To check the fines you have against your vehicle or driving licence you can call the Dubai Traffic Police Information Line (268 5555, Arabic & English) or visit their Website: www.dxbtraffic.gov.ae – a handy thing to know rather than being faced with an unexpectedly large bill when you renew your car registration!

Office location: For payment of traffic fines, Traffic Fines Section, Traffic Police HQ – near Galadari roundabout, Dubai-Sharjah Road (269 2222, Map Ref 15-B1). It is also possible to pay road fines at other locations around Dubai. These include Al Safa Union Co-operative, Al Tawar Union Co-operative and Jumeirah Town Centre. You can pay fines online using your credit card (www.dxbtraffic.gov.ae), but this service carries a small processing fee.

Tinted Windows

Currently, the government allows you to avoid the sun somewhat by tinting your vehicle's windows up to 30 percent. Some areas have facilities where you can get your car windows tinted as dark as you like – but don't get carried away and remember to stick to the limit. Random checks take place and fines are handed out to those caught in the dark! Tinting in Sharjah is allowed for a fee of Dhs.100 and Ajman residents may tint for Dhs.200 per annum, but only if they are women.

Breakdowns

In the event of a breakdown, you will usually find that passing police cars stop to help, or at least to check your documents! We recommend that you keep water in your car at all times - the last thing you want is to be stuck in the middle of summer with no air conditioning while you wait for assistance. Dubai Traffic officers recommend, if possible, that you pull your car over to a safe spot. If you are on the hard shoulder of a highway you should pull your car as far away from the yellow line as possible and step away from the road until help arrives.

Off-Road Explorer
Experience the UAE's delights off the beaten track. Designed for the adventurous, a brilliant array of outback route maps, satellite images, step by step guidance, safety information, details on flora and fauna, and stunning photography make this outdoor guide a perfect addition to your four wheeler.

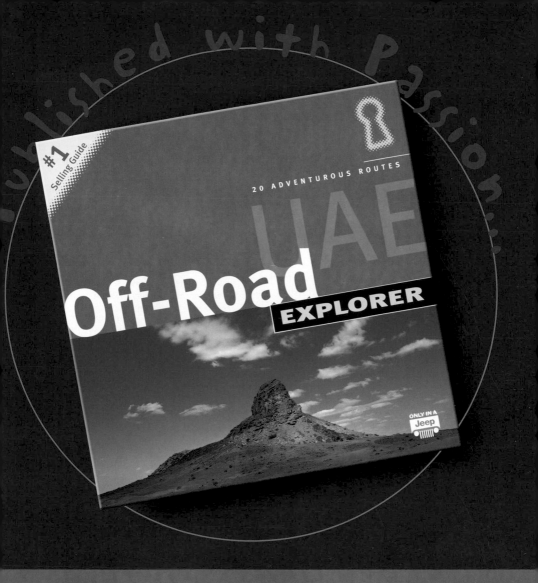

Head for the Hills!

While the UAE may be fast becoming the Middle East's most modern metropolis there still remain a vast desert and mountainous expanse waiting to be explored. While you might be able to take yourself out of the city you can't always take the city out of you, so getting lost in the UAE's 'outback' could be a problem. Or not... when equipped with this off-road route guide that has easy to follow instructions, satellite imagery, distances, landmarks, points of interest and driving tips for difficult terrain.

- Satellite Maps & GPS Coordinates
- Driving & First Aid
- Wildlife Guide
- Outdoor Activities
- Archaeology & Heritage

Passionately Publishing...

The Arabian Automobile Association (AAA) (266 9989 or 800 4900, www.aaa-uae.com) offers a 24 hour roadside breakdown service for an annual charge. This includes help in minor mechanical repairs, battery boosting, or help if you run out of petrol, have a flat tire or lock yourself out. Mashreq Bank Visa card holders receive AAA membership free of charge. The more advanced service includes off-road recovery, vehicle registration and a rent a car service. It's a similar concept to the RAC or AA in Britain, or AAA in the States.

Traffic Accidents

Other options ➔ Cars [p.214]

Licensed to spend

The '2' licence plate was bought in 2001 for Dhs.1,240,000 in an two day auction of personalised licence plates which brought in a staggering total Dhs.44,000,000 in revenue! Check out the Traffic Police's Website for current auction details www.dxbtraffic.gov.ae/en.

Be very careful on the roads in Dubai as there are more than a few maniacs behind the wheel so be extra vigilant and remember to use your mirrors (and indicators) at all times. If, however you are involved in an accident, in serious cases dial 999 or in less critical cases, call Deira (266 0555), Bur Dubai (398 1111), or Sharjah (06 538 1111). The Dubai Traffic Police Information Line (268 5555, Arabic & English) gives the numbers of police stations around the emirate. The police will assess the accident and once they have apportioned blame they will give you a copy of the accident report, if it is green then the other party is at fault but if it is pink then you are to blame for the accident. You will need to submit this form to the insurance company in order to process the claim. For more details on traffic accidents and procedures see Accidents in General Information, [p.44].

Black Points

In addition to a system of fines for certain offences, a black points penalty system operates. If you have a permanent licence and receive 12 black points four times in one year, your licence is taken away and your car impounded. The first time you hit 12 points, you receive a fine and your licence is revoked for anything between two weeks and a month. For the next set of 12 points, the penalty is more severe, and so on.

If you are on a probationary licence and aged between 18 - 21, and receive 12 points within 12 months, your licence is revoked and you have to start the whole process of obtaining a licence from the beginning.

However, it seems that there are no hard and fast rules or amounts when it comes to black points. If you do something serious, your licence can be taken away immediately. If you run a red light, you receive nine black points instantly.

Repairs

By law, no vehicle can be accepted for major repairs without an accident report from the Traffic Police, although very minor dents can be repaired without a report. Usually, your insurance company has an agreement with a particular garage to which they will refer you. The garage will carry out the repair work and the insurance company will settle the claim. Generally, there is Dhs.500 deductible for all claims, but check with your insurance company for details of your policy. It is worth noting that if you purchase a new vehicle it is worth paying extra insurance for agency repairs if you want to maintain the maximum value of your car – check with your insurer for the difference in price.

Which way to the carwash?

The UAE's largest automotive group redefines used car standards.

Introducing Al-Futtaim Automall, the quality used car division of the Al-Futtaim Group.

Al-Futtaim Automall offers you the widest choice of globally renowned automotive brands: four wheel drives, sedans, coupes and station wagons. More importantly, they come with the assurance of quality and the trust of the Al-Futtaim Group. A five star service that makes it a cut above the rest.

★ 12 month warranty	★ Mileage Certificate	★ 99 point check	★ Automall Vehicle Club	★ 30 day Exchange Pledge
The world's most comprehensive Used Car Warranty, **identical** to that of a new car!	The **Km** reading of each car will be investigated and will carry an exclusive Al-Futtaim Automall Mileage Certificate.	Every car will undergo a rigorous 99 point service check at an Al-Futtaim workshop, before being offered for sale.	Each car will carry unique identification showing it to be a Quality Used Vehicle from the Al-Futtaim Automall Vehicle Club.	Our customers' peace of mind is so important, that each purchase carries the reassurance of the Al-Futtaim Automall 30 Day Exchange Pledge.

Call 800 4227

◆ **Al-Futtaim automall**

Dubai Airport Road (04) 8004227, Sheikh Zayed Road (04) 3472212, (050) 7482949,
Al Awir Municipality Complex (04) 3336870, (050) 5686587 **Sharjah** near Honda showroom (06) 5533155, (050) 4782623
Abu Dhabi Honda showroom, Electra Street (02) 6763300 **RAK** (07) 2352284
e-mail: automall@alfuttaim.ae www.al-futtaim.com

An **Al-Futtaim group** company

www.automalluae.com

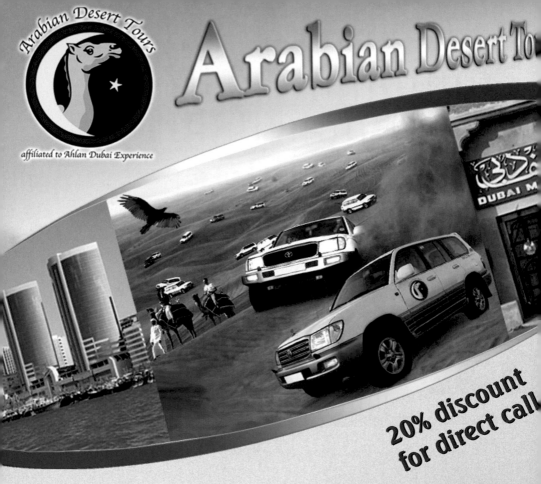

Arabian Desert Tours

affiliated to Ahlan Dubai Experience

20% discount for direct call

- ▼ Dubai City Tours
- ▼ Sharjah-Ajman Tours
- ▼ Al Ain Tours
- ▼ Abu Dhabi Tours
- ▼ Desert Safari
- ▼ Dune Drive
- ▼ Sand Skiing
- ▼ Overnight Safari

- ▼ Buggy Safari
- ▼ Hatta Mountain Trips
- ▼ Dhow Cruise Dinner
- ▼ Shopping Tours
- ▼ Fishing Trip
- ▼ East Coast Mountain Tour
- ▼ Burj Al Arab Restaurant Reservations

Tel: 04-268 2880, Fax: 04-268 2881, PO Box: 93349 Dubai UAE
E-mail: arabian7@emirates.net.ae, website: www.arabiandesert-dubai.ae
for 24 hour reservations 050-578 6632, 050-598 5935

Exploring

Exploring

What's new?

Visitor's Checklist

Page 152

Tickets - check! Passport - Check! Explorer - Check! If you can tear yourself away from the pool or the beach for long enough then we've compiled a handy list of places and activities you 'must see and do' during your stay in Dubai. Proof that there's more to this great city than just sun, sea, sand, and shopping

Living the High Lights!

Always striving to make your life easier we've provided bite-size guides to some of the main areas in and around Dubai, and told you what's hot and what's not. The car icon denotes accessibility - will you find any parking ... what's the traffic like? More 'dots' means more car-friendly. The camera icon denotes an area's 'tourist' value, and the clock gives you an idea of how long you might want to spend exploring..

 Car/Traffic

 Touristic Value

 Amount of Time

Escape from the City

Page 197

As much as we all love Dubai and its plethora of nooks and crannies to explore, sometimes you just need to wash that city air out of your hair. If you need to escape for a couple of days and sample a change of pace and scenery, then turn to the section on weekend breaks. All the best getaways are listed, so check it out before you check in!

Exploring

Known as the City of Gold or the City of Lights, Dubai is a world class destination and epitomises the meeting of East and West. The following section is aimed at everyone, whether you have chosen Dubai for a holiday, find yourself here on a long flight stopover, or work/live here and think you know it all. As well as being voted the safest holiday destination by Condé Nast Traveller magazine, Dubai has many reasons to be proud. From the highest hotel standards, including the famous Burj Al Arab and many other top hotels, to luxurious shopping malls, beach resorts, a varied night life and a plethora of entertainment and activities on offer, pretty much everything is covered. There are also numerous photographic opportunities: mosques, palaces, dhows, camel and horse racing, sunsets, architecture and windtowers, to name a few. Combining modern convenience with traditional Arabia, in Dubai you will find a wealth of places to explore where new and old meet.

This cosmopolitan city has something for everyone and just when you think you have heard it all, Dubai comes up with something fresh; whether it's the world's tallest building, the world's largest shopping mall, the first underwater luxury hotel or a ski slope in the desert! To see what you can cram into a one or two day stopover, refer to the Visitors Checklist, while for a leisurely week or two, refer to the Guide Checklist, or to explore it all, read on!

Also covered are places out of Dubai, although for more information on Abu Dhabi, the Sultanate of Oman and off the beaten track in the UAE, refer to the *Abu Dhabi Explorer*, the *Oman Explorer* and the *Off-Road Explorer (UAE)*, all by Explorer Publishing.

Dubai's heart is still considered to be the Creek, where early settlers built their mud and palm frond huts – difficult to imagine now when you see the Creek lined with skyscrapers. However, the modern city is developing into a linear coastal settlement, mainly spreading southwest towards Abu Dhabi. The 15 km long Creek is about 500 metres wide and has three main crossing points; the Al Shindagha Tunnel nearest the sea, then the Al Maktoum Bridge and furthest inland, the Al Garhoud Bridge. For each of the main geographical areas of Dubai, we have described the key activities and landmarks. Dubai Creek divides the city into two areas – to the south is known as Bur Dubai and to the north as Deira. On the Bur Dubai side of the city are Oud Metha (a recreational and commercial area), Satwa and Karama (both original suburbs of old Dubai), plus Jumeira and Umm Suqeim (originally fishing settlements) along the coast away from the Creek. Further past Umm Suqeim on the way to Abu Dhabi, is Jebel Ali, which is the most southerly point of the city, and famous for its port and free zone (these can be seen from space). The road leading to Jebel Ali and Abu Dhabi is the Sheikh Zayed Road, an eight lane highway shadowed by some of the most impressive skyscrapers in the city. Areas north of the Creek include Al Garhoud, the district close to the airport, and the developing residential area of Mirdif. The pull-out map at the back of this book will help you find your bearings wherever you decide to venture.

The mighty Burj Al Arab

Exploring

Dubai Visitor's Checklist

Dubai Visitor's Checklist

The following is our list of 'must dos' to help you make the most of your stay in Dubai. While this city isn't steeped in culture and heritage, there are still plenty of options other than shopping or lounging by the hotel pool. So while you're topping up on your tan, sit back, read on and tailor your own memorable tour of this fascinating city. If you're an extreme adventure buff, you can pop down to the beach and try a spot of kite surfing. For the kids, there's hours of endless fun at the Wild Wadi waterpark, while those with itchy feet can escape the city and experience all the thrills of a desert safari.

Madinat Jumeirah [p.242]

Inspired by traditional Arabian architecture, this stunning new souk is a must for shoppers and sightseers alike. Lose yourself exploring the maze of alleyways leading to intimate open-fronted boutiques, classy cafés, and charming waterfront bars and restaurants.

History and Heritage

Delve into Dubai's fascinating past at the Dubai Museum, and visit Sheikh Saeed Al Maktoum's House for a collection of evocative old photographs. Finish up at the Heritage and Diving Village to see traditional crafts, tribal dances and ceremonies.

Bastakiya [p.170]

Learn ancient facts at the Dubai Museum, stroll through historical streets and stop for a coffee at the Basta Art Café. Traditional wind towers, courtyard houses, museums and galleries accentuate this traditional part of the city.

Burj Al Arab [p.38]

Indulge in the glamour and luxury of the Burj. Order pre-dinner drinks and watch the sunset from the Juna Lounge. Then take the two minute submarine ride to the Al Mahara seafood restaurant for a delicious and hearty meal.

Jumeira Mosque [p.167]

Learn more about local culture through organised tours held here on Thursdays and Sundays (10:00 sharp). You don't need to book, but it would be wise to call beforehand to confirm (344 7755). You should also adhere to the dress code.

Open Top Bus [p.177]

Jump on the bus for a quick tour of Dubai's main attractions. Starting and finishing at Wafi City, the hop on/hop off tour includes traditional points of interest, such as the Dubai Museum and the Heritage & Diving Village.

Wonder Bus [p.177]

This amphibious bus offers a different way of experiencing Dubai. Each trip costs Dhs.95 (per adult) and Dhs.65 (per child). Dhs.290 buys a family package, which admits two adults and two kids.

Shop Till You Drop [p.201]

Keep fresh and cool at one of Dubai's many shopping malls. Skim through the Shopping section for detailed descriptions of each centre and choose the one that best suits your retail needs.

Souks [p.253]

Visit the Gold Souk and discover why Dubai is called the City of Gold. Diamonds, pearls and most other precious stones can also be found here. Better still, spoil yourself by designing your own piece of jewellery.

Dhows Unloading [p.156]

Check out dhows being unloaded at Deira creekside and be amazed by the trusting way in which boxes of electrical goods are left on the pavement.

Scenic Flying [p.178]

Catch an aerial view of Dubai. Book a scenic flight with a tour operator and see the city's new developments underway. Prices start from Dhs.250 for a 45 minute to one hour flight. Hot air balloons and helicopter rides are also available, but are more expensive.

Cable Car [p.180]

Take an exciting trip in a cable car at the Creekside Park. Suspended 30 feet in the air, this 45 minute ride travels the full length of the park, and is not advisable for those suffering from acrophobia.

Water Delights [p.257]

Parasailing, snorkelling, diving, and surfing - there's lots to do at the beach. Hotels run various in-house activities, but also check with tour operators or flip to the Activities section for independent facilities.

Desert Safari [p.182]

While in Dubai, a trip to the desert is a must. Ride a camel, climb a sand dune, sand ski, watch the stars, eat your fill and learn how to bellydance. Plenty of tour operators offer various excursions at competitive prices, so be sure to shop around first.

Water Taxi [p.154]

Soak up the panoramic views of the Creek in traditional abras. If you've already seen the sights of Bastakiya, visited the Dubai Museum and perused the textile souk, then catch an abra across the Creek to explore the spice and gold souks.

Shawarma [p.412]

Grab a tasty shawarma at any time of the day or night. Or, take a break from sightseeing with a thirst quenching fruit cocktail. If you're a health freak, you will know that watermelon juice is a great digestive tonic containing Vitamin A, B Complex and Vitamin C.

Wild Wadi [p.293]

Next door to the Burj Al Arab, this 12 acre water park has 23 rides in all, including the daunting 'Jumeirah Sceirah'. Dhs.110 and Dhs.130 (for adults) will give you full access for the day. Check opening times and discounted 'Sundowner' rates, as these vary from month to month.

Creek Dining [p.155]

Choose a sightseeing cruise and experience a memorable evening in Dubai. Dining options vary from lunch, sunset and dinner cruises, and on board entertainment is included (don't forget your camera).

A Day at the Races [p.56]

The Dubai World Cup will be held on the 26th of March 2005. This annual event is an expensive day out but it is the World's Richest Horserace and a rare opportunity for ladies to wear hats! An alternative is camel racing, popular during Oct - April. Dhs.2 for adults and Dhs.1 for children.

Dhow Building

Grab a taxi and ask the driver to take you to the dhow building yard by the Al Garhoud bridge. Watch the mesmerising procedures of dhows being constructed without the aid of drawings or modern equipment.

Fun & Games [p.258]

Encounter Zone at Wafi Mall has the popular Crystal Maze, a horror chamber and fascinating 3D films. Magic Planet at Deira City Centre is a kid's paradise, while WonderLand Family Fun Park offers endless exciting rides and water attractions.

Shisha [p.26]

Join in the social tradition of hanging out at a shisha café. A widely favoured pastime with the locals, shisha consists of tobacco, mixed with molasses and a variety of flavourings, smoked from a water pipe.

Exploring

Dubai Visitor's Checklist

Dubai – Main Areas

Dubai Creek

Map Ref → 8-C4

The Creek has played a pivotal role in the development of Dubai, dividing the city in two. The earliest Dubai settlement was near the mouth of the Creek, but when it was dredged to create a larger anchorage and encourage trade, the growing town gradually crept further inland.

Dubai Creek has three main crossing points – nearest to the sea is Al Shindagha Tunnel, next Al Maktoum Bridge and furthest inland is Al Garhoud Bridge. Both bridges can be raised to allow boats through to the boatyard inland, but this usually only happens late at night. There is also a pedestrian foot tunnel near Al Shindagha.

The layout of the roads combined with the soaring temperatures, especially in summer, mean Dubai isn't the easiest city to explore on foot, however, some parts are well worth the effort of walking around. In particular, these include the souks and the corniche areas on

Area Overview

both sides of the Creek, which you can cross in an 'abra' (water taxi) to experience a traditional side of Dubai that luckily lives on today. The word 'corniche' refers to any walkway by a stretch of water – in the UAE this can be along the seafront or around one of the creeks or lagoons.

A useful guide is the *Dubai Town Walk Explorer* (Dhs.10), which outlines two routes through the most interesting parts of the city. It is available from all good bookshops or directly from Explorer Publishing.

Taking an abra is not only a more leisurely way of crossing the Creek but it is also far more pleasurable than the congested bridges and tunnel. These water taxis ply between the two banks as they have done for decades, carrying around 15,000 people across the Creek each day. The abra crossing takes about ten minutes and can be made in either direction from the dhow wharfage area on the Deira side or Al Seef Road in Bur Dubai. The abras are basic wooden boats that seat about 30 people (huddled together) and are used as a convenient and cheap method of transport. For visitors, they are a great way to see the mirrored towers of Deira and traditional Arabic architecture of Bur Dubai, as well as get a real feel for the city. At 50 fils, it's probably the cheapest

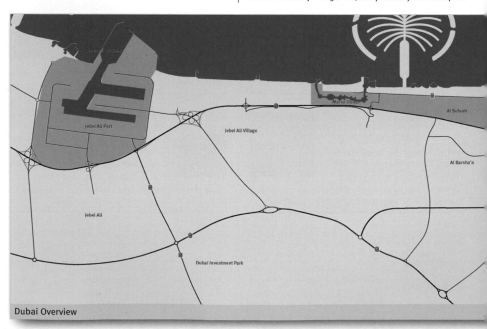

Dubai Overview

Exploring

Dubai – Main Areas

There are two sides to every creek

tour in the world! The steps down to the Creek are steep and can be slippery, so be careful when stepping across to your boat.

Alternatively, for Dhs.30 – 50 (depending on your haggling skills), you can hire an abra and driver for a half hour private Creek tour, just make sure you agree the price in advance.

Creek Tours

Creek Tours		
Bateaux Dubai	P.399	337 1919
Creekside Leisure	P.401	336 8406
Danat Dubai Cruises		351 1117

Creek Tours

Other options → **Boat & Yacht Charters [p.260]**
Dinner Cruises [p.400]

A more luxurious way of exploring the Creek is an organised Creek tour. It is a wonderful way to see new and old Dubai side by side, while enjoying a peaceful and relaxing journey. Prices per adult range from about Dhs.35 for a daytime trip to Dhs.260 for an evening cruise with dinner. Many of the tours are in a traditional wooden dhow (often with air conditioned decks to avoid the summer heat).

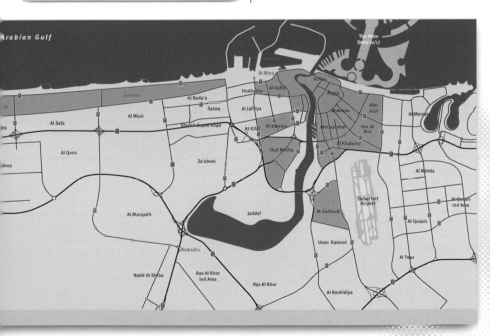

Deira

Map Ref → 8-C3

You can reach the Deira side of the Creek by abra and soak up the skyscraper scenery along the way, or to sample the local road-rage you can take a taxi! Narrow convoluted streets bustle with residential and commercial activity while gold, spices, perfumes and general goods are touted from the numerous souks. With rents generally less expensive on this side of the Creek the streets are full of people, especially in the evenings.

Take a stroll along the dhow wharfage where local traders are busy unloading wooden dhows tightly packed with everything from fruit and vegetables to televisions and if you're lucky even a car or two. This slice of local merchants' life is a reminder of Dubai's trading history and a photo opportunity not to be missed.

Area Overview

Bordering the Creek are some awe-inspiring buildings that almost seem to be years ahead of their time. A large golf ball that sits atop a high rise and pinpoints the Etisalat telecommunications building is testimony to the unique imagination of Dubai's modern architecture. The sparkling glass building housing the National Bank of Dubai (known locally as the 'pregnant lady') is a sculptural vision, standing tall like a magnificent convex mirror. At dusk, wander down the corniche on the Bur Dubai side (near the British Embassy) to get the best view of the stark contrast between ancient and modern Dubai, when moored trading dhows are reflected in the glass high rises and the water of the Creek.

Area Highlights

Souks, souks, souks!
Gold, spices, electronics - it''s all here. Walk along the streets and discover the various souks that pay tribute to the authentic trading methods of the Arab world.

Dhow Wharfage
Magnificent wooden dhows lazily docked by the water's edge provide excellent photo opportunities for happy snappers. Often you will find a stack of electrical goods trustingly left on the wharfage - a sight rarely seen elsewhere in the world.

Take the pedestrian underpass to the left of the abra station on the Deira side to enter the oldest market in Dubai, now mainly selling household items. Close by is the Spice Souk where the aroma of saffron and cumin entice and traders attempt to lure passers by with their exotic produce. You will find every spice under the sun as well as loose frankincense and other perfumed oils and dried herbs sold for medicinal purposes. The souk spreads over a large area between Al Nasr Square and the Gold Souk.

If it's rugs you want then Deira Tower on Al Nasr Square is worth a visit. About 40 shops offer a colourful profusion of carpets from Iran, Pakistan, Turkey and Afghanistan to suit everyone's taste and pocket.

Known as the 'City of Gold', Dubai is famed for its affordable gold and the Gold Souk is the Aladdin's Cave of gold shopping. Street after street is paved with gold shops whose windows are laden with 22 or 24 carat gold, so expect to make more than one visit. Bargaining is expected, and discounts depend on the season and the international gold rate. Dubai Shopping Festival and Dubai Summer Surprises are the main periods for low prices when huge discounts attract gold lovers from around the world. Be sure to haggle hard to get the 'best price'. Individual pieces can be made, or copies to your own specifications done, within a few days. Even if you aren't buying, an evening stroll through the gold souk in Deira, when it's all lit up and shiny, is worth the experience. For further information on carpets and gold, refer to the Shopping section of the book.

In this part of town, the earliest school in the city, Al Ahmadiya School, has been turned into the Museum of Education and is located next to the Heritage House. For further information on Al Ahmadiya School, refer to Museums, Heritage & Culture [p169].

Dubai Municipality has also reconstructed Murabba'at Umm Rayool (the name derives from the Arabic word for 'leg' as the building stands on seven pillars/legs). This was originally used as a weapons store, located on Baniyas Street, but the new building is on Union Square near the Deira taxi stand. This building style dates from 1894 - 1906.

Another cultural attraction is Dubai's largest and busiest fish market (near the Hyatt Regency hotel), where you can stock up on the freshest seafood in town at bargain prices. You can pay a 'wheelbarrow man' to follow you and carry your shopping, and someone else to gut your fish. Once you get used to the smell it's a lot of fun. A fish museum has recently been created at Deira Fish Market to give shoppers, and tourists, a better idea about the 350 species of fish in the Arabian Gulf, the history of the fishing trade in the UAE, and the types of fishing boats and equipment used by fishermen.

In true Dubai style, development plans are in the offing to reclaim land from the sea and transform the Deira seafront by building residential and commercial units, as well as public utilities and tourist attractions. The aim is to complete these in 2005.

Deira sights - all shiny and new

Bur Dubai

Map Ref → 8-A3

Once a flat, sandy area with a sprinkling of palm trees and barasti (palm) houses, this area of the city is now very much a bustling business hub, with modern buildings, shopping malls and restaurants. It is also a residential hotspot. There is a myriad of multi-storey apartment blocks furnished with gyms and rooftop pools and, despite the area being a bit of concrete jungle with soaring rents, it remains very popular with expats of all nationalities. As for its exploring value there's not much to see, except for near the Creek.

Just south is Port Rashid where the Dubai Ports Authority building is a large glass and chrome construction imaginatively designed like a paddle steamer, and all the paraphernalia of a port can be glimpsed over the surrounding fence.

Area Overview

🚗	●●○○○	
📷	●●●●●	
🕐	●●●○○	

Port Rashid

Al Mina | Al Saeed · Al Maktoum House

eiba | Al Raffa Rd

liya | Burjuman Centre

2.5km

Area Highlights

BurJuman Shopping Centre
Another Dubai venue not content with its already impressive status, this mall has undergone massive expansion to make it even bigger and better.

Textile Souk
Located just off the Creek, you can while away the hours browsing the array of stalls. Fashion victims can stock up on enough cheap material to start their own garment store.

Water Taxi (Abra)
Stroll down to the Creek and catch an abra. This traditional wooden boat will take you across the Creek for a very low fare or you pay a lot more for the scenic route and enjoy the sights and sounds of the Creek from a unique vantage point.

The area near the mouth of the Creek, known as Al Shindagha, is a good starting point to explore Bur Dubai. Here you can visit Sheikh Saeed Al Maktoum's House and the Heritage & Diving Village (a two minute walk from each other), before following the Creek inland to Dubai Museum. For further information, see Museums, Heritage & Culture.

Near the Astoria Hotel is the busy Al Faheidi Street [p.252]. Its narrow, bustling streets are a paradise for electrical goods. Close by, underneath wooden shaded walkways, every type of fabric imaginable can be bought at the Textile Souk.

Facing Dubai Museum is the Diwan, the Ruler's office, and the highest administrative body of the Dubai government. Built in 1990, the low white building is surrounded by black railings and combines modern materials with a traditional design, including examples of traditional windtowers.

Located near the Diwan, the Grand Mosque was recently renovated at an estimated cost of Dhs.15.5 million. It can accommodate 1,200 worshippers, and has 54 domes and a 70 metre minaret – presently the tallest in the city.

It is possible to walk inland along the edge of the Creek past the Diwan to the Bastakiya district of the city. The relaxed atmosphere of this walkway with its outdoor restaurants makes it a great place to stop and enjoy Arabic fare and a shisha pipe while watching the river traffic.

Near to the Diwan, the Bastakiya (also Bastakia) district is one of the oldest heritage sites in the city. Originally known as Bastakiya Chok (square), this intriguing neighbourhood dates back to the early 1900s when traders from Bastak in southern Iran were granted tax concessions by the then ruler of Dubai and encouraged to settle there. Here you can view one of the earliest forms of air conditioning in the shape of windtowers ('barajeel' in Arabic), which are distinctive rectangular structures on top of the traditional flat roofed buildings. These were built to catch the slightest of breezes and funnel them down into the rooms below. Amble down alleyways, visit the Majlis art gallery in a converted house, and another restored building next door, the Basta Art café makes a great pit stop. Behind the Majlis gallery is the beautifully restored XVA guesthouse & gallery. Bastakiya is gradually being reconstructed by the Dubai Municipality to pay homage to the traditional Arabian way of life with small winding alleys leading to over 50 houses.

Nearby, Bait Al Wakeel was built in 1934 as Dubai's first office building. It currently houses the fishing museum. Numerous embassies are located in this area, and further inland from the Creek is the popular BurJuman Shopping Centre [p.234]. Located on the busy crossroads of Khalid bin Waleed Road (or Bank Street, as it is popularly known), this already huge mall has recently been extended almost tripling in size.

The many faces of Bur Dubai

Al Garhoud

Map Ref → 14-D4

The area Al Garhoud (known as Garhoud) lies to the north of the Al Garhoud Bridge, between the Creek and Deira, and is bordered by the airport. It is primarily a commercial district that quietens down at night, although there are residential pockets.

There are places by the Creek that offer escape from the ever-increasing congestion. Almost under the bridge is a popular spot for fishing and nearby, along the Creek, is the site for Dubai Festival City, one of the city's latest shopping and entertainment complexes currently under construction. It is being developed at an estimated cost of six billion dirhams over the next three years. The first phase, which is due to open in 2005, will include a marina, a 3.2 km waterfront promenade, 40 water view restaurants and an amphitheatre. Subsequent phases will include hotels, restaurants, family entertainment venues, a 'global village', residential and office space, plus indoor and outdoor shopping.

In the middle of Garhoud is Dubai Tennis Stadium, which on occasion doubles as a concert venue. A couple of locations in Garhoud have al fresco licensed bars and restaurants overlooking pleasant landscaped courtyards. Two are Century Village and the Irish Village, which are built into the side of the tennis stadium, and The Cellar is nearby. There is also the Meridien Village at Le Meridien Dubai hotel near the airport.

One landmark in Garhoud that will catch your eye is a building shaped almost exactly like the front half of an aeroplane, which rather appropriately is the training centre for Emirates Airline. The main shopping centre in Garhoud is Deira City Centre. Not only is it a gigantic shopping mall but it also houses many restaurants and cafés and an 11 screen cinema. Usually referred to as City

Area Overview

Centre, it is always busy and gets particularly crowded at weekends and in the evenings, however there is plenty of underground parking, plus two adjacent multi storey car parks. Recent expansion has created 20 more outlets, and it is probably the most popular mall with visitors and residents alike.

Opposite City Centre and bordering the Creek for about 1½ km is an enticing stretch of carefully landscaped greenery, home to the Dubai Creek Golf & Yacht Club which re-opens in early 2005 after extensive landscaping and refurbishment. The impressive golf clubhouse is based on the shape of dhow sails (in fact the image of this famous building is found on the Dhs.20 note), while the yacht club is aptly in the shape of a yacht! This peaceful retreat from the bustle of the city offers night golf, a gym and swimming pool, plus several excellent restaurants that are open to non-members.

Located to the north east, Dubai International Airport has been voted Airport of the Year several times, and is currently undergoing a massive $4.1 billion expansion. Work is in progress for Terminal 3 and two additional concourses, which are due for completion in 2006.

Area Highlights

Century Village
A great place to chill out with friends at your choice of indoor or outdoor restaurant with quaint surroundings, then carry on the evening at the authentic Irish Village pub next door.

Dubai Creek Golf & Yacht Club
A prime spot to enjoy panoramic views of the Creek. The vistas, coupled with the architectural splendour of the club puts it on the must do list for avid photographers.

The Aviation Club Stadium

Oud Metha

Map Ref → 10-D4

The Oud Metha Road cuts diagonally through this part of Dubai and is bordered by the Creek to the north, Umm Hurair and Za'abeel roads to the west and Al Quta'eyat Road to the south. Within this residential area, you'll find recreational, social and educational facilities, as well as Lamcy Plaza, which offers great shopping and is also home to Loulou Al Dugong's, a fabulous play area for young children. Just off Oud Metha Road are a string of social clubs from various countries and two of Dubai's churches. Close by are Rashid Hospital, the American Hospital and Al Nasr Leisureland. This leisure complex offers a variety of facilities, including bowling and an indoor ice rink.

Near Al Maktoum Bridge are the Dubai Courts and Creekside Park. The manicured lawns of the park run for 2.5 km alongside the Creek to Al Garhoud Bridge. An minimal entrance fee is charged and facilities include an amphitheatre, mini 'falaj' (traditional irrigation system), children's play area, plus you can roller blade or hire two-seated bicycles to tour the expansive park. For an aerial view of your surroundings, travel high above the Creek in one of the cable cars. A popular attraction at Creekside Park is Children's City, the world's fifth largest 'infotainment' facility comprising 77,000 square metres of exhibits, which target children between the ages of five and 15 and are very educational. There is also a planetarium inside.

WonderLand Theme & Water Park at the Al Garhoud Bridge end of Creekside Park is a popular amusement park offering various rides, from bumper cars to a hot air balloon; there's even a rollercoaster and a log flume ride. Between WonderLand and the park is Paintball, an entertaining (and painful) way to de-stress and 'kill your enemies' with powerful paintball sub-machine guns. For further details see [p.286].

Near Al Garhoud Bridge is the Al Boom Tourist Village, which is popular with local couples who hire the hall for wedding functions. Tourists also visit to sample the local cuisine and to enjoy an evening cruising the Creek on one of the beautifully illuminated dhows.

Opposite Al Boom Tourist Village is a patch of land where, if you are lucky, you can observe a traditional wooden dhow being built. Mainly used for trade, these distinctive high bowed vessels take months to construct, but their lifespan is boasted at over a century.

Wafi City consists of several complexes, including a shopping mall, numerous popular restaurants, a nightclub and a health club and luxury spa with an ancient Egyptian theme. The health club and mall exteriors are impressive, with huge mock Egyptian statues and a row of crouching sphinxes guarding the entrances. Wafi Mall specialises in upmarket quality items from international brand names. This site is also home to Planet Hollywood (hard to miss, as it is housed in a giant blue globe).

Near Wafi City are the Grand Cineplex, an 11 screen cinema, and the impressive Grand Hyatt Hotel with its opulent lobby resembling a beautiful, lush tropical garden. Also in this area construction has started on Phase One of Dubai Healthcare City, a state of the art medical facility being developed in partnership with world leaders in medicine including Harvard Medical School, Johns Hopkins and the Mayo Clinic. Phase One is due for completion in 2005, with final completion scheduled for 2010.

The Oud Metha Neighbourhood Park covering an area of 1.34 hectares is still in the planning stages, but when complete will offer volleyball and basketball facilities, a jogging track, children's playgrounds, a small lake, shaded areas, and a cafeteria to meet the recreational needs of residents in this area.

Area Overview

🚗	●●●●○	
📷	●●●○○	
🕐	●●○○○	

Area Highlights

Wafi City
An Egyptian themed health spa, a plush shopping mall, nightclubs, restaurants... and more!

Lamcy Plaza
One of the many malls in Dubai, and a particular favourite with kids. Front door valet parking makes it easier for the mums and it has one of the few post offices in town.

Creekside Park
Great family venue overlooking Dubai Creek with numerous leisure activities in finely manicured gardens. The early birds can start the day with a relaxing yoga session in this peaceful scenic environment.

Al Karama

Map Ref → 10-D2

Al Karama is known for being cheap and cheerful, with something for everyone. It is primarily a residential area, consisting of multi-storey apartment blocks and street level shops. It is very built up, but unusually for Dubai, the layout of the pavements and streets encourages pedestrians.

Area Overview

2.3km

The heart of Karama is an open air shopping area consisting of two central streets lined with lots of small shops, all with their goods spilling out onto the pavements. This is a great area for buying anything from funky clothes or suitcases to kitsch fluffy camels and Omani silver jewellery and boxes. Many of the goods are cheap imitations of designer labels (usually easy to spot, although some of the fakes aren't too bad). Dubai Municipality has been strict in clamping down on the sale of counterfeit items, but that said, you're still likely to have a guy sidle up to you asking if you want to buy a 'Rolex'.

If all this shopping makes you hungry, there are numerous cafés offering shawarma, fruit juices, etc, or try one of the many Indian, Pakistani or Filipino restaurants.

The renovated fish and vegetable markets are also worth a visit for the atmosphere and some good cheap produce. If you are looking for second hand or inexpensive furniture, a street virtually devoted to furniture can be found near the Fruit and Vegetable Market, parallel to the main shopping drag. More expensive furniture can be found in the upmarket interior design showrooms that line the busy Za'abeel Road.

A foot bridge is currently under construction from Karama to the area near Trade Centre Roundabout where plans are underway to build the ambitious Zabeel Technology Theme park. At the park will be the Stargate Centre, a space-ship themed educational entertainment centre with a Dhs.120 million price tag that is due to cover 260,000 square feet, and aims to be completed in 2006.

Area Highlights

Al Karama Shopping Area
This open air shopping area is famous for its stock of good fake designer brands. A myriad of shops sells everything, from bags to shoes, sunglasses and clothes.

Fruit & Vegetable Market
This busy and very atmospheric marketplace is great for purchasing or for just taking in the sights and sounds.

Cheap Furniture
Parallel to the main shopping drag is a street entirely devoted to selling cheap or second hand furniture, and an ideal choice for decorating on a tight budget.

Karama nights

A great reason to get a coffee table!

A picture tells a thousand words, and this outstanding collection of stunning photography books speaks volumes. A corporate gift, festive present or interior accessory, discover life through the lens of gifted photographers with an eye for the awe-inspiring.

Abu Dhabi

Dubai

Dubai

Sharjah

Geneva

Sheikh Zayed Road

Map Ref → 9-B2

Another key area of Dubai, stretching southwest from Trade Centre Roundabout towards Abu Dhabi, parallel with the coast, is the infamous eight lane Sheikh Zayed Road (known for its numerous accidents, total lack of lane etiquette and crazy drivers!). The initial stretch after the roundabout is lined with modern high rise office and apartment blocks, hotels and shopping malls – a truly amazing forest of stunning buildings in various architectural styles.

Area Overview

3.2km

At the start of the Sheikh Zayed Road 'business district' is the landmark Dubai World Trade Centre and exhibition halls (illustrated on Dhs.100 banknotes). The 39 storey tower was once the tallest building in Dubai and although it has been surpassed in terms of size and grandeur by a multitude of statuesque skyscrapers it remains a prominent landmark on this ever-expanding skyline. For a great view, especially in winter when it is less hazy, try the guided tour to the observation deck (timings: 09:30 and 16:30 except Friday from the information desk in the lobby; cost: Dhs.10). At the top is an Arabic restaurant offering typical Lebanese /Arabic food and gorgeous views over the city. The conference and exhibition centre hosts many international exhibitions during the year, such as GITEX, the biggest annual IT exhibition in the Middle East.

Nearby, and towering above most other buildings in the city (but not for long), the Emirates Towers are an impressive address for international business, and pleasure, in Dubai. At 355 metres, the Office Tower is at present the tallest building in the Middle East. The smaller tower, at 305 metres and with 'only' 53 storeys, houses the Emirates Towers five star hotel. The views from the 51st floor cocktail bar are no less than spectacular, and the adrenaline pumping lift ride is not to be missed. Also in this area, construction has started on the Dubai International Finance Centre, a bold project involving all the big names in financial services. The ambition of DIFC is to transform Dubai into a global financial centre to rival Hong Kong and Singapore.

Work has commenced on the Burj Dubai, with completion due in 2008. This aims to be the world's tallest building, at 705 metres, and is being billed as 'the most prestigious square kilometre on the planet'! The building will reflect the UAE's heritage, and the three leaf design will ensure visitors have the ultimate view over Dubai.

Near Interchange One, known locally as Defence Roundabout, you will find the Dusit Dubai Hotel, the design of which is based on the image of hands praying, but to some it looks like a pair of trousers!

The area to the north of the Sheikh Zayed Road is mainly residential with a mix of villas and apartment towers. Between Sheikh Zayed Road and Al Wasl Road you can find Safa Park. To the south of the road, off Interchange Two, is Al Quoz Industrial Estate and tucked away here is the Courtyard. This building is home to a variety of retail outlets and art exhibitions are held on a regular basis; however, the main attraction is the imaginatively designed courtyard itself, which reflects a variety of building styles from around the world.

Even further south on the Sheikh Zayed Road between Interchanges Three and Seven there are a number of projects evolving, the largest of which is Dubailand. Comprising more than 45 separate projects, from a space exploration centre to a full-size dinosaur enclosure, and featuring the world's biggest shopping mall, Dubailand will be the world's largest theme park when it is completed in 2008. For an idea of its mind-boggling scale, Dubailand will be twice the size of Disneyworld and 100 times the size of Monaco!

If you travel inland from Interchange Two for about 5 km, you will find the Dubai Camel Racecourse where racing camels and

Area Highlights

World Trade Centre
This landmark is housed in the busy central business district of Dubai and is a popular venue for exhibitions; GITEX is one, taking place yearly and attracting a fair number of international visitors.

Emirates Towers
These two magnificent towers are a favourite with photographers. Venture inside for a drink or a bite at one of the many restaurants and bars, or indulge in some retail therapy at the Shopping Boulevard.

Architectural Marvels
There is no shortage of architectural monuments on this visually artistic highway. Its location just ten minutes away from the beach and other major city attractions makes this a hip place to stay.

their riders are put through their paces in the early morning [p.54, p.177]. A large floral roundabout proclaims the entrance to Nad Al Sheba, which has a golf course (excellent night golf available), but is mainly known for horse racing, including the richest horse race in the world, the Dubai World Cup [p56].

Architectural sculptures scrape the sky over Sheikh Zayed Road

Al Satwa

Map Ref ➔ 6-C4

One of the more bustling areas of Dubai, Satwa has plenty of low storey apartment blocks with small shops on the ground floor. In Arabic, Satwa means 'hold up' referring to its more adventurous past.

Area Overview

1.5km

The focal point of Satwa is Al Diyafah Street where residents can dodge the traffic and wander up the broad palm lined street checking out the shops, inexpensive restaurants and cafés.

At the western end of Al Diyafah Street, nearest the sea, is the Dar Al Ittehad (Union House) building. This is where the treaty to create the Arab world's first federation of states, the United Arab Emirates, was signed on 2 December 1971. It is also the site of the UAE's largest flag (40 x 20 metres) on top of a 120 metre reinforced column. This is floodlit at night and is noticeable from quite a distance.

At the other end of Al Diyafah Street (near the Rydges Plaza Hotel) is the permanently busy Al Satwa Road. Along here are numerous small shops selling mainly textiles, inexpensive clothes and general household items. There are tailors here who have a good reputation for copying designs very inexpensively. You will also find a small area full of car repair shops. If you need a tyre change, new battery, etc, and your car is more than five years old or no longer on the dealer's warranty, this place is worth a visit – they can fix just about anything and everything, and bargaining on price is expected.

Between Al Satwa Road and Al Wasl Road is a street known as 'Plant Street', with wider pavements and shops selling plants and flowers. You can buy fir trees in December, unusual artificial trees all year round and all sorts of fresh flowers. It also has numerous pet shops, selling exotic birds, fish and animals. Near this mini 'jungle' are art shops selling original paintings, drawings and prints. Many offer framing facilities at very reasonable rates.

On Al Wasl Road is the beautiful and intricate Iranian Mosque, with distinctive blue tiles, arches and pillars mirroring the similarly patterned Iranian Hospital opposite.

Area Highlights

Al Diyafah Street
Meander down this popular street to experience a diversity of shopping areas, outdoor cafés and restaurants (the traffic noise level can be a little distracting though).

Plant Street
Sample a more down to earth way of trading amongst the hustle and bustle of this colourful street. Plants are strewn across the pavement to attract shoppers and you'll find bargains galore.

Tailors & Textiles Area
The choice of material shops is never ending, and a wide variety of fabrics are on display. Pick up your chosen fabric and then pop into one of the many tailors' shops. These crafty devils can conjure up a designer outfit for you at splendidly low costs.

The UAE national flag

Jumeira

Map Ref → 6-B3

On the Bur Dubai side of the city, stretching south for about 10 km along the coast from Satwa's borders towards Umm Suqeim, is Jumeira. In English, it translates as 'burning embers'. Once a fishing village, it is now a highly desirable residential area hence the popular expression 'Jumeira Jane', referring to the stereotypical well heeled female resident of this district.

Area Overview

There are lots of medical practices catering to the needs of the population along the two main roads in the district – Jumeira Beach Road (also known as the Beach Road) and Al Wasl Road. Jumeira Beach Road is fast becoming a shopping mall alley, along with exclusive beauty salons, several flower shops and numerous cafés and restaurants.

The Jumeira Mosque, located at the beginning of the Beach Road, is easily the most beautiful mosque in the city, as well as the best known (it features on the Dhs.500 bank note) and is especially breathtaking at night when lit up.

Between Al Wasl Road and Sheikh Zayed Road is the 51 hectare oasis of Safa Park. Facilities here include a big wheel, various games pitches and plenty of barbecue sites. The tennis courts are generally busy and it's a popular place in the early evening with joggers who trot around the perimeter, which features a sprung running track. Nearby, construction has started on a 7.2 hectare neighbourhood park with games courts, elevated walkways, jogging track, and a central fountain with shaded seating, to cater to the recreational needs of local residents.

The public beach, Jumeira Beach Corniche, quickly fills with tourists and unfortunately a few voyeurs – if you want some peace, try one of the beach parks. The nearest is Jumeira Beach Park, which is off the Beach Road in a beautiful tropical paradise setting.

Area Highlights

Jumeira Mosque

This beautiful landmark is a visual delight, particularly in the evenings when lit up. Although sightseeing in mosques is usually prohibited, the Jumeira Mosque opens its doors to organised tours.

Jumeira Beach Park

Sections of the park are open to the public for an entrance fee (Dhs.20 per car or Dhs.5 per person) and Saturdays are set aside for ladies only. Public beaches can be found past the park but for some women it may feel a bit uncomfortable and exposed.

Shopping Malls

There is no shortage of shopping areas on the Jumeira strip; scores of retail outlets are found here. This is however, not a place for the bargain hunter.

Exploring

Dubai – Main Areas

The coolest coast in town

Other Areas

Umm Suqeim
Map Ref → 4-E4

Umm Suqeim is mostly residential, stretching from Jumeira towards Al Mina Al Seyahi (Al Sufouh). The area was hit by the plague at the beginning of the 20th century and most of the residents passed away, hence the name Umm Suqeim, which, when translated, means 'mother of sickness'.

Today, Umm Suqeim is a pleasant family neighbourhood and boasts some of Dubai's most prominent attractions. The summer residence of the late Sheikh Rashid bin Saeed Al Maktoum is now the Majlis Ghorfat Um Al Sheef – a small park with an excellent museum reflecting Arabic tradition.

Dubai's famous international landmark, the Burj Al Arab, stands 280 metres off the coast; the atrium alone is large enough to fit the Dubai World Trade Centre inside. The Jumeirah Beach Hotel, dwarfed in the Burj's shadow, complements the famous sail with its own shape of a breaking wave. The popular water adventure park, Wild Wadi, is also located here. Nearby, the new exclusive hotel and residential complex, Madinat Jumeirah is styled as an ancient Arabian citadel, and is a great place to come for sundowners and a stunning view of the Burj.

Al Sufouh
Map Ref → 3-E3

Al Sufouh is the coastline area that stretches from Black Palace Beach (named after one of the palaces visible from the road), to the borders of Jebel Ali Port.

The coast is home to a number of stunning five star hotels, such as The Ritz-Carlton and One&Only Royal Mirage. The Hilton Dubai Jumeirah, Sheraton Jumeirah, and Le Meridien Mina Seyahi, are also here. Massive construction is underway to create the Jumeirah Beach Residence, comprising 36 residential towers and four hotels. With the entrance to the manmade Palm Island added to this address, and with Dubai Marina and Madinat Jumeirah as neighbouring developments, this area will continue to be regarded as a high prestige residential locale, but for the next year or two remains a huge construction site.

Emirates Hills
Map Ref → 2-E4

A number of luxurious residential complexes have been constructed around the Emirates Golf Club (before the Jebel Ali Interchange). These are part of the massive Emaar project, Emirates Living, which consists of The Lakes, The Greens, The Meadows, The Springs and, of course, the very opulent Emirates Hills. This mixture of apartments, villas, and townhouses comprises luxurious family residential areas, landscaped gardens, parks and water features. The first class Montgomerie Golf Estate is perhaps the most prestigious address here.

Up the road, Nakheel Properties have launched another residential development: fifty islands will accommodate villas, apartments and townhouses, all surrounded by unique waterways in the form of landscaped canals, waterfalls, gardens and marinas. Two Brazilian style islands will be the main feature of this complex. Eventually, Jumeirah Islands Village will complete this visionary self-contained environment with retail and leisure facilities.

Further inland is the proposed Dubailand site, and another exceptional residential villa development, Arabian Ranches. Stemming from Sheikh Mohammed's love of horses (he personally donated 200 thoroughbreds to the project), the Ranches will feature equine activities, a world-class golf course, lakes and the attractive Gazelle project, a community-style townhouse development boasting schools and numerous leafy parks.

Marsa Dubai
Map Ref → 2-D2

Commonly known as Dubai Marina, Marsa Dubai is located past Al Sufouh on the Jumeira beach side and is currently under extensive construction. Offering panoramic views of the ocean, the Dubai Marina project by Emaar is aiming to be a residential community for 40,000 people, with five star hotels, residential apartments, townhouses, villas and shopping malls, all enhanced by the tranquil surrounding marina.

Jebel Ali
Map Ref → 1-B2

Situated south of the city, this area is chiefly known for its free zone and port. Jebel Ali was the first free zone in Dubai and an extremely attractive one for foreign investors with the luring temptations of 100% business ownership exempt of all tax and customs duties.

Jebel means 'mountain' in English, which seems to be a dramatic exaggeration for this slight rise in the land (it's barely even a hill!). Contrary to its reputation of being a busy industrial area, it is not all factories and workers. Many residential and scenic developments are coming up, including the Palm Island Jebel Ali project, a larger version of the Jumeira Palm. Jebel Ali also boasts its own quaint village with beautiful residential apartment complexes aptly named 'The Gardens'. With seemingly natural floral surroundings and the architecturally splendid Gardens shopping mall due for completion in February 2005, this area is fast evolving into a highly desirable residential neighbourhood.

Museums, Heritage & Culture

Art Galleries

Other options → Art [p.207]
Art Supplies [p.208]

While there's nothing like the Tate Gallery or the Louvre in Dubai, there are a number of galleries that have interesting exhibitions of art and traditional Arabic artefacts. Most simply operate as a shop and a gallery, but some also provide studios for artists and are involved in the promotion of art within the emirates. The Majlis Gallery, The Courtyard and the XVA Gallery are all worth visiting in their own right as examples of traditional or unusual architecture. They provide striking locations in which you can enjoy a wide range of art, both local and international.

XVA Gallery

Creative Art Centre

Location → Nr Choithrams · Jumeira
Hours → 08:00 - 18:00   Fri closed
Web/email → www.arabian-arts.com

344 4394

Map Ref → 5-E2

A large art gallery with eight showrooms set in two villas. The gallery has a wide range of fine art, Arabian antiques and gifts, and a team of in-house framers, artists and restorers work on-site. The range of antiques includes Omani chests, old doors, weapons and silver. Lynda Shephard, the managing partner, is a well known artist in both Oman and Dubai. Location: in two villas set back from Jumeira Beach Road. Take the turning inland between Choithram supermarket and Town Centre shopping mall.

Four Seasons Ramesh Gallery

Location → Al Karama Shopping Complex
Hours → 09:00 - 21:00   Fri 17:00 - 21:00
Web/email → www.fourseasonsgallery.com

334 9090

Map Ref → 10-D2

This large gallery is in Karama, near the main post office. Opened in 1970, it is one of the largest galleries in Dubai, exhibiting and selling a mixture of work by local and international artists. There are different exhibitions of art throughout the year, and it's a great place to purchase a unique gift. Their range has also been expanded to include furniture, making this a one stop home decorating shop.

Green Art Gallery

Location → Villa 23, St 51, Beh Dubai Zoo · Jumeira
Hours → 09:30 - 13:30 & 16:30 - 20:30 Fri closed
Web/email → www.gagallery.com

344 9888

Map Ref → 6-A2

The Green Art Gallery features original art, limited edition prints and handcrafted work by artists from all over the world. In particular, the gallery draws on those influenced and inspired by the heritage, culture and environment of the Arab world and its people. The gallery also encourages local artists by guiding them through the process of exhibiting and promoting themselves. Seasonal exhibitions are held from October to May.

Hunar Art Gallery

Location → Villa 6, Street 49 · Al Rashidiya
Hours → 09:00 - 13:00 & 16:00 - 20:00 Fri closed
Web/email → hunarart@emirates.net.ae

286 2224

Map Ref → 15-A4

This gallery exhibits fine art by international artists. Beautifully decorated Japanese tiles, Belgian

Exploring

Museums, Heritage & Culture

pewter and glass pieces fill the spaces between traditional Persian paintings and contemporary art. Often on display is work by the well known artists Rima Farah and Abdul Quadir Al Rais.

Majlis Gallery, The

Location → Al Faheidi Street · Bur Dubai **353 6233**
Hours → 09:30 - 13:00 & 16:00 - 20:00 Fri closed
Web/email → majlisga@emirates.net.ae   Map Ref → 8-A2

Set in traditional surroundings in the old Bastakiya area of the city, the Majlis Gallery is a converted Arabic house, complete with windtowers and courtyard. Small whitewashed rooms lead off the central garden area and host a variety of exhibitions by contemporary artists. In addition to the fine art collection, there's an extensive range of handmade glass, pottery, fabrics, frames, unusual pieces of furniture and bits and bobs. The gallery hosts, on average, ten exhibitions a year, but is worth visiting year round for both the artwork and the atmospheric surroundings.

Total Arts

Location → Courtyard, The · Al Quoz **228 2888**
Hours → 10:00 - 13:00 & 16:00 - 20:00 Fri closed
Web/email → www.courtyard-uae.com   Map Ref → 4-D4

Dubai's biggest gallery occupies two floors of The Courtyard. The gallery generally exhibits works of art from a variety of cultures and continents, however, there is a bias towards Middle Eastern talent, particularly Iranian artists. There are over 300 paintings on permanent display, and regular shows of traditional handicrafts and antique furniture. One of the main attractions here is the cobbled courtyard itself, which is surrounded by different façades combining a variety of building styles from around the world.

XVA Gallery

Location → Bastakiya · Bur Dubai **353 5383**
Hours → 09:00 - 21:00 Fri closed
Web/email → www.xvagallery.com   Map Ref → 8-B3

This interesting property is an original windtower house, restored to its former glory, and is worth a visit for its architecture and displays of local and international art. It is also one of the most unusual and evocative places to stay – guests can paint their own canvas, dine on traditional UAE food, chill out in rooftop rocking chairs, and gaze over

the mosque-tops to the lights of Bur Dubai. Book early as capacity is limited. The gallery focuses primarily on paintings, and hosts many different exhibitions throughout the year.

Heritage Sites - City

Other options → **Art [p.207]**
Mosque Tours [p.178]
Museums – City [p.172]

There are many fascinating places to visit in old Dubai, that offer glimpses of life as it was when the city was nothing more than a small fishing and trading port. Most of the pre-oil Dubai heritage sites have been carefully restored, paying close attention to traditional design, and using original building materials. The Bastakiya area is probably the most ambient place to take a stroll and experience old Dubai (see Bastakiya in the Bur Dubai section [p.158]). The best of the rest are listed below.

Bastakiya

Location → nr Diwan & Al Faheidi R/A · Bur Dubai **na**
Hours → na
Web/email → na   Map Ref → 8-B3

The Bastakiya (also spelt Bastakia) area is one of the oldest heritage sites in Dubai. This intriguing neighbourhood dates back to the early 1900's when traders from Bastak in southern Iran, encouraged by the tax concessions granted by the then ruler of Dubai, settled there. Here you can

Traditional windtower

Exploring

Museums, Heritage & Culture

view one of the earliest forms of air conditioning in the shape of windtowers ('barajeel' in Arabic), which are distinctive rectangular structures on top of the traditional flat roofed buildings. These were built to catch the slightest of breezes and funnel them down into the rooms and courtyards of the houses below.

Amble down alleyways, step into a converted house, which is now an art gallery, and picture yourself living in a bygone era. An ongoing reconstruction project is gradually turning the area into a pedestrian conservation area, with over 50 houses due for restoration by early 2005. Eventually there will be a museum, a cultural centre and a restaurant. See also: Majlis Gallery, The [p.168].

Heritage & Diving Village

Location ➔ Nr Al Shindagha Tunnel · Al Shindagha | 393 7151
Hours ➔ 07:30 - 22:00 Fri 16:00 - 22:00
Web/email ➔ www.dubaitourism.ae   Map Ref ➔ 8-B1

Located near the Creek mouth, the Heritage & Diving Village focuses on Dubai's maritime past, pearl diving traditions and architecture. The museum is staffed by real live potters and weavers, who display their craft, and is ideal for family visits (camel and pony rides are available some afternoons. During Eid holidays and the Shopping Festival, traditional ceremonies such as sword dancing are performed. Local Arabic women serve up traditionally cooked dishes for visitors to try. The village is close to Sheikh Saeed Al Maktoum's House and has several shops and a cafeteria. It is also at the centre of plans to develop the Shindagha area into a cultural microcosm, recreating traditional life in Dubai as it was before its miraculous transformation into the metropolis it is today.

Majlis Ghorfat Um Al Sheef

Location ➔ Beach Rd · Jumeira | 394 6343
Hours ➔ 08:30 - 13:30 & 15:30 - 20:30 Fri 13:30 – 20:30
Web/email ➔ www.dubaitourism.ae   Map Ref ➔ 8-A2

Constructed in 1955, this simple building was used by the late Sheikh Rashid bin Saeed Al Maktoum as a summer residence. The ground floor is an open veranda (called 'leewan' or 'rewaaq'), while on the second floor, the majlis (Arabic for 'meeting place') is decorated with carpets, lanterns and rifles. The roof terrace was used for sleeping – ideal to catch the slightest breeze – and it originally offered an

uninterrupted view right to the sea. Dubai Municipality has added a garden, which includes the traditional 'falaj' irrigation system.

Location: look for the brown Municipality historical places signposts for Majlis Al Ghoraifa, off Jumeira Beach Road, past Jumeira Beach Park, next to HSBC Offshore and Jumbo Electronics.

Entrance fees: Dhs.2 adults; under 6 yrs free

Sheikh Saeed Al Maktoum's House

Location ➔ Nr Al Shindagha Tunnel · Al Shindagha | 393 7139
Hours ➔ 07:30 - 21:00 Fri 15:00 - 21:00
Web/email ➔ www.dubaitourism.ae   Map Ref ➔ 8-A1

The modest home of Dubai's much loved former ruler was once strategically located at the mouth of Dubai's lifeline, the Creek, but now lies close to the Bur Dubai entrance to Al Shindagha Tunnel. Dating from 1896, this carefully restored house turned museum is built in the traditional manner of the Gulf coast, from coral covered in lime and sand coloured plaster. The interesting displays include rare and wonderful photographs of Dubai pre-oil, plus an old currency and stamp collection. Worth combining with a visit to the nearby Heritage & Diving Village.

Entrance fees: Dhs.2 adults; Dhs.1 children; under 5 yrs free.

Sheikh Saeed Al Maktoum's House

Heritage Sites - Out of City

Other options → Tours & Sightseeing [p.181]
Museums – Out of City [p.173]

Al Hisn Kalba

Location → Coast Rd · Kalba | 09 277 4442
Hours → 09:00 - 13:00 17:00 - 20:00
Web/email → www.sdci.gov.ae   Map Ref → UAE-E2

As you drive along the coast road in Kalba town, you come to the restored house of Sheikh Sayed Al Qassimi, overlooking the sea. It's located at the end of a large grassy expanse with swings and small rides for children. On the opposite side of the road is Kalba's Al Hisn Fort, which houses the town's museum and contains a limited display of weapons.

Entrance fee: Dhs.3 single entrance; Dhs.6 family entrance

Fujairah Heritage Village

Location → Nr Fujairah Fort · Fujairah | 09 222 7000
Hours → 07:30 - 14:30   Tue & Fri closed
Web/email → na   Map Ref → UAE-E2

Opened in 1996, this 6,000 square metre heritage village depicts life in the UAE pre-oil, with displays of fishing boats, simple dhows, clay, stone and bronze implements and pots, and hunting and agricultural tools. The heritage village is close to Ain Al Madhab Gardens, which are situated in the foothills of the Hajar Mountains just outside Fujairah City. The gardens are fed by mineral springs and this warm sulphur laden water is used in two swimming pools (separate for men and women). Private chalets with large wooded gardens can be hired and on public holidays an outdoor theatre is used for festivals that include traditional singing and folklore dances.

Entrance fee: Dhs.5

Hatta Heritage Village

Location → Hatta Town · Hatta | 852 1374
Hours → 08:00 - 20:30   Fri 14:00 to 20:30
Web/email → www.dubaitourism.ae   Map Ref → UAE-D3

Opened to the public in early 2001, Hatta Heritage Village is located an hour's drive south east of Dubai City and a few kilometres from the Hatta Fort Hotel. It is constructed around an old settlement and was restored in the style of a traditional mountain village. Explore the tranquil oasis, the narrow alleyways and discover traditional life in the mud and barasti houses.

Hatta's history goes back over 3,000 years and the area includes a 200 year old mosque and the fortress built by Sheikh Maktoum bin Hasher Al Maktoum in 1896, which is now used as a weapons museum. Entry is free.

Dar al Dhyafa al Arabia

Location → Souk Al Arsah · Heritage Area | 06 569 6111
Hours → na
Web/email → daraldhyafa@liberty.ae   Map Ref → UAE C2

Nestled in the heart of the Heritage Area is a gem of a location, the 'Dar al Dhyafa al Arabia'. This tiny boutique hotel is modelled completely on the traditional way of living in the Emirates, and it has the feel of a museum, but the comfort level of one's own home. The staff are welcoming, the surroundings quaint, and the location fabulous. Step out of the front door into the Souk al Arsah or take in their rooftop café views of the UAE's only round windtower, the surrounding Heritage Area, and the bustling nearby port. Highly recommended.

Sharjah Heritage Area

Location → Btn Al Hisn Ave & Corniche Rd | 06 569 3999
Hours → 09:00 - 13:00 & 17:00 - 20:00 Fri 17:00 - 20:00
Web/email → www.sharjah-welcome.com   Map Ref → UAE-C2

The beautifully restored heritage area in Sharjah is a great place for individuals with an interest in local history. The area includes a number of old buildings: Al Hisn Fort (Sharjah Fort); Sharjah Islamic Museum; Sharjah Heritage Museum (Bait Al Naboodah); the Majlis of Ibrahim Mohammed Al Midfa and the Old Souk (Souk Al Arsah). Here you will see traditional local architecture and home life depicted as it was over 150 years ago. Toilets can be found at each venue and there's an Arabic coffee shop in the shady courtyard of Souk Al Arsah. The Majlis of Ibrahim Mohammed Al Midfa is situated between the souk and the waterfront. This peaceful majlis is famous for its round windtower, the only one of its kind in the UAE. Closed on Mondays. See also: Museums – Out of the City section [p.173].

Museums - City

Other options → Art [p.207]
Heritage Sites – City [p.170]
Mosque Tours [p.178]

For residents and visitors alike, a visit to one of the museums or heritage sites is a great opportunity to discover the culture and history of the UAE, as well as to catch a glimpse of a fast disappearing way of life. Dubai Municipality has an active role in preserving Dubai's past and is currently overseeing a huge renovation project on over 230 of Dubai's old buildings. Completion is expected sometime in 2009. As of the end of 2004, renovation has finished on about half the buildings, including six mosques: Al Shoyookh, Al Mulla, Bin Zaywed, Abdul Qader, Al Mur bin Hiraiz and Al Otaibat. Entrance fees are minimal and information is given in both Arabic and English. Note that opening times often change during the summer months, Ramadan, Eid, and public holidays, so check before leaving home to avoid disappointment. Refer also to Dubai Areas [p.151] for further information on what there is to do in these areas.

Al Ahmadiya School & Heritage House

Location ➔ Al Khor St, Al Ras · Deira | 226 0286
Hours ➔ 08:00 - 19:30   Fri 14:00 - 19:30
Web/email ➔ www.dubaitourism.ae   Map Ref ➔ 8-C2

Al Ahmadiya School, or the Museum of Education, was the earliest regular school in the city and a visit here is an excellent opportunity to see the history of education in Dubai. Established in 1912 by Mr Ahmadiya for Dubai's elite, it closed in 1962, until its restoration and conversion into a museum in March 2000. The school is located next to the Heritage House, the former home of Mr Ahmadiya, which dates back to 1890. Touch screens take you on a guided tour of the two museums. Admission is free.

Dubai Museum

Location ➔ Nr Bastakiya · Bur Dubai | 353 1862
Hours ➔ 08:30 - 20:30   Fri 15:00 - 20:30
Web/email ➔ www.dubaitourism.ae   Map Ref ➔ 8-B3

This is no stuffy museum and is well worth a visit, even if museums aren't your scene. Built in 1787 for sea defence and as the residence of the ruler of Dubai, Al Faheidi Fort was renovated in 1970 to house the museum. The site has been expanded to include a large area under the courtyard of the old fort. Everything is represented in a highly creative way: spy on a typical bride preparation scene, step off a dhow unloading its wares, enter a souk from the 1950s and walk through a labyrinth of shops... you can even discover an Islamic school. Then enter the world of an oasis, a tribute to the sea and archaeological finds from the area. Tour guides are available and there's also a restaurant and children's playground. Highly recommended.

Entrance fees: adults Dhs.3; children under 10 Dhs.1.

Godolphin Gallery

Location ➔ Nad Al Sheba Racecourse · Nad Al Sheba | 336 3031
Hours ➔ 09:00 - 17:00 Race nights 09:00 - 20:00 Fri closed
Web/email ➔ www.godolphin.com   Map Ref ➔ 17-A3

A great location for horse racing fans, the Godolphin Gallery celebrates the Maktoum family's private racing stable, and houses the world's finest collection of horse racing trophies. The gallery was refurbished in 2002 and incorporates interactive touch screen consoles, photographs, video presentations and memorabilia from the first nine years of the Godolphin racing stable. Adjacent to the Nad Al Sheba Club, the gallery is open throughout the horse racing season until April 30.

Gold & Diamond Museum

Location ➔ Gold & Diamond Park · Al Quoz | 347 7788
Hours ➔ 10:00 - 22:00   Fri 16:00 - 22:00
Web/email ➔ www.goldanddiamondpark.com   Map Ref ➔ 4-B4

An interesting feature of the Gold & Diamond Park is the visitors' centre, which includes a museum and a themed café. Showcases display traditional Arabian jewellery and explain its history, and there are guided tours of the manufacturing plant (Saturdays and Mondays, 10:00 - 13:00) to see how jewellery is made. Then of course, there's the chance to flex your plastic and buy from the numerous retail outlets in the complex. Alternatively, watch your own design being made on the spot. The tour takes approximately 30 minutes. Entrance is free. An extension is underway, due for completion in October 2005, which will add another 30 retail units as well as 154 manufacturing units and showrooms to the park.

Museums - Out of City

Other options ➔ **Tours & Sightseeing [p.181]**
Heritage Sites – Out of City [p.172]

Ajman Museum

Location ➔ Opp Etisalat · Ajman | 06 742 3824
Hours ➔ 09:00 - 13:00 & 16:00 - 19:00 Fri 16:00 - 19:00
Web/email ➔ ajmuseum@emirates.net.ae   Map Ref ➔ UAE-C2

Ajman Museum, like most museums in the Emirates, is interesting and well arranged, with displays described in both English and Arabic. The fort guide is well worth the Dhs.4 charge. The museum has a variety of exhibits, including a collection of passports (Ajman used to issue its own). It is housed in one of the former residences of

Museums, Heritage & Culture

the ruler of Ajman – a fortress dating back to around 1775. In 1970, it became the main police station, before becoming the museum in the early 1980s. Closed Saturdays.

Entrance fees: *Adults Dhs.4; children under 6 years Dhs.2; students Dhs.1. Evening timings: 17:00 - 20:00 summer; 16:00 - 19:00 winter.*

Fujairah Museum

Location → Opp Ruler's Palace | 09 222 9085
Hours → 08:30 - 13:30 & 16:00 - 18:00 Fri 16:00 – 18:00
Web/email → www.gia.gov.ae   Map Ref → UAE-E2

Situated near Fujairah Fort, this museum offers an insight into Fujairah's history and heritage. It has displays of the traditional way of life and artefacts found in archaeological excavations throughout the emirate. Work by local and foreign archaeologists has yielded items dating back over 4,500 years, including Bronze and Iron Age weapons, finely painted pottery, delicately carved soapstone vessels and pre-Islamic silver coins. The museum was enlarged during the summer of 1998 to permit more finds to be displayed. Closed on Saturdays.

Fujairah Fort

Fujairah Fort has been going through a major renovation programme over the past few years and once complete (sometime in 2005) it is expected that the Municipality will use it as a museum. Carbon dating estimates the main part of the fort to be over 500 years old, with other sections being built about 150 years later. Several buildings nearby are also being renovated.

Entry fee: adults Dhs.3; children Dhs.1.

National Museum of Ras Al Khaimah

Location → Old town · Beh Police HQ | 07 233 3411
Hours → See below
Web/email → www.rakmuseum.gov.ae   Map Ref → UAE-D1

Located in a fort, and former home of the present ruler of Ras Al Khaimah, this museum mainly has local natural history and archaeological displays, plus a variety of paraphernalia from pre-oil life. Upstairs you can see an account of the British naval expedition against Ras Al Khaimah in 1809, a model of a 'baggala', a typical craft used in the early 1800s, and excellent examples of silver Bedouin jewellery. Look out for fossils set in the rock strata of the walls of the fort – these date back 190 million years!

Entrance fees: *Adults Dhs.2; children Dhs.1. Photo permits are Dhs.5.*

Location: *Behind Police Headquarters in the old town close to the bridge. From Dubai, turn left at the second roundabout after the Clock roundabout and the museum is 100 metres on your right.*

Hours: *Sep-May 09:00 - 17:00 Daily; Closed Tues. June-Aug 08:00 – 12:00 & 16:00 – 19:00 Daily; Closed Tues*

Al Hisn Fort/Heritage Museum

Location → Al Hisn Ave, Bank St · Sharjah | 06 568 5500
Hours → 09:00 - 13:00 & 17:00 - 20:00 Fri 17:00 – 20:00
Web/email → www.sharjah-welcome.com   Map Ref → UAE-C2

Built in 1820, this fort was originally the home of Sharjah's ruling family, the Al Qassimi. It was renovated in 1996 - 97 and includes an interesting display of old photographs and an introductory video (English and Arabic) covering Sharjah's history. The fort is built in the traditional courtyard style with three towers on the surrounding walls. Enclosed by modern buildings, it's hard to imagine that once it was an isolated building on the edge of the Creek. The fort links Sharjah's main heritage and arts areas. Closed on Mondays.

Discovery Centre

Location → Opp Sharjah Airport · Al Dhaid Rd | 06 558 6577
Hours → Sat - Wed 09:00 - 14:00; Wed - Fri 15:30 - 20:30
Web/email → www.sharjah-welcome.com   Map Ref → UAE-C2

This colourful scientific centre offers everything toddlers to under 13s love to see and do in safe, supervised surroundings. Based on themed areas, children can touch, experiment, run and have fun. Of course, the underlying aim is to teach youngsters about the biological, physical and technological worlds in a practical way. A soft play area is available for the very young. Pushchair access is good and the centre has a café and a shop, as well as ample parking.

Costs: *children under 2 years free; ages 2 - 12 mornings Dhs.4, evenings Dhs.7; 13+ years mornings Dhs.5, evenings Dhs.10. For families (maximum two adults, three children) mornings Dhs.15, evenings Dhs.30.*

Sharjah Archaeological Museum

Location → Nr Cultural R/A · Sharjah | 06 566 5466
Hours → 09:00 - 13:00 & 17:00 - 20:00 Fri 17:00 – 20:00
Web/email → www.archaeology.gov.ae   Map Ref → UAE-C2

This hi-tech museum offers an interesting display of antiquities from the region. Linked to a conference centre and used as an educational

Exploring

Museums, Heritage & Culture

venue for local schoolchildren, the museum has installed computers in each hall to provide in-depth information on the exhibits. The museum traces man's first steps and progress across the Arabian Peninsula through the ages using well-designed displays and documentary films. One area features the latest discoveries from excavation sites in the Emirates. Worth a visit for archaeology and history lovers.

Costs: *Admission is free. Wednesday evenings are for ladies only; closed on Sundays.*

Sharjah Art Museum

Location ➜ Sharjah Arts Plaza Area · Sharjah | 06 568 8222
Hours ➜ 09:00 - 13:00 & 17:00 - 20:00
Web/email ➜ www.sharjah-welcom.com   Map Ref ➜ UAE-C2

Opened in April 1997, Sharjah Art Museum dominates the arts plaza area. It was purpose built in a traditional style, chiefly to house the personal collection of over 300 paintings and maps of the ruler, HH Dr Sheikh Sultan. Permanent displays include the work of 18th century artists, with oil paintings and watercolours depicting life from all over the Arab world, while other exhibits in the 72 small galleries change frequently. There's also an art reference library, bookshop and coffee shop, and the museum hosts various cultural activities. The museum is closed on Mondays and Friday mornings; Wednesday afternoons are for ladies and children only. There is no entry fee.

Al Hisn Fort

Sharjah Heritage Museum

Location ➜ Sharjah Arts Plaza Area · Sharjah | 06 569 3999
Hours ➜ 09:00 - 13:00 & 17:00 - 20:00 Fri 17:00 - 20:00
Web/email ➜ www.sharjah-welcome.com   Map Ref ➜ UAE-C2

This two storey building was once owned by the late Obaid bin Eesa Al Shamsi, nicknamed Al Naboodah, and is a reconstruction of a typical family home (bait) about 150 years ago. Originally home to the Al Naboodah family (three generations of the family lived here until 1972), it is built around a traditional courtyard. The various rooms display items such as clothing, weapons, cooking pots and goatskin water bags. A visit here includes a short documentary film, and in true Arabic style, coffee and sweets are offered. There is no entry fee. Closed on Mondays.

Sharjah Islamic Museum

Location ➜ Nr Cultural R/A · Sharjah | 06 568 3334
Hours ➜ 09:00 - 13:00 & 17:00 - 20:00
Web/email ➜ www.sharjah-welcome.com   Map Ref ➜ UAE-C2

Sharjah Islamic Museum is home to an unrivalled collection of Islamic masterpieces and manuscripts, representing the cultural history of Muslims over 1,400 years. On display are examples of Islamic crafts such as ceramics, jewellery and textiles. There's also an impressive collection of gold plated Korans and a replica of the curtain that covers the Ka'aba Stone at Mecca. Housed in a 200 year old building, the display is from HH Dr Sheikh Sultan's private collection. The museum is open during holy days and public holidays. Wednesday afternoons are for ladies and children only. Closed on Mondays and Friday mornings. There is no entry fee.

Sharjah Natural History Museum

Location ➜ Jct 8 - Sharjah - Al Dhaid Rd · Sharjah | 06 531 1411
Hours ➜ 09:00 - 19:00; Thu 11:00 - 19:00; Fri 14:00 - 19:00
Web/email ➜ www.sharjah-welcome.com   Map Ref ➜ UAE-C2

This fascinating museum which combines learning with entertainment unfolds through five exhibition halls to expose you to the earth's secrets. Exhibits include a 35 metre diorama of the UAE's natural habitat and wildlife; a stunning geological UV light display; a hall showing the interaction between man and his environment – including the museum's best known exhibit... a mechanical camel; plus a botanical hall, and the marine hall, where replicas of Gulf and Indian Ocean sea creatures can be viewed as if from the bottom of the sea.

Museums, Heritage & Culture

The site also incorporates the Arabian Wildlife Centre (06 531 1999), which is a breeding centre for endangered species; most famously, the Arabian leopard (note: photography is forbidden – if you are caught taking photos, your camera will be confiscated).

There is also a Children's Farm (06 531 1127) where animals, such as donkeys, camels and goats, can be fed and petted. The facilities are state of the art and offer an enjoyable, interactive and educational day out. Picnic areas are available, plus cafés and shops. Great fun for all ages, and a place that you will want to visit again and again. Closed on Mondays.

Entrance fees: Dhs. 15 per person, Dhs. 30 for families. Includes entrance to desert park. Last tickets 17:30.

Sharjah Science Museum

Location → Nr TV station · Halwan | **06 566 8777**
Hours → 09:00 - 14:00 Wed-Fri 15:30 - 20:30
Web/email → www.sharjah-welcome.com   Map Ref → UAE-C2

Opened in 1996, this museum offers visitors interactive exhibits and demonstrations, covering subjects such as aerodynamics, cryogenics, electricity and colour. There's also a children's area where the under fives and their parents can learn together. Those who are inspired to learn more can visit the Learning Centre, which offers more in-depth programmes on many of the subjects covered in the museum. There is also a café and gift shop. School groups are more than welcome.

Entrance fees: Under 2's free. Ages 2 - 12 Dhs.2, ages 12+ Dhs.5; families (two adults and four kids) morning Dhs.8, afternoon Dhs.15; groups of 15+ are given a 20% discount.

Zoos

Arabia's Wildlife Centre

Location → Sharjah Natural History Museum | **06 531 1411**
Hours → 09:00 - 19:00 Thu 11:00 - 19:00, Fri 14:00 - 19:00
Web/email → www.sharjah-welcome.com   Map Ref → UAE-C2

Please see the review under the 'Sharjah Natural History Museum' [p.175].

Children's Farm

Location → Sharjah Natural History Museum | **06 531 1127**
Hours → 09:00 - 19:00   Thu 11:00 - 19:00 Fri 14:00 - 19:00
Web/email → www.sharjah-welcome.com   Map Ref → UAE-C2

Please see the review under 'Sharjah Natural History Museum' [p.175]. Closed on Mondays.

Dubai Zoo

Location → Beach Rd · Jumeira | **349 6444**
Hours → 10:00 - 17:00   Tue closed
Web/email → www.dubaitourism.ae   Map Ref → 6-A2

Dubai Zoo was created from a private collection of animals housed in a large private garden, but is now owned by the Municipality. This is an old fashioned type of zoo with caged lions, tigers, giraffe, monkeys, deer, snakes, bears, flamingos, giant tortoise and other animals that are well cared for by Dr Rezi Khan, the dedicated manager, and his staff. However, animals are in small, limiting cages, although attempts have been made to send some to other zoos around the world to increase the space for the remaining inmates. In order to give the animals more space the zoo is to be relocated in Mushrif Park near the airport, but dates are not finalised. Those with a more 'modern' approach to animal welfare may prefer to pass on a visit here.

Cost: Dhs.3 per person.

Local Attractions

Birdwatching

Other options → **Birdwatching Groups [p.300]**

As a destination for birdwatchers, Dubai's reputation has grown considerably over the years. With ever-increasing greenery many species which are not easily found in Europe or in the rest of the Middle East have been attracted here. Over 80 species breed locally, and during the spring and autumn months, over 400 species have been recorded on their migration between Africa and Central Asia. Within the city, the best bird watching sites would be the many parks and golf clubs, where parakeets, Indian rollers, little green bee eaters and hoopoe can easily be spotted.

The Khor Dubai Wildlife Sanctuary at the end of the Creek is the only nature reserve within the city. Although entrance to the reserve is prohibited you can easily spot flamingos and if you're lucky other shore birds and waders from the road as you drive past. Other species that are found in the Emirates include the Socotra cormorant, striated scops owl, chestnut bellied sandgrouse, crab plover, Saunders' little tern and Hume's wheatear. Other good places for birdwatching include the mangrove swamps in Umm al Quwain and Khor Kalba on the East Coast. Khor Kalba is the only place in the world where you can spot the rare white collared kingfisher. Birdwatching tours through the mangroves in a canoe can be arranged through Desert Rangers.

In addition, falconry, the sport of sheikhs, has a deep rooted tradition here. The best opportunity for enjoying these beautiful and powerful birds is on an organised tour, where you can see the birds in flight. (See also, Birdwatching Groups [p.300]).

Bus Tours

Big Bus Company, The

Location → Wafi City · Umm Hurair | 324 4187
Hours → Various
Web/email → www.bigbus.co.uk   Map Ref → 13-D2

It's not a mirage, there really are eight open air London double decker buses roaming the streets of Dubai! There's a live commentary in English, with little known facts such as in 1968 there were only 13 cars in Dubai. It's wise to break the tour at their recommended stops and then hop on the following bus once you've finished exploring. Overall, visually very interesting and informative.

Prices: adults Dhs.120; children Dhs.75 (ages 5 - 15); free for under 5s; families Dhs.315 (two adults and two children).

Timings: – Daily departures every hour from 09:00 – 17:00

Wonder Bus Tours

Location → BurJuman Centre · Bur Dubai | 359 5656
Hours → See below
Web/email → www.wonderbusdubai.com   Map Ref → 11-A1

Another first in Dubai is the Wonder Bus, an amphibious bus that is capable of doing 120 kph on the road and seven knots on water (life jackets are supplied, if you're nervous). The trips are two hour mini tours of Dubai, concentrating on the Creek, and covering Creekside Park and Dubai Creek Golf Club, under Maktoum Bridge towards Garhoud Bridge, then up the boat ramp and back to BurJuman. The bus is air conditioned and can take 44 passengers.

Prices: adults Dhs.95; children Dhs.65 (ages 3 - 12).

Timings: Three departures daily: 11:30, 14:30, 17:00

Camel Racing

Other options → **Camel Rides [p.263]**

Camel racing followed by a freshly cooked campfire breakfast... is there a better way to start the day?

For the young and old alike, a morning at the races is a memorable experience. This extraordinary sport involves large numbers of camels, the owners and their families, and the jockeys, all congregated to form a great atmosphere.

For visitors, this is an opportunity to see a truly traditional local sport and to visit the 'shops' selling camel paraphernalia (blankets, rugs, beads etc). Races take place during the winter months, usually on a Thursday and Friday morning, at the tracks in Dubai, Ras Al Khaimah, Umm Al Quwain, Al Ain and Abu Dhabi. Often, additional races are held on National Day and certain other public holidays. Races start very early (by about 07:30) and are usually over by 08:30, and admission is free.

Ras Al Khaimah has one of the best racetracks in the country at Digdagga, situated on a plain between the dunes and the mountains, about 10 km south of the town. There are some beautiful campsites in the big red dunes that overlook the racetrack, just five minutes away.

Camel rides are available at various heritage sites, and also within the city of Dubai during the Dubai Shopping Festival. The local press also has information on dates and times. Also check with tour operators who organise camel rides in the desert, very often at their desert camps.

Horse Racing

Other options → **Horse Riding [p.280]**

Dubai Racing Club

Location → Nad Al Sheba Racecourse · Nad Al Sheba | 332 2277
Hours → 19:00 - 22:00   Thurs & Fri only
Web/email → www.dubairacingclub.com   Map Ref → 17-A3

A visit to Dubai during the winter months is not complete without experiencing Race Night at Nad al Sheba. This racecourse is one of the world's leading racing facilities, with top jockeys from Australia, Europe and the USA regularly competing throughout the season (October - April). Racing takes place at night under floodlights and there are usually six to seven races each evening. The start time is 19:00 (except during Ramadan when it is 21:00). The clubhouse charges day membership on race nights; prices change, so check the Website for details. Everyone can take part in various free competitions to select the winning horses, with the ultimate aim of taking home prizes or cash. Hospitality suites, with catering organised on request, can be hired by companies or private

Exploring

Local Attractions

individuals. The dress code to the public enclosures is casual, while race goers are encouraged to dress smart/casual in the clubhouse and private viewing boxes. General admission and parking are free and the public has access to most areas with a reserved area for badge holders and members.

Location: Nad Al Sheba is approximately 5 km south east of Dubai, signposted from Sheikh Zayed Road at the Metropolitan Hotel junction and then from the roundabout close to the Dubai Polo Club and Country Club.

Mosque Tours

Other options → **Museums - City [p.170]**

Sheikh Mohd Centre for Cultural Understanding

Location → Bastakiya · Bur Dubai | 353 6666
Hours → 09:00 - 15:30; Thu 09:00 - 13:30
Web/email → smccu@emirates.net.ae   Map Ref → 8-B3

This non profit organisation was established to bring down the barriers between different nationalities and to help visitors and residents understand the customs and traditions of the UAE through various activities. These include free visits to a mosque, usually Jumeira Mosque (Thursday and Sunday morning 10am, limited numbers only. Remember to cover up/dress conservatively). There are also opportunities to visit the home of a UAE National for a traditional lunch. Arabic courses are offered, usually during the Shopping Festival, and visits by school groups can be arranged.

Powerboat Racing

Dubai International Marine Club

Location → DIMC · Al Sufouh | 399 5777
Hours →   Check Website
Web/email → www.dimc-uae.com   Map Ref → 3-A2

The UAE is well established on the world championship powerboat racing circuit – in Abu Dhabi with Formula One (inshore) and in Dubai and Fujairah with Class One (offshore). Family and friends take a picnic to these events and settle in to be armchair sports fans for the day. The Dubai Creek also provides a stunning setting for national events in Formulas Two and Four. The local Victory Team of Dubai continues to compete in Class One and is ranked amongst the best in the world. Traditional dhow sailing races are held once a month, and all action usually takes place on a Friday.

Scenic Flights

Other options → **Flying [p.271]**
Hot Air Ballooning [p.280]

What better way to view the sights of Dubai than from the air? Just book a plane, helicopter, or hot air balloon and soar into the skies for a lofty perspective of the city. Within a short sightseeing tour, you have the chance to get an aerial view of the impressive parks, traditional dhows, the Creek, beaches and much more. For more information, refer to Flying [p.271] in the Activities section.

Stable Tours

Other options → **Horse Riding [p.280]**
Polo [p.286]

Nad Al Sheba Club

Location → Nr Bu Kidra Interchange · Nad Al Sheba | 336 3666
Hours → Tour starts at 07:00 sharp
Web/email → www.nadalshebaclub.com   Map Ref → 17-A3

An early morning visit to the world's top racehorse training facilities at Nad Al Sheba is inclusive of a cooked breakfast, a behind the scenes glimpse of the jockey's facilities and a view over the racecourse from the Millennium Grandstand, plus the chance to see horses training. The tour ends with a visit to the Godolphin Gallery where the Dubai World Cup is on display. The tour costs Dhs.140, which includes breakfast.

The Millenium Grandstand at Nad Al Sheba

Parks & Beaches

Beaches

Other options → Beach Clubs [p.300]
Parasailing [p.286]

Beach lovers will find a number of options in Dubai. Choose between the public beaches, which usually have limited facilities but no entrance charge, and the beach parks, which charge for entrance, but have a variety of facilities, including changing rooms and play areas. If none of these appeal, try the beach clubs, which are normally part of a hotel or resort (refer to [p.300]). If you want to explore by yourself, map pages 1-6 clearly show Dubai's southwestern coastline where there are several beaches, although public access is restricted in some areas.

Options for public beaches include the lagoon at Al Mamzar (Map Ref 12-E2), which has a roped off swimming area, chalets and jet skis for hire. Travelling south, you'll come to Jumeira Beach Corniche (Map Ref 5-C1) (known locally as Russian Beach), which is a great favourite with tourists for soaking up the sun, swimming and people watching. Moving further south brings you to the small beaches near the Dubai Offshore Sailing Club (Map Ref 4-E2, immensely popular with the kite surfers) and the Jumeirah Beach Hotel (Map Ref 4-B2). Die hard beach lovers frequent the area past the Jebel Ali Hotel, where there is a 10 km expanse of beach (Map Ref 1-A1). This is a great spot for barbecues and camping, but only if you have a permit (available free of charge) from the Municipality (221 5555).

Regulations for the public beaches are gradually becoming stricter. Currently, dogs are banned from the beaches, as is 4 wheel driving, but this is often ignored. Officially, other banned beach activities include barbecues on sand, camping (without a permit the fine is Dhs. 3000), and holding large parties. Contact the Public Parks and Recreation Section (336 7633) for clarification. New regulations with far more restrictions on what you can and cannot wear operate in Sharjah; so if you are planning a trip there, ensure that you are aware of the latest rules. Refer to the Decency Law.

> **Warning!**
>
> *Although the waters off the coast of Dubai generally look calm and unchallenging, very strong rip tides can carry the most confident swimmer away from the shore very quickly and fatalities have occurred in the past. Take extra care when swimming off the public beaches where there are no lifeguards.*

Beach Parks

Other options → Parks [p.180]

A visit to one of Dubai's beach parks is an enjoyable way to spend the day and a perfect break from city life where you can soak up a tropical paradise experience with lush greenery, palm trees and stretches of sandy beach!

Both of Dubai's beach parks are very busy at weekends, especially in the cooler months, although Al Mamzar Park covers such a large area that it rarely feels overcrowded. They both have a ladies day when men are not admitted (except for young boys with their family). Dress wise, it is fine to wear swimsuits and bikinis (top and bottom

Sunset over Dubai's shoreline

halves please!). During Ramadan park timings change, usually opening and closing later in the day. Al Mamzar has an amphitheatre and often stages concerts on special occasions or public holidays with details appearing in the newspapers 2 - 3 days in advance.

Both of the beach parks have lifeguards on duty during the day. A raised red flag means that it is unsafe to swim, and you are strongly advised to heed the warning however calm and unchallenging the waters may look.

Al Mamzar Beach Park

Location → Nr Hamriya Port · Al Hamriya | 296 6201
Hours → 08:00 - 23:00
Web/email → www.dm.gov.ae   Map Ref → 12-E2

Four beaches, open grassy spaces and plenty of greenery make this beach park a popular spot. A large amphitheatre is located near the entrance and paths wind through picnic areas and children's playgrounds. The well maintained beaches have sheltered areas for swimming and changing rooms with showers. Kiosks sell food and other small necessities you may have left at home. Chalets complete with a barbecue area can be hired for Dhs.150 - 200. There are also two swimming pools and lifeguard patrols.

Entrance fees: Dhs.5 per person; Dhs.30 per car, including all occupants.

Pool fees: Dhs.10 per adult; Dhs.5 per child.

Timings: Wednesdays are for women and children only.

Jumeira Beach Park

Location → nr Jumeirah Beach Club · Jumeira | 349 2555
Hours → 08:00 - 23:00
Web/email → www.dm.gov.ae   Map Ref → 5-C1

With azure seas, palm trees and a long, narrow, shady stretch of beach, this is a popular park with plenty of grassy areas for all ages to run around on. Barbecue pits are available for public use, as well as a volleyball area for ball games. Lifeguards are on duty along the beach between 08:00 to sunset and swimming is not permitted after sunset. No adult bicycles or rollerblades are allowed in the park.

Entrance fee: Dhs.5 per person; Dhs.20 per car. Saturdays are for women and children only.

Parks

Other options → **Beaches [p.179]**
Parks [p.180]

Dubai has a number of excellent parks and visitors will be pleasantly surprised by the many lush green lawns and the variety of trees and shrubs which make the perfect escape from the concrete jungle of the city. In the winter months, the more popular green parks can be very busy at weekends. Most have a kiosk or café selling snacks and drinks; alternatively take a picnic or use the barbecue pits provided (remember to take your own wood or charcoal, and food!). Creekside Park has an amphitheatre and often holds concerts on public holidays or special occasions (details are announced in the newspapers two or three days before).

Regulations among the parks vary, with some banning bikes and rollerblades, or limiting ball games to specific areas. Pets are not permitted and you should not take plant cuttings. Most have a ladies day, when entry is restricted to women, girls and young boys (check the individual entries). As with the beach parks, timings change during Ramadan. Entrance to the smaller parks is free, while the larger ones charge Dhs.5 per person, except for Safa and Mushrif parks, which cost Dhs.3 per person.

Creekside Park

Location → Nr Wonderland · Umm Hurair | 336 7633
Hours → 08:00 - 23:00
Web/email → www.dm.gov.ae   Map Ref → 14-A1

Situated in he heart of the city but blessed with acres of gardens, fishing piers, jogging tracks, BBQ sites, children's play areas, restaurants and kiosks, this is the ultimate in park life. There's also a mini falaj and a large amphitheatre. Running along the park's 2.5 km stretch of Creek frontage is a cable car system allowing visitors an unrestricted view from 30 metres in the air. Alternatively, near Gate One, visit the amazing Children's City, a new interactive museum for children. From Gate Two, four wheel cycles can be hired (Dhs.20 per hour; you can't use your own bike in the park). Rollerblading is allowed, and there are no ladies only days.

Entrance fee: Dhs.5. Cable car: adults Dhs.25; children Dhs.10. Children's City: adults Dhs.15; children Dhs.10.

Mushrif Park

Location → Al Khawaneej Rd, 9 km past Dxb Airport | 288 3624
Hours → 08:00 - 23:00
Web/email → www.dm.gov.ae   Map Ref → 16-D4

The largest park in Dubai, Mushrif Park is a little out of town, but popular with families owing to its unusual features and extensive grounds (you may prefer to take your car in to get around). Wander around miniature houses or take the train, which tours the park in the afternoons (Dhs.2 a ride), then visit the camel and pony areas (afternoon rides cost Dhs.2). Separate swimming pools are available for men and women. No bikes or rollerblades are allowed and there are no ladies only days.

Entrance fees: Dhs.3 per person; Dhs.10 per car. Swimming pools: Dhs.10 per adult; Dhs.5 per child (a membership scheme is available).

Rashidiya Park

Location → Nr Bin Sougat Centre, Off Airport Rd · Al Rashidiya | na
Hours → 08:00 - 23:00
Web/email → www.dm.gov.ae   Map Ref → na

This is a surprisingly clean and pretty park with attractive flowerbeds and brightly coloured children's play areas. It is mainly used by local residents, although it would also suit mothers with pre-school children. Shaded grassy areas are ideal for picnics. Saturdays to Wednesdays are for ladies and children only.

Safa Park

Location → Nr Union Co-op & Choithrams · Al Wasl | 349 2111
Hours → 08:00 - 23:00
Web/email → www.dm.gov.ae   Map Ref → 5-C3

Spot the giant Ferris wheel opposite Jumeira Library and you've found Safa Park. Artistically divided, this large park offers electronic games for teenagers, plus bumper cars and the big wheel (at weekends). It also has volleyball, basketball and football pitches, tennis courts, an obstacle course, barbecue sites and expanses of grassy areas. Bicycles can be hired inside (the use of personal bikes is not allowed). Rollerblading is allowed and Tuesday is ladies day.

Entrance fee: Dhs.3 per person, free for children under three years. Bike hire: Dhs.100 deposit; Dhs.20 - 30 for one hour.

Tours & Sightseeing

Other options → **Out of Dubai [p.186]**
Activity Tours [p.186]
Weekend Breaks [p.197]

An organised tour can be a great way to discover the UAE, especially if you are only here for a short time or do not have ready access to a vehicle, and Dubai has plenty of tour operators offering an exciting range of city and safari trips. The following information is not exhaustive, but covers the most popular tours given by the main operators. Refer to Tour Operators [p.184] for the largest and most reputable companies operating out of Dubai.

Tours range from a half day city tour to an overnight safari visiting the desert or mountains and camping in tents. On a full day, evening or overnight tour, meals are generally provided, while on a half day city tour you will usually return in time for lunch. Generally all tours include soft drinks and water as part of the package, but check what is included when you book. Expect to pay anything from Dhs.35 for a 30 minute tour of the Creek to Dhs.110 for a half day city tour, and about Dhs.350 for an overnight desert safari.

Most tours group four to six people together and if you want a tour or car to yourself, you will probably have to pay for four or more people, even if there are less of you. It is advisable to book three or four days in advance. A deposit of up to 50% is normal, with the balance payable when you are collected. Cancellation usually means loss of your deposit, unless appropriate notice is given.

On the day of the tour you can be collected from either your hotel, residence, or from a common meeting point if you are part of a large group. Tours usually leave on time and if you're late then don't expect a

Shaded paths through a Deira park

refund. It's advisable to wear cool, comfortable clothing, plus a hat and sunglasses. Desert or mountain tours require strong, flat soled shoes if there is the possibility of walking. The temperature can drop considerably in the desert after sunset, especially in winter, so take warm clothing. Other necessities include suncream and a camera.

The desert safaris are a must for anyone who hasn't experienced dune driving before, especially good for friends and relatives visiting the Emirates. You can request an easier route if there are young children, the elderly, or anybody who doesn't want to experience extreme dunes. Most companies have excellent safety records, but there is an element of risk involved when driving off-road. However, you are the client and if the driver is going too fast for your group then tell him to slow down.

City Tours – Dubai

Dubai by Night

This is a tour around the palaces, mosques and souks of the city, whilst enjoying the early evening lights. See the multitude of shoppers in their national dress, and streets alive with traditional charm, then enjoy dinner at one of Dubai's many restaurants (half day).

Dubai City Tour

This is an overview of old and new Dubai. Usual sights include souks, the fish market, mosques, abras, Bastakiya windtower houses and thriving commercial areas with striking modern buildings. (half day)

City Tours – Out of Dubai

Abu Dhabi Tour

The route from Dubai passes Jebel Ali Port, the world's largest manmade seaport, on the way to Abu Dhabi, capital of the United Arab Emirates. Founded in 1761, the city is built on an island. Visit the Women's Handicraft Centre, Heritage Village, Petroleum Exhibition and Abu Dhabi's famous landmark – the Corniche. (full day)

Ajman & Sharjah Tour

Ajman is the place to visit to see wooden dhows being built today just as they were hundreds of years ago. Take in the museum before driving to the neighbouring emirate of Sharjah, where you can shop to your hearts content at the souks.

Finish with a wander around the restored Bait Al Naboodah house to see how people lived before the discovery of oil. (half day)

Al Ain Tour

Known as the 'Garden City', there are many historical attractions here, from one of the first forts to be built by the Al Nahyan family over 175 years ago, to prehistoric tombs at Hili, said to be over 5,000 years old. Other attractions include Al Ain Museum, the camel market, the falaj irrigation system, which is still in use, and the obligatory souk. (full day)

Ras Al Khaimah Tour

Drive up country along the so called Pirate Coast through Ajman and Umm Al Quwain. Explore ancient sites and discover the old town of Ras Al Khaimah and its museum. The return journey passes natural hot springs and date groves at Khatt, via the striking Hajar Mountains. (full day)

Shopping Tour

Known as the 'shopping capital of the Middle East', Dubai is a shopper's paradise! From almost designer clothes at incredibly low prices to electronics, watches or dazzling bolts of cloth in the Textile Souk, everything is available at prices to suit every budget – don't forget to bargain your way through the day! Then there are the malls... (half day) See also: Bargaining [p.204], Shopping Malls [p.234].

Safari Tours

Dune Dinners

Enjoy some thrilling 4 wheel desert driving before settling down to watch the sun set behind the dunes. Departing at around 16:00, the route passes camel farms and fascinating scenery, which provide great photo opportunities. At an Arabic campsite, enjoy a sumptuous dinner and the calm of a starlit desert night, and return around 22:00. (half day)

East Coast

Journey east to Al Dhaid, a small oasis town known for its fruit and vegetable plantations. Catch glimpses of dramatic mountain gorges before arriving at Dibba and Khor Fakkan on the East Coast. Have a refreshing swim, then visit the oldest mosque in the UAE. This tour usually visits the

Discover the best in you... Go outward bound with...

Desert Rangers.

Desert Rangers is an exiting and innovative company that offers a variety of outward-bound activities and adventure safaris, providing exclusive opportunities for you when in the UAE to try something totally different.

Overnight Safari   **Dune Buggy Safaris**   **Sandboarding Safari**

Mountain Safari   **Tailor-made Packages**   **Canoe Expeditions**

Hatta pool Safari   **Trekking**   **Dune Dinner Safari**

Desert Driving Course   **Camel Trekking**

Desert Rangers
TOURS & ADVENTURE SPORTS

PO Box 37579, Dubai, UAE · Tel (+971 4) 3402408 · Fax (+971 4) 3402407

rangers@emirates.net.ae

DESERT GROUP

Friday Market for a browse through cheap carpets, clay pots and fresh local produce. (full day)

Full Day Safari

This day long tour usually passes traditional Bedouin villages and camel farms in the desert, with a drive through sand dunes of varying colours and heights. Most tours also visit Fossil Rock and the mesmerising Hajar Mountains, the highest in the UAE. A cold buffet lunch may be provided in the mountains before the drive home. (full day)

Hatta Pools Safari

This authentic town is nestled in the foothills of the Hajar Mountains, famed for the fresh water rock pools, where you can swim. The trip generally includes a stop at the Hatta Fort Hotel, where you can enjoy the pool, landscaped gardens, archery, clay pigeon shooting and 9 hole golf course. Lunch is served either in the hotel, or in the mountains. (full day)

Mountain Safari

Travelling north along the coast and heading inland at Ras Al Khaimah, you enter the spectacular Hajar Mountains at Wadi Bih. Rumble through rugged canyons onto steep winding tracks, past terraced mountainsides and old stone houses. It leads to Dibba where a highway quickly returns you to Dubai, stopping at Masafi Market on the way. Some tours operate in reverse, starting from Dibba. (full day)

Overnight Safari

This 24 hour tour starts at about 15:00 with a drive through the dunes to a Bedouin style campsite. Dine under the stars, sleep in the fresh air and wake to the smell of freshly brewed coffee, then head for the mountains. The drive takes you through spectacular rugged scenery, along wadis (dry riverbeds), before stopping for a buffet lunch and then back to Dubai. (overnight)

Tour Operators

Tour operators in Dubai are fast evolving with new companies finding their feet in order to cater for the growing number and needs of tourists in the region. While some struggle to get off the ground others have become more established and offer a good range of activities. Listed in the table are a selection of the more reputable tour operators.

Apart from the usual tours, Arabian Desert Tours specialises in corporate events - if you want to arrange a company Christmas party with a difference, or a team building event, this is the tour operator to call. Even though they are relatively new to the market, they have already hosted TV programmes for the BBC and organised the entertainment for visiting international rugby teams.

Tour Operators	
Arabian Adventures	303 4888
Arabian Desert Tours `P.148`	268 2880
Arabianlink Tours	06 572 6666
Charlotte Anne Charters	050 670 9430
Creek Cruises	393 9860
Creekside Leisure `P.401`	336 8406
Danat Dubai Cruises	351 1117
Desert Rangers `P.183`	340 2408
Dubai Travel & Tourist Services	336 7727
East Adventure Tours `P.187`	335 5530
Escapades	353 4444
Gulf Ventures	209 5568
Khasab Travel & Tours	266 9950
Lama Desert Tours	334 4330
Leisure Time	332 7226
Net Tours	266 8661
North Star Expeditions LLC	332 8702
Off-Road Adventures `P.185`	343 2288
Orient Tours	282 8238
Planet Travel Tours & Safaris	282 2199
Quality Tours	297 4000
Relax Tourism	345 0889
Sunflower Tours	334 5554
SNTTA Travel & Tours (L.L.C.)	282 9000
Turner Travel & Tourism	345 4504
Voyagers Xtreme	345 4504

Quad bike daredevils take on Big Red

Activity Tours

Other options → **Tours & Sightseeing [p.181]**

In addition to the city and safari tours, some companies offer more specialised activities. For adrenaline junkies there are desert driving courses, dune buggy desert safaris, mountain biking and hiking or for something a little more peaceful there is a canoe tour of Khor Kalba. Note that a basic level of fitness may be required. Refer to the Activities chapter of the book for other activities that you can enjoy in the Emirates.

Desert Rangers

Location → Dubai Garden Centre · Al Quoz | 340 2408
Hours → 09:00 - 18:00
Web/email → www.desertrangers.com   Map Ref → 4-B4

Desert Rangers are one of only a few companies in the UAE to specialise in outdoor adventure activities. In addition to the standard range of desert and mountain safaris, they offer something a little different, visiting locations that you are unlikely to see with other tour companies. With camel riding, sand boarding, canoeing, raft building, camping, hiking, mountain biking, desert driving courses or dune buggying to choose from, your weekends should never be dull! They also specialise in initiative tests and team building as well as multi-activity trips for children, especially schools and youth groups.

Timings: most tours start around 08:00; afternoon tours start around 14:30; evening tours start around 16:00.

East Adventure Tours

Location → 64B Zomorrodah Building · Al Karama | 335 5530
Hours → 10:00 - 19:00
Web/email → www.holidayindubai.com   Map Ref → 10-E1

East Adventure Tours offer city discovery tours with a personal guide/driver as an escort. Trips can include a Bedouin desert safari, dhow dinner cruise and camel safari, as well as activities such as horse riding and golf, and the service extends to after dark. This unique chauffeur/escort service is available 24 hours a day. For further information, visit the website or contact Mr Ali (050 644 8820).

Mountain High

Location → Le Meridien Mina Seyahi · Marsa Dubai | 318 1420
Hours → na
Web/email → jules@mountainhighme.com   Map Ref → 3-A2

For the adventure seeker, Mountain High has a whole host of adrenaline pumping activities for novices and experts alike. Founder Julie Amer organises an exhilarating range of adventure challenges including worldwide mountain treks, cycling holidays, walking, cycling and outdoor circuit sessions and Himalayan Expeditions to Nepal, Tibet & India. If all that excitement tires you out she also offers holistic and well-being treatments.

Off-Road Adventures

Location → Metropolitan Hotel · Burj Dubai | 343 2288
Hours → Timings on request
Web/email → www.arabiantours.com   Map Ref → 5-C4

Please see review [p.308]

Voyagers Xtreme

Location → Dune Centre · Al Satwa | 345 4504
Hours → 09:00 - 18:00
Web/email → www.turnertraveldubai.com   Map Ref → 6-E3

Voyagers Xtreme (VX) provides a range of adventurous activities over land, air and sea. On offer is everything from hot air ballooning, dune driving, a Mussandam cruise, dive charters, skydiving, sailing, rock climbing, plus outdoor team building programmes. They also offer a two day self drive desert expedition to the Empty Quarter – the world's largest sand desert.

Out of the City

Other options → **Weekend Breaks [p.197]**

If you have access to a car, it's worth spending some time exploring places outside the city. To the east of Dubai lies the town of Hatta; just over an hour's drive away. It is the only town of any notable size in the emirate of Dubai, apart from the capital itself. South of Dubai is Abu Dhabi, the largest of all the emirates, covering 87% of the total area of the country and with a population close to one million. Abu Dhabi is also the capital of the UAE. Al Ain is this emirate's second city.

To the north of Dubai are Sharjah, Ajman, Umm Al Quwain and Ras Al Khaimah, known collectively as the Northern Emirates. Also covered in this section is Fujairah, the only emirate located entirely on the East Coast of the peninsula. This region is a mix of rugged mountains and golden beaches, and is one of the most interesting areas to explore. For further information on exploring the UAE's 'outback', refer to the *Off-Road Explorer (UAE)*, published by Explorer Publishing.

east
ADVENTURE TOURS & SAFARI
DESERT ROSE TOURISM L.L.C.

With 14 years of **experience** , we offer:

* Dune Buggy self drive Safari

* Dune Bashing and Sand Boarding

* Desert Safari to Ali Baba's bedouin village

* Desert Driving Course

* Dhow Cruise Dinner with return Transfer

* Private City Tours

* Hatta Trek, Dunes and Wadies

* 10 to 10 Full Day Adventure Tour

Any Tour any day!!

call us and get 25% discount with the below reference no.: Ali1001.

Tel: 04 - 3350950
    04 - 3555677
24 hours tel.no:
    050-6448820
E-mail:
tourism@emirates.net.ae

Hatta

Other options → **Weekend Breaks [p.197]**

Hatta nestles at the foot of the Hajar Mountains, about 100 km from Dubai and 10 km from the border with Oman, but remains within the emirate of Dubai. Hatta is the site of the oldest fort in the emirate (built in 1790), and there are several watchtowers on the surrounding hills. The town has a sleepy, relaxed feel about it and beyond the ruins and the Heritage Village, there is little to see or do. However, past the village and into the mountains are the Hatta Pools where you can see deep, strangely shaped canyons that have been carved out by rushing floodwater.

The Hatta Fort Hotel is an ideal weekend destination. Spacious bungalow style luxury rooms sit in tranquil gardens with a mountainous backdrop making it the perfect antidote to Dubai's city living.

On the way to Hatta, just off the main road, is the famous 'Big Red' sand dune. Estimated to be over a hundred metres high, it's a popular spot for practising dune driving in 4 wheel drives or quad bikes, as well as attempting sand skiing. Alternatively, take a walk (if you have the energy) to the top for a great view. For further information on the area around Hatta, refer to the *Off-Road Explorer (UAE)*. See also: Dune Buggies [p.269]; Sand Boarding/Skiing [p.288] ; Tour Operators [p.184] .

Liwa Oasis

Abu Dhabi Emirate

Other options → **Weekend Breaks [p.197]**

Only 50 years ago, Abu Dhabi consisted of little more than a fort surrounded by a modest village of just a few hundred date palm huts. However, with the discovery of oil in 1958 and subsequent exports starting five years later, life changed beyond recognition. The dramatic rise in income enabled the growth of a modern infrastructure and a 21st century city was born, resplendent with high-rise buildings, multi-lane highways, a large port and numerous luxury hotels.

The airport is located on the mainland, 35 km from the city. The city itself lies on an island, which became home to the Bani Yas Bedouin tribe in 1761 when they left the Liwa Oasis in the interior. Being an island, it offered security, but the tribe also found excellent grazing, fishing and fresh water supplies. The descendants of this tribe have in fact, in alliance with other important families in the region, governed the emirate ever since. If you have access to a car, it's worth spending some time exploring places outside the city.

Liwa Oasis

To the south of Abu Dhabi lies the Liwa Oasis situated on the edge of the infamous Rub Al Khali desert, also known as the Empty Quarter. This region stretches from Oman, through southern UAE into Saudi Arabia, and throughout history was regarded as the edge of civilisation.

Al Ain

Al Ain is the second most important city in the emirate and lies on the border with Oman and shares the Buraimi Oasis. The shady oasis is a pleasant stretch of greenery amidst the harsh surroundings, and the palm plantations have plenty of examples of the ancient 'falaj' irrigation system. Al Ain has a variety of sights to interest visitors including a museum, a couple of forts, livestock and camel souks, while visits to the nearby Jebel Hafeet, Hili Fun City and archaeological site are also worthwhile. Jahili Fort and Park, located near the Public Garden, is famous for being the birthplace of the late ruler of the UAE, HH Sheikh Zayed bin Sultan Al Nahyan, who died in November 2004. Also worth checking out is the Ain Al Fayda resort (02 783 8333) built around a natural hot spring and located in a dramatic setting at the foot of the Hafeet Mountain. The *Off-Road Explorer (UAE)* gives details of four interesting trips around Al Ain/Buraimi. For detailed information on the emirate of Abu Dhabi, refer to the *Al Ain & Abu Dhabi Explorer*.

Exploring · Out of the City

An Exclusive Mountain Retreat
Awaits You

فندق حصن حتا
HATTA FORT HOTEL

P.O. Box 9277, Dubai, U.A.E.
Tel. +971 4 852 3211 Fax +971 4 852 3561
E-mail: hfh@jaihotels.com
www.jebelali-international.com

A MEMBER OF

جبل علي الدولية للفنادق
JEBEL ALI INTERNATIONAL
HOTELS
A TRADITION OF HOSPITALITY AND EXCELLENCE

In the heart of the majestic Hajar Mountains lies the Hatta Fort Hotel, an 80-acre 'Relais & Chateaux' retreat that is a refreshing getaway from bustling city life. Our Exclusive Mountain Retreat is the perfect place to unwind and recharge, relax in beautiful pools, enjoy al fresco or gourmet dining, and retire to our chalet-style suites and rooms that offer a breathtaking view from their private patios.

Ajman

Other options → Museums - Out of City [p.173]
Weekend Breaks [p.197]

The smallest of the seven emirates is Ajman, the centre of which lies about 10 km from Sharjah, although the two towns merge along the beachfront. Ajman also has two inland enclaves, one at Masfut on the edge of the Hajar Mountains and one at Manama between Sharjah and Fujairah. This emirate has one of the largest dhow building centres in the UAE, which offers a fascinating insight into a traditional skill.

Investment in this small emirate is growing, with the opening of the Ajman Kempinski Hotel & Resort and a popular shopping and entertainment complex, Ajman City Centre, sister to the busy Dubai mall.

Ras Al Khaimah

Other options → Museums - Out of City [p.173]
Weekend Breaks [p.197]

The most northerly of the seven emirates, Ras Al Khaimah (RAK) is refreshingly lush with greenery and has possibly the best scenery of any city in the UAE. It lies at the foot of the Hajar Mountains, which can be seen rising into the sky just outside the city. As with all coastal towns in the region, pearling, trading and fishing were once primary commercial activities. Like many of the emirates it has a split personality – the old town (Ras Al Khaimah proper) and across the creek, the newer business district (Al Nakheel).

Visit the souk in the old town and the National Museum of Ras Al Khaimah, which is housed in an old fort, and is also a former residence of the Sheikh. The large shopping and leisure complex, Manar Mall has a cinema complex, family entertainment centre and water sports area.

The town is quiet and relaxing, and is a good starting point for exploring the surrounding countryside and visiting the ancient sites of Ghalilah and Shimal. Also worth quick stops are the hot springs at Khatt or the camel racetrack at Digdagga. One town in the emirate, Masafi, is home to the country's favourite bottled spring water of the same name and has become the UAE's answer to Evian. RAK is the starting or finishing point for a spectacular trip through the mountains via Wadi Bih to Dibba on the East Coast and is also the entry point to the Mussandam Peninsula, Oman. Refer to the *Off-Road Explorer (UAE)* for further information on exploring these areas. See also: Wadi & Dune Bashing [p.292].

Sharjah

Other options → Weekend Breaks [p.197]
Other options → Museums - Out of City [p.173]

Historically, Sharjah was one of the wealthiest towns in the region, with settlers earning their livelihood from fishing, pearling and trade, and to a lesser extent, from agriculture and hunting. It is believed that the earliest settlements date back over 5,000 years. Today, while Sharjah remains a centre for trade and commerce it has been surpassed by the impressive metamorphosis of neighbouring Dubai. Sharjah's city grew inland from the original creek side town, but the creek remains a prominent landmark today, and while it may only be a 20 minute drive from Dubai, commuter traffic at peak times can double (if not triple) the journey time.

> ### Decency Law
>
> *Visitors should be aware that a decency law has been implemented in Sharjah. Leaflets have been distributed in all public places to make people aware of the codes of moral behaviour and dress that are expected. This essentially means that there is now little freedom in this emirate for men and women who are not related or married to mix, or even be in a car together. In addition, to avoid offence (and attracting the interest of the police) you should dress much more conservatively than in Dubai. Basically, avoid wearing tight or revealing clothing. Also alcohol is forbidden in Sharjah.*

The emirate is worth a visit for its various museums if nothing else. In 1998, UNESCO named Sharjah the cultural capital of the Arab world due to its commitment to art, culture and preserving its traditional heritage. Sharjah is the only emirate with a coastline on both the Arabian Gulf and the Gulf of Oman and a trip from the city centre to its territory on the East Coast (approximately one to two hours drive), heads through the spectacular Hajar Mountains. The towns of Dibba, Khor Fakkan and Kalba are all part of Sharjah.

A useful guidebook to refer to for further information on this emirate is *Sharjah The Guide*.

Sharjah Creek

Sharjah is built around Khalid Lagoon, (popularly known as the Creek), and the corniche surrounding it is a popular spot, especially with families, for a stroll in the evening. In the middle is a huge fountain, allegedly the second highest in the world. From three points on the lagoon, small dhows can be hired to see the lights of the city from the water. It is also a great photo opportunity during daylight hours. Trips cost Dhs.30 per dhow for 15 minutes.

Sharjah Corniche

Al Qasba Canal

A Dhs.80 million project links the Khalid Lagoon with the Al Khan Lagoon area via the 1,000 metre long Al Qasba Canal. The aim is to create a 'Little Venice' tourist attraction along the canal, complete with bridges and boat rides, amusement parks, plus art galleries and restaurants, making it a destination in itself. The development is in keeping with the Sharjah government's desire to develop the tourism industry on a cultural and educational basis.

Al Dhaid

Al Dhaid is a green oasis town on the road from Sharjah to the East Coast, and is the second most important town in the Sharjah emirate. Thanks to an extensive irrigation system, above and below ground, the area is fertile and agricultural produce includes a wide range of fruit and vegetables. On the outskirts, shoppers will find roadside stalls selling pottery, carpets, fruit and vegetables. During the winter, camel racing is held at the racetrack on the road to Mileiha.

Sharjah Blue Souk	
Location → Nr Corniche · Sharjah	na
Hours → 09:00 - 13:00 16:00 - 22:00	
Web/email → www.sharjah-welcome.com	Map Ref → UAE-C2

Consisting of two long, low buildings running parallel to each other and connected by footbridges, the exterior of Sharjah Blue Souk (or New Souk) is

intricately decorated and imaginatively built in Arabian style. Each building is covered and air conditioned to protect shoppers from the hot sun. Bargain hunters will find about 600 shops here selling everything from furniture and carved wood to clothing, jewellery and souvenirs, plus a fabulous range of carpets from all over the world.

Souk Al Arsah	
Location → Nr Bank St · Heritage Area	na
Hours → 09:00 - 13:00 16:30 - 21:00	
Web/email → www.sharjah-welcome.com	Map Ref → UAE C2

This is probably Sharjah's oldest souk, and has been renovated in the style of a traditional market place using shells, coral, African wood and palm leaves. There are almost 100 small shops, set in a maze of peaceful alleyways, selling goods such as traditional silver jewellery, perfumes, spices, coffee pots and wedding chests, plus numerous other items, old and new. There is also a small coffee shop where you can get Arabic coffee and sweets.

Umm Al Quwain

Other options → **Weekend Breaks [p.197]**

Further north along the coast, between Ajman and Ras Al Khaimah, is the emirate of Umm Al Quwain. On a superficial level, not much has changed here over the years and it gives visitors an idea of how life in the UAE was a few decades ago. The emirate has six forts that are still standing and a few old watchtowers around the town, but otherwise there is not a lot to see or do here.

However, the lagoon, with its mangroves and birdlife, is a popular weekend spot for boat trips, windsurfing and other water sports. Just north of Umm Al Quwain, near the Barracuda Hotel (and grey market liquor store) is a growing fun park, Dreamland Aqua Park. Together with the UAQ Flying Club, UAQ Shooting Club, UAQ Equestrian Centre and the opportunity to try karting and paintballing, this is fast becoming the 'activity centre' of the Northern Emirates.

East Coast

Other options → **Weekend Breaks [p.197]**
Museums – Out of City [p.173]

A trip to the East Coast of the Emirates is well worth making, even if you are only in the UAE for a short time. The coast can be reached in under two hours and the drive takes you through the rugged Hajar Mountains and down to the Gulf of Oman.

Breathtaking views

LE MERIDIEN
AL AQAH BEACH RESORT

On a stretch of white beach, nestled between the mountains and the blue Indian Ocean, you'll discover the new Le Méridien Al Aqah Beach Resort.

- Diving in the UAE's best sites
- Deep sea fishing
- Watersports
- Desert Safaris
- Health Cub
- Kids Penguin Club
- Spa Treatments
- Tennis Courts
- UAE's largest free-form swimming pool
- Wide choice of restaurants, bars and clubs

All this, just 90 minutes from Dubai.

To find out more or make a reservation just call **+971 9 244 9000** or visit www.lemeridien-alaqah.com

re to do on land, and in the water.

led between the mountain and the sea   All rooms are sea facing

AL AQAH BEACH RESORT
www.lemeridien.com
In Partnership with Nikko Hotels International

J DHABI • AHMEDABAD • AL KHOBAR • AMMAN • BANGALORE • BEIRUT • CHENNAI • COCHIN • DAMASCUS
BAI • HAMBURG • JEDDAH • KOVALAM • KUWAIT • LATTAKIA • MADINAH • MAKKAH
BOURNE • MUMBAI • NEW DELHI • NEW YORK • PARIS • PUNE • TASHKENT • TAIF • TOKYO

Take the road through the desert to Al Dhaid and Masafi. On reaching Masafi, you can do a loop round, either driving north to Dibba and then along the coast to Fujairah and Kalba and back to Masafi, or the other way round.

The mountains and East Coast are popular for camping, barbecues and weekend breaks, as well as various sporting activities. Snorkelling is excellent, even near the shore, and locations such as Snoopy Rock are always popular. In addition, the diving on this coastline is usually good, with plenty of flora and fauna to be seen on the coral reefs. Check out the *Underwater Explorer (UAE)* for further information.

For off-road driving fans, the route to the East Coast has a number of interesting diversions, check out the *Off-Road Explorer (UAE)*. See also: Camping [p.263]; Diving [p.267] ; Snorkelling [p.290] .

In Dibba, the Holiday Beach Motel is situated opposite Dibba Island and is good for diving and snorkelling. Immediately opposite is Northstar Adventures, a company that specifically offers activities for kids. Close by is Al-Fujairah Royal Beach, which offers bungalow chalets. The small village of Al Aqah is home to the impressive five star Le Meridien beach resort and spa, and opposite Snoopy Island is the less salubrious but ever-popular Sandy Beach Hotel.

Badiyah

The site of the oldest mosque in the UAE, Badiyah is located roughly half way down the East Coast, north of Khor Fakkan. The mosque is made from gypsum, stone and mud bricks finished off with white washed plaster and its design of four domes supported by a central pillar is considered unique. It was restored in 2003 and is officially called Al Masjid Al Othmani. It is thought to date back 1,400 years, in the Islamic calendar, having been built in the year 20 Hijra (1446 AD). The mosque is still used for prayer, so non-Muslim visitors have to satisfy themselves with a photo from the outside. Built into a low hillside with several recently restored watchtowers on the hills behind, the area is now lit up at night with lovely sodium coloured light. The village of Badiyah itself is one of the oldest settlements on the East Coast and is believed to have been inhabited since 3000 BC.

Wadi Bih is Back!

While there have been many rumours that the much loved Wadi Bih was closed indefinitely for 'security' reasons, it is in fact open for business. There is, however a security check and you will have to provide identification for all vehicle occupants, such as a passport or driver's licence and number plates are noted. A 4 wheel drive is recommended but it can be accessed by cars, although maybe not after heavy rains when the roads can be rough.

Bithna

Set in the mountains about 12 km from Fujairah, the village of Bithna is notable mainly for its fort and archaeological site. The fort once controlled the main pass through the mountains from east to west and is still impressive. The village can be reached from the Fujairah - Sharjah road and the fort through the village and wadi. The archaeological site is known as the Long Chambered Tomb or the T-Shaped Tomb, and was probably once a communal burial site. It was excavated in 1988 and its main period of use is thought to date from between 1350 and 300 BC, although the tomb itself is older. Fujairah Museum

Escape from the city to the mountains

has a detailed display of the tomb that is worth seeing since the site itself is fenced off and covered against the elements. The tomb can be found by taking a right, then left hand turn before the village, near the radio tower.

Dibba

Located at the northern most point of the East Coast, on the border with the Mussandam, Dibba is made up of three fishing villages. Unusually, each part comes under a different jurisdiction: Dibba al Hisn is part of Sharjah, Dibba Muhallab is Fujairah and Dibba Bayah is Oman! The three Dibbas share an attractive bay, fishing communities, and excellent diving locations – from here Dhow trips can take you to unspoilt dive locations in the Mussandam. The Hajar Mountains provide a wonderful backdrop to the village, rising in places to over 1,800 metres. Dibba is the starting or finishing point for the stunning drive to the West Coast through the mountains via Wadi Bih. Allegedly there is a vast cemetery on the outskirts of town where over 10,000 headstones can still be seen. This is the legacy of a great battle fought in 633 AD, when the Muslim armies of Caliph Abu Baker were sent to suppress a local rebellion and to re-conquer the Arabian Peninsula for Islam. See also: Dhow Charters. [p.266].

Fujairah

Fujairah is the youngest of the seven emirates since it was part of Sharjah until 1952. Its independence makes it the only emirate located entirely on the East Coast and its golden beaches bordered by the Gulf of Oman on one side and the Hajar Mountains on the other make it worthy of a place on even the most jam packed of itineraries. The town is a mix of old and new; overlooking the atmospheric old town is the fort, which is reportedly about 300 years old, and will eventually house the artefacts currently on display in the Fujairah Museum, when restoration is complete. The surrounding hillsides are dotted with ancient forts and watchtowers, which add an air of mystery and charm. Most of these also appear to be undergoing restoration work.

Off the coast, the seas and coral reefs make a great spot for fishing, diving and water sports. It is also a good place for birdwatching during the spring and autumn migrations since it is on the route from Africa to Central Asia. The emirate has started to encourage more tourism by opening new hotels and providing more recreational facilities. Since Fujairah is close to the mountains and many areas

of natural beauty, it makes an excellent base to explore the countryside and see wadis, forts, waterfalls and even natural hot springs. An excellent tourist map has been produced by the Fujairah Tourism Bureau (09 223 1554); to get a copy of this map, visit the Tourism Bureau at Fujairah Trade Centre, 9th Floor, Office #901, on Sheikh Hamad Bin Abdullah Rd (call ahead for opening times, as these are subject to change).

Off-Road Explorer Experience the UAE's delights off the beaten track. Designed for the adventurous, a brilliant array of outback route maps, satellite images, step by step guidance, safety information, details on flora and fauna, and stunning photography make this outdoor guide a perfect addition to your four wheeler.

During the winter months, late on a Friday afternoon, between the Hilton Hotel and Khor Kalba area, crowds gather to watch 'bull butting'. This ancient Portuguese sport consists of two huge bulls going head to head for several rounds, until after a few nudges and a bit of hoof bashing, a winner is determined. A new wire fence protects spectators from angry runaways.

Kalba

If you go on an outing to the East Coast, don't turn back at Fujairah, as just to the south lies the tip of the UAE's Indian Ocean coastline. Here you will find Kalba, which is part of the emirate of Sharjah and renowned for its mangrove forest and golden beaches. The village is a pretty, but modern, fishing village that retains much of its historical charm. A road through the mountains linking Kalba to Hatta has recently been completed, creating an interesting alternative to returning to Dubai on the Al Dhaid - Sharjah road.

Khor Kalba

South of the village of Kalba is Khor Kalba, set in a beautiful tidal estuary (khor is the Arabic word for creek). This is the most northerly mangrove forest in the world, the oldest in Arabia and is a 'biological treasure', home to a variety of plant, marine and birdlife not found anywhere else in the UAE. Although it has been proposed to make this a fully protected nature reserve, it is still waiting for Federal protection.

The mangroves flourish in this area thanks to the mix of saltwater from the sea and freshwater

Exploring

Out of the City

from the mountains, but they are receding due to the excessive use of water from inland wells. For birdwatchers, the area is especially good during the spring and autumn migrations when special species of bird include the reef heron and the booted warbler. It is also home to the rare white collared kingfisher, which breeds here and nowhere else in the world. There are believed to be only 55 pairs of these birds still in existence. A canoe tour by Desert Rangers is an ideal opportunity to reach the heart of the reserve and you can regularly see over a dozen kingfishers on a trip. There is also the possibility of seeing one of the region's endangered turtles. The reserve is a unique area so please treat it with respect. See also: Desert Rangers – Canoeing [p.264]; Birdwatching [p.176].

Khor Fakkan

Khor Fakkan lies at the foot of the Hajar Mountains halfway down the East Coast between Dibba and Fujairah. It is a popular and charming town, set in a bay and flanked on either side by two headlands, hence its alternative name 'Creek of the Two Jaws'. It is a favourite place for weekend breaks or day trips and has an attractive waterfront and beach. The iconic 70's style Oceanic Hotel is a popular choice, and there are plenty of good fishing and diving sites nearby. Above the Oceanic, the Ruler of Sharjah's Palace is visible high up on the hilltop. Part of the emirate of Sharjah, it has an important modern port; ships discharging their cargo here don't have to suffer a further 48 hour journey through the Strait of Hormuz to the West Coast. Nearby is the old harbour, which is an interesting contrast to the modern port. Set inland in the mountains is the Rifaisa Dam. Local legend has it that when the water is clear, a lost village can be seen at the bottom of the dam.

Wahala

This site is inland from Khor Kalba and is notable for a fort, which archaeologists judge to be over 3,000 years old. It is believed that the fort once protected the resources of the mangrove forests for the local population. A complete renovation program started in late 2003 and was due for completion at the end of 2004.

Mussandam

Other options → **Weekend Breaks [p.197]**

The Mussandam Peninsula is the Omani enclave located to the north of the UAE. It has only been

opened to tourists relatively recently and is a beautiful, unspoilt region of Arabia. The capital is Khasab, a quaint fishing port largely unchanged by the modern world. The area is of great strategic importance since its coastline gives control of the main navigable stretch of the Strait of Hormuz, with Iran only 45 km across the water at the narrowest point. The region is dominated by the Hajar Mountains, which run through the UAE and the rest of Oman.

The views along the coast roads are stunning. Inland, the scenery is equally as breathtaking, although to explore properly, a 4 wheel drive is useful. It is sometimes called the 'Norway of the Middle East', since the jagged mountain cliffs plunge directly into the sea and the coastline is littered with inlets and fjords. Just metres off the shore are beautiful coral beds with an amazing variety of sea life, including tropical fish, turtles, dolphins, occasionally sharks, and even whales on the eastern side.

To reach the Mussandam from Dubai, follow the coast road north through Ras Al Khaimah. At the roundabout for Shaam turn right and follow the road to the UAE exit post. The Omani entry point is at Tibat, then basically follow the road until it runs out. See the Omani Visa's section below for visa details.

Refer to the *Off-Road Explorer (UAE)* and the *Oman Explorer* for further information on this fascinating area.

Sultanate of Oman

Other options → **Weekend Breaks [p.197]**

The Sultanate of Oman is a peaceful and breath-taking place to visit, with a friendly laissez faire approach that is quite refreshing especially after the big city feel of Dubai. Visitors have two options – either go east and explore Oman fully or north to visit the Omani enclave of the Mussandam. Both areas can be visited either by plane or car. If you are driving into Oman, there are two main border crossing points; at Hatta (if you want to travel to Muscat) or through the Buraimi Oasis, near Al Ain (if you are driving towards Ibb, Nizwa or Al Salalah). At both places your vehicle will be searched, so it's advisable not to include prohibited items (alcohol, for instance) in your luggage. The journey from Dubai to Muscat by car takes 4 - 5 hours, although crossing the border at the start or end of a public holiday can sometimes be tediously slow, with a 1 - 2 hour wait.

Flying takes about 45 minutes to Muscat. There are flights daily by Emirates and Oman Air. Regular flights direct to Salalah from Dubai are a new service. Salalah, in the south of Oman, is a 'must do' location for visitors.

The local currency is the Omani Riyal (referred to as RO), which is divided into 1,000 baisa (or baiza). The exchange rate is usually about Dhs.10 = RO.1.

Note that talking on hand held mobile telephones whilst driving is illegal in Oman, as is driving a dirty car (no joke)! For further information on what Oman has to offer both visitors and residents, refer to the Oman Explorer.

Omani Visas

Visas for Oman are required whether entering by air or road, and different regulations apply depending on your nationality and how long you want to stay in Oman. Nationalities are split into two groups - check out the Royal Oman Police website, www.rop.gov.om/services_passports for full lists. People in group one can get a visit visa for no charge at the border - it's free for visitors but Dubai residents may incur a charge (about Dhs. 60). Residents from group two however will need to get a visa from the Oman consulate or embassy in advance for a Dhs.60 charge, which may take a few days to process. The visit visa is valid for one month. Remember that regulations in this part of the world often change virtually overnight, so check details before you leave to avoid disappointment.

Note that special clearance is required if you have 'journalist' or 'photographer' as a profession in your passport. The consulate in Dubai issues visit visas, but these cost more than just arriving at the border. Alternatively, let your sponsor (hotel, tour operator, Omani company) do the paperwork for you. If you are travelling to the Mussandam from Dibba port, the tour company will arrange a special pass for the day, usually for no additional cost. However, if you are travelling to the Mussandam from Ras Al Khaimah to visit the Khasab side, the standard visit visa is needed, either from the consulate or by applying at the border (if you fulfil the criteria).

Weekend Breaks

Other options → Hotel [p.34]
Out of Dubai [p.186]
Tours & Sightseeing [p.181]

For residents or visitors, escaping the city rat race is a balm for the soul and an entire catalogue of peaceful mini-holiday spots are right on Dubai's doorstep. With distances in the UAE being relatively small, it's easy to get well away from home without having to drive for hours – you can even check into a beach hotel up the road and feel that you have entered another world! The alternative to staying in a hotel is to camp, and this is a very popular, well established pastime in the UAE. See Camping – Activities [p.263].

The main travel agents in Dubai often have special offers for people wanting something a little further a field – such as a trip to Zanzibar, Bahrain or India. These offers are sometimes only available to GCC residents, and the travel agents listed in the table are some of those that provide good advice, and exciting, yet affordable itineraries. Last minute deals can often be found on the Internet.

If you decide to stay in a hotel and are booking with them directly, remember that (if asked) they will often give a discount on their 'rack' rate or published price. In the quieter summer months there are some incredible bargains available at five star hotels, but always check whether breakfast is included. Typically, for a weekend in the peak season or for corporate rates, expect a 30% discount. Off peak this can be as much as 60%.

For a list of places to stay, check out the Weekend Break table [p.198]. This has a guide to the room costs at the hotels; however, these may be discounted further. For more detailed information on Abu Dhabi and the Sultanate of Oman, refer to the *Abu Dhabi Explorer* and the *Oman Explorer*; both books are part of the Explorer series of guidebooks. For camping options, see the *Off-Road Explorer (UAE)*, and if you're looking to really get away from it all, including dry land, refer to the *Underwater Explorer (UAE)*.

Travel Agencies	
Airlink	282 1050
Al Futtaim Travel	228 5470
Al Naboodah Travel	294 5717
Al Tayer Travel Agency LLC	223 6000
Africa Connection	339 0232
Belhasa Tourism Travel & Cargo Co.	391 1050
DNATA	295 1111
Emirates Holidays	800 5252
Kanoo Travel	393 5428
MMI Travel	209 5527
SNTTA Travel & Tours (L.L.C.)	282 9000
Thomas Cook Al Rostamani	295 6777
Turner Travel & Tourism	345 4504

Exploring

Weekend Breaks

Weekend Break Summary

United Arab Emirates (+971)

Emirates	Hotel	Phone	Email	Rate
Abu Dhabi	Abu Dhabi Hilton	02 681 1900	auhhitw@emirates.net.ae	900 (+16%)
180km	Beach Rotana	02 644 3000	beach.hotel@rotana.com	1,050 (+16%)
	InterContinental	02 666 6888	auhha-reservation@interconti.com	950 (16%)
	Le Meridien	02 644 6666	meridien@emirates.net.ae	1,300 (+16%)
	Mafraq Hotel	02 582 2666	mafraq@emirates.net.ae	550 (+16%)
	Millennium	02 626 2700	sales.abudhabi@mill-cop.com	550 (+16%)
	Sheraton Abu Dhabi	02 677 3333	reservations.abu-dhabiuae@sheraton.com	720 (+16%)
Al Ain	Al Ain Rotana	03 754 5111	alain.hotel@rotana.com	700 (+16%)
130km	Al Ain Hilton	03 768 6666	alhilton@emirates.net.ae	350 (+16%)
	InterContinental	03 768 6686	aanha@icalain.ae	696 (+16%)
	Mercure Grand	03 783 8888	resa@mercure-alain.ae	520 inc
Jazira 60km	Al Diar Jazira Beach	02 562 9100	reservations@jaziraresort.net	750 (+16%)
Liwa 365km	Liwa Hotel	02 882 2000	liwahtl@emirates.net.ae	290 (+16%)
Ajman 20km	Ajman Kempinski	06 745 1555	ajman.kempinski@kemp-aj.com	1,080 inc
Dubai	Al Maha Desert Resort	04 832 9900	almaha@emirates.net.ae	5,880 inc
	Al Qasr Hotel	04 366 8888	reservations@madinatjumeirah.com	2,500 (+20%)
	Bab Al Shams	04 832 6699	info@babalshams.com	2,040 inc
	Jumeirah Beach Hotel	04 348 0000	reservations@thejumeirahbeachhotel.com	1,850 (+20%)
	Mina A' Salam	04 366 8888	reservations@madinatjumeirah.com	1,850 (+20%)
	One&Only Royal Mirage	04 399 9999	reservations@one&onlyroyalmirage.ae	1,560 (+20%)
	Ritz-Carlton Dubai, The	04 399 4000	rcdubai@emirates.net.ae	2,150 inc
Hatta 110km	Hatta Fort	04 852 3211	hfh@jaihotels.com	780 inc P.189
Jebel Ali 50km	Jebel Ali Resort	04 883 6000	jagrs@jaihotels.com	1,890 inc
Fujairah	Al Diar Siji	09 223 2000	sijihotl@emirates.net.ae	750 (+16%)
130km	Fujairah Hilton	09 222 2411	rm_fujairah@hilton.com	700 (+15%)
Al Aqah	Le Meridien Al Aqah	09 244 9000	reservations@lemeridien-alaqqah.com	900 (+15%) P.193
175km	Sandy Beach Motel	09 244 5555	sandybm@emirates.net.ae	385 inc
Ras Al Khaimah	Al Hamra Fort	07 244 6666	sales@alhamrafort.com	800 inc
75km	Ras Al Khaimah Hotel	07 236 2999	rakhotel@emirates.net.ae	440 inc
	RAK Hilton	07 228 8888	reservations.rak@hilton.com	550 inc
Khor Fakkan	Oceanic Hotel	09 238 5111	oceanic2@emirates.net.ae	450 (+15%)
Umm Al Quwain	Flamingo Beach Resort	06 765 1185	flaming1@emirates.ne.ae	300 inc

Sultanate of Oman (+968)

Emirates	Hotel	Phone	Email	Rate
Barka 250km	Al Sawadi Resort	+968 895 545	sales@alsawadibeach.com	230 (+17%)
Muscat	Al Bustan Palace	+968 799 666	albustan@interconti.com	1,290 (+17%)
450km	Chedi Muscat, The	+968 505 035	chedimuscat@ghmhotels.com	823 (+17%)
	Crowne Plaza	+968 560 100	cpmct@omantel.net.om	580 (+17%)
	Grand Hyatt Muscat	+968 602 888	hyattmct@omantel.net.om	880 (+17%)
	Holiday Inn Muscat	+968 687 123	mcthinn@omantel.net.om	590 (+17%)
	InterContinental	+968 600 500	muscat@interconti.com	700 (+17%)
	Mercure Al Falaj	+968 702 311	accorsales@omanhotels.com	420 (+17%)
	Radisson SAS	+968 685 381	sales@mcdzh.rdsas.com	550 (+17%)
	Sheraton Oman	+968 799 899	sheraton@omantel.net.om	650 (+17%)
Mussandam				
Khasab 150km	Golden Tulip Khasab	+968 830 777	info@goldentulipkhasab.com	459 inc
	Khasab	+968 830 271	khoman@omantel.net.om	340 inc
Nizwa 350km	Falaj Daris	+968 410 500	fdhnizwa@omantel.net.om	295 inc
Salalah	Holiday Inn Salalah	+968 235 333	hinnsll@omantel.netcom	574 (+17%)
1,450km	Salalah Hilton Resort	+968 211 234	sllbc@omantel.net.om	660 (+17%)
Sohar 250km	Sohar Beach	+968 841 111	soharhtl@omantel.net.om	350 (+17%)
Sur 650km	Sur Mercure	+968 443 777	reservationssur@omanhotels.com	430 (+17%)

Note   Rate = Price in dirhams of one double room; +xx% = plus tax; B = Inclusive of breakfast.
The above prices are peak season rack rates. However, many hotels will offer a discount off the rack rate if asked.

It's all abou
good living

DEIRA TAXI STAND

AL GHURAIR CENTRE

FISH R/A

ETISALAT

AL MAKTOUM ROAD

AL RIGGA ROAD

MARKS & SPENCER

SALAHUDDIN ROAD

RENAISSANCE HOTEL

MURAQABAT ROAD

MURAQABAT POLICE STATION

MARRIOTT HOTEL

SPINNEYS

MAKTOUM BRIDGE

CLOCK TOWER R/A

MAKTOUM BRIDGE

WAFI

EPPCO

DEWA

GRAND H'

GR. CIN

CITIBANK

GARHOUD BRIDGE

MARKS & SPENCER

MARKS & SPENCER

Shopping

EXPLORER

What's new?

Shopaholics Scream For Joy!

Three new retail developments have reconfirmed Dubai's status as THE number one destination for incurable shopaholics: Souk Madinat Jumeirah, with its charming boutiques and water-front eateries, is a 'must-do' for any Dubai tourist or resident. The Gardens mall is a welcome addition at the Jebel Ali end of town, with scores of well-known retailers, a hypermarket and Imax cinema, and Reef Mall is Deira's latest landmark, with big brand names and a Fun City promising something for all the family.

It's Party Time...

Everybody loves a good party, whether it's little kids or grown-ups who should know better, and Dubai has plenty of shops selling all you need - from balloons to bouncy castles - to make sure yours goes with a bang. You could even maximise the fun factor by going in fancy dress. You'll find all the details inside, but for even more info on children's parties and entertainment check out the Family Explorer from Explorer Publishing.

Clothing Sizes

Women's Clothing							Women's Shoes						
Aust/NZ	8	10	12	14	16	18	Aust/NZ	5	6	7	8	9	10
Europe	36	38	40	42	44	46	Europe	35	36	37	38	39	40
Japan	5	7	9	11	13	15	France only	35	36	38	39	40	42
UK	8	10	12	14	16	18	Japan	22	23	24	25	26	27
USA	6	8	10	12	14	16	UK	3.5	4.5	5.5	6.5	7.5	8.5
							USA	5	6	7	8	9	10

Men's Clothing							Men's Shoes						
Aust/NZ	92	96	100	104	108	112	Aust/NZ	7	8	9	10	11	12
Europe	46	48	50	52	54	56	Europe	41	42	43	44.5	46	47
Japan	S	-	M	M	-	L	Japan	26	27	27.5	28	29	30
UK	35	36	37	38	39	40	UK	7	8	9	10	11	12
USA	35	36	37	38	39	40	USA	7.5	8.5	9.5	10.5	11.5	12.5

Measurements are approximate only; try before you buy

Shopping

Table of Contents

Dubai is renowned for its shopping, and for good reason as virtually every item under the sun is available, be it cheap and cheerful or designer and decadent. However, despite its tax-free status you won't find bargains galore stocking the shelves of every store. Although prices on certain speciality items, such as carpets, textiles and gold, are extremely competitive, many imported goods are generally similar in price to any other major city in the world. The key to shopping like a pro in Dubai is to bargain hard where possible and remember that the best deals are to be found in and amongst the souks, see [p.252].

What this city can be justifiably proud of, however, is the sheer plenitude of purchasing opportunities. From an array of grandiose shopping malls with international brand names and local boutiques to souks selling Arabian treasures and jewellery, not forgetting the hidden gems such as furniture warehouses in Al Barsha, [p.220], you'll find a number of 'great buys' in Dubai. The following section provides information on all that is relevant for shoppers – from what to buy to where to buy it, plus a few tips on how to make those dirhams go a long way.

Refunds & Exchanges

In general, faulty goods are more easily exchanged than refunded at the shop of purchase. If, however, you have simply changed your mind about a recently purchased item, many retailers are not so obliging. Most will only exchange or give credit notes; very few will refund, although the international stores in the shopping malls are likely to be the most cooperative. To be successful returning unwanted items, make sure that they are unworn, unused and in their original packaging. Always check the refund and exchange policy when buying something, always keep your receipt and if there is a problem ask to see the manager. As a customer it may be nice to be important it is also important to be nice and getting hot under the collar is unlikely to get you your desired result. Instead keep your cool and appeal to the good nature of the retailer and if all else fails check your consumer rights.

Consumer Rights

There are no real specific laws, codes or regulations in Dubai that protect consumers which means that stores can do what they please. However, there is an excerpt in the UAE Civil and Commercial code, which states that the customer is entitled to recover the price paid for faulty goods (although unless you are prepared to take the shop to court, an exchange will have to do). Dubai Chamber of Commerce & Industry is, however, negotiating to introduce a Federal arbitration law that will cater for such commercial disputes. In the meantime, any complaints are best dealt with by the Commercial Protection division of the Department of Economic Development (202 0200 or 222 9922) or visit www.dubaided.gov.ae. You can send your complaint by email, fax or visit the department in person, but make sure you can produce your receipt. The department will in turn commence proceedings based on the complaint. Alternatively you can contact the Emirates Society for Consumer Protection (06 556 7333). In recent years the society has been active in campaigning for clearer food labelling, but they are also worth approaching if you feel that you have been badly treated as a consumer.

Shipping

Getting purchases home can be a tedious business, but there are a number of shipping and cargo agencies to make the experience plain sailing. Most companies operate globally and are quite reliable. Prices can vary considerably and depend on weight, destination and route, whether it is air or sea freight, and the airline. Air freight takes between a couple of days and a week while sea freight can take anywhere between two weeks and a month, although it is significantly cheaper. It's advisable to shop around for prices from shipping companies such as Ferns Shipping (352 1999) who arrange only sea freight and First Gulf Shipping LLC (335 1350), Gulf Agency Co Dubai LLC (345 7555), Inchcape Shipping Services (303 8593) and Westport Shipping Services LLC (337 7160) who will arrange both air and sea freight. DNATA Sky Cargo are based in Cargo Village at Dubai Airport (211 1111) and offer immediate quotes mainly for air freight although

> **No Going Back?**
>
> *Buying a gift to send back home? Marks & Spencer [p.200] is one of the few international retailers that allows refunds and exchanges on goods bought overseas. So if granny in Scotland would have preferred a woolly scarf to those flip-flops you bought her, she can take them back to her local store, providing she has the receipt.*

they will arrange sea freight if need be. During the Dubai Shopping Festival and Dubai Summer Surprises, some courier and shipping companies offer special rates so check them out if you are planning to export your shopping frenzy. See also: Moving Services [p.100].

How to Pay

While credit and debit cards are accepted in Dubai cash payment still dominates and you will have no problems exchanging or withdrawing money. ATMs (otherwise known as automatic teller machines, service tills or cash points) can be found in all shopping malls, most supermarkets, a few petrol stations and a growing number of bank branches around the city. Most cards are accepted by the plethora of banks in Dubai, which offer international access through CIRRUS or PLUS.

Credit cards are widely accepted, the exception being small traders in the souks and local convenience stores. Accepted international credit cards include American Express, Visa, MasterCard and Diners Club. To soften the high rates of interest you have to pay, local banks reward their credit card users with a number of promotions, competitions and discounts. US currency is also widely accepted, even by the ubiquitous 'corner shops', and since the dirham is pegged to the US dollar, the exchange rate is broadly the same throughout Dubai. However the best bargains can be had by using local currency. There are numerous money exchange bureaus in major shopping areas and the souks, and being equipped with dirhams makes shopping a whole lot quicker and hassle free. It can also, potentially, translate into some cash discounts. See also: Local Currency [p.49]

Bargaining

Although for many bargaining is an alien way of doing business, it is a time-honoured tradition in this part of the world. Vendors will often drop the price quite substantially for a cash sale, especially in the souks. So, relax, be friendly and enjoy the experience, most sellers are very receptive and bargaining can be a lot of fun. The key to bargaining is to decide what you are happy paying for the item and to walk away if you don't get it for that (it's not uncommon for shop assistants to chase after you to secure a purchase!). Always be polite and amiable, and never use rudeness or aggression as bargaining tools. Ask the shop assistant how much, and when he tells you, look shocked or indifferent. In the souks, a common rule is to initially offer half the quoted price. Once you've agreed to a price, that's it – it's a verbal contract and you are expected to buy. Remember, storekeepers are old pros at this and have an instinct for a moment's weakness!

Away from the souks, bargaining is not common practice, although many stores operate a set discount system, saying that the price shown is 'before discount'. Offering to pay cash can be beneficial, so it won't hurt to ask for a further discount.

> ### Buyer Beware
>
> Note: Traps for the unwary shopper exist in Dubai, as elsewhere. Some of the international stores sell items at prices that are far more expensive than in their country of origin (you can even still see the original price tags). This can be as much as 30% higher - so beware!

Window shopping

ZEN
INTERIORS

Furniture for the body
mind and soul

What & Where to Buy

Dubai's stores sell an abundance of goods and you should have few problems finding what you need. The following section covers the main categories of products that can be bought in the city, from carpets to cars and electronics to gold, as well as where you'll find them.

Alcohol

Other options → Drinks [p.321]
Liquor Licence [p.74]
On the Town [p.416]

Anyone aged over 21 years can buy alcohol at licensed bars, restaurants and some clubs for consumption on the premises. However, to buy alcohol for consumption at home it's not just a case of popping into your local supermarket but rather requires a liquor licence. Only non-Muslim residents can apply for a liquor licence. For information on how to obtain a licence and the restrictions that apply, refer Liquor Licences, [p.74] . Note that residents who have a liquor licence from another emirate are not permitted to use it in Dubai (except for old Sharjah licences, which are no longer valid in Sharjah, but can be endorsed by Dubai Police). Once you have a licence, it's easy enough to purchase alcohol from the special stores that are strategically scattered around Dubai. Especially useful are those located near supermarkets such as Spinneys, so you can do all your shopping in one trip. There is one catch to be aware of; when you get to the checkout, expect to pay 30% more than the sale price as tax.

Booze Run

There are ways of bucking the system... the UAE has a few 'hole in the wall' stores selling tax-free alcohol to unlicensed patrons; great if you don't mind the trek. The Barracuda Beach Motel (next to Dreamland Aqua Park near Umm Al Quwain) is one of those most frequented by Dubai residents.

Another store is opposite the Ajman Kempinski, which literally is a hole in the wall and has a limited selection. Bear in mind that it is illegal to transport alcohol over the border of an emirate, and in particular, through Sharjah. Police often turn a blind eye to this practice, but if you get busted with booze in your car, don't say you weren't warned.

Alcohol

African & Eastern Ltd		
Nr Clock Tower	Deira	222 2666
Spinneys	Dubai Marina	368 3981
Spinneys	Umm Suqeim	394 2676
Nr Choithrams	Al Karama	334 8056
Spinneys	Ramada	359 0730
Maritime & Mercantile Int P.75		
Al Maskan Bldg	Al Karama	335 1722
Behind Spinneys	Trade Centre Rd	352 3091
Emirates Group HQ	Deira	294 0390
Khalid Bin Waleed Street	Bur Dubai	393 5738
Next to Spinneys	Umm Suqeim	394 0351
Saeed Tower 2	Trade Centre 1	321 1223

Arabian Souvenirs

Other options → Carpets [p.212]

For visitors and residents alike, many items from this part of the world make novel souvenirs, gifts or ornaments for the home. The price and quality of cultural items varies enormously and the souks usually offer the best bargains, although there is something to suit all budgets here. Today, many of the items are mass produced in India or Oman.

Shopping malls have many shops specialising in Arabian artefacts - the wooden wedding chest is especially popular and has been widely copied. Traditional wooden doors are also sought after, and can be either used as intended, hung against a wall as art or turned into furniture (usually tables with glass tops so you can still see the intricacies of the carving). If you're a visitor and want something for your home, but can't fit a door in your suitcase, carpets are a good buy here too, [p.212]. Try to do a bit of research before you shop, so you'll have some idea of what makes a bargain. Don't forget to take your time and see as many choices as possible, build up a rapport with the carpet seller and haggle, haggle, haggle.

A symbol of Arabic hospitality, the coffee pot and cups (usually crafted out of beaten copper) are a popular purchase. Arabic coffee can be bought from many supermarkets and really is worth trying. The traditional method of preparing it is still practised today; coffee beans are roasted, ground and boiled, then cardamom, rosewater, saffron and cloves are added to create a wonderful aroma. The final coffee is quite refreshing, especially when served with dates.

Another favourite souvenir is the *khanjar*, which is the traditional dagger, a short curved knife in an elaborate sheath. Many people choose to display these in frames, and in some shops you will be

Shopping

What & Where to Buy

able to buy them already framed. Don't make the mistake of carrying your khanjar home with you in your hand luggage – it is still a dangerous item and you won't get it past airport security.

Traditional wedding jewellery made of heavy silver and crafted into engraved (and extremely chunky) necklaces, bracelets, earrings and rings are coveted forms of historical art, especially as many of the larger pieces make excellent pictures when framed. However, since you're in the 'City of Gold' you should seize the opportunity to buy gold items. Even if you are not buying, The Gold Souk (see [p.253]) is well worth a visit just to see the astounding range of jewellery on offer – there is so much gold here that it actually casts a yellow glow onto the pavement.

Trinkets and treasures

You will either love or hate the smell of incense and the heavy local perfumes, but they make a great gift. Take a walk among the many stalls in the Perfume Souk for the smell of frankincense and myrrh. In the Middle East, frankincense has been traded for centuries and was at one time considered more desirable than gold.

Shisha or hubbly bubbly pipes are a fun souvenir and can be bought with various flavours of tobacco, such as apple or strawberry. Both working and ornamental ones are available and some come with a protective carrying case – handy

if you are taking it to the desert or beach. For edible souvenirs look out for delicious Lebanese sweets, often made from pastry, honey, ground nuts and dates, or fresh dates supplied by the main producers from around the world. Iranian caviar is widely available and very good value, and is sold without import duty or a valued added tax.

Even though there are so many classy souvenirs available, you'll still find the usual touristy things, like fluffy camels (the snoring ones are the best), pictures made out of the seven sands of the UAE, Persian carpet mousepads, and the tackiest of the tacky; a mosque alarm clock, which comes in a variety of garish colours and plays the wailing sound of the *azzan* (prayer call) to wake you up in the morning.

As the saying goes, a picture is worth a thousand words, and a good coffee table book full of beautiful pictures of this fascinating land makes a wonderful souvenir. Grab a copy (or two!) of *Images of Dubai and the United Arab Emirates* to take home with you.

Arabian Souvenirs		
Al Jaber Gallery	Deira City Centre	295 4114
	Opp Hamarain Centre	266 7700
Creative Art Centre	Nr Choithrams	344 4394
Falcon Gallery	Nr 4x4 Motors	337 5877
Showcase Antiques	Opp Dxb Municipality	348 8797

Art

Other options → Art Classes [p.304]
Art Galleries [p.169]
Art Supplies [p.208]

A growing and avid interest in art is being displayed in the region, and many local and international artists are setting up base here. Most shops selling art also double up as gallery space, so, flick back to Art Galleries [p.169] in the Exploring section of the book for a listing of the available options.

Art		
Aquarius	Jumeirah Plaza	349 7251
Art Space Gallery	Fairmont Dubai, The	332 5523
Five Green	Nr Dubai TV, Oud Metha	336 4100
Art & Culture	Htl Inter-Con Dubai	222 7171
Jadis	Courtyard, The	347 4233
Profile Gallery	Jumeira	349 1147
Sharjah Arts	Sharjah Arts Area	06 568 8222
Total Arts	Courtyard, The	228 2888

Shopping

What & Where to Buy

Art Supplies

Other options → Art [p.207]
Art Classes [p.304]
Art Galleries [p.169]

Creative types who like to dabble in arts and crafts can find tools of the trade at any of the following stores.

Art Supplies		
Al Hathboor	Al Karama	286 5965
Art Source	Rashidiya	285 6972
Art Stop	Jumeirah Plaza	349 0627
Chinese Trading	Hor Al Anz	266 3384
Crafters Home	Mazaya Centre	343 3045
Dubai Int. Art Centre	Nr Town Centre	344 4398
Elves & Fairies	Jumeirah Centre	344 9485
Emirates Trading	Nr Al Nasr Cinema	337 5050
Talent Stationery	Shk Zayed Rd, Al Wasl	343 2734

Beach Wear

Other options → Clothes [p.214]
Sporting Goods [p.230]

Since many Dubai residents spend their weekends basking by the pool or on the beach it's not surprising that some people spend as much money on a designer swimming togs as they do on a suit for work. Generally, prices are pretty high in the specialist beach wear boutiques that stock everything from French and Italian designer wear to the hippest Californian and Australian surfing

Totally babelicous beach wear

labels. Since there is no real 'off' season, these shops often have sales at strange times of the year – ask to be added to their mailing lists so you can be first to snap up the bargains.

Dubai's many sports shops also stock a decent range of swimwear, from no-nonsense styles for competitive swimmers to teeny weeny bikinis for die-hard beach babes. You'll also find a good selection in department stores such as BHS in Bur Juman [p.234], Woolworths and Debenhams in Deira City Centre [p.236] and Marks & Spencer in Wafi [p.244] all sell beach wear, plus all the related paraphernalia like hats, sarongs and beach bags at prices that won't break the bank.

Beach Wear		
Al Boom Marine	Jumeira Beach Rd	394 1258
P.209	Ras Al Khor, nr Coca Cola	289 4858
Bare Essentials	Jumeirah Centre	344 0552
Beyond the Beach	Mercato	349 0105
P.209	Palm Strip	346 1780
	Souk Madinat Jumeirah	368 6037
	Spinneys, Umm Suqeim	394 2977
Heat Waves	Le Meridien Dubai	399 3161
Oceano	Palm Strip	346 1961
Westwood	Deira City Centre	295 5900

Books

Other options → Libraries [p.312]
Second-Hand Items [p.230]

Literature lovers will find a reasonable selection of English language books on sale in Dubai, covering a broad range of subjects, from travel or computing to children's books, best selling fiction, and coffee table books. Most of the larger hotels also have small bookshops offering a limited choice. However, you are unlikely to find as extensive a range of books and bookshops as in your home country, although the number and size of outlets is increasing all the time.

Foreign newspapers and magazines are flown in regularly, but are always more expensive than at home. For all males out there who enjoy their monthly racy blokes' mags, be warned: due to censorship laws, any pictures of semi-naked women are always disguised by a giant black pen mark.

Good shops with wide-ranging selections are Book Corner, Books Plus and Magrudy's. Carrefour, Spinneys, Choithrams and Park'n'Shop supermarkets also carry a decent range of books and magazines.

There are several second-hand bookshops too, and many will offer a 50% 'refund' should you wish to return a book once you've read it. Alternatively there are plenty of charities that appreciate book donations, while Medecins Sans Frontieres holds an annual second-hand book bazaar. For more information on this and other events, visit www.msfuae.ae.

Books

Al Jabre Al El Miah	BurJuman Centre	351 6740
Book Corner	Al Ghurair City	228 2835
	Deira City Centre	295 3266
	Dune Centre	345 5490
Book Worm	Beh Park & Shop	394 5770
Books Plus P.213	Lamcy Plaza	336 6362
	Oasis Centre	339 4080
	Spinneys, Umm Suqeim	394 0278
Carrefour P.237	Al Shindagha	393 9395
	Deira City Centre	295 1600
House of Prose	Jumeirah Plaza	344 9021
Kids Plus	Town Centre	344 2008
Magrudy's Bookshop	BurJuman Centre	359 3332
P.211	Deira City Centre	295 7744
	Magrudy's Centre	344 4193
Spinneys	Mazaya Centre	321 2225
	Mercato	349 6900
	Nr. BurJuman Centre	351 1777
	Umm Suqeim	394 1657
	Nr Ramada Htl	355 5250
Titan Book Shop	Holiday Centre	331 8671
	Hotel Inter-Continental	227 1372
Virgin Megastore	Mercato	344 6971
White Star Bookshop	Beach Centre, The	344 6628

Buy the book

Other options → Electronics & Home Appliances [p.216]

Camera Equipment

For those who enjoy photography as a hobby, the latest cameras are widely available in Dubai. Bab Al Salam Electronics and Grand Stores are the two main shops for cameras and related equipment. Grand sells Nikon, Fuji and Mamiya. However, if you want Canon then JK National Stores is the agent. For serious photographers, Salam and Grand have the best selection for everything from darkroom equipment and filters to tripods and studio equipment. Salam also sells brands such as Pentax, Leica, Minolta, Bronica and Noblex, although purchasing professional equipment in Dubai is expensive Prices from the agents are usually fixed and reasonable, although many famous brands can be found for less on Al Faheidi Street and the surrounding area in Bur Dubai. Here prices can be negotiated, but watch out for 'parallel' imports. With the introduction of the trademark and copyright law the counterfeit market has been reduced, but not eradicated.

Camera film is available in supermarkets, local shops and hotel foyer shops. Film UCF stocks Kodak, while Grand Stores supply Fuji and Ilford. Both outlets refrigerate the film - vital in Dubai's climate.

Opinion is divided as to whether it's cheaper to buy cameras in Dubai than elsewhere. Due to low import costs, cameras here are less expensive than in the UK for instance, but you may find better deals in Hong Kong or Singapore, if you know what you're looking for. Before you go out shopping for an expensive piece of equipment, it pays to know your stuff. There are several Websites where you can get advice from experts; try www.godubai.com, www.uae-photo.com, www.betterphoto.com or www.bhphoto.com. Buying online can also be a cheaper alternative from companies such as B&H Photo in New York – this is a reputable company with excellent prices, and often you can get a better deal even after you include the shipping costs.

If you are purchasing in Dubai to take back home, check out the tax implications of your home country. Your 'bargain' camera may not turn out to be such a great deal if you have to pay added import duty. It is also important to get a stamped and dated international warranty, otherwise the agent in your home country will not honour any future defects. Sony UK refuses to honour any Sony products bought abroad, claiming that they are not an international company.

Shopping

What & Where to Buy

"And they lived happily ever after"

The tale of customers and books at **MAGRUDY'S**.

MAGRUDY'S

MAGRUDY ENTERPRISES LLC

Jumeirah Beach road   04 3444 193

Deira City Centre   04 295 77 44

Burjuman   04 359 333 2

Camera Equipment

Grand Stores	282 3700
Jacky's Electronics	881 9933
M.K. Trading Co. L.L.C.	222 5745
National Stores	353 6074
Salaam Studios	324 5252
UCF	336 9399

Cards & Stationery

Other options → Art Supplies [p.208]
Books [p.208]

Most supermarkets carry a limited supply of greeting cards, wrapping paper and stationery. However, there are a number of speciality stores mainly in the shopping malls, offering everything from Christmas and Easter to Mother's Day and Eid cards.

If you prefer your greeting cards a little risqué then you may be disappointed - the more daring cards tend not to slip through Dubai's censors, although if you look hard enough the odd one may be found.

Shop around for greeting cards, as some shops are more expensive than others, and the range differs with each outlet. If you're looking for something with local flavour, you'll find a range of locally produced cards in most shops. Wrapping paper ranges in price from scandalously expensive to reasonable, depending on the shop. Shops like THE One, IKEA and Woolworths stock a range of reasonably priced gift wrap, as do many independent stationery shops.

Cards & Stationery

Al Fahidi Stationery	Al Faheidi St	353 5861
	Opp Al Khaleej Hotel	222 8641
Carlton Cards	Deira City Centre	294 8707
	Lamcy Plaza	336 6879
Carrefour P.237	Deira City Centre	295 1600
Emirates Trading Est.	Nr Al Nasr Cinema	337 5050
Farook Int'l Stationary	Meena Bazaar	352 1997
Gulf Greetings	Al Bustan Centre	263 2771
	BurJuman Centre	351 9613
	Deira City Centre	295 9627
	Oasis Centre	339 1810
	Spinneys	394 0397
	Wafi Mall	324 5618
IKEA P.IBC	Deira City Centre	295 0434
Office 1	Za'abeel Rd	335 9929
THE One	Nr Jumeira Mosque	342 2499
Titan Book Shop	Holiday Centre	331 8671

Carpets

Other options → Arabian Souvenirs [p.206]
Bargaining [p.204]

In Dubai, carpets originate from countries such as Iran, Pakistan, China and Central Asia, and there is a truly exquisite array of designs and colours on the market.

To ensure that you are buying the genuine article at a good price, it's advisable to do some research first. Information on the intricacies of carpet origins and designs can be found on the Internet (try www.persiancarpethouse.com). Don't rush into actually buying your carpets online, unless you are an absolute pro - it is probably better to visit a number of shops, getting a feel for price, quality and traditional designs, before you make your decision.

As with most goods, carpets differ in quality and this is reflected in the price. Silk is more expensive than wool, and rugs from Iran are generally more valuable than their equivalent from Turkey or Kashmir. Always check if a carpet is machine or handmade; handmade carpets are never quite perfect and the pile is slightly uneven, although they are much more valuable. A good tip is to decide in advance the maximum you are prepared to spend, and begin the bargaining by offering half of that amount. Bargaining is expected in most shops; prices vary from a few hundred to many thousand dirhams, but are always negotiable. If you are new to the haggling game, check our guide to bargaining, [p.204].

Deira Tower shopping mall in Al Nasr Square has the largest number of carpet outlets under one roof – the majority of traders being from Iran. The annual Dubai Shopping Festival (see [p.56]) features the 'Carpet Oasis', usually located in the Airport Exhibition Centre, where you'll find an overwhelming choice of carpets at excellent prices.

Carpets

Afghan Carpets	Airport Rd	286 9661
	Oasis Centre	339 5786
Al Orooba Oriental	BurJuman Centre	351 0919
Carpetland	Opp Al Nasr Cinema	337 7677
Feshwari P.221	Nxt to Oasis Centre	344 5426
Kashmir Gallery	Al Ghurair City	222 5271
Persian Carpet House	Crowne Plaza	332 1161
Quem Persian Carpets	Sheraton Htl & Towers	228 1848
Red Sea Exhibition	Beach Centre, The	344 3949

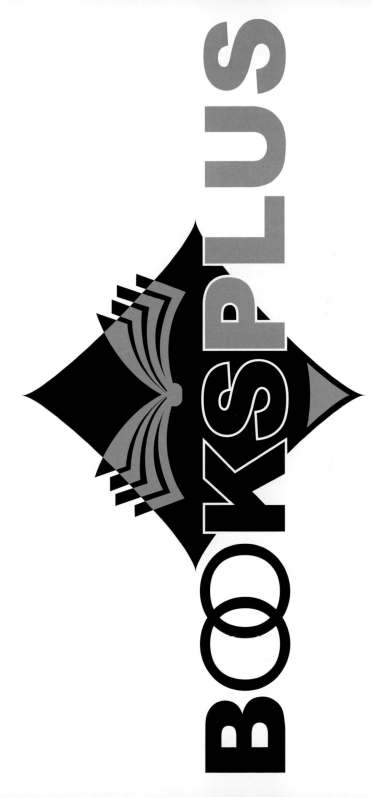

9 great stores. <u>One great name.</u>

BOOKSPLUS

• Lamcy Plaza Dubai • Reef Mall Deira • Spinneys Mall - Jumeirah • Town Centre - Jumeirah
• Oasis Center - Sheikh Zayed Road • Greens Centre - Sheikh Zayed Road • Knowledge Village
• Dubai Marina Towers • Jimi Mall Al Ain

You'll also find a number of road side carpet sellers on the way to Hatta (close to the Hatta Fort Hotel) - for the best bargains this is the place to carpet shop. However, be aware that what the seller says about the origin or material of the carpet may not be strictly true so don't buy if you're looking for an investment. That said, these stalls are an excellent place to stock up on a few rugs to insulate Dubai's regulatory marble floors in villas and apartments.

Cars

Other options → Buying a Vehicle [p.138]

One of the best things about Dubai is the fact that cars are usually much cheaper than they are in your home country, and so you should be able to upgrade. That's the good news. The even better news is that banks and dealers tend to offer very attractive interest rates for auto loans. From Audi to Volkswagen, you'll find all the major car dealers here if you're looking for a new car. The best times of year to get a discount on your new car is during the Shopping Festival (see [p.56]) or at the end of the year when next year's model is due.

The second-hand car market is a thriving industry, and you'll find an abundance of used car dealerships all over Dubai. Whether you want to look smooth in a Porsche or rugged in a Jeep, you'll find your dream car at a dream price. And don't forget to bargain! Alternatively, you can always browse through the classifieds section of the newspaper or search the supermarket noticeboards for used cars being sold privately, if you don't mind going through the hassle of the registration process yourself (normally the dealer would do this for you). Also, it's a good idea to have the vehicle vetted by a reputable garage before you take the plunge and buy.

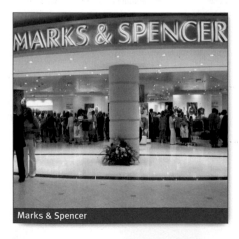

Marks & Spencer

Clothes

Other options → Beach Wear [p.208]
Kids' Items [p.224]
Lingerie [p.226]
Shoes [p.230]
Sporting Goods [p.230]
Tailoring [p.231]

In Dubai, fashion lovers will find everything from the priciest designer shops and up-to-the-minute boutiques to 'pile it high, sell it cheap' bargain basement stores. Most malls will have a good selection of quality clothing and you'll find quite a few shops that you recognise from back home (but you might find the prices a bit higher).

The really upmarket, designer label shops are found mainly in malls and hotel boulevards, although you'll still find a handful on Al Maktoum Street in Deira. You'll also find a number of shops along the Deira side of the Creek (near the Twin Towers) selling men's suits, jackets and casuals. Many offer permanent sales on 'designer' suits. For more info on finding your way around this area refer to Deira in the Exploring section [p.156].

The shopping outlets in Satwa and Al Karama offer countless outlets selling cheap clothing of varying quality – on a good day you'll find some real bargains, but on other days you'll find nothing worth buying, unless you're going to a 'bad taste' party!

Clothing sizes can be confusing here - the difference in UK, US, European and Asian sizes is quite significant. Ask the shop assistant for advice – most will know what size you need, or they'll have a conversion chart handy. Or take along your *Dubai Explorer* and refer to the conversion table on [p.202].

An alternative to buying clothes off the rack is to have pieces tailor made, and you'll find hundreds of tailors around Dubai. They can usually knock up a garment from a picture or by copying an original – they'll even be able to tell you how much material you should buy. The end result may vary from one tailor to another (word of mouth is usually the best starting point), but once you find one you are happy with, it's a great way to get original items at very reasonable prices.

If you love rummaging through sales and finding some excellent bargains, you're in the right place – Dubai is the cut-price capital and you'll find something on sale virtually every day of the year.

Clothes

Amichi	Mercato	349 0999		Jennyfer	Lamcy Plaza	337 2924
Armani Jeans	Deira City Centre	295 1165		Karen Millen	Deira City Centre	295 5007
	Mercato	344 2118			Palm Strip	345 6703
Bargains	Al Diyafah St.	398 3929		Kookai	Al Rigga Street	223 8500
Benetton	Al Ghurair City	221 1593			Deira City Centre	295 2598
	Deira City Centre	295 2450			Wafi Mall	324 9936
	Jumeirah Centre	349 3613		Lacoste	Deira City Centre	295 4429
	Lamcy Plaza	334 7353		Levi's	BurJuman Centre	351 6728
Bershka	Deira City Centre	295 8440			Deira City Centre	295 9943
	Mercato	344 8645		Levi's Outlet	Al Khaleej Centre	359 6770
Bhs	Al Ghurair City	227 6969		Liwa	BurJuman Centre	351 5353
	BurJuman Centre	282 2555			Deira City Centre	295 3988
	Lamcy Plaza	335 8334		Mango	BurJuman Centre	355 5770
Bossini	Al Ghurair City	221 5917			Deira City Centre	295 0182
	Beach Centre, The	349 0749			Palm Strip	346 1826
	BurJuman Centre	351 6917		Marks & Spencer	Salah Al Din Rd	222 2000
	Lamcy Plaza	305 9417		P.200	Wafi Mall	324 5145
	Meena Bazaar	352 4817		Massimo Dutti	BurJuman Centre	351 3391
Burberry	BurJuman Centre	351 3515			Deira City Centre	295 4788
	Deira City Centre	295 0347			Mercato	344 7158
Calvin Klein	BurJuman Centre	352 5244		Max Mara	BurJuman Centre	351 3140
	Deira City Centre	295 0194		Mexx	BurJuman Centre	355 1881
Cartoon Fashion	Al Ghurair City	221 6461			Deira City Centre	295 4873
Century 2000	Nr Al Nasr Cinema	336 6654		Mexx for Less	Lamcy Plaza	334 0096
Cerruti	Twin Towers	227 2789		Miss Sixty	Mercato	349 9199
Chanel	BurJuman Centre	355 7388			Wafi Mall	324 1998
	Wafi Mall	324 0464		Moka	Jumeirah Centre	349 3800
Christian Lacroix	BurJuman Centre	351 7133		Monsoon	Deira City Centre	295 0725
Custo Barcelona	Emirates Towers	330 0564		Next	BurJuman Centre	351 0026
Debenhams	Deira City Centre	294 0011			Deira City Centre	295 2280
Diesel	Deira City Centre	295 0792		Oasis	Nr Emirates Exchange	334 4227
DKNY	BurJuman Centre	351 3788			Wafi Mall	324 9074
	Deira City Centre	295 2953		Oui	Deira City Centre	295 3906
DKNY Jeans	Town Centre	349 7693		Part Two	Deira City Centre	295 0261
Donna Karan	BurJuman Centre	351 6794		Pierre Cardin	Twin Towers	224 7774
Escada	BurJuman Centre	359 1117		Polo Ralph Lauren	BurJuman Centre	352 5311
Esprit	BurJuman Centre	355 3324			Deira City Centre	294 1200
Etoile	Wafi Mall	324 0465		Pull & Bear	Deira City Centre	295 3525
Evans	Deira City Centre	294 0011		Replay	BurJuman Centre	355 3324
FCUK	Deira City Centre	295 0413		River Island	Deira City Centre	295 4413
Five Green	Oud Metha	336 4100		Rodeo Drive	Al Bustan Hotel	282 4006
Fleurt	Mercato	342 0906			Emirates Towers	330 3500
G2000	BurJuman Centre	355 2942		Sana Fashion	Al Karama	337 7726
Gerry Webber	Deira City Centre	295 4914		SP & Co.	Deira City Centre	294 8481
	Wafi Mall	324 3899		Splash	Nr Maktoum Bridge	335 0525
Giordano	Al Ghurair City	223 7904			Oasis Centre	339 0511
	BurJuman Centre	351 3866		Top Shop	Deira City Centre	295 1804
	Deira City Centre	295 0959			Mercato	344 2677
	Al Karama Centre	336 8312		Truworths	Deira City Centre	295 5900
	Wafi Mall	324 2852		Verri	Twin Towers	228 2262
Givenchy	Wafi Mall	324 2266		Villa Moda	Emirates Towers	330 4555
Guess	Deira City Centre	295 2577		Westwood	Deira City Centre	294 9292
Hang Ten	BurJuman Centre	351 9285		Woolworths	Deira City Centre	295 5900
	Deira City Centre	295 5449		XOXO	BurJuman Centre	355 3324
Hugo Boss	Deira City Centre	295 5281		Zara	BurJuman Centre	351 3332
Jaeger	Wafi Mall	324 9838			Deira City Centre	294 0839
JC Penney (Liwa)	BurJuman Centre	351 5353				

Shopping

What & Where to Buy

Not only is there the fabulous annual Dubai Shopping Festival (a month of sales held from 15th January to 15th February), but you'll get slashed prices in the end-of-season stock clearance sales too (the best times for these are August/September and January). And then after Ramadan, there's the Dubai equivalent of the post-Christmas sales back home, when the Eid sales begin.

Designer label fans should refer to the table in this section on [p.215]; it will guide you to the best places to find your favourite brands.

Computers

Other options → Electronics & Home Appliances [p.216]

Dubai is on track when it comes to the latest technology so purchasing a computer should be no problem. Many outlets sell computers and accessories, and there are even shopping malls devoted to computers and computer products such as the Al Ain Centre next to Spinneys Ramada or the Al Khaleej Centre across the road. Both these malls cater to IT boffins, and sell anything and everything related to computers and accessories. Or take a stroll along 'Computer Street' (at the other end of 'Bank Street', where you'll find many smaller outlets that specialise in selling in bulk. The price quoted is often a cash price only.

The UAE government, together with the BSA (Business Software Alliance) is clamping down heavily on the sale of pirated software. As a result, most computer shops are reputable and only sell genuine software and high quality hardware. If you have a problem with sub-standard computer equipment, and you don't achieve a satisfactory outcome after complaining directly to the shop, the Consumer Protection Cell in the Department of Economic Development should be able to assist. This can include arranging and overseeing meetings between the two parties, implementing fines and even arranging for the payment of refunds to be made at the Economic Department, leaving 'dodgy' shopkeepers little room for manoeuvre. Call 222 9922 or visit the Department's Website at www.dubaided.gov.ae.

Every October, Dubai is host to GITEX, the largest IT exhibition in the Middle East, [p.57]. This is the place to visit if you're really serious about the latest technology, and you'll find all the big names of the industry represented here. The

retail arm of the GITEX exhibition is the GITEX Computer Shopper, held at the Airport Expo Centre. So once you've cruised the stands at GITEX and written up your wish list, you can pop along to Computer Shopper and buy whatever gadgets your heart desires. You'll have to pay an entrance fee (around Dhs.15), but this is a small price to pay for access to a computer geek's paradise of special offers and amazing discounts. As with any 'special offer' though, it helps if you know the market before you buy – it's easy to get sucked in by offers of free mobile phones, printers or gift vouchers, only to find out later that you didn't get such a great price on that state of the art laptop after all.

Computers		
Al Faris Computers	Bur Dubai	393 3444
Aptec Gulf LLC	Al Safi	336 6885
Compu-Me	Al Garhoud	282 8555
Explorer Computers	Bur Dubai	393 4080
GBM Distribution	Jebel Ali	883 5652
Interdev Info Systems	Computer Street	351 4153
Jumbo Electronics	Media City	336 7999
PACC	Al Karama	337 0070
Plug-ins	Deira City Centre	295 0404
Redington Middle East	Khalid Bin Walid	359 0555
Seven Seas Computers	Opp. Al Nasr Cinema	308 3555

Electronics & Home Appliances

Other options → Camera Equipment [p.210]
Computers [p.216]

Both household names and less renowned manufacturers of electronics and home appliances can be found in Dubai. Prices are usually lower than in many parts of the world, although it might be worth comparing a few prices before you leave home, especially if you are buying a major item. There are so many shops here selling the same or similar items, so prices are pretty competitive. A bit of bargaining will reduce the price even further, although you probably won't have much luck trying to knock down the prices in the bigger shops, such as supermarkets. Warranties, after-sales service, delivery and installation should always be finalised before you hand over your cash. And if you're planning on taking an electronic appliance back to your home country, check first whether you are buying a model that will work there – televisions, for example, sometimes operate on different frequencies so what works in Dubai won't necessarily work in other countries, and vice versa.

Shopping

What & Where to Buy

Electronics & Home Appliances

Aftron	Al Futtaim Electronics	359 9979
	Deira City Centre	295 4545
Aiwa	Al Sayegh Bros	227 4142
Bang & Olufsen	BurJuman Centre	355 1162
	Town Centre	342 2344
Black & Decker	Jashanmal	324 4800
Bosch	Mohd Hareb Al Otaiba	269 1575
Bose	G & M International LLC	266 9000
Bowers & Wilkins	Archimedia	337 0181
Braun	The New Store LLC	353 4506
Elekta	Elekta Gulf	883 7108
General Electronics	Juma Al Majid	266 0640
Grundig	Agiv (Gulf)	223 2228
Hitachi	Eros Electricals	266 6216
Ignis	Universal Electricals	282 3443
JVC	Oasis Enterprises (LLC)	282 1375
Kenwood	Jashanmal	266 5964
Lenox	Eros Electricals	266 6216
Marantz	VV & Sons	353 2444
Palm P.xxx	Axiom - City Centre	295 1888
	Plug-ins	295 0404
	Jumbo	352 3555
Panasonic	Jumbo Electronics	352 3555
	Viking Electronics	223 8167
	Oman National Electronics	351 0753
Phillips	Agiv (Gulf)	223 2228
	Al Ghandi Electronics	337 6600
Pioneer	Agiv (Gulf)	223 2228
Popular Brands	Carrefour	295 1600
	Jacky's Electronics	282 1822
	Plug-ins	295 0404
	Radio Shack	295 2127
Russel Hobbs	Jashanmal National	266 5964
Samsung	Eros Electricals	266 6216
	Juma Al Majid	266 0640
	Samsung Electronics	222 5747
Sansui	V.V & Sons	353 2444
Sanyo	Agiv (Gulf)	223 2228
	Al Futtaim Electronics	359 9979
Sharp	Agiv (Gulf)	223 2228
	Cosmos	352 1155
Siemens	Scientechnic	266 6000
Simpson	Universal Electrical	282 3443
Sony	Jumbo Electronics	352 3555
Thomson	G & M International	266 9000
Toshiba	Al Futtaim Electronics	359 9979
Whirlpool	Al Ghandi Electronics	337 6600
Yamaha	Agiv (Gulf)	223 2228

Eyewear

Other options → Opticians [p.122]
Sporting Goods [p.230]

The sun shines throughout the year in these parts, so a good pair of sunglasses will become a very necessary accessory. You'll find just about every brand name here, as well as lots of cheap rip-offs – although these may look the part, they may not provide adequate protection for your eyes. You're better off spending a bit more for a pair of sunglasses with good quality lenses; make sure that they give UVA and UVB protection and are dark enough to shield your eyes from the sun's glare. If you need glasses for vision, most shopping malls have opticians that can perform eye tests, make prescription lenses and advise you on contact lenses. Some opticians will do an eye test for free, while others may charge you anything between Dhs.20 and Dhs.50.

Eyewear

Al Adasat Opticals	Lamcy Plaza	335 4006
Al Jaber Optical Centre	Al Ghurair City	224 9444
	Deira City Centre	295 4400
	Lamcy Plaza	336 0773
	Mercato	349 3938
	Town Centre	342 9933
Al Sham Optic	Oasis Centre	339 1193
City Optic	Deira City Centre	295 1400
Dubai Opticals	BurJuman Centre	351 0051
	Deira City Centre	295 4303
Fashion Optics	Jumeirah Beach Htl	348 6559
Grand Optics	Carrefour (Al Shindagha)	393 6133
	Deira City Centre	295 4699
Grand Sunglasses	Deira City Centre	295 5334
Lunettes	Jumeirah Centre	349 2270
Lutfi Opticals Centre	Wafi Mall	324 1865
Opic Gallery	Deira City Centre	295 3825
Optic Art	BurJuman Centre	352 8171
Sunglass Hut	Wafi Mall	324 4277
Top Visions Optics	Al Diyafah St	398 4888
Yateem Opticians	Al Ghurair Centre	228 1787
	BurJuman Centre	352 2067
	Emirates Towers	330 3301

Flowers

Other options → Gardens [p.218]

Dubai is home to a reasonable selection of florists, many of which sell dried flowers as well as fresh. Larger supermarkets (in particular Spinneys, Carrefour and Lifco) have in-house florists where you can buy anything from a few stems to an elaborate arrangement. Prices vary according to establishment, and the minimum order for local delivery is usually Dhs.100 per bouquet. If you need flowers delivered internationally (great for if you've forgotten all about Mother's Day), refer to the Yellow Pages, look for an Interflora sign in the window of your local florist, or get on the Internet and make someone's day with the click of a mouse. Try www.interflora.com or www.World-Florists.com.

Flowers

Blooms	Near Dubai Zoo	344 0912
City of Flowers	Jaddaf	324 3525
Desert Flowers	Nr Iranian Hospital	349 7318
Dubai Garden Centre	Sheikh Zayed Road	340 0006
Floramex		267 5850
Flower Box Intl.	DIC, Bldg # 13	390 1144
Gift Express	Jumeirah Centre	342 0405
	Magrudy's Centre	342 0568
Intraflora P.219	Sheikh Zayed Road	332 5333
Oleander	Next Mercato	344 0539
Planters	Opp Hamrain Centre	266 6427
Sentiments	Safestway	349 8969

Food

Other options → **Health Food [p.220]**

The groceries and supermarkets of Dubai have to feed many different nationalities, and most stock wide varieties of food items from all over the world. Prices vary dramatically; fresh produce is imported from other countries, and some items are double (or even triple!) what they would cost back home. However, standard, everyday items are usually reasonably priced, and if you're prepared to shop around or visit the markets, you'll find certain items very cheap. In particular, you should visit the Fish Market in Deira, [p.253] and the Fruit and Vegetable Market (now in its brand new location near Al Aweer) for good prices on fresh produce.

There are plenty of 'corner shops' in residential areas, which are handy for picking up milk and bread (although it's amazing how much they manage to cram into these tiny shops). Many shopkeepers will take orders on the phone for home deliveries. A lot of people do their grocery shopping at supermarkets like Spinneys and Choithrams (both have multiple branches), or Lifco, which has branches on Sheikh Zayed Road and in Al Garhoud. Spinneys is regarded as the most 'upmarket' of the supermarkets and stocks a range of products from the UK based high quality supermarket, Waitrose.

Park 'n' Shop, near Safa Park, stocks lots of goodies from the UK and USA and even if you don't live in the area, it's worth visiting for the excellent bakery and butchery. Carrefour, the French hypermarket chain, currently has two Dubai branches (Deira City Centre and Al Shindagha) and they sell everything from groceries and shoes to electronics and hardware, and Lulu's Supermarkets sell a similarly huge range of items.

Daiso, Lals or Fuji Mart (near Lamcy Plaza) are the places to go for Asian or Japanese food, and for a mouth watering selection of Lebanese treats, head straight for Goodies in Wafi City. Union Co-operative (Trade Centre Road) is a great bargain hunters paradise with clothes, food and homewares at discount prices. You can buy pork in Dubai, although only in designated sections of certain shops such as Spinneys and Choithrams.

Gardens

Other options → **Flowers [p.217]**
Hardware & DIY [p.220]

It's amazing how many plants can actually thrive in such harsh conditions, but with a bit of tender loving care and a whole lot of water, you can maintain a beautiful garden throughout the year. As more and more people start buying property in Dubai, and invest more time and money in their own gardens, you can reasonably expect the gardening industry to expand. The Dubai Garden Centre along Sheikh Zayed Road is a paradise of indoor and outdoor plants, garden furniture and accessories, plant pots, water features and irrigation equipment. Outside there is 2,000 square metres of shaded space, overflowing with plants and show gardens. Dubai Municipality Nursery, located just before the Garhoud Bridge towards Sharjah, is well worth a visit. It features lots of individual nurseries tightly packed into one big area, but don't worry if you don't know where to start, as they all sell pretty much the same things at identical prices. It's surprising how many varieties of plants can thrive in such arid conditions and the nursery sellers can advise you which plants and trees will suit your garden space or balcony. You'll also find a few roadside stalls, selling a variety of colourful pots and plants, along the Jumeira Beach Road.

Garden furniture can be bought at Royal Gardenscape (off Int. 4 on Sheikh Zayed Road), as well as at all the major furniture shops (see Home Furnishings, [p.220]), and certain supermarkets.

Add a little *colour* *to someone's life…*

Gardens

Dubai Garden Centre	Al Quoz	340 0006
Dubai Municipality Nursery	Al Jaddaf	na
Floramex	Al Qusais	267 5850
Pagoda House	Al Satwa	345 1963
Royal Gardenscape	Al Quoz	340 0648
Stone Gallery L.L.C.	Al Quoz	347 2525

Hardware & DIY

Other options → Outdoor Goods [p.228]

It is often cheaper and easier to simply hire a handy man (you'll find lots of guys waiting for work by their trucks near the back of Spinneys on Trade Centre Road) to do jobs around the house . But if you prefer doing it yourself, you'll be able to get all the tools you need to finish the job from hardware shops in Dubai. Ace Hardware stocks all the basics and much, much more - you'll find customised paints, glazes, electronic tools, gardening accessories, electric fittings and all the nuts, bolts, screws, nails and plugs you'll ever need. Alternatively, check out the main supermarkets (like Carrefour) and the various smaller DIY shops in Satwa or Deira.

Hardware & DIY

Ace Hardware	BurJuman Centre	355 0698
	Nr Oasis Centre	338 1416
Carrefour P.237	Al Shindagha	393 9395
	Deira City Centre	295 1600
Speedex	Nr Oasis Centre	339 1929

Health Food

Other options → Food [p.218]
Health Clubs [p.300]

Dubai is home to a high ratio of 'beautiful people' who swear by healthy eating. Specialist health food shops are becoming more common, and even regular pharmacies usually stock a range of supplements and vitamins. Major supermarkets sell some health food, and while you might not find everything you need under one roof, if you shop around you'll be able to collect all kinds of wheat-free, fat-free, gluten-free or organic items. In particular, try Choithrams for gluten-free bread, and Park 'n' Shop for a range of wheat-free breads (spelt or rye flour is used instead of wheat flour) and Spinneys has an organic vegetable range. If you're in need of a spring clean, you'll find a limited number of herbal liver, kidney and blood cleansing products, as well as some detoxifying products and a range of herbal teas in the dedicated health and

nutrition stores. Vitamins and minerals may be cheaper in your home country, so it's a good idea to bring a stockpile with you when you arrive.

Many of Dubai's sports shops now stock supplements for sports performance or slimming, from shakes to pills and energy bars to rehydration drinks.

Health Food

GNC	BurJuman Centre	352 6771
Healthy Eating	Nr Princeton Hotel	286 5777
Nutrition Centre	Jumeirah Centre	344 7464
Nutrition Palace	Crowne Plaza	332 8118
Nutrition World	Palm Strip	345 0652
Nutrition Zone	Jumeirah Town Centre	344 5888
Planet Nutrition	Deira City Centre	294 5889
	Spinneys	394 4108

Home Furnishings & Accessories

Other options → Furnishing Accommodation [p.100]
Hardware & DIY [p.220]

As the construction boom continues in Dubai and new villas and apartment blocks appear magically overnight (as do the people to fill them), it's high times for the home décor industry. IKEA needs no introduction as everybody knows that they cover just about all your furnishing and decorating needs. Other retailers that you are probably familiar with are Debenhams and Woolworths (the South African chain, not the British), both of which have small home décor sections. But Dubai is also home to other excellent furniture shops catering to all tastes, whether glitzy, gaudy, girly, glamorous or grand. The area between the third and fourth interchanges on Sheikh Zayed Road is where you'll find some interesting furniture warehouses, such as Stone Gallery, Pride of Kashmir, Nostalgia, Design People, The Loft, Cottage Furniture, Habitat, The Warehouse and Exotica. A must visit is

Making your house a home...

Home Furnishings & Accessories

Aati	Al Manzil Building	337 7825
Al Huzaifa Furniture	Zomoroddah Bld	336 6646
Al Jaber Gallery	Deira City Centre	295 4114
	Opp Hamarain Centre	266 7700
And So To Bed	Nr Burjuman Centre	396 2022
Antique Museum	Al Quoz	347 9935
Apollo Furniture	Sh Zayed Rd	339 1358
Art Of Life	Courtyard, The	340 6755
Bafco Trading LLC	Trade Centre Rd	335 0045
Bayti	Deira City Centre	294 9292
Bhs	BurJuman Centre	282 2555
	Lamcy Plaza	335 8334
Bombay	Wafi Mall	324 5255
Cane Craft	Al Karama	337 4572
Carpe Diem	Villa 145 A	344 4734
Carre Blanc	Deira City Centre	295 3992
Carrefour P.237	Deira City Centre	295 1600
Casa Marakesh	Wafi Mall	342 0981
Chen One	Century Plaza	342 2441
Cottage Furniture	Behind Gold &	
	Diamond Park	347 8228
Daiso	Lamcy Plaza	335 1532
Desert River P.415	Mazaya Centre	050 658 1641
Ethan Allen	Beach Rd, Jumeira	342 1616
Ethniture	Al Barsha	340 6515
Exotica	Al Quoz	340 2966
Fauchar	Wafi Mall	324 6769
Feshwari P.221	Nxt to Oasis Centre	344 5426
Georg Jensen	Wafi Mall	324 0704
Grand Stores	Al Garhoud	282 3700
Guess Home	BurJuman Centre	355 3324
Habitat	Jumeirah Plaza	344 7456
	Near Spinneys	340 4996
Harvest Home	Jumeirah Centre	342 0225
Home Centre	Mercato	344 2266
	Oasis Centre	339 5218
Homes r Us	Mazaya Centre	321 3444
ID Design	Sharjah Road	266 6751
IKEA I.B.C.	Deira City Centre	295 0434
Indian Village	Shk Zayed Rd	347 8335
Interiors	Al Karama	337 0116
JC Penney (Liwa)	BurJuman Centre	351 5353
Jotun Paints	Al Quoz	339 5000
Kas	Mercato	344 1179
Lalique	Wafi Mall	324 2556
Living Zone, The	Mercato	344 5994
Liwa	Deira City Centre	295 3988
Loft, The	Al Quoz	347 4255
Marina Gulf Trd	Al Barsha Rd P.iv	347 8940
Pan Emirates	Nr Oasis Centre	339 1910
Persepolis	Al Karama	334 2824
Petals	Courtyard, The	340 2201
Pier Import	Mazaya Centre	343 2002
Pride of Kashmir	City Centre P.xv	295 0655
	Mercato	342 0270

Home Furnishings & Accessories

Sara - Villeroy & Boch	Deira City Centre	295 0408
	Wafi Mall	324 0100
Showcase Antiques	Opp Dxb Municipality	348 8797
Tanagra	Deira City Centre	295 0293
	Wafi Mall	324 2340
THE One	Nr Jumeira Mosque	342 2499
	Wafi Mall	324 1224
Warehouse, The	Jumeirah Plaza	344 0244
Western Furniture	Nr Maktoum Bridge	337 7152
Westwood	Deira City Centre	295 5900
Wicker	Za'abeel Road	337 8888
Woolworths	Deira City Centre	295 5900
Zen Interiors P.205	Al Barsha	340 5050

Marina Gulf Trading in Al Barsha, which has grown from a dusty warehouse into a stunning showroom in the space of a few years. They specialise in wooden furniture, but have an excellent range of accessories too, and will arrange shipping if required. If you don't mind a hot and cramped environment, you can shop for Indian teak and wrought iron items, at reasonable prices, at Khans, Pinkies and Luckys in Sharjah. For something really original, Feshwari can custom make furniture according to your design (visit their Website at www.feshwari.com).

Of course, if you're on a tighter budget, you can always buy some items second-hand; Dubai's large expat population is very transient and there are always people wanting to sell their furniture when they leave. Look through the newspaper Classifieds, or

Interior Desires

If your interior design is lacking inspiration, then there are some excellent glossy magazines available to lend a hand. Emirates Home, Identity and Inside Out may just help you transform your home into a palace fit for a Sheikh!

check the supermarket noticeboards (where you'll often be able to see photographs of items for sale).

Kitchenware and linen can be bought at any of the main furniture shops, but you'll also find these items in certain supermarkets (like Carrefour and Lulu's) or department stores (like Debenhams, which offers a free personal shopping service if you book in advance; call 294 0011).

If you're getting married and then setting up home, register for gifts and avoid the 'six toasters' nightmare. Debenhams have a wedding service (although items can only be purchased at the store here and not via international outlets). THE One also offers a wedding gift registry service, all you have to do is pick out what you want, and they'll do the rest (345 6687)

The Fusion of Consumer Electronics and Personal Computing

Spectra

Entertainment PC
The Future of
Entertainment, Today

CE PC

Media Centre PC
The PC Revolution
Has Begun

PDA-Pocket PC
The World's Smallest PC,
GSM Phone & Camera

E500
PDA

Jewellery, Watches & Gold

Other options → Souks [p.252]

Dubai is renowned for its gold and the sheer amount of jewellers in the shopping malls and souks are evidence of this. Gold is available in 18, 21, 22 or 24 carats and is sold according to the international daily gold rate. In addition to the weight of a piece of jewellery you'll also be charged for craftsmanship, depending on the intricacy of the design. Jewellery comes in many shapes and forms, from Japanese cultured pearls to complex ethnic creations from India or Pakistan. Don't reach for your wallet until you've had a go at bargaining – if nothing else it's pure entertainment to watch the salesman whip out his calculator with a flourish and tap away like a mathematical genius to produce a discount of five percent! For a different shopping experience you should try the Gold Souk in Deira, [p.253], or the Gold and Diamond Park on Sheikh Zayed Road [map ref. 9-B2]. Most jewellery outlets can make up an original design for you, based on a photo or sketch. Check in advance whether there is any obligation to buy the finished item or whether you have the chance to opt out if you are not satisfied with the result.

Gallons of gold

Kids' Items

Other options → Clothes [p.214]
Family Explorer

A variety of goods can be found in Dubai for children of all ages, from nursery equipment and

Jewellery, Watches & Gold

Al Fardan Jewels	Deira City Centre	295 4238
	Hamarain Centre	269 9882
	Twin Towers	222 1222
Al Futtaim Jewellery	Deira City Centre	295 2906
Al Liali	Mercato	344 5055
Bin Hendi Jewellery	Deira City Centre	295 2544
	Jumeirah Beach Htl	348 7030
Breitling Watches	Deira City Centre	295 4109
Cartier	Emirates Towers	330 0333
Chopard	Wafi Mall	324 1010
Citizen	Nr Fish RA	271 5607
Damas Jewellery	BurJuman Centre	352 5566
	Deira City Centre	295 3848
	Gold Centre Bldg	226 6036
Espace Omega	Deira City Centre	295 3623
Fossil	BurJuman Centre	352 8699
	Deira City Centre	295 0108
Gold Souk	Nr Hyatt Regency Htl	na
Golden Ring	Deira City Centre	295 0373
Guess	Deira City Centre	295 2577
Mahallati Jewellery	Mercato	344 4771
Mansoor Jewellery	BurJuman Centre	355 2110
Paris Gallery	Golden Tower Shj	06 574 4000
Philippe Charriol	BurJuman Centre	351 1112
Prima Gold	BurJuman Centre	355 1988
	Deira City Centre	295 0497
Pure Gold	Mercato	349 2400
Raymond Weil	Deira City Centre	295 3254
Rivoli Group	BurJuman Centre	351 2279
Rossini	Deira City Centre	295 4977
	Wafi Mall	324 0402
Silver Art	Deira City Centre	295 2414
Swarovski	Wafi Mall	324 0168
Swatch	BurJuman Centre	359 6109
	Deira City Centre	295 3932
Tag Heuer	Wafi Mall	324 3030
Tiffany & Co	BurJuman Centre	359 0101
Watch House, The	Deira City Centre	295 0108

toys to the latest computer games and mini designer fashions. Toys range from very expensive to very cheap, but if you're buying toys for younger children you should probably stick to the reputable shops that are less likely to sell sub-standard items. The Bear Factory in Deira City Centre (295 9751) will definitely be a big hit with kids – here they can pick out a fluffy animal (from a variety including bears, camels, dogs, lions, cats, gorillas and giraffes), stuff it, insert a 'voicebox' (that plays a tune or even a recorded voice message), pick an outfit and accessories and even fill out the birth certificate. For more information on shopping for kids' items and other aspects of family life in the UAE pick up a copy of the Family Explorer guidebook.

Camel caravan

at affordable prices. Woolworths (the South African chain) and Debenhams in Deira City Centre stocks a good range of lingerie at excellent value. Marks & Spencer has stores in Deira, Wafi Mall, and Sharjah's Sahara Centre. Lastly, as long as you don't mind standing at the cash till with your smalls nestled among the weekly shop, well-regarded European labels Sloggi and Dim are available in many supermarkets. Park'n'Shop and the larger branches of Choithrams stock a range of styles at great value for money.

Lingerie

Bare Essentials	Jumeirah Centre	344 0552
Carrefour P.237	Al Shindagha	393 9395
	Deira City Centre	295 1600
Inner Lines	Deira City Centre	294 0011
Janet Reger	Emirates Towers	330 0660
La Belleamie	Beach Centre, The	349 3928
La Perla	BurJuman Centre	355 1251
La Senza	BurJuman Centre	351 5353
Marks & Spencer P.200	Salahudin Rd, Deira	222 2000
	Wafi Mall	324 5145
My Time	BurJuman Centre	351 3881
Triumph	Deira City Centre	295 2756
	Mercato	344 4707
Womens Secret	Deira City Centre	295 9665

Luggage & Leather

With the warm climate, leather clothing is not exactly in demand, but Dubai is a retail oasis and attracts international designer brands selling leather accessories from gloves and wallets to handbags, shoes and suitcases. The more expensive malls, like Wafi, house specialised

Luggage & Leather

Aigner	BurJuman Centre	351 5133
	Deira City Centre	295 4149
Aristocrat	BurJuman Centre	355 2395
Bally	BurJuman Centre	351 8129
Calonge	Al Ghurair City	228 4232
Chanel	BurJuman Centre	355 7388
	Wafi Mall	324 0464
Francesco Biasia	Mercato	349 9622
Furla	BurJuman Centre	352 2285
La Valise	Deira City Centre	295 5509
Leather Palace	Al Ghurair City	222 6770
	BurJuman Centre	351 5251
	Hamarain Centre	266 7176
Louis Vuitton	BurJuman Centre	359 2535
Mohd Shareif	BurJuman Centre	355 3377
Porsche Design	Deira City Centre	295 7652
Sacoche	Deira City Centre	295 0233

Kids' Items

Adams 0 - 10	BurJuman Centre	355 2205
Baby Shop 0 - 9	Al Karama	335 0212
Baby Shop, The	Deira & Oasis Centre	266 1519
Dar Al Tasmim Uniforms	Rashidiya Factory	285 9624
	Spinneys	394 1477
Early Learning Centre	Deira City Centre	295 1548
Kids R Us	Oasis Centre	339 1817
Little Me	Palm Strip	345 6424
Mothercare	Al Ghurair City	223 8176
	BurJuman Centre	352 8916
	Deira City Centre	295 2543
	Spinneys	394 0228
Ovo Kids	Deira City Centre	295 5900
Prémaman	BurJuman Centre	351 5353
Toys 'R' Us	Salahudin Rd, Deira	222 5859

Lingerie

Other options → Clothes [p.214]

Every designer name in lingerie is healthily represented in Dubai. So, if you are on the lookout for a few decent additions to a bridal trousseau, and money is no object, you'll find a proliferation of frilly and frighteningly expensive lingerie boutiques.

However, if you veer towards function rather than glamour, there are several noteworthy alternatives. In the past year or so, lingerie chain La Senza has opened branches in shopping malls throughout the Emirates, offering decent underwear and nightwear

Shopping

What & Where to Buy

leather shops such as ST Dupont's (324 2340), a Parisian boutique with exclusive prices. Louis Vuitton (359 2535) and Tod's (355 4417) are both found in the BurJuman Centre along with other expensive brand names, although prices are similar to the rest of the world. A more realistically priced range of luggage can be found in Carrefour. However, Dubai is near to places such as Pakistan, where the leather trade is known for its excellent quality and cheap deals. A good starting place for tracking down these bargain imports is Al Karama [p.162]. Designer copies can also be found in some stores, and although the quality can vary, if you find a good one you can hardly tell the difference. Always check the inside as well as the outside of the product for tears or snags and remember, the chances of an exchange or refund at a later date are pretty slim.

Maternity Clothes

Other options → Maternity [p.118]

Whilst Dubai doesn't have a huge choice for fashion conscious mums-to-be there are a few specialist shops worth visiting such as Jenny Rose (349 0902) and Great Expectations (345 3155). Branches of Mothercare, Marks and Spencer, Debenhams and Next also stock a range of maternity wear. For more information on all matters maternal check out the Family Explorer from Explorer Publishing - available at all good bookshops!

Maternity Clothes		
Formes	Wafi Mall	324 4856
Great Expectations	Palm Strip	345 3155
Jenny Rose	Beach Centre, The	349 0902

Medicine

Other options → General Medical Care [p.116]

In the UAE you are able to buy most prescription drugs over the counter. If you know what medicine you need it can save you the expense and hassle of going to a doctor, and pharmacists themselves are always willing to listen to symptoms and suggest a remedy. Remember to check the expiry date of medicines before purchasing, as well as the contradictions as pharmaceuticals are often given too freely. Most pharmacies also carry a variety of beauty products, baby care items, sunscreens, vitamins and perfumes. Each emirate has at least one pharmacy open 24 hours a day – the location

and phone numbers are listed in the daily newspapers. In addition, a Municipality emergency number (223 2323) gives the names and locations of 24 hour pharmacies.

Mobile Phones

Other options → Telephone [p.112]

A mobile phone is an essential accessory for almost every Dubai resident, and most shopping areas and malls seem to have at least two or three outlets selling a wide range of the latest models. All of the big electronics stores sell mobiles, as do Carrefour supermarkets. There are also many dedicated retailers such as Axiom Telecom with various branches. If you're in the mood to shop around and haggle there are bargains to be had in Bur Dubai around Al Fahidi Street and along Al Naif Road in Deira, but you may feel happier buying from a retailer with recognised after-sales service.

Mobile Phone Retailers		
Axiom Telecom	Deira City Centre	295 1888
Carrefour	Deira City Centre	295 1600
Jackys	Al Garhoud	282 2093
Jumbo Electronics	Wafi Mall	324 2077
Plug-ins	Deira City Centre	295 0404

Music, DVDs & Videos

Other options → Music Lessons [p.313]
Musical Instruments [p.228]

From boy bands to Britney, Arabic to Alternative, Bollywood to Hollywood, most music genres are available in Dubai. While the censors might stop anything too unsavoury coming in, you'll still find a surprising range of music and movies in the shops, although some of the less mainstream bands and films may be hard to find so there is always Amazon. Your first stop, particularly if you're looking for the latest releases or something a little more unusual, should be Virgin Megastore, which has several branches in Dubai. Alternatively, supermarkets often stock CDs, DVDs and Videos - in particular you should check out the range at Carrefour in Deira City Centre.

Although the Dubai Authorities are clamping down on piracy, you'll find plenty of shady characters selling fake DVDs. While the quality of some copies may be good, others are terrible so you just have to try your luck.

Videos are in PAL format, so make sure your VCR has a multi-format capability. You can rent videos and DVDs from rental shops around Dubai - you'll have to pay a hefty deposit but the actual cost of hiring is Dhs.4 - 10 for videos, and Dhs.10 for DVDs.

Music, DVDs & Videos

Al Mansoor	BurJuman Centre	351 3388
	Wafi Mall	324 4141
Al Meher Recordings		353 1278
Carrefour P.237	Al Shindagha	393 9395
	Deira City Centre	295 1600
Diamond Palace	BurJuman Centre	352 7671
Ohm Records	Opp. Burjuman Centre	397 3728
Plug-ins	Deira City Centre	295 0404
Spinneys P.225	Al Ghurair City	222 2886
	Mazaya Centre	321 2225
	Mercato	349 6900
	Nr Ramada Htl	355 5250
	Nr BurJuman Centre	351 1777
	Spinneys Centre	394 1657
Virgin Megastore	Deira City Centre	295 8599
	Mercato	344 6971

Musical Instruments

Other options → Music Lessons [p.315]
Music, DVDs & Videos [p.227]

Musicians may be disappointed with the limited number of outlets selling instruments in Dubai, but with the continuing retail boom each week seems to herald the opening of a new mall, so things are looking up. Sadek Music in the Souk Madinat Jumeirah stocks a good selection of both Western and Eastern instruments, as well as all the relevant accessories. The Music Room in the Beach Centre (Jumeira Beach Road) has a very wide range of sheet music for all instruments and styles, and the owner (an experienced British music teacher) will be happy to give advice on instruments and tuition. They also deal in Kawai and Steinway pianos, should you have an empty corner in your villa.

Musical Instruments

Fann Al Sout Music	Nr Fish R/A	271 9471
House of Guitar	Al Karama	334 9968
Melody House Musical Instruments	Opp. Hamarain Centre	227 5336
Mozart Musical Instruments	Al Karama	337 7007
Music Room, The	Beach Centre, The	344 8883
Popular Music	Wafi Mall	324 2626
Sadek Music	Souk Madinat Jumeirah	368 6570
Sound of Guitar	Naif Rd	222 1508
Thomsun Music	Nr. Mashreq Bank	266 8181
Zak Electronics	Za'abeel Rd	336 8857

Musical instruments

Outdoor Goods

Other options → Camping [p.263]
Hardware & DIY [p.220]
Sporting Goods [p.230]

Despite the humidity, sand and a few creepy crawlies, residents of the UAE are lucky to be able to spend most of the year outdoors, and off-roading and camping are popular pastimes for many. A weekend away is a peaceful escape from the chaos of the city although new camping regulations require permits, [p.74]. For most people, the lack of heat and humidity make the winter

Off-Road Explorer
Experience the UAE's delights off the beaten track. Designed for the adventurous, a brilliant array of outback route maps, satellite images, step by step guidance, safety information, details on flora and fauna, and stunning photography make this outdoor guide a perfect addition to your four wheeler.

months the best time to go. However, if you choose your location carefully – at altitude or by the sea – the summer months aren't always completely

Outdoor Goods

Ace Hardware	BurJuman Centre	355 0698
	Nr Oasis Centre	338 1416
Carrefour P.237	Al Shindagha	393 9395
	Deira City Centre	295 1600
Harley-Davidson	Shk Zayed Rd	339 1909
Picnico General Trdg	Jumeira Beach Rd	394 1653
ULO Systems Ltd	Sharjah	06 531 4036

Shopping

What & Where to Buy

unbearable. To kit yourself out with the basics for a night under the stars or just some gear to enjoy a few hours in the great outdoors, check out the following list of shops. You can get a good range of stuff, but specialised equipment might need to ordered online.

Party Accessories

Most major supermarkets and stationery stores sell basic party paraphernalia and if you go to specialised shops you'll find an even wider range. From cards, balloons, candles, table settings and room decorations to gift-wrapping and fancy dress outfits, bouncy castles and entertainers, the choice for both children and adult parties is comprehensive. If you want some inspiration for a child's birthday the Family Explorer guidebook has a dedicated Birthday Parties chapter.

Party Services (MMI)

Everything you need to get your party going! Wine or pint glasses, ice buckets, coasters, etc, are available from Maritime & Mercantile International LLC (MMI), which offers this service free of charge (no liquor licence required). Leave a Dhs.500 refundable deposit to use all the items listed below. A minimal breakage charge of Dhs.5 per glass will be deducted from the deposit, and items must be returned within five days. A party pack includes 24 pint beer glasses, 24 wine glasses, two ice buckets, two waiter trays, three bar towels and 24 coasters.

Party Accessories

Balloon Lady, The	Jumeirah Plaza	344 1062
Card Shop	Al Diyafah St	398 7047
Elves & Fairies	Jumeirah Centre	344 9485
Flying Elephant	Al Quoz P.273	347 9170
Gulf Greetings	BurJuman Centre	351 9613
In Disguise	Near Iranian Hospital	342 2752
Magrudy's	BurJuman Centre	359 3332
P.211	Deira City Centre	295 7744
	Magrudy's Centre	344 4193
	Spinneys	351 1777
Papermoon	Mina Rd, off Diyafah St	345 4888
Toys 'R' Us	Salahudin Rd, Deira	222 5859

Costumes/Fancy Dress

At present there is a limited number of costume and fancy dress shops. In Disguise, Satwa (342 2752) and Too Much Fun, Jumeira Plaza (344 1062), specialise in costumes and accessories, but why not make the most of Dubai's wonderfully skilled tailors? Let those artistic juices flow and

design your own costume; you never know, it could be the start of a whole new career as a fashion designer. Alternatively you may find a few gems in Al Karama markets - in fact 'Karama' fancy dress parties are all the rage!

Perfumes & Cosmetics

Other options → Souks [p.252]

Beauty in Dubai is big business, and whether the temperature goes up or down, there's always a busy trade in perfumes and cosmetics. You will find the latest additions to the market available in most main shopping malls. For a personalised fragrance, look out for the local perfumeries that are in every shopping area. Beware, however, many of these scents are rather powerful and only the slightest dab is needed – unless you want to ward off unwanted advances!

Perfumes & Cosmetics

Ajmal Perfumes	Al Ghurair City	222 7991
	BurJuman Centre	351 5505
	Deira City Centre	295 3580
	Emirates Towers	330 0600
	Hamarain Centre	269 0102
Areej	Emirates Towers	330 3340
	Mercato	344 6894
	Oasis Centre	339 1224
	Souk Madinat Jumeirah	368 6097
Body Shop	Deira City Centre	295 0701
	Jumeirah Centre	344 4042
Debenhams	Deira City Centre	294 0011
Jashanmal	Wafi Mall	324 4800
Lush	Deira City Centre	295 9531
MAC	Deira City Centre	295 7704
	Mercato	344 9536
	Wafi Mall	324 4112
Make Up Forever	Wafi Mall	324 2364
makeup etc.	Mazaya Centre	343 3531
Mikyajy	Deira City Centre	295 7844
Nature Shop, The	Deira City Centre	295 4181
Paris Gallery	Al Bustan Centre	261 1288
	BurJuman Centre	351 7704
	Deira City Centre	295 5550
	Hamarain Centre	268 8122
	Lamcy Plaza	336 2000
	Town Centre	342 2555
	Wafi Mall	324 2121
Rasasi	Al Ghurair City	222 9109
	BurJuman Centre	351 2757
Red Earth	Al Ghurair City	227 9696
	Deira City Centre	295 1887
	Mercato	344 9439
Virgin	Wafi Mall	324 4233

Shopping

What & Where to Buy

Second-Hand Items

Other options → Books [p.208]
Cars [p.214]

Rather than throwing out your unwanted clothes, shoes, books, kitchen equipment etc, why not take them to one of the second-hand shops in Dubai? Some of these shops operate on a charity basis, so you are doing a good turn, as well as clearing out your cupboards. For buying or selling second-hand items such as furniture, cookers etc, refer to the Classifieds section of the newspapers, supermarket noticeboards and the following table. For clothes, Dubai Charity Shop and In Disguise are worth a visit for their abundant selection of designer items for sale – most in excellent condition and at bargain basement prices.

Second-Hand Items

Al Noor Charity Shop		397 9989
Dubai Charity Assoc	Al Rigga Rd	268 2000
Holy Trinity Thrift Shop	Holy Trinity, School Rd	337 0247
House of Prose	Jumeirah Plaza	344 9021
In Disguise	Nr Iranian Hospital	342 2752

Shoes

Other options → Beach Wear [p.208]
Clothes [p.214]
Sporting Goods [p.230]

Whether your penchant is for Doc Martins, flip-flops or kitten-heeled mules, shoes come in as many shapes and sizes as feet do. Training shoes tend to be more reasonably priced in Dubai than elsewhere, although fashionistas may find that the styles are one season behind. All major brands are available at decent prices, but be warned - if you're shoe shopping in Al Karama and think you've just stumbled on the deal of a lifetime, remember this is the area for fakes.

Dubai: Tomorrow's City Today

A photography book that sheds light on the beauty and functionality of contemporary Dubai. Pages and pages of stunning images showcase the city's historical highlights, municipal successes and civic triumphs, making you wonder of the grandeur in store for the future.

Shoes

Shoes		
ALDO	Al Ghurair City	223 8851
	Deira City Centre	295 7885
	Mercato	344 7995
Aqua Shoes	Al Ghurair City	221 3340
Bally	BurJuman Centre	351 8129
	Deira City Centre	295 0240
Cesare Paccioti	Wafi Mall	324 3227
Domino	Al Ghurair City	221 0298
	BurJuman Centre	351 2321
	Mercato	344 9407
Ecco	Al Ghurair City	221 3340
	Mercato	344 3374
Escada	BurJuman Centre	359 1117
Florsheim	BurJuman Centre	351 5353
	Deira City Centre	295 3988
Marelli	Al Ghurair City	227 0933
Mario Bologna	BurJuman Centre	352 9726
Milano	Al Ghurair City	222 8545
	Deira City Centre	295 7492
	Mercato	344 9517
Nine West	Al Ghurair City	221 1484
	BurJuman Centre	351 6214
	Deira City Centre	295 6887
	Lamcy Plaza	337 4575
	Mercato	349 1336
	Oasis Centre	339 1779
	Town Centre	344 0038
Philippe Charriol	BurJuman Centre	351 1112
Rockport	Deira City Centre	295 0261
Shoe Bazar	Al Faheidi St	353 0444
Shoe City	Deira City Centre	295 0437
Shoe Mart	Lamcy Plaza	337 9811
	Nr Jumbo Showroom	351 9560
	Oasis Centre	338 0440
Valencia	Baniyas Centre	223 2772
	Deira City Centre	295 0990
	Jumeirah Centre	344 2032
	Twin Towers	221 6104

Sporting Goods

Other options → Off-Road Explorer
Outdoor Goods [p.228]
Underwater Explorer

Dubai is a great location for a variety of sports, from the popular activities such as tennis, sailing, golf or football to more unusual ones like sand skiing (check out the Activities chapter, [p.254] for more wacky and wonderful sports). Try the general sports shops listed below for items like squash racquets or sports clothing. Alternatively, there's a range of specialist sports shops around the city. Unless yours is an unusual sport in the Emirates or you require a more specialised piece of equipment, you shouldn't have too much difficulty in finding what you require.

See also: Canoeing (ULO Sharjah); Cycling (Carrefour, Future Bikes, Magrudy's, Pascal's, Trek, Wheels); Diving (see dive centres); Golf (Golf House); Ice Skating (ice rinks sell some equipment); Jet Skiing (Al Boom Marine, ULO Sharjah); Motor Sports (various shops on Al Awir Road); Sailing (Dubai Offshore Sailing Club, Jebel Ali Sailing Club, ULO Sharjah); Snorkelling (dive centres, Carrefour); Water skiing (Al Boom Marine); Windsurfing (Al Boom Marine, ULO Sharjah).

Sporting Goods

360 Sports	BurJuman Centre	352 0106
Adidas	Deira City Centre	295 4151
Al Boom Marine P.209	Jumeira Beach Rd	394 1258
	Ras Al Khor	289 4858
Alpha Sports	Deira City Centre	295 4087
Body Glove	Oasis Centre	339 0511
Carrefour P.237	Al Shindagha	393 9395
	Deira City Centre	295 1600
Dubike	Shk Zayed Rd	343 4741
Emirates Sports	Wafi Mall	324 2208
Golf House	BurJuman Centre	351 4801
	Deira City Centre	295 0501
	Lamcy Plaza	334 5945
Magrudy's Centre	Nr Spinneys	344 4192
Royal Sporting House	Deira City Centre	295 0261
Skechers	BurJuman Centre	352 0106
Sport One Trading	BurJuman Centre	351 6033
Studio R	Deira City Centre	295 0261
Sun & Sand Sports	Al Ghurair Retail City	222 7107
P.261	BurJuman Centre	351 5376
	Deira City Centre	295 5551
	Jumeirah Centre	349 5820
	Oasis Centre	339 5866
	Souk Madinat Jumeirah	368 6120
Trek Shop	Jumeira Beach Rd	394 6505
ULO Systems Ltd	Sharjah	06 531 4036
Wheels Trading	Shk Zayed Rd	331 7119
Wolfi's Bike Shop	Shk Zayed Rd	339 4453

Tailoring

Other options → **Arabian Souvenirs [p.206]**
Bur Dubai [p.156]
Clothes [p.214]
Textiles [p.232]

If you have all the creative flair of a fashion designer but none of the sewing skills, you can take your fabric to one of Dubai's many tailors and have something made to your specifications. Many tailors also provide an alteration service, sometimes while you wait depending on how busy they are. If you are new in Dubai, ask around for recommendations of good tailors, or some fabric shops can point you in the right direction. Most tailors can create an item by copying a picture or an original garment. When trying a tailor for the first

time, it's advisable to order only one piece to check the quality of the work. They will advise on how many metres of material are needed (buy a little extra to be on the safe side), and most provide the extras such as buttons, cotton and zips. Confirm the price (obviously the more complex the pattern, the pricier it will be) before committing, and make sure that it includes the cost of the lining, if appropriate. A good tailor should tack it all together so that you can have a trying on session before the final stitching. When it is finished, try it on again. Don't be bashful about asking them to put something right if you are not completely happy.

In addition to the numerous tailors are specialist embroidery shops catering mainly for the heavily decorated Arabic version of the Western style white wedding dress, although some will design more subtle specifications if instructed. The cost for embroidery depends largely on the intricacy of the work.

Tailoring

Al Aryam Tailor	Al Satwa	349 2434
Ali Eid Al Muree	Jumeira Beach Rd	348 7176
Couture	Deira	269 9522
Dream Girl	Meena Bazaar	352 6463
Eves	Nasser Square	228 1070
First Lady	Al Faheidi St	352 7019
Future Tailors	Al Satwa	349 8723
Garasheeb	Al Karama	396 8900
Hollywood Tailors	Bur Dubai	352 4243
Kachins	Meena Bazaar	352 1386
La Donna	Al Wahida Rd	266 6596
Ma Belle	Opp Buy & Save, Deira	269 6500
Monte Carlo	Behind York Hotel	352 0225
Oasis	Nr Emirates Exchange	334 4227
Regency Tailors	Bur Dubai	352 4732
Royal Fashions	Al Karama	396 8282
Sheema	Nr Astoria Hotel	353 5142
Tailorworks	Al Satwa	349 9906
Vanucci Fashions	Al Ghusais	263 2626

Textiles

Other options → **Arabian Souvenirs [p.206]**
Tailoring [p.231]

On both sides of the Creek you'll find plenty of fabric shops selling everything from the cheapest to the finest textiles. In particular, Cosmos Lane and Al Faheidi Street in Bur Dubai have an excellent choice of shops. The main road through Satwa also has a good selection. However, if you can't face busy, non-airconditioned areas of the city, most of the shopping malls have textile shops, although prices are generally higher.

Shopping

What & Where to Buy

Textiles

Abdulla Hussain	Al Ghurair City	221 7310
Al Masroor (Gents)	Deira City Centre	295 0832
Damas (Ladies)	Al Ghurair City	221 6700
Deepak's	Plant Street, Satwa	344 8836
Yasmine (Ladies)	Al Diyafah St	398 8476

Fabric shops in Satwa

Places to Shop

The following section includes Dubai's main shopping malls as well as a selection of some of the favoured smaller malls. It also covers the main shopping streets or areas in the city and the best souks.

Shopping Malls

The attractive, and often imaginatively designed, modern shopping malls in Dubai are one of the highlights of shopping here. They are generally spacious and airconditioned, offering a welcome escape from the heat. Here you will find virtually every kind of shop that you can imagine, from supermarkets or card shops, to clothes emporiums and specialist perfume shops. However, malls are more than just a place to buy goods; in the evenings and on weekends especially, the more popular malls are abuzz as people window shop, meet friends, drink coffee and people watch.

During the Dubai Shopping Festival and Dubai Summer Surprises, the larger malls are venues for special events such as dancing or magic shows. These performances are always popular and involve acts from all around the world. The malls also feature numerous raffles during these months – the prize for the lucky few is usually a car.

Most malls have foodcourts offering a wonderful variety of cuisine, from the ubiquitous hamburger to Arabic meze, Japanese or Mexican food. Some malls also have children's play areas, arcade games, and cinemas and most have convenient, extensive and free parking. The following are the largest and most popular malls in town. For more information about Dubai's shopping malls, visit www.dubaishoppingmalls.com.

Holiday crowds at Deira City Centre

Shopping

Places to Shop

Shopping Malls - Main

BurJuman Centre

Location ➔ Trade Centre Rd · Bur Dubai | 352 0222
Hours ➔ 10:00 - 22:00   Fri 16:00 - 22:00
Web/email ➔ www.burjuman.com   Map Ref ➔ 11-A1

This stylish centre has just raised shopping mall standards with the opening of its new extension (it's now nearly four times its original size and impressive in its design). BurJuman already had a reputation for being a superior host to many designer shops and the new space brings even more big name designer brands to the region. Joining the list are Hugo Boss, Christian Dior and Kenneth Cole to name a few, plus the anchor tenant Saks Fifth Avenue.

While it is definitely the place to go for pricey designer outfits, there are also shops of a more everyday nature such as BHS, Giordano, Next, Zara and Mango. There are also electronics, home décor and lifestyle shops. Two foodcourts offer diverse eating options, plus a big kids' area.

Dome Café on the ground floor of the original mall is a popular hangout for both residents and tourists, and in cooler months you can sit outside and watch the world go by. Within the mall, there are plenty of other cafés, all perfectly positioned for optimal people watching. Four basement levels provide plenty of underground parking.

BurJuman Centre

Books, Cards & Gifts

Al Jabre Al Elmiah Bookshop
Gulf Greetings
Magruly's Bookshop
Virgin Megastore

Clothes

Alain Manoukian
Banana Republic
Bhs
Burberry
Calvin Klein
Chanel
D&G & Dolce & Gabanna
Diesel
DKNY & Donna Karan
Elle
Escada & Escada Sport
Gap
Giordano
Guess
Kenzo
Levi's
Liz Claiborne
Mango
Massimo Dutti
Max Mara
Mexx
Morgan
Next
Paul & Shark
Paul Smith
Salsa Jeans
Zara

Department Stores

Grand Stores
Mohd Sharief & Bros
Saks Fifth Avenue

Electronics

Bang & Olufsen
Jumbo Electronics
Plug-Ins

Eyewear

Magrabi Optics
Optic Art
Yateem Optician

Food

Al Baiq (Lebanese)
Barista Café
Bateel
Belladonna
Chinese Palace (Chinese)
Dome Café
Fish & Co
Fujiyama (Japanese)
Gloria Jeans Coffee
Hediard Café
Japengo
Johnny Carinos
La Gaufrette
Lipton T Junction
Patchi
Paul Café
Sala Thai
Shamiana (Indian)
Starbucks
Subway
YoSushi

Furniture & Household

Ace Hardware
Kas Australia
Tavola
THE One
Villeroy & Boch

Jewellery & Gold

Damas Jewellery
Mansour Jewellery
Tiffany & Co.
Van Cleef & Arpels

Kids' items

Adams
Bear Factory
Du Pareil Au Meme
Early Learning Centre
Mothercare
Okaidi

Leather & Luggage

Aigner
Furla
Leather Palace
Louis Vuitton

Lingerie

Ines de la Fressange
La Perla
La Senza

Music & Videos

Al Mansoor
Diamond Audio Visuals
Virgin

Perfumes & Cosmetics

Ajmal Perfumes
Lush
MAC
Paris Gallery
The Body Shop

Services

Al Ghurair Int'l Exchange
BurJuman Pharmacy
Champion Cleaners
DNATA
Etisalat Payment Machine
Fun City
Fun World
National Bank of Dubai
Seconds (key cutting)
Xerox Emirates

Shoes

Aldo
Bruno Magli
Cesare Paciotti
Domino Shoes
Kenneth Cole
Nine West
Prada
Salvatore Ferragamo
Tods

Sporting Goods

360 Sports
Adidas
Nike
Sport One Trading
Studio R
Sun & Sand

Watches

Baume & Mercier
Cartier
Omega
Rivoli
Swatch
TAG Heuer
The Watch House

THE
FASHION
DESTINATION

Over 300 stores including: Saks Fifth Avenue, Christian Dior,
Hermes, Loewe, Versace, Christian Lacroix, Etro, Rodeo Drive,
Salvatore Ferragamo, Just Cavalli, Emanuel Ungaro, Moschino,
Van Cleef & Arpels, Baume & Mercier, Kenzo, Calvin Klein,
Celine, Tod's, Armand Basi, Marlboro Classic, Rolex, Zara, Mango,
Bang & Olufsen, THE One, Diesel, Laura Ashley, Virgin Megastores.

BURJUMAN

Deira City Centre

Location → Opp Dubai Creek Golf Club · Deira | **295 1010**
Hours → 10:00 - 22:00 Fri 14:00 - 22:00
Web/email → www.deiracitycentre.com   Map Ref → 14-D1

This is a major stop on every tourist bus route and attracts shoppers of all nationalities. Tourists will love the Arabic shopping experience in Arabian Treasures, which is well stocked with all the classic souvenir items like Arabian perfumes, pashminas, Arabic coffee sets, wooden carvings, carpets and the like. At one end of this mammoth mall is Debenhams, which is the only outlet to herald three shopping floors and has a great hidden away Starbucks on the third floor for a peaceful coffee.

The centre of the mall is dominated by a huge Carrefour hypermarket, which sells such a variety of items that you feel like you could spend half a day just browsing. The other end of the mall

houses IKEA, Arabian Treasures, Virgin Megastore and an 11 screen cineplex. There are two main food areas; a massive foodcourt on the first floor, specialising in fast food, and a strip of restaurants and cafés on the second floor offering slightly more comfortable sit-down dining.

There is also Magic Planet - a fantasy land of flashing lights, arcade games and fun rides for the little ones. The jewellery court features a whole row of reputed jewellers selling all things sparkly and also offering services such as jewellery design, manufacturing and cleaning/repairs. The rest of the outlets make up a perfect mix of fashions, stationery, gifts, designer outlets, shoes and sports, plus you'll also find several large electronics stores. Be warned though, this mall is so popular that thronging crowds are almost guaranteed and even though there is plenty of undercover parking, you'll still need luck on your side to find a spot at busy times.

Books, Cards & Gifts
Book Corner
Carlton Cards
Gulf Greetings
Magrudy's

Cinema
Cinestar

Clothes
Armani Jeans
Banana Republic
Bershka
Burberry
Calvin Klein
Diesel
DKNY
Forever 21
GAP
Gerry Webber
Giordano
Guess
In Wear
Karen Millen
Kookai
Levi's
Mango
Massimo Dutti
Mexx
Monsoon
Morgan
Next
Oasis
Olsen
Old Navy
River Island
SP & Co
Stefanel
Truworths
Westwood
Zara

Department Stores
Debenhams
Woolworths

Electronics
Aftron
Harman House
Jacky's Electronics
Jumbo Electronics
Plug-Ins
Radio Shack

Eyewear
Al Jaber Optical
City Optic
Grand Optics
Grand Sunglasses

Food
Al Safeer (Lebanese)
Cactus Cabana (Tex-Mex)
Chilis (American)
China Times (Chinese)
Cinnabon
Coco's
Costa Coffee
Fujiyama (Japanese)
Hatam (Persian)
L'Auberge (Lebanese)
Panda Chinese
Pizzeria Uno
Shamiana (Indian)
Starbucks
Subway

Furniture & Household
Al Jaber Gallery
Carre Blanc
IKEA
Liwa Home

Marina Gulf Trading
Pride of Kashmir

Hypermarket
Carrefour

Jewellery & Gold
Al Futtaim Jewellery
Al Mansour Jewellery
Damas Jewellery

Kids' Stuff
Early Learning Centre
Magic Planet
Mothercare

Leather & Luggage
Aigner
Aristocrat
La Valise
Porsche Design
Sacoche

Lingerie
Inner Lines
La Senza
Triumph
Womans' Secret

Medicine
New Ibn Sina Pharmacy

Music & Videos
Virgin Megastore

Perfumes & Cosmetics
Ajmal
Arabian Oud

Body Shop
Lush
MAC
Mikyajy
Nature Shop, The
Paris Gallery
Red Earth

Services
Al Futtaim Travel
Al Ghurair Exchange
Digiphoto
Minutes Shoe Repair
National Bank Of Dubai

Shoes
Aldo
Bally
Brantano Shoe City
Clarks
Ecco
Maria Pino
Milano
Nine West
Pretty Fit
Valencia

Sporting Goods
Golf House
Reebok
Royal Sporting House
Studio R
Sun & Sand Sports

Watches
Breitling
Raymond Weil
Omega
Swatch
The Watch House

Shopping

Places to Shop

WELCOME TO
UAE

8 Hypermarkets at your service!
....and more in 2005

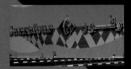

Deira City Centre
Since 1995
Tel.: 04-2951600,
Fax: 04-2951601

Ajman City Centre
Since 1998
Tel.: 06-7434111,
Fax: 06-7435200

Al Saqr Mall
Since 2000
Tel.: 02-4494300,
Fax: 02-4494364

Al Manar Mall
Since 2000
Tel.: 07-2285555,
Fax: 07-2270525

Sharjah City Centre
Since 2001
Tel.: 06-5332333,
Fax: 06-5398891

Marina Mall
Since 2001
Tel.: 02-6817100,
Fax: 02-6814266

Al Jimi Mall
Since 2001
Tel.: 03-7620044,
Fax: 03-7624151

Shindagha Market
Since 2002
Tel.: 04-3939395,
Fax: 04-3935604

A Majid Al Futtaim Group Company

Low Prices and So Much More!

www.carrefourme.com

Lamcy Plaza

Location ➜ Nr EPPCO HQ · Oud Metha
Hours ➜ 10:00 - 22:00   Fri 10:00 - 22:30
Web/email ➜ lamcydxb@emirates.net.ae

| 335 9999

Map Ref ➜ 10-D4

Lamcy is a five-storey mall with a variety of open plan shops selling fashions, shoes, sports equipment, books, jewellery and children's items all at affordable prices. Don't be deterred if on your first visit you can't even find the escalator to the second floor - once you get to know your way around the Lamcy labyrinth you'll love the fact that you can literally buy everything under one roof.

A recent addition to the mall is Japanese retailer Daiso, where everything costs just Dhs.5 (you do have to sort through a few tacky items, but there are some real bargains to be found here). The foodcourt is extensive and offers most cuisines, plus there is a Starbucks on the first floor and a stylish café on the second floor.   The entire fourth floor is a hypermarket selling everything from groceries to household items and linens.

An outlet worth particular mention is LouLou Al Dugong's on the ground floor; this children's play area is one of the best in Dubai. Lamcy also seems to have more sales than other malls and when they have a sale, they do it in price-slashing style.

The centre tends to get quite congested during peak times, and parking can be problematic (parking spaces are incredibly tight here, so if you have a large 4 wheel drive, you might need two spaces).

Lamcy Plaza

Books, Cards & Gifts	Food	Lingerie	Gift Wrap & Balloon Shop
Books Plus	Arrabiatta (Italian)	Daffodils	Traffic Fine Payment Machine
Carlton Cards	Bombay Chowpatty (Indian)	Dim	
	China Grill (Chinese)	La Senza	**Shoes**
Clothes	Hardees	Nayomi	Aldo
Benetton	KFC		Hush Puppies
Bhs	Kwality (Indian)	**Medicine**	Nine West
Bossini	Mongolian BBQ	Lamcy Pharmacy	Shoe Mart
Dorothy Perkins	Pizza Hut		Shoe Studio
Giordano	Starbucks	**Music & Videos**	
Guess	Thai Express	Al Mansoor Video	**Sporting Goods**
G2000			Athlete's Foot
Hang Ten	**Jewellery & Gold**	**Perfumes & Cosmetics**	City Sports
Jenyfer	Damas Jewellery	Paris Gallery	Golf House
Mexx for Less	Clio Jewellery		
Mr. Price		**Services**	**Supermarkets**
	Kids' Stuff	Al Ansari Exchange	Daiso
Eyewear	Adams	ATM Machines	Lamcy Hypermarket
Al Adasat Opticals	Giordano Junior	Emirates Driving Institute	
Al Jaber Optical Centre	Loulou Al Dugong's	Empost (Postal Services)	**Watches**
	Mothercare	Etisalat Bill Payment Machine	Rivoli
Electronics	Next for Kids		Swatch
Plug-Ins	Pumpkin Patch	Flower Shop	Watch House

Percept Gulf

Explore a world of international brands and new lifestyles at Lamcy

• More than 150 International Brands • 16 Multi-cuisine Food Court
• Host of services - Etisalat Bill Payment, Driving Institute, Postal Services, Money Exchange, Florist and more

The only
Air Miles Mall
in Dubai

**Open on
Friday Morning**

Get it all at Lamcy

Timings: Sat to Tue: 9.30am - 10pm, Wed to Fri: 9.30am - 10.30pm, **Food Court Timings:** 10am - 12 midnight, **Tel: 04-335 9999**

Mercato

Location → Jumeira Beach Road · Jumeira
Hours → 10:00 - 22:00   Fri 14:00 - 22:00
Web/email → www.mercatoshoppingmall.com/   Map Ref → 5-E1

|344 4161

This Renaissance style shopping centre certainly adds a bit of colour to the Beach Road, and is a worthwhile stop for those who love shopping. It contains over 90 upmarket outlets, as well as a Spinneys, a Home Centre and a Virgin Megastore. Other smaller outlets sell a range of items including accessories, lingerie, designer clothing and shoes. There is even a whole shop dedicated to Barbie. There is also a number of Arabian gift outlets and a large Early Learning Centre. Several entertainment options are crammed in too, such as a multi-screen cineplex and a children's play area, as well as several food outlets (Paul Café is worth visiting for a rest from shopping and a delectable treat from their patisserie).

Mercato Mall

Books, Cards & Gifts

Hallmark
Virgin Megastore

Cinema

Century Cinemas

Clothes

Amichi
Armani Jeans
Bershka
Diesel Jeans
Energie
Fleurt
Gianfranco Ferre
Hugo Boss
Mango
Massimo Dutti
Miss Sixty
Next
Polo Jeans Co.
Promod
Pull & Bear
Top Shop
Trussardi

Electronics

G&M International

Food

Chinese Palace (Chinese)
Cinnabon
Dolce Antico (Italian)
McDonald's
PAUL
Starbucks

Home Accessories

Bodum
Home Centre
KAS Australia
Pride of Kashmir
Susan Walpole
The Zone

Jewellery & Gold

Damas
Mahallati
Pure Gold

Kids' Stuff

Adams
Armani Junior
Early Learning Centre

Leather & Luggage

Francesco Biasia

Lingerie

Beyond the Beach
Nayomi
Triumph

Music & Videos

Virgin Megastore

Perfumes & Cosmetics

Areej
MAC
Red Earth
The Body Shop

Services

Al Wasl Pharmacy
ATM machines
Dubai Police Fine Payment Machine
Etisalat Payment Machine
Minutes Cobblers Shop
The Nail Spa

Shoes

Aldo
Ecco
Milano
Nine West
Pretty Fit

Supermarkets

Spinneys

Watches

Hour Choice
Rivoli

Get on the Bridgewalk at Mercato.

tep into another world at Mercato, with over 90 shops, restaurants, afés and entertainment outlets, including:

Spinneys • Century Cinemas • Virgin Megastore • Zone, Bodum, Bombay • Home Centre • Starbucks
Mango • Promod • Areej • Massimo Dutti • Fun City • Hugo Boss • Cerruti • Patchi • PAUL • GF Ferre
Pull & Bear • T. Store Trussardi • Armani Jeans • Diesel • Polo Jeans • Damas • Armani Junior
Francesco Biasia • Rivoli • Next • Argento • Topshop • Bella Donna/Second Cup • Milano • Nine West
MAC • Al Liali Jewellery • Bershka • Aldo • Pablosky • AGMC • ECCO • Early Learning Centre
prettyFIT • Energie • Miss Sixty • Red Earth • Costa • Costa/Mercato Nursing Room • Adams • Hip Hop
Mahallati • Pure Gold Jewellers • Hour Choice • Claire's • Rossini • TWS • Triumph • Pride of Kashmir
DOMINO • Fiesta • G&M International • Barbie Avenue • Hallmark • Beyond the Beach • Moda Brazil
KAS Australia • Fleurt • Nemo • Susan Walpole • Nayomi • Michie • Ivy • Maestro • Charabia • Mexar
Arabian Treasure • The Nail Spa • C'est L'amour • Tahran Persian Carpets & Antiques • VIP
Crystalline Trading • Dolce Antico • Le Mystique • Kashan Emporium Trading LLC • Syed Junaid Alam
National Iranian Carpets • Al Wasl Pharmacy • Al Thawb Al Watani • Cinnabon • McDonald's
Hardee's • Pizza Hut • Kentucky Fried Chicken • Chinese Palace • Subs & Salads • Milky Lane
Juicy Lucy • Castanea • Nutrition World • Champion Cleaners • Central Exchange • Photo One
Super Trim • Spinneys Book Shop • Spinneys Audio/Video Shop • Showtime Pay TV Service
Crepes de France Paris • The Body Shop • Al Jaber Sunglasses • Aqua Massage • Minutes "Cobblers Shop"
HSBC-Customer Service Centre and many other services.

MERCATO
The Good Life

meirah Beach Road, P.O. Box 755, Dubai, UAE. Tel: 04-344 4161, e-mail: mercato@emirates.net.ae
ww.MercatoShoppingMall.com

Souk Madinat Jumeirah

Location ➔ Souk Madinat Jumeirah · Umm Suqeim | 366 8888
Hours ➔ 10:00 - 23:00
Web/email ➔ www.jumeirahinternational.com   Map Ref ➔ 4-A2

Souk Madinat Jumeirah is an authentic recreation of an ancient marketplace with traditional Middle Eastern design, style and ambience. Shoppers enter a world of winding alleys and Arabian charm in this traditional bazaar-like atmosphere. It's great for souvenir shopping, and you'll also find electronics and furniture. Definitely check out the stands scattered throughout the mall – they offer everything from traditional Arabian sweets to jewelled purses.

Within and outside the souk are more than 20 waterfront cafés, restaurants and bars, plus 75 boutique-style shops and galleries. This is currently THE place to go in Dubai in the evening - especially during the cooler winter months, when the outdoor food and beverage outlets are filled to the brim with both residents and tourists. A nightclub, music club, amphitheatre and an indoor theatre located in the souk also host a broad range of entertainment options, including the annual Dubai International Film Festival.

Souk Madinat Jumeirah

Books, Cards & Gifts

The Camel Company
Gallery One (Photography)

Clothes

Beyond The Beach
Cotton Club
Crew Clothing
Ounass
Oxbow
Rodeo Drive Casuals
Tommy Bahamas

Electronics

Plug Ins

Eyewear

Yateem Optician

Food

Agency, The
Al Makan (Traditional Local)
Anar (Persian)
Barzar
Costa Coffee
Dome Café
Japengo

Left Bank
Meat Company, The
Noodle House
Pisces (Seafood)
Seattle's Best Coffee & Cinnabon
Shoo Fee Ma Fee (Moroccan)
Starbucks
Times of Arabia (Lebanese)
Toscana (Italian)
Trader Vic's
Trilogy (Nightclub)

Home Accessories

Al Jaber
Indian Emporium
Kashmir Cottage Arts
Marina Gulf Trading
Orient Spirit
Pride of Kashmir
Toshkhana

Jewellery & Gold

Damas
La Marquise Diamonds & Watches
Pure Gold

Kids' Stuff

Early Learning Centre

Leather & Luggage

Un Jour Un Sac

Medicine

Lifestyle Pharmacy

Music & Videos

Sadek Music

Perfumes & Cosmetics

Arabian Oud
Areej
Mikyajy

Services

Fotofun
National Bank of Dubai
N-Style Nail Bar

Sporting Goods

Sun & Sand Sports

Watches

Hour Choice
Rivoli

The Tale Of The New Arabian Legend.

It is said there is a place so lavish and so majestic that legends are born and you can experience tomorrow's history today. They call it Madinat Jumeirah – a stunning Arabian beach resort in Dubai. A monumental destination where the natural beauty of the region is captured in a re-creation of ancient Arabia. One kilometre of beautiful private beach borders two magnificent grand boutique hotels, Mina A' Salam and Al Qasr including 29 stand-alone Dar Al Masyaf traditional courtyard summer houses, the pinnacle of luxury and sun drenched spaciousness. At the vibrant heart of the resort, Souk Madinat Jumeirah, a shopping and dining experience unique in the world and a sanctuary of serene care and relaxation, the region's first Six Senses Spa.

Madinat Jumeirah®

المنتجع العربي · دبي
THE ARABIAN RESORT · DUBAI

Come Live The Legend.

جميرا انترناشـــونال
JUMEIRAH
INTERNATIONAL®

Experience authentic Arabia visit www.madinatjumeirah.com

Wafi Mall

Location ➜ Wafi City · Umm Hurair	**324 4555**
Hours ➜ 10:00 - 22:00 Fri 16:30 - 22:00	
Web/email ➜ www.waficity.com	Map Ref ➜ 13-D2

Possibly the most exclusive mall in Dubai, Wafi's four floors and maze of walkways are packed with trendy boutiques, luxury gift shops, coffee shops, designer food stores, home furnishings and many other smart retail outlets. A recent addition to the mall is a large Marks & Spencer, and a Pan Emirates Furniture will open early 2005. The large complex is topped by three distinctive glass pyramids and one wall frames a stunning stained glass window. The size of the mall can be a bit daunting, but there are plenty of location charts, so take your time. It can also be a little quiet, but possibly because there are so many other attractions just around the corner in Wafi City, such as restaurants, nightclubs, a health spa and a cinema.

For the kids, there's the popular Encounter Zone offering excellent activities, and children are well looked after if you want to leave them while you browse. Christmas is a particular favourite with shoppers as Santa welcomes the little ones and the decorations are spectacular - well worth a visit in their own right.

Wafi Mall

Books, Cards & Gifts
Gulf Greetings
Living Zone
Patchi
Petals
Sara - Villeroy & Boch
Swarovski
Tanagra

Clothes
Betty Barclay
Cerruti
Etoile
Gas
Gerry Weber
Giordano
Givenchy
Jaeger
Kookai
Marina Rinaldi
Miss Sixty
Olsen
Tally Weijl
Verri
Versace

Department Stores
Marks & Spencer
Jashanmal
Salam Studio & Stores

Electronics
Jumbo Electronics

Eyewear
Lutfi Optical Centre
Rivoli

Food
Asha's
Biella Caffé Pizzeria Ristorante
Elements
Renoir
Square, The
Starbucks

Furniture & Household
Fauchar
Frette
Pan Emirates
Petals
THE One

Jewellery & Gold
Chopard
Damas Jewellery
Mont Blanc

Kids Stuff
Imaginarium
Miki House
Osh Kosh B'gosh

Lingerie
Caresse
La Senza

Medicine
Al Sham Pharmacy

Music & Videos
Al Mansoor
Popular Music Institute

Perfumes & Cosmetics
MAC
Make Up Forever
Paris Gallery

Services
Al Ansari Exchange
Encounter Zone
Photo Magic

Sporting Goods
Emirates Sports

Supermarkets
Goodies

Watches
Chopard
Hour Choice
Omega Boutique
Rivoli
Swatch
Tag Heuer

Shopping

Places to Shop

Shopping Malls - Other

Al Ghurair City

Location → Al Rigga Rd · Deira | 222 5222
Hours → 10:00 - 22:00   Fri 14:00 - 22:00
Web/email → www.alghuraircity.com   Map Ref → 11-D1

This mall was first built in 1981 and started a shopping trend that would be followed at a furious pace in Dubai. It was refurbished in 2003, and now it houses an eight screen cinema, a Spinneys, a good range of shops (including several designer names) and four new restaurants. Hungry shoppers can choose their sustenance from a range of outlets offering seafood, Arabic, International or Oriental cuisine. For entertainment (aka something to keep the kids occupied), there's a huge Fun Corner. The multi-storey undercover car park holds up to 2,000 cars.

Other outlets include: Book Corner, Benetton, Bossini, Esprit, FCUK, Guess, Mexx, BHS, La Senza, Triumph, Plug-ins, Red Earth, Paris Gallery, Aldo, Nine West, Sun & Sand Sports, Swatch, Starbucks.

Beach Centre, The

Location → Nr Dubai Zoo · Jumeira | 344 9045
Hours → 09:30 - 13:00   16:30 - 21:30
Web/email → na   Map Ref → 6-B2

This is a large, airy mall featuring over 50 outlets selling goods ranging from books and furniture to jewellery, knick knacks and carpets, plus there is a pharmacy and an optician. There is also an Internet corner called Cyber Café – Training Zone (surfing and playing games cost Dhs.7.50 per hour). The Beach Centre is a good place to meet friends, shop and then sit and chat in the central coffee shop area, where the atmosphere is pleasantly sociable. Look for the blue glass building, to distinguish it from the 'pink' plaza (Jumeira Plaza) and Jumeira Centre further along the road.

Other outlets include: Bossini, Crystal Gallery, Dubai Desert Extreme, Hobby Land, Jenny Rose, Kids to Teens, Kuts 4 Kids, Music Room, Party Zone, Photo Magic, Sports House, World of Art, Yateem Opticians.

Boulevard at Emirates Towers, The

Location → Emirates Towers · Trade Centre 2 | 319 8999
Hours → 10:00 - 22:00   Fri 16:00 - 22:00
Web/email → www.jumeirahinternational.com   Map Ref → 9-C2

The Boulevard at Emirates Towers links two of Dubai's most impressive buildings, the Emirates Towers Hotel and Emirates Towers Offices. This exclusive, spacious and striking mall is home to a number of quality retail outlets, from expensive international jewellery stores to exclusive fashion boutiques. The evenings are more crowded with the novelty of licensed restaurants such as Scarlett's and The Noodle House, while The Agency is a definite after work hangout for the suave 'suited and booted' crowd. Back to the shopping, you can certainly give your wallet a work out with outlets such as Giorgio Armani, Bvlgari and Gucci to name but a few.

Other outlets include: Ajmal, Areej, Azza Fahmy, Bottega Veneta, Cartier, Custo Barcelona, Damas, D. Porthault, Ermenegildo Zegna, Europcar, Flowers@the towers, Galerie Hamadan, Emporio Armani, Grand Stores, Janet Reger, Jimmy Choo, La Casa del Habano, Lanvin, Michael Kors, My Fair Lady, N-Bar, Patchi, Persian Carpet House, Rivoli, Rodeo Drive, Safari Gems, Telefonika, Fron Fron, Villa Moda, Yateem Opticians, Yves Saint Laurent, Sergio Rossi, and the 1847 Male Spa,

Ibn Battuta Shopping Mall (Gardens Mall)

Location → Gardens, The · Jebel Ali | 882 1414
Hours → tbc
Web/email → www.gardensshoppingmall.ae   Map Ref → 2-A3

This shopping extravaganza (near the 6th interchange) due to open February 2005 will encompass 5.4 million square feet. Imitating Arabic folklore, shopping zones will honour the famous Arab explorer, Ibn Battuta, reflecting his travels through Egypt, Morocco, Persia, India and China. The mall will also feature the world's largest maze, encompassing over 1,200 metres, plus the region's first IMAX cinema alongside 20 other screens. There will be the usual host of international retail names as well as a hypermarket.

Jumeirah Centre

Location → Nr Jumeira Mosque · Jumeira | 349 9702
Hours → 09:00 - 13:00   16:00 - 22:00   Fri 16:00 - 21:00
Web/email → www.dubaishoppingmalls.com   Map Ref → 6-C2

This mall has exclusive ladies boutiques side by side with The Body Shop and Baskin Robbins. It's popular with Jumeira residents and prices are not the cheapest, but not overly expensive either. Stationery stores are well stocked and toyshops keep youngsters occupied, while adults shop for the latest watch designs, get their cameras repaired or browse for Persian rugs and unusual art. For those interested in natural healing, Essensuals on the first floor offers professional advice on aromatherapy. Elves & Fairies, a craft

and hobbies shop, is also located here and the Coffee Bean is great for a coffee to relax after all that shopping.

Other outlets include: Benetton, Blue Cactus, Caviar Classic, Cut Above, Flower Box, Kazim Gulf Traders, Lunnettes, Mothercare, Nutrition Centre, Photo Magic, Rivoli, Sun & Sand Sports, Sunny Days, The Barber Shop, Thomas Cook, Toy Magic.

Jumeirah Plaza

Location → Nr Jumeira Mosque · Jumeira | **349 7111**
Hours → 09:30 - 13:00 16:30 - 21:30 Fri 16:30 - 21:30
Web/email → www.dubaishoppingmalls.com   Map Ref → 6-C2

Commonly called the 'pink plaza', this pink stone and glass building along the Beach Road contains some hidden away gems that are definitely worth a good browse. Right in the middle of the ground floor you'll find a children's play area and a Dome Café, surrounded by some interesting home décor shops full of beautiful trinkets from around the world. There is also Brush N Bisque-it, where you can handpaint ceramic items, and House of Prose, an excellent second-hand bookshop. The Plaza hosts regular art exhibitions and houses a Dubai International Arts Centre outlet. You can even renew your driver's licence and pay your traffic fines at a small branch of the Dubai Police here (good for avoiding the queues at the main branch).

Other outlets include: Balloon Lady, Girls' Talk Beauty Centre, Heatwaves, Kashmir Craft, Susan Walpole and Safeplay.

Oasis Centre

Location → Oasis Centre · Al Quoz | **339 5459**
Hours → 10:00 - 22:00   Fri 16:00 - 22:00
Web/email → www.landmarkgroupco.com   Map Ref → 5-A4

One of the calmer malls in terms of parking and shopping, the Oasis Centre nevertheless offers a good range of shops in its compact design. It has a number of huge superstores, but is probably best known for Home Centre, The Baby Shop (a good and cheaper alternative to Mothercare), Lifestyle (a gift shop with a vast range of items at fantastic prices) and a large Shoe Mart, which is guaranteed to satisfy even the strongest shoe fetish. The mall is a good family venue with two excellent children's areas; Fun City for youngsters, and Cyborg – a busy (noisy) cave-like area that boasts a ten-pin bowling alley and several karaoke booths among its neon attractions. If you're peckish, choose between the small Jungle food court or La Fontana, which is open plan and ideal for those who like to watch the world go by.

Other outlets include: Books Plus, Areej, Petland, Gulf Greetings, Nine West, Splash, Sun & Sand Sports.

Palm Strip

Location → Opp Jumeira Mosque · Jumeira | **346 1462**
Hours → 10:00 - 22:00   Fri 13:30 - 22:00
Web/email → www.dubaishoppingmalls.com   Map Ref → 6-D2

Located on the Beach Road, this open fronted mall is a small but pleasant place for a stroll around the shops or to catch up on emails over a coffee at F1 Net Café. The shady frontage has easy access to a range of upmarket stores, mainly selling designer labels and other familiar fashion names, such as Mango. It also features N-Bar, Dubai's first walk-in nail bar, where you can get a quick manicure or pedicure without having to make an appointment (although sometimes you may have to wait). If you don't manage to get a parking in the front of the mall, try the underground car park which has an entrance round the side. Although Palm Strip is fairly quiet during the day, it perks up a bit in the cooler evenings when Japengo Café becomes an ideal location for alfresco dining and to enjoy the magnificent view of the Jumeira Mosque.

Other outlets include: Escada Sport, Giano Franco Ferre Studio, Oceano, Little Me, Beyond the Beach, Elite Models, Barcelona Shoes and Starbucks.

Sales abound in Dubai

Reef Mall

Location → Salahuddin Street · Deira | **224 2240**
Hours →   na
Web/email → infodesk1@reefmall.ae   Map Ref → 11-E1

The Reef Mall is Deira's newest landmark, having opened in late 2004. It is conveniently located next

Shopping

Places to Shop

Who's place will you visit next?

Home Centre, Glitter, Mr. Price, The Athlete's Foot, Splash...

...Shoe Mart, Lifestyle, Babyshop, Bossini, Karisma or Al Maya Supermarket. Yes, all your favourite brands have moved in next door to you at the new Reef Mall, Deira. Looks like it's time to pay your neighbour a visit.

REEF MALL
Your neighbour in Deira
Salahuddin Street, Tel: 04 2242240

to Marks & Spencer and Toys R Us, and features well known shops such as Home Centre, Lifestyle, Splash and The Baby Shop. There is also a huge Fun City play centre for the kids.

Other outlets include: Damas, Grand Optics, Oriental Stores, Karisma, Oasis Greetings, Hour Choice, Plug-ins, Jumbo Electronics, The Athlete's Foot, Bossini, Nine West, McDonald's and Dome Café.

Town Centre

Location → Jumeira Beach Road · Jumeira | **344** 0111
Hours → 10:00 - 22:00 Fri 17:00 - 22:00
Web/email → www.towncentrejumeirah.com   Map Ref → 5-E1

The shops within this community mall sell everything from clothes to jewellery. One of the more interesting outlets is Café Ceramique, where adults can enjoy a coffee while kids concentrate on painting their own piece of pottery. If you're looking for an unforgettable gift for grannies and granddads, this is where you should go to get mugs featuring hand or footprints of their treasured grandchildren. The mall is a haven for those needing some relaxation and pampering - it houses a Nail Station, Kaya Beauty Centre and Feet First (reflexology for both men and women). On a practical level there's an Empost, an electronic Etisalat machine for paying phone bills, and a payment machine for traffic fines.

Other outlets include: Al Jaber Optical, Bang & Olufsen, Bateel, Books Plus, Bayti, Calonge, Café Moka, Damas, DKNY, Marie Claire, Nine West, Nutrition Zone, Papermoon, Paris Gallery, Simply Healthy, and World of Pens.

Town Centre

Shopping Malls - Other

Al Ain Centre	Nr Ramada Htl	351 6914
Al Bustan Centre	Nr Al Mulla Plaza	263 0000
Al Ghurair City	Al Rigga Rd	222 5222
Al Hana Centre	Al Mankhool Rd	398 2229
Al Khaleej Centre	Opp Ramada Htl	355 5550
Al Manal Centre	Deira, Naif Road	227 7701
Al Mulla Plaza	Dubai - Sharjah Rd	298 8999
Al Rais Centre	Opp Ramada Htl	352 7755
Beach Centre, The	Nr Dubai Zoo	344 9045
Bin Sougat Centre	Airport Rd	286 3000
Boulevard at Emirates Towers, The		319 8999
BurJuman Centre P.235	Trade Centre Rd	352 0222
Century Mall	Al Mamzar area	296 6188
Century Plaza	Jumeirah Beach Rd	349 8062
Deira City Centre P.xix	Al Garhoud	295 1010
Galleria	Hyatt Regency	209 6000
Gold & Diamond Park	Shk Zayed Rd	347 7788
Hamarain Centre	Nr JW Marriott Htl	262 1110
Holiday Centre	Trade Centre 1 & 2	331 7755
Jumeirah Centre	Nr Jumeira Mosque	349 9702
Jumeirah Plaza	Nr Jumeira Mosque	349 7111
Al Karama Centre	Al Karama	337 4499
Lamcy Plaza P.239	Nr EPPCO HQ	335 9999
Magrudy's Centre	Jumeira Beach Rd	344 4192
Mazaya Centre	Mazaya Centre	343 8333
Mercato P.241	Jumeira Beach Road	344 4161
Oasis Centre	Oasis Centre	339 5459
Palm Strip	Opp Jumeira Mosque	346 1462
Reef Mall P.249	Salahuddin Street	224 2240
Souk Madinat Jumeirah P.243	Umm Suqeim	366 8888
Spinneys	Spinneys Centre	394 1657
Town Centre	Jumeira Beach Road	344 0111
Twin Towers	Nr Htl Inter-Continental	221 8833
Village Mall, The P.251	Beach Road	344 7714
Wafi Mall P.245	Oud Metha	324 4555

Village Mall, The

Location → Beach Road · Jumeira | **344 7714**
Hours → na
Web/email → enquiries@thevillagedubai.com   Map Ref → 6-C2

The Village is Jumeira Beach Road's latest shopping addition, but with a twist - rather than being just a run-of-the-mill mall, it has more of a community feel with niche boutiques and cobble-stoned corridors. Great for those in hot pursuit of cool beachwear, funky interior designs and materials, or a good dose of pampering, The Village also features healthy eats at Shakespeare & Co, Thai Time, The Village Kitchen or Tony's New York Deli. One floor up from the shops is the Better Homes office, the French Medical Clinic, Gulf American Clinic, Jumeirah American Clinic and SensAsia Urban Spa.

The القرية Village

Mediterranean city boutiques in a continental setting.

The Mediterranean people are famous for their high quality of life and cosmopolitan passion for all things good. Inspired by this, The Village brings the Mediterranean to your doorstep. The finest selection of shops and dining to match your lifestyle. Select clothing, eclectic home furnishings, health facilities and international cuisine.

The Village, Beach Road, Jumeirah
email: enquiries@thevillagedubai.com
tel: (04) 344 7714 fax: (04) 349 6026

betterhomes
and properties

Other outlets include: Books Gallery, Candella Clothing, Edouard Rambaud Designs, Emilio Robba Flowers, Exotica Flowers, Irony Home, Julian Hairdressing for Men, Magrabi Optical, Offshore Legends, OXBOW Sportswear, Peekaboo, S*uce, Sisters Beauty Lounge, Tayyiba Beachwear.

Streets/Areas to Shop

Other options → **Al Karama [p.162]**
Al Satwa [p.166]
Bur Dubai [p.158]

Al Diyafah Street

Location → Nr Jumeira Rotana Htl · Al Satwa | na
Hours → 09:00 - 14:00 16:00 - 21:30
Web/email → na   Map Ref → 7-A3

Al Diyafah Street is fondly known as 'uptown Satwa' to residents, as opposed to the cheaper shopping area around the corner ('downtown Satwa'). You can buy lots of things here, from silk carpets to unusual gift items. Just be prepared though; for some reason this area has a high shop turnover and what was there yesterday may not be there tomorrow. This is the street to be on if you need to hire formal evening wear (men's or ladies'). You can try either Elegance or Formal Wear, or if you have time to have something made, downtown Satwa has numerous fabric shops and tailors who can knock something up for you. On cooler evenings, this is a great place for a window-shopping stroll and a bite to eat; you can enjoy some of the best Lebanese food in Dubai at Al Mallah, savour the delicious pizzas in Round Table, or sample the fare in one of the other numerous food outlets along the road.

Al Faheidi Street

Location → Nr Astoria Htl · Bur Dubai | na
Hours → 08:00 - 13:30 16:00 - 21:30
Web/email → na   Map Ref → 8-A2

This busy street in Bur Dubai is definitely the place to visit when you're looking for electronic goods. Here you'll find brand names such as Canon, Sony, Panasonic, JVC, Sharp, Phillips, Grundig, and GEC, at negotiable prices. Don't make your purchase at the first shop you come to, instead take time to look around and discover the best range and price. It gets busy in the evenings, especially with tourists hunting for bargains, so you may have a bit of difficulty when it comes to parking. The Thomson shop has a large choice of cheap original cassettes and inexpensive CDs. Thomas Cook Al Rostamani is the place to go to change your currency at a favourable rate, and plenty of restaurants are on hand to replenish you after a hectic session of haggling. These include Talk of the Town for Chinese and Indian food, Bananas for a decent pizza, as well as the various outlets at the nearby Astoria and Ambassador hotels.

Al Karama Shopping Complex

Location → Shopping Area · Al Karama | na
Hours → 08:30 - 14:00 16:00 - 22:00
Web/email → na   Map Ref → 10-D2

This long street running through the middle of Al Karama has veranda covered shops on both sides enticing you to 'buy, buy, buy' cheap goods at below average prices. Browse through mix n' match ideas direct from the Far East – there's sports apparel, t-shirts, shorts, sunglasses, shoes, gifts and all the usual souvenirs (fluffy camels, shisha pipes, pashminas, etc). Or dive into a sea of fake designer accessories – stores are packed to the gills with faux Gucci, Prada and Chanel handbags for the women, and Rolexes and Breitlings galore for the men. The sale of fake watches is a particularly clandestine affair, and if you show interest you'll be whisked into a back room to view the goods! Several small restaurants in the area offer Indian, Pakistani, Filipino and Arabic cuisine – it's good food at amazingly cheap prices. For the daring, the fish market offers fresh hammour and other varieties of fish, prawns, and crabs, while at the fruit and vegetable shops you can choose from a variety of regular and special items.

Souks

Other options → **Bargaining [p.204]**
Bur Dubai [p.158]
Deira [p.156]

Souks are Arabic markets where all kinds of goods are bought, sold and exchanged. Traditionally, dhows from the Far East, China, Ceylon and India would offload their cargoes, and the goods would be haggled over in the souks adjacent to the docks. Over the years, the items on sale have changed dramatically from spices, silks and perfumes to include electronic goods and the latest kitsch consumer trends. Although Dubai's souks aren't as fascinating as others in the Arab world, such as Marrakech in Morocco or Mutrah in Oman, they are worth a visit for their bustling atmosphere, the eclectic variety of goods and the traditional way of doing business.

Shopping

Places to Shop

The myriad of souks are located on both banks of the Creek, but predominantly in Deira (it's worth exploring both sides if you have the time). You can cross between the two banks of the Creek in about ten minutes on an abra (a small wooden water-taxi); it only costs 50 fils. Alternatively, most taxi drivers know where to go if you ask for a specific souk and the fares are reasonable. If you have the time, why not brave the public transport. Bus numbers 5, 16, 19 and 20 run frequently throughout the day and stop at all of the souks, both sides of the Creek.

It is wise to visit when the weather is a little cooler in the late afternoon, but for early birds the souks open 07:00 - 12:00. They then re-open around 17:00 - 19:00, every day except Friday, when they only open in the afternoon. Thursday and Friday evenings are the busiest times. This is a great time to see the souk trading at full throttle, but if you are more interested in exploring at a leisurely pace then these evenings are best avoided.

Fish Market

Location ➜ Nr Shindagha Tunnel · Deira	na
Hours ➜ 07:00 - 23:00	
Web/email ➜ na	Map Ref ➜ 8-C2

It may be a little on the smelly side but the fish market is worth a trip for a few snapshots to show the folks at home. The variety of fresh fish is amazing and you will most likely come across some species that you've never seen (let alone eaten) before. It isn't just the display of fish; the cleaning and gutting activity and the bargaining process is quite fascinating too. The market has undergone a revamp in a bid to accentuate the fishing heritage of the region and also to educate tourists. Besides a seafood restaurant, a museum explains the history of the fishing village Dubai once was.

Gold Souk

Location ➜ Nr Hyatt Regency Htl · Deira	na
Hours ➜ 09:30 - 13:00 16:00 - 22:00	
Web/email ➜ na	Map Ref ➜ 8-C2

Even if you're not interesting in buying the Gold Souk is still worth a visit. The souk is a labyrinth of back streets lined with shops selling all that glitters. In the past it was worth buying gold in the souk for the bargain prices, although these days you're just as likely to get the same price at the jewellery shops located in Dubai's shopping malls. Your bargaining power is greater at the souk though, so brush up on your negotiating skills.

Apart from gold, you'll also find diamonds, rubies, emeralds, opals, amethysts and pearls, which can be bought as they are or in a variety of settings.

Souk Madinat Jumeirah

Location ➜ Umm Suqeim	366 8888
Hours ➜ na	
Web/email ➜ www.jumeirahinternational.com	Map Ref ➜ 4-A2

Please see review under Main Shopping Malls [p.234].

Spice Souk

Location ➜ Deira	na
Hours ➜ na	
Web/email ➜ na	Map Ref ➜ 8-C2

The Spice Souk has narrow streets and an aroma so unique, it's like walking into another era. The place seems to have downsized in the past few years, and the rows of stalls displaying spice laden sacks are fast diminishing. Although spices are still available in a few shops, the souk is now home to an increasing number of cheap electronic goods and wholesale shoes. Perhaps the slow demise is due to more and more supermarkets supplying a wider range of spices. Carrefour in Deira City Centre has a whole section dedicated to exotic spices, and although the choice is good, it lacks the atmosphere of the souk. The souk vendors are only too happy to chat endlessly, advising you on the various spices and herbs. Although most of the stalls stock the same basic items, you'll be able to pick up expensive spices, such as saffron, at bargain prices.

Textile Souk

Location ➜ Nr Creekside · Bur Dubai	na
Hours ➜ 09:00 - 13:00 16:00 - 22:00	
Web/email ➜ na	Map Ref ➜ 8-A2

The Textile Souk in Bur Dubai is a treasure trove of colours, textures and weaves from around the world. You'll find thin voile adorned with shimmering threads, broderie anglaise, satin, silk and velvet in abundance, although good drill cottons are sometimes harder to come by. Shop around as the choice is virtually unlimited and prices are negotiable. Sales occur quite frequently in this area, particularly around major holidays and the Dubai Shopping Festival.

Shopping

Places to Shop

MacKenzie Associates

SPECIALIST DECORATION

MURALS • SPECIALIST PAINTING • CREATIVE COMMISSIONS

PO Box 34275, Dubai, UAE • Tel +971 50 453 4232

Activities
EXPLORER

Activities

Table of Contents

Activities

What's new?

Fore!
Page 274

It seems that Dubai's developers have a checklist when it comes to new construction projects - housing, a shopping mall, and a new golf course. As a result there are more and more opportunities for golfers of all abilities to hit the fairways. With championship courses on virtually every doorstep, if you haven't got into the swing of all things golf yet, it's about time you start!

Sports & Activities

Despite first impressions, life in Dubai is not all shopping malls, restaurants, and five star hotels. No matter what time of year, visitors and residents can try their hand at a wide range of activities. Warm winters provide the perfect environment for all manner of outdoor activities, while a host of diversions are available to take your mind off the extreme heat and humidity of the summer. From climbing on an indoor training wall to flower arranging or yoga classes, the fun doesn't have to stop when the tarmac starts melting. Even the heat of the summer doesn't stop some sports enthusiasts sailing the Gulf or hitting the greens regardless of the 48° C temperature.

When the weather does start to cool, Dubai and the surrounding emirates are ideal for athletes and outdoor enthusiasts, with every sport under the sun (or the sports hall roof) being played by would-be professionals and those out for a bit of fun. Traditional favourites such as tennis, golf (on idyllically manicured courses), rugby and cricket are enjoyed, both informally by friends and families and more competitively in local clubs. For the more adventurous there's always skydiving, rock-climbing, mountain biking, hashing and caving, with all the necessary equipment available in sports shops, refer to Sporting Goods [p.230].

With a sprawling coastline of crystal clear waters and a plethora of exhilarating water parks, as well as the endless luxurious hotel pools, it's no surprise that Dubai embraces aqua life. Scuba diving is probably the most popular water sport, followed by sailing, surfing, water-skiing, and the new kiteboarding craze. Keep in mind that while the Gulf waters often seem tranquil, rip tides do occur and there are a few stingrays and jellyfish. At beach parks, pay attention to the lifeguard's flag (if it's red, stay out of the sea), but if you're at one of the public beaches be aware of possible dangers.

While the azure shoreline of the Arabian Gulf is one of Dubai's main attractions, the endless desert plains and mountainous wilderness add to the appeal of this unique emirate. Whether you decide to go desert driving, wadi-bashing, camping, hiking, rock climbing or all of the above, the *Off-Road Explorer (UAE)* will keep you in good stead. It has 20 detailed routes, stunning photographs, detailed satellite imagery, GPS co-ordinates and information and photos of the flora and fauna you can expect to see along the way.

With so many different nationalities and cultures at play in Dubai, most interests are covered. Sometimes word of mouth is the best way of discovering that there are others that share your passion. If you can't find an existing club, you could always start your own. We are always looking for new activities, so if you belong to any club, organisation, or group - official or unofficial - we'd love to hear from you. See the Reader Profile Survey on our Website (www.Explorer-Publishing.com) and give us your comments and details - it's free.

Oops!

Did we miss anything out? If you have any thoughts, ideas or comments for us to include in the Activities section, drop us a line. If your club or organisation isn't in here, let us know and we'll shout your name from the rooftops (or at least include your details in our next edition). Visit www.Explorer-Publishing.com and say whatever's on your mind... we're listening!

Fitness Help

Can't seem to take out time for the gym? Why not hire a personal trainer. There are plenty of fitness gurus advertising privately. They will pop over and set you on the road to body sculpting success with your very own tailor made fitness programme. For information and contacts, check out the classifieds of the daily newspapers, or refer to any of Dubai's monthly magazines.

Aerobics

Other options → Aqua Aerobics [p.260]
Sports and Leisure Facilities [p.300]
Dance Classes [p.307]

If you want to shed unwanted weight or just stay fit, aerobics is a great way to exercise. Step, pump, aqua and conventional aerobics classes are offered at many beach, health and sports clubs. For a complete list of up to date classes, times and instructors, check with the clubs, and book in advance for popular sessions. Prices vary from club to club but average around Dhs.25 per class for members and Dhs.30 for nonmembers.

Off-Road Explorer

Experience the UAE's delights off the beaten track. Designed for the adventurous, a brilliant array of outback route maps, satellite images, step by step guidance, safety information, details on flora and fauna, and stunning photography make this outdoor guide a perfect addition to your four wheeler.

Amusement Centres

Other options → Amusement Parks [p.258]

Adventureland

Location → Sahara Centre · Sharjah | 06 531 6363
Hours → 10:00 - 24:00, Fri 14:00 - 23:00
Web/email → www.adventureland-sharjah.com Map Ref → UAE-C2

With so many amusement centres in Dubai you may think the drive to Sharjah unnecessary, but Adventureland is worth the trip for its sheer size and variety of rides. It caters for people of all ages and offers one of a kind rides for toddlers, kids, teenagers and adults, and prices vary from Dhs.3 – Dhs.8.50. The centre also features 100 video games and simulators, an Internet café, party room, billiards, bowling and a sports café.

City 2000

Location → Hamarain Centre · Deira | 266 7855
Hours → 10:00 - 23:00 Fri 16:30 - 23:00
Web/email → city2000@emirates.net.ae Map Ref → 12-A4

City 2000 has a range of video games and rides where you can enjoy a variety of gaming simulators. Entrance is free and food is available at the food court. Arcades are operated by Dhs.1 tokens and all machines take two tokens, except for adult simulator games, which that take three.

Encounter Zone

Location → Wafi Mall · Umm Hurair | 324 7747
Hours → 10:00 - 23:00, Wed/Thu 10:00 - 23:00, Fri 13:00 - 22:00
Web/email → ezone@emirates.net.ae Map Ref → 13-D2

Encounter Zone offers a range of activities for people of all ages. Galactica, for teenagers and adults, features a themed inline skateboarding park. Lunarland, for kids aged one to eight, hosts activities designed for younger children. Prices range from Dhs.5 – Dhs. 25, and you can get a day pass package for Dhs.45.

Fantasy Kingdom

Location → Al Bustan Centre · Al Qusais | 263 2774
Hours → 10:00 - 23:00 Fri 14:00 - 23:00
Web/email → www.al-bustan.com Map Ref → 15-C2

Themed as a medieval castle, Fantasy Kingdom offers adventure and excitement for the little ones. The centre has a 24,000 square foot indoor play area, which is divided into sections for different age groups. Younger children can enjoy the merry-go-around, while older ones can play interactive games, bumper cars, pool and air hockey.

Magic Planet

Location → Deira City Centre · Deira | 295 4333
Hours → 10:00 - 24:00 Fri 12:00 - 24:00
Web/email → www.deiracitycentre.com Map Ref → 14-D1

At Magic Planet you can enjoy various rides, including a merry-go round and train there is also a large activity play gym and a small soft area for toddlers, as well as bumper cars and the latest video games. Entrance is free, and you pay as you play using Dhs.2 cards. For unlimited entertainment you can buy a Dhs.50 special pass. There are also over a dozen outlets at the food court that surrounds Magic Planet.

Amusement Parks

Other options → Amusement Centres [p.258]
Water Parks [p.293]

Fruit & Garden Luna Park

Location → Al Nasr Leisureland · Oud Metha | 337 1234
Hours → 09:00 - 23:00
Web/email → www.alnasrleisureland.ae Map Ref → 10-E4

This park offers rides that are suitable for everyone from four to 60 years old and is an ideal venue for a birthday party. Activities include go-karts, bumper cars, helicopter and a roller coaster. Entrance fees are set at Dhs.10 for adults and Dhs.5 for children under the age of five.

Park 'n slide

PLEASE FASTEN YOUR SEAT BELTS
THE TRAIN IS ABOUT TO TAKE OFF

Quantum Leap

The roller coaster train that takes you around hairpin bends and turns at speeds that make your head spin. It's one of the 20 thrilling rides found only at Adventureland.

WonderLand Theme & Water Park

Location → Nr Creekside Park · Umm Hurair | **324 1222**
Hours → 16:00 - 23:00 Thu / Fri 15:00 - 23:00
Web/email → www.wonderlanduae.com   Map Ref → 14-A3

Both an amusement theme park and a water park, Wonderland will keep the most demanding of youngsters happy. Indoor and outdoor rides for people of all ages, including The Space Shot, Freefall and Action Arm. Parties and events can be catered for and paintball and go-karting are also available. See Water Parks [p.293] for more information.

Aqua Aerobics

Other options → Aerobics [p.257]

Jumeirah Beach Club Resort & Spa	344 5333
Nautilus Academy, The	397 4117
Pharaohs Club	324 0000

Archery

Dubai Archers Club

Location → Dubai Country Club · Al Awir | **344 2591**
Hours → Thu/Fri 15:00
Web/email → linton@emirates.net.ae   Map Ref → 3-C2

Small, friendly and informal, members of the Dubai Archers Club gather at Dubai Country Club on Thursday and Friday afternoons from 15:00 until dark. Coaching is available and club equipment is on hand for novices. There's a target charge of Dhs.20 per session, with an equipment rental fee that ranges between Dhs.5 - Dhs.10.

Hatta Fort Hotel

Location → Hatta Fort Hotel | **852 3211**
Hours → Timings on request
Web/email → www.jebelali-international.com Map Ref → UAE-D3

Hatta Fort Hotel's archery range is 25 metres long and has eight targets. Archery fans can enter the hotel's annual archery competition, and the Dubai Archery Club also holds its annual archery tournament at this venue. Assistance is available at the hotel for this challenging sport, and prices are available upon request.

Jebel Ali Shooting Club

Location → Nr Jebel Ali Golf Resort & Spa | **883 6555**
Hours → 13:00 - 22:00
Web/email → www.jebelali-international.com   Map Ref → 1-A2

Apart from excellent clay shooting facilities, The Jebel Ali Shooting Club also boasts an archery range with equipment for both men and ladies. Instructions are given to beginners who have never tried archery before. Prices are available upon request.

Basketball

Basketball courts can be rented at the Aviation Club and Dubai Country Club, or you can go down to Safa Park (349 2111) and get regular pick up games on Wednesday, Thursday and Sunday evenings. Organised club basketball is, however, limited.

Boat & Yacht Charters

Other options → Dhow Charters [p.266]
Dinner Cruises [p.400]
Speedboating [p.290]

Bateaux Dubai

Location → Nr British Embassy · Bur Dubai | **337 1919**
Hours → Timings on request
Web/email → www.bateauxdubai.com   Map Ref → 8-C4

Bateaux Dubai ensures parties of up to 300 people unobstructed sightseeing from all seats, and offers charters for corporate events and private parties. The vessel can be chartered daily with advance bookings, including weekends and holidays.

Sail away into the sunset

SUN & SAND SPORTS
LLC

Charlotte Anne Charters

Location ➜ Various
Hours ➜ Timings on request
Web/email ➜ www.charlotteannecharters.com   Map Ref ➜ UAE-E1

| 050 670 9430

The Charlotte Anne was built in Denmark in 1949 and has been chartering in Arabian Gulf waters for more than a decade. Built entirely of oak, the ship is available for cruises to the Mussandam Peninsula for scuba diving or corporate use.

The Charlotte Anne sets sail

Danat Dubai Cruises

Location ➜ Nr British Embassy · Bur Dubai
Hours ➜ 08:00 - 18:30
Web/email ➜ www.danatdubaicruises.com   Map Ref ➜ 8-C4

| 351 1117

Boasting a top speed of 18 knots, this 34 metre catamaran is available for group charters, product launches and wedding receptions, and has a capacity of 300 passengers (170 for sit down functions). Onboard facilities include a dance floor, music system, video monitors, sun deck and two enclosed air conditioned decks.

Dusail

Location ➜ Jumeirah Beach Hotel Marina, The
Hours ➜ Timings on request
Web/email ➜ www.dusail.com   Map Ref ➜ 4-B2

| 311 6770

Dusail Yacht Charter provides coastline tours aboard their 50ft flagship luxury yacht, Andorra,

deep sea, reef or fly fishing packages and rentals of motor and rigid inflatable boats. They also have custom designed thrill rides that include wave jumping and fast turns at speeds of up to 100 km/h.

El Mundo

Location ➜ DIMC · Al Sufouh
Hours ➜ Various
Web/email ➜ www.elmundodubai.com   Map Ref ➜ 3-A2

| 343 4870

El Mundo is a 60 foot catamaran that can be chartered to watch dhows on Dubai's Creek or to have romantic dinner cruises around Palm Island. Longer charters for snorkelling, dolphin watching or trips to the Mussandam are also available.

Jebel Ali Golf Resort & Spa

Location ➜ Jct 9 · Jebel Ali
Hours ➜ Timings on request
Web/email ➜ www.jebelali-international.com   Map Ref ➜ 1-A1

| 883 6000

Club Joumana, at the Jebel Ali Golf Resort and Spa, can arrange one or two hour boat trips for up to seven people on its 36ft fishing boat. Departure is from the private marina at the resort in the morning or afternoon, and prices are available upon request.

Le Meridien Mina Seyahi Beach Resort & Marina

Location ➜ Le Meridien Mina Seyahi · Al Sufouh
Hours ➜ Timings on request
Web/email ➜ www.lemeridien-minaseyahi.com   Map Ref ➜ 3-A2

| 399 3333

Le Meridien Mina Seyahi operates a variety of charter cruises from their marina. A number of boats are available for trips of different lengths and activities include deep-sea fishing, trawling and sightseeing. Prices are available on request and all rates include a skipper and equipment.

Yacht Solutions

Location ➜ Jumeirah Beach Htl · Umm Suqeim
Hours ➜ Timings on request
Web/email ➜ www.yacht-solutions.com   Map Ref ➜ 4-B2

| 348 6838

Yacht Solutions can arrange anything from short blasts aboard high speed sports boats to exclusive overnight stays on their 20 metre Princess yacht. Myriad cruising options are available and they provide full catering selections. Corporate enquiries are also welcome.

Bowling

Al Nasr Leisureland

Location → Beh American Hospital · Oud Metha | **337 1234**
Hours → 09:00 - 24:00
Web/email → www.alnasrleisureland.ae   Map Ref → 10-E4

Al Nasr Leisureland has an eight lane bowling alley with various fast food outlets and a bar that serves alcohol. Booking is recommended since there are regular league games that take place during the week. The entrance fee is Dhs.10, and each game costs Dhs.7 - this includes shoe rental.

Bungee Jumping

For adrenaline junkies, bungee jumping is available in Dubai at certain times of the year. During the Dubai Shopping Festival (DSF) it is one of the attractions on the Bur Dubai side of the Creek and is offered by an organisation hailing from Australia. For more information, check the daily press for details as DSF approaches.

Camel Rides

Other options → **Camel Racing [p.177]**

When in Arabia, riding a camel is like riding a London bus - it's a must-do, and a bumpy ride. You can opt for short camel rides that are often offered as part of a desert tour or hotel and beach resort package. For a more memorable experience you should go on a longer guided camel ride in the sand dunes. On such tours there are stops for rests, refreshments and photos, so that you can remember your experience long after the aches subside.

Catch the seaside camel train

Al Ain Golden Sands Camel Safaris

Location → Hilton Al Ain | **03 768 8006**
Hours → 09:00 - 13:00 17:30 - 20:00
Web/email → na   Map Ref → UAE-D4

Al Ain Golden Sands Camel Safaris offer a selection of tours that include a camel ride over the dunes of Bida Bint Saud. The rides usually last one to two and a half hours, and all tours include transfers from Al Ain, Arabic coffee and dates.

Camping

Other options → **Off-Road Explorer**
Outdoor Goods [p.228]
Wadi & Dune Bashing [p.292]

Persistent sunshine and an awe-inspiring array of locations make camping a much loved activity in Dubai. In general, warm temperatures and next to no rain mean you can camp with much less equipment and preparation than in other countries and many first timers or families with children of any age, find camping, despite the accompanying mosquitoes, becomes their favourite weekend break. For most the best time to go is between October and April, as in the summer it can get unbearably hot sleeping outside.

Choose between the peace and stillness of the desert or camp amongst the wadis and mountains next to trickling streams in picturesque oases. Many good campsites are easily accessible from tarmac roads so a 4 WD is not always required.

Although the UAE has low rainfall, care should be taken in and near wadis during the winter months as flash floods can occur (remember, it may be raining in the mountains miles from where you are and when it rains it pours)

For most people, a basic amount of equipment will suffice. This may include:

- Tent
- Lightweight sleeping bag (or light blankets and sheets)
- Thin mattress (or air bed)
- Torches and spare batteries
- Cool box for food
- Water (always take too much)
- Camping stove, or BBQ and charcoal if preferred
- Firewood and matches
- Insect repellent and antihistamine cream
- First aid kit (including any personal medication)

Bowling | Camping

Activities

- Sun protection (hats, sunglasses, sunscreen)
- Jumper / warm clothing for cooler evenings
- Spade
- Toilet rolls
- Rubbish bags (ensure you leave nothing behind.)
- Navigation equipment (maps, compass, Global Positioning System (GPS))

For the adventurous with a 4 WD, there are endless possibilities for camping in remote and beautiful locations all over the UAE. The many sites in the Hajar Mountains (in the north near Ras Al Khaimah or east and south near Hatta or Al Ain), and the huge sand dunes of Liwa, in the south, are recommended. Each require some serious off-road driving but offer a real wilderness camping experience. For more information on places to visit, refer to the *Off-Road Explorer (UAE)*.

Life's a beach - with new regulations

Canoeing

Other options → Kayaking [p.282]
Outdoor Goods [p.228]
Tour Operators [p.184]

Canoeing is a great way to access hidden places of natural beauty and to get close to marine and bird life in the UAE. At Khor Kalba Nature Reserve on the east coast, tours are available and canoes can be hired. If you have your own canoe, other worthwhile areas to visit include the coastal lagoons of Umm Al Quwain, selected areas around Ras Al Khaimah and mangrove covered islands north of Abu Dhabi. Many of these areas are on

their way to becoming protected reserves, so treat them with respect and do not litter. Adventurous kayakers occasionally go to the Mussandam in sea touring canoes where it is possible to visit secluded bays and view spectacular rocky coastlines with fjord like inlets and towering 1,000 metre cliffs. For further information refer to the Hatta to Kalba Route in the *Off-Road Explorer (UAE)*. Also see Khor Kalba [p.195].

Desert Rangers

Location → Dubai Garden Centre · Al Quoz | 340 2408
Hours → 09:00 - 18:00
Web/email → www.desertrangers.com   Map Ref → 4-B4

Desert Rangers offers trips through the mangroves at Khor Kalba Reserve. Only a basic level of fitness is required and this is a suitable activity for people of all ages. A guide accompanies you on your trip and rates are Dhs.300 per person.

Caving

Other options → Out of Dubai [p.186]

The cave network in the Hajar Mountains is extensive and much of it is yet to be explored. Some of the best caves are located near Al Ain, the Jebel Hafeet area and in the Hajar Mountains just past Buraimi, which is near the Omani border. Many of the underground passages and caves have spectacular displays of curtains, stalagmites and stalactites, as well as gypsum flowers.

At this point in time there are no companies offering guided tours, and caving is limited to unofficial groups of dedicated cavers. Within the region, caving ranges from fairly safe to extremely dangerous, but either way you should always be well-equipped and accompanied by an experienced leader.

Check weather forecasts to find out about recent rainfalls and be warned that flash floods occur regularly at certain times of the year. The Hajar Mountain range continues into the Sultanate of Oman, where it is higher and even more impressive. In Oman, the range includes what is believed to be the second largest cave system in the world, as well as the Majlis Al Jinn Cave - the second largest chamber in the world. A word of warning though, no mountain rescue services exist, therefore anyone venturing out into mountains should be reasonably experienced, or go with someone who knows the area.

Climbing

For those who feel at home on vertical cliffs or hanging from rocky precipices, excellent climbing can be found in a various locations around the UAE, including Ras Al Khaimah, Dibba, Hatta and the Al Ain/Buraimi region. The earliest recorded rock climbs were made near Al Ain/Buraimi in the late 1970s; since then more than 200 routes have been climbed and named. These vary from short outcrop routes to difficult and sustained mountain routes of alpine proportions. New routes are generally climbed 'on sight', with traditional protection. Most routes are in the higher grades - ranging from (British) Very Severe, up to extreme grades (E5). Due to the nature of the rock, some climbs can feel more difficult than their technical grade would suggest. Many routes, even in the easier grades, have loose rock, poor belays and difficult descents, often by abseil, making them unsuitable for total novices. However, there are some excellent easier routes for new climbers, especially in Wadi Bih and Wadi Khab Al Shamis. To meet some like-minded people head along to Wadi Bih where you're sure to find some climbers nearly every weekend, or go to the indoor climbing wall (Pharaoh's Club) where most of the UAE climbing fraternity congregates at some point during the week.

There are no formal climbing or mountaineering clubs in the UAE but unofficial meetings do take place at Dubai's only indoor climbing wall at Pharaoh's Club. While new climbers are welcome, this group does not run courses for beginners. For more information contact John Gregory on 050 647 7120 or email arabex@emirates.net.ae.

Pharaoh's Club	
Location → Pyramids · Umm Hurair	324 0000
Hours → 07:00 - 22:00 Fri 09:00 - 21:00	
Web/email → www.pyramidsdubai.com	Map Ref → 13-D2

Dubai's only indoor climbing wall at Pharaoh's Club lets climbing enthusiasts improve their skills. The wall comprises of varied climbing routes and crash mats are present for low level climbs - pricing starts at Dhs.35 per hour. During the winter climbing trips are sometimes organised to Ras Al Khaimah.

Crab Hunting

Lama Desert Tours	
Location → Nr Lamcy Plaza · Al Karama	334 4330
Hours → 09:00 - 18:00	
Web/email → www.lamadubai.com	Map Ref → 12-A2

This unusual tour takes you to Umm Al Quwain where you head out to sea to hunt crabs, and the buffet dinner comprises of your own catch of the day. The cost is Dhs.220 per person (minimum six people required) and includes return transfer, soft drinks, snacks and traditional buffet dinner.

Cricket

Bringing together Brits and Ozzies, Kiwis and South Africans, Indians and Pakistanis, cricket is a passion shared across many communities living in Dubai. Car parks and grassy parks sprout stumps on weekends and evenings and neighbourhood teams partake in their favourite game. Many organisations have their own cricket teams for inter company competitions and the sport is becoming more popular in schools. Coaching is also widely available.

International matches are regularly hosted in the Emirates, especially at the grounds in Sharjah, where it's possible to see some of the world's best teams in action.

Batting on the beach

Darjeeling Cricket Club

Location ➜ Nr Dubai Country Club · Al Awir
Hours ➜   Timings on request |333 1746
Web/email ➜ darjeelingdubai@yahoo.com   Map Ref ➜ 17-B3

Every Thursday and Friday 25-over matches take place at the Darjeeling Cricket Club. The clubhouse, complete with bar, is open from Tuesday to Sunday and is available for private functions. Membership costs Dhs.750 per playing member and Dhs.300 per social member.

Croquet

A classic croquet lawn is available for a game on Jebel Ali Golf Resort and Spa's grounds. For more information, call Club Joumana on 883 6000.

Cycling

Other options ➜ Mountain Biking [p.284]
Out of Dubai [p.186]
Sporting Goods [p.230]

Dubai is not a very bicycle friendly city but there are plenty of areas where you can ride, and it can be a great way to explore as well as keep fit. The pedestrian areas on both sides of the Creek are pleasant places for a spin, especially in the evening, and riding through the souks can also be an experience. Clubs and groups of cyclists generally ride at the weekends, early mornings and evenings when roads are quieter and the temperatures are cooler. If you have no choice but to ride in busy areas, exercise a lot of care and attention. Although helmets are not legally required, it is recommended that you wear one considering how crazy Dubai traffic can be. Outside the city limits the roads are flat until you near the mountains. Jebel Hafeet near Al Ain, the Hatta area of the Hajar Mountains and the central area in the mountains near Masafi down to the coast at either Fujairah or Dibba offer interesting paved roads with better views. The new road from Hatta through the mountains to Kalba on the East Coast is probably one of the most scenic routes in the country.

Dubai Roadsters

Location ➜   Various locations
Hours ➜   Timings on request |339 4453
Web/email ➜ wolfisbs@emirates.net.ae   Map Ref ➜ na

The only criteria for joining Dubai Roadsters are a safe bike, cycling helmet, pump and spare tubes.

The average distance covered on a Friday ride is 65 - 100 km, while weekday rides are about 30 km. There are no membership fees, and you can email the club to get added to their newsletter mailing list.

Dhow Charters

Other options ➜ Boat & Yacht Charters [p.260]
Creek Tours [p.155]
Dinner Cruises [p.400]

An evening aboard a dhow, either on the Creek or sailing along the coast, is a wonderfully atmospheric and memorable experience. Contact one of the companies below to find out more about dhow charters. Alternatively, large independent groups can charter a dhow from the fishermen at Dibba to travel up the coast of the Mussandam. If you're prepared to haggle you can usually knock the price down substantially, especially if you know a bit of Arabic - try saying your proposed price followed by 'Mafi Mushkila' ('no problem'). Expect to pay around Dhs.2,500 per day for a dhow large enough to take 20 - 25 people, or Dhs.100 per hour for a smaller one. You'll need to take your own food and water, as nothing is supplied onboard except for ice lockers that are suitable for storing supplies. Conditions are basic, but you'll have the freedom to plan your own route and to see the beautiful fjord-like scenery of the Mussandam from a traditional wooden dhow. The waters in the area are beautifully clear and turtles and dolphins can often be seen from the boat, although sometimes unfavourable weather conditions can seriously reduce visibility for divers.

If you leave from Dibba (or Dabba), Omani visas are not required, even though you enter Omani waters. It is also possible to arrange stops along the coast and it's worth taking camping equipment for the night, although you can sleep on board. This kind of trip is ideal for diving but you should hire any equipment you may need before you get to Dibba (refer to the *Underwater Explorer* for dive shop rentals or Diving [p.267]). If diving is not your thing, you can just spend the day swimming, snorkelling and soaking up the sun, and for an extra Dhs.500 you can even hire a speedboat.

Al Boom Tourist Village

Location ➜ Nr Al Garhoud Bridge · Umm Hurair
Hours ➜   20:00 - 22:30 |324 3000
Web/email ➜ www.alboom.ae   Map Ref ➜ 14-A3

Al Boom Tourist Village is a dhow boat operator on the Creek, that operates seven dhows ranging in capacity from 20 - 280 passengers. They offer a range of international menus, and prices range from Dhs.500 per hour for an Al Taweel (single deck, 20 passenger), to Dhs.3,000 for a Kashti (double deck, 150 passenger).

Al Madhani Sea Tourism & Diving

Location ➔ Various	050 690 508
Hours ➔ Timings on request	
Web/email ➔ na	Map Ref ➔ UAE-E2

Al Madhani Sea Tourism and Diving offers dhow cruises from Dibba to Mussandam. There are trips for one or more days, including overnight stays and romantic dinners on the dhow or on the beach (Dhs.300 per day). The company also offers dhow cruises on the Creek (Dhs.250), desert safaris (Dhs.250) and mountain tours in Fujairah (Dhs.250).

Al Marsa Charters

Location ➔ East Coast	06 544 1232
Hours ➔ 08:00 - 13:00 15:00 - 18:00 Fri closed	
Web/email ➔ www.musandamdiving.com	Map Ref ➔ UAE-E1

Al Marsa has two purpose built dhows that are suitable for divers and tourists. You can relax on the sundeck for a day trip and discover fishing villages or you can go on an overnight voyage and explore fjords. Prices start at Dhs.370 for divers and Dhs.300 for non-divers.

Creek Cruises

Location ➔ Nr DCCI · Deira	393 9860
Hours ➔ 20:30 - 22:30	
Web/email ➔ www.creekcruises.com	Map Ref ➔ 11-C2

The Malika Al Khor and Zomorrodah dhows can be chartered for any occasion, and are suitable for groups of 20 - 200 people. Facilities include an air-conditioned deck, majlis, sound system and dance floor. The charter fee is Dhs.1,500 per hour (minimum two hours) and catering can be provided from Dhs.80 per person.

Creekside Leisure

Location ➔ Opp Dubai Municipality HQ · Deira	336 8406
Hours ➔ Timings on request	
Web/email ➔ www.tour-dubai.com	Map Ref ➔ 11-C1

Creekside Leisure offers a variety of charter packages that range from romantic dinners for two, to corporate hospitality for up to 50 guests. The

dhows are licensed and offer catering, live entertainment and business facilities. A two hour dinner cruise costs Dhs.175 and includes food, a welcome drink, water and belly dancing.

Khasab Travel & Tours

Location ➔ Warba Centre · Deira	266 9950
Hours ➔ Timings on request	
Web/email ➔ www.khasab-tours.com	Map Ref ➔ na

Sailing north from Dibba (no Omani visa is required) the cruise follows the coastline from steep rocky cliffs rise out of the sea. You'll also pass small fishing villages that are accessible only by boat and see dolphins and turtles swimming alongside the dhow. Prices start at Dhs.150 per adult for a four hour cruise with refreshments.

Diving

Other options ➔ Snorkelling [p.290]
Underwater Explorer

The UAE's coastal waters are home to a variety of marine species, coral life and even shipwrecks. You'll see some exotic fish, like clownfish and seahorses, and possibly even spotted eagle rays, moray eels, small sharks, barracuda, sea snakes and stingrays. This rich underwater world, and the fact that the warm seas are perfect for year-round diving, makes the UAE a diving hotspot. The UAE is also fortunate to have two coastlines - to the west, covering Abu Dhabi, Dubai and Sharjah, and to the east, covering Fujairah, Khorfakkan and Dibba. Most of the wrecks are on the western coast, while the beautiful flora and fauna of coral reefs can be seen on the eastern coast.

There are many dive sites on the west coast that are easily accessible from Dubai and provide some great diving opportunities. Visibility ranges from five to 20 metres, depending on conditions. MV Sarraf – Three, Cement Barge, MV Dara, Port Rashid Wrecks and Sheikh Mohammed Barge are some of the more popular dive sites. Off the east coast, a well known dive site is Martini Rock, a small, underwater mountain covered with colourful soft coral, with a depth range of three to 19 metres. North of Khorfakkan is the Car Cemetery, a reef that has thrived around a number of cars placed 16 metres below water. Visibility off the east coast ranges from five to 20 metres.

Another option for diving enthusiasts is to take a trip to the area north of the UAE, the Mussandam. This area, which is part of the Sultanate of Oman, is often described as the 'Norway of the Middle East' due to the numerous inlets and the way the sheer cliffs plunge directly into the sea. It offers some spectacular dive sites. Sheer wall dives with strong currents and clear waters are more suitable for advanced divers, while the huge bays, with their calm waters and shallow reefs, are ideal for the less experienced. Visibility ranges from ten to 35 metres. If you plan to travel to Khasab, the capital of the Mussandam, you may not be able to take your own air tanks across the border and will have to rent from one of the dive centres there. You will not require an Omani visa. Alternatively, from Dibba on the UAE east coast, you can hire a fast dive boat to take you anywhere from five to 75 kilometres up the coast. The cost ranges between Dhs.150 and Dhs.500, for what is usually a two dive trip. During winter, you may be lucky enough to spot a few whale sharks, and you'll usually see dolphins playing in the bow waves of your boat.

There are plenty of dive companies in the UAE where you can improve your diving skills, whether you are an absolute beginner who wants to learn the ropes, or an experienced diver wanting to become an instructor. Courses are offered under the usual international training organisations, such as PADI, CMAS, NAUI, IANTD and HAS. For more information on diving in the UAE and the Mussandam, refer to the *Underwater Explorer*. See also The Mussandam – Sultanate of Oman [p.196].

7 Seas Divers

Location → Nr Khorfakkan Souk | **09 238 7400**
Hours → 08:00 - 20:00
Web/email → www.7seasdivers.com   Map Ref → UAE-E2

This PADI dive centre offers day and night diving trips to a variety of sites in Khorfakkan, Mussandam and Lima Rock. Training is provided at beginner and instructor level in Arabic, English or Russian. The centre arranges diving equipment that you can buy or rent.

Al Boom Diving

Location → Nr Iranian Hospital · Al Wasl | **342 2993**
Hours → 10:00 - 20:00   Fri closed
Web/email → www.alboomdiving.com   Map Ref → 6-C3

Daily dive courses are offered at Al Boom Dive Centre (399 2278). Their Aqua Centre on Al Wasl Rd (342 2993) is a purpose built school with a fully outfitted diving shop. Their PADI Gold Palm Resort at Le Meridien Al Aqah Beach Resort (09 204 4912) also offers daily courses.

Divers Down

Location → Oceanic Hotel | **09 237 0299**
Hours → 08:30 - 18:00
Web/email → www.diversdown.tk   Map Ref → UAE-E2

Divers Down is a PADI five star Gold Palm Resort that offers divers and non-divers a chance to plunge into the tropical waters of the Indian Ocean and explore the marine life it has to offer. The centre is open seven days a week.

Emirates Diving Association

Location → Heritage & Diving Village · Al Shindagha | **393 9390**
Hours → 08:00 - 15:00
Web/email → www.emiratesdiving.com   Map Ref → 8-B1

This group's aim is to conserve, protect and restore the UAE's marine resources by promoting the importance of the environment. The association looks after the well-being of UAE corals as part of their coral monitoring project, and hope to establish a marine park using artificial reefs.

Pavilion Dive Centre, The

Location → Jumeirah Beach Htl · Umm Suqeim | **406 8827**
Hours → 09:00 - 18:00
Web/email → www.jumeirahinternational.com   Map Ref → 4-B2

This centre is run by qualified PADI instructors offering an extensive range of courses for beginners and instructors. Daily excursions for certified divers leave at 10:00 (weather permitting), and trips to the Mussandam are also

Wreck diving

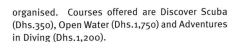

organised. Courses offered are Discover Scuba (Dhs.350), Open Water (Dhs.1,750) and Adventures in Diving (Dhs.1,200).

Sandy Beach Diving Centre

Location → Sandy Beach Motel **09 244 5050**
Hours → 08:00 - 18:00
Web/email → www.sandybm.com   Map Ref → UAE-E2

This dive centre is managed by Sandy Beach Hotel and offers a qualified team of instructors and support staff. It is open all year round for diving and accommodation, and the retail store stocks diving gear. The famous Snoopy Island is alive with hard corals and marine life, and is an excellent spot for snorkelling and scuba diving.

Scuba 2000

Location → Al Badiyah Beach **09 238 8477**
Hours → 09:00 - 19:00
Web/email → www.scuba-2000.com   Map Ref → UAE-E2

This East Coast Dive Centre is open all year round and provides daily trips to dive sites at Dibba and Khorfakkan. Standard courses are available for beginners and advanced divers. Costs range from Dhs.300 for Discover Scuba to Dhs.1,600 for Open Water to Dhs.1,000 for Advanced.

Scuba Dubai

Location → DWTC Appts, Block C · Trade Centre 2 **331 7433**
Hours → 09:00 - 13:00   16:00 - 20:30   Fri closed
Web/email → www.scubadubai.com   Map Ref → 9-D2

For those wishing to arrange their own diving and snorkelling trips, equipment can be rented from Scuba Dubai on a 24 hour basis, collecting one day and returning the next. Rates for Thursday, Friday and Saturday are the same as renting for one day because the shop is closed on Fridays. Note that original diving certification must be shown for all scuba equipment rentals.

The shop will be moving sometime around June 2005, check by phone, e-mail or keep an eye on their website for their new location.

Scuba International

Location → Fujairah Int'l Marine Club **09 222 0060**
Hours → 09:00 - 17:00
Web/email → www.scubainternational.net   Map Ref → UAE-E2

Scuba International (PADI Five Star) offers activities for both divers and non-divers that include recreational dive charters, snorkelling trips and diver training (Discover Scuba dive costs Dhs.250). Scuba International also offer modern dhow excursions, sundowner cruises, day trips and large group bookings.

Scubatec

Location → Sana Bld · Al Karama **334 8988**
Hours → 09:00 - 13:30   16:00 - 20:30
Web/email → scubatec@emirates.net.ae   Map Ref → 10-C1

Scubatec is a five star centre that's licensed by PADI and TDI. Lessons are provided in Arabic, English, German or Urdu, and the company offers a full range of courses from beginner to instructor level. Dubai, East Coast and shipwreck dive trips are available.

Sharjah Wanderers Dive Club

Location → Sharjah Wanderers Sports Club **06 566 2105**
Hours →   Timings on request
Web/email → www.sharjahwanderers.com   Map Ref → UAE-C2

Sharjah Wanderers Dive Club is part of Sharjah Wanderers Sports Club, which means that members automatically get to benefit from other sporting and social activities. The club is a member of the British Sub Aqua Club and follows its training, certification and diving practices. Clubhouse facilities include a training room, social area, equipment room, compressors, dive gear and two dive boats.

Dune Buggy Riding

Other options → **Karting [p.281]**
Quad Bikes [p.286]

Bouncing over the dunes in a buggy is exhilarating, addictive, and definitely one of the best ways to experience the desert. Desert Rangers in Dubai offers dune buggy tours where you can enjoy all the thrills and spills of this extreme sport in the safest possible way – they provide training, all the safety equipment you'll need, and an experienced leader to guide you through the dunes. Alternatively, you can hire a quad bike from independent companies, most commonly found at the 'Big Red' area on the road from Dubai to Hatta. A variety of quads are available on an hourly basis, but unlike dune buggies, quad bikes have no roll bar, so be careful. The area around this landmark sand dune gets pretty crazy on Fridays, when off-roading enthusiasts head there in large numbers for a bit of dune bashing. Hang around after your ride and watch the locals two wheeling their huge Nissan Patrols down the dune.

Diving | Dune Buggy Riding

Activities

Desert Rangers

Location ➔ Dubai Garden Centre · Al Quoz	**340 2408**
Hours ➔ 09:00 - 18:00	
Web/email ➔ www.desertrangers.com	Map Ref ➔ 4-B4

After a brief safety lecture you will be taken on a buggy ride through a series of desert dunes. Desert Rangers promise to make this an unforgettable experience while ensuring safety is a top priority. Not to be mistaken with quad biking which has clocked up a few unsurprising accidents over the years. Safaris can be combined with a BBQ dinner at an Arabic campsite. Costs are Dhs.375 per person.

A bit of peace and quiet

Fencing

Dubai Fencing Club

Location ➔ Mina A'Salam · Umm Suqeim	**050 794 4190**
Hours ➔ Timings on request	
Web/email ➔ www.dubaifencingclub.com	Map Ref ➔ 4-A2

The Dubai Fencing Club provides individual and group training sessions in Epee and Foil for juniors and adults. All beginners receive the necessary basic equipment such as masks, gloves and weapons. For advanced fencers, the club offers three fencing paths with electrical scoring systems and electrical weapons.

Fishing

Other options ➔ Boat & Yacht Charters [p.260]
Crab Hunting [p.265]

Fishing has become increasingly popular in the region in recent years, and subsequently the government has introduced regulations to protect fish stocks off the UAE coast. However, you can still fish, as long as you have the right permit or you charter a licensed tour guide. The most productive fishing season lasts from September to April, although it is still possible to catch sailfish and queenfish in the summer months. Fish commonly caught in the waters off Dubai are king mackerel, tuna, trevally, bonito, kingfish, cobia and dorado or jacks.

Beach or surf fishing is popular along the UAE coast, and in season you can even catch barracuda from the shore. Any beach along the Dubai coastline will be a reasonable fishing spot, and you should definitely try fishing from the end of the promenade on the Jumeira Beach Corniche. The Creek front in Creekside Park is also popular, although you may want to think twice before putting these fish on the barbie! Alternatively, on a Friday, you could hire an abra for the morning (either at the Bur Dubai or Deira landing steps) and ask your driver to take you out to the mouth of the Creek for a bit of fishing. Always agree on a price before you leave. If you want to splash out you could consider a deep-sea fishing trip with one of the charter companies listed below.

Bounty Charters

Location ➔ Various locations	**348 3042**
Hours ➔ Timings on request	
Web/email ➔ bountycharters@hotmail.com	Map Ref ➔ na

Bounty Charters is a fully equipped 36 foot Yamaha Sea Spirit game fishing boat captained by Richard Forrester, an experienced game fisherman from South Africa. The company offers full day sailfish sessions, half day bottom fishing or night fishing charters as well 3 - 5 day trips to the Mussandam Peninsula.

Club Joumana

Location ➔ Jebel Ali Golf Resort & Spa	**883 6000**
Hours ➔ Timings on request	
Web/email ➔ www.jebelali-international.com	Map Ref ➔ 1-A1

Four and eight hour fishing trips are available for up to seven people per boat. The captain, tackle, equipment, soft drinks, water, Danish pastries and croissants are included as part of the package as you try and catch barracuda, lemonfish, trevally, hammour and kingfish. Prices available upon request.

Dubai Creek Golf & Yacht Club

Location → Opp Deira City Centre Mall · Al Garhoud | 295 6000
Hours → 06:30 - 19:00
Web/email → www.dubaigolf.com   Map Ref → 14-C2

Take a trip on the club's Sneakaway Yacht into the Arabian Gulf and experience big game sports fishing. The fully equipped 32ft Hatteras carries up to six passengers and rates include tackle, bait, ice, fuel and a friendly crew. Rates: four hours Dhs.1,875; five hours Dhs.2,125; six hours Dhs.2,375; eight hours Dhs.2,850; thereafter each additional hour is Dhs.250.

Fun Sports

Location → Various | 399 5976
Hours → 09:00 - 17:00
Web/email → www.funsport-dubai.com   Map Ref → na

Fun Sports offer fishing, sailing, windsurfing, water skiing, wakeboarding, knee boarding, banana rides, kayaking, power boat rides, parasailing and sunset cruises. Tuition is available for all levels of ability, with specialised courses in sailing, windsurfing, water skiing and kite surfing.

Le Meridien Mina Seyahi Beach Resort & Marina

Location → Le Meridien Mina Seyahi · Al Sufouh | 399 3333
Hours → Timings on request
Web/email → www.lemeridien-minaseyahi.com   Map Ref → 3-A2

Fishing trips take place on the custom built Ocean Explorer and Ocean Luhr. Sailfish are the main prize, and Le Meridien Mina Seyahi supports the tag and release scheme. While you are welcome to bring your own gear, the boats are fully equipped with 20, 30 and 50 lb class tackle.

Oceanic Hotel

Location → Beach Rd, East Coast | 09 238 5111
Hours → Timings on request
Web/email → www.oceanichotel.com   Map Ref → UAE-E2

Fishing trips from here are to a favourite local spot where catches are guaranteed. After you're done, you can watch the sunset as you return to the

hotel. The catch can be cooked by the hotel chef, who will prepare it according to your taste. The cost is Dhs.100 per person (minimum of six people per boat) for three hours.

Yacht Solutions

Location → Jumeirah Beach Htl · Umm Suqeim | 348 6838
Hours → Timings on request
Web/email → www.yacht-solutions.com   Map Ref → 4-B2

Yacht Solutions offers the opportunity to experience fishing on board one of their sports fishing vessels. With modern tackle you have the chance to catch sailfish, kingfish, tuna and barracuda. Experienced skippers guide you to the best fishing spots, and for the less experienced there is plenty of advice to make your fishing experience memorable.

Flying

Other options → Helicopter Flights [p.278]
Hot Air Ballooning [p.280]
Plane Tours [p.286]
Scenic Flights [p.178]

Dubai Flying Association

Location → Dubai International Airport · Al Garhoud | 351 9691
Hours → Timings on request
Web/email → www.dfadxb.com   Map Ref → 14-D3

The Dubai Flying Association (DFA) is a registered, non-profit group that aims to provide flying to members at cost price. The DFA has also taken up operations at Umm Al Quwain Airfield. Membership costs Dhs.500 per annum and the association welcomes UAE private pilot licence holders to join.

Emirates Flying School

Location → Terminal 2, Dubai Int'l Airport · Al Twar | 299 5155
Hours → 08:30 - 17:30
Web/email → www.emiratesaviationservices.com Map Ref → 15-B2

Emirates Flying School is the only approved flight training institution in Dubai and operates six Piper aircraft. The school offers private and commercial pilot licences, and will convert international licences to UAE licences. Gift vouchers (Dhs.500) are available for those interested in experiencing flying for the first time.

Fishing | Flying

Activities

Fujairah Aviation Centre

Location ➜ Fujairah Int'l Airport
Hours ➜ Timings on request
Web/email ➜ www.fujairah-aviation.ae

09 222 4747

Map Ref ➜ UAE-E2

Fujairah Aviation Centre is accredited with Civil Aviation Authorities in the UAE and UK. Facilities include twin and single engine training aircraft, an instrument flight simulator and workshop for repairs. Training is offered for private and commercial pilot licences, instrument rating and multi-engine rating. For information on different flights and costs contact the centre.

Umm Al Quwain Aeroclub

Location ➜ 17km North of UAQ on RAK Rd
Hours ➜ 09:00 - 17:30
Web/email ➜ www.uaqaeroclub.com

06 768 1447

Map Ref ➜ UAE-D1

The Umm Al Quwain Aeroclub offers flying, skydiving, skydive boogies, paramotors and helicopter training. The facilities include a variety of small aircraft, two runways, eight hangars with engineering services, a pilot's shop and a briefing room. Sightseeing tours are available in Cessna aircraft, and prices start at Dhs.300 for 30 minutes.

Football

Like most places around the world, football is a much loved sport here in the Emirates. At evenings and weekends, parks, beaches and open areas play host to football games. Even remote villages have informal teams kicking a ball around on sandy and rocky pitches. Formal outdoor and indoor pitches exist in Dubai and coaching (mainly for kids) is offered at a number of sports centres and health clubs.

Dubai Celts GAA

Location ➜ Dubai Exiles Rugby Club · Bukadra
Hours ➜ 20:00 - 22:00   Mon & Wed
Web/email ➜ www.dubaicelts.com

na

Map Ref ➜ 17-B3

Dubai Celts GAA Club holds games and organises training in men's and ladies' Gaelic football, hurling and camogie. In addition to monthly matches within the UAE, international tournaments are held in Bahrain (November) and Dubai (March) each year. Training sessions are held every Saturday and Tuesday at 19:00.

Dubai Irish Village Football Club

Location ➜ Dubai Exiles Rugby Club· Bukadra
Hours ➜ Call for timings
Web/email ➜ callowjd@emirates.net.ae

050 551 9250

Map Ref ➜ 17-B3

Dubai Irish Village is one of the most recent teams to join The Budweiser Expat League. The team consists of many different nationalities that come together to enjoy football at a competitive level. Games are usually played between Saturdays and Wednesdays.

Emirates Golf Club

Location ➜ Emirates Hills
Hours ➜ 06:00 - 24:00
Web/email ➜ www.dubaigolf.com

380 2222

Map Ref ➜ 3-A3

Emirates Golf Club is home to the Reebok Soccer Academy and has over 140 enrolled juniors. The academy sports two polyurethane pitches alongside their grass five-a-side facilities. The academy operates regular squad coaching, as well as camps during school holidays and half terms.

UAE English Soccer School of Excellence

Location ➜ Various locations
Hours ➜ Various
Web/email ➜ masty57@hotmail.com

050 476 4877

Map Ref ➜ na

Emirates Golf Course and Emirates Lakes are home to UAE E.S.S.E. and presently have over 450 students on their books. All coaches at the academy are English F.A. qualified, and the school organises camps during holidays and half terms.

Showing off your ball skills

Flying | Football

Activities

Corporate Family Days
Theme Decoration • Birthday Parties

Golf

Dubai is becoming one of the world's premier golfing destinations, with excellent weather and top class facilities. There are already quite a few international standard golf courses around the city, with plenty more at planning stage. In a place where it hardly ever rains the golf courses are a welcome splash of colour in the desert. The Desert Course at Arabian Ranches is Dubai's newest golf course, designed with input from golfing great Jack Nicklaus. The Al Badia Golf Course, situated within Dubai Festival City on the banks of the Creek, is due to open in mid 2005. In January 2005, the ever-popular Dubai Creek Golf and Yacht Club course reopens after extensive redevelopment.

Each year the city is host to the prestigious Dubai Desert Classic golfing tournament, which is part of the European PGA Tour. Tiger Woods, Ernie Els, Ian Woosnam, Colin Montgomerie and Seve Ballesteros are just some of the golfing heroes who have teed off in this tournament, which is played at the Emirates Golf Club. There are also several local monthly tournaments and annual competitions that are open to all, such as the Emirates Mixed Amateur Open, the Emirates Ladies' Amateur Open (handicap of 21 or less), and the Emirates Men's Amateur Open (handicap of five or less).

Dubai Golf operates a central reservation system for those wishing to book a round of golf on any of the major courses in the emirate. For further information, visit their Website at www.dubaigolf.com, send an email to booking

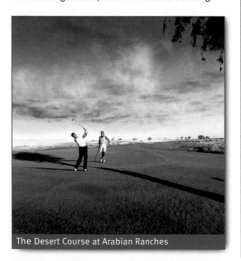
The Desert Course at Arabian Ranches

Al Badia Golf Resort

Location → Al Rabat Street, Ras Al Khor · Deira | **285 5772**
Hours → Timings on request
Web/email → www.albadiagolfresort.com   Map Ref → 14-B4

Due to open in mid-2005, the Al Badia Golf Course is situated within Dubai Festival City on the banks of Dubai Creek, and is designed around 11 lakes and waterfalls feeding into the Creek. For further information please contact the club or visit www.albadiagolfresort.com.

Desert Course, The

Location → Arabian Ranches · Dubai | **884 6777**
Hours → 07:00 - 17:30
Web/email → www.thedesertcourse.com   Map Ref → 4-A4

The Desert Course is open to all players with an official handicap and offers practice facilities on its floodlit driving range. The club employs the Golfplus System that uses GPS technology to inform players of the exact distance from their cart to the centre of the green, which makes club selection easier.

Dubai Country Club

Location → Nr Bukadra Interchange · Bukadra | **333 1155**
Hours → 08:00 - 22:00
Web/email → www.dubaicountryclub.com   Map Ref → 17-B3

Dubai Country Club boasts two sand courses that provide a unique golfing experience for beginners and seasoned players are used to playing on grassy fairways. The club hosts the Dubai Men's Open, and includes facilities such as a 24 bay floodlit driving range, practice putting browns and corporate day packages.

Dubai Creek Golf & Yacht Club

Location → Opp Deira City Centre Mall · Al Garhoud | **295 6000**
Hours → 06:30 - 19:00
Web/email → www.dubaigolf.com   Map Ref → 14-C2

This par 71 championship golf course is open to all players holding a valid handicap certificate. Those who are new to the game are encouraged to join the Golf Academy. The floodlit facility offers a challenging par 3 course, thirty six bay driving range, three practice greens and a golf studio featuring state-of-the-art swing analysis software. PGA qualified golf instructors are also available to answer questions.

Golf

Activities

THE DESERT
COURSE

A NATURAL DESERT OASIS.
AN UNFORGETTABLE GOLFING EXPERIENCE.

A DESERT TERRAIN YOU'LL WANT TO PLAY AGAIN AND AGAIN.

Test yourself. The Desert Course at Arabian Ranches is a new breed of golf course.
Designed by Ian Baker-Finch, in association with Nicklaus Design, it doesn't get much better than this.
18 holes of lush greens and manicured fairways carved out of a ruggedly beautiful desert landscape.
The spectacular Desert Course will be the ultimate golfer's challenge.
To make a booking call us on +(971) 4 8846777 and get ready to exceed your personal best.

EMAAR

www.thedesertcourse.com   Email: teetime@thedesertcourse.ae

Emirates Golf Club

Location → Emirates Hills | 380 2222
Hours → 06:00 - 24:00
Web/email → www.dubaigolf.com   Map Ref → 3-A3

The Majlis Course was the first grass course in the Middle East and plays host to the Dubai Desert Classic. There are two 18 hole championship courses to choose from: Majlis (Dhs.525) and Wadi (Dhs.280 - 340). The club also offers the Peter Cowen Golf Academy, along with two driving ranges and dedicated practice areas.

Montgomerie Golf Club

Location → Emirates Hills | 390 5600
Hours → 05:30 - 20:00
Web/email → www.themontgomerie.com   Map Ref → 2-E4

The course is set on 200 acres of land and was designed by Colin Montgomerie and Desmond Muirhead. This 18 hole, par 72 course has some unique characteristics, including the world's largest green (which is in the shape of the UAE). Other facilities include a driving range, putting greens, par 3 course and a swing analysis studio.

The Montgomerie Golf Club

Nad Al Sheba Club

Location → Nr Bukadra Interchange · Nad Al Sheba | 336 3666
Hours → 07:30 - 24:00
Web/email → www.nadalshebaclub.com   Map Ref → 17-A3

This Scottish Links style golf course is the only floodlit 18 hole course in the Middle East. The back nine are situated inside the Nad Al Sheba horseracing track, and golf is prohibited on race nights. The club sports a 50 bay floodlit driving range and coaching is available from British PGA professionals.

Resort Course, The

Location → Jebel Ali Golf Resort & Spa | 883 6000
Hours → 06:30 - 00:00
Web/email → www.jebelali-international.com   Map Ref → 1-A1

Situated in the landscaped gardens of the Jebel Ali Golf Resort and Spa, this nine hole, par 36 golf course offers golfers the opportunity to play alongside peacocks and with views of the Gulf. Renowned for its good condition all year round, the Resort Course is also home to the Jebel Ali Golf Resort and Spa Challenge, the curtain raiser for the annual Dubai Desert Classic.

UAE Golf Association

Location → Creek Golf Club · Al Garhoud | 399 5060
Hours → 09:00 - 17:00
Web/email → www.uagolf.com   Map Ref → 14-C2

This non-profit organisation is the governing body for amateur golf in the UAE. It is overseen by the General Authority of Youth & Sports and actively supports junior players and the development of the national team. Affiliate membership starts at Dhs.200 a year, and members can get a Council of National Union of Golf or Ladies Golf Union handicap for Dhs.595.

Hashing

Other options → Pubs [p.430]
Running [p.287]

Sometimes described as drinking clubs with a running problem, the Hash House Harriers are a worldwide family of social running clubs. The aim of running in this setup is not to win, but to merely be there and to take part. The club was formed in Kuala Lumpur in 1938 and is now the largest running organisation in the world with members in over 1,600 chapters in 180 countries.

Hashing consists of running, jogging or walking around varied courses, often cross-country, laid out by a couple of 'hares'. It's a fun way to keep fit and meet new people, since clubs are invariably very sociable and the running component is not competitive.

Golf | Hashing

Activities

Designed by Colin Montgomerie, in association with Desmond Muirhead, The Montgomerie, Dubai is an integral part of Troon Golf's expanding

EXPERIENCE THE LUXURY OF THE MONTGOMERIE, DUBAI.

international network of upscale golf properties. Covering over two hundred acres, this spectacular course boasts 79 bunkers, sparkling waterways and a host of unique features including the world's single largest green. The Montgomerie, Dubai is also home to The Academy by Troon Golf with world-class practice facilities and state-of-the-art coaching programmes. Located in the prestigious Emirates Hills Estate, The Montgomerie, Dubai has established itself as the Middle East's premier luxury golf destination.

THE
MONTGOMERIE
DUBAI

PO Box 36700, Dubai, United Arab Emirates. Tel (+971) 4 3905600 Fax (+971) 4 3905700
info@themontgomerie.ae www.themontgomerie.com www.troongolf.com

A PROJECT BY
EMAAR

EXPERIENCE TROON GOLF®

Barbie Hash House

Location ➜ Various locations	348 4210
Hours ➜ See Website	
Web/email ➜ www.deserthash.net	Map Ref ➜ na

Meeting on the first Tuesday of every month (except in summer), this is a girls only gathering with a Barbie theme, which means pink dress code with a tiara. 20 - 25 members get together for a social evening that involves hashing, champagne, a meal and singing their Barbie song. Cost is Dhs.10.

Creek Hash House Harriers

Location ➜ Various locations	050 451 5847
Hours ➜ Various	
Web/email ➜ www.creekhash.net	Map Ref ➜ na

This is a men only hash that meets each Tuesday in a different location. Start times are usually 45 minutes before sunset and runs last 40 - 50 minutes. Further information can be obtained from Ian Browning on the above number or Richard Holmes (050 644 4285). Information on weekly runs can be obtained at www.creekhash.net.

Desert Hash House Harriers

Location ➜ Various locations	050 454 2635
Hours ➜ Sun evenings	
Web/email ➜ www.deserthash.net	Map Ref ➜ na

The Desert Hash House Harriers meet every Sunday evening at various locations around Dubai. Runs

Ain't no mountain high enough

start an hour before sunset and last about 50 minutes. Fees are Dhs.50 for men and Dhs.30 for women and include food and beverages. Contact Stuart Wakeham (050 454 2635) or Alan Permain (050 457 1603) for more details.

Moonshine Hash House Harriers

Location ➜ Various locations	050 452 3094
Hours ➜ Once a month	
Web/email ➜ www.deserthash.net	Map Ref ➜ na

Moonshine Hash House Harriers run once a month on the night of the full moon. The run/walk creates a thirst, which is then quenched upon return to the alehouse for traditional hash ceremonies. The Moonshine is a small friendly hash with an emphasis on being sociable not competitive. Fees are Dhs.10 per hash.

Helicopter Flights

Other options ➜ Flying [p.271]
Plane Tours [p.286]

Aerogulf Services Company

Location ➜ Dubai Intl Airport · Al Garhoud	220 0331
Hours ➜ 07:00 - 19:30	
Web/email ➜ aerogulf@emirates.net.ae	Map Ref ➜ 15-A2

Viewing Dubai from the air is an exhilarating experience and it's an ideal way to get a unique perspective of the city. Helicopter tours will show you dhows, parks, the Creek, palaces and beaches, and rides are available between 10:30 and 17:00.

Hiking

Other options ➜ Off-Road Explorer
Out of Dubai [p.186]
Outdoor Goods [p.228]

Although Dubai is mostly flat desert, spectacular locations can be found an hour outside its city limits. To the north, the Ru'us Al Jibal Mountains contain the highest peaks in the area and stand proud at over 2,000 metres. To the east, the impressive Hajar Mountains form the border between the UAE and Oman, stretching from the Mussandam Peninsula, north of Ras Al Khaimah, to the Empty Quarter Desert, which is several hundred kilometres to the south.

Most of the terrain is heavily eroded and crumbling due to the harsh climate, but there are still places where you can walk through shady palm plantations and lush oases. Routes range from short easy walks leading to spectacular viewpoints, to all day treks over difficult terrain and can include major mountaineering. Some hikes follow centuries old Bedouin and Shihuh mountain paths, a few of which are still being used as the only means of access to remote settlements.

One of the nearest and easiest places to reach is the foothills of the Hajar Mountains on the Hatta Road, about 100 Km from Dubai, near the border of Oman. After passing through the desert and the flat savannah-like plains, stark, rugged outcrops transform the landscape on either side of the road. Explore any turning you like, or take the road to Mahdah, along which you will find numerous wadis, paths and scaleable hills.

Other great areas for hiking and exploring include Al Ain and its surroundings, many places in Wadi Bih (the mountainous route from Ras Al Khaimah to Dibba), and the mountains near the east coast. The mountains in the UAE don't generally disappoint, and the further off the beaten track you get, the more likely you are to find interesting villages where residents live much the same way as they did centuries ago.

For more information on hiking routes refer to the *Off-Road Explorer (UAE)*. This is a handy manual and includes information on health and safety, off-road driving, flora and fauna and GPS co-ordinates as well as details of interesting hikes. For somewhere a bit further afield see *Trekking in Oman*, a new series of pocket sized books produced in cooperation with the Omani Government that cover all the major signed routes in Oman.

Off-Road Explorer
Look out for the all-new *Off-Road Explorer* with fully updated routes, maps and satellite images. This indispensable guide to the UAE's 'outback' also features safety information and driving tips. Available early 2005, it's the ultimate accessory to any 4x4.

As with any trip into the UAE 'outback', take sensible precautions. Tell someone where you're going and when you should be back and don't forget to take a map, compass, GPS equipment and robust hiking boots. Don't underestimate the strength of the sun - take food for energy, sunscreen, and most importantly, loads of water.

For most people, the cooler and less humid winter months between November and April are the best season for serious mountain hiking. Be particularly careful in wadis (dry riverbeds) during the wet season as dangerous flash floods can immerse a wadi in seconds. Also note that there are no mountain rescue services in the UAE, so anyone venturing out into the mountains should be reasonably experienced or accompanied by someone who knows the area.

Desert Rangers

Location → Dubai Garden Centre · Al Quoz | 340 2408
Hours → 09:00 - 18:00
Web/email → www.desertrangers.com   Map Ref → 4-B4

Desert Rangers offer hikes for individuals and groups of up to 100 people by dividing them into smaller teams and taking different trails to the summit. A variety of routes are offered according to age and fitness. Locations include Fujairah, Dibba, Masafi, Ras Al Khaimah and Al Ain, and prices start at Dhs.275 per person.

Hockey

Other options → Ice Hockey [p.280]

Dubai Hockey Club

Location → Emirates Golf Club · Emirates Hills | 050 624 8185
Hours → Various
Web/email → www.dubaihockey.com   Map Ref → 3-A3

DHC is a club with players of all abilities and has a strong social component. Members include people from South Africa, UK, Netherlands and Australia. The club competes in 11-a-side matches against other clubs and often enters UAE tournaments. Annual international tours are also organised.

Sharjah Wanderers Hockey Club

Location → Sharjah Wanderers Sports Club | 06 566 2105
Hours → Timings on request
Web/email → www.sharjahwanderers.com   Map Ref → UAE-C2

The club was born as a part of the Sharjah Contracts Club in 1976. The hockey section became the first mixed team in the Gulf, and has always retained a strong mixed club atmosphere. The approach at the club is to play sport within a friendly, but competitive, environment.

Horse Riding

Other options → Polo [p.286]
Stable Tours [p.178]

Club Joumana

Location → Jebel Ali Golf Resort & Spa	883 6000
Hours → Timings on request	
Web/email → www.jebelali-international.com	Map Ref → 1-A1

Located at Jebel Ali Golf Resort and Spa, this riding centre has five horses, air-conditioned stables and a paddock overlooking the Arabian Gulf. Keith Brown, the resident riding instructor, gives half hour private lessons from Tuesday to Sunday. One hour desert rides can be arranged for experienced riders and the stables are closed during the summer months.

Emirates Riding Centre

Location → Nr Camel Race Track · Nad Al Sheba	336 1394
Hours → Timings on request	
Web/email → emrc@emirates.net.ae	Map Ref → 17-A3

The Emirates Riding Centre has 147 horses and facilities include an international sized floodlit arena, riding school, dressage and lungeing ring. The club hosts at least two competitions and three riding school shows per month, as well as gymkhanas from October to May. The centre also has regular clinics and stable management courses.

Jebel Ali Equestrian Club

Location → Jebel Ali Village · Jebel Ali Village	884 5485
Hours → 08:00 - 11:30 16:00 - 19:00 Fri closed	
Web/email → na	Map Ref → 10-E3

Fully qualified instructors teach children and adults, from beginner to advanced levels, at Jebel Ali Equestrian Club. For more experienced riders, dressage, jumping and hacking are on offer, and gymkhana games, with competitions are held on a regular basis. Registration fees are Dhs.120 per rider or Dhs.300 per family.

Sharjah Equestrian & Racing Club

Location → Jct 6, Al Dhaid Rd	06 531 1155
Hours → 07:00 - 10:00 16:00 - 20:00	
Web/email → www.forsanuae.org.ae	Map Ref → UAE-C2

This riding centre was built in 1984 under the supervision of Sheikh Sultan bin Mohammed Al-Qassimi, member of the Supreme Council and Ruler of Sharjah. Facilities include a floodlit sand arena and paddock, a grass show jumping arena and hacking trails into the desert. The club houses 250 horses and riding at the club is only done by appointment and approval.

Hot Air Ballooning

Other options → Flying [p.271]
Plane Tours [p.286]

Voyagers Xtreme

Location → Dune Centre · Al Satwa	345 4504
Hours → 09:00 - 18:00	
Web/email → www.turnertraveldubai.com	Map Ref → 6-E3

This is a great way to celebrate birthdays, anniversaries or product launches. Daily flights for up to 12 people operate every morning over the city, mountains or desert, taking off from Dubai Internet City or Fossil Rock with a fully certified pilot. Trips are weather permitting.

Ice Hockey

Other options → Ice Skating [p.281]

Dubai Mighty Camels Ice Hockey Club

Location → Al Nasr Leisureland · Oud Metha	050 450 0780
Hours → Timings on requst	
Web/email → www.dubaimightycamels.com	Map Ref → 10-E4

Ice hockey has been a fixture on the local sports scene ever since Al Nasr Leisureland opened in 1979. The club presently has over 120 members and has regular social get-togethers from September to May. The club also hosts an annual tournament in April, which will be attended by 15 - 20 teams from the Gulf, Europe and the Far East in 2005.

Dubai Sandstorms Ice Hockey Club

Location → Al Nasr Leisureland · Oud Metha	344 1885
Hours → Sat 16:30 - 21:00	
Web/email → rproctor@emirates.net.ae	Map Ref → 10-E4

This club was established to provide boys and girls (six to 18 years) with the opportunity to learn how to play ice hockey. The club's emphasis is on teamwork and sportsmanship, and no previous experience is required. Practices are held twice a week and matches are played against teams from Dubai, Abu Dhabi, Al Ain and Oman.

Horse Riding | Ice Hockey

Activities

Ice Skating

Other options → Ice Hockey [p.280]

Al Nasr Leisureland

Location → Beh American Hospital · Oud Metha | 337 1234
Hours → 09:00 - 24:00
Web/email → www.alnasrleisureland.ae   Map Ref → 10-E4

Open to the public (except when in use by clubs), the rink is part of the Leisureland complex that comprises a bowling alley, fast food outlets, arcade games and shops. Entrance fees are Dhs.10 for adults and Dhs.5 for children under 10, while skate rental charges are Dhs.10 for two hours.

Galleria Ice Rink

Location → Hyatt Regency · Deira | 209 6550
Hours → 10:00 - 13:30 14:00 - 17:30 18:00 - 21:00
Web/email → www.dubai.regency.hyatt.com   Map Ref → 8-D2

Located in the centre of a shopping mall, the Galleria Ice Rink is a busy place. Fees for public sessions are Dhs.25 per person (including skate hire) or Dhs.15 if you have your own skates. Membership rates start at Dhs.300 per month, or Dhs.1,200 per year, and members are entitled to unlimited skating. Lessons are available for non-members and start at Dhs.80 per half hour.

Jet Skiing

Other options → Beach Clubs [p.300]

Every weekend, and on most afternoons, you will see trailer loads of jet skis parked near Al Garhoud Bridge, from the opposite side of Dubai Creek Golf Club and at the first lagoon between Dubai and Sharjah, near Al Mamzar Beach Park. The cost to hire a jet ski is approximately Dhs.100 for half an hour. Additional places where you can now also hire jet skis includes the Ritz-Carlton and Le Royal Meridien Beach Resort and Spa, as well as the public beach near the Jumeirah Beach Hotel.

With all the aquatic traffic you may find the waters of Dubai Creek a little bit too murky and dirty. Locations on the Gulf offer a cleaner environment, as well as stricter controls and better safety records. It may also be worth checking that your medical insurance covers you for this potentially dangerous sport – broken legs are apparently not all that uncommon.

Jet setter making waves

Karting

Other options → Dune Buggy Riding [p.269]

Emirates Kart Centre

Location → Jct 9, nr Jebel Ali Golf Resort & Spa | 282 7111
Hours → Timings on request
Web/email → www.emsf.ae   Map Ref → 1-A1

At Emirates Karting Centre you can experience real motor racing and it's an ideal activity for family, friends and corporate clients. Pro and junior karts are available and you can take part regularly without buying any equipment. The outdoor circuit is floodlit and includes a track that's 0.8 kms long.

Formula One Dubai

Location → Dubai Exiles Rugby Club | 338 8828
Hours → 15:00 - 22:00
Web/email → f1dubai@emirates.net.ae   Map Ref → 14-A3

Formula One Dubai offers a range of racing opportunities for individuals, groups and corporate clients, and no experience is required to take part in this exciting activity. The club also caters for corporate entertainment, children's parties, individual practice sessions and specialised outdoor functions. For information on prices contact the club office.

Ice Skating | Karting

Activities

Kayaking

Other options → **Canoeing [p.264]**
Tours & Sightseeing [p.181]

Beach Hut, The

Location → Sandy Beach Motel
Hours → 08:00 - 17:30
Web/email → www.sandybm.com   Map Ref → na

09 244 5050

The Beach Hut offers a variety of water sports equipment for rent or sale. For those who want to paddle out to Snoopy Island and explore, kayaks are available for hire at Dhs.30 per hour. You can also try your hand at windsurfing. Diving and snorkelling equipment is also available.

Kitesurfing

Other options → **Beaches [p.179]**
Windsurfing [p.294]

Kitesurfing is a fast growing extreme sport that's swiftly gaining popularity. It's not windsurfing, it's not wakeboarding, it's not surfing and it's not kite flying. In fact, it's a fusion of all these disciplines, with a few other influences thrown in for good measure.

Dubai Kite Club, The

Location → Kitebeach beh Wollongong Uni
Hours → 18:00 - 20:00 Timings on request
Web/email → www.dubaikiteclub.com   Map Ref → 4-E2

884 5912

The Dubai Kite Club regulates the sport of kite surfing, mountain board kiting, power kiting and display kiting. While the beach behind the old site of Wollongong

Have kite, will travel

University was once a popular site for kite surfers the future of the club is uncertain due to new regulations so check with the website for more information. Recommended brands for use in the Arabian Gulf are Naish, Flexifoil and Peter Lynn. Contact Fatima Sports on 050 455 5216 for more information.

Fun Sports

Location → Various
Hours → 09:00 - 17:00
Web/email → www.funsport-dubai.com   Map Ref → na

399 5976

Wakeboarding or windsurfing experience is helpful if you're new to kite surfing, because it is a sport that requires knowledge of the wind. For those taking up this sport up for the first time, there's an hour session on the sand before you take to the sea.

Martial Arts

Whether you're a black belt Bruce Lee wannabe or just fancy trying your hand at karate there are various fitness centre in Dubai where you can hone your martial arts skills. Be it judo, which is a great form of self defence or aikido, which combines joint locks and throws with the body movements of sword and spear. Check with the club to find out what disciplines they teach.

Al Majaz

Location → Trade Centre Rd · Al Karama
Hours → 09:00 - 13:00 16:00 - 21:00 Fri closed
Web/email → www.goldenfistkarate.com   Map Ref → 10-D1

335 3563

Al Majaz offers a variety of self improvement and fitness classes, as well as swimming lessons. Ladies and girls can practice yoga, aerobics or take self defence classes. In addition, separate classes for adults, girls and boys are available in karate, kung fu, taekwondo and ju-jitsu. Contact Golden Fist Karate Club (355 1029) for more details. Transport can also be provided.

Dubai Aikido Club

Location → Dubai Karate Centre · Al Wasl
Hours →   Timings on request
Web/email → www.aikido-uae.net   Map Ref → 6-A4

344 7797

Aikido is a self defence martial art that also trains the mind. The Dubai Aikido Club was established in 1995 and is affiliated with the International Aikido Association. Classes are held on Sundays

Kayaking | Martial Arts

Activities

and Tuesday. For further information contact John Rutnam, chief instructor.

Dubai Karate Centre

Location → Nr Emirates Bank, Al Wasl Rd · Al Wasl | **344 7797**
Hours → Timings on request
Web/email → www.dubaikarate.com   Map Ref → 6-A4

At the Dubai Karate Centre a team of black belt, JKA qualified instructors teach shotokan, aikido and judo. The club is a member of the Japanese Karate Association (JKA) and offers tuition for everyone from beginners to black belts. There is a Dhs.100 registration fee and Dhs.200 monthly membership fee.

Golden Falcon Karate Centre

Location → Beh Sony Jumbo · Al Karama | **336 0243**
Hours → 08:30 - 12:00 16:30 - 22:30
Web/email → www.goldenfalconkarate.com   Map Ref → 10-C3

Established in 1990, this karate centre is affiliated to the International Karate Budokan and UAE Judo, Taekwondo and Karate Federation. The centre is open throughout the week and students can choose class times that suit their schedules. Official certificates are issued from international headquarters to successful grading candidates.

House of Chi & House of Healing

Location → Musalla Towers · Bur Dubai | **397 4446**
Hours → 09:00 - 22:00 Fri 10:00 - 22:00
Web/email → www.hofchi.com   Map Ref → 8-A4

Shotokan karate and aikido are among the martial arts offered by this school. Shotokan karate is an unarmed combat system that employs kicking, striking and defense blocking with arms and legs, while aikido is a traditional Japanese martial art based on the blend of ancient sword, staff and body techniques.

Taekwondo

Location → Ballet Centre, The · Jumeira | **344 9776**
Hours → Sun & Tue 15:30 - 21:00 Thu 10:00 - 13:00
Web/email → www.balletcentre.com   Map Ref → 6-C3

The Ballet Centre's taekwondo arm is run by Fabun, a 7th dan black belt. This form of martial art teaches children and adults mental calmness, courage, strength and humility, courtesy, integrity, perseverance, self-control and indomitable spirit.

Mini Golf

Other options → Golf [p.274]

Aviation Club, The

Location → Nr Tennis Stadium · Al Garhoud | **050 624 0162**
Hours → 06:00 - 23:00
Web/email → www.cftennis.com   Map Ref → 14-C3

This nine hole pitch and putt course is located between the tennis stadium and the clubhouse. With manicured fairways and greens, each hole is a reasonable challenge for beginners as well as accomplished golfers. The course offers putting variety and holes differ in distance from 40 to 82 yards. This activity is open to members only.

Hatta Fort Hotel

Location → Hatta Fort Hotel | **852 3211**
Hours → Timings on request
Web/email → www.jebelali-international.com Map Ref → UAE-D3

Set against the backdrop of the Hajar Mountains, the Hatta Fort Hotel offers a crazy golf experience. The hotel also features a driving range where golfers can practice their swings. Prices are available upon request and activities can be combined with an outing to the pool or with a barbeque.

Hyatt Golf Park

Location → Hyatt Regency · Deira | **209 6802**
Hours → 08:00 - 23:00
Web/email → www.dubai.hyatt.com   Map Ref → 8-D2

The Hyatt offers a nine hole pitch and putt grass course (Dhs.15 for one round) or an 18 hole crazy golf course (Dhs.10 per person). Clubs are provided and golf balls are sold at Dhs.8 each. The park is floodlit in the evenings and the clubhouse overlooks a small lagoon.

Moto-Cross

Other options → Motorcycling [p.284]

Dubai Youth Moto-Cross Club (DMX)

Location → Beh Kart Club | **050 452 7844**
Hours → Timings on request
Web/email → www.dubaimotocross.net   Map Ref → 1-A1

DMX runs classes for Cadets, Juniors, 65s, 85s, 125s and adults. The new Jebel Ali Motocross

Martial Arts | Moto-Cross

Activities

Park features two tracks (one for juniors and one for seniors) along with other facilities that make it fun for the whole family to enjoy a day at the track.

Motorcycling

Other options → Moto-Cross [p.283]

Al Ramool Motorcycle Rental

Location → Big Red, on Hatta Rd
Hours → 07:00 - 18:30
Web/email → na

050 453 3033

Map Ref → UAE-D3

Al Ramool rents LT50, LT80, 125cc, 350cc and 620cc motorcycles, as well as quad bikes and safari vehicles. Rental costs vary between Dhs.20 - 100 for 30 minutes. The company also offers tailor made packages such as camel rides, falcon hunting and baby camel feeding.

UAE Motorcycle Club

Location → Al Muraqqabat Street · Deira
Hours → 09:00 - 17:00   09:00 - 14:00
Web/email → www.uaedesertchallenge.com

266 9002

Map Ref → 11-E2

The UAE Motorcycle Club is the UAE's FIM representative. Regular Moto-X and off-road enduros are held between September and April, and activity centres at the DMX Club and in Umm al Quwain host quad and drag races. Call the UAEMC office for details on upcoming events.

Motor Sports

Emirates Motor Sports Federation

Location → Nr Aviation Club · Al Garhoud
Hours → Timings on request
Web/email → www.emsf.ae

282 7111

Map Ref → 14-D4

For rally enthusiasts in the UAE, the Federation organises a variety of events throughout the year ranging from the 4 WD 1000 Dunes Rally to the Champions Rally for saloon cars. Other events include road safety awareness campaigns and classic car exhibitions. Federation membership stands at Dhs.750 and a professional competition licence is required to participate.

Mountain Biking

Other options → Cycling [p.266]
Off-Road Explorer
Out of Dubai [p.186]

The UAE interior has a lot on offer for outdoor enthusiasts, especially mountain bikers. On a mountain bike it's possible to see the most remote and untouched places that are not even accessible in four wheel drives. For hardcore, experienced mountain bikers there is a good range of terrain, from the super technical rocky trails in areas like Fili and Siji, to mountain routes like Wadi Bih, which climb to over a thousand metres and can be descended in minutes.

The riding is mainly rocky, technical and challenging. Even if you are an experienced biker, always be sensible and go prepared – the sun is strong, you will need far more water than you think, and it is easy to get lost. Not to mention the pain caused by a fall on such rocky terrain! For further information on mountain biking in the UAE, including details of possible routes, refer to the *Off-Road Explorer (UAE)*.

Biking Frontiers

Location → Various locations
Hours → Timings on request
Web/email → www.bikingfrontiers.com

050 450 9401

Map Ref → na

Biking Frontiers is an active club of enthusiasts who ride every weekend, all year round. The group also camps, hikes and barbecues. You will need your own bike, helmet and other essential gear.

Uh-oh - where did the ground go?

THE BEST REASON YET TO RIDE RED

It's the many years of experience, advanced 4-stroke technology and unparalleled reliability that have made Honda off-road bikes the finest on earth! Choose from one of the widest range of off-road bikes and ATVs, including the class leading CRF450R3 and TRX400EX.

Experience a piece of the action - visit your local Trading Enterprises - Honda showroom and 'Ride Red'.

HONDA
PERFORMANCE FIRST

trading enterprises

An *Al-Futtaim group* company

Dubai Airport Road (04) 2954246, Sheikh Zayed Road (04) 3472212, Fleet Sales (04) 3472212 **Sharjah** (06) 5597833 **Ajman** (06) 7446543 **RAK** (07) 2351881 **Al Ain** (03) 7211838 **Fujairah** (09) 2223097 **Abu Dhabi** (02) 6763300 **UAQ** (06) 7666694
e-mail: tradingent@alfuttaim.ae   www.tradingenterprises.com   www.al-futtaim.com

www.**honda**uae.com

Netball

Dubai Netball League

Location ➜ Dubai Exiles Rugby Club · Bukadra | 050 450 6715
Hours ➜ Timings on request
Web/email ➜ jon37@emirates.net.ae   Map Ref ➜ 17-B3

There are over 18 teams in three divisions at the club, and players range from beginners to experts. Matches are played from September to May on Wednesday nights. During the season, players are selected for the Inter Gulf Netball Championships, a tournament that features teams from Abu Dhabi, Bahrain, Dubai, Kuwait, Oman and Saudi Arabia.

Paintballing

Other options ➜ Shooting [p.289]

Pursuit Games

Location ➜ WonderLand · Umm Hurair | 324 1222
Hours ➜ Timings on request
Web/email ➜ paintbal@emirates.net.ae   Map Ref ➜ 14-A3

This is a fun game for teenagers and adults where bullets are replaced with paint balls. Club experts break groups up into two teams and give safety demonstrations before equipping participants with overalls, facemasks, special guns and paintballs. Costs start at Dhs.70 for a two hour game, and include 100 paintballs, gun and gas.

Paintballing

If you want to maintain a great work environment, why not take your office mates on a team building exercise? Paintballing [p.286] is sure to improve, boost or destroy relations in the office. Find out if you're brave enough to smoke out the 'silent but deadly' types.

Note of caution: It is advisable for the boss to wear extra padding.

Parasailing

Experience the thrill of parasailing in the Gulf and enjoy spectacular views to boot. Most of the major coastal hotels offer parasailing off the beach. Flights last for about eight minutes and there's no need to run down the beach during take off or landing – it all happens on the back of a boat. Availability of this activity is naturally subject to weather conditions.

Plane Tours

Other options ➜ Flying [p.271]
Helicopter Flights [p.278]
Hot Air Ballooning [p.280]

Fujairah Aviation Centre

Location ➜ Fujairah Int'l Airport | 09 222 4747
Hours ➜ Timings on request
Web/email ➜ www.fujairah-aviation.ae   Map Ref ➜ UAE-E2

A bird's eye view of the coastline, rugged mountains, villages and date plantations is available from the Fujairah Aviation Centre. Flights last from 30 minutes (Dhs.100 per person) to four hours, while longer tours for one to three people cost Dhs.480 per hour. Rates are subject to change without prior notice.

Polo

Other options ➜ Horse Riding [p.280]

Ghantoot Polo & Racing Club

Location ➜ Shk Zayed Rd towards Abu Dhabi | 02 562 9050
Hours ➜ Timings on request
Web/email ➜ na   Map Ref ➜ UAE-A4

With six international standard polo fields (three of which are floodlit), two stick and ball fields, three tennis courts, swimming pool, gym, sauna and a restaurant, this club has first class facilities for the entire family. Nonmembers are welcome to dine at the restaurant or to watch polo matches that take place between October and April.

Quad Bikes

Other options ➜ Dune Buggy Riding [p.286]

Quad bikes are available at Big Red on the Dubai Hatta road, but beware - unlike Dune Buggies, Quad bikes have no roll cages and there are no instructors. For more information, refer to Dune Buggy Riding [p.269].

Rollerblading & Roller Skating

Other options ➜ Beaches [p.179]
Parks [p.180]

Dubai's many parks provide some excellent locations for rollerblading. The Creekside Park and Safa Park offer wide pathways, few people and enough slopes and turns to make it interesting.

Alternatively, check out both sides of Dubai Creek, the seafront near the Hyatt Regency Hotel or the promenade at the Jumeira Beach Corniche, where the view is an added bonus.

Roller Blade Runner

Rugby

Other options → **Sporting Goods [p.230]**

Dubai Exiles Rugby Club

Location → Nr Dubai Country Club · Bukadra | **333 1198**
Hours → Timings on request
Web/email → www.dubaiexiles.com   Map Ref → 17-B3

The Exiles is Dubai's most serious rugby club and has become a bastion for the sport. 1st and 2nd XV practices take place on Sundays and Wednesdays, while veterans train on Tuesdays and Saturdays. The Exiles also host the annual Dubai International Rugby Sevens Tournament, which attracts international teams from all the major rugby playing nations.

Dubai Hurricanes

Location → Country Club · Bukadra | **333 1155**
Hours → Timings on request
Web/email → hurricanepauly@hotmail.com   Map Ref → 17-B3

Originally formed as a purely social outfit, Dubai Hurricanes now compete in the Dubai Sevens tournament. The club sports a ladies team and invites new players of all abilities to join their ranks. Training sessions are held on Sunday and Tuesday evenings. Contact club captain, Dominic Parker (050 766 2658), for more details.

Running

Other options → **Hashing [p.276]**

For over half the year Dubai's weather is perfect for running and many groups and clubs meet up for runs on a regular basis. There are several major running events, usually held annually, such as the Round the Creek Relay Race, the Dubai Marathon, and the epic Wadi Bih Race. In the latter, each runner in a five member team runs a portion of the 70 km route between Ras Al Khaimah on the west coast to Dibba on the east. The terrain is arduous, featuring mountains that top out at over a thousand metres. For more information on the Round the Creek Relay Race, contact Ian Colton (050 658 4153) and for more information on the Wadi Bih Race, call John Gregory (050 647 7120). The Dubai Marathon is usually run in January every year, and aside from the official marathon-distance run around the city of Dubai, there is also a 10 km road race and a 3 km fun run. For more information, or to register online, visit www.dubaimarathon.org.

Dubai Creek Striders

Location → Opp Exhibition hall no 4 · Trade Centre 1 | **321 1999**
Hours → Fri 06:30
Web/email → www.dubaicreekstriders.com   Map Ref → 9-E2

This medium to long distance running club organises weekly outings on Friday mornings. Distances and routes differ each week, but normally consist of 10 km runs during the summer and 32 km winter training runs that form part of the build up to the annual 42.2 km Dubai Marathon that takes place in early January.

Dubai Road Runners

Location → Safa Park · Al Wasl | **340 3777**
Hours → Sat 18:30
Web/email → www.dubai-road-runners.com   Map Ref → 5-C3

Come rain or shine, 100% humidity or 50°C temperatures, Dubai Road Runners meet every Saturday at 18:30 at Safa Park outside gate 4, and the objective of the meeting is to run a 3.5 or 7 km track around the park. A Dhs.5 entrance fee is charged, and most people try to run this course against the clock.

Sailing

Temperatures in winter are perfect for sailing and water sports, and taking to the sea in summer serves as an escape from the scorching heat that prohibits some land-based sports. Sailing is a popular pastime in Dubai and many people are members of the Jumeirah Beach and Mina Seyahi clubs. Membership allows you to participate in club activities and to rent sailing and water sports equipment. You can also use the leisure facilities and the club's beach, and moor your boat at an additional cost.

There's a healthy racing scene for a variety of boat types, as well as long distance races such as the annual Dubai to Muscat race which is held in March. The traditional dhow races are also a spectacle and many companies will take you out on a cruise for pleasure or fishing, where times can range from a couple of hours to a full day. You can also charter your own boat for periods ranging from one morning to several weeks. See Dhow Racing – Annual Events [p.54] for more details.

Dubai Offshore Sailing Club

Location → Jumeira
Hours →   Timings on request
Web/email → www.dosc.org   Map Ref → 4-E2

| 394 1669

DOSC is recognised by the Royal Yachting Association and runs dinghy, keelboat and windsurfing courses throughout the year. The Thursday and Friday Cadet Club is great for younger sailors, and the club provides mooring, storage, launch facilities, and sail training along with a full yachting and social calendar.

Sailing off Jumeira Beach

Fun Sports

Location → Various
Hours → 09:00 - 17:00
Web/email → www.funsport-dubai.com   Map Ref → na

| 399 5976

Offering multi-hull sailing with professional sailing instructors available to teach beginners and improvers. For bookings contact Suzette on the above number or 050 453 4828.

Locations: The company operates at the following beach clubs: Hilton Dubai Jumeirah, Metropolitan Resort & Beach Club, Oasis Beach Hotel, Ritz-Carlton Beach Club and Le Meridien Mina Seyahi

Jebel Ali Sailing Club

Location → Nr Le Meridien Mina Seyahi · Al Sufouh
Hours → 09:00 - 22:00
Web/email → www.jebelalisailingclub.com   Map Ref → 2-E2

| 399 5444

This club is recognised by the RYA to teach and certify sailing, windsurfing and powerboat licences, and instruct in kayaking. Races are held on most Fridays for toppers, lasers, catamarans and cruisers. Topper coaching takes place every Wednesday afternoon, while cadet club takes place on Thursdays.

Sand Boarding/Skiing

Other options → Tour Operators [p.184]

Sandboarding is not as fast or smooth as snowboarding but it can be a lot of fun. Head out into the desert in your 4 WD, climb a big dune and feel the wind rush past you as you carve down the sandy slopes. A popular sandboarding spot is the huge dune halfway to Hatta, which is affectionately known as Big Red.

Boards are usually standard snowboards, but as the sand wears them down they end up being good for nothing else. Some sports stores sell sandboards, but they are really nothing more than cheap, basic snowboards. As an alternative for children, a plastic sledge or something similar can do the trick.

All major tour companies offer sandboarding experiences at the highest dunes, along with basic instructions on how to surf, and also provide 4 WD taxi services back to the top of dunes. Sandboarding can be done as part of another tour or you can opt for a half day session, which will cost between Dhs.175 and Dhs.200.

Shooting

Other options → Paintballing [p.286]

Hatta Fort Hotel

Location → Hatta Fort Hotel | 852 3211
Hours → Timings on request
Web/email → www.jebelali-international.com   Map Ref → UAE-D3

Clay pigeon shooting is one of many activities offered by Hatta Fort Hotel, which is located less than an hour's drive from Dubai. More frequently visited as an overnight retreat from the hustle and bustle of Dubai, the Hatta Fort Hotel also features a rock pool and Friday barbeque for guests or day visitors. See Hatta in Exploring for more information [p.188].

Jebel Ali Shooting Club

Location → Nr Jebel Ali Golf Resort & Spa | 883 6555
Hours → 13:00 - 22:00
Web/email → www.jebelali-international.com   Map Ref → 1-A2

The Jebel Ali Shooting Club has five floodlit clay shooting ranges that consist of skeet, trap and sporting, and there are also two fully computerised indoor pistol ranges. Professional shooting instructors provide lessons and experienced member or non-member shooters can try their hand at clay or pistol shooting - a variety of calibres will soon be available.

Ras Al Khaimah Shooting Club

Location → Al Dehes - 20 min from RAK Airport | 07 236 3622
Hours → 15:00 - 20:00
Web/email → na   Map Ref → UAE-D1

This club welcomes interested parties that want to learn how to shoot any type of gun, from 9mm pistols to shotguns and long rifles. The club boasts a 50-metre indoor and 200-metre outdoor rifle range. A canteen sells snacks and soft drinks, and the club is open on Mondays for women and children only.

Skiing & Snowboarding

Ski Dubai

Location → Mall of the Emirates · Dubai | 884 4888
Hours → Opening June 2005
Web/email → na   Map Ref → 3-E4

The Middle East's first indoor ski resort is set for its grand opening in June 2005. The resort, which will feature over 6,000 tons of snow, will be part of the Mall of the Emirates. The snow dome will boast a 400 metre ski run with a 62 metre vertical drop, quarter pipe for snowboarding and a number of other slopes.

Skydiving

Umm Al Quwain Aeroclub

Location → 17km North of UAQ on RAK Rd | 06 768 1447
Hours → 09:00 - 17:30
Web/email → www.uaqaeroclub.com   Map Ref → UAE-D1

In addition to pilot training, helicopter flying, hangar/aircraft rental, paramotors and microlights, the club also operates as a skydive school and boogie centre. You can enjoy an eight level accelerated free fall parachute course (Dhs.5,200) and train for your international parachute licence. Alternatively, try a tandem jump with an instructor from 12,000 feet for Dhs.720.

Snooker

Dubai Snooker Club

Location → Nr Post Office · Al Karama | 337 5338
Hours → 09:00 - 02:00 Fri 15:00 - 01:00
Web/email → www.dubaisnooker.com   Map Ref → 10-E2

The Dubai Snooker Club has 15 snooker tables and eight pool tables, along with three private snooker rooms that can be rented by groups. Tables are rented out at Dhs.20 per hour and, the club organises five tournaments a year.

Rack 'em up

Millennium Avenue

Location → Nr Galadari R/A · Hor Al Anz | **266 6844**
Hours → 10:00 - 02:00   Fri 14:00 - 03:00
Web/email → www.uaebilliard.com   Map Ref → 12-B4

The Millennium Avenue has 18 billiard tables in spacious surroundings and two private snooker tables. The club organises annual inter-club leagues as well as international tournaments, and they are also the official organiser of the Billiards Championships in Dubai. Other facilities include computer games and an Internet café.

Snooker Point

Location → Nr Al Nasr Cinema · Al Karama | **337 7997**
Hours → 10:00 - 03:00   Fri 14:00 - 03:00
Web/email → na   Map Ref → 10-D3

At Snooker Point you can hire one of eight full size snooker tables or nine pool tables at Dhs.4 for 15 minutes. There is a bar in the pool room that sells fruit cocktails, coffees and teas, and food is available at the newly opened fast food restaurant.

Snorkelling

Other options → Diving [p.267]
Underwater Explorer

Snorkelling is a great way to see the varied marine life in the Gulf or on the east coast at popular places such as Snoopy Island, near Sandy Beach Motel, Dibba. Another good spot is the beach north of Dibba village where the coast is rocky and coral can be found close to the shore. Closer to home, the sea off Jumeira Beach has a fair amount of marine life. Most hotels or dive centres rent equipment (snorkel, mask and fins) but costs vary greatly so shop around. Check out the *Underwater Explorer* guidebook for further information on where to go snorkelling in the UAE.

Beach Hut, The

Location → Sandy Beach Motel | **09 244 5050**
Hours → 08:00 - 17:30
Web/email → www.sandybm.com   Map Ref → na

For those who want an exhilarating snorkelling experience, the Beach Hut is a good place to start. Snoopy Island, the house reef, is just off their private beach and is an excellent place to enjoy the underwater world. Equipment is available for sale or you can rent an entire set for Dhs.50. Kayaking and windsurfing are also offered.

Oceanic Hotel

Location → Beach Rd, East Coast | **09 238 5111**
Hours → Timings on request
Web/email → www.oceanichotel.com   Map Ref → UAE-E2

The Oceanic Hotel, on the UAE's east coast, offers a boat ride to Shark Island or guests can snorkel and swim from the hotel beach to Hidden Beach. Equipment hire is Dhs.30 per hour for hotel guests and visitors are obliged to pay an entrance fee of Dhs.45 for adults and Dhs.25 for children.

Scuba 2000

Location → Al Badiyah Beach | **09 238 8477**
Hours → 09:00 - 19:00
Web/email → www.scuba-2000.com   Map Ref → UAE-E2

This east coast Centre offers snorkelling from the beach or by boat ride to Snoopy Island, Shark Island or Al Badiyah Rock. Snorkelling trips to these destinations cost Dhs.120 and are inclusive of fins, mask, snorkel and boots. The centre also has other water sports facilities, including diving, jet skiing, pedal boats and canoes.

Softball

Dubai Softball League

Location → Metropolitan · Shk Zayed Rd | **050 650 2743**
Hours →   Wed & Sat 19:00 - 23:00
Web/email → www.dubaisoftballleague.com   Map Ref → 5-C4

The Dubai Softball League runs from September till December and from January till May, and the only criteria is that you are over 16 years of age. Dubai usually hosts the bi-annual Middle East Softball Championships, held in November and April. It attracts 30 teams with over 500 players from around the Gulf. Entrance is free and food and beverages are available.

Speedboating

Other options → Boat & Yacht Charters [p.260]

Fun Sports

Location → Various | **399 5976**
Hours → 09:00 - 17:00
Web/email → www.funsport-dubai.com   Map Ref → na

Speed boating in the Gulf is a great weekend activity. You can hire a boat, which is handled by a captain, and you can go wherever you please, even up close to the Burj al Arab. Trips are based on prior bookings as well as weather conditions.

Squash

Other options → Sports and Leisure
Facilities [p.300]

Dubai Squash League	
Location → Dubai & Sharjah	343 5672
Hours → Timings on request	
Web/email → meshrakh@emirates.net.ae	Map Ref → na

The squash league has been active in Dubai and Sharjah since the 70s and is run by the UAE Squash Rackets Association. About 300 competitors play three 10 week seasons at over 30 clubs. The league meets every Monday evening and each team fields four players. Contact Shavan Kumar (343 5672), Chris Wind (333 1155) or Andy Staines (339 1331) for more details.

Surfing

Other options → Beaches [p.179]
Kitesurfing [p.282]

Dubai is a respectable surfing location, and while it doesn't compare to hot spots like Indonesia or Hawaii, there is a dedicated group of surfers keeping their eye on the weather and tides from November to June. Swells are generally on the small side (two to four foot), but every now and again conditions are right and bigger waves hit the Gulf coast. The sport's popularity has increased in the last few years and more boards are available on the market. Check out the Surfers of Dubai Website (www.surfersofdubai.com) for information on the best surfing locations, current conditions, where to buy boards and where to meet to watch surfing videos.

Swimming

Other options → Sports and Leisure
Facilities [p.300]
Beaches [p.179]

Dubai is situated on the Arabian Gulf and the sea is easily accessible. The water is relatively clean on Dubai's coast and maintains pleasant swimming temperatures throughout the year, but during the blazing summer months the water in the sea reaches bath-like temperatures. Dubai's white sandy beaches make for great swimming spots,

whether it's at a public beach, beach club or one of the beach parks. Ladies, remember to be modest in your choice of swimming costume. Also be warned that when swimming in the sea, do not underestimate the strength of the tides and currents. Even on the safest looking beaches rip tides have been known to carry people out to sea.

Most hotels have swimming pools that are open for public use for a day entrance fee. This charge varies, starting from Dhs.60 on weekdays and increases at weekends. Swimming lessons are widely available from health and beach clubs, and many clubs offer the services of swimming coaches.

Table Tennis

Other options → Sports and Leisure
Facilities [p.300]

A game of ping pong may not be a high energy sport, but it is a lot of fun. Finding a table is the biggest obstacle but the best place to start is the beach, health and sports clubs, see p.300.

Tennis

Other options → Sports and Leisure
Facilities [p.300]

Dubai has firmly established itself on the international tennis circuit with the $1,000,000 Dubai Duty Free Tennis Open that takes place each year in February.

There are plenty of venues around Dubai to enjoy a game of tennis. Outdoor courts are available at most health and beach clubs, many of which are floodlit and this allows matches to take place in the evenings if the daytime summer heat gets too much. There are also indoor courts at InSportz (347 5833) and they can be hired out for between Dhs.25 – 50 on weekdays, and as much as Dhs.100 at weekends. Group or individual coaching is also widely available.

Aviation Club, The	
Location → Nr Tennis Stadium · Al Garhoud	050 624 0162
Hours → 06:00 - 23:00	
Web/email → www.cftennis.com	Map Ref → 14-C3

The Clark Francis Tennis Academy at The Aviation Club offers a variety of lessons (14 week course – Dhs.540) and activities for all ages and abilities. The club boasts a range of modern facilities, including eight floodlit Decoturf tennis courts. It also hosts The Aviation Cup and the

Speedboating | Tennis

Activities

annual ATP, WTA and Dubai Duty Free Tennis Open each February.

Dubai Tennis Academy

Location → American University · Al Sufouh | **344 4674**
Hours →   Timings on request
Web/email → na   Map Ref → 3-A3

The Academy offers world class training with experienced internationally qualified coaches all year round for tennis players of all ages and abilities. The Academy's full time adult and junior programmes include private lessons, group clinics, competitions, ladies tennis mornings and school holiday sports camps. A personal progress report and video analysis are also available.

Emirates Golf Club

Location →   Emirates Hills | **380 2222**
Hours → 06:00 - 24:00
Web/email → www.dubaigolf.com   Map Ref → 3-A3

The Emirates Tennis Academy (located at Emirates Golf Club) is open to members and non-members, and offers coaching for all ages and skill levels. The centre has six courts, and coaching is provided by qualified USPTR (United States Professional Tennis Registry) professionals. The academy also has two teams in the ladies' Spinneys League and one in the men's Prince League.

Ever get that sinking feeling?

Thai Boxing

Other options → **Martial Arts [p.282]**

Colosseum

Location → Za'abeel Rd · Al Karama | **337 2755**
Hours → 06:00 - 22:00
Web/email → na   Map Ref → 10-E3

This health and fitness club was the first to introduce the martial art of Muay Thai (Thai Boxing) to the UAE. Classes are held on Monday, Wednesday and Saturday evenings from 20:00 – 21:00. Personal training sessions for Muay Thai are also available for children over the age of 8.

Triathlon

Dubai Triathlon Club

Location →   Various locations | **050 654 7924**
Hours →   Timings on request
Web/email → www.dubaitriclub.com   Map Ref → na

During the winter season (October to April) the Dubai Triathlon Club organises the Dubai Triathlon Series that comprises three or four triathlons, aquathons or duathlons. Weekly training sessions take place on Thursday mornings from 07:00 – 08:00 at Umm Suqeim Beach. All interested participants are invited to register via email and no membership is required.

Wadi & Dune Bashing

Other options → **Camping [p.263]**
Desert Driving Courses [p.308]
Off-Road Explorer
Tour Operators [p.184]

With the vast areas of virtually untouched wilderness in the UAE, wadi and dune bashing are very popular pastimes. To protect the environment from damage, you should try to stick to existing tracks rather than create new tracks across virgin countryside. While it may be hard to deviate from the track when wadi bashing, dunes are ever changing so obvious paths are less common. Although the sandy dunes and rocky wadis may look devoid of life, there is a surprising variety of flora and fauna that exists in a delicate balance.

Dune bashing, or desert driving, is one of the toughest challenges for both car and driver, but once you have mastered it, it's also the most fun.

Driving in the wadis is usually a bit more straightforward. Wadis are (usually dry) gullies, carved through the rock by rushing floodwaters, following the course of seasonal rivers. The main safety precaution to take when wadi bashing is to keep your eyes open for developing thunder storms – the wadis can fill up quickly and you will need to make your way to higher ground pretty quickly to avoid flash floods.

If you want a wilderness adventure but don't know where to start, contact any of the major tour companies (see Tour Operators, [p.184]). All offer a range of desert and mountain safaris. For further information and tips for driving off-road, check out the *Off-Road Explorer (UAE)*. This fabulous book features 20 detailed routes, stunning satellite imagery, striking photos and a useful off-road directory.

Wakeboarding

Other options → Water Skiing [p.293]

Dubai Water Sports Association

Location → Nr Shipyard · Al Jaddaf	324 1031
Hours → 09:00 - 18:00	
Web/email → www.dwsa.net	Map Ref → na

Wakeboarding was pioneered by Dubai Water Sports Association (DWSA) and they produced one of the top junior wakeboarders in the world. This sport is an aquatic equivalent of snowboarding: strap your feet onto a large board, weigh the back of the boat down to create a bigger wake, and jump over it. Contact DWSA for more details.

Water Parks

Other options → Amusement Parks [p.258]

Dreamland Aqua Park

Location → 17km North of UAQ on RAK Rd	06 768 1888
Hours → Timings on request	
Web/email → www.dreamlanduae.com	Map Ref → UAE-D1

Dreamland Aqua Park brings you four million gallons of fresh water and over 60 acres of fun, making it one of the largest aqua parks in the world. Dreamland recently launched a water attraction called Aqua Play that includes 12 different water games, and five news slides have also been added. Admission costs Dhs.40 for adults and Dhs.20 for children.

SplashLand

Location → WonderLand · Umm Hurair	324 3222
Hours → 10:00 - 19:00	
Web/email → www.wonderlanduae.com	Map Ref → 14-A3

Try any of the nine water rides or relax by the pool and sunbathe. There's an adults' swimming pool and a children's activity pool with slides, bridges and water cannons. Lockers and changing rooms are available. Refer to WonderLand Theme & Water Park for more details [p.260].

Wild Wadi Water Park

Location → Wild Wadi · Umm Suqeim	348 4444
Hours → Timings on request	
Web/email → www.wildwadi.com	Map Ref → 4-A2

Wild Wadi is a world-class water park themed around the adventures of Juha, Sinbad's mythical friend. The park offers a variety of rides, including Jumeirah Sceirah (the tallest and fastest freefall slide outside North America), Juha's Journey that allows you to float serenely through a changing landscape and Juha's Dhow and Lagoon for younger visitors. All day admission: Dhs.120 for adults and Dhs.100 for children.

Water Skiing

Other options → Beach Clubs [p.300]
Jet Skiing [p.281]
Wakeboarding [p.293]

Club Joumana

Location → Jebel Ali Golf Resort & Spa	883 6000
Hours → Timings on request	
Web/email → www.jebelali-international.com	Map Ref → 1-A1

Water skiing can be arranged at the Aqua Hut which is located on Jebel Ali Golf Resort and Spa's private beach. Prices are available upon request.

Dubai Water Sports Association

Location → Nr Shipyard · Al Jaddaf	324 1031
Hours → 09:00 - 18:00	
Web/email → www.dwsa.net	Map Ref → na

The Dubai Water Sports Association promotes waterskiing and wakeboarding, and organises competitions. The association has two tournament ski boats, slalom course and a full sized jump for hire. The club is open seven days a week, and memberships are available. Entrance fees for non-members are Dhs.20 on weekdays and Dhs.30 on Fridays and public holidays.

Water Sports

Club Joumana

Location → Jebel Ali Golf Resort & Spa | 883 6000
Hours → Timings on request
Web/email → www.jebelali-international.com Map Ref → 1-A1

Located on Jebel Ali Golf Resort and Spa's private beach, the Aqua Hut operates a variety of water sports that range from water skiing and banana boat rides to windsurfing, catamarans, laser sailing and kayaking. Special rates are available for guests and club members. Non-residents of the hotel are charged an additional fee for day access to the beach and swimming pools.

Windsurfing

Other options → Kitesurfing [p.282]
Water Sports [p.294]

Club Joumana

Location → Jebel Ali Golf Resort & Spa | 883 6000
Hours → Timings on request
Web/email → www.jebelali-international.com Map Ref → 1-A1

Windsurfing and other non-motorised water sports can be arranged by the staff at the Aqua Hut, which is located on Jebel Ali Golf Resort and Spa's private beach. Prices are available upon request.

Fun Sports

Location → Various | 399 5976
Hours → 09:00 - 17:00
Web/email → www.funsport-dubai.com Map Ref → na

Fun Sports is one of the leading water sports companies in Dubai. For information on what activities they have to offer, refer to their review under Sailing [p.288].

Well-Being

Dubai is renowned for its luxury services and spas, and treatments and well-being activities are no exception. Be it pampering sessions at health spas

to receiving meditation guidance from a guru or energetic Pilates workouts, whatever your definition of leisure, there's a good chance that someone in town will provide you with the relaxation services you're looking for.

Beauty Salons

Other options → Beauty Training [p.305]
Hairdressers [p.124]
Perfumes & Cosmetics [p.229]

Beauty is big business in Dubai. Salons are very popular and there is a huge variety to choose from offering every type of treatment imaginable. Services range from manicures, pedicures, waxing and henna, to the latest haircuts, styles and colours. Alternatively, you can arrange for a stylist to come to your house if you want to be truly decadent. The quality and range of treatments vary greatly, so trial and error or word of mouth is probably the best way to find a good salon.

In hotels you'll find both male and female stylists working alongside each other, but in establishments located outside hotels, only female stylists are permitted to work in ladies' salons. These salons are good for privacy and men are not permitted inside – even the windows are blacked out.

There are also numerous salons aimed primarily at Arabic ladies and they specialise in henna designs, so look out for a decorated hand poster in salon windows. The traditional practice of painting henna on the hands and feet, especially for weddings or special occasions, is still very popular with UAE nationals. For tourists, a design on the ankle or shoulder can make a great memento – it will cost about Dhs.30 and the intricate brown patterns fade after two to three weeks.

Health Spas

Other options → Sports and Leisure Facilities [p.300]
Health Spas [p.294]
Reflexology/Massage Therapy [p.124]

Assawan Spa and Health Club

Location → Burj Al Arab · Umm Suqeim | 301 7600
Hours → 06:30 - 22:00
Web/email → www.burj-al-arab.com Map Ref → 4-A1

Located on the 18th floor of the Burj Al Arab, this spa allows you to relax using the latest treatments to invigorate your body. You can make use of the health club that features a gymnasium and studio that's equipped with the latest fitness gear. The

Fundamentally fun!

ld Wadi is a trading name of Jumeirah Beach Resort LLC. Company with Limited Liability. Registration Number 45069. Share Capital Dhs. 300,000 fully paid up.

club also offers aerobics, yoga, and other personalised exercise programmes.

Ayoma Spa

Location → Taj Palace Hotel · Deira
Hours → 10:00 - 22:00
Web/email → www.tajpalacehotel.ae

223 2222

Map Ref → 11-D2

With a focus on Ayurvedic therapy and treatments, Ayoma Spa sets out to relax the body, mind and soul. Treatments start with foot therapy and set the tone for the rest of your experience, while facilities include saunas and steam rooms, a swimming pool and Jacuzzi. A recommended treatment is the Abyanga, a full body massage performed with a combination of strokes and oils.

Chi Spa

Location → Shangri-La Hotel · Trade Centre 1
Hours → 06:00 - 24:00
Web/email → www.shangri-la.com

405 2441

Map Ref → 9-A2

The Spa at Shangri-La aims to impress with its elegant and luxurious facilities. Embracing a holistic approach to physical and spiritual well-being, its healing philosophies and treatments are based on the principal of restoring balance and harmony to the mind and body. A cosy shop with oils, aromatic herbs and spices is also on hand.

Cleopatra's Spa

Location → Pyramids · Umm Hurair
Hours → Timings on request
Web/email → www.waficity.com

324 7700

Map Ref → 13-D2

This spa offers a range of exotic treatments ranging from facials to wraps to hydro baths to massages. Cleopatra's Spa has its own consultant specialising in Ayurveda and who can recommend suitable treatments. The spa also features a sports injury clinic for the treatment and prevention of sport related injuries. Call the spa for male and female timings.

Crossroads Massage & O2 Bar

Location → Dubai Media City · Al Sufouh
Hours → 09:30 - 21:30   Fri 16:00 - 21:30
Web/email → crossroads@sahmnet.ae

367 1684

Map Ref → 3-A2

Crossroads Massage & O2 Bar is the region's first oxygen parlour where you can fill your lungs with pure oxygen that's been infused with essential oils. Crossroads suggests a minimum

of two sessions per week, for three months, to get optimum results. Treatments cost Dhs.50 for 20 minutes.

Givenchy Spa

Location → One&Only Residence & Spa · Al Sufouh
Hours → See below
Web/email → www.oneandonlyresort.com

399 9999

Map Ref → 3-A2

The Givenchy Spa offers a vast range of treatments and therapies, and they have become well known in Dubai for their deep cleansing facials. The spa is open to ladies only between 9:30 - 13:00, and gentlemen are allowed on the premises from 13:30 – 20:00. .

Oasis Retreat

Location → Oasis Beach Hotel · Marsa Dubai
Hours → Timings on request
Web/email → www.jebelali-international.com

399 4444

Map Ref → 2-D2

The Oasis Retreat offers holistic treatments at one of Dubai's friendliest beach hotels. Pamper yourself with an innovative facial or body treatment designed to help you relax and alleviate stress, which will leave you feeling content and re-energised.

Oriental Hammam

Location → One&Only Residence & Spa · Al Sufouh
Hours → See below
Web/email → www.oneandonlyresorts.com

399 9999

Map Ref → 3-A2

The Hammam & Spa is architecturally impressive in traditional Arabic style. The Hammam offers services that are dedicated to nurturing beauty and to the pursuit of well being. The traditional oriental Hammam offers massages, steam baths and Jacuzzis in serene settings.

Ritz-Carlton Spa

Location → Ritz-Carlton, The · Marsa Dubai
Hours → 09:00 - 21:00
Web/email → www.ritz-carlton.com

399 4000

Map Ref → 2-E2

A Balinese theme runs through this spa, from its treatments to the décor. The facilities include eight treatment rooms, a hair and beauty salon, Jacuzzi, sauna, steam room and a ladies gym complete with toning tables. A popular treatment is the Balinese massage, where you can instruct the masseur how much pressure you'd like them to apply.

Royal Waters Health Spa

Location → Al Mamzar Centre · Deira | 297 2053
Hours → 09:00 - 24:00   See below
Web/email → therwspa@emirates.net.ae   Map Ref → 12-C4

This spa features a gym, rooftop swimming pool, café, sauna and steam room. The focus is on holistic healing and the spa offers different memberships and programmes such as stress management and nutrition, Reiki, Pilates, spa and beauty treatments, and consultations with their in-house doctor.

Satori Spa

Location → Jumeirah Beach Club Resort & Spa | 344 5333
Hours → 09:00 - 21:00
Web/email → www.jumeirahinternational.com   Map Ref → 5-D1

Sheltered by lush foliage and serene surroundings a visit to Satori Spa is a euphoric experience from the moment you stroll along the undulating paths of the tranquil Jumeirah Beach Club Resort and Spa until the time you return to reality. The Satori Signature Treatments are the ultimate in indulgence and will transport your mind, body and soul to paradise. The spa is exclusive to Jumeirah Beach Club members and guests as well and is also accessible through special day packages.

So spa so good

Six Senses Spa

Location → Souk Madinat Jumeirah | 366 6818
Hours → 09:00 - 22:00
Web/email → www.jumeirahinternational.com   Map Ref → 4-A2

A quick abra ride from the bustling Madinat Souk takes you a world away to the tranquil, luxurious Six Senses Spa. With incredible attention to detail in the overall design, therapies and personalised service, this spa offers a range of holistic treatments that pamper, heal and energise. Stroll to your individual or twin treatment bungalow, located amid the landscaped grounds, and prepare to relax and be rejuvenated. Senses is a refreshingly healthy restaurant, serving from 9:00 to 18:00, where you can relax on the terrace. Credit cards are accepted.

Spa at Palm Tree Court, The

Location → Jebel Ali Golf Resort & Spa | 883 6000
Hours → 09:00 - 20:00
Web/email → www.jebelali-international.com   Map Ref → 1-A1

Set amidst serene gardens, swaying palm trees and unspoiled golden sandy beaches, The Spa at Palm Tree Court couldn't be more tranquil. The spa offers a variety of treatments and holistic experiences to calm the soul and soothe the mind.

Spa Thira

Location → Opp Jumeira Beach Park · Al Wasl | 344 2055
Hours → 09:00 - 20:00   Thu 09:00 - 14:00
Web/email → amalchachaa@hotmail.com   Map Ref → 5-C2

Spa Thira is located in a converted double story villa, where music filters through the rooms and creates a sense of peace. The spa offers a full range of beauty therapies including facials, manicures, semi-permanent makeup, Moroccan baths, Chinese massages and soft-light laser treatments for safe hair removal.

Willow Stream Spa

Location → Fairmont Dubai, The · Trade Centre 1 | 311 8800
Hours → 06:00 - 24:00
Web/email → www.fairmont.com   Map Ref → 9-E1

In keeping with the décor of the Fairmont, Willow Stream is decorated in the style of a luxurious Roman bath. Consisting of a men's and ladies' spa, gym and pool complex, Willow Stream offers full and half day packages. Facial care, waxing, eye care, hydrotherapy, and hand and nail treatments are available.

Health Spas

Activities

Massage

Other options ➔ Sports and Leisure Facilities [p.300]
Health Spas [p.294]

Soothing for the body, mind and soul, a massage could be a weekly treat, a gift to someone special, a relaxing way to unwind or to get you through a trying time at work. Numerous massage techniques are available, but prices and standards vary, so it's worth doing your research into what's on offer. A full body massage will cost in the range of Dhs.100 - 300 for a one hour session. Massages, in addition to a variety of other treatments, are available at most spas in Dubai. For further details on health spas refer to [p.294].

Pilates

Other options ➔ Yoga [p.298]

House of Chi & House of Healing

Location ➔ Musalla Towers · Bur Dubai
Hours ➔ 09:00 - 22:00   Fri 10:00 - 22:00
Web/email ➔ www.hofchi.com | 397 4446
Map Ref ➔ 8-A4

The balance of the mind, body and spirit is the maxim of this alternative therapies outlet. The surroundings inspire peace and well-being, while a team of professional practitioners teach traditional Chinese medicine, yoga, Karate, Aikido, Xiang Gong and meditation. A variety of methods, including Pilates, are offered to alleviate health problems and promote inner harmony.

Pilates Studio, The

Location ➔ Nr Thunder Bowl · Al Wasl
Hours ➔ 08:00 - 20:00   Thu 08:00 - 16:00
Web/email ➔ www.pilates.ae | 343 8252
Map Ref ➔ 5-E3

Pilates is an effective and safe way to tone and strengthen muscles. It was introduced to the UAE in 1998 by the owner of this studio, Catherine Lehmann, a physiologist with years of experience in teaching Pilates. The studio offers mat and reformer classes for beginners and advanced students.

Reiki

Reiki is a healing technique based on the belief that energy can be channelled into a patient by means of touch. Translated as 'universal life force energy', Reiki can, like meditation, emotionally cleanse, physically invigorate and leave you more focused. You can learn Reiki to practice on yourself or others, directly or remotely.

Archie Sharma Reiki

Location ➔ Nr Police College · Umm Suqeim
Hours ➔ 16:00 - 20:00
Web/email ➔ NA | 348 8190
Map Ref ➔ 14-D4

Archie Sharma is a Reiki master who has been practising for over ten years and is involved in teaching and healing. She also conducts Zen meditation, is a qualified herbalist and reflexologist, and when time permits, advises on matters pertaining to Feng Shui.

Pookat Suresh Reiki

Location ➔ Various locations
Hours ➔ 08:00 - 13:00   16:00 - 19:00
Web/email ➔ na | 285 9128
Map Ref ➔ na

The Pookat Suresh Reiki centre offers various degrees of attunement. In the first degree, a series of four attunements are taught by a traditional master to channel a higher amount of universal life force energy. The second degree level teaches powerful absentee healing. For more details contact Reiki master Pookat Suresh Babu (050 453 9643).

Stress Management

Other options ➔ Support Groups [p.128]

Holistic Healing & Life Source Energy

Location ➔ Trade Centre 13th floor · Trade Centre 1
Hours ➔ 09:00 - 18:00
Web/email ➔ www.sesam-omniverse.com | 344 9880
Map Ref ➔ 4-D3

Karin Meyer-Reumann is a counsellor, holistic healer and family display practitioner who helps people 'break patterns'. With 30 years experience, she creates individual grids (a combination of forms and colours) that are transferred into auras so that people will attract new options into their lives while providing ways to lift energy levels.

Yoga

Other options ➔ Pilates [p.298]

Al Karama Ayurvedic centre

Location ➔ 109, Karama Centre · Al Karama
Hours ➔ 09:00 - 22:30   Fri 09:00 - 14:00
Web/email ➔ almadxb@emirates.net.ae | 337 8921
Map Ref ➔ 10-D2

Operating for over 18 years, this centre is run by qualified professionals with expertise in the

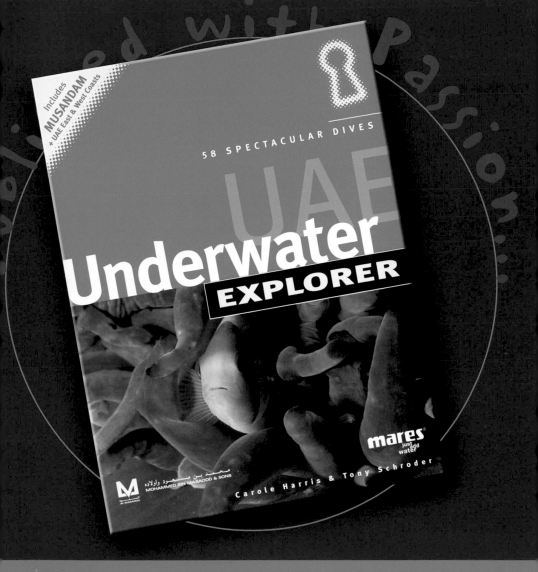

58 Spectacular Dives

Detailing 58 top dive sites covering both coastlines and the Mussandam, this dedicated guidebook contains suggested dive plans, informative illustrations, shipwreck stories and marine life photographs. Written by avid divers who want to share their passion and local knowledge with others, the **Underwater Explorer** includes all the crucial information diving enthusiasts need to know about diving in the UAE.

- East Coast (UAE)
- West Coast (UAE)
- Mussandam Peninsula (Oman)
- Maps & GPS Co-ordinates
- Shipwreck Histories & Illustrations
- UAE Visitor Overview
- First Aid

Passionately Publishing...

Phone (971 4) 335 3520 • **Fax** (971 4) 335 3529 • **Email** Info@Explorer-Publishing.com

Insiders' City Guides • Photography Books • **Activity Guidebooks** • Commissioned Publications • Distribution

EXPLORER

www.Explorer-Publishing.com

traditional systems of Ayurveda, herbal beauty care, yoga and meditation. This is a one stop institution that has all the necessary facilities to take care of healing, rejuvenation and beauty care. Separate areas are available for men and women.

Al Majaz

Location → Trade Centre Rd · Al Karama | 335 3563
Hours → 09:00 - 13:00 16:00 - 21:00 Fri closed
Web/email → www.goldenfistkarate.com   Map Ref → 10-D1

Ladies and girls can practice yoga, aerobics and take self defence classes.

Gems of Yoga

Location → Wht. Crown Bld · Trade Centre 1 | 331 5161
Hours → 06:30 - 13:30 15:00 - 22:00 Fri 16:00 - 22:00
Web/email → www.gemsofyogadubai.com   Map Ref → 9-D2

Gems of Yoga mixes yoga and art through yogasanas, mudras, pranayam, meditation and other stress release techniques. The centre also offers classes such as weight-watchers, desktop yoga, prenatal and postnatal yoga, therapeutic yoga and animal yoga for children. Packages range from Dhs.550 - Dhs.1,500, and home yoga packages are available.

House of Chi & House of Healing

Location → Musalla Towers · Bur Dubai | 397 4446
Hours → 09:00 - 22:00   Fri 10:00 - 22:00
Web/email → www.hofchi.com   Map Ref → 8-A4

Hatha yoga teaches you to control stress on a physical and spiritual level. Most illnesses are a result of an accumulation of toxins in our body, and yoga asanas helps eliminate these toxins. Pranayama plays a vital role in learning how to control the life force through breathing exercises. These forms of yoga are all taught at House of Chi & House of Healing.

Sports & Leisure Facilities

Whether on the beach or near the Creek there are a wide variety of exercise facilities available in Dubai. As well as health clubs in hotels, there are many local neighbourhood gyms, and they are often filled with serious workout fanatics (mostly beefy men), and while facilities offered tend to be mixed, prices are generally a fraction of health club membership fees. Refer to the Club Facilities table on [p.302] for full details on various clubs in Dubai, including their membership rates and amenities offered.

Beach Clubs

Other options → Beaches [p.128]

Beach clubs are similar to health clubs (see below) but have the added bonus of beach access.

A date on the beach?

Health Clubs

Beach Clubs [p.300]
Sports Clubs [p.304]

Health clubs generally offer workout facilities: machines and weights, plus classes varying from aerobics to yoga, some also have swimming pools and tennis courts. See the Health Club table [p.302].

Swing and swim

Yoga | Health Clubs

Activities

Club Membership Rates & Facilities

Beach Clubs

Caracalla Spa & Health Club	Le Royal Meridien Beach Resort & Spa	Al Sufouh	2-E2	399 5555
Club Joumana	Jebel Ali Hotel & Golf Resort	Jebel Ali	1-A1	804 8058
Club Mina	Le Meridien Mina Seyahi	Al Sufouh	3-A2	399 3333
Dubai Marine Beach Resort & Spa	Dubai Marine Beach Resort & Spa	Jumeira	6-D2	346 1111
Jumeirah Beach Club Resort & Spa	Jumeirah Beach Club Resort & Spa	Beach Rd, Jumeira	5-D1	344 5333
Jumeira Health & Beach Club	Sheraton Jumeirah Beach Resort & Towers	Al Sufouh	2-D2	399 5533
Metropolitan Beach Club	Metropolitan Resort & Beach Club Htl	Marsa Dubai	2-E2	399 5000
Oasis Beach Club	Oasis Beach Hotel	Al Sufouh	2-D2	315 4029
Pavilion Marina & Sports Club	The Jumeirah Beach Hotel	Umm Suqeim	4-B2	406 8800
Ritz-Carlton Health Club & Spa	The Ritz-Carlton, Dubai	Marsa Dubai	2-E2	399 4000

Health Clubs

Al Nasr Fitness Centre (m/f separate)	Al Nasr Leisureland	Oud Metha	10-E4	337 1234
Assawan Health Club	Burj Al Arab	Umm Suqeim	4-A1	301 7777
Aviation Club P.301 ▶	Aviation Club	Al Garhoud	14-C3	282 4122
Ayoma Health Club	Taj Palace Hotel	Deira	11-D2	223 2222
Big Apple, The,	Boulevard at Emirates Towers, The	Trade Centre 1&2	9-C2	330 0000
Body Connection Health Club	Rydges Plaza Hotel	Al Satwa	7-A4	398 2222
Bodylines Jumeira	Jumeira Rotana Hotel	Al Satwa	6-E3	345 5888
Bodylines Leisure & Fitness	Towers Rotana Hotel	Trade Centre 1&2	9-B2	343 8000
Bodylines Leisure & Fitness	Al Bustan Rotana Hotel	Al Garhoud	14-E3	705 4571
Club Olympus	Hyatt Regency Hotel	Deira	8-D2	209 6802
Club, The	Dubai International Hotel Apartments	Trade Centre 1&2	9-D2	306 5050
Colosseum	Za'abeel Road, Montana Building	Za'abeel, Karama	10-E3	337 2755
Creek Health Club	Sheraton Dubai Hotel & Towers	Creekside, Deira	11-C1	207 1711
Dimensions Health & Fitness Center	Metropolitan Hotel	Jct 2, Shk Zayed Rd	5-C4	407 6704
Dubai Country Club P.73 ▶	Al Awir Rd	Bukadra	17-B3	333 1155
Dubai Creek Golf Resort	Dubai Creek Golf & Yacht Club	Al Garhoud	14-C2	205 4567
Fitness Planet (mixed & ladies)	Al Hana Centre	Al Satwa	7-A4	398 9030
Griffins Health Club	JW Marriott	Deira	12-A3	607 7755
Health Club, The	Emirates Towers Hotel	Trade Centre 1&2	9-C2	330 0000
Hiltonia Health Club	Hilton Dubai Jumeirah	Al Sofouh	2-D2	399 1111
Inter Fitness Dubai	Hotel Inter-Continental Dubai	Deira	8-C4	222 7171
Lifestyle Health Club	City Centre Residence	Deira	14-D1	603 8825
Natural Elements	Le Meridien Dubai	Al Garhoud	14-E3	702 2430
Nautilus Health Centre	Metropolitan Palace Hotel	Deira	11-D2	227 0000
Pharaohs (mixed & ladies)	Pyramids	Umm Hurair (2)	13-D2	324 0000
Platinum Club	Atrium Suites	Hor Al Anz	12-C4	266 9990
Quay Healthclub	Madinat Jumeira	Umm Sequim	4-A2	366 8888
u Concept Centre	Village Mall, The	Jumeira	6-C2	344 9060
Willow Stream	Fairmont Hotel	Trade Centre 1&2	9-E1	332 5555

Sports and Leisure Facilities

Activities

Membership Rates					Gym						Activity				Relaxation				
Male	Female	Couple	Family	Non-Members (peak)	Treadmills	Exercise bikes	Step machines	Rowing machines	Free weights	Resistance machines	Tennis courts	Swimming Pool	Squash courts	Aerobics/Dance Exercise	Massage	Sauna	Jacuzzi	Plunge pool	Steam room
8,800	8,800	12,100	13,750	–	8	6	6	3	✔	16	4FL	✔	2	✔	✔	✔	✔	✔	✔
3,300	2,200	5,500	5,500+	100	1	1	1	1	✔	✔	4FL	✔	2	–	✔	✔	✔	–	✔
6,500	6,500	10,000	10,000	–	10	4	1	2	✔	18	4FL	✔	–	✔	✔	✔	✔	✔	✔
6,000	4,500	8,000	8,000	–	5	5	2	1	✔	13	2FL	✔	✔	✔	✔	–	–	✔	✔
8,500	8,500	12,250	16,000	150	8	9	3	2	✔	12	7FL	✔	3	✔	✔	✔	✔	✔	✔
4,800	4,800	6,500	On req.	80	3	4	3	2	✔	11	2FL	✔	2	✔	✔	✔	–	✔	✔
6,500	6,500	7,750	8,750	–	3	2	1	1	✔	✔	2FL	✔	0		✔	✔	✔	✔	✔
4,500	4,500	5,400	6,000	88	2	2	2	1	✔	✔	1FL	✔	–	–	✔	✔	✔	✔	✔
On req.	On req.	On req.	On req.	On req.	9	8	2	3	✔	23	7FL	✔	3	✔	✔	✔	✔	✔	✔
12,000	12,000	15,000	19,000	–	3	6	3	2	✔	10	4FL	✔	2		✔	✔	✔	✔	✔
1,300	1,000	1,800	2,300	–	4	5	–	–	✔	4	✔	✔	✔	–	–	✔	–	–	–
On req.	On req.	On req.	On req.	–	5	8	3	2	✔	15	–	✔	1	✔	✔	✔	✔	✔	✔
5,000	3,750	6,500	7,500	–	9	5	3	3	✔	16	6FL	✔	2	✔	✔	✔	✔	✔	✔
3,500	3,000	5,250	7,250	85	5	3	1	1	✔	7	–	✔	–	✔	✔	✔	✔	✔	✔
2,600	2,600	4,400	–	30	8	3	4	2	✔	11	–	✔	–	✔	–	–	–	✔	✔
2,500	2,500	3,800	4,000	–	2	2	2	2	✔	9	–	✔	–	✔	✔	✔	✔	✔	✔
1,900	1,600	2,500	2,850	50	1	1	–	–	✔	2	–	✔	–	✔	✔	✔	–	✔	–
2,600	2,000	3,600	4,000	55	3	1	2	1	✔	9	–	✔	–	✔	✔	✔	✔	✔	✔
3,250	2,750	4,250	4,750	75	6	6	2	2	✔	9	3	✔	2	✔	✔	✔	✔	✔	✔
3,500	2,000	4,200	On req.	60	8	4	2	2	✔	10	3	✔	2	✔	✔	✔	✔	✔	✔
3,500	3,000	4,500	5,700	35	6	3	2	2	✔	12	4FL	✔	3	✔	–	✔	✔	✔	✔
1,890	1,590	2,590	2,690+	–	5	3	–	2	✔	10	–	✔	–	✔	✔	✔	✔	✔	✔
2,500	2,500	3,400	4,500	50	2	2	2	–	✔	1	1	✔	2	✔	✔	✔	✔	✔	✔
2,400	2,000	3,500	4,000	55	6	4	2	2	✔	19	1	✔	–	✔	✔	✔	✔	✔	✔
3,200	2,400	4,850	5,150	60	4	3	2	2	✔	✔	7FL	✔	3	✔	–	–	–	–	✔
4,500	4,500	–	6,500	60	4	3	2	3	✔	13	7 FL	✔	3	✔	✔	✔	✔	✔	✔
2,350	2,350	–	–	30	7	7	5	2	✔	25	–	–	–	✔	✔	✔	✔	✔	✔
3,575	2,530	5,060	On req.	80	7	6	4	2	✔	4	–	✔	2	✔	✔	✔	✔	✔	✔
4,000	4,000	6,500	On req.	100	8	3	2	2	✔	11	–	✔	–	–	✔	✔	✔	✔	✔
5,500	5,500	7,000		90	4	2	2	2	✔	2	–	✔	–		✔	✔	–	–	✔
4,300	3,500	5,800	–	80	5	4	2	2	✔	10	1FL	✔	2	✔	✔	✔	✔	✔	✔
2,900	2,600	4,400	4,400	50	8	6	2	1	✔	14	1FL	✔	2	✔	✔	✔	–	✔	✔
3,200	3,200	4,600	On req.	50	3	4	1	2	✔	15	–	✔	2	✔	✔	✔	✔	✔	✔
4,750	3,600	6,250	7,250	100	10	4	2	3	✔	22	3FL	✔	2	✔	✔	✔	✔	✔	✔
5,500	5,500	8,000	10,000	60	7	8	4	2	✔	18	3	✔	2	✔	✔	✔	✔	✔	✔
3,000	3,000	5,000	–	–	10	9	2	2	✔	36	–	–	–	✔	✔	✔	✔	–	✔
10,230	10,230	13,090	–	–	9	8	3	3	✔	12	5FL	✔	✔	✔	–	✔	–	–	✔
–	–	–	–	250	2	2	–	1	✔	5	–	–	–	–	✔	–	–	–	–
4,500	4,500	7,500	–	150	5	4	2	2	✔	13	–	✔	–	✔	✔	✔	✔	✔	✔

Sports and Leisure Facilities

Activities

Sports Clubs

Beach Clubs [p.300]
Health Clubs [p.300]

The following clubs offer a range of sporting activities, and feature a variety of facilities like swimming pools, tennis and squash courts, and golf courses. Most also have workout facilities. For details of individual sports refer directly to listings in this section of the guide.

Dubai Country Club

Location → Nr Bukadra Interchange · Bukadra | 333 1155
Hours → 08:00 - 22:00
Web/email → www.dubaicountryclub.com   Map Ref → 17-B3

Dubai Country Club's sports facilities are excellent and include seven floodlit tennis courts, a 25m swimming pool, two squash courts, two badminton courts inside the sports hall, and a floodlit football/rugby field, along with two sand golf courses and a fully equipped gym. Indoors, the club offers two championship sized snooker tables, darts and pool tables.

India Club

Location → Nr. Indian High School · Oud Metha | 337 1112
Hours → 06:00 - 22:00
Web/email → www.indiaclubdubai.com   Map Ref → 10-E4

Opened in 1964, this club currently has 6,500 members and seeks to provide facilities for sports, entertainment and recreation, and to promote business. Facilities include a gym, with a separate steam room and sauna for men and women, badminton, squash and tennis courts, snooker, table tennis, basketball, a swimming pool, and a variety of indoor games.

LG InSportz

Location → Jct 3, Shk Zayed Rd · Al Quoz | 347 5833
Hours → 09:30 - 21:30
Web/email → www.insportzclub.com   Map Ref → 4-C4

LG InSportz Club is Dubai's first indoor sports centre and features five multi-purpose courts, a cricket coaching net and cafeteria, all within the comfort of air conditioned surroundings. Sports available include cricket, football, basketball and hockey, and there's a complete coaching programme for juniors. Prices (inclusive of equipment) start from Dhs.20 for children and Dhs.25 for adults.

Sharjah Wanderers Sports Club

Location → Nr Sharjah English School | 06 566 2105
Hours → 08:00 - 24:00
Web/email → www.sharjahwanderers.com   Map Ref → UAE-C2

This is a popular club that's supported by the expat community in Sharjah, Dubai and the Northern Emirates. Facilities include floodlit tennis courts, football, rugby and hockey fields, squash courts, swimming pool, gym, library, snooker, darts, aerobic classes, yoga, dancing for kids, netball and a kids' play area.

Expand Your Horizons

If it's a hobby you want you're certainly in the right place to add a few strings to your bow. From music schools and art classes to dance groups and arabic language lessons whatever your skill set you're after you will probably find it in Dubai whether in a workshop, month-long course or special interest group. Learning opportunities are abundant and flexible enough to fit into your schedule.

Art Classes

Other options → Art Galleries [p.169]
Art Supplies [p.208]

Café Ceramique

Location → Town Centre · Jumeira | 344 7331
Hours → 08:00 - 24:00
Web/email → www.café-ceramique.com   Map Ref → 5-E1

Combine ceramic painting with coffee and cake. Café Ceramique also run classes, refer to the review under Cafés & Coffee Shops in the Going Out Section [p.404].

Creative Modern Centre

Location → Opp Audio Workshop · Al Rashidiya | 285 9925
Hours → 08:30 - 13:00 16:00 - 19:30 Thu 08:30 - 14:00 Fri closed
Web/email → mdrnart@emirates.net.ae   Map Ref → 16-A2

The Creative Modern Centre offers women and children the chance to be artistic by partaking in a variety of courses that include painting, drawing, calligraphy, sculpture, fabric painting, flower arranging, ceramic flower making and cookery. Ladies can also join aerobics, aqua aerobics or karate classes.

Mind your lip

Dubai International Art Centre

Location ➜ Nr Town Centre · Jumeira | **344 4398**
Hours ➜ 08:30 - 19:00 Thu 8:30 - 16:00
Web/email ➜ artdubai@emirates.net.ae Map Ref ➜ 6-C2

The Arts Centre is a haven of artistic tranquility. Classes are offered in over 70 subjects, including all types of painting and drawing, Arabic, dressmaking, etching, pottery and photography. Courses last six to eight weeks, and prices vary according to the materials required. Annual membership fees start at Dhs.250, but classes are open to non-members with a 30% premium.

Elves & Fairies

Location ➜ Jumeirah Centre · Jumeira | **344 9485**
Hours ➜ 09:30 - 13:30 15:30 - 20:30
Web/email ➜ jmeadows@emirates.net.ae Map Ref ➜ 6-C2

This craft shop for adults and children specialises in stencils, rubber stamps and face painting. They also deal in decorative paint effects and stock paints, glazes, colourwashes, varnishes and brushes, as well as cross-stitch, mosaics and decoupage. They run regular workshops for children and adults on all things crafty.

Ballet Classes

Other options ➜ Dance Classes [p.307]

Ballet Centre, The

Location ➜ Beh Jumeira Plaza · Jumeira | **344 9776**
Hours ➜ 09:00 - 12:30 15:00 - 18:30
Web/email ➜ www.balletcentre.com Map Ref ➜ 6-C3

For a full review of the Ballet Centre see [p.307].

Beauty Training

Other options ➜ Beauty Salons [p.294]

Cleopatra & Steiner Beauty Training Centre

Location ➜ Wafi Residence · Umm Hurair | **324 0250**
Hours ➜ 08:30 - 17:30
Web/email ➜ www.cleopatrasteiner.com Map Ref ➜ 13-D2

This is the Middle East's first internationally endorsed training facility, and offers long and short term courses in health, beauty and holistic therapy. Courses include anatomy and physiology, body massage, nail and skin treatments, reflexology, hairdressing and aromatherapy. Qualifications are recognised by CIDESCO, CIBTAC, and City & Guilds.

Belly Dancing

Other options ➜ Dance Classes [p.305]

Belly dancing is not only an ancient Arabic art but also great fun and a good way to keep fit. The Ballet Centre holds belly dancing lessons on various mornings and evenings (check for timings on 04 344 9776) suitable for beginners. Helene from the Nautilus Fitness Centre at the Crowne Plaza teaches oriental belly dancing on Sunday and Tuesday evenings, call her on 050 784 7703 for more details.

Birdwatching Groups

Other options ➜ Birdwatching [p.176]
Environmental Groups [p.310]

Birdwatching Tours

Location ➜ Various locations | **050 650 3398**
Hours ➜ Timings on request
Web/email ➜ www.arabianwildlife.com Map Ref ➜ na

Colin Richardson, author of *The Birds of the United Arab Emirates*, has been organising bird watching trips since 1993. Tours include Khor

Dubai, where thousands of Arctic shore birds and flamingos winter, Umm Al Quwain with its crab plovers and Socotra cormorants, and Khor Kalba with the threatened white-collared kingfisher, Indian rollers and bee-eaters. Prices start at Dhs.250 per person.

Emirates Bird Records Committee

Location → None	050 642 4358
Hours → Timings on request	
Web/email → www.uaeinteract.com	Map Ref → UAE-A4

The Emirates Bird Records Committee puts together information about birds in the UAE and maintains a checklist. A weekly round up of bird sightings and a monthly report is available via email upon request. For more information contact the Committee chairman, Simon Aspinall (050 642 4358).

Bridge

Dubai Bridge Club

Location → Country Club · Bukadra	050 658 6985
Hours → Timings on request	
Web/email → olavo786bridge@yahoo.com	Map Ref → 17-B3

The Dubai Bridge Club is a non-profit organisation and has members from the UAE, Poland, Iran, France, India, Syria, Turkey, Pakistan and the UK. The club organises monthly tournaments and you should contact Olavo D'Sousa (050 658 6985) if you have any questions.

Checkmate

Dubai Ladies Bridge Club

Location → Nad al Sheba	050 645 4395
Hours → Sun & Wed 08:45 - 13:00	
Web/email → na	Map Ref → 17-A3

Ladies only bridge mornings are held at 09:00 on Sundays and Wednesdays at the Nad Al Sheba Millennium Stand. Registration ends at 08:45, and games start promptly at 09:00. For further details, contact Marzie Polad (050 659 1300) or Jan Irvine (050 645 4395).

Chess

Other options → Scrabble [p.315]

Dubai Chess & Culture Club

Location → Nr Al Shabab Club · Hor Al Anz	296 6664
Hours → 10:00 - 13:00 16:00 - 22:00 Fri 17:00 - 23:00	
Web/email → www.dubaichess.com	Map Ref → 12-C3

This club is involved in all aspects of chess and cultural programmes. Members can play chess at the club seven nights a week and competitions are organised on a regular basis. International competitions are also promoted including the Dubai International Open, Emirates Open and Dubai Junior Open, attracting representatives from Asia, Arabia and Europe. Annual membership: Dhs100 for nationals and Dhs 200 for expats.

Clubs & Associations

Other options → Scouts & Guides [p.314]

Australia New Zealand Association	394 6508
British Community Assistance Fund	337 1413
Club for Canadians, The	355 6171
Egyptian Club	336 6709
German Speaking Women's Club	332 5797
Indian Association	351 1082
Italian Cultural Association	050 453 5422
Norwegian Centre	337 0062

Cookery Classes

Many hotels and restaurants hold occasional cookery demonstrations or classes, so look out for special events advertised in the media. The Shangri-La hotel run Kraft Korner where for Dhs.60 you can join in a weekly cookery class with an expert chef and try cooking a variety of cuisines. Call the hotel for more details on 343 8888.

Activities   Birdwatching Groups | Cookery Classes

Dance Classes

Other options → Belly Dancing [p.305]
Music Lessons [p.313]
Salsa Dancing [p.314]

Whether it's the Polka, Salsa or Bharatnatyam, all dancing tastes are catered for in Dubai. Dance has a universal appeal that breaks down barriers and inhibitions, and is being great way to exercise for people of all ages. In addition to established dancing institutions, many health clubs, restaurants and bars hold weekly sessions in flamenco, salsa, samba, jazz dance, ballroom and more. Some health clubs also offer dance based aerobic classes that are energetic and exhausting.

Al Naadi Club

Location → Al Ghurair City · Deira | 205 5229
Hours → 06:00 - 23:00
Web/email → wilson@alghurairgroup.com | Map Ref → 11-D1

Ballet lessons leading to Royal Academy of Dancing examinations are taught by Sally Bigland, who also teaches Latin American dance to adults. Indian dance, as well as Karate for boys and girls aged six and older, are also on offer. Tennis and squash is available seven days a week.

Ballet Centre, The

Location → Beh Jumeira Plaza · Jumeira | 344 9776
Hours → 09:00 - 12:30 15:00 - 18:30
Web/email → www.balletcentre.com | Map Ref → 6-C3

The Ballet Centre offers Royal Academy Ballet and Imperial Society of Teachers Tap classes. The centre also has classes for modern, Spanish, Irish and jazz dancing. For aerobics fans, there are various sessions for all levels of fitness.

Ceroc Dubai

Location → Various locations | 367 2217
Hours → Timings on request
Web/email → www.cerocdubai.com | Map Ref → na

Ceroc is a modern partner dance and is a great way to socialise and keep fit. Its style is comparable to modern jive and has similar moves to salsa and swing. Evenings start with a beginners' class led by Des, a certified instructor and UK champion, and are followed by intermediate freestyle dancing sessions. There's no need to bring a partner and no special footwear is required. Call Des (050 428 3061) for details on class timings.

Dance Centre, The

Location → Various locations | 286 8775
Hours → 09:00 - 17:00
Web/email → www.dance-centre-dubai.com | Map Ref → na

The Dance Centre offers classes in ballet, ISTD tap, jazz, modern and Irish dance to children over the age of 3, and GCSE dancing lessons to children over the age of 14. The centre is affiliated to the Royal Academy of Dance in London and enters students for RAD graded examinations each year.

Dubai Liners

Location → Various locations | 050 654 5960
Hours → Tue & Sat, 19:00 - 22:00
Web/email → difromdubai@yahoo.com | Map Ref → na

The Dubai Liners was started over five years ago by Diana and although traditional line dancing involves a strong country western music theme, Diana teaches a more modern version of line dancing to a wide variety of music including disco, rock 'n roll, salsa, jazz, R&B, waltz, and ballads. There are line dance classes for beginners and intermediate students on Saturday and Tuesday evenings, from 19:00 to 22.00. Contact Diana on the above number for more details.

Indian Classical Dances

Location → Nr MMI & Pioneer Bld · Al Karama | 335 4311
Hours → 16:30 - 20:00
Web/email → www.nrityaupadesh.com | Map Ref → 10-C3

Indian classical dances have their own style with fast rhythmic footwork and facial expressions. Geetha Krishnan, a respected Bharatnatyam and Kuchipudi teacher, holds classes for anyone aged six and older. On completion of the course (takes about four years), the pupil performs an Arangetam, which is a presentation in front of dance maestros. Dance workshops and choreography on Indian and Bollywood dances are also offered.

Savage Garden

Location → Capitol Hotel · Al Satwa | 346 0111
Hours → 19:00 - 03:00
Web/email → caphotel@emirates.net.ae | Map Ref → 7-A2

Savage Garden is a Latin American restaurant and nightclub that sports a Latino band and food. You can also partake in Salsa and Merengue dance classes that are run by Marcela and Javier.

Dance Classes

Activities

Daily classes (except Fridays) are offered from 20:00 - 21:00 for beginners and 21:00 - 22:00 for intermediate and advanced dancers. Classes cost Dhs.35.

Swing Dancing

Location → Various locations | 367 2217
Hours → Timings on request
Web/email → www.megajive.com | Map Ref → na

Swing into the 40s and relive a bygone era. Des will get you up to speed, teaching you the funkiest moves to the hottest swing music. Learn partnered moves with fancy footwork such as the swing-out, Charleston and Suzi-Q, or learn solo stroll routines like the Shim-Sham and Madison. No partners are required.

Desert Driving Courses

Other options → Camping [p.263]
Off-Road Explorer
Wadi & Dune Bashing [p.292]

For those who want to master the art of driving a 4 WD in the desert without getting stuck (and getting yourself out when you do), several organisations offer desert driving courses with instruction from professional drivers. Vehicles are provided on some courses, while others require participants to bring their own. Courses vary widely in terms of price, but expect to pay around Dhs.250 - 300 for the day. Picnic lunches and soft drinks are sometimes included as part of the package.

Al Futtaim Training Centre

Location → Opp Municipality Garage · Al Rashidiya | 285 0455
Hours → 08:00 - 17:00   Thu half day
Web/email → www.traininguae.com | Map Ref → na

The Desert Campus Training Course gives off-road driving enthusiasts the knowledge and experience to venture safely into the desert. It starts with a three hour classroom session covering the basics of your vehicle and is followed by five hours of supervised off-road driving where you take your own 4 WD up and down dunes. Costs are Dhs.300 per person or Dhs.450 for two people in one car.

Desert Rangers

Location → Dubai Garden Centre · Al Quoz | 340 2408
Hours → 09:00 - 18:00
Web/email → www.desertrangers.com | Map Ref → 4-B4

Desert Rangers offer lessons for anyone wanting to learn how to handle a car in the desert. If you are starting out you get taught the basics of venturing off-road. There are also advanced classes that tackle challenging dune scenarios.

Emirates Driving Institute

Location → Beh Al Bustan Centre · Al Qusais | 263 1100
Hours → 09:00 - 16:00
Web/email → www.edi-uae.com | Map Ref → 15-D2

The Emirates Driving Institute offers a one day desert driving course for Dhs.175 (Saturday to Thursday), or Dhs.200 on Fridays, and this fee includes lunch. The institute also offers a one day defensive driving course for Dhs.300 (Saturday to Thursday), or Dhs.350 on Fridays. Participants receive certificates on completion of all courses. Call the number above to find a branch that's nearest to you.

Off-Road Adventures

Location → Metropolitan · Shk Zayed Rd | 343 2288
Hours → 08:00 - 20:00
Web/email → www.arabiantours.com | Map Ref → 5-C4

With 17 years off-road experience in the UAE, Off-Road Adventures provides exciting safari tours with a focus on safety, exclusivity and expert instructors. In addition to off-road driving courses, the company also arranges fun drives, treasure hunts, camping tours, camel safaris and sand boarding. 24/7 hotline: 321 1377.

Voyagers Xtreme

Location → Dune Centre · Al Satwa | 345 4504
Hours → 09:00 - 18:00
Web/email → www.turnertraveldubai.com | Map Ref → 6-E3

Voyagers Xtreme offers lessons for anyone wanting to learn how to handle a 4 WD in the desert. The one day introductory course covers basic skills required for off-roading, including dos and don'ts, negotiating dunes, how to avoid getting stuck and recovery techniques. Individual, group and advanced courses are available.

The Dance Centre

Ballet
Modern
Jazz
Tap
Irish Dancing
G.C.S.E. Dance

Drama Groups

Dubai Drama Group

Location → Country Club · Bukadra
Hours → Timings on request
Web/email → www.dubaidramagroup.org   Map Ref → 17-B3

| 050 769 8963

The Dubai Drama Group has been entertaining Dubai audiences for thirty years. Members range from those on the stage like actors, singers and dancers, to behind the scenes personnel like directors, costumiers, painters and gaffers. This amateur drama society stages four productions each year including its famous pantomime at Christmas. Annual membership costs Dhs.100 and includes the monthly newsletter.

Environmental Groups

People don't generally chain themselves to palms or dunes here, but over the last few years environmental issues have gradually become more important in the UAE. However, as is always the case, far more needs to be done by all sections of the community. Leading the way, HH Sheikh Mohammed bin Rashid Al Maktoum, Crown Prince of Dubai, has established a prestigious international environmental award in honour of HH Sheikh Zayed bin Sultan Al Nahyan, late President of the UAE. The award, which was first presented in 1998, goes to an individual or organisation for distinguished work carried out on behalf of the environment.

On an everyday level there are increasing numbers of glass and plastic recycling points around the city. The Khaleej Times sponsors bins for collecting newspapers for recycling; these are easily spotted at a variety of locations, but mainly outside shopping centres.

In addition, the government of Dubai is gradually taking action with school educational programmes and general awareness campaigns. However, overall, there seems to be very little done to persuade the average person to be more active environmentally, for instance by encouraging the reduction of littering.

If you want to take action contact one of the environmental groups that operate in the Emirates. These range from the Emirates Environmental Group to the flagship Arabian

Leopard Trust. They always need volunteers and funds.

Dubai Natural History Group

Location → Emirates Academy · Jumeira
Hours → Timings on request
Web/email → na   Map Ref → 5-B3

| 349 4816

Dubai Natural History Group was formed to promote interest in flora, fauna, geology, archaeology and the natural environment of the Emirates. Meetings are held on the first Sunday of each month and speakers give lectures on a range of natural history topics. Regular trips are organised and the group maintains a library of natural history publications. Annual membership: Dhs.100 for families or Dhs.50 for individuals.

Emirates Environmental Group

Location → Crowne Plaza · Trade Centre 1
Hours → 09:00 - 18:00   Thu 09:00-14:00
Web/email → www.eeg-uae.org   Map Ref → 9-D2

| 331 8100

This is a voluntary, non-governmental organisation devoted to protecting the environment through education, action programmes and community involvement. Current members include individuals and corporate members, schools and government organisations. Activities include regular evening lectures on environmental topics, and special events such as recycling collections and clean-up campaigns. Annual membership: adults Dhs.50 and students Dhs.20 - 30.

Flower Arranging

Other options → Flowers [p.217]
Gardens [p.218]

Ikebana Sogetsu Group

Location → Nr Syrian Consulate · Al Hamriya
Hours → 09:30 - 18:00
Web/email → fujikozarouni@hotmail.com   Map Ref → 12-C3

| 262 0282

Ikebana is the art of Japanese flower arranging. Dubai's Ikebana Sogetsu Group was formed by Sogetsu members in 2000, and attempts to deepen cultural understanding in the city's multinational society through exhibitions, demonstrations and workshops. Classes are taught by Fujiko Zarouni, a qualified teacher from Japan.

Gardening

Other options → Gardens [p.218]

Dubai Gardening Group

Location → Various locations
Hours → Timings on request
Web/email → bomi@emirates.net.ae
| 344 5999
Map Ref → 5-C2

The Dubai Gardening Group was established in 2000 and aims to share its love and knowledge of gardening in a friendly and informal atmosphere. During the cooler months, trips to greenhouses, nurseries and member's gardens are arranged. Speakers, who are experts in various fields, address the meetings and, where possible, give practical demonstrations.

Kids Museums

Museums - City [p.172]
Museums - Out of City [p.173]

Children of all ages have plenty to keep them occupied in Dubai, even during the blazing summer months when outside activities are not possible. There are numerous play sites and activities devoted specifically to children, and include 'discovering' dinosaur bones buried in the sand, planetarium visits, or trips to a bouncy castle. Amusement for the little ones is never far away.

For more details on children's activities in Dubai and the Northern Emirates, refer to the *Family Explorer*. This handbook offers a wealth of information for the whole family and covers everything from medical care, education and birthday parties, to eating out and other fun activities.

Children's City

Children's City

Location → Creekside Park · Umm Hurair
Hours → 09:00 - 21:30   Fri 16:00 - 21:30
Web/email → www.childrencity.ae
| 334 0808
Map Ref → 14-A1

Children's City is an educational project that offers kids their own learning zone and amusement facilities, by providing hands-on experiences relating to theory they have been taught at school. Children's City focuses on five to 12 year olds, although items of interest are included for toddlers and teenagers.

Sharjah Science Museum

Location → Nr TV station · Halwan
Hours → 09:00 - 14:00   Wed-Fri 15:30 - 20:30
Web/email → www.sharjah-welcome.com
| 06 566 8777
Map Ref → UAE-C2

It might be a museum, and a science one at that, but kids will love the interactive displays. See the review under Museums - Out of Town [p.176] for more details.

Language Schools

Other options → Learning Arabic [p.136]

Alliance Française

Location → Opp American Hospital · Umm Hurair
Hours → 09:00 - 13:00   16:00 - 20:00   Thu & Fri closed
Web/email → www.afdubai.com
| 335 8712
Map Ref → 13-E1

The Alliance Française is a non-profit organisation that promotes the French language and culture. The Alliance Française in Dubai has started French language classes in the evenings for adults, while courses in Sharjah take place at the French School, Lycée Georges Pompidou. Terms run from September to June and an intensive course is held during the summer for adults and children.

Arabic Language Centre

Location → Trade Centre · Trade Centre 2
Hours → 08:30 - 18:30   Thu & Fri closed
Web/email → alc@dwtc.com
| 308 6036
Map Ref → 10-A2

A division of the Dubai World Trade Centre, this language school was established in 1980 to teach Arabic as a foreign language. Courses, from beginner to advanced levels, are held five times a year, last 30 hours, and cost Dhs.1,650 (inclusive of all materials). Specialist courses can be designed to meet the requirements of the hotel, banking, hospital, motor and electronic industries.

Berlitz

Location ➜ Nr Dubai Zoo · Jumeira
Hours ➜ 08:00 - 20:00   Thu 08:00 - 14:00 Fri closed
Web/email ➜ www.berlitz.ae   Map Ref ➜ 6-B2
344 0034

The Berlitz method has helped more than 41 million people acquire a new language. A variety of courses are offered and can be customised to fit specific requirements such as English for banking or technical English. Instruction is in private or small groups, with morning classes for women and children's classes on Thursdays. Additional training includes translation and self-teaching.

British Council

Location ➜ Nr Maktoum Bridge · Umm Hurair
Hours ➜ 08:00 - 20:00
Web/email ➜ www.britishcouncil.org/uae   Map Ref ➜ 11-A3
337 0109

The British Council has teaching centres in Dubai, Abu Dhabi, Sharjah and Ras Al Khaimah, and offers English language courses for adults, children (three - 16 year olds) and company groups. There are also business English courses aimed at professionals who need to improve their language skills for the workplace. Fees: English courses (36 hours) Dhs.1,650.

Dar El Ilm School of Languages

Location ➜ Exhibition Hall 4 · Trade Centre 1
Hours ➜ 09:00 - 19:00   Thu 09:00 - 13:00
Web/email ➜ darelilm@emirates.net.ae   Map Ref ➜ 9-A2
331 0221

Now entering its sixteenth year, Dar El Ilm offers language courses to students of all ages and abilities, with an emphasis on making learning fun. Adult and children's tuition is offered in English, French, German, Italian, Spanish and Arabic. Adult courses last 15 hours and run eight times during the academic year. Fees start at Dhs.850 for adults and Dhs.58 per hour for children.

El Ewla Language Academy

Location ➜ Knowledge Village, Block 2B · Al Sufouh
Hours ➜ 08:30 - 21:30
Web/email ➜ www.elewla.com   Map Ref ➜ 3-B2
391 1640

EL Ewla, meaning 'the first' in Arabic, is a language and training institute. EL Ewla's language programmes (Arabic, English, French) are offered to individuals, companies and government institutions. Classes focus on every language aspect including grammar,

vocabulary, use of idioms and improving your accent and pronunciation. Special exam programmes and corporate packages are also available.

Polyglot Language Institute

Location ➜ Al Masaeed Bld, beh Inter-Con · Deira
Hours ➜ 09:00 - 13:00 16:30 - 21:00
Web/email ➜ www.polyglot.ae   Map Ref ➜ 8-C4
222 3429

Polyglot Language Institute offers courses in modern languages, as well as secretarial and computer skills for individuals and companies. Courses offered include Arabic, general and business English, French, Spanish, Italian, German, TOEFL preparation, office skills, typing, and secretarial and computer studies. Courses last 6 - 10 weeks and all materials are provided. Courses range between Dhs.1,350 - 1,500.

Libraries

Other options ➜ Books [p.208]
Second-Hand Items [p.230]

Alliance Française

Location ➜ Opp American Hospital · Umm Hurair
Hours ➜ 09:00 - 13:00 16:00 - 20:00 Thu & Fri closed
Web/email ➜ www.afdubai.com   Map Ref ➜ 13-E1
335 8712

The Alliance Française multimedia library has over 12,000 books (including a children's section), plus 50 daily, weekly and monthly French newspapers and magazines, 2,000 videotapes, 150 CD-ROMs and 250 DVDs.

The book borrowers

Archie's Library

Location → Pyramid Bld, nr BurJuman · Al Karama | **396 7924**
Hours → See timings below
Web/email → abcl180@hotmail.com   Map Ref → 10-E1

Archie's Library is stocked up with 45,000 English fiction, nonfiction, classic, cooking, health and fitness, and management books. A selection of children's books and comics are also available, along with the latest magazines. The annual membership fee of Dhs.75 (plus Dhs.100 refundable deposit) entitles you to borrow four books for ten days. Reading charges vary from Dhs.1 - Dhs.7. Sharjah branch: 06 572 5716.

British Council Library

Location → Nr Maktoum Bridge · Umm Hurair | **337 0109**
Hours → 09:00 - 20:00
Web/email → www.britishcouncil.org/uae   Map Ref → 11-A3

The British Council Library offers English courses and is the centre for UK-based examinations and assessments. The library is used by students who attend the courses, and is also open to non-members who can use the reference collection. The service includes a wide selection of fiction and nonfiction materials, as well as videos and CD-ROMs. Membership fee: Dhs.350.

Juma Al Majid Cultural & Heritage Centre

Location → Nr Dubai Cinema · Deira | **262 4999**
Hours → 08:00 - 19:30   Fri closed
Web/email → na   Map Ref → 12-A4

This is a non-profit reference library and research institute that focuses on Islam and has a collection of 500,000 cultural media items that range from heritage to current world issues, plus 3,000 periodicals and out of print publications. Books cannot be taken home, but you can use the reading room or make photocopies. There's no fee to use the library.

Old Library, The

Location → Int Art Centre · Jumeira | **348 6683**
Hours → 10:00 - 12:00   16:00 - 18:00
Web/email → scamouna@emirates.net.ae   Map Ref → 6-C2

The Old Library has been around since 1969 and is run entirely by volunteers. The library has a collection of over 13,000 adult fiction and reference books including specialist science fiction, romance, biographies and Middle East sections. The library also boasts a children's section and a German

language collection has been recently added. Call the library for information on annual membership rates.

Public Library

Location → Nr St George Htl · Bur Dubai | **226 2788**
Hours → 08:00 - 21:00   Thu 08:00 - 14:00 Fri closed
Web/email → www.dpl.gov.ae   Map Ref → 8-B2

This is one of the oldest libraries in the Gulf and has an Arabic and English section, plus a reading room for magazines and newspapers. Books can be taken out for two week stints, with a limit of three books per person. You'll need one passport photo, copy of your passport and visa, and Dhs.200 (Dhs.150 is refundable) to apply.

Music Lessons

Other options → **Dance Classes** [p.307]
Singing [p.315]

Crystal Music Institute

Location → Al Karama | **396 3224**
Hours → 08:30 - 12:00   15:30 - 21:00
Web/email → www.crystalmusicdubai.com   Map Ref → 10-E2

Recognised by the UAE Ministry of Education, the Crystal Music Institute aims to promote fine arts. Courses are designed mainly for children and are available for a variety of instruments. Children take periodic examinations, which are conducted by the Trinity College of Music (London) in Dubai.

Dubai Music School

Location → Stalco Bld, Zabeel Rd · Al Karama | **396 4834**
Hours → 09:00 - 13:00   15:00 - 20:00
Web/email → www.glennperry.net   Map Ref → 10-D3

Dubai Music School offers guitar, piano, organ, violin, brass, drums, singing and composing lessons for beginners and serious amateurs. Lessons last for one hour, and students take Trinity College of London examinations to get certification. Monthly fees range from Dhs.200 – Dhs.395, and there's a Dhs.50 registration fee.

Gymboree Play & Music

Location → Al Mina Rd · Al Satwa | **345 4422**
Hours → 08:00 - 18:00
Web/email → www.gymboree.com   Map Ref → 7-A2

Set in a colourful area, filled with state-of-the-art child-safe gym equipment, classes are

Libraries | Music Lessons

Activities

designed to build confidence, imagination, social skill and physical abilities. The music classes combine rhythm, movement and use of basic musical instruments while exploring styles of music that change every three weeks. Gymboree also organises birthdays, baby showers and theme parties.

Shruthi Music & Dance Training Center

Location → Sana Fashion Bld · Al Karama | 337 7398
Hours → 08:00 - 12:00 16:00 - 21:00
Web/email → www.crystalmusicdubai.com   Map Ref → 10-C1

Education is available for a variety of instruments including piano, electric organ, guitar, drums, violin, accordion and tabla, and students can register with Trinity College of Music (London) and take exams in Dubai. Lessons are also offered in Carnatic and Hindustani vocals, as well as dance from Indian styles such as Bharatnatyam or Kathak, to western dance styles like disco and jive.

Vocal Studio, The

Location → Dubai & Abu Dhabi | 050 698 0773
Hours → 10:00 - 20:00 by appointment only
Web/email → www.bravoproductionsdubai.com   Map Ref → na

The Vocal Studio offers vocal instruction and a range of singing related activities for adults and youngsters. The centre offers ABRSM and Trinity College (London) syllabus exam preparations, and grades range from beginner to advanced. Students are also encouraged to take part in recitals and concerts, and are also featured in musical productions with visiting international guest artists.

Orchestras/Bands

Other options → Music Lessons [p.313]
Singing [p.315]

Dubai Chamber Orchestra

Location → Various locations | 349 0423
Hours → Timings on request
Web/email → dubaichamberorchestra@hotmail.comMap Ref → na

The Dubai Chamber Orchestra was founded by a group of musicians residing in the UAE. The group comprises many different nationalities and meets regularly to rehearse. Its aim is to give at least two public performances a year. For more information, contact Linda Brentano (050 625 2936).

Dubai Wind Band

Location → American School of Dubai · Al Wasl | 394 1011
Hours → Tue 19:30 - 21:00
Web/email →   Map Ref → 6-A3

This is a gathering of over 50 woodwind and brass musicians. Abilities range from beginners to grade eight plus, and all levels and ages are welcome. The band is in popular demand during December for seasonal singing and music engagements at clubs, malls and hotels. For further information, contact Peter Hatherley-Greene (050 651 8902).

Salsa Dancing

Other options → Belly Dancing [p.305]
Dance Classes [p.307]

Malecon

Location → Dubai Marine Beach · Jumeira | 346 1111
Hours → 19:30 - 03:00
Web/email → www.dxbmarine.com   Map Ref → 6-D2

Learn to Salsa to the beat of resident band, Los Naipes, every Tuesday night between 20:00 - 22:00. Lessons are Dhs.30, but if you dine at the restaurant, they're free. On Saturdays, it's Salsa all night, so you can show off all your moves.

Salsa Dubai

Location → Various locations | 050 848 7188
Hours → See timings below
Web/email → www.salsanight.com   Map Ref → na

Salsa Dubai is fronted by Phil, who has over ten years experience in Cuban, New York and Spanish dance styles. Classes are tailored to the individual, so everyone can progress at their own speed. Members also have the opportunity to learn the famous La Rueda Cuban dance. Nights out are organised at Latin venues to enjoy live bands. Call to find out more about classes.

Scouts & Guides

Rainbows, Brownies, Guides, Young Leaders & Rangers

Location → Various locations | 02 642 1777
Hours → Timings on request
Web/email → pchuuat@emirates.net.ae   Map Ref → na

Various groups for girls of different age ranges include Rainbows (5 – 7), Brownies (7 – 10), Guides

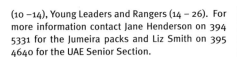

(10 −14), Young Leaders and Rangers (14 − 26). For more information contact Jane Henderson on 394 5331 for the Jumeira packs and Liz Smith on 395 4640 for the UAE Senior Section.

Scouts Association (British Groups Abroad)

Location → Various locations | 050 654 2180
Hours →   Timings on request
Web/email → tumbles@emirates.net.ae   Map Ref → na

The Scout Association aims to encourage the development of youngsters through weekly activities and outings. The scout groups are broken up by age: Beavers (6 - 8), Cubs (8 - 10½), Scouts (10½ - 14), Explorer Scouts (14 − 18) and Scout Network (18 − 25). Activities for younger groups include games, badge activities, sports, competitions and outings. For general enquiries contact UAE District Commissioner Susan Jalili (349 3982) or Dawn Tate (050 654 2180).

Scrabble

Other options → Chess [p.306]

Dubai Scrabble League

Location → Al Maskam Bldg · Al Karama | 050 653 7992
Hours →   Mon 19:00
Web/email → alicoabr@emirates.net.ae   Map Ref → 10-D2

If you're looking for a game of scrabble, this club meets once a week for friendly games between players of all levels. Regular competitions are held, and players also attend competitions in Bahrain, Singapore and Bangkok. The UAE Open (held every year in March/April) is the qualifier for the Gulf Open held in Bahrain. For more information, contact Selwyn Lobo (050 653 7992).

Singing

Other options → Music Lessons [p.313]

Dubai Harmony Chorus

Location → Various locations | 348 9395
Hours →   Tue 19:00 - 22:00
Web/email → seewhy@emirates.net.ae   Map Ref → na

Barbershop style singing varies greatly from other kinds of group singing. Finding the right part for your voice is the initial step, but any woman with average singing ability, with or without music or vocal training, will find a part that fits her vocal range. Dubai Harmony Chorus has 50 female members who get together for weekly rehearsals.

Dubai Singers & Orchestra

Location → Various locations | 349 1896
Hours →   Mondays 20:00 - 22:00
Web/email → www.dubaisingers.tripod.com   Map Ref → 11-A3

This is a group of amateur musicians who meet regularly to create music in a variety of styles, including requiems, choral works, Christmas carols, musicals and variety shows. Membership is open to everyone and no auditions are required, except for solo parts. Membership fees are low and sheet music is provided.

Social Groups

Other options → Clubs & Associations [p.306]
Support Groups [p.128]

With its cosmopolitan population, it's hardly surprising that Dubai has a large number of social and cultural groups, from the ubiquitous Irish contingent to mothers' meetings, each with their own events agenda. Some groups are linked to an embassy or business group and can be an excellent way of meeting like-minded people or even business networking. See the Business Councils & Groups table in New Residents for more details [p.82].

However, if your particular interest or background is not covered, now is the perfect opportunity to fine tune your organisational skills and to start something new. You can rest assured that there will always be someone out there who will join.

The 'expat mum' population is also alive and well in Dubai with various Mother and Toddler groups, check www.ExpatWoman.com for more information. And get your hands on a copy of the *Family Explorer*, which has tons of information on where to find the best 'mums and tots' groups.

DSSN

Location → Various locations | 050 654 1319
Hours →   Timings on request
Web/email → pleides@emirates.net.ae   Map Ref → na

An informal group for single professionals to socialise and network with likeminded people. Meetings happen on the last Sunday of every month and locations vary.

Dubai Caledonian Society	394 9110
Dubai Irish Society	345 6873
Dubai Manx Society	394 3185

Scouts & Guides | Social Groups

Activities

Dubai Adventure Mums

Location ➜ Various locations
Hours ➜ Timings on request | 390 4053
Web/email ➜ www.dubaiadventuremums.com   Map Ref ➜ na

Once a month this group of women sets off without their children or partners to test themselves in new and challenging ways. The aim of this non-profit group is to offer women a wide range of recreational activities that they may not have experienced before. Qualified instructors offer advice and teach the safest way to enjoy these new activities.

Dubai Round Table

Location ➜ Country Club · Bukadra | 050 456 1068
Hours ➜ 1st Mon every month 20:00
Web/email ➜ www.geocities.com/artag_2000   Map Ref ➜ 17-B3

Round Table has been around for 76 years and is a descendant of Rotary, which is present in over 60 countries. In the Arabian Gulf there are 12 Tables with a membership that represents a broad cross-section of professions within your locality. The Dubai Anchorage Ladies Circle and 41 Club are also active. For more information, contact Richard Miles.

Dubai Toastmasters Club, The

Location ➜ Al Futtaim Training Centre · Al Rashidiya | 694 2913
Hours ➜ 07:15 - 21:30
Web/email ➜ www.toastmasters.org   Map Ref ➜ na

Through member clubs, Toastmasters International helps men and women learn the art of listening, thinking and speaking, all of which are vital skills that enhance leadership potential

and foster human understanding. The clubs provide a supportive and positive learning environment that foster self-confidence and personal growth. Contact Pallavi Shevade (050 694 2913) for more details.

Summer Camps & Courses

While the summer used to see a mass exodus of expatriate women and their children to their home countries today less and less people head for cooler climates and instead stay put despite the heat. With more kids in Dubai during the summer holidays many hotels, clubs and organisations have added summer camps and activities to their annual schedule. Most language schools run summer courses for kids, see Language Schools [p.311], and tour operators have a good range of family-orientated activities during the summer, see Tour Operators [p.184], not forgetting Dubai Summer Surprises which is packed with fun for all the family, see [p.56]. Also places like the Dubai Country Club, Dubai Tennis Academy and Futurekids offer good summer classes, check out the *Family Explorer* for more details.

Alliance Française

Location ➜ Opp American Hospital · Umm Hurair | 335 8712
Hours ➜ 09:00 - 13:00 16:00 - 20:00 Thu & Fri closed
Web/email ➜ www.afdubai.com   Map Ref ➜ 13-E1

EduFrance was founded by Alliance Française to promote training in French and international educational exchange programmes. It enhances the French educational system by co-ordinating with French universities and grandes écoles to offer higher education courses to foreign students.

Little monkeys

Social Groups | Summer Camps & Courses

Activities

...We put the FUN in function.

Corporate Family Days
Theme Decoration • Birthday Parties

Tel: 04 347 9170   www.flyingelephantuae.com

Hospitality At It's Best

AL FALAJ HOTEL

MUSCAT

P.O. Box 2031, P.C. 112
Ruwi, Sultanate of Oman
Tel: (968) 2470 2311
Fax: (968) 2479 5853

E-mail: sales@omanhotels.com

فندق
الفلج

مسقط

ص.ب: ٢٠٣١، الرمز البريدي: ١١٢
روي، سلطنة عمان
هاتف: ٢٣١١ ٢٤٧٠ (٩٦٨)
فاكس: ٥٨٥٣ ٢٤٧٩ (٩٦٨)

RUWI HOTEL

MUSCAT

P.O. Box 2195, P.C. 112
Ruwi, Sultanate of Oman
Tel: (968)2470 4244
Fax: (968) 2470 4248

E-mail: reservationruwi@omanhotels.com

فندق
روي

مسقط

ص.ب: ٢١٩٥، الرمز البريدي: ١١٢
روي، سلطنة عمان
هاتف: ٤٢٤٤ ٢٤٧٠ (٩٦٨)
فاكس: ٤٢٤٨ ٢٤٧٠ (٩٦٨)

SUR PLAZA HOTEL

SUR

P.O. Box 908, P.C. 411
Sur, Sultanate of Oman
Tel: (968) 2554 3777
Fax: (968) 2554 2626

E-mail: resvnsur@omantel.net.om

فندق
الفلج

ضور

ص.ب: ٩٠٨، الرمز البريدي: ٤١١
ضور، سلطنة عمان
هاتف: ٣٧٧٧ ٢٥٥٤ (٩٦٨)
فاكس: ٢٦٢٦ ٢٥٥٤ (٩٦٨)

AL WADI HOTEL

SOHAR

P.O. Box 459, P.C. 311
Sohar, Sultanate of Oman
Tel: (968) 2684 0058
Fax: (968) 2684 1997

E-mail: gmalwadi@omanhotels.com

فندق
الوادي

صحار

ص.ب: ٤٥٩، الرمز البريدي: ٣١١
صحار، سلطنة عمان
هاتف: ٠٠٥٨ ٢٦٨٤ (٩٦٨)
فاكس: ١٩٩٧ ٢٦٨٤ (٩٦٨)

OMAN HOTELS & TOURISM COMPANY SAOG
Sultanate of Oman

شركة عمان للفنادق والسياحة ش.م.ع.ع.
سلطنة عمان

Going Out

Going Out

What's new?

Dinner Dilemmas?   Page XXX

There are more restaurants in Dubai than you can shake a chopstick at, and our review section is bursting with over 300 eateries listed by cuisine type. But what if you're in a hurry for a curry and simply don't have time to read every write-up? Well fear not just turn to our Top Picks. There's the best al fresco, fine dining and romantic restaurants as well as those with the best views.

Table Of Contents | What's new?

Going Out

Going Out

If you're out and about in Dubai, you will soon find there is a surprising variety of places to go and things to do. It might not be Ibiza but with more and more hotels springing up the nightlife is constantly improving with enough choice to entertain even the most passionate pleasure seeker. The following section has been divided into two; restaurants are listed under Eating Out, while cafés, bars, pubs, nightclubs and 'cultural' entertainment such as theatre, cinema and comedy clubs, are under On the Town [p.416].

Eating Out

Cosmopolitan and vibrant, Dubai has an excellent variety of restaurants. From Arabic to Vietnamese, Indian to Italian and everything in between, there really is something to suit every taste and budget, and eating out is extremely popular with all segments of the Dubai community.

Most places open early in the evening at around 18:00, but generally aren't busy until about 21:00. A lot of Dubai's most popular restaurants are in hotels, and these are virtually the only outlets that can serve alcohol with your meal (if you want booze, check for the Alcohol Available icon in individual reviews). However, remember that there are several superb independent restaurants around town that shouldn't be ignored just because they are unlicensed.

Theme nights with different types of cuisine than usual are popular in Dubai. Many restaurants also have weekly buffet nights when you can eat, and sometimes drink, as much as you like for a great value, all-inclusive price. See [p.414] for details.

Delivery

Many of the restaurants you would expect offer a free home delivery service but you can also get your hands on à la carte dishes from hotel restaurants. Room Service offers a delivery service from some of Dubai's top restaurants, their brochure has the menus of the participating restaurants and they deliver to your door. The delivery time is between 30 minutes and an hour, and a minimum order of Dhs.60 applies. Delivery charges range from Dhs.10 to Dhs.20. Call 345 5444 or visit the Website (www.roomservice-uae.com).

Drinks

Other options → Alcohol [p.206]

Although Dubai is about the most liberal state in the GCC, alcohol is only available in licensed restaurants and bars that are within hotels, plus a few non hotel outlets, such as golf clubs and some government owned establishments. The mark-up can often be considerable – it's not unknown for a Dhs.11 bottle of indifferent wine to be charged at Dhs.90 plus. While most independent restaurants are unable to serve alcohol, don't let it put you off, since the food is often just as good, and sometimes even better.

Like alcohol, a bottle of house water can also be outrageously marked up, especially for premium brands. Imported water can be charged at up to Dhs.30 a bottle and if you object to this, we suggest you send it back and ask for a local bottled water (but not tap water). A standard one litre bottle of water usually costs Dhs.1.50 in a supermarket and is in no way inferior to imported brands.

Hygiene

All outlets in Dubai are regularly checked by the Municipality for hygiene, and they are strict on warning places to improve and, when necessary, closing them down. Bear this in mind when you are considering eating at a little shawarma shop by the side of the road or a small independent restaurant. It will be perfectly safe to eat there and you're very unlikely to get food poisoning. Indeed, you'll probably have an excellent cheap and atmospheric meal.

Tax & Service Charges

On top of the basic bill, there can be a 15 - 16% service charge and 10% municipality tax, which apparently only applies to 'rated' hotels. These taxes are required to be incorporated into the bill, but are often indicated as being an addition to prices by ++. This information must be clearly indicated somewhere on the menu.

Service charge, perhaps incorrectly named, is not often passed on to staff, and can't be withheld for poor service, so tips are still the best way to reward good service.

Tipping

Tipping is another grey area, but following the standard rule of 10% will not be out of line. It's not necessarily expected, but will be appreciated. Few waiters seem to realise that there's a direct correlation between good service and the size of the tip!

Independent Reviews

We undertake independent reviews of all restaurants and bars that we include in this book. The following outlets have been visited by our freelance reporters and the views expressed are our own. However, if we have unwittingly led you astray, please do let us know. We appreciate all feedback, positive, negative and otherwise. Please log on to www.EatOutSpeakOut.com and share your views. Your comments are never ignored.

Ratings

Rating restaurants is always a highly subjective business. We ask our reviewers to summarise their experiences (the scores are at the end of each entry) in terms of Food, Service, Venue, and Value. You may notice that a local café has the same summary rating as a premium gourmet restaurant. This is not to say that they are equal to one other but rather that their score is in relation to their category, to help you find the best venue be it for a fine dining experience or a café snack.

Each rating is out of five - one dot means poor, two and a half means acceptable and five means fab:

Food ●●●●○ Serv ●○○○○ Venue ●●●●● Value ●●●●○

Venues scheduled to open late 2004 received 'na' ratings, (not available) as a review could not be carried out:

Food – na   Service – na   Venue – na   Value – na

Restaurant Listing Structure

With the ever-increasing size of Dubai the choice of venues for eating out is massive so the *Dubai Explorer* lists only the best selection of restaurants in each category, highlighting those that are recommended as must-dos.

Featuring reviews for over 300 outlets, Going Out provides a comprehensive listing of the places to check out. Listed alphabetically by cuisine styles, as much information as possible is given on the individual outlets.

In order to categorise the restaurants by cuisine we have placed restaurants that serve varying cuisines or styles either under their prominent cuisine or under international if the mix is truly varied. In addition, as we have listed restaurants by cuisine and not theme there is a list of Explorer Top Picks [p.324] if you are looking for a great alfresco restaurant, or one for a romantic evening. If, however you want to know what outlets are in a particular hotel you can flip to the index at the back of the book and look up the hotel, under which there will appear a list of all the outlets with their corresponding page numbers.

To avoid any confusion concerning a particular restaurant's listing, as a rule, any non English names retain their prefix (ie, Al, Le, La and El) in their alphabetical placement, while English names are listed by actual titles, ignoring prefixes such as 'The'. Bon appetit!

Icons - Quick Reference

The price guides are calculated as the cost of a starter, main course and dessert for one person. This includes any relevant taxes, but excludes the cost of drinks. The Dhs.150 icon indicates that an average meal should cost Dhs.150 (plus or minus Dhs.25). Another good cost indication is whether the outlet is licensed, the restaurant location (in a hotel or not), type of cuisine, etc.

Quick Reference Explorer Icons	
	Explorer Recommended!
100	Average price ± Dhs.25 (3 courses per person, including Tax & Service)
	NO Credit Cards Accepted
	Live Band
	Alcohol Available
	Have a Happy Hour
	Will Deliver
	Kids Welcome
	Reservations Recommended
	Dress Smartly
	Outside Terrace
	Vegetarian Dishes

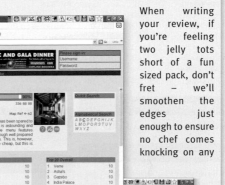

Explorer Publishing is quite proud to be a bit of a 'people's publisher'. We understand your hangovers, your need for excitement, your boredom thresholds and your desire to be heard, and we're always striving to make our publications as interactive with our loyal readership as possible. In the past, our Food Correspondent's telephone has been ringing constantly with people wanting to add their two pennies' worth to the reviews in our guidebooks.

Hence, our most ingenious solution for a satisfied diner, accurate food reporting and lower decibels in the work place, is **EAT OUT SPEAK OUT**.

This Website provides the opportunity to pen down all of your comments, frustrations, tips and tantrums about specific dining experiences at any of the restaurants listed in our guide. Not only will we publish your thoughts online, we'll also pass on your review (anonymously, of course) to the outlet concerned and take your views into consideration for next year's edition of our guidebook.

Now that you know what it's all about, we will restrain you no longer...

Once logged on to **www.EatOutSpeakOut.com**, select the restaurant you wish to review by typing in the outlet name. Alternatively, you can search for your restaurant alphabetically, by cuisine or area/location.

Once you've found the object of your wrath or praise, simply scroll through people's previously penned prose and then enter your own. Don't forget to put in those all important ratings too.

When writing your review, if you're feeling two jelly tots short of a fun sized pack, don't fret – we'll smoothen the edges just enough to ensure no chef comes knocking on any

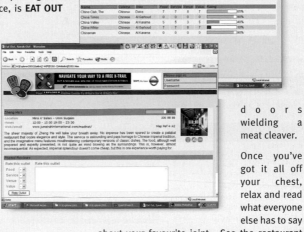

doors wielding a meat cleaver.

Once you've got it all off your chest, relax and read what everyone else has to say about your favourite joint. See the restaurant rated by 'Venue' and also skim through the 'Best Overall' category.

Come on, let's hear what you have to say to improve, or reward the service here!

Explorer Area Top Picks

Al Garhoud

Blue Elephant	Thai	396
India Palace	Indian	358
Cellar, The	International	362
Irish Village	Pubs	431
Legends	Steakhouses	393
Meridien Village	Buffet	341
Boardwalk	International	360
M's Beef Bistro	Steakhouses	393
Rodeo Grill	Steakhouses	393
Come Prima	Italian	368
Cafe Chic	French	338

Al Karama

Midnight Café	International	365

Al Satwa

Il Rustico	Italian	371
Kitchen	Indian	359
Boston Bar, The	American Bars	417

Al Sufouh

Rooftop Lounge	Cocktails	421
Eauzone	Far Eastern	350
Beach Bar & Grill	Seafood	389
Tagine	Moroccan	384
Retro	European	347
Barasti Bar	Beach Bars	418
Hard Rock Café	American	326

Al Wasl

Sea World	Seafood	390

Bur Dubai

Kwality	Indian	359
Yakitori	Japanese	378
Mr. Chow	Chinese	344
Basta Art Café	Cafés	404
Rock Bottom Cafe	American Bars	418
Waxy O'Conner's	Pubs	432
Troyka	Russian	388
Fatafeet	Egyptian	346
Chinese Kitchen	Chinese	343

Deira

Palm Grill	Steakhouses	393
Shabestan	Persian	386
Glasshouse	European	347
Ashiana	Indian	357
Al Dawaar	Buffet	338
Market Place, The	Buffet	341
Verre	French	354
Junction, The	International	365
Cucina	Italian	370
Creekside	Japanese	374
Miyako	Japanese	375
Fish Market, The	Seafood	390

Hor Al Anz

Spice Island	Buffet	342

Jumeira

Prasinos	Mediterranean	382
Lime Tree Cafe	Cafés	406

Marsa Dubai

Lobby Lounge, The	Afternoon Tea	410
BiCE	Italian	367
Chandelier	Arabic	335
Pachanga	Latin American	379
Blues	Seafood	389
Grill Room, The	Steakhouses	392
Ossigeno	Italian	371
Oregano	Mediterranean	382
Amazeena	Arabic	334
Rupee Room, The	Indian	359

Oud Metha

Lemongrass	Thai	396
Lan Kwai Fung	Chinese	344
Fakhreldine	Arabic	335
Khazana	Indian	358
Jimmy Dix	Nightclubs	433

Trade Centre 1

Bacchus	Italian	367
Exchange Grill, The	Steakhouses	392

Marrakech	Moroccan	383
Hoi An	Vietnamese	400
Spectrum on One	International	366
Sumo	Japanese	376
Spectrum on One	General Bars	424
Tangerine	Nightclubs	436
Al Tannour	Arabic	334
Cascades	Buffet	340
Teatro	International	366
Long's Bar	General Bars	423

Trade Centre 2

Al Nafoorah	Arabic	332
Bistro 21	Cafés	404
Vu's	Mediterranean	382
Vu's Bar	General Bars	426
Blue Bar	Jazz Bars	426
Al Safadi	Arabic	332

Umm Hurair

Asha's	Indian	357
Panini	Cafés	406
Ginseng	Cocktails	420
Sphinx	European	348
Vintage	Wine Bars	430
MIX	Nightclubs	434
Seville's	Spanish	392
Peppercrab	Singaporean	391

Umm Suqeim

Villa Beach Rest.	International	366
Left Bank	General Bars	423
Segreto	Italian	372
Bahri Bar	Cocktail	420
Uptown	General Bars	426
Apartment, The	French	352
Al Mahara	Seafood	388
Zheng He's	Chinese	345
Go West	American	326
Dhow & Anchor	Pubs	431
La Parrilla	Argentinean	338
Al Muna	Buffet	340
Koubba	General Bars	422
Arboretum	International	360
Napa	American	328
Pierchic	Seafood	390

Enjoy the View

Al Dawaar	338
Al Muntaha	360
Boardwalk	360
Fatafeet	346
Uptown	426
Vu's (Bar and Rest.)	382

Arabic Experience

Al Hadiqa Tent	418
Fatafeet	346
Khaymat Al Bahar	365
Shabestan	386
Al Mallah	412
Fakhreldine	335

Cheap Chow

Al Mallah	412
Karachi Darbar	384
Kitchen	359
Mr. Chow	344
Open House	344
Golden Fork	390

Family Friendly

Applebee's	326
Café Ceramique	404
Chili's	326
India Palace	358
Planet Hollywood	328
Sea World	390

Explorer Top Picks

Going Out

Explorer Category Top Picks

American

Napa	Jumeira	328
Shooters		330
Go West	Umm Suqeim	326
Hard Rock Café	Al Sufouh	326

Arabic/Lebanese

Al Nafoorah	Trade Centre 2	332
Chandelier	Marsa Dubai	335
Amazeena	Marsa Dubai	334
Al Tannour	Trade Centre 1	334
Fakhreldine	Oud Metha	335
Al Safadi	Trade Centre 2	332

Buffet

Meridien Village	Al Garhoud	341
Al Dawaar	Deira	338
Market Place, The	Deira	341
Spice Island	Hor Al Anz	342
Al Muna	Umm Suqeim	340
Cascades	Trade Centre 1	340

Chinese

Zheng He's	Umm Suqeim	345
Lan Kwai Fung	Oud Metha	344
Mr. Chow	Bur Dubai	344
Chinese Kitchen	Bur Dubai	343

European

Glasshouse	Deira	347
Sphinx	Umm Hurair	348
Retro	Al Sufouh	347

French

Signatures	Jebel Ali	354
Verre	Deira	354
Apartment, The	Umm Suqeim	352
Cafe Chic	French	338

Indian

Asha's	Umm Hurair	357
India Palace	Al Garhoud	358
Ashiana	Deira	357

Kitchen	Al Satwa	359
Kwality	Bur Dubai	359
Rupee Room, The	Marsa Dubai	359
Khazana	Oud Metha	358

International

Villa Beach Rest.	Umm Suqeim	366
Arboretum	Jumeira	360
Midnight Café	Al Karama	365
Cellar, The	Al Garhoud	362
Junction, The	Deira	365
Spectrum on One	Trade Centre 1	366
Teatro	Trade Centre 1	366

Italian

BiCE	Marsa Dubai	367
Bacchus	Trade Centre 1	367
Il Rustico	Al Satwa	371
Segreto	Umm Suqeim	372
Ossigeno	Marsa Dubai	371
Come Prima	Al Garhoud	368
Cucina	Deira	370

Japanese

Sumo	Trade Centre 1	376
Yakitori	Bur Dubai	378
Creekside	Deira	374
Miyako	Deira	375

Mediterranean

Vu's	Trade Centre 2	382
Oregano	Marsa Dubai	382
Prasinos	Jumeira	382

Moroccan

Marrakech	Trade Centre 1	383
Tagine	Al Sufouh	384

Seafood

Blues	Marsa Dubai	389
Al Mahara	Umm Suqeim	388
Beach Bar & Grill	Al Sufouh	389
Sea World	Al Wasl	390
Fish Market, The	Deira	390
Pierchic	Jumeira	390

Steakhouses

Palm Grill	Deira	393
Exchange Grill, The	Trade Centre 1	392
Grill Room, The	Marsa Dubai	392
Legends	Al Garhoud	393
M's Beef Bistro	Al Garhoud	393
Rodeo Grill	Al Garhoud	393

Thai

Blue Elephant	Al Garhoud	396
Lemongrass	Oud Metha	396

Cafés & Coffee Shops

Bistro 21	Trade Centre 2	404
Panini	Umm Hurair	406
Lime Tree Cafe	Jumeira	406
Basta Art Café	Bur Dubai	404

Cocktail Lounges

Rooftop Lounge	Al Sufouh	421
Trader Vic`s	Umm Suqeim	421
Ginseng	Umm Hurair	420
Bahri Bar	Umm Suqeim	420

General Bars

Left Bank	Umm Suqeim	423
Koubba	Jumeira	422
Vu's Bar	Trade Centre 2	426
Spectrum on One	Trade Centre 1	424
Long's Bar	Trade Centre 1	423

Pubs

Irish Village	Al Garhoud	431
Waxy O'Conner's	Bur Dubai	432
Dhow & Anchor	Umm Suqeim	431

Nightclubs

MIX	Umm Hurair	434
Tangerine	Trade Centre 1	436
Jimmy Dix	Oud Metha	433

Explorer Top Picks

Going Out

High-Class Hangouts

Koubba	422
Library & Cigar Bar	419
Vu's Bar	426
Blue Bar	426
Verre	354
Celebrities	362

Al Fresco Favourites

Boardwalk	360
Cellar, The	362
Century Village	na
Fatafeet	346
Irish Village	431
Madinat Jumeirah	na

Romantic

Cellar, The	362
Il Rustico	371
Khaymat Al Bahar	365
Oregano	382
Villa Beach Rest.	366
Tagine	384

Off the Beaten Track

Al Shera'a	412
Basta Art Café	404
Fatafeet	346
Maria Bonita	382
More	406
Signatures	354

American

Other options → **American Bars [p.417]**
Tex Mex [p.394]

Applebee's

Location → Sheikh Issa Tower · Trade Centre 1 | **343 7755**
Hours → 11:00 - 24:00 Wed, Thu, Fri 11:00 - 01:00
Web/email → www.anemco.com | Map Ref → 9-C2

This Tex-Mex newbie is a fine addition to the bustle of Sheikh Zayed Road. The menu is full of choices (some menu items can be altered by request to suit vegetarian tastes), and to accompany your meal you can order a 'bottomless' soft drink (free refills) or choose from a range of exotic non-alcoholic cocktails. Go hungry, as the portions are Texan in size. Kids will enjoy the special children's menu, which comes with an activity sheet and free coloured pencils. The decor is pleasant (the walls are packed with fascinating memorabilia) and the waitresses are some of the friendliest in town.
Food●●●●○Serv●●●●○Venue●●●●○Value●●●●○

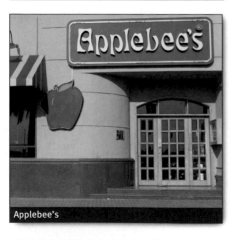
Applebee's

Chili's

Location → Nr Le Meridien Fairway · Al Garhoud | **282 8484**
Hours → 11:00 - 23:00 Thu 11:00 - 24:00 Fri 13:00 - 23:00
Web/email → www.chilis.com | Map Ref → 14-D2

A real family favourite, Chili's has a great menu, fun atmosphere and the staff are extremely helpful and amiable. The menu caters to all tastes, including a number of 'guiltless' and 'low carb' recipes for those counting calories. The burgers are famous but to really get your taste buds going, try the steak and fish dishes. With roaring trade during lunchtime, soup and salad combos are popular. Children are well catered for, and doted over, with activities (such as colouring pencils and sheets) to keep them occupied and a varied kids' menu.

Other Locations: Jumeirah Beach Centre (344 1300); Deira City Centre,(295 9559); BurJuman (352 2900); Dubai Internet City, (390 1496); Sahara Centre, Sharjah (06 531 8890); Dubai Home Delivery (282 8303).
Food●●●●○Serv●●●●○Venue●●●●○Value●●●●○

Go West

Location → The Jumeirah Beach Hotel · Umm Suqeim | **406 8181**
Hours → 12:30 - 15:00 18:00 - 23:30
Web/email → www.jumeirahinternational.com | Map Ref → 4-B2

Reminiscent of a kitsch Colorado steak joint with saddles, wagons and servers in plaid shirts, Go West completes the Western experience with great North American chow. For starters, the buffalo wings are enough for two, chicken fajitas arrive sizzling with all the trimmings, and the BBQ ribs are rich and tender. Children get their own menu and colouring book, and mum and dad get a great live band, an impressive range of beers and half price happy hour from 18:00 - 19:00.
Food●●●●○Serv●●●●○Venue●●●●○Value●●●●○

Hard Rock Café

Location → Jct 5 Shk. Zayed Rd · Al Sufouh | **399 2888**
Hours → 12:00 - 01:30
Web/email → www.hardrock.com | Map Ref → 3-A3

Classic rock songs, a lively crowd and a huge bar selection just might have you dancing on the tables with the staff. Big portions of American-style food and drinks are available for all palates, from fajitas and pasta to vegetarian choices, but burgers are the heart and soul of the menu. The atmosphere rocks, literally, from Pink Floyd to Pink and the food is good but remember the Hard Rock Café is loud and not really for the faint hearted.
Food●●●○○Serv●●●●○Venue●●●○○Value●●●○○

Johnny Rockets

Location → Opp Jumeirah Centre · Jumeira
Hours → 12:00 - 24:00
Web/email → www.johnnyrockets.com   Map Ref → 6-C2

Can't get Happy Days on cable? Shake, rock and roll your way to a shake, burger and fries at this 50's style diner. Jam packed with energy and almost always a good crowd, Johnny Rockets' straightforward menu offers big burgers, tasty floats and the best chilli cheese fries in town. 50's tunes perfectly match the décor – red vinyl seats and a counter for the ultimate diner experience. Leather jackets optional.

Food●●●○○Serv●●●○○Venue●●●●○Value●●●○○

Napa

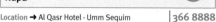

Location → Al Qasr Hotel · Umm Sequim
Hours → 12:00 - 15:00 19:00 - 23:30
Web/email → www.jumeirahinternational.com   Map Ref → 4-A2

Adventurous diners ought to savour the imaginative and refreshingly light flavours of Californian cuisine at Napa. A tantalising menu is offset by a relaxed ambience and inviting décor. Sit inside and watch the chefs at work, or dine alfresco on the wide terrace with famous views of the Madinat Jumeirah waterways. Don't leave here before tucking in to the stunning deserts, some are sinful but there's also some less calorific temptations if you're feeling too guilt-ridden.

Food●●●●○Serv●●●●○Venue●●●●○Value●●●●○

Planet Hollywood

Location → Wafi City · Umm Hurair
Hours → 12:00 - 24:00
Web/email → www.planethollywood-dubai.com Map Ref → 13-D2

Planet Hollywood is the archetypal American experience and a haven for movie hounds. The walls are covered in film memorabilia, your meal is soundtracked by theme music and accompanied by video clips. Big burgers and giant desserts are definite 'Oscar nominees', but stray from the basics and you're in 'straight to video' territory. Some dishes suffer from a lack of culinary care and have a synthetic, pre-packaged feel. A great novelty venue that's cool for kids, not connoisseurs.

Food●●○○○Serv●●●●○Venue●●●●○Value●●○○○

Scarlett's

Location → Boulevard at Emirates Towers, The
Hours → 12:30 - 03:00
Web/email → www.jumeirahinternational.com   Map Ref → 9-C2

The decadence of the Deep South lives on at Scarlett's, where the festive mood and consistent crowds testify to its continuing popularity. The dining area downstairs gives way to a busy dance floor (playing the latest top 40 hits) and well stocked bar upstairs. There are plenty of drinks specials, as well as ladies' nights on Tuesdays and Sundays. A terrace (located in the shopping mall, rather than outdoors) provides respite from the festivities inside. A strict dress code is in force.

Food●●●○○Serv●●●●○Venue●●●○○Value●●●○○

Planet Hollywood

Scarlett's Fever!

Shooters

Location ➜ Jebel Ali Shooting Club ·   **883 6555**
Hours ➜ 19:00 - 23:00   Tue closed
Web/email ➜ www.jebelali-international.com   Map Ref ➜ 1-A2

   150

A touch of Texas marks Shooters, a friendly steakhouse that serves up mouth-wateringly juicy cuts of prime Angus beef. Country music keeps the place jumping in Western style and a complimentary glass of Sangria at the door will help ease you into the feast of a menu awaiting you. Careful not to fill up too much on the main course because the deserts here are delectable. And yes, the Mississippi mud pie is definitely worth the guilt.

Food●●●●○Serv●●●○○Venue●●●●○Value●●●●○

TGI Friday's

Location ➜ Holiday Centre · Trade Centre 1   **331 8010**
Hours ➜ 11:00 - 01:00
Web/email ➜ tgifdxb@emirates.net.ae   Map Ref ➜ 9-D2

   100

This famous chain has typical American offerings in most of its outlets: loud music, a bar, a dance floor and Hollywood memorabilia. The menu of enormous burgers, sizzling Tex Mex fajitas, speciality salads, appetisers, pasta and ribs, are more than generous in size. The sinful dessert of Oreo cookies and vanilla icecream is a calorie watcher's nightmare. Extremely helpful – if sometimes manic – staff keep the pace moving. TGI Friday's appeals to many despite the lack of alcohol, and is a particular treat for the kids.

Food●●○○○Serv●●●○○Venue●●○○○Value●●●○○

Americas, The

Lumping together Central, North and South America may seem strange, but there is method to the madness. Generally speaking, this is hearty fare with an emphasis on portion size and is especially good for meat lovers. American restaurants offer the ubiquitous burgers alongside ribs and steaks, often prime quality meat especially flown in from the States to be cooked to your preference.

Mexican and Tex-Mex cooking usually have a wider range of tastes, a lot of the time spicier but offering a much better choice for vegetarians. Some options include refried beans, guacamole, salsa, nachos (small, hard tortillas topped with melted cheese, peppers and chilli), fajitas (a soft tortilla, wrapped around sizzling vegetables and cheese or meat) and enchiladas (a tortilla filled with meat or cheese and served under a rich sauce), plus some great salads.

Further south and the cuisine is still meat based - in particular, Argentinean cooking is noted for serving high quality steaks.

Desserts vary widely in this category, but old favourites like Mississippi mud pie, apple pie or chocolate cake with lashings of ice-cream can usually be found somewhere on the menu - to the delight of those who like to finish with a dish that is sweet, filling and calorie laden!

Arabic/Lebanese

Other options ➜ **Egyptian [p.346]**
Emirati [p.346]
Middle Eastern [p.383]
Moroccan [p.383]
Persian [p.386]
Turkish [p.399]

Al Diwan

Location ➜ Metropolitan Palace · Deira   **227 0000**
Hours ➜ 19:30 - 03:00
Web/email ➜ www.methotels.com   Map Ref ➜ 11-D2

    150

Early in the evening Al Diwan is a quiet venue serving traditional Lebanese meze and grills, with extensive set menus, fabulously large portions and all at good value. Around midnight the lights dim and the live music starts, but not even the hypnotic gyrations of the belly dancer can distract you from noticing the

Dubai Eye 103.8 FM

alk Radio... Classic Hits

DVBAI EYE 103.8

steeply increased prices. Set menu diners may feel distinctly unwelcome as bigger spending punters arrive, but the food quality is good, the shisha excellent and the service is right on the money, despite you spending lots of it here. ⓙⓚ

Food ●●●○○ Serv ●●○○○ Venue ●●●○○ Value ●●●○○

Al Khayal

Location → The Jumeirah Beach Hotel · Umm Suqeim | **406 8181**
Hours → 20:00 - 03:00
Web/email → www.jumeirahinternational.com   Map Ref → 4-B2

    (150)

This plush restaurant with its Bedouin tent themed dining area is going to be a hit for Lebanese food connoisseurs. The menu is vast but not too pricey. Try a mixture of mezes to share with your friends or go for one of the signature dishes cooked by Chef Ibrahim, either way, you won't leave disappointed. The Omani lobster or the Babaganoush for vegetarians come highly recommended. The evening's belly-dancing kicks off at around 10pm, and you'd be wise to book in advance to avoid disappointment. ⓔⓐⓣ

Ramadan Timings

During Ramadan, opening and closing times of restaurants change considerably. Be sure to call and check before arriving somewhere, only to find all the lights off and nobody home. While many nightclubs remain open, the dance floor is closed and foot tapping is off the menu.

Food ●●○○○ Serv ●●●○○ Venue ●●●●○ Value ●●●○○

Al Koufa

Location → Nr Cyclone · Oud Metha | **335 1511**
Hours → 18:30 - 02:00
Web/email → na   Map Ref → 10-D4

 (50)

Al Koufa offers good Arabic food (including Emirati dishes), great people watching and pretty decent shisha. The look has evolved over the years from a temporary looking tent into something of a 'mock fort' with polystyrene walls and even proper tables. In comparison to the décor, the food and service are better. Before 23:00, the place is almost deserted. After that, the band starts up and people pack in. Expect a pleasant enough dining experience, although popularity is flagging with the abundance of new places opening up. ⓣⓜ

Food ●●●●○ Serv ●●●●○ Venue ●●●○○ Value ●●●○○

Al Mijana

Location → Le Meridien Dubai · Al Garhoud | **282 4040**
Hours → 12:30 - 15:00 20:00 - 24:00
Web/email → www.lemeridien-dubai.com   Map Ref → 14-E3

   (200)

Located at the end of Le Meridien Village, Al Mijana serves Lebanese cuisine at a cut above the competition. The set menus offer feast like portions of all the usual Arabic offerings prepared to a particularly high standard. A highlight is the freshly cooked Arabic bread, which arrives puffy and warm at your table. Excellent service, delicious food, and live entertainment make this a great place to spend an evening. Various connoisseurs will enjoy the extensive shisha menu or the cognac and cigar list. ⓐⓑⓗ

Food ●●●●○ Serv ●●●●○ Venue ●●●●○ Value ●●●●○

Al Nafoorah

Location → The Boulevard at Emirates Towers | **319 8088**
Hours → 12:30 - 15:00 20:00 - 23:30
Web/email → www.jumeirahinternational.com   Map Ref → 9-C2

(100)

Armed with no gimmick other than a succulent presentation of complimentary desserts, this elegant Lebanese restaurant offers deliciously prepared food in an opulent setting. Chef Ali specialises in classic dishes with a twist, giving you fresh appreciation for some of your old favourites. The chicken livers, drizzled in pomegranate sauce, are undoubtedly the best in town. This vibrant, modern day Aladdin's cave is highly recommended for a wonderful evening at a surprisingly reasonable price. ⓐⓟ

Food ●●●●○ Serv ●●●●● Venue ●●●●○ Value ●●●●●

Al Safadi

Location → Al Kawakeb Bld · Trade Centre 2 | **343 5333**
Hours → 10:00 - 02:00 Fri 08:00 - 02:00
Web/email → na   Map Ref → 9-A2

 (50)

Like most restaurants in this category, the service is good, the food copious and tasty, and the value for money, fantastic. Perhaps the menu is not so vast here, but the good news is that what's listed is likely to be very deliciously prepared. The lights are bright and the customer turnover high, but relaxed dining is available outside to watch the world go by while you eat, especially pleasant at the Al Rigga Road branch. ⓣⓜ

See also: Al Rigga Road, Deira (227 9922)

Food ●●●●○ Serv ●●●○○ Venue ●●●○○ Value ●●●●○

Arabic/Lebanese

Going Out

Variety is the spice of life.

Beachcombers

Carnevale

The Apartment

Al Khayal

La Parrilla

Der Keller

For Dubai's finest selection of world class cuisine, it has to be The Jumeirah Beach Hotel.
To reserve your table at any of our 20 restaurants, bars and cafés, simply call 04 406 8181.

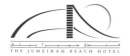

THE JUMEIRAH BEACH HOTEL

جميرا انترناشيونال
JUMEIRAH
INTERNATIONAL
www.jumeirahinternational.com

Al Tannour

Location ➔ Crowne Plaza · Trade Centre 1 | **331 1111**
Hours ➔ 20:30 - 03:00
Web/email ➔ www.crowneplaza.com   Map Ref ➔ 9-D2

Doubling as a serious restaurant in the early evening and a live entertainment venue later on, Al Tannour offers excellent Lebanese fare. Meze dishes are generally simple and expertly prepared, while grills served in stay-hot salvers reflect their high standards and attention to detail. Attentive service and a pleasant candlelit ambience add further appeal, and draw attention away from the large, open, and fairly plain room. As with many restaurants of this kind, hefty cover charges kick in after 11:00, so come early to enjoy a fabulous meal at reasonable prices.⬤

Food⬤⬤⬤⬤⬤Serv⬤⬤⬤⬤⬤Venue⬤⬤⬤◯◯Value⬤⬤⬤⬤◯

Ali Baba

Location ➔ Regent Palace Hotel · Bur Dubai | **344 4120**
Hours ➔ 19:00 - 03:00
Web/email ➔ www.ramee-group.com   Map Ref ➔ 11-A1

Ali Baba is an intimate, atmospheric place with a mixed menu that offers traditional Lebanese treats, along with 'International' fare including pizza, pasta and Mexican dishes. Book ahead and ask for a table overlooking the sea – you can enjoy the sunset and a game of backgammon while the friendly staff set about preparing your order. Add the sultry strummings of the oud player, and you've got the makings of a relaxing, agreeable night out in a charming venue.⬤

Food⬤⬤⬤◯◯Serv⬤⬤⬤◯◯Venue⬤⬤⬤⬤◯Value⬤⬤⬤◯◯

Amazeena

Location ➔ Ritz-Carlton, The · Marsa Dubai | **399 4000**
Hours ➔ 19:30 - 00:30 Thu 19:30-01:30 Tue closed
Web/email ➔ www.ritzcarlton.com   Map Ref ➔ 2-E2

Set in the impressive Ritz-Carlton, Amazeena is one of the better poolside restaurants in Dubai. With a varied and very well priced selection of meze on offer, this is one of the best places to relax and enjoy traditional Arabic cuisine. Excellent hummus and saj are delightful ways to enjoy dining under the stars or in your own little tent. Sampling the shisha

while the oud player plucks away will definitely lead you from the dining chairs to the lounge areas.⬤

Food⬤⬤⬤⬤◯Serv⬤⬤⬤⬤◯Venue⬤⬤⬤⬤⬤Value⬤⬤⬤◯◯

ARZ Lebanon

Location ➔ Trade Centre Rd · Al Karama | **396 4466**
Hours ➔ 08:00 - 01:00 Fri 12:00- 01:00
Web/email ➔ abci1@emirates.net.ae   Map Ref ➔ 10-E1

This beautifully decorated Lebanese restaurant has seating for about 70, including a romantic little terrace outside. The menu has so much to offer that you'll welcome the help of your friendly waiter in making your choice. If you're not in the mood for Lebanese, ARZ also offers a small range of Italian pastas and continental dishes. The highlight is the piping hot Lebanese bread, freshly baked in an open oven while you watch.⬤

Food⬤⬤⬤⬤◯Serv⬤⬤⬤⬤◯Venue⬤⬤⬤◯◯Value⬤⬤⬤⬤◯

Automatic

Location ➔ Beach Centre, The · Jumeira | **349 4888**
Hours ➔ 11:00 - 01:00
Web/email ➔ na   Map Ref ➔ 6-B2

For more than 25 years the Automatic chain of restaurants has set the benchmark for Arabic food in Dubai. With a large number of branches throughout the city and delivery options available, the food is not only reasonably priced and tasty, it is also convenient. Good portions of grilled meat, fish and salads are served fresh and hot to your table by the efficient and friendly waiting staff. The atmosphere is more minimalist in style but still clean and bright, with family friendly amenities attracting a mixed clientele.⬤

Food⬤⬤⬤⬤◯Serv⬤⬤⬤⬤◯Venue⬤⬤◯◯◯Value⬤⬤⬤⬤⬤

Awafi

Location ➔ JW Marriott Hotel · Deira | **262 4444**
Hours ➔ 20:00 - 24:00
Web/email ➔ www.marriott.com   Map Ref ➔ 12-A3

The best thing about Awafi is the alfresco atmosphere it offers around the rooftop pool of the Marriott. This is at its best late at night, when the live entertainment and the shishas come to the fore. Early diners may be compromised by having to share the pool and toilets/showers with swimmers.

The menu is limited to the standard Arabic fare and while the service is excellent, prices are higher than the competition. Open only during the cooler months of the year.

Food●●●●○ Serv●●●○○ Venue●●●●● Value●●●○○

Awtar

Location → Grand Hyatt Dubai · Umm Hurair
Hours → 12:30 - 15:00 19:30 - 03:00 Sat closed
Web/email → www.dubai.grand.hyatt.com

317 2222

Map Ref → 13-E3

   150

This upmarket Lebanese restaurant features a warm and comfortable interior, including cosy booths. Service is good and the food menu expansive, with very good meze and desserts (share the Grand Desert, there's plenty to go around and it's all good). Unfortunately the same cannot be said for the mains, particularly the seafood. Band and belly dancers shake at ten. Awtar will impress patrons, especially if they just stick to starters and sweets.

Food●●●○○ Serv●●●●○ Venue●●●●○ Value●●●●○

Ayam Zaman

Location → Ascot Hotel · Bur Dubai
Hours → 19:30 - 03:00
Web/email → www.ascothoteldubai.com

352 0900

Map Ref → 7-E3

150

The Ascot Hotel houses Ayam Zaman and its rather distinctive Lebanese kitchen. Friendly waiters are proud of what they serve. As they should be, especially when they spread out the eleven delicious cold mezes followed by eight mouth-watering hot ones. The unusually fine stuffed grape leaves deserve a mention, as do the juicy chicken livers and crunchy sesame cakes. Belly dancers and beverages raise the cost of an evening, but Ayam Zaman repays much of the price with wholly satisfying fare.

Food●●●●○ Serv●●●●○ Venue●●●○○ Value●●●●○

Chandelier

Location → Marina Walk · Marsa Dubai
Hours → 08:30 - 01:00
Web/email → www.chandelier-uae.com

366 3606

Map Ref → 2-E2

100

Combine funky tunes, chic décor with nouveau Lebanese cuisine (if there's such a thing), and you have the scintillating Chandelier. Situated in the up and coming Marina Walk, you can enjoy an

Arabic experience with a twist. The menu offers a wide variety of traditional and eclectic Middle Eastern fare. Generous portions, delightful presentation and palate pleasing flavours, make for an outstanding dining experience. Finish your evening with drinks upstairs in the lounge or shisha on the outdoor waterfront terrace.

Food●●●●○ Serv●●●●● Venue●●●●○ Value●●●●●

Fakhreldine

Location → Mövenpick Hotel · Oud Metha
Hours → 12:30 - 15:30 19:30 - 03:00
Web/email → www.movenpick-hotels.com

335 0505

Map Ref → 10-D4

     100

If you think all hummus is created equal, you're in for a pleasant surprise at this top notch Lebanese venue. Better yet, be daring and opt for something out of your norm since the rest of the menu is extensive and equally delicious. Fakhreldine is beautifully decorated and the band and belly dancer add even more charm to your evening. Throw in the good service by knowledgeable waiters, and you have yourself an unforgettable Arabian night.

Food●●●●○ Serv●●●○○ Venue●●●○○ Value●●●●●

Fakhreldine

Going Out

Arabic/Lebanese

Kan Zaman Restaurant

Location → Heritage & Diving Village · Al Shindagha | **393 9913**
Hours → 10:00 - 01:30
Web/email → www.dubaitourism.ae   Map Ref → 8-B1

  50

Aptly located at the Al Shindagha Heritage Village and offering some of the best night views of the creek, Kan Zaman brings to Dubai an excellent Arabic menu, with a few Western alternatives, to tickle the taste buds. Big sized portions come with little sized price tags. Iranian, Chinese and continental dishes are also available, but stick to the Arabic and local dishes for a more 'authentic' experience. The fact that parking is plentiful is also a bonus, especially in this part of town.

Food●●●●○Serv●●●○○Venue●●●●○Value●●●●○

L'Auberge

Location → City Centre · Deira | **295 0201**
Hours → 12:00 - 24:00   Fri 13:00 - 24:00
Web/email → www.deiracitycentre.com   Map Ref → 14-D1

  50

L'Auberge offers decent Arabic food within the mall. Seating options include social booths, open tables or small alcoves that can be curtained off for private dining, and the service is good and not too rushed. Like most Lebanese restaurants, Arabic bread and a huge garden salad arrive at your table first, with which you can enjoy a selection of meze or other starters, and main meals consist mostly of grills. Overall, this a surprisingly pleasant restaurant, particularly suited for an escape from consumer mania.

See also: Hamarain Centre (262 6965); Al Rigga Rd (295 0208); Town Centre (349 9110)

Food●●●○○Serv●●●○○Venue●●○○○Value●●●○○

Mays El Reem

Location → JW Marriott Hotel · Deira | **262 4444**
Hours → 18:00 - 03:00
Web/email → www.marriott.com   Map Ref → 12-A3

    100

A popular late night entertainment venue, Mays Al Reem's cavernous interior is reminiscent of a faded Ottoman palace, replete with gurgling stone waterfall and large softly-cushioned alcoves. The restaurant only comes alive after 23:00 when the band and belly dancer appear, so early diners munch in silence and solitude. You could take comfort in the extensive menu, except that most

dishes are fairly ordinary. Coupled with indifferent service, this place does not inspire a repeat visit – except maybe to experience the festive shisha-filled party atmosphere later on.

Food●●○○○Serv●●○○○Venue●●○○○Value●●○○○

Mays El Reem

Mazaj

Location → Century Village · Al Garhoud | **282 9952**
Hours → 12:00 - 03:00
Web/email → www.aviationclubonline.com   Map Ref → 14-C3

      100

If you crave the fruity aroma of shisha pipes in the night air, then Mazaj is the place to go. This authentic venue offers alfresco Arabic cuisine among the fairy lit palms of Century Village. The menu comprises an attractive range and with its location, this is a great place for shisha after a meal at Century Village. If you are here for food stick to the starters (which are wonderful) and the shisha. The main courses (although generous) are average kebab house fare.

Food●●●○○Serv●●○○○Venue●●●●○Value●●●○○

Reem Al Bawadi

Location → Nr HSBC · Jumeira | **394 7444**
Hours → 09:00 - 03:00
Web/email → aymanshj@emirates.net.ae   Map Ref → 5-B2

50

With its authentic décor and curtained majlises, Reem Al Bawadi has a definite Arabian buzz, attracting expats looking for a taste of local culture. Customers linger over Turkish coffee, Arabic sweets and shisha, or sample the meze and mains including tasty salads, dips, kibbehs and koftas.

BEACH HOTEL MUSCAT

BEACH HOTEL

Since it has been established in 1997 The Beach Hotel has tried to gain customers satisfaction, who seek simplicity and quietness; taking advantage from its charming situation in the heart of Muscat city and between its most luxurious and harming districts, which are only 200m far from its enhancing beach.

- 24 – Hour Room Service
- Soft-bar in each room
- Safe deposit boxes at front desk
- Satellite T.V.
- Restaurant
- Direct dial telephone
- Same day laundry and dry cleaning services
- Car hire, tour information
- Booking & ticket confirmation
- Daily local paper (Arabic / English)
- Ample car parking area
- Doctor on call

A Home Away From Home

Contact Details :

Beach Hotel
Muscat
P O Box - 678, P C - 116, Mina Al Fahal
Sultanate of Oman
Tel : (968) 24696601, Fax : (968) 24697686
www.omanbeachhotel.com
Email : info@omanbeachhotel.com

The menu also embraces a range of international entrées ranging from seafood platters and burgers to Moroccan style chicken. Service is relaxed, the quality of food can vary but is generally reasonable, the portions are generous and the prices typical of this type of restaurant.
Food●●●○○ Serv●●●○○ Venue●●●●○ Value●●●○○

Argentinean

Other options → Latin American [p.379]

La Parrilla

Location → The Jumeirah Beach Hotel · Umm Suqeim | 406 8181
Hours → 19:00 - 01:00
Web/email → www.jumeirahinternational.com   Map Ref → 4-B2

La Parilla offers wonderful décor, food and service like many a successful restaurant. But add some Argentinean spice, lively entertainment and a sensational view of Dubai's night lights, and you have a venue that's a 'must do' on the city's fine dining circuit. Steak lovers should not miss the signature meaty treats on the menu, which also offers vegetarian and seafood options. It's all delicious and you could easily be enticed into becoming a regular, were it not for the prices that relegate this to a 'special occasion' restaurant.
Food●●●●○ Serv●●●●○ Venue●●●●○ Value●●●○○

Buffet

Other options → All You Can Eat & Drink [p.414]
Friday Brunch [p.412]

Al Dawaar

Location → Hyatt Regency · Deira | 209 1100
Hours → 12:30 - 15:30 19:00 - 23:30
Web/email → www.dubai.regency.hyatt.com   Map Ref → 8-D2

Being Dubai's only revolving restaurant is but one unique element of Al Dawaar. The International buffet is magnificent and features top quality European, Arabic and Indian fare. Favourites include the Fresh Oysters, authentic Arabic Meze, Grilled Omani Lobster Tails and Moroccan Lamb & Date Tagine - all exquisite, as is the delicious assortment of sweets and deserts. Discreet service, ultra stylish décor, soft lighting and chilled tunes all enrich the panoramic dining experience. Welcome to the only stress-free roundabout in town.
Food●●●●○ Serv●●●●○ Venue●●●●● Value●●●○○

Al Iwan

Location → Burj Al Arab · Umm Suqeim | 301 7600
Hours → 12:30 - 15:30 19:00 - 24:00
Web/email → www.jumeirahinternational.com   Map Ref → 4-A1

With breathtaking views of the Arabian Gulf and an intimate dining space make this spectacular restaurant, adjacent to the tallest atrium in the world, the perfect place to be pampered with traditional Arabic and international cuisine. The buffet alternates between international and local delicacies but quantity doesn't replace quality. The service is somewhat formal but the staff remain friendly. Dining at its most elegant and restaurant décor at its most opulent make this venue the perfect choice for a special occasion.
Food●●●●○ Serv●●●●○ Venue●●●●○ Value●●●○○

Al Muna

Location → Mina A'Salam · Umm Suqeim | 366 8888
Hours → 12:30 - 15:00 19:00 - 23:30
Web/email → www.jumeirahinternational.com   Map Ref → 4-A2

Immersed in good company (given the Burj Al Arab is literally a stone's throw away), the ambience within this restaurant is subtle and unpretentious. The terrace offers a suitably intimate setting amid the magical atmosphere of the Madinat. Serving international cuisine, a menu plus buffet option caters to all and the à la carte menu is available around the clock. The staff are extremely friendly and eager to please, but do choose your company carefully – many words are needed to fill the extended gaps between courses.
Food●●●○○ Serv●●●●○ Venue●●●●○ Value●●●●○

Antigo

Location → Le Meridien Dubai · Al Garhoud | 282 4040
Hours → 05:30 - 23:45
Web/email → www.lemeridien-dubai.com   Map Ref → 14-E3

Antigo offers a varied menu and exceptional service quality, although prices are high and the restaurant's identity seems a little confused. However, there are regular special deals and a large buffet option available, which can make the bill as palatable as the food. The wine list and cocktail menu are both extensive and expensive. While the décor is more pleasure than business Antigo is still a good option for corporate dining.
Food●●●●○ Serv●●●●● Venue●●●○○ Value●●○○○

experience

A million different flavours, styles and impressions await you …
Come and experience a mélange of restaurants offering fresh and authentic cuisines from east and west,
only at Hyatt Regency Dubai.

FEEL THE HYATT TOUCH®

PO Box 5588, Dubai, UAE

TELEPHONE: +971 4 209 1234 FACSIMILE: +971 4 209 1235 www.dubai.regency.hyatt.com

Bella Vista

Location ➜ Jumeira Rotana · Al Satwa
Hours ➜ 11:00 - 15:30 19:00 - 23:00
Web/email ➜ www.rotana.com

345 5888

Map Ref ➜ 6-E3

Theme nights are what Bella Vista does best. There's Carvery and Jazz on Sunday, Mexican on Monday, Taste of Asia on Wednesday and Curry Night on Thursday. The atmosphere is cheery, the variety of dishes on offer plentiful and the staff are quick to replenish. The venue layout is a little bewildering with random function rooms taking up much of the restaurant's entrance, but past the puzzlement lies a fabulous view and a casual Mediterranean layout.

Food●●●●○Serv●●●●○Venue●●●●○Value●●●●○

Boulvar

Location ➜ Hotel Inter-Continental · Deira
Hours ➜ 00:00 - 24:00
Web/email ➜ www.interconti.com

205 7333

Map Ref ➜ 8-C4

Compared to the many buffet themed restaurants in town, this is no prize winner. The restaurant's international buffet includes the usual array of soups, salads, a variety of meats and fish, a limited selection of sushi and desserts. The service is attentive. With little excitement here, Boulvar is, as expected, mainly visited by hotel guests.

Food●●○○○Serv●●●●○Venue●●○○○Value●●●○○

Cascades

Location ➜ Fairmont Dubai, The · Trade Centre 1
Hours ➜ 00:00 - 24:00
Web/email ➜ www.fairmont.com

311 8000

Map Ref ➜ 9-E1

The artsy waterfall feature with rotating colourful lights is the opening feature of Cascades. But the impressing don't end there, as the staff do all they can to make a first class impression. The cuisine is mainly Arabic, Mediterranean and Seafood with an excellent à la carte menu to choose from. Friday is brunch day but any day of the week is worth a visit to Cascades, if for nothing more than their sinful, yet mouth-watering desert options.

Food●●●●○Serv●●●●○Venue●●●●○Value●●●●○

Cascades

Gozo Garden

Location ➜ Millennium Airport Hotel · Al Garhoud
Hours ➜ 06:00 - 24:00
Web/email ➜ www.millenniumhotels.com

282 3464

Map Ref ➜ 14-D3

Gozo Garden is one of the many Dubai restaurants offering themed meal deals, ranging from Mediterranean to British, Indian to Hawaiian and everything in between. The food is average and the service is a little overstretched, but after a few too many of the all inclusive unlimited house beverages you won't mind so it won't matter! Very good for a cheap night out.

Food●●●○○Serv●●○○○Venue●●●○○Value●●●○○

La Cité

Location ➜ Sofitel City Centre · Al Garhoud
Hours ➜ 12:00 - 15:00 19:30 - 23:30
Web/email ➜ www.accorhotels.com

603 8200

Map Ref ➜ 14-D1

La Cité is a typical catch all hotel restaurant. Daily international buffet theme nights satisfy hunger, but not always taste buds. An à la carte menu is on hand for a sense of something special, with a variety of European styled options and the odd themed dish that changes regularly enough to stave off boredom. While food and standard of service are mediocre, both are still amenable set against mid-range hotel prices. Perhaps merits a visit if you're in and around Deira City Centre but hardly worth a trip out especially.

Food●●○○○Serv●●○○○Venue●●○○○Value●●○○○

Buffet

Going Out

Market Café, The

Location → Grand Hyatt Dubai · Umm Hurair
Hours → 12:30 - 15:30 19:00 - 23:30
Web/email → www.dubai.grand.hyatt.com

317 1234

Map Ref → 13-E3

 100

The bustling Market Café cuts right through the opulent lower lobby of the Grand Hyatt. This glorified food court offers diners the choice of Italian, Arabic, Indian, Japanese and a grill station. Guests are obliged to 'shop' for their meal using personal swipe cards, an interesting new concept though doubtful an idea that will take off in other venues. The great choice of food is only let down by an atmosphere that is far too casual to accommodate a special meal.

Food ●●●●○ Serv ●●●●● Venue ●●●○○ Value ●●●●●

Market Place, The

Location → JW Marriott Hotel · Deira
Hours → 12:30 - 15:00 19:30 - 23:30
Web/email → www.marriott.com

262 4444

Map Ref → 12-A3

 150

A good 'all you can eat' concept with a range of cuisines, from Italian to Chinese to BBQ grill plus beverages (and at a very reasonable price). The venue has a marketplace feel with strategically placed 'shop shelves' of goodies and fare piled high. The ambience is perfect for lunch and just intimate enough for a cosy dinner. A diverse buffet suits every taste; the unusual and delicious hors d'oeuvres are highly recommended. The staff are jovial and helpful, making for a relaxed atmosphere and a leisurely bite.

Food ●●●●○ Serv ●●●●● Venue ●●●●○ Value ●●●●○

Meridien Village Terrace

Location → Le Meridien Dubai · Al Garhoud
Hours → 20:00 - 23:00 Oct to April only
Web/email → www.lemeridien-dubai.com

282 4040

Map Ref → 14-E3

 100

Okay so we know Dubai loves buffets, but don't shy away from the Meridien Village Terrace just because you are all buffeted out. Firstly the surroundings, tranquil greenery and soothing waterfalls, are exotically inviting and secondly the food is quite simply delicious. Eight enticing stations (six with their own cooks) offer Salmon with Ginger, Lamb Roast, Fish Thermidor, Roasted Quail, Grilled Vegetables and more while cheerful staff ceaselessly replenish beverages – all for Dhs.110

during the week and Dhs.130 on Thursdays. Reservations are essential.

Food ●●●●○ Serv ●●●●○ Venue ●●●●○ Value ●●●●●

La Cite

Oceana

Location → Hilton Jumeirah · Marsa Dubai
Hours → 07:00 - 23:00
Web/email → www.hilton.com

399 1111

Map Ref → 2-D2

 150

Don't expect your average hotel foyer dining experience at Oceana. Every night of the week, changing themed buffets offer a well chosen array of fresh, vibrant fare. Dishes are colourful and impeccably prepared, particularly the carvery meats, which are cooked to perfection and utterly delicious. Head Chef Yash Amir is a man who takes obvious pride in his work. The presence of the holidaymaking tribes goes largely unnoticed due to the relaxed ambience and generous interior layout. Staff are friendly and attentive and the place offers a welcome respite from the ordinary.

Food ●●●●○ Serv ●●●●○ Venue ●●●○○ Value ●●●●○

Spice Island

Location → Renaissance Hotel · Hor Al Anz
Hours → 07:00 - 23:30
Web/email → www.renaissancehotels.com

262 5555

Map Ref → 12-A3

 100

Can't decide between Mexican, Indian, Italian, Chinese, Japanese, Mongolian? Why not have them all! This spacious venue is self serve, apart from drinks, and has specific areas for each cuisine with food themes spread out in different alcoves throughout the restaurant. An added bonus is the live cooking stations where chefs can accommodate the fussiest of diners. Buffets range from Dhs.99 - Dhs.189. Its popularity means that making reservations is often essential, particularly over the weekend.

Food●●●●○ Serv●●●●○ Venue●●●●○ Value●●●●○

Spice Island

Waves

Location → Le Meridien Mina · Al Sufouh | **399 3333**
Hours → Open 24 hours
Web/email → www.lemeridien-minaseyahi.com   Map Ref → 3-A2

Waves is the recently renovated lobby level restaurant in the classy Le Meridien Mina Seyahi. On first sight little sets it apart from many of the other restaurants in town, but its themed buffet deals six nights of the week (Thursdays are the only exception) are enough to make it worth your while. For Dhs.125 per head you can expect to enjoy good quality food and drink - and plenty of it. Reservations are only necessary for the more popular dining hours.

Food●●●○○ Serv●●●●○ Venue●●●○○ Value●●●○○

Chinese

Other options → **Far Eastern [p.348]**

China Club, The

Location → Hotel Inter-Continental · Deira | **222 7171**
Hours → 11:00 - 15:30 19:00 - 23:00
Web/email → www.interconti.com   Map Ref → 8-C4

China Club is an elegant, modern affair, where the yin of innovation blends in perfect harmony

with the yang of tradition. High and provincial cuisine, prepared by "eleven Chinese master chefs", is inspired and delectable. The restaurant exudes high class eastern design chic, while retaining a vestige of Chinese philosophy, evident in the prominent use of imperial red, and intimate screened booths. The food and ambience, coupled with service smooth as proverbial silk, makes dining at China Club a truly Nirvana-like experience.

Food●●●●○ Serv●●●●○ Venue●●●●○ Value●●●●○

China Sea

Location → Al Maktoum Rd · Deira | **295 9816**
Hours → 12:00 - 15:00 19:00 - 24:00
Web/email → na   Map Ref → 11-D3

The occasional set of plastic flowers and golden dragons, mixed with traditional décor, fit the restaurant's origins, as do the large number of Chinese patrons who authenticate the food. China Sea is one of the more original Chinese restaurants in Dubai. The extensive menu includes pictures to help identify the differences in the dishes and help decipher some of the wording and spelling. One side of the restaurant includes fish tanks and cooler cabinets that display the fresh ingredients used in the preparation. Perhaps not the place for a romantic dinner, but instead for simple, good fresh Chinese fare.

Food●●●○○ Serv●●●○○ Venue●●●○○ Value●●●●○

Chinaman

Location → Nr Pyramids Bldg, Block 10 · Al Karama | **396 9685**
Hours → 12:00 - 15:00 19:00 - 23:30
Web/email → na   Map Ref → 10-E1

Offering a standard Chinese menu, the Chinaman is great value compared to most, but bypasses some of those extra touches you may have come to expect and appreciate including a washroom. The restaurant is small with the cosy feeling of a converted front room. The sounds and smells of your meal being freshly prepared in the kitchen next door are effective in helping you to develop an appetite. For all of its lows, the Chinaman still hits all the right highs – good food at good prices with basic but amiable service, all in an uncompromisingly real atmosphere.

Food●●●○○ Serv●●●○○ Venue●○○○○ Value●●●●●

Buffet | Chinese

Going Out

Chinese Kitchen

Location ➜ Nr Union Co-op · Jumeira
Hours ➜ 12:00 - 15:00 18:00 - 24:00
Web/email ➜ chinkit@emirates.net.ae

394 3864

Map Ref ➜ 5-B2

This creative kitchen offers tasty, inventive Chinese cooking. The décor is bright and colourful with authentic touches, and the food on offer is inspired chiefly from the Szechuan and Canton regions. Favourites include lemon chicken, garlic prawns and Shanghai rice, all fresh and perfectly cooked. The chef prides himself on his home-made sauces and individually made spring rolls and wontons. The duck with pineapple also shouldn't be missed. Outside catering and free delivery are available.

Other Locations: *Al Wasl Road, Jumeira (394 3864)*

Food●●●●○Serv●●●●○Venue●●●●○Value●●●●○

Chinese Pavilion

Location ➜ Beach Centre, The · Jumeira
Hours ➜ 12:30 - 15:00 19:00 - 23:15
Web/email ➜ na

344 4432

Map Ref ➜ 6-B2

For a no frills, hearty Chinese meal, make a beeline for Chinese Pavilion. Tucked away in an almost obscure corner of the Jumeirah Beach Centre, this understated venue offers ample choice at decent prices. An easy interior offsets a tasty menu, with favourites including the Singapore Chicken and Shanghai Squid. The restaurant has no licence to sell alcohol, but it's no bad thing since the hot jasmine tea will complement your meal perfectly.

Food●●○○○Serv●●○○○Venue●●○○○Value●●●○○

Chinese Treasure

Location ➜ Opp American Hospital · Oud Metha
Hours ➜ 19:00 - 24:00
Web/email ➜ www.chinesetreasuredubai.com

336 2525

Map Ref ➜ 10-D4

If you're looking for a relaxed atmosphere, a wide choice of Chinese food and pleasant service then this is the venue for you. The menu is extensive with a large choice of fish and meat dishes, as well as the traditional and scrumptious Peking Duck. Vegetarians are also well catered for and the lettuce wraps are certainly recommended. The husband and wife team is only too willing to listen to ideas and certainly make you feel at home

within this well laid out family friendly restaurant. Check out the all you can consume buffets for a value night out.

Food●●●●○Serv●●●●○Venue●●●○○Value●●●●○

Dynasty

Location ➜ Ramada Hotel · Bur Dubai
Hours ➜ 12:30 - 15:00 19:00 - 23:30
Web/email ➜ www.ramadadubai.com

351 9999

Map Ref ➜ 7-E3

Bur Dubai is perhaps an unlikely location for one of Dubai's best top notch Chinese restaurants, but try it once and we promise, you'll be heading to the Ramada on a regular basis. The food appears to be from Canton, Beijing and Szechwan provinces (though they aren't marked as such on the menu). From the excellent, attentive service and the tranquil ambience to the tasteful décor and the outstanding selection of dishes Dynasty makes for a delightful dining experience.

Food●●●●●Serv●●●●●Venue●●●●○Value●●●●○

Golden Dragon

Location ➜ Trade Centre Rd · Al Karama
Hours ➜ 12:00 - 15:00 19:00 - 01:00
Web/email ➜ www.goldendragondubai.com

396 7788

Map Ref ➜ 10-D1

This popular Chinese restaurant beckons you with neon flashing dragons and promising aromas from within. Much bigger than expected (on two floors with 'private dining rooms' upstairs), the Golden Dragon is both spacious and welcoming. A huge menu offers all the old favourites, accommodating even those choices that aren't listed. Not quite the venue for a romantic sojourn, but befitting those craving authentic Chinese food at good prices.

Food●●●●○Serv●●●●○Venue●●●○○Value●●●●○

Lan Kwai Fung

Location ➜ Nr Lamcy Plaza · Oud Metha
Hours ➜ 12:00 - 15:00 19:00 - 24:00
Web/email ➜ na

335 3680

Map Ref ➜ 10-D4

Newcomer Lan Kwai Fung serves up authentic, delicious Hong Kong style Chinese food to those in the know. Its semi industrial feel, with open ceiling and large Chinese characters plastered on the red and silver walls, gives extra character to the place – this is not a five star hotel venue and that's

Chinese

Going Out

the charm. Watch your meal being skillfully prepared behind the kitchen's glass wall (select from the menu or invent a dish – the chef will happily make it for you) and be sure to have at least one order of the Crispy Beef in Golden Basket.

Food●●●●○ Serv●●●●○ Venue●●●●○ Value●●●●○

Long Yin

Location → Le Meridien Dubai · Al Garhoud |282 4040
Hours → 12:30 - 14:45 19:30 - 23:45
Web/email → www.lemeridien-dubai.com   Map Ref → 14-E3

  100

Intimate and classy describes the setting of this premier Chinese restaurant, complete with traditional décor and ubiquitous goldfish ponds. The menu is interesting and not restricted to the standard, obvious fare. Highly recommended are the prawns, 'Bi-Fong' style if you like it hot. The wine list is impressive – but not particularly suited to the budget conscious. The dessert selection could be the only flaw, lacking anything truly decadent for those with a serious sweet tooth.

Food●●●●○ Serv●●●●○ Venue●●●○○ Value●●●○○

Mini Chinese

Location → Al Diyafah Street · Al Satwa |345 9976
Hours → 12:00 - 24:00
Web/email → www.binhendi.com   Map Ref → 7-A3

 50

Lighting up the Satwa strip is this bright beacon of a Chinese restaurant. Fresh, quick Chinese cuisine satisfies the many hungry patrons who fill this venue till the very wee hours, every night of the week. Expect huge servings of great food served quickly and at a modest price. Modern prints adorn the walls and loud colours liven the mood. The open glassed kitchen allows you to multi-task – keep an eye on your chef but happily people watch. A good stop for a group outing.

Food●●●○○ Serv●●●○○ Venue●●●●○ Value●●●●○

Mr. Chow

Location → Imperial Suites Rd · Bur Dubai |351 0099
Hours → 12:00 - 02:30 Fri am closed
Web/email → openhouse_rest@yahoo.com   Map Ref → 7-E3

 50

Mr. Chow is all about good, cheap food and lots of it, and in a setting more charming than many of its competitors. The menu features a long list of Chinese dishes along with some Thai favourites. The food is

---

anything but bland, and portions are generous enough to share with a friend. For a different take on chicken wings, try the melodiously named Drums of Heaven starter. Service is quick, making this a good stop for a tasty workday lunch.

Food●●●●○ Serv●●●○○ Venue●●●○○ Value●●●●○

Nanking Chinese

Location → Beh Regent Palace Htl · Al Karama |396 6388
Hours → 12:00 - 15:00 18:30 - 24:00
Web/email → na   Map Ref → 11-A1

   50

Handily located behind the infamous Rock Bottom Café, the front door is bordered by waterfall windows and opens to a little wooden bridge giving you an authentic oriental initiation. From then on in the restaurant is a little shabby chic (the toilets are an experience) but the food makes up for any interior misgivings. Cheap and very cheerful, the menu is varied with all your favourites and a few surprises. Ask for Andre and he'll devise a delicious cacophony of dishes for your pleasure.

Food●●●○○ Serv●●●●○ Venue●●●○○ Value●●●○○

Open House

Location → Nr Pyramid Bld · Al Karama |396 5481
Hours → 12:00 - 02:30
Web/email → openhouse@emirates.net.ae   Map Ref → 10-E1

  50

Welcoming and colourful, Open House will tickle your taste buds with mouth-watering morsels. While it may be famous for its Indian specialities (being the sister restaurant of Satwa's Kitchen), Open House also has a good Chinese menu. Big smiles and attentive, thoughtful service complement the excellent food, while the artfully decorated, incensed atmosphere ensures a feeling of relaxed contentment. Recommended for dining in or takeaway. Open House also has a busy branch in Mirdif (288 6601), although this is suitable for takeaway only.

Food●●●●○ Serv●●●●○ Venue●●●●○ Value●●●●○

Peacock Chinese Restaurant

Location → Sheraton Jumeirah Beach · Marsa Dubai |399 5533
Hours → 12:00 - 15:00 19:00 - 24:00
Web/email → www.starwood.com   Map Ref → 2-D2

150

Perched on a balcony overlooking the busy lobby restaurant, Peacock offers traditional Chinese fare in a bright, minimalist setting. Thoroughly attentive service and thoughtful presentation of tasty, well prepared dishes are plus points, but uncomfortable seating, a distinctly family-oriented atmosphere, and shrieking kids below are not conducive to a relaxing or intimate dining experience. Reasonable prices would make this place good value if only the environment was more inviting.

Food ●●●●○○ Serv ●●●●○ Venue ●●○○○ Value ●●●○○

Shang Palace

Location → Shangri-La Hotel · Trade Centre 1 | **343 8888**
Hours → 12:30 - 15:00 20:00 - 24:00
Web/email → www.shangri-la.com   Map Ref → 9-A2

  100

With a view over the lobby and some interesting artwork scattered around, Shang Palace delivers some of the finest Chinese food in Dubai. Deliciously delicate dumplings and other Dim Sum are so good that they are almost obligatory and are among the best found locally. Wok Fried Scallops and Peking Duck are favourites of the mainly Cantonese menu, though its variety may confuse the hungry diner. The plush, comfortably lit surrounds and quite imperious chairs are well complemented by welcoming staff whose care and attentiveness is assured.

Food ●●●●○ Serv ●●●○○ Venue ●●●●○ Value ●●●●○

Places for Pork

Remember that you are in a Muslim country. Nevertheless, all you pork freaks out there curbing your fetish, know that, although rare, you can still find pork on the menu. Understandably, the local, independent outlets are unlikely to serve any, but hotel restaurants are more accommodating and will state dishes that contain pork. Most supermarkets also have a pork section so if all else fails you can always enjoy a bacon butty at home.

Summer Place, The

Location → Metropolitan · Shk Zayed Rd | **343 0000**
Hours → 12:30 - 15:30 19:00 - 23:30
Web/email → www.methotels.com   Map Ref → 5-C4

 150

Years ago, when this venue was the Summer Palace, diners flocked here for the only upmarket Chinese dining experience in town. Today, the Summer Place still impresses with its elegant dining room, and polished, attentive service. And while the name has changed, some things have stayed the same. The menu remains heavy on the bland meal options, expensive for what you get and not in the least bit innovative. Its one saving grace - the Peking Duck pancakes are still delicious.

Food ●●●○○ Serv ●●●●○ Venue ●●●○○ Value ●●○○○

Zheng He's

Location → Mina A'Salam · Umm Suqeim | **366 8888**
Hours → 12:00 - 15:00 19:00 - 23:30
Web/email → www.jumeirahinternational.com   Map Ref → 4-A2

 150

Zheng He's is much more than a simple Chinese restaurant. In fact the word 'simple' could not have been in their vocabulary when they created both the interior and the menu. Jaw-dropping in its opulence, the elegance and style are certainly not understated whilst the service and food live up to the palatial atmosphere. Contemporary versions of classic dishes pay homage to Chinese imperialism and not a taste-bud goes untantalised. Imperial splendour, however, doesn't come cheap.

Food ●●●●○ Serv ●●●●● Venue ●●●●○ Value ●●●○○

Cuban

Other options → **Latin American [p.379]**

Malecon

Location → Dubai Marine Beach Resort · Jumeira | **346 1111**
Hours → 19:30 - 03:00
Web/email → www.dxbmarine.com   Map Ref → 6-D2

    150

With its high turquoise walls (covered in graffiti), low lighting and big windows overlooking a tranquil lagoon, Malecon welcomes you in true Cuban style. The sultry atmosphere builds up slowly during the course of the evening, helped along by the live music and some of Dubai's best Salsa dancers. The small but ample menu includes all the best Cuban specialities, and the Paella, Malecon's signature dish, is highly recommended. If you're a Salsa fan, the music played here and the lessons on some nights will appeal.

Food ●●●●○ Serv ●●●●○ Venue ●●●○○ Value ●●●●○

Chinese | Cuban

Going Out

Egyptian

Other options → **Arabic/Lebanese [p.330]**

Fatafeet

Location → Nr British Embassy · Bur Dubai
Hours → 10:30 - 24:00
Web/email → na   Map Ref → 8-C4

397 9222

Fatafeet is perfect for great shisha, Arabic coffee and a wonderfully atmospheric view of the Creek. Additional offerings are the usual batch – fruit juices, meze, salads and so forth, plus some good Egyptian dishes. The service can be extremely leisurely (consider it part of the 'cultural' experience) and, although parking seems ample, it does fill up quickly. Alternatively, park further along the Creek and enjoy the stroll. This venue is ideal in the cooler months as the setting is delightful. Evenings are recommended over a daytime visit for a better overall experience.

Food ●●●○○ Serv ●●○○○ Venue ●●●●● Value ●●●○○

Fatafeet

Emirati

Other options → **Arabic/Lebanese [p.330]**

Al Areesh

Location → Al Boom Tourist Village · Umm Hurair
Hours → 12:00 - 16:00 19:00 - 24:00
Web/email → www.alboom.ae   Map Ref → 14-A3

324 3000

Set in traditional Arab sailing style and with the Creek as stunning backdrop, Al Areesh offers fine

alfresco dining. For a reasonable price you can indulge in an extensive buffet of local fare. But if you ask them what they are best at, the folks at Al Areesh will tell you that they specialise in catering for large parties, weddings and the odd local Sheikh – in which case save the intimate dinner for two for somewhere else. Still, for a taste of local culture and delicious dishes, Al Areesh is a safe bet.

Food ●●●●○ Serv ●●●●○ Venue ●●●●○ Value ●●●●○

Local House

Location → Bastakiya · Bur Dubai
Hours → See below
Web/email → na   Map Ref → 8-B3

353 9997

Emirati cuisine seems to be sadly overshadowed by the hub of international flavours rife in Dubai. Recently renovated and ideally located in vintage Bastakiya, Local House fills the gap with a dedicated Emirati menu. Sit inside or outside on Arabic style seating, and feast away. Harees, magly and amouesh are among the authentic dishes served, and if you want to find out more... you'll just have to go and see for yourself.

> **Cultural Meals**
>
> *Bastakiya is a great place to eat and simultaneously soak up local culture. This traditional part of the city is best experienced by strolling in the streets, visiting the museums and dining at one of the many cafés. A cultural and fuel boost injection rolled into one.*

Contact: Maria 050 774 6207.

Food ○○○○○ Serv ○○○○○ Venue ○○○○○ Value ○○○○○

European

Other options → **French [p.352]**
German [p.356]
Italian [p.367]
Mediterranean [p.379]
Pizzerias [p.387]
Portuguese [p.387]
Russian [p.388]
Spanish [p.392]

European cuisine is as varied as the number of languages spoken. From German sausages (wurst) or Greek moussaka to Spanish tapas or English beef Wellington, there really is a style to suit every preference and mood. Most European restaurants are located in hotels with an upmarket ambience, a liquor licence and commensurate prices. In Dubai, the most dominant of the European cuisines is Italian. Numerous independent restaurants are springing up around the city, offering good value for money, but sadly, no chance to indulge in a glass of Chianti with your cannelloni.

Dubai offers diners more than a handful of genuinely world class restaurants that match – in terms of food, wine, décor, service and price – anything that the European capitals have to offer.

Glasshouse - Brasserie

Location → Hilton Creek · Deira	227 1111
Hours → 07:00 - 24:00	
Web/email → www.hilton.com	Map Ref → 11-C2

 150

This restaurant has a relaxed and informal open space with well set out tables and a semi stark but comfortable interior. Windows, a concept so rare in many of Dubai's hotels, offer a pleasant enough view of the Creek but the glass floor can be a little disconcerting. Friendly meals and comfort food such as 'Bangers and Mash' are complemented by Asian inspired dishes and excellent meats and seafood from the grill. After your meal, Glasshouse transforms into a trendy nightclub so you can dance those extra kilos away.

Food ●●●●○ Serv ●●●●○ Venue ●●●●○ Value ●●●●○

Glasshouse

Retro

Location → Le Meridien Mina · Al Sufouh	399 3333
Hours → 19:00 - 23:00	
Web/email → www.lemeridien-minaseyahi.com	Map Ref → 3-A2

200

With a regularly changing menu of seasonal international dishes, this restaurant has one of the best reputations along the beach. Gallic flair leaps off the modern European plates as meats and fishes are transformed by stunning presentation. The serving staff is friendly and genuinely knowledgeable. Mood and music are chilled and relaxed, the design is contemporary with an obvious edge towards modern art, and the warm lighting gives each table a feeling of intimacy. Indoor or alfresco options are available.

Food ●●●●○ Serv ●●●●○ Venue ●●●●○ Value ●●●●○

Sphinx

Location → Pyramids · Umm Hurair	324 4100
Hours → 19:30 - 23:30	
Web/email → www.waficity.com	Map Ref → 13-D2

      200

For an evening of great food and exotic ambience, Sphinx is a must. The atmosphere is elegant and chic, the furnishing large and impressive and the service warm and pleasant. As for the food, expect nothing but glamorous mouth-watering dishes uniquely designed and impeccably presented. Resident musicians treat diners to an evening of good jazz and their own interpretations of some golden oldies. From the over-the-top entrance to the last bite of your dinner, this restaurant is the gem in Wafi's crown.

Food ●●●●○ Serv ●●●●○ Venue ●●●●○ Value ●●●●○

Valet it

Still single because you're always late for your date? In Dubai, finding a parking space can be a time consuming task. If you're dining at a restaurant in a hotel, don't stress for a spot. Boldly drive your beaten up bandwagon to the main entrance, and hand over your keys to a valet. It's quick, easy and you can feel like a movie star!

Far Eastern

Other options → **Chinese [p.342]**
Filipino [p.352]
Japanese [p.374]
Korean [p.378]
Polynesian [p.387]
Singaporean [p.391]
Thai [p.396]
Vietnamese [p.400]

For lovers of light, generally healthy food, Far Eastern cuisine includes an amazing array of styles, providing a multitude of excellent choices for either dining out or takeaway. Seafood, vegetables and the staples, rice and noodles,

European | Far Eastern

Going Out

dominate menus, with an emphasis on steamed or stir-fried cooking methods. The food can be spicy, but usually less so than a fiery, denture melting Vindaloo curry. Tastes are more commonly enhanced by the use of delicate and fragrant herbs and spices such as ginger and lemon grass, and coconut milk.

With the exception of Chinese outlets, Far Eastern restaurants are generally located in hotels in more upmarket surroundings, with prices that match. The décor of Thai and Polynesian restaurants often reflects a stereotypically exotic view of the Far East, with bamboo, beach huts and 'demure' oriental waitresses. Sometimes this combines to create a tasteful, relaxing and classy ambience, and sometimes it doesn't quite make it.

Hidden Charges

When the bill arrives, subtly check out the dreaded small print (slyly lurking at the bottom of the bill) that says 'INCLUSIVE +15% +5%'. Be careful what you touch, as you may find that even the most innocent eye contact with a nut bowl can result in surplus charges.

Japanese restaurants usually offer a choice of seating options, from teppanyaki tables where the entertainment is provided by the chefs as they juggle, dice and slice, to private tatami rooms, or the sushi option, where dishes pass before your eyes on a conveyor belt. Any way you like it, the standard of Japanese food in Dubai is high, but, again, with prices to match.

Dubai also has a great number of Chinese restaurants, and standards vary greatly from MSG-laden, taste killing dishes to light and delicious cuisine. Many of the independents (i.e. those not linked to a hotel or club) offer good value for money, with large portions of quality food. As with Indian outlets, many Chinese restaurants offer tasty takeaway and home delivery, giving Dubai residents even less incentive to learn how to use their wok.

Bamboo Lagoon

Location ➜ JW Marriott Hotel · Deira | **262 4444**
Hours ➜ 19:30 - 24:30
Web/email ➜ www.marriott.com   Map Ref ➜ 12-A3

   100

This restaurant offers an almost bewildering range of Asian–Pacific cuisine in one location. You'll be faced with a rather difficult decision thanks to the extensive range of dishes on offer. With a tropical garden theme running throughout, walk along the paths and around ponds to discover even more

enticing food corners and live cooking stations. The food quality is excellent and almost exactly what you'd expect from a restaurant housed within the plush Marriott hotel. Five star food from a five star location.

Food ●●●○○ Serv ●●●●○ Venue ●●●○○ Value ●●●○○

Beachcombers

Location ➜ The Jumeirah Beach Hotel · Umm Suqeim | **406 8181**
Hours ➜ 12:00 - 16:30 19:00 - 24:00
Web/email ➜ www.jumeirahinternational.com   Map Ref ➜ 4-B2

 150

Located right on the beach, with fantastic views of Burj Al Arab, this bedecked, breezy seaside shack hosts atmospheric Far Eastern buffets every night. Live cooking stations for stir-fry, noodle and Peking duck, curry hot pots and satay stalls offer great variety, and there's plenty more to chose from in the starter and seafood salad section. While the food doesn't disappoint and the staff are certainly attentive it is the prime location of this restaurant that scores the most points.

Food ●●●○○ Serv ●●●●○ Venue ●●●●○ Value ●●●○○

Eauzone

Location ➜ One&Only Arabian Court · Al Sufouh | **399 9999**
Hours ➜ 12:00 - 15:30 19:00 - 23:30
Web/email ➜ www.oneandonlyroyalmirage.com   Map Ref ➜ 3-A2

 200

Eauzone's ability to successfully mix intimate dining with contemporary surroundings is unsurpassed. One of the best in poolside indoor/outdoor dining, the tables overlook beautifully lit water and

Eauzone

Far Eastern

Going Out

Life's a Journey... Take a Guide

Ain't no mountain high enough (even the Hajar) or riverbed wide enough (even Wadi Bani Khalid) to keep us from bringing this book to you. From Arabian charm to the call of the wilderness, get ready to explore. It's Oman, it's breathtaking and it's time you bought this book!

gardens and are in great demand when the weather is good. The menu manages to offer a fusion style choice in dishes which would tickle the most discerning of taste buds. Teppanyaki tables are well worth a visit but be sure to leave room for the outstanding desserts. Also watch out for the fancy water!

Food ●●●●○ Serv ●●●●○ Venue ●●●●● Value ●●●●○

Fusion

Location ➜ Le Royal Meridien · Marsa Dubai | 399 5555
Hours ➜ 19:00 - 24:00
Web/email ➜ www.leroyalmeridien-dubai.com   Map Ref ➜ 2-E2

   150

With an elegant combination of service, fresh ingredients, artistic presentation and tranquil surroundings, Fusion rates highly. The tasty and creative selection of Thai, Malay and Indonesian dishes are offered with a mix of seafood and meat. Particularly proud of their authentic Thai curries, they can make dishes as spicy or mild as you like, and can custom make vegetarian dishes on request. The ultra chic décor, with the choice of bar, terrace or indoor dining affords plenty of options. The staff are discreet and unassuming, mirroring the minimalist nature of the surroundings.

Food ●●●●○ Serv ●●●●○ Venue ●●●●○ Value ●●●●○○

Noodle House, The

Location ➜ The Boulevard at Emirates Towers | 319 8088
Hours ➜ 12:00 - 24:00
Web/email ➜ www.jumeirahinternational.com   Map Ref ➜ 9-C2

150

Bustling and full of life, The Noodle House provides a refreshingly informal dining experience in the sleek and shiny surroundings of The Boulevard at Emirates Towers. No bookings are taken, just turn up and wait for free seats either on the long communal tables, the more private areas or at the bar (where you'll get a good view of the chefs in action). The comprehensive Chinese and Thai menu offers a range of starters, soups, noodles and main courses. Tick your choice and sit back and wait for your meal, though not for long. Portions are generous, dishes are fresh, authentic and tasty and the service is friendly and prompt - impressive how the orders flying out of the kitchen always make their way to the right place.

Food ●●●●○ Serv ●●●●○ Venue ●●●●○ Value ●●●●○

Noodle House, The

Location ➜ Souk Madinat Jumeirah · Umm Suqeim | 366 8888
Hours ➜ 12:00 - 01:00
Web/email ➜ www.jumeirahinternational.com   Map Ref ➜ 4-A2

150

Placing an order at the new and glamorous Noodle House in the Madinat Jumeirah means generous portions of the most sumptuous cuisine available in Dubai. Though similar and indeed a franchise of the same Noodle House in the Emirates Tower, the décor of this version has a far more up-market look and feel. For added charm the restaurant opens onto a beautiful dining terrace beside the canal. Everything on this self ticking menu is made to perfection and delivered with panache.

Food ●●●●○ Serv ●●●○○ Venue ●●●○○ Value ●●●●○

Noodle House

Yum!

Location ➜ Hotel Inter-Continental · Deira | 222 7171
Hours ➜ 12:00 - 01:00
Web/email ➜ www.interconti.com   Map Ref ➜ 8-C4

 100

An upmarket noodle bar with the maxim "Live fast, eat fast", YUM! delivers tasty dishes in a stylish, contemporary setting, where you can watch the chefs chop, flip and fry your Thai, Vietnamese, Chinese, Japanese, Laotian or Malay selections in the central glass-walled kitchen. With such a diverse melting pot of cuisines available, it's perhaps unsurprising that some dishes are more authentic than others, and the youthful service lacks a little seasoning. However, if you're in the area and crave some quick chow in a funky setting, this is a good option.

Food ●●●○○ Serv ●●○○○ Venue ●●●○○ Value ●●●○○

Far Eastern

Going Out

WITH ELEVEN *success*
STORIES,
IT'S THE *perfect* SETTING
FOR DINING OUT.

There are many restaurants in Dubai. But only a few can claim to be the best in their class. You'll find them at Emirates Towers - your first choice for world class cuisine. **To reserve your table, simply call 04 319 8088.**

The Agency • ET Sushi • Harry Ghatto's • Mosaico • Al Nafoorah • The Noodle House • The Rib Room • The Cigar Lounge • Scarlett's • tokyo@thetowers • Vu's

EMIRATES TOWERS
hotel

JUMEIRAH
INTERNATIONAL®
www.jumeirahinternational.com

Emirates Towers Hotel is a trading name of Emirates Towers LLC. Company with Limited Liability. Registration No. 54356. Share Capital Dhs. 300,000 fully paid.

Filipino

Other options → **Far Eastern [p.347]**

Tagpuan

Location → Al Karama Shopping Centre · Al Karama | **337 3959**
Hours → 09:30 - 24:00
Web/email → na | Map Ref → 10-D2

This small but cosy restaurant lives up to its name ('meeting place' in Tagalog), attracting a regular clientele of Filipino residents. Tagpuan is an excellent value for money experience, offering a wide choice of both Chinese and Filipino dishes. A complimentary bowl of soup arrives with each main, and portions are generous. The Formica tables, TVs and free karaoke give this working man's diner an unpretentious atmosphere that genuinely welcomes visitors.

Food●●●○○Serv●●●○○Venue●●○○○Value●●●●○

Fish & Chips

There might not be a 'chippy' on every corner in Dubai but if you're really hankering after some good old fish and chips there are a few choices at your disposal. Fryer Tuck and The Chippy are both 'home away from home' chip shops, where the interior may be a little drab but the food is just what you'd expect – crispy battered fish and great chips. The Plaice (next door to the Irish Village) is great for its location and has a nice outside area, a varied menu (fish and chips are the main event, but you'll also find pies, prawns, chicken and even haggis), and you can wash your meal down with a nice cold beer, since they serve alcohol.

Fish & Chip Restaurants

Chippy, The	343 3114
Fryer Tuck	344 4228
Plaice, The	286 8233

French

Apartment, The

Location → The Jumeirah Beach Hotel · Umm Suqeim | **406 8181**
Hours → 19:00 - 23:30
Web/email → www.jumeirahinternational.com | Map Ref → 4-B2

If you want to feel like a superstar then a night at The Apartment will have you well on your way to celebrity status. Hidden beneath the ground level of the Jumeirah Beach Hotel this French restaurant has all the trimmings of an exclusive Paris eatery. Upon entry, you can indulge in complimentary cheese and wine in the cellar alcove, before being escorted to your romantically set table under intimate lighting. The food surpasses expectations (for starters try the deliciously understated lobster salad), and the service is knowledgeable and efficient. As a unique fine dining experience The Apartment has few adversaries in Dubai.

Food●●●●○Serv●●●●○Venue●●●●○Value●●●●○

Café Chic

Location → Le Meridien Dubai · Al Garhoud | **282 4040**
Hours → 12:30 - 14:45 20:00 - 23:45 Fri lunch closed
Web/email → www.lemeridien-dubai.com | Map Ref → 14-E3

Café Chic has a sophisticated bistro-esque charm, featuring an eclectic mix of traditional dishes with a modern twist. The Goat's Cheese and Potato Salad is noteworthy and the Oriental take on the Seared Tuna Fillet creates a deliciously pink and tender bite. The artistic presentation and imaginative content of the dishes reflect international chef, Michel Rostang's close influence. Whilst it's a little too bright and airy to be truly intimate, Café Chic brings a welcomed slice of French fine dining to Dubai and therefore reservations are essential.

Food●●●●○Serv●●●●○Venue●●●●○Value●●●○○

Café Chic

jazzy jacuzzis

A good jacuzzi design incorporates the various components of your lifestyle. Our team gives you the freedom to create distinctive and unique jacuzzis. Whatever your taste, Jacuzzi By Design offers the team to create a jacuzzi to meet your needs.

Contact us for a speedy hassle free, no obligation estimate. No job too small and no job too large!

PO Box 28174, Dubai
Phone 347 7193 Fax 347 7946
Email info@jacuzzi-by-design.com Web www.jacuzzi-by-design.com

La Baie

Location → Ritz-Carlton, The · Marsa Dubai
Hours → 19:00 - 23:00
Web/email → www.ritzcarlton.com   Map Ref → 2-E2

| 399 4000

 150

La Baie is spacious, quiet and dignified with none of the stiffness that can make dining a trying task rather than the simple pleasure it should be. Chef Simon Barber's ever exciting and surprising French inspired menu can leave you a little spoilt for choice but fear not, it's all very, very good. An excellent wine list traverses the continents and matches the dishes on offer. The service is attentive, measured and very friendly and, in the cooler months, the spectacular views from the terrace are worth a trip alone.
Food●●●●○Serv●●●●○Venue●●●○○Value●●●●○

Le Classique

Location → Emirates Golf Club · Emirates Hills
Hours → 12:00 - 15:30 19:00 - 22:30 Fri closed
Web/email → egc@dubaigolf.com   Map Ref → 3-A3

| 380 2222

 200

Food at Classique is what you would expect from a place that makes you wear a jacket and tie. A good selection of wine is available, with many reds oddly displayed in a chilled compartment. The varied menu has something for everyone - set menus and flambéed foods put the F in French cuisine. A view of the golf course is visible behind the constantly hovering staff and delicate piano music in the background offsets the whole evening.
Food●●●●○○Serv●○○○○Venue●●●●○○Value●●●○○

Signatures

Location → Jebel Ali Golf Resort & Spa
Hours →   Wed, Thu, Fri 19:00-23:00
Web/email → www.jebelali-international.com   Map Ref → 1-A1

| 883 6000

 200

Gourmet dining reaches its peak here at Signatures with some of Dubai's most inspired and innovative cuisine making up much of the menu. Everything at this venue is achieved to the highest standard with no small detail overlooked. From the freshest ingredients to the perfect preparation and from the beautiful presentation to the elegant décor, this is handsome dining at its very best. The best things in life are, in fact, not free and a meal at Signatures will prove just that. Expensive, but worth it.
Food●●●●●Serv●●●●○Venue●●●●○Value●●●●○

St Tropez Bistro

Location → Century Village · Al Garhoud
Hours → 12:30 - 24:00
Web/email → sttropez@emirates.net.ae   Map Ref → 14-C3

| 286 9029

 100

A tasty French Bistro conveniently set in the heart of Century Village, with indoor and outdoor dining for your convenience. The menu is concise, while remaining mouth-wateringly tempting with a variety of dishes to choose from. House specials, and a must-have, are the New Zealand steaks perfectly cooked to your liking and the juicy lamb rack. Expect your quick bite visit to last a couple of hours so you can savour the experience.
Food●●●●○○Serv●●●●○Venue●●●●○Value●●●●○

Verre

Location → Hilton Creek · Deira
Hours → 19:00 - 24:00
Web/email → www.hilton.com   Map Ref → 11-C2

| 212 7551

250

Gordon Ramsay's first foray out of Britain is undoubtedly one of Dubai's finest dining experiences. The menu features well constructed dishes with unusual combinations of flavours that confound, yet unexpectedly delight. You can choose from the à la carte or surprisingly good value set menus, in which courses can be matched by just the right wine. An elegant room, a well selected wine list and measured staff add to the special occasion.
Food●●●●●Serv●●●●●Venue●●●●○Value●●●○○

Gordon Ramsay's Verre

Hilton

Dubai, another Hilton city.

Rooms with Views

Choose between the beach or the city.
The Hilton Dubai Jumeirah, a spectacular beachfront hotel with restaurants,
meeting and recreational facilities on the exclusive Jumeirah strip.
The Hilton Dubai Creek, a unique lifestyle hotel featuring contemporary design
and dining options, in the heart of the city,

Hilton
Dubai Jumeirah

For Hilton Information & Reservations
Tel: +971 (4) 318 2111
www.hilton.com

Hilton
Dubai Creek

German

Brauhaus

Location → Jumeira Rotana · Al Satwa
Hours → 18:00 - 01:00 Thu & Fri 12:00 - 24:00
Web/email → www.rotana.com

345 5888

Map Ref → 6-E3

It seems that Brauhaus have taken a few hints about their musical tastes and have toned down the background sounds. However the food makes up for any newfound subtleties by remaining big and bold. The no nonsense menu includes sausages aplenty, a delicious horseradish-salmon, first class peppersteak, goulash soup, perfect Spätzle, apple strudel, and cheesecake. Vegetarian options, however, are sparse and if you get to the desserts your appetite must be truly hearty.●GER●
Food●●●○○Serv●●●○○Venue●●●○○Value●●●○○

Der Keller

Location → The Jumeirah Beach Hotel · Umm Suqeim
Hours → 18:00 - 23:30
Web/email → www.jumeirahinternational.com

406 8181

Map Ref → 4-B2

Der Keller (meaning 'the cellar'), gives you a warm welcome and hearty food along with an unexpected but fantastic view of the sea. The red bricked walls, carefully planned lighting and soft background music create a relaxed family atmosphere, regardless of whether you sit at the restaurant or sip at the bar. Do try the speciality veal dishes and the sauerkraut, not to mention the fondue to share. Service here is always with a smile, but beware the Germanic sized portions – this is not a place for light eaters.●●
Food●●●●○Serv●●●●○Venue●●●●○Value●●●●○

Hofbrauhaus

Location → JW Marriott Hotel · Deira
Hours → 19:30 - 24:30
Web/email → www.marriott.com

262 4444

Map Ref → 12-A3

A German franchise, the Hofbrauhaus name is usually synonymous with steins of delectable hand crafted beer, and mouth-watering man-sized portions of steaming 'fleisch'. Hofbrauhaus Dubai looks the part, and is most definitely a great place to sample a few authentic dishes, or a bottle from the expansive wine. However, time-honoured options from the meat-oriented menu are reproduced in a somewhat lacklustre fashion here. Despite the warm rustic atmosphere, and piped oompah music, the overall impression is that this is Hofbrauhaus in name only. Nice try though.●GER●
Food●●●○○Serv●●●●○Venue●●●●○Value●●●○○

Hofbrauhaus

Indian

Other options → **Pakistani [p.384]**

Antique Bazaar

Location → Four Points Sheraton · Bur Dubai
Hours → 19:30 - 03:00
Web/email → www.starwood.com

397 7444

Map Ref → 8-A4

This weirdly, but aptly named restaurant is full of antique marble, ivory, silver and wooden furniture, all crammed into an intimate candlelit space. The staff are proud of their place, and will happily describe the various artefacts around the room if you show an interest. Long lists of exotic kebab and curry dishes sound appealing, but it's the live Indian music and dance that makes the Bazaar so popular. If the food were not so oily, this place would be a real winner.●●
Food●●●○○Serv●●●●○Venue●●●●●Value●●●○○

Asha's

Location → Pyramids · Umm Hurair
Hours → 12:30 - 15:00 19:30 - 24:30
Web/email → www.asharestaurants.com   Map Ref → 13-D2

 150

Well loved Indian singing legend Asha Bhosle's eponymous restaurant is a real treat for lovers of fine food, great voices and old vinyl. A very funky interior with young, cheery and snappily dressed staff makes for a welcoming and relaxed atmosphere. The menu offers better than standard Indian fare mixed with some of the diva's personal family recipes ensuring that Asha's is positioned far and beyond a regular curry house. A great selection of cocktails will ensure that it's not just food you're coming here for.

Food●●●●● Serv●●●●○ Venue●●●●○ Value●●●●●

Ashiana

Location → Sheraton Hotel & Towers · Deira   228 1707
Hours → 12:30 - 15:30 19:30 - 01:00 Fri am closed
Web/email → www.starwood.com   Map Ref → 11-C1

   100

Tucked away in the corner of the Sheraton, Ashiana is a delight for lovers of Indian food and comfortable spaces. With a menu that covers the entire sub-continent, there are many options for meat lovers and vegetarians alike. Some dishes, such as the Black Dhal, are meticulously prepared overnight and the long cooking time is definitely worth it. The mains are quite a bit larger than you may be used to so order judiciously.

Food●●●●○ Serv●●●●○ Venue●●●●● Value●●●●○

Bikanervala

Location → Beh Bombay Chowpatty · Al Karama   396 3666
Hours → 09:00 - 24:00   Fri during prayers closed
Web/email → bikanodb@emirates.net.ae   Map Ref → 10-E1

 50

Famous for its Indian sweets and namkeens (salty snacks), its authenticity and great value for money, this restaurant prides itself on traditional Rajasthani recipes passed down through generations. Pani Puri (a savoury dish) and Ras Malai (a sweet dish) are two of the many mouth-watering delights on offer. Simply grab a voucher and move towards the cooking stations to watch your order come to life. Banquet tables as well as smaller settings satisfy all customers.   Home bodies have the option of takeaway.

Food●●●●○ Serv●●●○○ Venue●●●○○ Value●●●●○

Chhappan Bhog

Location → Trade Centre Rd · Al Karama   396 8176
Hours → 09:00 - 24:00 Fri 09:00-11:00, 13:30-24:00
Web/email → na   Map Ref → 10-E1

 50

One of the more refined vegetarian restaurants in town judging by the popularity of the place, Chhappan Bhog is a favourite in Al Karama. The tastefully decorated dining room is clean and bright while uniformed waiters competently present colourful and satisfying meals. The food tastes great and the value is amazing. Of particular note is the lunch thali - endless servings of the curries of the day for only Dhs.12.

Food●●●○○ Serv●●●○○ Venue●●●○○ Value●●●●○

Coconut Grove

Location → Rydges Plaza Hotel · Al Satwa   398 3800
Hours → 12:00 - 15:00 19:00 - 24:30
Web/email → www.rydges.com   Map Ref → 7-A4

 100

Vibrant colours and tastes combine to form a wonderful and surprising cuisine. The chef prepares unique dishes, using spices and a mixture of Indian and Sri Lankan tastes, to bring the best from Kerala, Tamil Nadu, Goa and old Ceylon. Make sure you taste the Nadea Kai Kara Kozhambu (crab curry in tamarind sauce), sample any of the cocktails or order the saffron flavoured rice, all are sublime and come highly recommended. There is a huge lunch buffet every Friday, with themed spreads from each region on the ancient spice route.

Food●●●○○ Serv●●●●○ Venue●●●○○ Value●●●○○

Foodlands

Location → Opp Ramada Continental Htl · Bur Dubai   268 3311
Hours → 07:30 - 15:30 19:00 - 24:00
Web/email → na   Map Ref → 7-E3

 50

Expect a dazzling range of Indian, Persian and Arabic delicacies, in a relaxed, family-friendly atmosphere. The food preparation is visible through the large window between the kitchen and the restaurant. At the end of this process your meal is brought fresh and sizzling hot to your table by the attentive waiters. The kebabs, fresh naans and vegetarian dishes are particularly recommended from the menu, although buffets and breakfast dishes also make for good value. Foodlands is recommended for all those looking for quality, tasty food at good prices.

Food●●●●○ Serv●●●●○ Venue●●●●○ Value●●●●○

Gazebo

Location → Al Karama
Hours → 12:00 - 15:30 19:00 - 24:00
Web/email → na

397 9930

Map Ref → 10-E1

Indian food just doesn't get better than this as Gazebo impresses with spicy, authentic cuisine that is low on lard and high on flavour. Charcoal grilled specialities, such as the chunky chicken kebabs and mouth-watering marinated leg of lamb are second to none, and the salads and side dishes are bursting with zingy freshness. Try and leave room for a fresh fruit kulfi – it's exquisite. The staff here are genuinely friendly and the service, top notch.

Food●●●●○ Serv●●●●○ Venue●●○○○ Value●●●●○

Handi

Location → Taj Palace Hotel · Deira
Hours → 12:00 - 15:00 19:00 - 23:30
Web/email → www.tajpalacehotel.ae

223 2222

Map Ref → 11-D2

Among the impressive number of reliable Indian restaurants in Dubai, Handi at the Taj Palace Hotel stands tall. An opulent setting staffed by friendly and informative waiters, Handi offers dishes of North India, though familiar, made magical by Chef Rasheed Qureshi. Diners may argue about what is best - the succulent Biryani, the captivating Carrot Halva, the luscious Tandoori fish, the perfect Naan - but disputes end with the realisation that the best is simply dining at Handi.

Food●●●●● Serv●●●●○ Venue●●●●○ Value●●●●○

India Palace

Location → Opp Sofitel City Cen. Htl · Al Garhoud
Hours → 12:00 - 16:00 19:00 - 01:00
Web/email → na

286 9600

Map Ref → 14-D2

Enter a virtual India where the culinary experience is close to perfection and it gets even better when the bill arrives (you'll be pleasantly surprised at just how far your Dirhams have stretched). The cuisine is mouth-watering and authentic and the service absolutely first-rate. The interior is appealing and tasteful – booths upstairs provide intimacy while the subtle sounds of the skilled tabla and sitar players downstairs truly add to the

experience. Children are more than welcome, but for those fearing a brat attack the atmosphere remains very nicely balanced.

Food●●●●● Serv●●●●● Venue●●●●○ Value●●●●●

Indian Pavilion, The

Location → Spinneys · Umm Suqeim
Hours → 12:30 - 15:00 18:45 - 23:15
Web/email → pavillion@emirates.net.ae

394 1483

Map Ref → 5-A3

This hidden gem remains a staple favourite amongst Jumeira residents, and for good reason. Although the décor, with its pastel green wicker chairs and stylised windows may scream simplicity, the same can't be said for its culinary content, which rivals any five star Indian alternatives. Recommended dishes include the butter chicken, tandoori and charcoal grilled specialities. Whether you decide to dine in or takeaway, the Indian Pavilion guarantees an experience that's good for your tummy, and your wallet!

Food●●●●● Serv●●●○○ Venue●●●○○ Value●●●●○

Kamat

Location → Opp BurJuman · Al Karama
Hours → 10:30 - 15:30 19:00 - 24:00
Web/email → na

396 7288

Map Ref → 10-E1

The bright lighting and utilitarian décor of Kamat reflect the no–nonsense approach of this venue. The service is attentive and efficient, and the wait staff will be all too happy to talk you through the almost daunting variety of selections on offer. The food is served fresh, hot and tasty, representing very good value for money. With a wide variety of dosas, idlis, lunchtime thalis and takeaway chaat and bil-puris also available downstairs, Kamat is a good option for a cheap and cheerful meal in a rush.

Food●●●○○ Serv●●●○○ Venue●●○○○ Value●●●●●

Khazana

Location → Cyclone Bld · Oud Metha
Hours → 12:30 - 14:30 19:00 - 23:00 Fri am
Web/email → na

336 0061

Map Ref → 10-D4

Celebrity chef Sanjeev Kapoor's spacious, popular family venue specialises in North Indian cuisine. The ambience is all bamboo gazebos, low partitions and an abundance of plants. Waitresses in national dress

Indian

Going Out

are ready to recommend dishes from the extensive range of vegetarian and non-vegetarian options, and have a knack of choosing dishes that complement each other. Meat and fish portions are plentiful with gravies optional, served with abundant rice and bread. Service is efficient and friendly. Consider this great value and good quality Indian food.

Food●●●●○ Serv●●●●○ Venue●●●●○ Value●●●●○

Kitchen

Location → Beh Hardees · Al Satwa | 398 5043
Hours → 10:00 - 02:30
Web/email → openhouse_rest@yahoo.com   Map Ref → 7-A3

  100

A small, friendly Indian restaurant located in the heart of Satwa that starts early and closes late. You'll be spoilt for choice with an extensive menu of meat, fish and chicken dishes and an outstanding vegetarian selection – all of which are delicious. Service is friendly and there's even a guest book, a glory testimony from diners to the food, service and total satisfaction. Fancy a little bit of India? Get yourself to Satwa (or phone for delivery).

Food●●●●○ Serv●●●●○ Venue●●●●○ Value●●●●○

Kohinoor

Location → Sea View Hotel · Bur Dubai | 355 8080
Hours → 12:00 - 15:00 20:00 - 03:00
Web/email → www.seaviewhoteldubai.com   Map Ref → 7-E2

100

When you go to Kohinoor, be prepared for more than just a meal. True, the food is good, generous and affordable, but the lights are low enough to encourage you to focus on the stage show. Three dancers provide different interpretations of ghazal music while you dine or drink at this restaurant/nightclub. The live music demands your attention, so don't expect to have a deep discussion. As the evening excitement builds and the revellers arrive, you'll have to bear the go-go with your aloo gobi.

Food●●●○○ Serv●●●○○ Venue●●●●○ Value●●●○○

Kwality

Location → Opp Ascot Htl · Bur Dubai | 393 6563
Hours → 12:30 - 15:00 19:30 - 23:45
Web/email → na   Map Ref → 7-E2

 50

This Indian restaurant is better than average. Popular for many years, Kwality offers a

bewildering array of dishes in a friendly setting. Downstairs is for bachelor diners and takeaway clients, but upstairs is where family customers sit and savour. Big portions, very reasonable prices, good service and endless options attract hoards. Novice Indian food diners will appreciate the somewhat westernised flavours. The restaurant is busiest from 21:30 onwards and it is advisable to book on weekends and holidays.

Food●●●●○ Serv●●●●● Venue●●●○○ Value●●●○○

Nina

Location → One&Only Arabian Court · Al Sufouh | 399 9999
Hours → 19:00 - 23:30 Fri closed
Web/email → www.oneandonlyroyalmirage.com   Map Ref → 3-A2

      150

In line with the Royal Mirage, the décor is as opulent and luxurious as one would expect. Though big and lavishly furnished, it still manages a warm and friendly ambience matched by a sumptuous Indian menu. The seemingly limitless choice means decision making is an effort. Luckily for you the waiting staff on hand are only too happy to talk you through the menu. The range of food caters to a variety of tastes, and the portions are small but adequate. A top choice for a special occasion.

Food●●●○○ Serv●●●●○ Venue●●●●● Value●●●●○

Rupee Room, The

Location → Dubai Marina · Marsa Dubai | 390 5755
Hours → 12:00 - 15:00 18:00 - 23:30 Fri am closed
Web/email → www.therupeeroom.com   Map Ref → 2-E2

    50

Making its debut in Scotland in 1999, this authentic British curry house is set for further success in it's new up and coming venue - the Marina. In a contemporary setting, attentive staff guide 'first timers' through the extensive menu of Indian delights - from mild kormas to an imaginative Tandoori selection deriving from the North region of India. Daily buffets along with a stylish private dining room make this ideal for business lunches, and the kids menu ensures that families are more than welcome at this swank venue. Also the venue promises to have an alcohol licence for the bar from January 2005.

Food●●●●○ Serv●●●●○ Venue●●●●○ Value●●●●○

Going Out

Indian

International

Other options → **Buffet [p.338]**

Al Muntaha

Location → Burj Al Arab · Umm Suqeim
Hours → 12:30 – 15:00 19:00 – 24:00
Web/email → www.jumeirahinternational.com   Map Ref → 4-A1

 250

From the décor to the delectables, Al Muntaha aims to impress, and with drama the order of the day you can expect to be overwhelmed. The menu is sophisticated with a wide range of European cuisine, and your mouth will water just from reading it, while the wine list is a connoisseur's dream. Your palate will be pampered with delicious delights and every dish is presented as an individual sculpture, but like fine art you can expect to pay for it.

Food●●○○○ Serv●●○○○ Venue●●●○○ Value●●○○○

Arboretum

Location → Al Qasr Hotel · Umm Suqeim
Hours → 12:30 – 15:00 19:00 – 23:30
Web/email → www.jumeirahinternational.com   Map Ref → 4-A2

 150

The Arboretum at Al Qasr may be the world's most lavish 24 hour restaurant. For extended periods each day beautiful buffets supplement the intelligent menu and complement the opulent red and cream interior. While buffets sometimes get bad press for their lack of creativity the Arboretum's offerings are simply delicious, especially the fish selection. The salmon, oysters and shrimp are glorious, the salads spectacular and the desserts, particularly the red raspberry mousse, hard to resist. As is the Arboretum itself.

Food●●●●○ Serv●●●●● Venue●●●●● Value●●●●●

Bab Al Yam

Location → Burj Al Arab · Umm Suqeim
Hours → 07:00 – 23:00
Web/email → www.jumeirahinternational.com   Map Ref → 4-A1

 250

Overlooking the ocean, Bab Al Yam combines gleaming glass walls with wood and chrome to convey a modern yet naturally blessed atmosphere. Which also applies to the menu, where an inventive mix of dishes arouse the curiosity. Rather than saving the best for last, the appetisers are superior featuring fresh seafood, salads and meze, while the bread could turn a carb-free fanatic's eye. The rest of the menu, while professionally executed, doesn't impress as much as the price tag would suggest but overall Bab Al Yam is worthy of its iconic host.

Food●●●○○ Serv●●●●● Venue●●●○○ Value●●○○○

Boardwalk

Location → Creek Golf Club · Al Garhoud
Hours → 08:00 – 24:00
Web/email → www.dubaigolf.com   Map Ref → 14-C2

 **100**

Definitely an essential destination, the views from this waterfront eatery are sublime, with panoramic views of the Creek from each of its three decks and its inside bar. The stylish wooden menus list equally stylish cuisine, with a mix of European, Arabic and Asian fare to choose from. Dishes are hit and miss, ranging from the delicious to the bland, and the quality of service is equally unpredictable. But the Boardwalk is still a winner for the stunning views – everything else is just a bonus.

Food●●●●○ Serv●●●●○ Venue●●●●● Value●●●●○

Boardwalk

Going Out   International

Dubai Creek

More than just golf...

Sneak Away

And what's more.... everyone is Welcome!

Celebrities

Location ➜ One&Only Palace · Al Sufouh
Hours ➜ 19:00 – 23:30 Sat closed
Web/email ➜ www.oneandonlyroyalmirage.com Map Ref ➜ 3-A2

|399 9999

 250

A formal though cosy setting – in keeping with the opulent surroundings of this hotel – Celebrities is without doubt one of the best examples of fine dining in Dubai. Additionally the beautifully landscaped and perfectly lit pool and gardens provide an exceptional backdrop for the outside terrace tables. The menu is broadly international, every selection is well thought out, and when it comes, the food is so well presented you will want to eat slowly and savour every morsel.🅰🅷

Food●●●●○Serv●●●●○○Venue●●●●●Value●●○○○

Cellar, The

Location ➜ Aviation Club, The · Al Garhoud
Hours ➜ 12:00 – 15:30 19:00 – 23:30
Web/email ➜ www.aviationclubonline.com Map Ref ➜ 14-C3

|282 4122

 100

The Cellar at the Aviation Club resembles a modish chapel with arched ceiling and stained glass. But no chapel ever cellared such sinfully satisfying beverages or provided such tantalising fare. An extensive wine list complements the delectable and innovative menu. Look out for the monthly wine tasting dinners, an enticing night out in itself for under Dhs.150, or even the Dhs.60 weekend brunch.🅐🅟

Food●●●●○Serv●●●●●Venue●●●●○Value●●●●○

The Cellar

Club Mille Miglia

Location ➜ API Tower · Trade Centre 1
Hours ➜ 09:00 – 01:00
Web/email ➜ na

|331 6288

Map Ref ➜9-E1

 100

Mille Miglia offers a café/restaurant menu (coffees, cake, shisha & good food) with three choices of dining location. The interior is modern electric, and there's alfresco seating available by the pool or in the inviting gardens surrounded by trees and bushes adorned with sparkling lights. The international menu, offering Italian, Lebanese and some Asian cuisine, has some creative touches, and the service is friendly.🆃🅼

Food●●●●○Serv●●●●○Venue●●●●○Value●●●○○

Clubhouse, The

Location ➜ Jumeirah Beach Club Resort & Spa
Hours ➜ 07:00 – 23:00
Web/email ➜ www.jumeirahinternational.com Map Ref ➜ 5-D1

|344 5333

 200

After an ocean swim, a dip in the pool or a game of tennis The Clubhouse offers a welcome spot where you can relax for breakfast, lunch, dinner or a coffee. You can tuck into a wide variety of delicious salads, sandwiches, Asian dishes, pasta, grilled fish and meat, or the impressive selection of Arabian meze. As the palm trees gently sway to the calming sounds of the sea lapping on the shore, you could easily forget that the hustle and bustle of the Beach Road is not far away.🅶🅱

Food●●○○○Serv●●●○○Venue●●●●○○Value●●○○○

Colonnade, The

Location ➜ The Jumeirah Beach Hotel · Umm Suqeim
Hours ➜ 24 hours
Web/email ➜ www.jumeirahinternational.com Map Ref ➜ 4-B2

|406 8181

 100

The open, stylish setting and the variety of international cuisine make this venue popular. The ever changing buffet offers delights from around the world such as Thai soups and salads, Arabian meze, Indian hot pots, Mongolian grill, and even an American soda fountain. The Colonnade is open 24 hours and apart from serving breakfast, lunch and dinner, it also has an all night snack menu. Good food, efficient service and an outside terrace help create a comfortable dining experience for both family and friends. 🆁🅲

Food●●●●○○Serv●●●●●○Venue●●●○○○Value●●●○○

International

Going Out

Stylish and relaxed ambience.

International cuisine.

Dubai's best stocked cellar.

Excellent value.

Friendly staff to guide you to the best selection.

For Reservations call 04 - 2829333

Entre Nous

Location → Novotel · Trade Centre 2
Hours → 12:00 – 24:00
Web/email → www.novotel.com

332 0000

Map Ref → 9-E3

Contemporary sophistication greets you as you enter this lobby level restaurant but it's not the décor that you will remember. You'll probably be impressed with the attention to detail in both how the food is cooked and how it is presented. Chef Marcus Gregs brings something rather unique to Dubai – Australian cuisine. The à la carte menu offers numerous meat dishes straight from the Outback, while the buffet offers a more traditional array of dishes. Either choice is a good one.
Food●●●●○Serv●●●●○Venue●●●○○Value●●●●○

Entre Nous

Fountain, The

Location → Mövenpick Hotel · Oud Metha
Hours → 12:00 – 15:00 18:00 – 24:00
Web/email → www.movenpick-hotels.com

336 6000

Map Ref → 10-D4

Friday brunch or the fondues are the main reasons you'll make your way into the Mövenpick's lobby restaurant. Try the traditional Swiss fondue nights where you can get as cheesy as you like. Definitely worth a taste is the Bourguignon meat fondue, or the lusciously indulgent, waist bulging chocolate fondue. Good selections of Arabic and International treats are also available with sushi, freshly shucked oysters, and a pasta cooking station dotted around the lobby. Don't forget to ask for your complimentary drink.
Food●●●●○Serv●●●●○Venue●●●○○Value●●●○○

Gardinia

Location → Towers Rotana · Trade Centre 1
Hours → 12:00 – 15:00 19:00 – 23:00
Web/email → www.rotana.com

343 8000

Map Ref → 9-B2

Always crowded, Gardinia offers a marvellous buffet on an 'all-inclusive' basis. The restaurant has five theme nights, including 'Spit Roast Night' where succulently roasted meats follow fantastic buffet starters such as poached salmon and guacamole. You'll have to remember to leave some room for the delicious dessert buffet, led by apple ginger tart and delectable chocolate cake topped with pureed raspberries.
Food●●●●○Serv●●●●○Venue●●○○○Value●●●●○

IKEA

Location → City Centre · Deira
Hours → 10:00 – 22:00 14:00 – 22:00
Web/email → www.ikeadubai.com

295 0434

Map Ref → 14-D1

In the middle of epic IKEA excursions, don't forget the calm café nestled inside the IKEA universe. Reasonable, tasty and most of all relatively quiet, this self service food bar offers dozens of food options, including a daily vegetarian special. Fresh 'Swedish' food is the theme: try the prawn mayonnaise open sandwich or the heartier Swedish meatballs. The cappuccino and hot chocolate is surprisingly good, but in this climate, why bother? A clearly superior option to the chaos of the food court.
Food●●●○○Serv●●●○○Venue●●○○○Value●●●●○

Japengo Café

Location → Oasis Tower · Trade Centre 2
Hours → 07:30 – 24:30
Web/email → www.binhendi.com

343 5028

Map Ref → 9-B2

Japengo Café offers a Japanese-Western hybrid menu that impresses with top notch food and drink in a bright, minimalist setting. The meals are excellent and include sushi, salads, sandwiches, hot dishes and fresh juices. Crab cakes and chicken dumplings are a treat and the assorted yakitori is superb – even better washed down with a fresh Kiwi juice. The portions are generous and the prices reasonable, although drinks and water are a bit more expensive. Crowds descend on the terrace, particularly at the Palm Strip branch.

Other branches: Palm Strip Mall, Beach Road (345 4979)
Food●●●●○Serv●●●●○Venue●●○○○Value●●●○○

Junction, The

Location → Traders Hotel Dubai · Deira
Hours → 12:30 – 15:30   19:30 – 24:00
Web/email → www.shangri-la.com
Map Ref → 12-A4

The Junction is a seriously classy buffet restaurant, complete with stylish, tasteful décor. The staff are immaculately smart and display attention to detail that puts the best à la carte restaurants to shame. The self-service buffet is beautifully presented with salads and sushi to start, an eclectic mix of European and Asian main courses and simply sumptuous desserts. Although you might question the point of a 'posh' buffet, Junction is excellent value, and well worth a try for the puddings alone.

Food ●●●●○ Serv ●●●●○ Venue ●●●●○ Value ●●●●○

Khaymat Al Bahar

Location → Al Qasr Hotel · Jumeira
Hours → 12:30 – 15:00   19:00 – 23:30
Web/email → www.jumeirahinternational.com
Map Ref → 4-A2

Like the Madinat itself, Khaymat Al Bahar aims to impress, and doesn't do a bad job. The restaurant ceilings are created like tents (khaymat), the décor is elegant and simple in cream and beige with marble and ceramics, and the small but delicious menu offers the usual dishes but served creatively and exquisitely. Not to be missed, so ensure you make a reservation well in advance.

Food ●●●●○ Serv ●●●●○ Venue ●●●●○ Value ●●●●○

Kitchen, The

Location → Hyatt Regency · Deira
Hours → 24 hours
Web/email → www.dubai.regency.hyatt.com
Map Ref → 8-D2

If you get a kick out of watching chefs hard at work, then The Kitchen at the Hyatt Regency is sure to satisfy on many different levels. The dynamic open kitchen allows for culinary voyeurism, while the inspired menu offers delicious combinations from Middle Eastern, Asian and European style cuisine. Get comfortable in the contemporary surroundings and appreciate the smells coming straight from the tandoor oven, lava stone grill, bakery oven and traditional burners. Elasticised waistbands are highly recommended since this is a 24 hour venue.

Food na   Serv na   Venue na   Value na

Lakeview

Location → Creek Golf Club · Al Garhoud
Hours → 06:30 – 23:30
Web/email → www.dubaigolf.com
Map Ref → 14-C2

Lounge by the Creek, watch the boats go by, and indulge in elegant pub food. This is Lakeview, one of the lesser expensive spots at the Club, with food that is just as good.   Sections of the menu are infused with Asian flavour; the rest is above average pub fare and pastas.   The venue encourages an intimate evening with someone special, or a quiet catch up with old friends over a seafood salad and a chocolate orange layered cake.   The house wine (both red and white) is recommended.

Food ●●●●○ Serv ●●●●○ Venue ●●●●○ Value ●●●●○

Midnight Café

Location → Opp Municipality · Al Karama
Hours → 10:30 – 15:00   17:00 – 24:45
Web/email → na
Map Ref → 10-E2

Rightfully claiming to be 'The Little Café with a Lot', Midnight Café comprises two tables and four chairs on the pavement, but offers a great Indian meets Western fast food menu bursting with flavour. The vast majority of their business is delivery and takeaway within Bur Dubai and Deira. Specialities include Frankeez, (rolled chapattis filled with spicy chicken tikka, vegetable or mutton), 'Chicken Looks Good', subs, garlic bread that melts in your mouth and dates with banana in cream.

Food ●●●●○ Serv ●●●●○ Venue ●●●●● Value ●●●●○

Promenade

Location → Four Points Sheraton · Bur Dubai
Hours → 12:30 – 15:00   19:30 – 23:00
Web/email → www.starwood.com
Map Ref → 8-A4

While this venue leaves much to be desired in terms of ambience, once you're over the lack of atmosphere the food is pretty good. Experience cooking stations every night of the week, except for Fridays, which is only open for brunch between 06:30 and 10:30. Meat – in all its various guises – comes highly recommended, whether you visit on BBQ night or simply indulge in any of the carnivorous dishes on offer. Good food, little flair, fewer sparks.

Food ●●○○○ Serv ●●●●○ Venue ●●●○○ Value ●●○○

International

Going Out

Seasons

Location → Century Village · Al Garhoud
Hours → 07:00 – 01:00
Web/email → www.mmidubai.com
286 9216
Map Ref → 14-C3

Seasons is a little tucked away to benefit from the usual festive atmosphere of the Century Village. However, it would be a shame not to give it a try, since the food and service are both surprisingly good, and the prices (especially of beverages) are excellent value for money. The international menu offers the usual array of soups, salads and sandwiches, but also a range of items from the grill that are elegantly served. Regular theme nights, such as couples' night on Wednesdays, buddies' night on Saturdays and corporate night on Mondays, keep the traffic flowing through this quiet little bistro.

Other branches: Dubai Internet City (04 391 8711)

Food●●●○○ Serv●●●○○ Venue●●●○○ Value●●●●○

Sketch

Location → Metropolitan Palace · Deira
Hours → 12:00 – 15:00 19:00 – 01:00
Web/email → www.methotels.com
227 0000
Map Ref → 11-D2

With so many fabulous places opening up on the beach strip, this stylish new kid on the Deira block should put a smile on the faces of those who live on the 'other side'. Sketch is split into two areas; a small but fashionable restaurant serving an interesting selection of international fare, and a heavenly chill-out area that's all about comfy seating, low lighting and good music. It's still early days, but Sketch has the potential to become a significant Deira nightspot for the young and trendy.

Food○○○○○ Serv○○○○○ Venue○○○○○ Value○○○○○

Spectrum on One

Location → Fairmont Dubai, The · Trade Centre 1
Hours → 17:30 – 19:00
Web/email → www.fairmont.com
311 8101
Map Ref → 9-E1

The menu here is a mind-boggling maze of Japanese, Thai, Chinese and Indian with a few European favourites thrown in. The massive variety sometimes means you take far too long in choosing and therefore are lucky to be eating within the hour of being seated. With impressive views of the kitchen and efficient and friendly staff, it's only

another pleasure that your meal is superbly presented and deliciously tasty. A must have is the amazing dessert platters that let you can sample a bit of everything – perfect for those with eyes bigger than tummies. Also see On the Town – General Bar Section [p.424].

Food●●●●○ Serv●●●●○ Venue●●●●○ Value●●●○○

Teatro

Location → Towers Rotana · Trade Centre 1
Hours → 18:00 – 24:00
Web/email → www.rotana.com
343 8000
Map Ref → 9-B2

Eclectic décor and subdued lighting set the tone for a memorable dinner at Teatro. The versatile menu is truly 'fusion' in its variety, with European, Asian and Indian flavours being the most obvious choices. Should your indecision get the better of you, the friendly waiters are happy to make recommendations. The quality of the food, the reasonable prices and the beautiful atmosphere make this arguably one of the best restaurants in Dubai.

Food●●●●○ Serv●●●●○ Venue●●●○○ Value●●●●○

Villa Beach Restaurant

Location → The Jumeirah Beach Hotel · Umm Suqeim
Hours → 12:00 – 17:00 19:00 – 23:00
Web/email → www.jumeirahinternational.com
406 8181
Map Ref → 4-B2

Follow the signs to perhaps the most romantic and isolated of all the restaurants at The Jumeirah Beach Hotel, where a truly outstanding dining experience awaits you. While the view of the Burj and its changing colours is unparalleled, the fine service and excellent food at Villa Beach will soon capture all your attention. Don't miss the lobster starter and be sure to save room for dessert, but remember to go slow and savour the beautifully presented and exquisitely prepared Mediterranean cuisine.

Food●●●●● Serv●●●●● Venue●●●●○ Value●●●●●

Wavebreaker

Location → Hilton Jumeirah · Marsa Dubai
Hours → 10:00 – 20:00
Web/email → www.hilton.com
399 1111
Map Ref → 2-D2

Lounging by the beach at the Hilton and have the munchies? If so, Wavebreaker is the obvious

International

Going Out

place to kick back. The limited (and slightly pricey) menu of sandwiches, salads, and burgers is adequately compensated for by the idyllic patio setting near the ocean. Kids can play on the nearby slides, while adults can pass the time (waiting and waiting for the food) on one of the inviting hammocks.

Food ●●○○○ Serv ●○○○○ Venue ●●●○○ Value ●●○○○

Windtower

Location → Country Club · Bukadra
Hours → 19:00 – 23:00 Fri pm closed
Web/email → www.dubaicountryclub.com

333 1155

Map Ref → 17-B3

 100

The Windtower is well worth the trip out into 'the country'. The décor may be a little past its prime, but the food more than makes up for it. A compact menu contains an eclectic array of delicious, yet very reasonably priced, dishes. The beetroot carpaccio for starters, and the Seafood Trilogy for mains, both deserve special mention. Get a taxi so you can take advantage of the exceptionally well priced wine list. Nonmembers of the club will need to book ahead.

Food ●●●○○ Serv ●●●○○ Venue ●●●○○ Value ●●●●○

Italian

Other options → **Mediterranean [p.379]**
Pizzerias [p.387]

Andiamo!

Location Grand Hyatt Dubai · Umm Hurair
Hours 12:30 – 15:00 18:00 – 23:30
Web/email www.dubai.grand.hyatt.com

317 2222

Map Ref → 13-E3

 100

Surrounded by the excellent Vinoteca, where you can sample Italy's finest wines and spirits and Panini, selling some of Dubai's finest Italian produce, Andiamo! completes an Italian culinary trinity. Colourful tiles and brightly coloured furniture are offset by over-sized lava lamps, and make for a rare and interesting ambience. The menu covers all the regions of Italy. Great pizzas, pastas and risottos, deliciously light main courses and traditional decadent desserts, including fine homemade gelato, should please all those who eat here. ●

Food ●●●●○ Serv ●●●○○ Venue ●●●●○ Value ●●●●○

Bacchus

Location Fairmont Dubai, The · Trade Centre 1
Hours 11:00 – 15:30 19:00 – 23:00
Web/email → www.fairmont.com

311 8000

Map Ref → 9-E1

 100

Bacchus falls between the Fairmont's two marbled pools, but graceful Italian design saves it from a fate of being a poolside snack joint. Bringing only the finest ingredients to its kitchens, guests can look forward to mouth-watering pasta and main courses, or sample any of the creative pizza choices. Never mind the calorie watching, a visit to this haven of indulgence demands a taste of anything on the dessert menu since it's all good, very, very good. ●

Food ●●●●● Serv ●●●●● Venue ●●●●○ Value ●●●●○

Bella Donna

Location Mercato · Jumeira
Hours 11:00 – 23:30
Web/email www.binhendi.com

344 7701

Map Ref → 5-E1

 50

If you want a great bowl of pasta before a stroll around the shops, or a pizza after your movie, this place is a good option. Tucked away in the upstairs corner of Mercato Shopping Mall, the open kitchen and classy monochrome décor make this a very stylish eatery. The menu is simple Italian fare, but the choice is delicious and healthy. Try the salmon and cream cheese pizza, served cold, and sit outside on the terrace watching the best of Jumeira going about their business. ●

Food ●●●○○ Serv ●●●○○ Venue ●●●●○ Value ●●●●○

BiCE

Location → Hilton Jumeirah · Marsa Dubai
Hours → 12:00 – 24:00
Web/email → www.hilton.com

399 1111

Map Ref → 2-D2

 150

An upmarket experience with exceptional food and terrific service, BiCE is undoubtedly a solid choice for Italian food fanatics. The place is tastefully decorated in bistro style, with quietly efficient staff whose knowledge of the menu is well above average. The broad range of choice includes fresh and perfectly cooked pasta, delicious pizza and a tantalising choice of specials, all presented with imagination and panache. ●

Food ●●●●○ Serv ●●●●● Venue ●●●●● Value ●●●●○

BiCE terrace

Biella Caffé Pizzeria Ristorante

Location → Wafi Mall · Umm Hurair | **324 4666**
Hours → 12:00 – 23:45
Web/email → www.waficity.com   Map Ref → 13-D2

Biella is a casual Italian café/restaurant serving top quality wholesome food at good prices. The indoor and terrace facilities create a relaxed ambience and the outstanding service is prompt, efficient and knowledgeable. The menu provides a host of mouth-watering options and includes an extensive range of pizza, pasta, meat, fish and excellent vegetarian specials. Try their delicious range of non-alcoholic cocktails too. A popular place, well worth a visit.
Food●●●●○Serv●●●●○Venue●●●●○Value●●●●○

Carnevale

Location → The Jumeirah Beach Hotel · Umm Suqeim | **406 8181**
Hours → 12:30 – 15:00 19:00 – 23:00
Web/email → www.jumeirahinternational.com   Map Ref → 4-B2

Carnevale offers a personalised, intimate and homey Italian ambience rare to Dubai. A rich and impressive à la carte menu comprises a range of pasta, poultry and red meat (pizzas are not included), but fish dishes seem to be the focus. The wine selection has some Italian gems that are rarely seen in this part of the world. Sit on the balcony if the climate permits, and let the eloquent and attentive staff guide you through a pleasurable authentic Italian experience.
Food●●●○○Serv●●●●○Venue●●●●○Value●●●○○

Casa Mia

Location → Le Meridien Dubai · Al Garhoud | **282 4040**
Hours → 12:30 – 14:45 20:00 – 23:30
Web/email → www.lemeridien-dubai.com   Map Ref → 14-E3

Casa Mia isn't the biggest of restaurants, but to its advantage the intimate space and dark wooden beams gives it a traditional trattoria feel. A varied menu with the usual Italian offerings, mixed with numerous meat dishes such as the Fillet of Beef with Duck Liver (which is exquisite but needs a salad or vegetable side order to satisfy). The service is certainly efficient if not a little sombre. The outdoor space for alfresco dining in the pleasant winter months is a definite selling point and reservations are essential most nights of the week.
Food●●●●○Serv●●●○○Venue●●●○○Value●●●●○

Ciro's Pomodoro

Location → Le Meridien Mina Seyahi · Al Sufouh | **399 3333**
Hours → 19:00 – 01:00
Web/email → www.lemeridien-minaseyahi.com   Map Ref → 3-A2

More bar than restaurant, Ciro's offers decent Italian food and live entertainment. The menu has a wide selection of pizzas, salads, pastas, and grilled main courses, although the starters seem to be the tastiest choices. After dinner, you can burn off the calories on the small dance floor. While you won't find top-notch Italian cuisine here, it is a lively venue and they also have theme nights, such as Karaoke and Boogie Nights, so check with the venue before going to ensure what theme they've got on offer is what you're in the mood for.
Food●●○○○Serv●●●○○Venue●●○○○Value●●○○○

Come Prima

Location → Al Bustan Hotel · Al Garhoud | **282 0000**
Hours → 12:00 – 15:00 19:00 – 23:00
Web/email → www.rotana.com   Map Ref → 14-E3

Come Prima is one of Dubai's hidden Italian gems. While the modern surroundings result in a slightly cold atmosphere (the fridge-like air conditioning doesn't help), the service and fresh Northern Italian food, prepared by their talented chef, are consistently excellent. Recommended is the Dhs.99 net Sunday and Monday night à la carte promotion: select one

WHERE THE WORLDS' GREAT CUISINES MEET.

Enter Le Méridien Dubai and you enter a culinary adventure with a wide variety of fifteen restaurants and bars where you have all the choice in the world.

Whether you dine indoors or al fresco each venue offers an atmosphere unique to its cuisine.

From Far East to Far West, we have flavours to tempt every one of your taste buds.

FOR FURTHER INFORMATION and reservations call +971 4 7022455 now, or log onto www.dubai.lemeridien.com

ABU DHABI • AMSTERDAM • BANGALORE • BRUSSELS • CAIRO • CHICAGO
COLOGNE • DAKAR • DOUALA • DUBAI • HONG KONG • LATTAKIA
LISBON • LONDON • MELBOURNE • MILAN • MINNEAPOLIS • PARIS • ROME

Le MERIDIEN
DUBAI

dubai.lemeridien.com
www.lemeridien.com
In Partnership with Nikko Hotels International

each from the starters, mains and desserts; house wine is included. The menu changes seasonally and any of the chef's recommendations is guaranteed to be mouth-watering.

Food●●●●○Serv●●●●○Venue●●●○○Value●●●●○

Come Prima

Cubo

Location → Ibis World Trade Centre · Trade Centre 2 | **332 4444**
Hours → 12:00 – 15:00 19:00 – 24:00 none
Web/email → www.accorhotels.com   Map Ref → 9-E3

Interestingly enough, in this Italian restaurant there is scarcely an Italian to be seen and this should be the telling tale. Still, Cubo fulfils the expectations of patrons (new and returning) with its good pasta and paper napkins. Although some may consider the pasta dishes over-sauced, they ought to thank their stars, especially when pitted against the restaurant's flat salads and bland main courses, served by enthusiastic yet temperamental staff. Only time will tell if the current departure from a thoroughly Italian menu will rebuild Cubo.

Food●●○○○Serv●○○○○Venue●●○○○Value●●○○○

Cucina

Location → JW Marriott Hotel · Deira | **607 7903**
Hours → 12:30 – 15:00 19:30 – 23:30
Web/email → www.marriott.com   Map Ref → 12-A3

With its faux Tuscan farm décor, Cucina adds a touch of the rustic to Dubai's usual glitz. A

solidly traditional Italian menu gives you all the Italian culinary standards and a reasonably priced wine list, with decent house wine, helps you keep the budget in check. The pizzas are very good and pasta dishes, while not exemplary, are still honest to Italian kitchens. If you like an old fashioned sing-a-long, then be sure to get there in time for the staff's renditions of Italian classic tunes.

Food●●●●○Serv●●●●○Venue●●●●○Value●●●●○

Da Vinci's

Location → Millennium Airport Hotel · Al Garhoud | **282 3464**
Hours → 12:00 – 24:00
Web/email → www.millenniumhotels.com   Map Ref → 14-D3

A popular mid-range Italian restaurant that boasts an impressively versatile menu, as well as a 20% discount on food for diners visiting between 17:00 and 21:00. The spacious, Italian country house style setting still manages to pull off great ambience without bypassing on the intimacy of dinnertime. Expect the usual in traditional Italian cuisine, served in great big portions and all reasonably priced. Couple this with spot on service, and you have a reliable restaurant that delivers good value for money.

Food●●●○○Serv●●●●○Venue●●●○○Value●●●○○

Cucina

Il Rustico

Location ➜ Rydges Plaza Hotel · Al Satwa |398 2222
Hours ➜ 12:00 – 15:00 18:00 – 24:00
Web/email ➜ www.rydges.com   Map Ref ➜ 7-A4

 100

Finally, a restaurant that does rustic charm and good value Italian fare with flair. Bare wooden floorboards, beamed ceilings and intimate candlelit tables make for a cosy atmosphere in which diners can enjoy the selection of tasty pasta and delicious wood fired pizzas, amongst other things. The menu is enticing with everything featured bordering on decadent if not plain indulgent. Booking in advance is advisable since this little gem of a restaurant is very popular.

Food●●●●○Serv●●●●○Venue●●●○○Value●●●●○

Italian Connection

Location ➜ Nr Lamcy Plaza · Oud Metha |335 3001
Hours ➜ 12:30 – 15:30 19:30 – 24:00
Web/email ➜ na   Map Ref ➜ 10-D4

50

Despite the absence of a wine list, Italian Connection still manages to offer a reasonable authentic Italian experience. It is worth asking whether the homemade pasta is available, which is served with a standard range of sauces. Pizzas are also a good choice (and the choice is extensive), and should not be dismissed as a potential starter to share amongst your table. Salads too are plentiful and quite imaginative. Table service can be a little lethargic, particularly at busy times. Prices are very reasonable for the results that are achieved both in terms of taste and volume.

Food●●●○○Serv●●○○○Venue●●●●○Value●●●●○

La Moda

Location ➜ Hotel Inter-Continental · Deira |205 7333
Hours ➜ 13:00 – 15:00 20:00 – 02:30
Web/email ➜ www.interconti.com   Map Ref ➜ 8-C4

 200

Centrally located on the Deira side of the Creek, La Moda at the Intercontinental makes for a fun night out, especially for larger groups. Waiting staff dressed in orange 'pit crew' outfits take good care of the patrons. In addition to the warm, freshly baked bread that greets you upon arrival, there is a wide choice of pizzas, pastas, antipasti, mains and desserts, which are a little over priced

(but then you're here for the ambience as well as the food!). For atmosphere and being seen out in Dubai, La Moda is worth a booking.

Food●●●○○Serv●●●●○Venue●●●●○Value●●●●○

La Vigna

Location ➜ Century Village · Al Garhoud |282 0030
Hours ➜ 11:30 – 01:00
Web/email ➜ dagama@emirates.net.ae   Map Ref ➜ 14-C3

 100

La Vigna is located within the hospitality precinct of Century Village, and offers a casual dining experience based around Italian style food. Seating is available both inside and out, depending on your mood and the weather. The menu consists of a broad range of pizzas, pastas, mains, antipasti and desserts but the quality of all the food is just average. Service is friendly and informative.

Food●●●○○Serv●●●○○Venue●●●○○Value●●●○○

Mosaico

Location ➜ Boulevard at Emirate Towers, The |319 8088
Hours ➜ 00:00 – 24:00
Web/email ➜ www.jumeirahinternational.com   Map Ref ➜ 9-C2

 200

Mosaico is a stylish and relaxed Italian venue boasting an intimate terrace and the largest mosaic in the Middle East. The menu offers a good choice, both for avid carnivores and voracious vegetarians, and the signature dishes (marked on the menu with a red 'm') are recommended, especially if you can't make your mind up! The cheesy aubergine stack starter is particularly good. The portions are adequate, the prices are reasonable, the staff are friendly and knowledgeable, and since Mosaico is open 24 hours a day, it's ideal for late night dining.

Food●●●●○Serv●●●●●Venue●●●○○Value●●●●○

Ossigeno

Location ➜ Le Royal Meridien · Marsa Dubai |399 5555
Hours ➜ 19:00 – 24:00
Web/email ➜ www.leroyalmeridien-dubai.com   Map Ref ➜ 2-E2

 150

Ossigeno is more than a cut above your average Italian restaurant. From its modern décor to its imaginatively conceived dishes, this is a classy act. The quality is evident in the ingredients

Italian

Going Out

(superb mozzarella, for example), and the wide selection of inventive combinations, all pleasingly presented. The superior nature of this modern establishment is somewhat reflected in the prices, but these should not deter you from making the journey - Ossigeno is an excellent restaurant.

Food●●●●○ Serv●●●●○ Venue●●●●○ Value●●●●○

Pax Romana

Location → Dusit Dubai · Trade Centre 2 | 343 3333
Hours → 12:00 – 15:00 19:00 – 23:30
Web/email → www.dusit.com Map Ref → 9-A2

 150

Delicious Italian food served in a relaxing atmosphere. Sit down on tables set in window alcoves overlooking the traffic on the Sheikh Zayed highway and try to remember to keep an eye on the time. Typical Italian fare includes pizzas and pasta, a variety of meats and seafood, as well as several interesting veggie options. The beef dishes are recommended, since the meat is incredibly tender and superbly succulent. Another favourite is the linguine with lobster and herbed tomato sauce, simply divine. Expect extra attentive service if the restaurant is not busy.

Food●●●●○ Serv●●●○○ Venue●●●●○ Value●●●●○

Pax Romana

Segreto

Location → Malakiya Villas · Umm Suqeim | 366 8888
Hours → 12:00 – 15:00 19:00 – 23:30
Web/email → www.jumeirahinternational.com Map Ref → 4-A2

 250

After arriving at Segreto by abra at its waterside location, nestled amid the Malakiya Villas, you receive a warm welcome from the exemplary staff. The venue is tasteful and refined, yet surprisingly relaxed – seating is designed to allow privacy for diners. The menu has a good selection of starters and pastas, slightly fewer main courses, but all dishes are beautifully presented and the tastes are sensational – although the main courses don't cater for vegetarians. Segreto offers fine dining for those looking for a leisurely, intimate atmosphere.

Food●●●●○ Serv●●●●● Venue●●●●○ Value●●●●○

Splendido Grill

Location → Ritz-Carlton, The · Marsa Dubai | 399 4000
Hours → 12:30 – 17:30 19:00 – 24:00
Web/email → www.ritzcarlton.com Map Ref → 2-E2

 150

Exactly what you would expect from the Ritz: no frills or fuss, just superbly classic dining in superbly classic surroundings. The dining room is small, with option to sit on the terrace outside. Splendido offers crisp white table linen, highly polished oak floors and staff that exude professionalism. The Antipasti will keep you occupied long after your main course is ready, and the varied wine list will take you the rest of the way. A very understated and tasteful dining experience.

Food●●●●○ Serv●●●●○ Venue●●●●○ Value●●●○○

Toscana

Location → Souk Madinat Jumeirah · Umm Suqeim | 366 8888
Hours → 12:00 – 00:30
Web/email → www.jumeirahinternational.com Map Ref → 4-A2

 100

This bright, bustling waterfront eatery serves up Italian fast food in picturesque surroundings. The outdoor terrace offers wonderful views of the Madinat in all its glory, especially at night, and beats the over bright, noisy dining room hands down. Toscana offers a limited menu featuring standard pizza and pasta dishes, and has a rapid turnover so wouldn't really suit the languorous, relaxed diner.

Italian

Going Out

Romantic

Dusit, the Thai way of life

PAX ROMANA

Open daily for lunch and dinner

Dusit Dubai
D U B A I
U . A . E .

Dusit Dubai, 133 Sheikh Zayed Road • P.O. Box 23335, Dubai, United Arab Emirates.
Tel: +971 (0)4 343 3333, Fax: +971 (0)4 343 4222, E-mail: foodbev@dusitdubai.com, Website: www. **Dusit.com**

No reservations are accepted, so if you want a terrace table, go early to avoid disappointment.
Food●●●○○ Serv●●●○○ Venue●●●○○ Value●●●○○

Trattoria La Piazza

Location → Ramada Hotel · Bur Dubai | **351 9999**
Hours → 18:00 – 24:00
Web/email → www.ramadadubai.com   Map Ref → 7-E3

  150

Located in the main lobby of the Ramada, Trattoria La Piazza offers more than its café appearance might suggest. Gracious service, delicious Italian favourites, and a substantial wine list all surpass expectations. The Grilled Shrimp and Rucola salad served in a parmesan cheese basket is delightful. Don't pass up the roasted garlic spread served with the fresh baked bread (just have a mint later).

Live piano music, a fountain, and cosy lighting help make this "piazza" a comfortable spot for dinner.
Food●●●●○ Serv●●●●○ Venue●●●○○ Value●●●●○

Venezia

Location → Metropolitan · Shk Zayed Rd | **343 0000**
Hours → 19:00 – 24:00
Web/email → www.methotels.com   Map Ref → 5-C4

 100

Flaming torches, stone lions and a pillared entry are your introduction to the scale and grandeur of Venezia, a massive themed dining room in the style of an outdoor piazza replete with canal, gondolas, an impressive Venetian street facade and twinkling starry, starry night ceiling. The simple, rustic menu offers well-prepared salads, pizza and pasta dishes, while operatic singers crooning from bridges and moody lighting add to the already authentic atmosphere. Exceptionally attentive and professional service is further evidence that Venezia has made quality improvements in recent times.
Food●●●●○ Serv●●●●○ Venue●●●●○ Value●●●○○

Vivaldi

Location → Sheraton Hotel & Towers · Deira | **207 1717**
Hours → 12:00 – 15:00 15:00 – 01:30 06:30 – 12:00
Web/email → www.starwood.com   Map Ref → 11-C1

     100

Vivaldi offers a rare Creek by night dining experience, from inside or on the balcony. Friendly, professional service guides you through a well paced evening in smart, yet unpretentious, surroundings. The menu offers traditional Italian standards prepared at the busy live cooking station. The ravioli with gorgonzola, mushrooms and walnuts or even the veal with Parma ham are definite winners. The adjoining bar with live music is a good pre-dining rendezvous.
Food●●●●○ Serv●●●●○ Venue●●●●○ Value●●●●○

Japanese

Other options → **Far Eastern [p.348]**

Benihana

Location → Al Bustan Hotel · Al Garhoud | **282 0000**
Hours → 12:00 – 15:00 19:00 – 23:30
Web/email → www.rotana.com   Map Ref → 14-E3

 100

Benihana is Japanese for the masses rather than for the connoisseur. You are guaranteed entertainment and a very social atmosphere at the Teppanyaki tables (book ahead) – the tables are one of Dubai's best locations for a group outing. Sushi is hit and miss, as is service in the restaurant's quiet front area away from the bustling Teppanyaki room. Excellent value for money is the Sunday all-you-can-eat Teppanyaki night (includes house wine, beer and soft drinks) all for Dhs.119. All-you-can-eat sushi on Tuesday and Saturday (also Dhs.119).
Food●●●○○ Serv●●○○○ Venue●●●○○ Value●●●○○

Creekside

Location → Sheraton Hotel & Towers · Deira | **207 1750**
Hours → 12:30 – 15:00 18:30 – 24:00 Fri am closed
Web/email → www.starwood.com   Map Ref → 11-C1

 100

So popular it has its own set of regulars, who keep coming back for the good stuff. Theme nights, like all you can eat sushi and all you can eat Japanese, take place on various nights and are definitely

Italian | Japanese
Going Out

money well spent. If it tickles your fancy, choose from the extensive menu that offers all you'd expect from a good Japanese place. The fresh sushi and sashimi come with the highest recommendation. The staff is very attentive and friendly. ●●●

Food ●●●●○ Serv ●●●●○ Venue ●●●○○ Value ●●●●○

ET Sushi

Location → The Boulevard at Emirates Towers | **319 8088**
Hours → 12:30 – 15:00 19:30 – 24:00
Web/email → www.jumeirahinternational.com   Map Ref → 9-C2

ET Sushi does conveyor belt sushi with class. There is table seating, but if you opt for the bar facing the conveyor belt you can pick up your favourite dishes as they roll past. If there's something you'd like that's not on the belt, ask the chefs to prepare it for you, or order off the à la carte menu (a pricier option though). You're guaranteed fresh, melt-in-your-mouth sushi here. Although the modern, minimalist tiled surroundings don't promote after dinner lingering, this is a great stop before joining the crowds at Scarlett's or The Agency. ●●●

Food ●●●●○ Serv ●●●●○ Venue ●●●○○ Value ●●●○○

Hana

Location → Riviera Hotel · Deira | **222 2131**
Hours → 12:00 – 15:00 19:00 – 23:00
Web/email → www.rivierahotel-dubai.com   Map Ref → 8-C3

Whether you are seeking a cosy evening in a private tatami room, or wish to be more publicly convivial at a teppanyaki table, you will find delicious food and exemplary service at Hana. A comprehensive menu offers a wide choice of Asian favourites, including stir fries, noodle soups and oriental salads. The sushi/sashimi platters are fresh and mouth-wateringly authentic, while the Early Birds' teppanyaki for Dhs.45 is incredible value. Allow time to conquer the Deira traffic and your journey will be richly rewarded. ●●●

Food ●●●●○ Serv ●●●●○ Venue ●●●●○ Value ●●●○○

Kiku

Location → Le Meridien Dubai · Al Garhoud | **282 4040**
Hours → 12:30 – 15:00 19:00 – 23:00
Web/email → www.lemeridien-dubai.com   Map Ref → 14-E3

A taste of Tokyo, the newly renovated Kiku's modern Japanese ambience is about as authentic as it gets. The staff, many of the clientele, menu, music and décor are genuine Japanese. Seating options include the teppanyaki bar, sushi counter, booths and private tatami rooms, but wherever you sit, you're guaranteed an excellent experience. Seafood is particularly good, as traditional dishes have been adapted to the local catch of the day. Kiku is a step above the run of the mill sushi joints. ●●●

Food ●●●●○ Serv ●●●●○ Venue ●●●●○ Value ●●●○○

Minato

Location → Hotel Inter-Continental · Deira | **222 7171**
Hours → 13:00 – 15:00 15:00 – 23:30
Web/email → www.interconti.com   Map Ref → 8-C4

You know the food will be both authentic and good when the diners are native to the cuisine. Minato allows you a brief glimpse into ancient Japan with Zen settings, a maze-like layout, Tatami rooms and a hoard of early evening Japanese diners. An impressive menu crosses the boundaries of popular oriental cuisine with a range of dishes that are prepared to near perfection. Ever tried ginger or bean flavoured icecream? For a broad selection, head down for the Monday or Wednesday buffets (Dhs.105 and Dhs.125 respectively) and let your palette loose. ●●●

Food ●●●●○ Serv ●●●●○ Venue ●●●○○ Value ●●●○○

Miyako

Location → Hyatt Regency · Deira | **209 6717**
Hours → 12:30 – 15:00 19:00 – 23:00
Web/email → www.dubai.regency.hyatt.com   Map Ref → 8-D2

Like a gleaming pearl inside an oyster, Miyako impresses – highly. A mind boggling array of dishes features everything you could possibly wish for in a Japanese restaurant, and the food is astoundingly good. Master chefs prepare perfect sushi, exquisite tempura prawns and superb yakitori, and the Shabu Shabu is a table cooked treat without equal. Exquisite Geisha style service

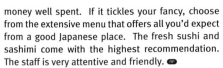

and an authentic, serene environment work their magic in easing the price conscious mind.

Food●●●●○Serv●●●●○Venue●●●○○Value●●●○○

Sho Cho's

Location ➜ Dubai Marine Beach Resort · Jumeira
Hours ➜ 19:30 – 02:00
Web/email ➜ www.dxbmarine.com   Map Ref ➜ 6-D2

  | 346 1111

  150

Sho Cho's may be a Japanese restaurant but while the food is delicate and imaginative, if not a little pricey for what you get, most people come for the party atmosphere that is more akin to a happening bar than an exquisite restaurant. Definitely slick and sophisticated but refreshingly unpretentious, the cocktail bar inside is inviting while the terrace has a chill out feel and great view. The in-house DJ, club nights and dance floor make this a place where you can start and finish your evening.

Food●●●○○Serv●●●○○Venue●●●●○Value●●●○○

Sumo

Location ➜ Jct1 – Nr Shangri-La · Trade Centre 1
Hours ➜ 11:00 – 23:00
Web/email ➜ www.sumosushi.net   Map Ref ➜ 9-A2

| 343 5566

  100

Sumo is a heavyweight contender for 'best independent Japanese joint' title. Skilled chefs serve up superb sushi and sashimi, as expected, but also deliver outstanding hot treats as well; the Yakitori, Tempura and Calamari are expertly cooked and delicious, and Bento meals are also fantastic – for those with a taste for delicacies, Unagi (BBQ eel) Bento is a top choice. Add friendly, welcoming staff, and an artfully decorated, spotlessly clean venue to the mix, and you have the makings of a champion.

Food●●●●●Serv●●●●○Venue●●●○○Value●●●●○

Sushi Bar

Location ➜ Grand Hyatt Dubai · Umm Hurair
Hours ➜ 12:30 – 15:00 19:00 – 23:30 Mon closed
Web/email ➜ www.dubai.grand.hyatt.com   Map Ref ➜ 13-E3

| 317 2222

 200

Sit yourself down at the bar and allow Chef Masuda to serve you till you're ready to pop. Food presentation is more minimalist than fancy, with the focus being entirely on the food itself. Regulars place special orders with Chef Masuda three days in advance, particularly for any uncommon fish otherwise difficult to find in Dubai. Sushi Bar won't appeal to those on a budget, or the strictly safe

California roll/Teppanyaki type of crowd, but this place is a haven for those in search of specialised, traditional sushi.

Food●●●○○Serv●●●●○Venue●●●●○Value●●●○○

Sushi Sushi

Location ➜ Century Village · Al Garhoud
Hours ➜ 12:30 – 24:00
Web/email ➜ www.aviationclubonline.com   Map Ref ➜ 14-C3

| 282 9908

   50

Fresh, funky décor and the best alfresco option of any Japanese in Dubai ensure this place remains popular. Seat yourself around the conveyor belt for a tempting view of the food passing before your eyes, or sink into one of the comfy chairs if you plan to linger. Either way the menu definitely encourages leisurely consideration with all traditional dishes well represented, along with some interesting new takes on old favourites. The adventurous sushi creations are particularly recommended, and the Dhs.95 dinner buffet (Tuesdays) continually draws the crowds.

Food●●●●○Serv●●●●○Venue●●●●○Value●●●●○

Sushi

tokyo@the towers

Location ➜ The Boulevard at Emirates Towers
Hours ➜ 12:30 – 15:00 19:30 – 24:00
Web/email ➜ www.jumeirahinternational.com   Map Ref ➜ 9-C2

| 319 8088

     150

If you plan to eat à la carte, follow the spacious corridors of tokyo@thetowers to the elegantly partitioned dining areas complete with traditional floor cushion seating. But the star of the show is definitely the teppanyaki, which features a range of soup and

SUSHI TRAY FOR JUST Dhs 99

FREE DELIVERY

SUMO IS THE IDEAL SPOT TO ENJOY DELICIOUS JAPANESE SPECIALITIES AT GREAT VALUE. ENJOY OUR DELECTABLE NIGIRI SUSHI COMBO TRAY FOR JUST DHS 99. WHAT'S MORE, WE ALSO DELIVER TO YOUR HOME OR OFFICE AND EVEN PROVIDE SUSHI FOR PARTIES AND GATHERINGS.

KH ZAYED ROAD, (NEXT TO SHANGRI LA HOTEL), TEL: 04 3435566

SUMO
SUSHI & BENTO

salad starters followed by delicious seafood, beef or chicken cooked in front of you by a skilful (and charismatic) chef. After dinner, continue the Japanese theme with a bit of karaoke at the adjoining bar. ●

Food●●●●○Serv●●●●○Venue●●●●○Value●●●○○

Wagamama

Location → Crowne Plaza · Trade Centre 1 | 305 6060
Hours → 12:00 – 24:00
Web/email → www.wagamama.ae   Map Ref → 9-D2

The latest international branch of this hip London chain is now open in Dubai, offering Japanese food with a healthy twist. Sitting on benches at communal tables amid the

Family Explorer

Written by Mums and Dads residing in the Emirates, this guidebook is the only essential resource for families with kids, providing you a multitude of indoor and outdoor activity options with your little ones. Make your life easier by following tips on practical topics, such as education and medical care.

lively throng of diners is a fun, social way of dining. Specialities are the noodle dishes, cooked a variety of ways, alongside other favourites such as gyoza, fried rice dishes and mild but tasty Japanese curry. Side orders go well with mains, with everything being brought when it's ready by the friendly and helpful staff. Sharpen up your chopstick skills and get slurping those noodles! ●

Food●●●●○Serv●●●●○Venue●●●●○Value●●●●○

Yakitori

Location → Ascot Hotel · Bur Dubai | 352 0900
Hours → 12:30 – 15:00 18:30 – 23:30
Web/email → www.ascothoteldubai.com   Map Ref → 7-E3

For advocates of real Japanese food, this is a hidden treasure trove. Walking into this true to life version of a Japanese everyman's diner, everything is Japanese; the chef, the chatter and the stylish red and black setting. The extensive menu offers an unrivalled choice of food, which clearly delights the regular Japanese clientele. Aficionados will enjoy the different food on offer, but the staff are helpful and informative so novices to this cuisine can seek guidance on unknown dishes. One may find venues with more subtle ambience but very rarely such choice of quality food. ●

Food●●●●○Serv●●●●○Venue●●●●○Value●●●●○

YO! Sushi

Location → BurJuman Centre · Bur Dubai | 336 0505
Hours → 11:00 – 23:00
Web/email → yo_sushi@emirates.net.ae   Map Ref → 11-A1

Park yourself on a stool and watch a wide variety of Japanese treats roll past on the conveyor belt that has become the trademark of this London based chain. Select dumplings, sushi, salad and sashimi to your heart's content. Dishes are expertly prepared, colour/price coded and set out for you to enjoy. Alternatively have the chefs cook up something hot and tasty while you watch. This semi industrial restaurant is brilliant for quick and easy peasy Japanese. ●

Food●●●●○Serv●●●○○Venue●●●○○Value●●●○○

Korean

Other options → **Far Eastern [p.348]**

Seoul Garden Restaurant

Location → Zomorodah Bld · Al Karama | 337 7876
Hours → 11:00 – 15:30 17:30 – 23:30 Fri 18:00-23:30
Web/email → seoulgarden@empal.com   Map Ref → 10-E3

Tucked away in your own private room, your group will set the pace for this delightful Korean experience. Each table is equipped with the traditional Korean barbecue and it's highly recommended that you put it to good use by opting for a beef dish or two. Typical of Korean dining, most main courses are served with an assortment of complimentary side dishes to offset the meal. Your waiters are literally at your fingertips as a table-mounted button brings a hospitable smile upon command. Cool ginger tea and sweet melon dessert accompany every meal and provide a unique and satisfying finish. ●

Food●●●●○Serv●●●●○Venue●●●○○Value●●●●○

Silla

Location → Ramada Continental · Hor Al Anz | 266 2666
Hours → 11:00 – 15:00 18:00 – 23:00
Web/email → www.ramadacontinental.com   Map Ref → 12-B4

Silla provides a straightforward introduction to Korean cooking. The owner carefully oversees his two dining rooms atop the Ramada Continental Hotel and insists on fresh, authentic vegetables to

Japanese | Korean

Going Out

complement the barbecued meat – to the delight of most diners. Seaweed in various guises and kimchi (undisguised) enliven the meal. The faint at heart should leave Silla to patrons seeking a fascinating gastronomic adventure. ⏺

Food●●◐○○Serv●●●◐○Venue●●◐○○Value●●○○○

Latin American

Other options → **Argentinean [p.338]**
Cuban [p.346]
Mexican [p.382]

Pachanga

Location → Hilton Jumeirah · Marsa Dubai | 399 1111
Hours → 18:00 – 24:00
Web/email → www.hilton.com   Map Ref → 2-D2

    V Y 150

Pachanga weaves threads of Argentinean, Brazilian, Mexican and Cuban cultures into a stunning tapestry. The decadent Cuban lounge opens out onto a rustic 'courtyard' replete with Corinthian columns and a trio of sizzling South American musicians. Traditional dishes are imaginatively transformed into things of wonder and are presented with flair and style. The overall effect is akin to being entertained in a royal hacienda. You'll pay for the Pachanga experience, but like all great works of art, price is somewhat irrelevant here. ™

Food●●●●○Serv●●●●○Venue●●●●●Value●●●●○

Mediterranean

Other options → **Italian [p.367]**
Spanish [p.392]

Café Insignia

Location → Ramada Hotel · Bur Dubai | 351 9999
Hours → 06:00 – 24:00
Web/email → www.ramadadubai.com   Map Ref → 7-E3

    150

A quaint restaurant with dimmed lighting and soft piano music provides for the ultimate in comfortable settings. Don't misjudge the restaurant by its basic décor; the open kitchen at the rear is a hive of activity with chefs rustling up some wonderful treats for your taste buds. Try the chef's special set menu (a firm favourite) or take a risk and go à la carte. Highly recommended is the delicious, tender steak, or tasty grilled prawns covered in herbs and chilli (generous portions) Don't be surprised if you don't have room for a sweet. ⏺

Food●●●●○Serv●●●◐○Venue●●●●○Value●●●●○

Focaccia

Location → Hyatt Regency · Deira | 209 1234
Hours → 12:30 – 15:00 19:30 – 23:30
Web/email → www.dubai.regency.hyatt.com   Map Ref → 8-D2

V Y 150

The faux Italian country house theme prevails here, as does great hospitality and even greater food. Tuck into warm focaccia bread with delicious

Pachanga

Going Out   Latin American | Mediterranean

looking (and tasting) accompaniments, pre warn your dinner buddies and slather on the grilled garlic cloves to your heart and stomachs content. The staff are beyond congenial and will happily guide you through the fresh and tasty antipasti, fish, meat and pasta. Every room has a different theme (the wine cellar is particularly spectacular) and can be booked out for private parties.⬛

Food⬤⬤⬤⬤○Serv⬤⬤⬤⬤○Venue⬤⬤⬤⬤○Value⬤⬤⬤⬤○

La Villa

Location ➜ Sofitel City Centre · Al Garhoud | 294 1222
Hours ➜ 12:30 – 15:30 19:00 – 23:30
Web/email ➜ www.accorhotels.com   Map Ref ➜ 14-D1

   150

About time your favourite waiter got a pat on the posterior for good service? Prompt a pay raise or promotion by shouting 'good service' from the rooftops! Eat Out Speak Out is the perfect way to get your 'pat' across. Not only will we publish your 'pat' online, we'll also make sure that it is transported straight from your hands to the 'back' of the establishment.

A sitting at La Villa will perhaps not have you reminiscing on your last romantic Mediterranean sojourn, as much you would have imagined. The menu attempts to marry 'a bit of this, a bit of that' from several Mediterranean countries, and sounds tantalising enough; but when served, dishes lack the expected zest associated with this kind of cuisine. The tacky, overly-bright dining area and expensive, predominantly French (this is Sofitel) wine list, give the feeling that this is a bit of a hotel-guest money trap.⬛

Food⬤⬤○○○Serv⬤⬤○○○Venue⬤○○○○Value⬤⬤○○○

Majlis Al Bahar

Location ➜ Burj Al Arab · Umm Suqeim | 301 7600
Hours ➜ 12:00 – 15:00 19:30 – 24:00
Web/email ➜ www.jumeirahinternational.com   Map Ref ➜ 4-A1

300

Opulent yet not ostentatious, the understated Majlis Al Bahar may well be the best way to visit the Burj Al Arab. A fantastic view of the hotel complements the delicious food and the Mediterranean menu offers a wide variety of dishes from pizzas, pastas and seafood to chicken, lamb, veal and more. A trio of excellent roaming musicians entertains diners with an eclectic mix of songs. Relaxing and welcoming, with amiable and informed waiters, the restaurant is luxurious yet comfortable. Non Burj Al Arab guests may only visit the restaurant for dinner.⬛

Food⬤⬤⬤⬤○Serv⬤⬤⬤⬤○Venue⬤⬤⬤⬤○Value⬤⬤○○○

Medzo

Location ➜ Pyramids · Umm Hurair | 324 4100
Hours ➜ 12:30 – 15:00 19:30 – 23:30
Web/email ➜ www.waficity.com   Map Ref ➜ 13-D2

    150

A stylish restaurant that subtly screams class, Medzo is fabulously popular with the chic Dubai set. The service is attentive and the Mediterranean menu offers a wide and creative range of vegetarian, meat and fish dishes to suit all tastes. If puddings are more your thing, then try the white chocolate Tiramisu – like a spoonful of heaven! The candlelit terrace offers a relaxed alfresco dining experience all year round, thanks to its new outdoor air-conditioning. Booking is recommended.⬛

Food⬤⬤⬤⬤○Serv⬤⬤⬤⬤○Venue⬤⬤⬤⬤○Value⬤⬤⬤⬤○

Medzo

Olive House

Location ➜ Nr One Tower · Trade Centre 1 | 343 3110
Hours ➜ 09:00 – 01:00
Web/email ➜ na   Map Ref ➜ 9-A2

 50

Set back from the bustle of Sheikh Zayed road, Olive House provides relaxing surroundings in which to enjoy a meal and good views of the activity of the area. The sofas tempt you to take your time over your food, which – being a mix of Mediterranean and Arabic – suits it perfectly. Try not to fill up on the tiny, fresh hot flat breads served with dips, as the menu offers a tasty and large range of salads,

CHURCHILLS
English Pub

1st floor
Sofitel City Centre Hotel
adjacent to Deira City Centre
Shopping Mall

• Entertainment
• Billiards
• Pub Menu

The only licensed
establishment
in the shopping centre.
(04) 603 8400
12 noon to 2am

Featuring our new
live band

RiX & ChiX
**every night
from 9pm onwards.**
(except Tuesdays)

SOFITEL
ACCOR HOTELS & RESORTS

Sofitel City Centre
HOTEL & RESIDENCE
DUBAI

ACCOR

fish, manesh, meze and other, more interesting dishes. The set meals are particularly good, offering a mix of dishes to share.

Food●●●●○Serv●●●●○Venue●●●●○Value●●●●○

Oregano

Location ➜ Oasis Beach Hotel · Marsa Dubai
Hours ➜ 18:00 – 23:00
Web/email ➜ www.jebelali-international.com   Map Ref ➜ 2-D2

  (150)

Oregano restaurant at the Oasis Beach Hotel is promoted as farmhouse fare with Mediterranean flair, but one meal there and you'll be convinced that this is so much more. The cosy atmosphere and attentive service makes you feel at home as soon as your evening begins. The food is excellent, with dishes from Italy, France and Spain and the choice is impressively dizzying. A pleasant surprise is Oregano's take on family feasting, they take the concept seriously enough to offer a separate menu for children. ●

Food●●●●○Serv●●●●○Venue●●●○○Value●●●●○

Prasinos

Location ➜ Jumeirah Beach Club Resort & Spa   344 5333
Hours ➜ 19:30 – 23:00
Web/email ➜ www.jumeirahinternational.com   Map Ref ➜ 5-D1

  (200)

While the space at Prasinos is airy the atmosphere remains intimate, especially on the terrace where stunning views of the exotic gardens and tranquil Arabian Gulf can be enjoyed. The modern Mediterranean menu blends traditional fare with inventive dishes that both delight and surprise. Favouring seafood, the Grilled King Scallops with Moroccan Tomato

Jam are simply spectacular while the vegetarian options don't compromise on taste. The Chilean musicians add to the authentic aura of this cosmopolitan yet traditional restaurant. ●

Food●●●●○Serv●●●●○Venue●●●●○Value●●●○○

Vu's

Location ➜ Boulevard at Emirate Towers, The   319 8088
Hours ➜ 12:30 – 15:00 19:30 – 24:00
Web/email ➜ www.jumeirahinternational.com   Map Ref ➜ 9-C2

 (250)

There is something about Vu's that makes it stand out from Dubai's fine dining crowd. Maybe it's the way you arrive at this exclusive restaurant, up on the 50th floor, that makes you feel like you're in a private members' club. It could be the intimate approach to lighting, with table lamps that are turned up to read the menu. Or it could just be the exquisite food, sculptured desserts and professional but unpretentious staff. Then there's the fact that it is the highest restaurant in the Middle East boasting a second to none view of Dubai's city lights. ●

Food●●●●○Serv●●●●○Venue●●●●●Value●●●○○

Mexican

Other options ➜ **Tex Mex [p.394]**

Maria Bonita

Location ➜ Nr Spinneys Centre · Umm Suqeim   395 5576
Hours ➜ 08:00 – 23:30
Web/email ➜ na   Map Ref ➜ 5-A2

  (150)

In the short space of time that Maria Bonita has been around, it's proved that real Mexican food

Maria Bonita

Going Out   Mediterranean | Mexican

Middle Eastern

There is no one distinct Middle Eastern or Arabic cuisine, but it is instead a blend of many styles of cooking from the region. Thus, an Arabic meal will usually include a mix of dishes from countries as far a field as Morocco or Egypt to Lebanon and Iran. In Dubai, modern Arabic cuisine tends to be based largely on Lebanese food. Typical ingredients include beef, lamb, chicken, seafood, rice, nuts (mainly pistachios and pine nuts), dates, yoghurt and a range of spices. The cuisine is excellent for meat eaters and vegetarians alike.

Meals usually start with 'meze' - a selection of appetisers served with pita bread, pickles and fresh vegetables, and quite often this can be a meal on its own. The choice can be vast, with as many as 30 on a menu or at a buffet. Popular dishes include 'hummus' (ground chickpeas, oil and garlic), 'tabbouleh' (parsley and cracked wheat salad, with tomato), 'fatoush' (lettuce, tomatoes and grilled Arabic bread), 'fattayer' (small, usually hot, pastries filled with spinach or cottage cheese) and falafel (small deep fried balls of chickpeas and beans).

Charcoal grilling is a popular cooking method, and traditionally dishes are cooked with many spices including ginger, nutmeg and cinnamon. An authentic local dish is 'khouzi' (whole lamb, wrapped in banana leaves, buried in the sand and roasted, then served on a bed of rice mixed with nuts), which is most often available at Ramadan for the evening meal at the end of the day's fast ('Iftar'). It would also have been served at the 'mansaf'; the traditional, formal Bedouin dinner, where various dishes were placed on the floor in the centre of a ring of seated guests.

Other typical dishes include a variety of kebabs and 'kibbeh' (deep-fried balls of mince, pine nuts and Bulgar (cracked wheat). Seafood is widely available, and local varieties include hammour (a type of grouper), chanad (mackerel), beyah (mullet), wahar and shrimps, which are often grilled over hot coals or baked in an oven.

Meals end with Lebanese sweets, which are delicious, but very sweet. The most widely known are 'baklava' (filo pastry layered with honey and nuts) and 'umm Ali' (mother of Ali in English), which is a rich, creamy dessert with layers of milk, bread, raisins and nuts - an exotic bread and butter pudding.

has little to do with Tex Mex. This is the ONLY authentic Mexican restaurant in the city. Recipes are true to tradition and stocked with flavour and fresh ingredients regularly flown in from the motherland. Tacos are made onsite in the noisy kitchen, and add to the homey atmosphere. Everything on the menu is highly recommended, from the freshly made guacamole and the prawn fajitas to the chicken burritos and the finger licking dessert menu. ⊕

Food ●●●●○ Serv ●●○○○ Venue ●●●○○ Value ●●●●○

Moroccan

Other options → **Arabic/Lebanese [p.330]**

Marrakech

Location → Shangri-La Hotel · Trade Centre 1   **343 8888**
Hours → 19:30 – 01:00
Web/email → www.shangri-la.com   Map Ref → 9-A2

Moroccan food may be a little under-represented in Dubai but the rather swish Marrakech proves that quality is better than quantity any day. Salads and perfectly light and flaky bastilla make way for the hearty, rich tagines and couscous dishes. The staff are pleasant and helpful and a reasonably priced wine list covers most continents and grape varieties. Low and cosy armchairs and refined crockery add to the general plushness of the Shangri-La and make for an elegant evening out. ⊕

Food ●●●●○ Serv ●●●●○ Venue ●●●●○ Value ●●●●○

Shoo Fee Ma Fee

Location → Souk Madinat Jumeirah · Umm Suqeim   **366 8888**
Hours → 12:00 – 15:00   19:00 – 23:30
Web/email → www.jumeirahinternational.com   Map Ref → 4-A2

Fine Moroccan food is served in the elegantly appointed interior or on the terrace with wonderful views across the Madinat's waterways. The friendly, authentically garbed staff and traditional music add to the authentic proceedings. The menu is of a very high standard, offering a range of tempting starters and time-honoured mains, alongside other options such as mixed grills. Relax upstairs after dinner for pastries, mint tea and shisha. Highly recommended although vegetarians may be a little disappointed. ™

Food ●●●●○ Serv ●●●●○ Venue ●●●●○ Value ●●●●○

Mexican | Moroccan

Going Out

Tagine

Location → One&Only Palace · Al Sufouh
Hours → 19:00 – 23:30 Mon closed
Web/email → www.oneandonlyroyalmirage.com
399 9999
Map Ref → 3-A2

 150

Tagine is not only a jewel in the crown of the *Royal Mirage*, it is a gem of a restaurant fit for kings. Traditionally garbed waiters are on hand to entertain as well as treat your taste buds with some of the most superb Moroccan fare available. Start with the 'pastilla bil hamam' (pigeon pie topped with cinnamon and icing sugar) or any of the other fabulous starters, then indulge in tagines (stews) or couscous (semolina) dishes. The dessert menu is slightly limited but the excellent 'kenaffa' will ensure you leave completely satisfied. The wine list, as with the place in general, is pricey – but it's not often you treat yourself and Tagine is the most heavenly way to do just that.

Food●●●●○Serv●●●●○Venue●●●●○Value●●●●○

Tagine

Pakistani

Other options → **Indian [p.356]**

Barbecue Delights

Location → Nr Lamcy Plaza · Oud Metha
Hours → 19:00 – 01:00
Web/email → na
335 9868
Map Ref → 10-D4

50

Serving predominantly North Indian, Pakistani and Afghani food, Barbecue Delights is a world away from the yee-ha steak place that its name conjures up. Nestled in what seems to be Oud Metha's growing restaurant strip, just across from Lamcy Plaza, you can slide into one of the sizeable booths and relax after your shopping spree. Deliciously tender kebabs, tea-towel sized naan breads and a variety of delicately spiced curries (the ginger chicken curry is a knockout) are all house specialities worth trying.

Food●●●●○Serv●●●●○Venue●●●○○Value●●●●○

Karachi Darbar

Location → · Various locations
Hours → 04:00 – 02:00
Web/email → na
334 7272
Map Ref → na

 50

A top option for tasty, friendly, and cheap Indo-Pakistani fare, this restaurant chain is a perennial favourite in Dubai. The simple décor, plain menus, and utilitarian settings may not pull visitors off the street, but that's their loss. The no-nonsense but very welcoming service, the range of high-quality food, and the generous portions make these restaurants exceptional. Amazingly, service and food are consistently good across the various branches, which further confirms that this is one local eatery that is worth seeking out.

Other Branches: Karama Shopping Centre, near the large car park (334 7434); Bur Dubai, near HSBC (353 7080); Qusais Road (261 2526); Naif Road, near Hyatt Regency Hotel (272 3755); Al Satwa (349 0202); Hor Al Anz, behind Dubai Cinema (262 5251); Al Qusais, Sheikh Colony (263 2266); Rashidiya (285 9464).

Food●●●●○Serv●●●○○Venue●●○○○Value●●●●●

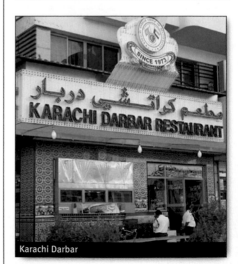
Karachi Darbar

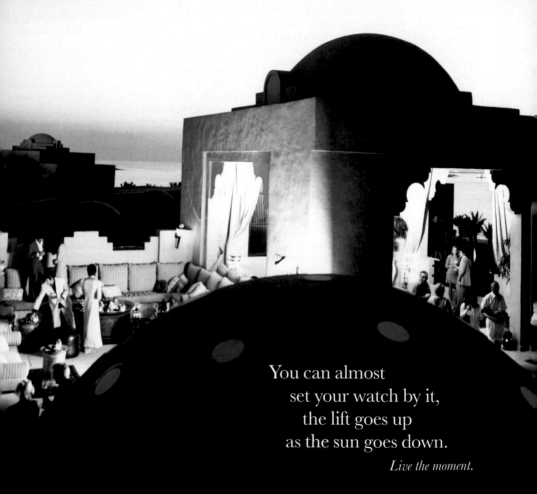

One&Only
Royal Mirage
Dubai

You can almost
set your watch by it,
the lift goes up
as the sun goes down.
Live the moment.

Ravi's

Location → Nr Satwa R/A · Al Satwa |331 5353
Hours → 24 hours
Web/email → na   Map Ref → 6-E4

Satwa's legendary Ravi's is probably the cheapest eatery in the book. This 24 hour Pakistani diner offers a delicious and not too spicy range of curried favourites, such as biryani, alongside more quirky dishes like fried brains. The venue is basic but there is the choice of eating outside in clement weather, dining in the main restaurant or in the quieter 'family' section. The clientele comprises a real mix of people after a quick cheap meal or collecting takeouts. Portions are shareable. Ravi's is perfect for generous curry in a hurry on a budget.⊕

Food●●●○○Serv●●●●○Venue●●○○○Value●●●●○

Persian

Other options → Arabic/Lebanese [p.330]

Al Borz

Location → Al Durrah Tower · Trade Centre 1 |331 8777
Hours → 11:00 – 24:00
Web/email → na   Map Ref → 9-D2

One of Tehran's best kebab houses has finally crossed the Gulf and set up shop on Sheikh Zayed Road, providing Dubai-ites the chance to sample their famous kebabs and rich rice specialities. The lunch buffet is an ideal introduction to Iranian cuisine, including soups and desserts, and is very moderately priced. A family setting and large portions make Al Borz especially popular among natives familiar with Persian fare. If lazy, opt for takeout – the delivery service is timely.⊕

Food●●●○○Serv●●●○○Venue●●●○○Value●●●●○

Pars Iranian Kitchen

Location → Nr Rydges Plaza · Al Satwa |398 4000
Hours → 18:00 – 02:00
Web/email → pars@emirates.net.ae   Map Ref → 7-A4

Pars Iranian Kitchen offers a casual Arabic atmosphere. Listen to Arabic music and enjoy a shisha while the staff bring you a host of appetisers and freshly baked bread. Start with the classics, such as hummus, moutabel, tabbouleh and soups before trying one of their tasty kebabs or grills, accompanied with rice or chips, from the slightly

limited Arabic main course menu. The restaurant has two branches; alfresco dining is available at the Al Diyafah St branch, the branch at the Wilson building (398 8787) offers more luxurious dining inside, with more variety of tasty Persian dishes.⊕

Food●●●○○Serv●●●○○Venue●●●●○Value●●●○○

Red Table

Location → Al Diyafah Street · Al Satwa |345 1222
Hours → 12:00 – 24:00
Web/email → na   Map Ref → 7-A3

Serving excellent Iranian cuisine in huge portions, the *Red Table* is a no-frills diner in the heart of Satwa. Wonderfully tender barbecued Chicken, Lamb and Prawn kebabs are great value, and are offered in a mind-boggling number of different guises. Secluded seating, and attempts at genuine décor are inviting, but the dreadful service, which attracts a 15% surcharge, leaves a bad aftertaste. A nightly Dhs.28 buffet means the crowds come forth nevertheless. Outstanding food makes this is a great option for home delivery.⊕

> ### Hidden Charges
>
> *When the bill arrives, subtly check out the dreaded small print (slyly lurking at the bottom of the bill) that says 'INCLUSIVE +15% +5%'. Be careful what you touch, as you may find that even the most innocent eye contact with a nut bowl can result in surplus charges.*

Food●●●●●Serv●○○○○Venue●●○○○Value●●●●○

Shabestan

Location → Hotel Inter-Continental · Deira |205 7333
Hours → 13:00 – 15:00 19:30 – 23:15
Web/email → www.interconti.com   Map Ref → 8-C4

Elegant and graceful, *Shabestan* welcomes discerning diners with genuine Persian hospitality and sumptuous cuisine. Expertly prepared dips, soups, kebabs and stewed specialities are traditional and authentic; sure to enchant even the most well-travelled palate. The Fesenjan-Ba-Morgh (roasted chicken in ground walnut and pomegranate sauce) is a sweet and savoury sensation, and salvers of tender roasted kebabs are delicious and plentiful. Genuinely warm and attentive service completes a truly memorable evening. If you're looking for a perfect Persian experience, you just found it.⊕

Food●●●●●Serv●●●●●Venue●●●●○Value●●●●○

Pakistani | Persian

Going Out

Shahrzad

Location ➜ Hyatt Regency · Deira | **209 1200**
Hours ➜ 12:30 – 15:30 19:30 – 23:00 Sat closed
Web/email ➜ www.dubai.regency.hyatt.com   Map Ref ➜ 8-D2

   (150)

Shahrzad has been open for seven years, and the dedication to good cooking is evident in the quality of the food, the excellent service and the authenticity of the venue. Beaming waiters can help you choose any one of the traditional dishes, while you enjoy the live music and the interesting appetisers. The menu is dominated by delicious stews and succulent kebabs, all served with mountains of buttery saffron rice. Sadly, the décor is just starting to look its age, although apparently a refurbishment is imminent. ●

Food●●●●●Serv●●●○○Venue●●●●○Value●●●●○

Discount Divas

Dedicated discount lovers should get a copy of The Entertainer, a book full of 'buy one, get one free' vouchers. It costs Dhs.225, but you could save thousands! Call 390 2866 for more information.

Pizzerias

Other options ➜ **Italian [p.367]**

Nothing beats a good pizza, and fortunately you'll find a variety of outlets in Dubai serving this tasty Italian treat. The following table lists places where you'll find great pizza – obviously you'll get pizzas at most Italian restaurants, but those listed below really stand out (marked with an 'R' on the table). Of course, the takeaway pizzas are pretty good too, and we've listed our favourites below (marked with a 'T').

Pizzerias

Biella Caffé Pizzeria (R)	Umm Hurair	324 4666
Casa Mia (R)	Al Garhoud	282 4040
Cucina (R)	Deira	607 7903
Il Rustico (R)	Al Satwa	398 2222
Italian Connection (R)	Oud Metha	335 3001
La Moda (R)	Al Sufouh	391 2550
Pastamania (R)	Al Sufouh	390 8672
Pizza Express (T/R)	Bur Dubai	355 2424
Pizza Express (T/R)	Al Rashidiya	285 2393
Pizza Express (T/R)	Jumeira	359 2463
Pizza Hut (T)	All over Dubai	800 6500
Pizzeria Uno Chicago (R)	Deira	294 8799
Round Table Pizza (T)	Al Satwa	398 6684
Round Table Pizza (T)	Jebel Ali	881 0808
Round Table Pizza (T)	Al Garhoud	282 0666
Round Table Pizza (T)	Al Karama	396 6999

Polynesian

Other options ➜ **Far Eastern [p.348]**

Tahiti

Location ➜ Metropolitan Palace · Deira | **205 1364**
Hours ➜ 12:00 – 15:00 19:30 – 23:30
Web/email ➜ www.methotels.com   Map Ref ➜ 11-D2

   (100)

A small, cosy, rattan decorated restaurant offering theme nights, accompanied by energetic entertainment from the Pacific Islands. Cross the rickety rattan bridge to the food island that consists of seafood, salad and sushi. The choices are quite limited in comparison to other buffet restaurants so opt for a little something special and have the chef cook up fresh fish or prawns the way you like it. The entertainment is a big plus but otherwise this is second rate to the competition. Check out the different theme nights, all you can eat & drink for Dhs.125●

Food●●●○○Serv●●●●○Venue●●●○○Value●●●●●

Trader Vic`s

Location ➜ Crowne Plaza · Trade Centre 1 | **331 1111**
Hours ➜ 12:00 – 15:00 18:00 – 01:30
Web/email ➜ tradervics@crowneplaza.co.ae   Map Ref ➜ 4-A2

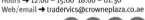 (150)

Please see review under Cocktail Lounges – On the Town [p.421].

Food●●●●○Serv●●●●●Venue●●●●○Value●●●●○

Portuguese

Da Gama

Location ➜ Century Village · Al Garhoud | **282 3636**
Hours ➜ 12:30 – 01:00
Web/email ➜ dagama@emirates.net.ae   Map Ref ➜ 14-C3

  (100)

Located in the courtyard next to Dubai's tennis stadium, Da Gama offers interesting alfresco dining as well as an indoor escape from the blistering summer heat. Although the Portuguese options are far more favourable, the restaurant's menu does include other international dishes and appetisers. The grilled skewers and seafood platter offer good value for money without scrimping on flavour. The efficient service is friendly and accommodating. Da Gama is probably best known for transforming itself into a Lebanese disco on Wednesday and Thursday nights.

Food●●●○○Serv●●●●○Venue●●●●○Value●●●●○

Nando's

Location ➜ Sheik Issa Tower · Trade Centre 1 | **321 2000**
Hours ➜ 12:00 – 02:00
Web/email ➜ headoffice@nandosuae.ae   Map Ref ➜ 9-C2

Nando's is famous for its flame-grilled Peri Peri chicken and sauces, a 'secret' recipe concocted by the Portuguese, with a kick of Africa. From lemon and herb for the novice to the extra-hot Peri Peri for the brave, there is something for everyone. The Chicken Espetada is a popular, fun and healthy choice. The service is speedy and the free top-up of soft drinks a bonus. Nando's provides a meal that is value for money and particularly suited to families.

Other Locations: nr Al Ghurair City (221 1992)
Food●●●○○Serv●●●●○Venue●●●○○Value●●●●○

Russian

Troyka

Location ➜ Ascot Hotel · Bur Dubai | **359 5908**
Hours ➜ 12:00 – 15:00 18:00 – 03:00
Web/email ➜ www.ascothoteldubai.com   Map Ref ➜ 7-E3

Walk into Troyka and it's as though you've walked through the doors to a mini Russia. The colourful wall murals and traditionally dressed staff give the impression of the motherland, and all without any pretension. The menu is extensive, and the staff both knowledgeable and well versed at explaining any queries you may have. Portions are bountiful and flavours traditional, from their fabulous borscht soup to the comfort of the homemade Chicken Kiev. With a diverse menu, interesting tastes and even late-night live entertainment, a unique dining experience awaits you here.

Food●●●○○Serv●●●●○Venue●●●○○Value●●●●○

Seafood

Al Bandar

Location ➜ Heritage & Diving Village · Al Shindagha | **393 9001**
Hours ➜ 12:00 – 01:00
Web/email ➜ na   Map Ref ➜ 8-B1

Its idyllic location on the edge of the Creek is score one for Al Bandar, a terrific venue offering good international seafood for a more dress down clientele. This is the perfect venue to ease guests and visitors into the Arabesque experience and certainly a breath of fresh air from the overwhelmingly plush restaurants in five star hotels that easily stifles Dubai residents. The choice of seafood is pleasantly varied and the prices all cheap and cheerful. Tradition is the theme with the added photographic thrill of the resident camels nearby.

Food●●●○○Serv●●●○○Venue●●●●○Value●●●●○

Al Dahleez

Location ➜ Bldg of Ministry of Justice · Al Garhoud | **282 3922**
Hours ➜ 08:00 – 01:30
Web/email ➜ abt@emirates.net.ae   Map Ref ➜ 8-B1

A refreshingly unpretentious mixture of competing television sets, shuffling playing cards, aromatic shishas, and a lantern-lit grotto where the friendly staff get your orders ready. To dine, the extensive and comprehensive menu offers hot and cold meze, an assortment of shish kebabs, fish dishes and stuffed vegetables. All will satisfy your belly without hurting your wallet. The highlight of this place comes in the guise of its juices, truly scrumptious.

Food●●●○○Serv●●●●○Venue●●●○○Value●●●●○

Al Mahara

Location ➜ Burj Al Arab · Umm Suqeim | **301 7600**
Hours ➜ 12:30 – 15:00 19:00 – 24:00
Web/email ➜ www.jumeirahinternational.com   Map Ref ➜ 4-A1

The experience of dining at Al Mahara begins with a simulated submarine ride that plunges you into a marine-themed wonderland – the

restaurant is curled around an enormous aquarium full of beautifully colourful and diverse fish. The menu is varied and offers some exciting seafood creations, all meticulously prepared by some of Dubai's top chefs. You can opt for a sampler menu, which lets you try all the brilliant dishes, or you can go for the traditional à la carte. An incredible wine list and staff that really care make this one of the Gulf's finest dining experiences. Gentlemen are required to wear a jacket for dinner.

Food ●●●●○ Serv ●●●●○ Venue ●●●●● Value ●●●○○

Amwaj

Location → Shangri-La Hotel · Trade Centre 1 | **343 8888**
Hours → 13:00 – 15:00 20:00 – 24:30
Web/email → www.shangri-la.com Map Ref → 9-A2

This seafood restaurant is everything you might expect from a five star hotel. The décor is a perfect combination of modern and understated, as is the service. Amwaj's menu offers an imaginative range of dishes (predominantly, but not exclusively, seafood), a variety of fresh fish can be done to your taste, with a selection of sauces and accompaniments. Prices are remarkably reasonable, given the quality of this operation. This is a welcome addition to the seafood restaurant fraternity in Dubai.

Food ●●●●○ Serv ●●●●○ Venue ●●●●○ Value ●●●●○

Aquarium

Location → Creek Golf Club · Al Garhoud | **295 6000**
Hours → 12:30 – 15:00 19:30 – 23:00
Web/email → www.dubaigolf.com Map Ref → 14-C2

A huge sparkling tube of coral and brightly coloured reef fish takes centre stage in this light and airy venue. Quality seafood exquisitely presented, efficient service and tranquil waterfront views all make for a memorable dining experience. Start with a lip-smacking lobster bisque, or tender five-spice scallops, then take on a robust seafood platter, or terrific Thermidor. Desserts are delicious and marvellously presented, so leave space! Unique, sophisticated and stylish.

Food ●●●●○ Serv ●●●●○ Venue ●●●●○ Value ●●●○○

Beach Bar & Grill, The

Location → One&Only Palace · Al Sufouh | **399 9999**
Hours → 12:00 – 15:30 19:00 – 23:30
Web/email → www.oneandonlyroyalmirage.com Map Ref → 3-A2

After a tranquil walk through the gardens to reach your destination, the main attraction is the tasteful Moroccan décor, unpretentious seating and thoughtful finishing touches, accompanied by a stunning view of the Arabian Gulf lapping almost at your feet. With an imaginative selection of seafood to choose from, all seafood delights are sampled in one portion of the Portuguese Cataplana – more than sufficient to satisfy two appetites.

Food ●●●●○ Serv ●●●●● Venue ●●●●○ Value ●●●●○

Blues

Location → Marina Walk · Marsa Dubai | **367 4747**
Hours → 11:30 – 23:30 Fri am closed
Web/email → www.damacgroup.com Map Ref → 2-E2

Blues Seafood restaurant is a gem waiting to be discovered at the Dubai Marina. Opened in the summer of 2004, the venue offers an incredible array of fresh seafood. Knowledgeable staff are on hand to advise you on your selection and entice you with a variety of ways to prepare your meal. The food, service and presentation are all top notch. During the cooler months, take advantage of the tables on the terrace, offering some spectacular views of the city.

Food ●●●●○ Serv ●●●●○ Venue ●●●●○ Value ●●●●○

Far East Seafood Market

Location → Regent Palace Hotel · Bur Dubai | **396 3888**
Hours → 12:00 – 15:00 19:00 – 01:00
Web/email → www.ramee-group.com Map Ref → 11-A1

Hook one of the helpful waiters and a basket to trawl the buffet for your ingredients, which will be cooked in the manner and sauce of your choosing. The range of seafood and options for preparation is impressive and the 'all you can eat' options are good value and simplify an otherwise unpredictable pricing process. Smokers get the best seats and the restaurant, in the *Regent Palace Hotel*, has a kind of faded grandeur which may extend to some of the choices on ice.

Food ●●○○○ Serv ●●●●○ Venue ●●●●○ Value ●●●●○

Seafood

Going Out

Fish Market, The

Location ➜ Hotel Inter-Continental · Deira | 205 7333
Hours ➜ 13:00 – 15:00 20:00 – 23:30
Web/email ➜ www.interconti.com   Map Ref ➜ 8-C4

The setting provides a close-up view of the Creek, which is equally spectacular day or night. Service is very personal and well-informed, which you will find is really rather important in fish market restaurants where one often needs some expert guidance on what to buy and how to cook it. They like to brag about their oyster sauce, and quite rightly so. It's simply exquisite, (as is the lobster Thai curry). If budget is not an issue then visits could become habitual (as long as you are immune to Deira traffic), but otherwise a great venue for intimate or special occasions.

Food●●●●○ Serv●●●●○ Venue●●●●○ Value●●●○○

Golden Fork

Location ➜ Various locations · Dubai | 228 2662
Hours ➜ 12:00 – 03:00
Web/email ➜ na   Map Ref ➜ na

If you're craving a healthy, but fast and cheap Asian meal, you'll find it here. The seafood is fresh and the noodles are delicious. For unbeatable value meals, try the omelette or the fried chicken sets for Dhs.7, including free soup. The chain has many locations, some with in-house bakery. Dine at the Diyafah Street location where you can watch the world go by, or try one of the numerous other venues around town. Otherwise, opt for a takeaway and enjoy your meal at home.

Locations: *Nasr Square (221 1895); nr Astoria Hotel (393 3081); Al Riqqa Street (222 9802); Satwa (398 3631)*
Food●●●○○ Serv●●●○○ Venue●●●○○ Value●●●●○

Marina Seafood Market

Location ➜ The Jumeirah Beach Hotel · Umm Suqeim | 406 8181
Hours ➜ 12:30 – 15:00 19:00 – 01:00
Web/email ➜ www.jumeirahinternational.com   Map Ref ➜ 4-B2

Whether you choose to look outside at views of the Burj Al Arab and the Marina, or inside at the interesting underwater world, this splendid seafood restaurant pleases. Fish, oysters and giant shrimp are displayed on ice as well as in tanks, which are also home to lobsters and other crustaceans. The menu extends to fish, scallops, crabs, prawns,

chicken, steak, duck and quail, and there are even some vegetarian options. Be daring and try the fish market, where you select the fresh ingredients for your meal, and then have it cooked to your liking.
Food●●●●○ Serv●●●●○ Venue●●●●○ Value●●●○○

Pierchic

Location ➜ Al Qasr Hotel · Umm Suqeim | 366 8888
Hours ➜ 12:00 – 15:00 19:00 – 23:30
Web/email ➜ www.jumeirahinternational.com   Map Ref ➜ 4-A2

Pierchic is simply a must-do restaurant, not because of the food, (first class seafood but with a little too much emphasis on artistic presentation rather than taste), or because of the service, (which is amiable but a little too relaxed). The main drawcard here is the location - a five minute stroll across a wooden pier, with a breath taking, and unobstructed, view of the Burj Al Arab, leads you to a restaurant which sits atop wooden stilts with the sea lapping beneath you. No words do it justice, you just have to see it to believe it.
Food●●●●○ Serv●●●○○ Venue●●●●● Value●●●○○

Pisces

Location ➜ Souk Madinat Jumeirah · Umm Suqeim | 366 8888
Hours ➜ 12:00 – 15:00 19:00 – 23:30
Web/email ➜ www.jumeirahinternational.com   Map Ref ➜ 4-A2

Tucked away amid the maze-like alleyways of the Souk Madinat, Pisces is a seafood aficionado's paradise. Erring on the side of ostentatious, this intimate modern restaurant embraces low lighting and dining formalities. Fish lovers may be in heaven but otherwise the menu is a little limited. The whole hammour baked in sea salt is gently dissected at your table and while it serves two you certainly won't go hungry. As for the deserts, the chocolate combo is deadly but delicious.
Food●●●●○ Serv●●●○○ Venue●●●○○ Value●●●○○

Sea World

Location ➜ Above Safestway · Al Wasl | 321 1500
Hours ➜ 12:00 – 16:00 19:00 – 23:00
Web/email ➜ www.seaworld-dubai.com   Map Ref ➜ 5-D3

You could be forgiven for thinking that a huge neon lobster on the outside equals tackiness inside, but you would be very, very wrong. This is a top quality venue that offers fresh seafood in clean and pleasantly decorated surroundings, with service to rival the best five star hotels. The concept is simple – choose from the huge iced market stall, and minutes later your Thai-inspired masterpiece appears, transformed from raw to 'give me more'. For a treat, try the Jumbo Prawns fried with Chilli and Garlic – astoundingly good.

Food●●●●○ Serv●●●●○ Venue●●●●○ Value●●●●○

Wharf, The

Location → Mina A'Salam · Umm Suqeim
Hours → 12:00 – 15:00 19:00 – 23:30
Web/email → www.jumeirahinternational.com   Map Ref → 4-A2

366 8888

     150

True to its name and capitalising on its waterside location, The Wharf is bordered by illuminated palm trees, Arabian windtowers and abras gliding by. A predominantly seafood restaurant, it offers innovative cuisine that is both superbly cooked and beautifully presented. While there is a good selection of vintage wines for the adults, the separate children's menu ensures its popularity with families and the pleasant staff aim to please. Inside, the classy restaurant is abuzz with activity while the terrace seems to have a slower pace.

Food●●●●○ Serv●●●●○ Venue●●●●○ Value●●●●○

Singaporean

Other options → **Far Eastern [p.348]**

Peppercrab

Location → Grand Hyatt Dubai · Umm Hurair
Hours → 19:00 – 23:30 Sun closed
Web/email → www.dubai.grand.hyatt.com   Map Ref → 13-E3

317 2222

 250

This place is all about relaxed, comfortable, culinary indulgence with great atmosphere and an open plan kitchen to marvel at the magic of Peppercrab's tasty food. Seafood dominates the menu and if you're not in the mood for crab, frog legs, squid or sushi then you may want to reconsider your choice of venue. Still, what is served here is awesome. Food presentation fits with the oriental theme and is beautifully designed. Service is quick and staff are friendly and attentive. Whether you are looking for a romantic night out, a sophisticated business dinner or an outing with friends, Peppercrab fits all.

Food●●●●○ Serv●●●●○ Venue●●●●○ Value●●●○○

Peppercrab

Singapore Deli Café

Location → Nr BurJuman Centre · Bur Dubai
Hours → 12:00 – 16:00 18:00 – 23:00
Web/email → singapuredeli@yahoo.co.uk   Map Ref → 11-A1

396 6885

  50

When it comes to good home cooking Singaporean style, there's no place like Singapore Deli Café. Each dish is freshly prepared and provides a range of authentic Asian dishes from bowls of steaming noodles to Nasi Goreng. The food is so good here it's not surprising that this place is so popular, particularly with local Indonesian and Malaysian customers. The venue is indeed a small café, creating a casual, intimate atmosphere. Waiting time between dishes is a little longer than usual but for a generous, well-cooked meal at a very reasonable price, give Singapore Deli Café a try.

Food●●●●○ Serv●●●○○ Venue●●●○○ Value●●●●○

Singapura

Location → Oasis Beach Hotel · Marsa Dubai
Hours → 18:00 – 23:00
Web/email → www.jebelali-international.com   Map Ref → 2-D2

399 4444

    100

Kitsch décor sets the pace for this friendly and incredibly casual restaurant. So casual in fact, that the menu doesn't strictly adhere to anything in particular, but Asian treats are European-ised and will suit easy-going taste buds to a T. The staff are incredibly friendly and are only too happy to stop for a chat about the souvenir-style furnishings or help you make your menu selection. They'll even provide both children and adults with traditional Singaporean games.

Food●●○○○ Serv●●○○○ Venue●●○○○ Value●○○○○

Spanish

Other options → **Mediterranean [p.379]**
Tapas Bars [p.429]

Al Hambra

Location → Al Qasr Hotel · Umm Suqeim
Hours → 12:00 – 15:00 19:00 – 23:30
Web/email → www.jumeirahinternational.com
Map Ref → 4-A2

| **366 8888** |

    250

Al Hambra serves Spanish cuisine in a venue reminiscent of an underground cavern, complete with bricks on the ceiling and soft lighting, creating a warm, welcoming mood. Meat lovers are well catered to and the focus is on superb presentation, and quality rather than quantity. With mains being on the smallish side, you should have room for something sweet and the dessert tapas are divine. The outdoor terrace is highly recommended in the winter months; reservations are essential particularly on weekends.

Food●●●●○ Serv●●●○○ Venue●●●○○ Value●●○○○

Seville's

Location → Wafi City · Umm Hurair
Hours → 12:00 – 02:00 Thu & Fri 12:00 – 03:00
Web/email → www.waficity.com
Map Ref → 13-D2

| **324 7300** |

    100

Please see review under Tapas Bars – Going Out [p.429].

Food●●●○○ Serv●●●●○ Venue●●●●○ Value●●●●○

Steakhouses

Other options → **American [p.326]**
Argentinean [p.338]

Exchange Grill, The

Location → Fairmont Dubai, The · Trade Centre 1
Hours → 19:00 – 01:00
Web/email → www.fairmont.com
Map Ref → 9-E1

| **311 8000** |

    250

For sumptuous dining at its best, The Exchange Grill located on the second floor of the Fairmont is the place to get dinner and service fit for a king (or queen). The food is fantastic with steaks cooked to perfection. For seafood lovers try the Oyster Thermidor and wash it all down with an expertly chosen bottle of Moet or an array of delicious wines. If you're not a meat lover expect to be

individually catered for with little room for disappointment. A beautifully set restaurant and superb menu, albeit a little on the pricey side.

Food●●●●● Serv●●●●● Venue●●●●● Value●●●○○

Grill Room, The

Location → Sheraton Jumeirah Beach · Marsa Dubai
Hours → 19:00 – 24:00
Web/email → www.starwood.com
Map Ref → 2-D2

| **399 5533** |

   150

Cosy and unassuming, this is a great alternative to the big name steakhouses in town. The simple menu offers a range of classic fare – the grilled goats cheese and walnut salad is excellent, and enough to share. Australian steaks are top quality, and perfect potato wedges add to your dining pleasure. Get used to plenty of complimentary snacks, and eager, attentive service. Plentiful portions and unpretentious pricing make this place excellent value.

Food●●●●○ Serv●●●●● Venue●●●●○ Value●●●●●

JW's Steakhouse

Location → JW Marriott Hotel · Deira
Hours → 12:30 – 15:00 19:30 – 23:30
Web/email → www.marriott.com
Map Ref → 12-A3

| **262 4444** |

   250

Widely regarded as one of the best in town, JW's Steakhouse impresses with stylish leather luxury and a welcoming, intimate atmosphere. US Angus cuts clearly have the right pedigree, but some are a tad toothsome – stay with fillet if you are intent on tenderness. Fish lovers with deep pockets can indulge in quality crustaceans, and atypical offerings

JW's Steakhouse

Going Out | Spanish | Steakhouses

such as Sako Tuna and Swordfish. Judging by the roll call of brass name plaques affixed to each table, JW's regular crowd of devotees are attached to this place in more ways than one. •JR

Food●●●○○ Serv●●●●○ Venue●●●●○ Value●●○○○

Legends

Location → Creek Golf Club · Al Garhoud | **295 6000**
Hours → 19:00 – 23:00 Fri closed
Web/email → www.dubaigolf.com   Map Ref → 14-C2

Situated on the first floor of the unique clubhouse with private tables upstairs, this modern steakhouse offers you the chance to try international cuisine at its finest. Exemplary standards of service complement the tempting and imaginative flair of the chefs. The venue's unique design, defined by the spectacular leaning tower in the centre of the sail-shaped building, makes the steakhouse a truly legendary dining experience. An impressive wine list and a live pianist add to the overall quality of this establishment. •JR

Food●●●●○ Serv●●●●○ Venue●●●●○ Value●●●●○

M's Beef Bistro
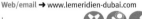

Location → Le Meridien Dubai · Al Garhoud | **282 4040**
Hours → 12:30 – 14:45 20:00 – 23:45 Fri lunch closed
Web/email → www.lemeridien-dubai.com   Map Ref → 14-E3

Meat lovers will be in heaven at M's Beef Bistro, especially with the finest steaks from New Zealand and the US dominating the menu. While there are other less carnivorous options, why come to a steakhouse if you don't want steak? And this cosy bistro arguably has the best tenderloin in town. Portions are generous and the staff very helpful as well as happy to make menu suggestions. All in all, if you love to eat meat, M's is right on the money. •AP

Food●●●●○ Serv●●●●○ Venue●●●●○ Value●●●●○

Manhattan Grill

Location → Grand Hyatt Dubai · Umm Hurair | 317 2222
Hours → 19:30 – 23:30 Fri closed
Web/email → www.dubai.grand.hyatt.com   Map Ref → 13-E3

This sleek, polished restaurant has undergone something of a transformation in recent times. A new chef has revitalised the previously disappointing food, transforming the Manhattan Grill into a truly fine dining venue. While quality cuts of beef are the

prime attraction, exquisite duck, lamb and fish dishes are also star performers. Classic training is evident in the earnest, attentive service, which is thankfully devoid of slick pretension. Choose a comfy red leather booth, start with a classic cocktail, and enjoy the dazzling production. •JR

Food●●●●○ Serv●●●●○ Venue●●●●○ Value●●●○○

Palm Grill

Location → Hotel Inter-Continental · Deira | **205 7333**
Hours → 19:30 – 00:45
Web/email → www.interconti.com   Map Ref → 8-C4

The newly opened Palm Grill at the Intercontinental Hotel knows how to buy, grill, and serve steaks. The meat from Australia, especially the 300-day grain-fed prime beef served as 200g and 300g centre-cut filet mignons, meets standards beyond the dreams of most ordinary meat eaters. The bill shares a similar disposition, so people hunting economy should steer clear. This is a place for those seeking an ethereal experience for what is arguably the best steak in town. •AP

Food●●●●● Serv●●●●● Venue●●●●● Value●●●●○

Rib Room, The

Location → Boulevard at Emirate Towers, The | 319 8088
Hours → 12:30 – 15:00 19:00 – 24:00
Web/email → www.jumeirahinternational.com Map Ref → 9-C2

The tasteful, trendy Rib Room is an obvious choice for red meat lovers, although there are some delicious vegetarian and seafood dishes on the menu too. All main courses are beautifully presented, expertly cooked, and accompanied by a choice of side dishes and succulent sauces. An excellent wine list complements the menu perfectly. The venue is stylish and versatile, and whether you're there for a romantic evening or a business meeting, your guest is sure to be impressed. •CG

Food●●●●○ Serv●●●●○ Venue●●●●○ Value●●●●○

Rodeo Grill

Location → Al Bustan Hotel · Al Garhoud | 705 4620
Hours → 12:00 – 15:00 19:00 – 24:00
Web/email → www.rotana.com   Map Ref → 14-E3

A classy upmarket venue, Rodeo grill is enormously popular for its consistently high food and service quality. Start with delectable chilli

Going Out | Steakhouses

chicken liver and rocket salad, and follow up with a prime hand-cut portion of rib eye, sirloin or tenderloin – guess the correct weight of your meat, and it's on the house! Otherwise choose from excellent pre-cut portions of pepper-crusted fillet, T-bone, or even bison and special Australian "Wagya" Beef, for those with a taste for the exotic. Decadent chocolate fondue rounds off a top quality evening, made even more enjoyable by personal and genuine attention. Top notch.●

Food●●●●●Serv●●●●●Venue●●●●○Value●●●●○

Rodeo Grill

Tex Mex

Other options → **American [p.326]**
Mexican [p.382]

Alamo, The

Location → Dubai Marine Beach Resort · Jumeira | 349 3455
Hours → 12:00 – 15:00 19:00 – 23:30
Web/email → www.dxbmarine.com   Map Ref → 6-D2

 100

If it's a fajita that you're after then coming to the Alamo will serve you well, since here they surpass good and move well into the realm of excellent fare. Heaped platters of beef, chicken, shrimp, or better yet, a combination, will satisfy the most discerning of Tex Mex connoisseurs. Large portions encourage sharing but it may take you a while to get to that stage since the menu is so

extensive, it's hard to choose. The place also pays attention to the finer details with good service, great salsa, superb margaritas and a fun live band. The Friday brunch buffet is famous and draws both families and the hangover crowd.●

Food●●●●○Serv●●●○○Venue●●●○○Value●●●○○

Cactus Cantina

Location → Rydges Plaza Hotel · Al Satwa | 398 2274
Hours → 12:00 – 01:00
Web/email → www.cactuscantinadubai.com   Map Ref → 7-A4

 100

This well known venue has lots to offer and is perfect if it's great Tex Mex fare you crave. Expect crowds on Thursdays with free margaritas for ladies. On other days, the drinks are cheap and Fridays are all about the 'two-for-one' food specials. The food is tasty but typically American style Mexican (refried beans and melted cheese with everything), and portions are *muy grandes*. Feeling the Tequila? In-house salsa classes on Saturday and Sunday nights help you shake it all down. ●

Food●●●●○Serv●●●○○Venue●●●●○Value●●●●○

Cactus Jacks

Location → Millennium Airport Hotel · Al Garhoud | 703 9167
Hours → 11:00 – 15:00 19:00 – 03:00
Web/email → www.millenniumhotels.com   Map Ref → 14-D3

 100

Bright colours and a liberal sprinkling of fake cacti give Cactus Jack's a cartoon-Mexican feel (although we suspect the Stetsoned customer at the bar was not a permanent fixture). The menu features good, if unoriginal, Mexican food, served by cheerfully competent staff and washed down with Margaritas (if you fancy) or something else from the bar (if you don't). There is a pleasant terrace, should the weather be nice. Well worth a try when those Mexican cravings start stirring.●

Food●●●○○Serv●●●●○Venue●●●○○Value●●●○○

Pancho Villa's

Location → Astoria Hotel · Bur Dubai | 353 2146
Hours → 12:00 – 15:00 19:00 – 02:00
Web/email → www.astamb.com   Map Ref → 8-A2

 100

Previously the king of Dubai nightlife, Pancho's has been eclipsed in the chase for the top spot, but still serves decent Mexican food and can be a

Going Out

Steakhouses | Tex Mex

Life's a journey... take a guide

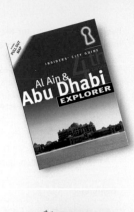

All the info you'll ever need, from where to eat, sleep, shop and socialise, to advice on cutting through red tape and negotiating bureaucracy minefields.

Explorer Insider's Guides are an absolute must for new residents, old residents, tourists and visiting business people alike.

Only available at the best bookstores with the right attitude, as well as hotels, supermarkets, hardware stores or directly from Explorer Publishing.

Passionately Publishing...

EXPLORER
www.Explorer-Publishing.com

Phone (+971 4) 335 3520 · Fax (+971 4) 335 3529
Email Info@Explorer-Publishing.com

lively venue later on for those venturing into the heart of Bur Dubai. The restaurant is usually quiet early in the evenings, when the room can seem a little too large. When it does eventually get going you can expect a quirky mix of guests at the bar. Good for groups and a no frills night of fun. ⚫

Food●●●○○Serv●●●●○Venue●●○○○Value●●●●○

Thai

Other options → **Far Eastern [p.348]**

Benjarong

Location → Dusit Dubai · Trade Centre 2 | 343 3333
Hours → 19:00 – 23:30
Web/email → www.dusit.com Map Ref → 9-A2

  150

Jangly Thai music and heavy furniture are all part and parcel of the Benjarong experience, as are the bright lights of Dubai that make for the perfect backdrop to a sumptuous dinner. A comprehensive menu offers up the usual Thai suspects and the Chef's specials – the Larb Gai (spicy ground meat and roasted rice) is particularly tasty – are all superbly presented, deliciously flavoursome and affordably priced. Complement your meal with any of the wide selection of beers or wines available. ⚫

> ### Privileged!
>
> *Dubai is a great place for discounts so it comes as no surprise that you can get privilege or discount cards. The benefits vary so call to find out what you get and whether you have to pay for the card. The Wafi Advantage Card is a particular favourite as it gives discounts on shopping and restaurants but check with the various hotels for what they offer in the way of privilege cards.*

Food●●●○○Serv●●●●○Venue●●●●○Value●●●●○

Blue Elephant

Location → Al Bustan Hotel · Al Garhoud | 705 4660
Hours → 12:00 – 15:00 19:00 – 23:30
Web/email → www.rotana.com Map Ref → 14-E3

 200

If you were looking for the best far eastern experience in town then you may have just found it. Tables overlooking the fish-filled lagoon add magic to the already buzzing ambience and even the *sawadee* ('welcome' in Thai) from the staff immediately transport you to an authentic oriental world. Expect food of superior quality but for a mind-blowing treat head straight to the Bangkok

Symphony or the Royal Thai Banquet. This place is a local favourite, so be sure to book in advance to avoid disappointment. ⚫

Food●●●●●Serv●●●●●Venue●●●●●Value●●●●○

Lemongrass

Location → Nr Lamcy Plaza · Oud Metha | 334 2325
Hours → 11:15 – 24:00
Web/email → na Map Ref → 10-D4

  100

At Lemongrass the subtle colours and seductive aromas alone justify crossing the street from Lamcy Plaza's jostling parking area. The serene Thai interior and gentle staff herald a splendid kitchen that fulfils its promise. Green papaya salad, crispy egg rolls, fried vegetables, and prawn cakes with tasty sauces; Tom Yam soup filled with prawns, lemon grass, and coriander; green, red, or yellow curry with chicken, prawns, or beef; irresistible smoothies and desserts—all make crossing to Lemon Grass an absolute imperative. ⚫

Food●●●●●Serv●●●●●Venue●●●●○Value●●●●○

Lotus One

Location → Dubai Int'l Convention Ctr · Trade Centre 2 | 329 3200
Hours → 12:00 – 15:00 19:00 – 23:30
Web/email → www.lotus1.com Map Ref → 9-E2

 150

Lotus One is all about the cool. Bucket swings over glass floors, big chichi sofas, split level floors, trendy fabric partitions and the hippest mood lighting you ever did see. But it isn't just the décor, the food is also ultra hip and fuses Thai, Vietnamese and Korean. Tapas or regular size portions of flavoursome, innovative and truly imaginative dishes (try the crispy chicken skins with banana sauce) scream 'tasty chic'. Even without a liquor licence, this place is still cool for cats. ⚫

Food●●●○○Serv●●●●○Venue●●●○○Value●●●●○

PaiThai

Location → Dar Al Masyaf · Umm Suqeim | 366 8888
Hours → 12:00 – 15:00 19:00 – 23:30
Web/email → www.jumeirahinternational.com Map Ref → 4-A2

     250

Set in the impressive surroundings of the Al Qasr hotel, at the Madinat Jumeirah, PaiThai offers contemporary Thai dining. Authentic Thai food lovers may not appreciate the presentation of traditional dishes, which have been infused with

A memorable experience....

...everytime

Over the past two years our restaurants have received over12 prestigous awards... need we say more?

AL BUSTAN ROTANA HOTEL
DUBAI

THERE'S ONE FOR YOU

For reservations and more information call 04-2820000

www.rotana.com

additional ingredients and cooked for Western palettes. However, the unique selling point of the restaurant is definitely the waterfront terrace – where diners can admire the charming Arabesque houses, waterways and bridges, under the sparkling Arabian night sky. While the location may be close to perfect you can expect to pay for it.●

Food●●●○○ Serv●●●○○ Venue●●●○○ Value●●○○○

Royal Orchid

Location → Marina Walk · Marsa Dubai |367 4040
Hours → 10:00 – 24:00
Web/email → orchido4@eim.ae   Map Ref → 2-E2

  50

Situated in Marina Walk, Royal Orchid offers decent, well-priced Thai and Chinese food in this up and coming part of town. Sister to the successful Abu Dhabi restaurant, waterside dining provides views over the marina while the interior is nicely done, with dining areas spread onto two floors. The full size windows provide inside diners with a view, so for more privacy sit more towards the interior. A good range of Chinese and Thai food doesn't disappoint, while the Mongolian barbecue allows diners to customise meals to their tastes.●

Food●●●○○ Serv●●●●○ Venue●●●●○ Value●●●●○

Discount Divas

Dedicated discount lovers should get a copy of The Entertainer, a book full of 'buy one, get one free' vouchers. It costs Dhs.225, but you could save thousands! Call 390 2866 for more information.

Sukhothai

Location → Le Meridien Dubai · Al Garhoud |282 4040
Hours → 12:30 – 14:45 19:30 – 23:45
Web/email → www.lemeridien-dubai.com   Map Ref → 14-E3

      150

Sukhothai offers one of the most authentic Thai experiences in Dubai. Staff don traditional silk costumes and delicately deliver the culinary artwork of award winning chef, Khun Chitlada Thanomsok. The Tom Yam Kung, Chicken in Pandan Leaf, and enormous River Prawns are irresistible, while the Red Duck Curry with Lychees is a savoury yet sweet sensation. Elegant teak décor and veritable South East Asian treasures add to your sensory experience. Save your airfare, Sukhothai is Dubai's very own Thai paradise.●

Food●●●●○ Serv●●●●● Venue●●●●○ Value●●●○○

Sukothai

Thai Chi

Location → Pyramids · Umm Hurair |324 4100
Hours → 12:00 – 15:00 19:30 – 24:00
Web/email → www.waficity.com   Map Ref → 13-D2

    100

A full Chinese and a full Thai kitchen, with ingredients freshly imported from their respective homelands, ensure delicious aromas and tastes at Thai Chi. Each kitchen has a separate dining room; the relaxed bamboo-filled Chinese room leads on to the more formal and luxurious Thai room. Both menus are available in each dining room, making Tai Chi the perfect place for indecisive groups. Set menus and sampler plates allow diners to experiment, and the friendly staff are happy to assist when it comes to making difficult decisions.●

Food●●●●○ Serv●●●●● Venue●●●●○ Value●●●○○

Thai House

Location → Al Ain Centre · Bur Dubai |351 8808
Hours → 11:30 – 23:30
Web/email → na   Map Ref → 8-A4

 50

Inspecting computers in Al Ain Centre clicks a direct link to Thai House. Rich rewards come from browsing a menu more satisfying than Microsoft's - superb salads, soups, and satays, fragrant red or green curries, crisply fried whole hammour, braised prawns in red curry paste and coconut milk, and, best of all, herbal marinated roasted duck with a perfect complementary sauce. Expect nothing fancy, just a clean, well-lit establishment pleasantly serving generous portions of wonderful Thai food.

Food●●●●○ Serv●●●○○ Venue●●●○○ Value●●●●●

Thai Time

Location → Village Mall · Jumeira
Hours → 11:00 – 23:00   Fri 12:30 – 23:00 Fri am closed
Web/email → enquiries@thevillagedubai.com   Map Ref → 6-C2

344 8034

Ⓥ 100

Don't be put off by Thai Time's somewhat unfortunate location in The Village Mall – while the venue may lack ambience, the delicious, authentic food is what will transport you away from the hectic activity of daily life. If you are a Thai food rookie, the heavenly tastes you'll find here could make an addict out of you; and seasoned connoisseurs won't be disappointed.

Food●●●●○ Serv●●●●● Venue●●●○○ Value●●●●○

White Orchid

Location → Jebel Ali Golf Resort & Spa
Hours → 19:00 – 23:00   Sun closed
Web/email → www.jebelali-international.com   Map Ref → 1-A1

883 6000

🔊 🍴 ✏ Ⓥ 🍷 100

Once considered almost another time zone, the spread of Dubai has now brought Jebel Ali and restaurants such as White Orchid within easy reach of the city. Enjoy top quality far eastern food in special surroundings and the resort style atmosphere. The terrace is especially recommended, as is a stroll around the gardens before your meal to set the mood. The menu comprises authentic and superb tasting Thai and Chinese dishes as well as other Asian faves.

Service is accomplished and super friendly, the whole experience very enjoyable and well worth the drive.

Food●●●●○ Serv●●●●● Venue●●●●○ Value●●●●○

Turkish

Other options → **Arabic/Lebanese [p.330]**

Topkapi

Location → Taj Palace Hotel · Deira
Hours → 12:00 – 16:00   19:00 – 23:30
Web/email → www.tajpalacehotel.ae   Map Ref → 11-D2

223 2222

🔊 Ⓥ 100

Located in the *Taj Palace Hotel*, a trip to Topkapi requires a bit of a road rage ride to get to the middle of downtown Deira. In its favour, this is the only Turkish restaurant in Dubai. The menu will seem familiar since this is more Arabic with a Turkish twist. The venue is only true to its roots with an Istanbul style interior and waiters in national Turkish dress. The food is average but the prices are certainly affordable and the everyday buffet is a particular bargain.

Food●●●○○ Serv●●●○○ Venue●●●○○ Value●●●●○

Vegetarian

Vegetarians should be pleasantly surprised by the range and variety of cuisine available in restaurants in Dubai. For its size, Dubai offers more choice than cities in most other countries. Arabic food, although dominated by meat in the

Sundown at the Boardwalk

main courses, offers a staggering range of meze, mostly vegetarian, and the general affection for fresh vegetables provides enough variety to satisfy even the most ravenous diner. Also, due to the large number of Indians who are vegetarian by religion, numerous Indian vegetarian restaurants offer so many styles of cooking and such a range of tasty dishes, that Indian cuisine is hard to beat.

In other restaurants, most outlets now offer at least one or two veggie dishes. Highlights include loads of excellent Italian, Mexican, Far Eastern and International restaurants all over the city, as well as Cafés, often the best chance of finding inventive and delicious vegetarian dishes.

A word of warning: if you are a strict veggie, confirm that your meal is completely meat free. Some restaurants cook their 'vegetarian' selection with animal fat or on the same grill as the meat dishes. Also, in some places you may need to check the ingredients of seemingly vegetarian items.

Vietnamese

Other options → Far Eastern [p.348]

Hoi An

Location → Shangri-La Hotel · Trade Centre 1 | 343 8888
Hours → 19:30 – 01:00
Web/email → www.shangri-la.com   Map Ref → 9-A2

One of the few Vietnamese restaurants in Dubai, though we suspect a little adapted for local taste, this restaurant is worth experiencing. An elegant environment with exceptionally well advised staff help guide you through the menu choice. The dishes are well presented with attention to detail, and the end result is both mouth watering and unusual. Definitely a place worthy of a visit if you fancy something that little bit different.

Food●●●●○ Serv●●●●○ Venue●●●●○ Value●●●●○

Indochine

Location → Grand Hyatt Dubai · Umm Hurair | 317 2222
Hours → 19:00 – 23:30   Mon closed
Web/email → www.dubai.grand.hyatt.com   Map Ref → 13-E3

This popular Vietnamese restaurant rates highly for its authentic cuisine and the bamboo décor brings out its oriental splendour. The staff are extremely genial and the service is quick and efficient. Expect a menu packed with excellent quality traditional Vietnamese fare. Worth a try

are any of the set menus, complete with starters, main courses, fresh fruits and an exquisite selection of teas; a deal that is fabulously good value for money. This venue's version of Vietnamese cooking is perfect for aficionados of pure Asian flavours.

Food●●●●○ Serv●●●●○ Venue●●●●○ Value●●●●○

Dinner Cruises

Other options → **Boat & Yacht Charters [p.260]**
Creek Tours [p.155]
Dhow Charters [p.266]

Al Boom Tourist Village

Location → Nr Al Garhoud Bridge · Umm Hurair | 324 3000
Hours → 20:00 – 22:30
Web/email → www.alboom.co.ae   Map Ref → 14-A3

Leaving from the Al Boom Tourist Village, the old dhow works its way languidly up and down the Creek. Assortments of Arabic appetisers are laid waiting at your table – hummus, fattoush and whatever else the chef has prepared – to whet your appetite. A fair size BBQ platter follows with something to tempt and please everyone; kebabs, chicken, fish, prawns and even lobster are served, followed by a colourful assortment of Arabic sweets and scrumptious desserts. Sitting on the deck provides a better view but it can get a little hot in summer. The regular Dinner Cruise costs just Dhs.100 per person and includes beverages.

Food●●○○○ Serv●●○○○ Venue●●●●○ Value●●●○○

Al Mansour

Location → Hotel Inter-Continental · Deira | 205 7333
Hours → 13:30 – 15:00   20:30 – 23:00
Web/email → www.interconti.com   Map Ref → 8-C4

Indulge in a nicely prepared Arabic buffet while cruising along the Creek. Diners board the well maintained, traditional wooden dhow at set sailing times in the afternoon and evening, and relax upstairs on the open-air deck or down below in the windowed buffet area. The views are spectacular, the food adequate. Friendly, almost eager, staff cater to all whims and live Arabic music, a majlis and shisha complete the experience. This is a fantastic option for newcomers or guests from out-of-town.

Food●●○○○ Serv●●●○○ Venue●●●○○ Value●●○○○

A Unique Dinner Cruise Experience

Step aboard the Bateaux Dubai for a voyage as inspiring as the city

Treat yourself to a stunning 360° view of the glimmering sights along the Dubai Creek while savouring your selection of freshly prepared specialities from an outstanding gourmet menu.

Experience a unique dinner cruise complemented by an extensive selection of beverages and personalised service amidst the modern décor, exquisite ambience, air-conditioned comfort and glass-enclosed splendour of the luxurious Bateaux Dubai.

For more information or table reservations please call +971 4 337 1919.

bateaux dubai

A MEMBER OF

JEBEL ALI INTERNATIONAL
HOTELS
A TRADITION OF HOSPITALITY AND EXCELLENCE

www.jebelali-international.com

Bateaux Dubai

Location → Nr British Embassy · Bur Dubai |337 1919
Hours → See below
Web/email → www.bateauxdubai.com   Map Ref → 8-C4

 200

Cutting through the creek in this shiny glass covered cruiser is a brilliant way to entertain out-of-towners or just to spoil yourself. The ex-Orient Express chef has swapped rail for sail and knows well how to work a small galley kitchen. The mainly French menu is small but still manages to confound you with tempting choices that are quite a few notches above the standard cruise buffets. Of course, the vistas are great but it's the food and service that will warrant a return trip. ●
Food●●●●○ Serv●●●●○ Venue●●●●● Value●●●●○

Creek Cruises

Location → Nr DCCI · Deira |393 9860
Hours → 20:30 – 22:30
Web/email → www.creekcruises.com   Map Ref → 11-C2

 150

Surf the Dubai waters as you delve into an authentic buffet meal catered for by a four star hotel, and enjoy the swaying rhythms of live musicians and a talented bellydancer. Then relax and take in the sights along the Creek. The cost of one such evening is Dhs.150 per person. The cruise starts at 20:30 and lasts for about two hours. Here's an idea – cater a private party (from 20 – 200 persons) and design your own genuinely remarkable dinner experience.●
Food●●●●○ Serv●●●●○ Venue●●●●○ Value●●●●○

Creekside Leisure

Location → Opp Dubai Municipality HQ · Deira |336 8406
Hours → Timings on request
Web/email → www.tour-dubai.com   Map Ref → 11-C1

 100

This floating majlis offers a unique view of Dubai by the Creek. Take in the marvellous city skyline while tucking into an international style buffet, and all at a reasonable price. Staff are prompt and friendly. Regardless of whether you're a resident or an out of towner, your stay in Dubai is not complete without the dinner cruise experience aboard Creekside Leisure. Certainly impressive!●
Food●●●●○ Serv●●●●○ Venue●●●●○ Value●●●●○

Danat Dubai Cruises

Location → Nr British Embassy · Bur Dubai |351 1117
Hours → 08:00 – 18:30
Web/email → www.danatdubaicruises.com   Map Ref → 8-C4

 50

Enjoy a sumptuous five star international buffet dinner under the stars and take in the sparkling lights of Dubai as you sail down the Creek. Evening cruises feature a range of dishes with a live cooking station and entertainment, including music and a dance floor. If you're looking for a non traditional Arabian dhow cruise experience, this is the one to choose.●

Costs: Dhs.195; children Dhs.120. (5 -12 years) Timings: Departs at 20:30; returns at 23:00. Otherwise choose the traditional Arabian dhow 'Taste of Arabia' dinner cruise.

Timings: Departs at 20:15; returns at 22:15
Food●●●●○ Serv●●●○○ Venue●●●●○ Value●●●○○

Al Boom Tourist Village

Cafés & Coffee Shops

Other options → **Afternoon Tea [p.410]**

Dubai is a wonderful city for those who love café culture – take a break from work or shopping, relax with the newspapers, a cup of tea and a croissant, or simply enjoy the chance to catch up on gossip with friends. The numerous cafés around the city vary from outlets that border on being a restaurant and serve an excellent variety of cuisine, to those that have more of a coffee and cake approach.

Due to the limitations on serving alcohol outside of hotels and certain clubs, plus the high number of people who do not drink alcohol, cafés enjoy a popularity here that they do not perhaps have in other parts of the world. The following section encompasses cafés, coffee shops, icecream parlours, and Internet and shisha cafés.

A'Rukn

Location → Souk Madinat Jumeirah · Umm Suqeim | 366 8888
Hours → 10:00 - 23:00
Web/email → www.jumeirahinternational.com   Map Ref → 4-A2

With indoor and outdoor seating next to the theatre at Madinat Jumeirah, A'Rukn makes a refreshing change from chain cafés. The beer and wine on the menu are ideal for an intermission tipple or after a stroll around the souk, and the huge variety of coffees is too good to pass up. They're perfect to complement the assortment of cakes, and you can choose from different syrups for a custom-made brew. Shisha is also available outdoors.⊙

Food●●●●○Serv●●●●○Venue●●●●○Value●●●○○

Axis

Location → Hilton Jumeirah · Marsa Dubai | 399 1111
Hours → 09:00 - 00:30
Web/email → www.hilton.com   Map Ref → 2-D2

Do yourself a favour and pop into the Hilton's Axis lounge lobby for a quick glass of grape or golden nectar followed by a light snack. Watch the busy human traffic in the lobby as you hide discreetly behind the palms dotted around its perimeter. Indulge in the cheesecake or chocolate brownie, but expect the guilt-trip that follows these sinful treats. While away a couple of hours people watching with soothing music and waterfall noises to help you forget whatever it was you had planned for later. ⊙

Food●●●○○Serv●●●●●Venue●●●○○Value●●●●○

Basta Art Café

Location → Bastakiya · Bur Dubai | 353 5071
Hours → 10:00 - 20:00
Web/email → bastaartcafe@yahoo.com   Map Ref → 8-B3

The courtyard of the Basta Art Café is a quiet sanctuary amidst the frenzy of the Bastakiya area. Sit on majlis style low cushions, or under one of the white cotton canopies while you look through the rustic menu. The food here really stands out from other Dubai cafés, since it's prepared with healthy eating in mind. Each menu item bears a description of what vitamins and minerals it contains, as well as the calorie count.

A new branch is opening in the Arabian Ranches in January 2005.⊙

Food●●●○○Serv●●●○○Venue●●●●○Value●●●●○

Bistro 21

Location → 21st Century Tower · Trade Centre 2 | 343 0777
Hours → 07:30 - 01:00
Web/email → bistro21@eim.ae   Map Ref → 9-B2

Its location on the constantly busy Sheikh Zayed Road makes this the perfect place to sit, relax and watch the world go by. The menu is as delicious as it sounds so expect your well intentioned quick coffee session to roll into a full on meal. Choose from burgers and bagels, focaccias and bouillabaisses, crab cakes and rasta pasta, and more. Though it gets busy the service never falters and the staff remain impressively attentive and quick to respond.⊙

Food●●●●●Serv●●●●○Venue●●●●○Value●●●●●

Café Ceramique

Location → Town Centre · Jumeira | 344 7331
Hours → 08:00 - 24:00
Web/email → www.café-ceramique.com   Map Ref → 5-E1

Regardless of whether you are an up-and-coming Van Gogh, or just searching for the perfect bagel, Café Ceramique adds an interesting twist to the typical café experience. Whether it is designer bagels, gourmet sandwiches, all-day breakfasts, or speciality teas, there is always something good to eat either on its own, or as you paint your ceramic masterpiece. While there are lots of special events for young and old, the service, perhaps like your art, is a work in progress.⊙

Food●●●●○Serv●●○○○Venue●●●●○Value●●●○○

Going Out | Cafés & Coffee Shops

Café Mozart

Location ➜ Nr Carlton Tower Htl · Deira
Hours ➜ 08:00 - 23:00
Web/email ➜ na

| **221 6565**

Map Ref ➜ 8-C4

Relaxed and calm, Café Mozart is a handy retreat from the busy streets of Deira. Set up by Austrian-born Suzan nine years ago, this café is quaint and welcoming, if a little kitsch, with Mozart-o-rama adorning the walls. Curiously, it also serves Thai food from a comprehensive menu, somewhat skewing the Vienna theme. Otherwise, there's a typical café range of sandwiches, salads, some main courses and cakes etc, the latter being most tempting. The café also undertakes private parties and outside catering.

Food●●●○○Serv●●●○○Venue●●●○○Value●●●○○

Costa

Location ➜ Mercato · Jumeira
Hours ➜ 08:00 - 22:00
Web/email ➜ www.mmidubai.com

| **344 5705**

Map Ref ➜ 5-E1

Though a chain of coffee shops, Costa is still able to offer patrons the perfect brew as well as an ideal location for a get together and a chat. Fashionable bucket seats allow you to take the weight off your feet and relax as your goodies arrive at your table. Fresh pastries, salads, sandwiches and other snacks complement the long list of trendy tea and coffee blends.

Other locations: *Bin Sougat Centre (286 1992); Century Village (286 9216); City Tower II, Shk Zayed Rd (331 2499); Deira City Centre (294 0833); DNATA Airline Centre, Shk Zayed Rd (321 0978); Dubai International Airport (Viewers Gallery - 220 0179 & Terminal 2 299 6358); Dubai International Airport (Concourse I 220 0224 & II - 220 0225); Dubai Internet City (391 8896); Madinat Jumeirah (368 6199); Ibn Battuta Shopping Mall (still to open); Greens Centre, The (368 3385)*

Food●●●○○Serv●●●○○Venue●●●○○Value●●●○○

Elements

Location ➜ Wafi City · Umm Hurair
Hours ➜ 10:00 - 02:00 Fri 12:00 - 02:00
Web/email ➜ www.thomaskleingroup.com

| **324 4252**

Map Ref ➜ 13-D2

Elements is a relaxed upmarket, minimalist venue with a tasteful, discreet air-conditioned terrace seemingly suspended amongst the palm trees. The broad menu offers a fusion of good café fare with sushi and tapas, all generously sized portions, packed with flavour. You can also select your choice

of fish, meat or pasta, pick a sauce and have a dish created to your taste. An equally vast drinks menu provides a choice including Moroccan teas, Turkish coffees and a great range of fruit cocktails. They also occasionally have special themed menus and even shisha pipes with fresh fruit.

Food●●●○○Serv●●●○○Venue●●●●○Value●●●●○

French Connection

Location ➜ Wafa Tower · Trade Centre 1
Hours ➜ 07:00 - 24:00 Fri breakfast all day
Web/email ➜ na

| **343 8311**

Map Ref ➜ 9-A2

Looking for a hotspot with your hot coffee? French Connection can even entice you to stay with a surprisingly good lunch menu. The sandwiches are served on gorgeous bread, reminding patrons that FC is a bakery at heart. There is a tempting variety of food to choose from, served to you in cool, bright surroundings. Indulge in the deliciously crumbly croissants and feel free to linger with anything from a newspaper to a laptop, convenient wireless access to the Internet is available here, as is an ample supply of magazines for technophobes.

Too much pepper in your prawn balls... and the muscle bound chef looks like he wouldn't take criticism lightly? Smile politely, go home, and log on to Eat Out Speak Out. Rant and rave to your heart's content! We'll not only publish your comments, we will also pass them on to the chef - anonymously of course...

Food●●●○○Serv●●●○○Venue●●●○○Value●●●○○

French Connection

Cafés & Coffee Shops

Going Out

Fresh

Location → Dubai Internet City · Al Sufouh
Hours → 08:00 - 17:00   Friday closed
Web/email → na

391 6768

Map Ref →3-B3

 50

A recent addition to Internet City's eateries, Fresh serves a tasty selection of wraps, salads and smoothies, as well as sushi prepared by the chefs at sister restaurant Sushi Sushi. There's ample indoor and outdoor seating, you can takeaway if you're in a hurry, or they deliver if you can't tear yourself away from your desk.⊙⊙⊙

Food   na   Serv   na   Venue   na   Value   na

Gerard

Location → Magrudy's Shopping Mall · Jumeira
Hours → 07:00 - 23:30
Web/email → gerard07@emirates.net.ae

344 3327

Map Ref → 6-C2

 50

If you're in the mood for a relaxing yet 'happening' spot to sit and watch the world go by, then grab yourself a seat at Gerard. This well located patisserie has a scrumptious showcase of flaky croissants, fruit-filled Danish pastries and chocolate covered dates - a display which is sure to satisfy. Grab a friend, or a good book, and enjoy a leisurely cappuccino and pastry at one of Dubai's oldest and best-known French patisseries.

Other locations: Al Ghurair City (222 8637)⊙⊙
Food●●●○○Serv●●●○○Venue●●●●○Value●●●●○

Lime Tree Café

Location → Nr Jumeira Mosque · Jumeira
Hours → 07:30 - 20:00
Web/email → limetree@emirates.net.ae

349 8498

Map Ref → 6-D2

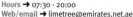 50

This funky café, an oasis of green both inside and out, is the buzzing hub of café culture in Jumeira. Always thronged with diners, the justifiably popular menu rotates daily to offer even regular patrons different choices from the tantalising selection of creative quiches, sandwiches, salads, savoury muffins and other delectables from the counter. For sweet-tooths, their smoothies, shakes and devilishly delicious cakes and cookies are all worth leaving room for. Vegetarians may need to check ingredients before ordering. A place that's definitely too good to leave just for Jane! ⊙⊙

Food●●●●○Serv●●●○○Venue●●●●○Value●●●●○

More

Location → Nr Welcare Hospital · Al Garhoud
Hours → 08:00 - 22:00
Web/email → www.morecafe.biz

283 0224

Map Ref → 14-D4

 50

Once seekers of More's great fare discover that 'next to Welcare' means hidden behind the supermarket, no obstacle to satisfaction remains. Take in and appreciate some of the most unique décor to Dubai in minimalist, industrial chic style. The food itself is in its own league. So-called starters – gallons of soup or bushels of basil dressed spinach almost concealed by roasted pumpkin and pine nuts – should be enough to convince anyone not captured by the More mantra. Don't be phased by the sometimes notorious service, the staff do try but during busy periods seem to suffer memory lapses.⊙⊙

Food●●●●○○Serv●●●○○Venue●●●●○Value●●●●○○

More

Panini

Location → Grand Hyatt Dubai · Umm Hurair
Hours → 08:00 - 01:00
Web/email → www.dubai.grand.hyatt.com

317 2222

Map Ref → 13-E3

 50

People hungry for sandwiches will do well to spend Dhs.28 at Panini in the Grand Hyatt. From a menu bursting with lists of meats, cheeses, vegetables, and condiments, the prospective

COSTA

Italian about Coffee

Ajman City Centre
Bin Sougat Centre
Carrefour, Airport Road, Abu Dhabi
City Tower 2, Sheikh Zayed Road
Deira City Centre
Dnata Travel Centre
Dubai International Airport – Departures Concourse
Dubai International Airport – Terminal 2
Dubai International Airport – Viewers Gallery
Dubai Internet City, Building 3
Gardens Shopping Mall
Souq Madinat Jumeirah
Mercato Mall
Sharjah City Centre
The Greens

COSTA
SINCE 1971
COFFEE

sandwich eater names the ingredients, and straight away they appear, enclosed between 200 square centimetres of a heavenly bun, manageably soft and flat, pleasantly substantial and crusty. Served with simply dressed greens, bearing tiny pickled onions and cucumbers, the sandwich extends the Italian notion of Panini far beyond its traditional excellence.●

Food●●●●○ Serv●●●●○ Venue●●●●○ Value●●●●●

Panini

Paul

Location → Mercato Mall · Jumeira
Hours → 08:00 - 23:00
Web/email → na

344 3505

Map Ref → 5-E1

Ⓥ 50

Paul Café raises the bar in terms of shopping mall eateries – the calmness of the European style interior is a welcome break from the hustle and bustle of Mercato. The food is hearty and healthy, with soups, salads and sandwiches topping the bill. Make sure you save plenty of room for Paul's speciality though – there is a huge selection of delectable French patisserie that are sinfully rich but irresistible. Service can be on the slow side, so give it a miss if you're in a hurry.●

Food●●●●● Serv●●●○○ Venue●●●●○ Value●●●●○

Pronto

Location → Fairmont Dubai, The · Trade Centre 1
Hours → 07:00 - 23:00
Web/email → www.fairmont.com

311 8000

Map Ref → 9-E1

Ⓨ 50

Pronto Deli is the perfect place for everything from power lunching to simply enjoying a coffee with

friends on the Sheikh Zayed strip. This gourmet café/deli offers a mouth-watering array of European meats and cheeses, patisserie, boulangerie, pralines, truffles, and market fresh dishes with a regional flair, for eating-in, or takeaway. A selection of beer and wine is also available and at reasonable prices. The opulent surrounds and excellent staff service make this a great place to indulge in true deli-style.●

Food●●●●○ Serv●●●●● Venue●●●●○ Value●●●●○

Shakespeare & Co.

Location → Al Attar Business Tower · Trade Centre 2
Hours → 07:00 - 01:30
Web/email → shakesco@emirates.net.ae

331 1757

Map Ref → 9-B2

🍴 Ⓥ 50

The only thing that this venue shares with its namesake in Paris is a truly eclectic concept. Something of an insider haunt, the food is good and the ambience relaxing. Choosing between the charmingly rustic interior and the terrace is the first challenge; choosing a meal from the diverse menu is another. Arabic, Moroccan, and some continental dishes appear (sometimes slowly) out of the smallish kitchen, destined to delight. Other branches are situated around town, and it's well worth visiting these to see if they maintain the same standards as the main restaurant.●

> **Flash Carry!**
>
> *If you're feeling flash, you can rent a stretch Hummer or Lincoln from Dubai Exotic Limo [p.45] to arrive at your destination in style.*

Other locations: *Gulf Towers (335 3335); Safa Centre nr Park n' Shop (394 1121); The Village Shopping Centre (344 6228).*

Food●●●●○○ Serv●●●●○ Venue●●●●○ Value●●●●○○

Square, The

Location → Wafi City · Umm Hurair
Hours → 10:00 - 23:00   Fri am closed
Web/email → www.waficity.com

324 2543

Map Ref → 13-D2

Ⓥ 50

Located bang in the middle of the upmarket Wafi City shopping mall, The Square is very much a place to see and be seen. A split level café/restaurant offers comfy chairs and coffee on the lower level with a more formal dining setting at the back. The quality on offer matches the upmarket chic you learn to expect from Dubai eateries. Not cheap for a bite to eat while shopping, but you get what you pay for. The Chicken and Mushroom pie is highly recommended.●

Food●●●●○ Serv●●●●○ Venue●●●●○ Value●●●●○○

Going Out   Cafés & Coffee Shops

T-Junction

Location ➜ The Boulevard at Emirates Towers | 330 0788
Hours ➜ 08:00 - 23:00
Web/email ➜ www.thomaskleingroup.com | Map Ref ➜ 9-C2

  50

The modern décor, bursting with orange and yellow tones, gives you a cheerful welcome to the T Junction. This tea bar leans heavily on the tea theme, and tea, in its many forms, finds its way into nearly every drink and dish on the menu. If you're peckish, try the salads or sandwiches, some of which feature chicken cooked in green tea (interesting and quite pleasant!). The signature drinks should not be missed - Spice Cha' (Assam tea infused with sweet spices), Cha'latte (Assam tea infused with ginger and orange) or Berry T Licious (a blend of teas and berry juices). ⓐⓟ

Food●●●◐○ Serv●●●●○ Venue●●●◐○ Value●●●◐○

T-Junction

THE One

Location ➜ Nr Jumeira Mosque · Jumeira | 342 2499
Hours ➜ 09:00 - 22:00   Fri 14:00 - 22:00
Web/email ➜ www.theoneme.com | Map Ref ➜ 6-D2

   50

With definitely one of the best reading menus of any eatery in town, this is fine dining, café style. Pleasantly appointed with decent views from the windows, the triple menu is an interesting concept and a mouth-watering read, offering a great variety of fantastic food from the clearly imaginative and talented chefs - far from just an in-store coffee shop. Vogue and Chic offer traditional or refined choices, while the Risque menu has to be sampled

with its unique versions of classic dishes. A meal from any menu will delight, definitely a place where one visit is not enough. ⓣⓜ

Food●●●●○ Serv●●●●○ Venue●●●◐○ Value●●●●○

West One

Location ➜ Jumeirah Centre · Jumeira | 398 7177
Hours ➜ 07:30 - 20:00
Web/email ➜ na | Map Ref ➜ 6-C2

   50

This refreshingly casual, café style eatery is a great place for a light meal or a quick sandwich on the run. The food is tasty and fresh, the service fast and friendly, and with a set lunch starting from Dhs.25, it's also good value. Now at a new location, the menu too has undergone a makeover, with kids' meals, a Friday brunch and 24 hour delivery. However, their speciality is outside catering – from corporate functions to private cocktail parties; they'll tailor make menus to suit any occasion. ⓣⓜ

Food●●●●○ Serv●●●●○ Venue●●●○○ Value●●●●○

Zyara Café

Location ➜ Nr Al Salam Tower · Trade Centre 1 | 343 5454
Hours ➜ 08:00 - 24:00
Web/email ➜ zyara@emirates.net.ae | Map Ref ➜ 9-B2

  50

The relaxed atmosphere, eclectic décor and laissez-faire service are all conducive to taking your time over a coffee or a light meal. Zyara is Arabic for 'visit', and a wide variety of magazines, books and games help you pass the time while you wait for your order. The mainly Arabic buffet attracts a largely Lebanese clientele and a predominantly sandwich and salad menu is popular with the business lunchers. Another branch of Zyara Café is located at Dubai Media City (391 8031). ⓣⓜ

Food●●●◐○ Serv●●●◐○ Venue●●●◐○ Value●●●◐○

Shisha Cafés

Other options ➜ **Arabic/Lebanese [p.330]**

Shisha cafés are common throughout the Middle East, offering relaxing surroundings and the chance to smoke a shisha pipe (aka 'hookah', 'hubble bubble' or 'narghile') with a variety of aromatic flavours. Traditionally the preserve of local men to play backgammon and gossip with friends, these venues are now popular with locals and visitors alike, especially in the cooler winter evenings.

Most cafés offer a basic menu of Arabic cuisine and a few international options, plus coffees, teas and fruit juices. So, choose your flavour of shisha, sit back and puff away – this is what life is all about! Prices are typically around Dhs.15 – 25 per shisha, and loads of cafés continue to spring up around town. Many literally offer door to car service, so you can roll up, wind down your window or smoke on the pavement next to your car – especially good if you want to impress that date on the back seat. Oud Metha's got some great (conveniently dark) areas for car shisha...

If you get 'hooked' (pun intended), and wish to have your own, Al Karama market (see [p.252]) and Carrefour, among many trinket shops all over the city, are particularly good places to get started, offering a variety of pipes and some of the basic tobacco flavours. It can be a very satisfying experience, puffing on a pipe around a campfire in the desert whilst watching the stars.

Shisha Cafés

Al Hadiqa	Sheraton Jumeira Beach
Al Hakawati	Sheikh Zayed Rd
Al Khayma	Dubai Marine Beach Resort
Al Koufa	Nr American Hospital
Aroma Garden	Nr Maktoum Bridge
Awafi	JW Marriott
Cosmo Café	Sheikh Zayed Rd
Courtyard	Royal Mirage Hotel
Fakhreldine	Holiday Inn Bur Dubai
Fatafeet	Next to Dubai Creek
QD's	Dubai Creek Golf & Yacht Club
Mazaj	Century Village
Shakespeare & Co	Sheikh Zayed Rd
Elements	Wafi City

Afternoon Tea

Other options → **Cafés & Coffee Shops** [p.404]

Lobby Lounge, The

Location → Ritz-Carlton, The · Marsa Dubai
Hours → 09:00 - 01:30   Thu 10:00-01:30 | 399 4000
Web/email → www.ritzcarlton.com   Map Ref → 2-E2

It's hard to keep up with the flash life of Dubai, but short of being a millionaire, tea at the Ritz is the essence of good living. The fabulous location, overlooking the beach, adds even more luxury to the art of sitting back with any of the 20 gourmet teas on offer. For a touch of something special choose the Royal Tea, which includes champagne, finger sandwiches and freshly baked scones with

clotted cream and homemade jams. Whether celebrating a special occasion or simply trying to outdo the Jones', the Lobby Lounge fits the bill without breaking the bank.

Food●●●●○ Serv●●●●● Venue●●●●● Value●●●●●

Sahn Eddar

Location → Burj Al Arab · Umm Suqeim | 301 7600
Hours → 07:00 - 02:00
Web/email → www.jumeirahinternational.com   Map Ref → 4-A1

From the lavish interior of the Burj to the enticing shores of the Arabian Gulf the mesmerising views from this decadent venue are just part and parcel of a once in a lifetime experience. You can order from the à la carte menu or sample the formidable Afternoon Tea. Sit back, relax and feel like aristocracy as personable staff serve up a feast of sweets, sandwiches, scones, chocolates and a pot of fragrant tea or coffee of your choice.

Food●●●○○ Serv●●●●○ Venue●●●●● Value●●●●○

Internet Cafés

Other options → **Internet** [p.114]

If you want to surf the Web, visit a chat room, email friends or play the latest game, but want to be a little bit sociable about it, or perhaps do not have your own facilities for being online, Internet cafés are perfect to visit. Over the last few years, this type of café has become a common feature throughout Dubai. The mix of coffee, cake and technology has proved an irresistible draw, and this particular niche of café will doubtless continue to expand. As always, facilities, ambience, prices and clientele vary considerably, so poke your head in the door and then make your decision. Prices are typically Dhs.5 - 15 per hour. Happy surfing!

About time your favourite waiter got a pat on the posterior for good service? Prompt a pay raise or promotion by shouting 'good service' from the rooftops! Eat Out Speak Out is the perfect way to get your 'pat' across. Not only will we publish your 'pat' online, we'll also make sure that it is transported straight from your hands to the 'back' of the establishment.

Current hotspot locations include: French Connection, Sheikh Zayed Road; Spot Café, Bank Street, Bur Dubai (Dhs.7/hour) and Al Jalssa Internet C@fe, Al Ain Centre (Computer Plaza) (Dhs.10/hour), but great cafés are springing up all the time, so check out what suits you.

Property World
The Arabian Gulf International Property Magazine
Middle East

The only dedicated international and local property magazine for the Arabian Gulf

ETA STAR presents Palladium a residential tower at Jumeirah Lake Towers, see above

Building Bahrain Tameer showcases Tala Island

The Pearl-Qatar profiled and defining Qatar's property laws

Dubai Property Investment Show the property event calendar continues from February 2005

www.propertyworldme.com

issue nine

Corinthian Publishing, PO Box 72280, 2nd Floor, Building 2, Dubai Media City, Dubai, United Arab Emirates, Tel: +971 4 3291425, Fax: +971 4 3420302 email: pworldme@eim.ae web site: www.propertyworldme.com

Food on the Go

Bakeries

In addition to bread, bakeries offer a wonderful range of pastries, biscuits and Lebanese sweets. Arabic foods include 'borek', flat pastries, baked or fried with spinach or cheese, and 'manoushi' (hot bread, doubled over and served plain or filled with meat, cheese or 'zatar' (thyme seeds)). Biscuits are often filled with ground dates. All are delicious, and must be tried at least once.

Fruit Juices

Other options → Cafés & Coffee Shops [p.404]

Fresh juices are widely available, either from shawarma stands or juice shops. They are delicious, healthy and cheap, and made on the spot from fresh fruits such as mango, banana, kiwi, strawberry and pineapple (have the mixed fruit cocktail if you can't decide).

Yoghurt is also a popular drink, often served with nuts, and the local milk is called 'laban' (a heavy, salty buttermilk that doesn't go well in tea or coffee). Arabic mint tea is available, but probably not drunk as widely as in other parts of the Arab world; however, Arabic coffee (thick, silty and strong) is extremely popular and will have you buzzing on a caffeine high for days!

Shawarma

Other options → Arabic/Lebanese [p.330]

Sidewalk stands throughout the city sell 'shawarma', which are rolled pita bread filled with lamb or chicken carved from a rotating spit, and salad. Costing about Dhs.3 each, these are inexpensive, well worth trying, and offer an excellent alternative fast food to the usual beefburger. The stands usually sell other dishes, such as 'foul' (a paste made from fava beans) and 'falafel' (or ta'amiya), which are small savoury balls of deep-fried beans. You can also buy a whole grilled chicken, salad and hummus for around Dhs.15.

While most shawarma stands offer virtually the same thing, slight differences make some stand out from the rest. People are often adamant that their particular favourite serves, for example, the best falafel in town. These can often be the first place you eat when you come to the UAE, however,

look around – every restaurant has its own way of doing things and you might find that the best is, surprisingly, the smallest, most low-key restaurant you happen on by chance.

Al Mallah

Location → Al Diyafah Street · Al Satwa | 398 4723
Hours → 06:30 - 03:30
Web/email → na   Map Ref → 7-A3

Among the throng of small Arabic joints, this one stands out. Situated on one of the busiest streets in town, it mainly offers pavement seating with a few tables and chairs inside. The shawarmas and fruit juices are excellent here, the cheese and zatar manoushi good and they have, possibly, the biggest and best falafel in Dubai. Grab an evening snack and watch the world drive by, or stay and order a bigger meal. Another branch of Al Mallah is located on Al Mateena Road, Deira (272 3431).

Food●●●○○ Serv●●●○○ Venue●●●○○ Value●●●●○

Al Shera'a Fisheries Centre

Location → Next to Marks & Spencer · Deira | 227 1803
Hours → 10:00 - 01:00
Web/email → na   Map Ref → 11-E1

We all know the lovely but ubiquitous shawarma that spins on spits everywhere in town. If you think you've tried them all, think again. This venue takes a winning concept and, well, let's say, adapts it. This is the only joint in town that serves fish shawarma, which is actually quite tasty and a pleasant change. A very casual shop that's worth a visit, if only for the novelty.

Food●●●●○ Serv●●●○○ Venue●●●○○ Value●●●●○

Friday Brunch

An integral part of life in Dubai, Friday brunch is a perfect event for a lazy start or end to the weekend, especially once the really hot weather arrives. Popular with all sections of the community, it provides Thursday night's revellers with a gentle awakening, and often much-needed nourishment. For families, brunch is a very pleasant way to spend the day, especially since many venues organise a variety of fun activities for kids, allowing parents to fill themselves with fine food and drinks, and to simply relax. Different brunches appeal to

Friday Brunch

Restaurant	Location	Phone	A La Carte	Kid Friendly	Alcohol	Outside Terrace	Cost Adult	Cost Child	Timings
Al Muntaha	Burj Al Arab	301 7777	–	–	✔	–	240	120	11:00 - 15:30
Al Shindagha	Metropolitan Palace hotel	227 0000	–	–	✔	–	89	u	11:00 - 15:00
Alamo	Dubai Marine Beach Resort	346 1111	–	–	✔	–	60	30	11:00 - 15:00
Antigo	Le Meridien Dubai	282 4040	–	✔	✔	✔	98	50	12:30 -15:30
Aquarium	Creek Golf & Yacht Club	295 6000	–	✔	–	–	75	35	11:30 - 15:00
Bazaar, The	Oasis Beach Hotel	399 4444	–	✔	–	✔	70	35	12:30 - 15:30
Bella Vista	Jumeirah Rotana Hotel	345 5888	–	✔	✔	–	75	37	11:30 - 15:30
Benjarong	Dusit Dubai	343 3333	–	✔	✔	–	95	u	12:30 - 15:00
Biggles	Millennium Airport Hotel	282 3464	–	–	–	✔	38	19	11:00 - 15:30
Boston Bar, The	Jumeirah Rotana Hotel	345 5888	–	–	✔	–	40	20	12:00 - 16:00
Brasserie	Le Royal Meridien	399 5555	✔	✔	–	✔	120	60	12:30 - 16:00
Cactus Jacks	Millennium Airport Hotel	282 3464	✔	–	–	✔	28	15	12:00 - 16:00
Café Boulvar	Hotel Inter-Continental	222 7171	–	–	✔	–	99	57	12:00 - 16:00
Café Insignia	Ramada Hotel	351 9999	–	✔	✔	–	110	38	12:00 -15:00
Carter's	Pyramids	324 0000	–	✔	✔	✔	65	30	11:30 - 15:00
Cascades	Fairmont Hotel	332 5555	–	–	–	–	95	45	09:00 - 15:15
Cellar, The	Aviation Club, The	282 4122	✔	–	✔	✔	60	u	11:30 - 16:30
Cheers	Lodge, The	337 9470	–	✔	–	–	40	20	11:30 - 15:30
Coconut Grove	Rydges Plaza Hotel	398 2222	–	–	–	–	30	15	12:30 - 15:00
Colonnade, The	Jumeirah Beach Hotel, The	348 0000	✔	–	✔	✔	130	65	12:00 - 15:30
Dubai Restaurant	Nad Al Sheba Racecourse	336 3666	–	✔	–	–	70	25	12:00 - 16:30
Dubliner's	Le Meridien Dubai	282 4040	✔	–	✔	–	40	40	11:00 - 23:45
Flnnegans	Palm Hotel Dubai, The	399 2222	–	✔	✔	✔	59	30	12:00 - 15:00
Fontana	Al Bustan Rotana Hotel	282 0000	–	✔	–	–	99	50	12:00 - 15:00
Gozo Garden	Millennium Airport Hotel	282 3464	✔	✔	–	✔	38	19	12:00 - 15:30
Handi	Taj Palace Hotel	223 2222	–	✔	–	–	88	44	12:00 - 16:00
Long's Bar	Towers Rotana Hotel	343 8000	–	–	✔	–	49	25	12:00 - 16:00
Market Place	JW Marriott Hotel	262 4444	–	✔	–	✔	99	m	12:30 - 16:00
More	Al Garhoud	283 0224	✔	–	–	–	65	35	11:00 - 16:00
New York Deli	Regal Plaza Hotel	355 6633	–	–	–	–	50	25	12:00 - 17:30
Oceana	Hilton Dubai Jumeirah	399 1111	✔	✔	✔	–	95	u	12:30 - 15:30
Olives	One&Only Royal Mirage, The	399 9999	–	–	–	✔	115	25	12:30 - 15:30
Pax Romana	Dusit Dubai	343 3333	–	–	✔	–	95	u	12:00 - 15:00
Planet Hollywood	Wafi City	324 4777	✔	✔	–	–	65	35	11:30 - 15:00
Prasino's	Jumeirah Beach Club Resort & Spa	344 5333	–	–	–	✔	130	65	12:30 - 15:00
Rainbow Room	Aviation Club, The	282 4122	–	–	–	–	30	15	12:00 - 16:00
Rock Bottom Café	Regent Palace Hotel	396 3888	–	✔	✔	–	49	u	12:00 - 15:30
Sakura	Taj Palace Hotel	223 2222	–	✔	–	–	88	44	12:30 - 16:00
Scarlett's	Emirates Towers Hotel	319 8768	–	✔	✔	✔	70	u	11:30 - 16:00
Spice Island	Renaissance Hotel	262 5555	–	✔	✔	–	91	71	12:00 - 14:30
Splendido	Ritz-Carlton	399 4000	–	✔	–	✔	140	70	12:30 - 15:30
Taverna	Dubai Marine Beach Resort	346 1111	–	✔	–	✔	125	70	12:30 - 15:30
Topkapi	Taj Palace Hotel	223 2222	–	✔	–	–	88	44	12:00 - 16:00
Verdi	Taj Palace Hotel	223 2222	–	✔	–	–	88	44	12:00 - 16:00
Vivaldi	Sheraton Dubai Creek Hotel	207 1717	–	–	–	✔	70	35	12:30 - 15:30
Waxy O'Conner's	Ascot Hotel	352 0900	–	–	✔	–	50	15	12:00 - 18:00
Windtower	Dubai Country Club	333 1155	–	✔	–	✔	49	20	12:00 - 16:00
Zyara Café	Sheikh Zayed Road	343 5454	–	–	–	✔	50	25	11:00 - 15:00

m - metre (charged by height)   u - under 12 is free

different crowds; some have fantastic buffets, others are in spectacular surroundings, while some offer all you can eat at amazing prices.

Parties at Home

Other options → **Family Explorer**
Party Accessories [p.228]

Entertaining at home is great, but it does involve a lot of hard work. Fortunately there are several companies in Dubai that can do all the cooking, decorating and cleaning up for you, leaving you with more time to tell witty after-dinner stories. In the tables below, we've listed party organisers and outside caterers, as well as who you can call to buy party supplies or hire party equipment. If you're planning a party for your children, refer to the Family Explorer which has a whole chapter dedicated to birthday parties.

Party Organisers

Other options → **Party Accessories [p.228]**

Flying Elephant

Location → Warehouse, Jct 3, Shk Zayed Rd · Al Quoz | **347 9170**
Hours → 08:00 - 18:00
Web/email → www.flyingelephantuae.com   Map Ref → 4-D4

Whatever your party planning needs, the folks at Flying Elephant will be only too happy to comply. The company offers everything from adding special effects to a product launch to providing a turnkey service for annual family days and even entertainment on your little one's first birthday party in your back garden. As quality organisers, the company will provide for a wide variety of

products to complete every occasion, be it balloons and decorations or the Gulf's largest outdoor confetti blaster. Flying Elephant also offers theme decoration, theme parties, balloon printing and balloon decoration/sculpting.

Caterers

A popular and easy way to have a party, special occasion or business lunch, outside catering allows you to relax and enjoy yourself, or to concentrate on ... anything but the cooking. Numerous places offer this service, so decide on the type of food you want – Chinese, Italian, Lebanese, Mexican finger food, etc, and ask at your favourite or local restaurant or café to see if they do outside catering.

India Palace

There are also specialist companies who provide a variety of services at very reasonable prices, while most of the larger hotels have outside catering

All You Can Eat & Drink		Other options → **Buffet [p.338]**	
Name	**Location**	**Cuisine**	**Phone**
Bamboo Lagoon	JW Marriott	Far Eastern	262 4444
Bella Vista	Jum. Rotana Htl	Asian, Carvery, Curry, German, Mexican	345 5888
Benihana	Al Bustan Rotana Htl	Sushi, Teppanyaki	282 0000
Brauhaus	Jumeira Rotana Htl	German	345 5888
Come Prima	Al Bustan Rotana Htl	Italian	282 0000
Creekside	Sheraton Hotel & Towers	Japanese Seafood, Sushi, Teppanyaki (food only)	207 1750
Fontana	Al Bustan Rotana Htl	Curry, Mexican & Seafood, Spanish	282 0000
Gardinia	Towers Rotana Htl	Asian, British, Seafood & Spit Roast, Pasta	343 8000
Gozo Garden	Millennium Airport Htl	BBQ, Chinese, Curry, European, Hawaiian, Seafood	282 3464
Le Meridien Terrace Village	Le Meridien Dubai	Arabic, Mediterranean, Singapore, Thai	282 4040
Market Place	JW Marriott	International	262 4444
Spice Island	Renaissance Htl	Asian, BBQ & Steak, Japanese, Mongolian, Seafood, Spice	262 5555
Sushi Sushi	Century Village	Sushi, Sashimi, Tempura, Teppanyaki (food only)	282 9908

Parties at Home | Caterers

Going Out

Moonlight

the original

Light up your event with our exclusive indoor and outdoor lighting.
Moonlights shed a pleasant and soothing light and can be coloured with a filter
to match any theme or environment. The full and half spheres are available in
various sizes from 250 to 750 mm. They are waterproof, sturdy, UV resistant
and can withstand temperatures of up to 80˚C.

Moonlights are available for purchase or rent.

UAE Distributor: Desert River LLC
Showroom at Centro Mall, Satwa, Dubai, 050 725 40 10 / 050 658 16 41, info@DesertRiver.com
www.DesertRiver.com

departments, usually capable of extravagant five-star functions. You don't even have to stay at home to order catering for a function – how about arranging a party in the desert? Depending on what you require, caterers can provide just the food or everything from food, crockery, napkins, tables, chairs and even waiters, doormen and a clearing up service afterwards. Costs vary according to the number of people, dishes and level of service etc, required.

For a list of hotel numbers, check out the hotel table in General Information. For restaurants and cafés, browse this section of the book. You can also refer to the catering section in the telephone books, especially the Hawk Business Pages.

Catering Services

Dubai World Trade Centre	308 6944
Emirates Abela	282 3171
Intercat	334 5212
Maria Bonita	395 5576
Metropolitan Catering Services	881 7100
Open House	396 5481
Sandwich Express	343 9922
Something Different	267 1639
West One	349 4500

Kids Video Services

Shooting Stars

Location ➔ Dubai Media City · Al Sufouh
Hours ➔ Timings on request
Web/email ➔ www.shootingstar.biz

394 1377
Map Ref ➔ 3-A2

Shooting Stars is an adventure video production company that produces keepsake videos of children in imaginative situations. Using the latest digital technology, they can turn children into the stars of their very own video blockbuster: a popular choice is 'My Arabian Adventure' (the background tape is filmed in the dunes at Hatta). It's a unique and unusual gift to send back to the grandparents. For more information contact the above number or 050 798 8209.

On the Town

If you're out on the town in Dubai, you'll soon find that there are a good many places to go and things to do. It may not be quite the buzzing city found in other parts of the world, but Dubai is without doubt the party capital of the Gulf, with enough choice to keep even the most ardent socialite happy. The following section covers the 'cultural' entertainment such as theatre and comedy clubs, as well as bars, pubs and nightclubs.

In Dubai people tend to go out late, usually not before about 21:00. Even on week nights, kick off is surprisingly late and people seem to forget, after about the tenth drink, that they really ought to be at work the next day. If you're venturing out to Arabic nightclubs or restaurants, you're likely to find them almost deserted before about 23:00.

Wednesday and Thursday, being the start of most peoples' weekend, are obviously busy, but you will also find that during the week many bars and restaurants offer promotions and special nights to attract customers and create a lively atmosphere. Particularly popular is Ladies' Night, which is traditionally on a Tuesday (and the busiest night of the week for some places). Women are given tokens on the door offering them free drinks – the number varies from one to an endless supply, and it may be limited to certain types of drink. This ploy certainly seems to attract male customers too! With men outnumbering women in Dubai (by two to one), it's an unbalanced world where women, for once, can take full advantage. The following are the main places that have a Ladies' Night at some point during the week:

Ladies' Nights

Boston Bar	21:30 - 02:30	Tue
Boudoir	22:30 - 03:00	Tue
Carters	22:00 - 24:00	Sun & Tue
Jimmy Dix	22:00 - 01:00	Sun & Tue
Lodge, The	20:00 - 01:00	Wed & Sun
Long's Bar	22:00 - 01:00	Tue & Wed
Oxygen	21:00 - 03:00	Mon & Wed
Planetarium	23:00 - 03:00	Tue & Wed
Rock Bottom	20:00 - 02:00	Everyday - not Fri, Wed
Scarlett's	21:00 - 23:00	Tue
Seville's	23:00 - 24:00	Tue & Fri
Waxy O'Conners	20:30 - 01:30	Thu
Zinc	19:00 - 23:00	Tue

Cafés and restaurants generally close between 23:00 and 01:00, with most bars and nightclubs split between those that close 'early' at 01:00 and those that stay open 'late' until 02:00 or 03:00. Not many places are open all night. To complement the bars and nightclubs, refer also to the information on Eating Out [p.321]. Many restaurants have a very good bar and some also have a dance floor which kicks in towards midnight. However, they are usually reviewed only once – as a restaurant. In this section, you will also find further information on, for instance, Dubai's alcohol laws.

Bars

Other options → **Nightclubs [p.432]**
Pubs [p.430]

Dubai has an excellent number of bars with a good variety of different styles. Most are located in hotels, and while many bars come and go, the more popular ones stick around and are always busy. In addition to the bars reviewed here, there are plenty of others (usually in the smaller hotels), which do not attract the regular crowds of the more popular venues. If you're looking for somewhere different... get out there and explore! The city's more upmarket locations range from terminally hip cocktail lounges to decadent wine bars, from jazz bars to cigar bars — all providing salubrious surroundings for those opulent and self-indulgent moments. For more details on where and when people in Dubai go to drink, refer to the start of the On the Town section. For information on the individual bars, read on.

Door Policy

Even with the mix of nationalities that makes up the cultural melting pot of Dubai, there are certain bars and nightclubs that have a selective entry 'policy'. Sometimes the 'Members Only' sign on the entrance needs a bit of explaining. Membership is usually introduced to control the clientele frequenting the establishment, but is often only enforced during busy periods. At quieter times, nonmembers may have no problems getting in, even if not accompanied by a member. Basically, the management uses the rule to disallow entry if they don't like the look of you or your group, and they will point to their sign and say 'Sorry'. Large groups (especially all males), single men and certain nationalities are normally the target. You can avoid the inconvenience, and the embarrassment, by breaking the group up or by going in a mixed-gender group.

If you find yourself being discriminated against, don't get mad – get even! In most cases it's not worth trying to discuss this rationally with the doorman – it won't work. Most companies hate bad publicity – try taking the issue up with some of the local media. Other possible solutions include taking out membership for that particular club, shamelessly trying to bribe the doorman, getting there early (around 19:00), going with Kylie Minogue, or staying at home.

Dress Code

Most bars have a reasonably relaxed attitude to their customers' dress sense. Some places, however, insist on no shorts or sandals, while others require at least a shirt with a collar and no jeans. Nightclubs generally have a dressier approach, so dress to impress. As Dubai is well on its way to becoming a trendy tourist destination, the dress code will continue to lean towards the fancy.

> **Hidden Charges**
>
> *When the bill arrives, subtly check out the dreaded small print (slyly lurking at the bottom of the bill) that says 'INCLUSIVE +15% +5%'. Be careful what you touch, as you may find that even the most innocent eye contact with a nut bowl can result in surplus charges.*

Specials

Many places hold occasional promotions with different themes and offers. These run alongside special nights, such as Ladies' Night, which are usually held weekly. For the promotions, you can find out what's coming up in the weekly and monthly entertainment publications and from the venues concerned. Special nights (such as the popular quiz nights), are mainly promoted in the bar or pub, and many attract quite a following. As a bonus, the prizes are often quite good.

American Bars

Boston Bar, The

Location → Jumeira Rotana · Al Satwa
Hours → 12:00 - 03:00
Web/email → www.rotana.com

345 5888

Map Ref → 6-E3

This handsome, well appointed bar is a welcome change from the usual homogenous Dubai pub experience; boasting an inspired menu, outstanding meals, reasonable drink prices and top-notch service. Start with one of the excellent warm salads, such as pan-seared tuna, before devouring a perfectly cooked, superior steak or salmon fillet cooked with your choice of spice rub and sauce. Classic pub dishes and burgers are also first-rate. A shade pricier, but streets ahead of the competition.

Food ●●●●○ Serv ●●●●○ Venue ●●●●○ Value ●●●●○

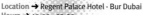

Rock Bottom Café

Location → Regent Palace Hotel · Bur Dubai | **396 3888**
Hours → 10:00 - 03:00
Web/email → www.ramee-group.com   Map Ref → 11-A1

    50

Rock Bottom Café has become a fixture of Bur Dubai nightlife with its ability to meet the requirements of just about anyone fancying a good night out. Earlier in the evening it appears to be a quiet restaurant, all candlelit tables, plenty of couples and families enjoying a good meal at reasonable prices. It's not until after 22:00 that Rock Bottom really rocks. A regular host of live music with its reasonably sized dance floor that becomes unnaturally crowded at the weekends. Rock Bottom also has two pool tables and big screen TVs to keep the sports fans happy.

Food●●●●○Serv●●●●○Venue●●●●●Value●●●●○

Scarlett's

Location → The Boulevard at Emirates Towers | **319 8088**
Hours → 12:30 - 03:00
Web/email → www.jumeirahinternational.com   Map Ref → 9-C2

    150

Please refer to the review under American [p.328].
Food●●●●○○Serv●●●●○Venue●●●○○Value●●●○○

Beach/Waterfront Bars

Barasti Bar

Location → Le Meridien Mina Seyahi · Al Sufouh | **399 3333**
Hours → 09:00 - 02:00
Web/email → www.lemeridien-minaseyahi.com Map Ref → 3-A2

   150

Barasti has had a loyal following for some years now and it's easy to understand why. The location is pretty impressive for starters - sitting directly over the beach with the waves lapping at the white sandy shore. The food may not be outstanding but satisfies nonetheless and sipping cocktails under the disappearing sun is far more important. The mixed grills and seafood are recommended and won't burn a hole in your beer budget. Fridays are favoured when Dubai's in-crowd comes out to play.

Food●●●●○Serv●●●●○Venue●●●●○Value●●●●○

Beach Bar, Al Hadiqa Tent, The

Location → Sheraton Jumeira Beach · Marsa Dubai | **399 5533**
Hours → 18:00 - 03:00
Web/email → www.starwood.com   Map Ref → 2-D2

   50

The tent is a small indoor Arabic themed restaurant, with an outdoor terrace that doubles as the Beach Bar. In the evenings, fairy lights and shisha pipes offer hotel guests a soothing setting on the candlelit terrace – a more atmospheric option than indoors. A limited selection of Arabic meze and grills are available, and are amply portioned. Though not the best example of Arabic cuisine or hospitality, it is nevertheless a peaceful way to unwind after a hard day on the beach.

Food●●●○○Serv●●○○○Venue●●●●○Value●●●○○

QD's

Location → Creek Golf Club · Al Garhoud | **295 6000**
Hours → 18:00 - 02:00
Web/email → www.dubaigolf.com   Map Ref → 14-C2

50

To contemplate Dubai's ever-changing skyline through a haze of fruity shisha smoke head down to QD's, a popular creek-side quarterdeck and regular hangout for those wishing to see and be seen. Attracted by live music, a range of sisha flavours and the option of majilis-style seating, the venue's clientele varies from the hip, rich and beautiful to rowdy teens enjoying a shared smoke. What staff lack in English they more than make up for with welcoming enthusiasm, but the food menu is not so accommodating and the falafel or fresh-baked pizza may be unavailable.

Food●●●○○Serv●●●●○Venue●●●●○Value●●○○○

Sunset Bar

Location → Jumeirah Beach Club Resort & Spa | **344 5333**
Hours → 17:00 - 22:00
Web/email → www.jumeirahinternational.com   Map Ref → 5-D1

   50

Sipping cocktails in front of a hedonistic horizon of blue azure seas and golden sandy shores, the Sunset Bar is the ultimate location for a superior sundowner. With chill out tunes, shisha and sunshine settings, Friday is the best day to sip the sun away amongst a beautiful crowd, and with a

Happy Hour to boot you may find yourself literally delirious! Seating may disappear with the sun as the bar fills up but then you can grab a spot on a beach carpet and relax with a giant cushion under the night sky.

Food●●●○○Serv●●●○○Venue●●●●○Value●●●●○

Sunset Bar

Wavebreaker

Location → Hilton Jumeirah · Marsa Dubai | 399 1111
Hours → 10:00 - 20:00
Web/email → www.hilton.com   Map Ref → 2-D2

  100

Please see the Wavebreaker review under International [p.366].

Food●●●○○Serv●●○○○Venue●●●●○Value●●●○○

Cigar Bars

Armoury Lounge

Location → Al Qasr Hotel · Jumeira | 366 8888
Hours → 12:00 - 02:00
Web/email → www.jumeirahinternational.com   Map Ref → 4-A2

100

If you love cigars and/or ancient weapons then the Armoury Lounge is the perfect place for an aperitif or after-dinner cocktail. The cocktail menu is impressive and the finger food tempting, however the opulent Arabic décor is let down by a lack of atmosphere, which could be easily cured by some soft background music and dimmed lighting. Give it time though and cigar

connoisseurs who are attracted by the Dhs.25 – 225 menu will no doubt bring their own atmosphere, albeit a smoky one.

Food●●●○○Serv●●○○○Venue●●●○○Value●●○○○

Cigar Bar

Location → Fairmont Dubai, The · Trade Centre 1 | 311 8000
Hours → 19:00 - 02:00
Web/email → www.fairmont.com   Map Ref → 9-E1

150

Conspiratorially low lighting, presidential leather armchairs and sofas, and the small sleek bar lend this smokers' den an air of intimate aristocracy, tempting you to wow your friends with your Humphrey Bogart and Winston Churchill impressions. The cigar menu reads like a collection of biographies, with detailed and informative history and trivia about each brand. The drinks selection is not vast, but prices are reasonable due to the absence of high-end connoisseur tipples (such as rare and/or expensive whiskeys and cognacs).

Zappy Explorer

Finally, life in Dubai made easy! This guide's your best chance of navigating through Dubai's administrative mysteries with over 100 step by step procedures on everything, from registering your car to getting a mortgage, or even just paying your phone bills.

Food●●●●○Serv●●●●●Venue●●●●○Value●●●●○

Library & Cigar Bar, The

Location → Ritz-Carlton, The · Marsa Dubai | 399 4000
Hours → 16:00 - 01:30
Web/email → www.ritzcarlton.com   Map Ref → 2-E2

 50

Moody and atmospheric, this cosy, captivating piano lounge will transport you into a Cluedo-esque world of opulent relaxation. Dark wood, Chesterfields, seductive lighting and moody 20s style jazz make this the perfect place for an early evening aperitif, or a late night snifter. Aficionados will be pleased with the huge array of classic stogies. As for the Scotch, single malt and cognac drinkers will be impressed. There are classy, classic cocktails available for the dames, and a range of wines by the glass. Inviting.

Food●●●●○Serv●●●○○Venue●●●●●Value●●●○○

Beach/Waterfront Bars | Cigar Bars

Going Out

Cocktail Lounges

Bahri Bar

Location ➜ Mina A'Salam · Umm Suqeim | **366 8888**
Hours ➜ 12:00 - 02:00
Web/email ➜ www.jumeirahinternational.com   Map Ref ➜ 4-A2

   (100)

Cocktail bars are ten a penny in this fair city so it's a pleasure that the Bahri stands head and shoulders above the rest. The view for a start, of the Venetian waterway, the lapping sea and the neighbouring Burj Al Arab, is reason enough to visit for a sundowner. The fact that the bar staff mix some of the most delicious drinks on this side of the world, serve great wines and pull a mean pint is a wonderful added incentive. Attentive service ensures that glasses are full at all times and the tasty nibbles never run out.●

Food●●●●○ Serv●●●●○ Venue●●●●○ Value●●●●○

Boudoir

Location ➜ Dubai Marine Beach Resort · Jumeira | **345 5995**
Hours ➜ 19:30 - 03:00
Web/email ➜ www.myboudoir.com   Map Ref ➜ 6-D2

  (150)

French Renaissance makes a revival at Boudoir, blending opulence and sophistication with slick crowds in one of the most 'exclusive' nightspots in Dubai. Deep colours, cool tunes and soft lighting set the mood for an experience which seemingly never fails to pack in the crowds. Door policy can be strict, especially so on the busiest nights. Theme nights promote different types of music including house, latino and R&B, in addition to great free drinks deals for ladies; champagne on Tuesdays and Fridays, and cocktails on Wednesdays before midnight ... tough luck guys!●

Food●●●○○ Serv●●●○○ Venue●●●●○ Value●●●○○

Ginseng

Location ➜ Wafi City · Umm Hurair | **324 8200**
Hours ➜ 19:00 - 02:00   Thu 19:00 - 03:00
Web/email ➜ www.ginsengdubai.com   Map Ref ➜ 13-D2

   (100)

If you want to impress or have a hip night out with your friends, you won't go wrong with Ginseng. An upmarket cocktail bar with décor and atmosphere that is trendy without the pretension, expect exotic drinks, fabulous champagne cocktails and an Asian tapas style menu to carry you through late into the night. Tuesday night is Gemini night – buy one cocktail, get one free. Resident DJ from 21:00 every night. Smart casual dress code applies.●

Food●●●●○ Serv●●●●○ Venue●●●●○ Value●●●●○

La Moda

Location ➜ Hotel Inter-Continental · Deira | **205 7333**
Hours ➜ 13:00 - 15:00   19:00 - 03:00
Web/email ➜ www.interconti.com   Map Ref ➜ 8-C4

      (50)

Please see La Moda review under Italian Restaurants [p.371].

Food●●●○○ Serv●●●○○ Venue●●●●○ Value●●●○○

Martini Lounge

Location ➜ Sofitel City Centre · Al Garhoud | **294 1222**
Hours ➜ 12:00 - 01:00
Web/email ➜ www.accorhotels.com   Map Ref ➜ 14-D1

(50)

Suffering from a shopping comedown? Need recharging? Head across to Martini Lounge and indulge yourself with a tipple from its quietly confident cocktail list. As you would imagine from its name, this bar teaches the old Martini a few new tricks, such as the Sweet Lips Martini with Baileys, angostura, and cinnamon, and the Midnight Martini with coffee liqueur and Cointreau. A handy place to unwind with a drink, whilst enjoying blue notes from the resident baby grand piano.●

Food●●●○○ Serv●●○○○ Venue●●○○○ Value●●○○○

Rooftop Lounge

Rooftop Lounge & Terrace

Location ➜ One&Only Arabian Court · Al Sufouh | **399 9999**
Hours ➜ 19:00 - 01:00
Web/email ➜ www.oneandonlyroyalmirage.com   Map Ref ➜ 3-A2

 50

This bar takes the concept of lounging and relaxation to new levels. Chill out on the circular couch surrounding a large spherical half moon, and rest your legs on the supplied pouffes. Sip a cocktail while taking in the stunning ocean vistas beyond and the stars above. If required, choose a more 'formal' seating option at one of the low Moroccan style tables. A wide selection of drinks includes non alcoholic beverages too, but their Arabian Comfort and Desert Dunes heighten the already romantic setting.●

Food ●●●●○ Serv ●●●●○ Venue ●●●●● Value ●●●●●

Trader Vic's

Location ➜ Crowne Plaza · Trade Centre 1 | **331 1111**
Hours ➜ 12:00 – 15:00 18:00 – 01:30
Web/email ➜ tradervics@crowneplaza.co.ae   Map Ref ➜ 4-A2

150

Take the lift to the third floor and step out into a Polynesian den of delight. The spacious, indoor veranda type bar area is complete with a wooden floor, cane chairs and plenty of artefacts to distract you. Cocktails are a speciality, with an extensive menu to choose from at the Mai Tai cocktail bar adjacent to the restaurant. Served in shrunken heads or adorned with feathered parrots, these potent concoctions are the same as those found in Trader Vic's worldwide. Not cheap, but worth every dirham. Try the bar menu for oriental snack delights such as satay, prawns with a selection of dipping sauces, crispy wontons and native Pacific finger food.

Other Locations: Madinat Jumeirah, Umm Suqeim (366 5646)
Food ●●●●● Serv ●●●●● Venue ●●●●○ Value ●●●●○

General Bars

Al Samar Lounge

Location ➜ Mina A'Salam · Umm Suqeim | **366 8888**
Hours ➜ 08:30 - 00:30
Web/email ➜ www.jumeirahinternational.com   Map Ref ➜ 4-A2

 50

Located in the lobby, the Al Samar Lounge is the meeting place of Mina A' Salam. Watch in comfort

amidst the bustle of this animated area, as the world and its people go by. The lounge features an extensive selection of non alcoholic and alcoholic cocktails, traditional high teas in the afternoon, and live entertainment in the evening. Adjacent is an outdoor shisha terrace overlooking the lagoon and beyond. Service is extra friendly and helpful and despite its transient location the atmosphere remains inviting.●

Food ●●●●○ Serv ●●●●● Venue ●●●●○ Value ●●●●○

Alamo, The

Location ➜ Dubai Marine Beach Resort · Jumeira | **349 3455**
Hours ➜ 12:00 - 15:30 19:00 - 24:00
Web/email ➜ www.dxbmarine.com   Map Ref ➜ 6-D2

 100

Please see The Alamo review under Tex-Mex [p.394].

Food ●●●●○ Serv ●●●●○ Venue ●●●○○ Value ●●●●○

Balcony Bar

Location ➜ Shangri-La Hotel · Trade Centre 1 | **343 8888**
Hours ➜ 12:00 - 03:00
Web/email ➜ www.shangri-la.com   Map Ref ➜ 9-A2

 50

Nestled in a corner of this classy hotel, Balcony Bar (as its name suggests) overlooks the lobby, providing a perfect opportunity for people-watching from a cosy setting. A wide range of drinks caters to the most discerning of palates and the atmosphere encourages indulging in a smooth cigar chosen from an impressive humidor. Just settle in, nibble on quaint oriental finger food and while away the hours as the world scurries by.●

Food ●●●○○ Serv ●●●●○ Venue ●●●○○ Value ●●●○○

Barzar

Location ➜ Souk Madinat Jumeirah · Umm Suqeim | **366 8888**
Hours ➜ 12:00 - 02:00
Web/email ➜ www.jumeirahinternational.com   Map Ref ➜ 4-A2

 50

Barzar is a funky split-level bar boasting a 'perfect spot' terrace that overlooks the bar below as well as the spectacular Madinat lagoon and the Mina 'A Salam. While so many venues attempt to be all things to all people, what is refreshing about Barzar is it is just that - a bar, albeit a very good one, and has unsurprisingly become popular with the after work crowd. Snacks are available but they play second fiddle to the six or nine pint beer towers!

Food●●●○○ Serv●●●○○ Venue●●●●● Value●●●○○

Bridges

Location → Fairmont Dubai, The · Trade Centre 1   **311 8000**
Hours → 09:30 - 01:45
Web/email → www.fairmont.com   Map Ref → 9-E1

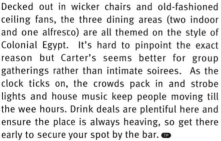

Slip into the fashionable swivel chairs or perch glamorously on the bar's high stools and choose from the fabulous array of cocktails (many with historical explanations in the menu). The suggestion of Art Deco, the quiet piano music, and the discreet service all work to create a comfortable, orderly space for civilised conversation. The generous cheese and fruit plate or mixed Arabic grill from nearby Fairmont restaurants sustain a hungry drinker, and the 50% saving on alcoholic beverages between 16:30 and 19:30 will excite the frugal.

Food●●●●○ Serv●●●●● Venue●●●●● Value●●●●○

Carter's

Location → Pyramids · Umm Hurair   **324 4100**
Hours → 12:00 - 01:00   Thu, Sun 12:00 - 02:00
Web/email → www.waficity.com   Map Ref → 13-D2

Decked out in wicker chairs and old-fashioned ceiling fans, the three dining areas (two indoor and one alfresco) are all themed on the style of Colonial Egypt. It's hard to pinpoint the exact reason but Carter's seems better for group gatherings rather than intimate soirees. As the clock ticks on, the crowds pack in and strobe lights and house music keep people moving till the wee hours. Drink deals are plentiful here and ensure the place is always heaving, so get there early to secure your spot by the bar.

Food●●●●○ Serv●●●○○ Venue●●●●○ Value●●●○○

Chameleon

Location → Traders Hotel Dubai · Deira   **265 9888**
Hours → 18:00 - 03:00
Web/email → www.shangri-la.com   Map Ref → 12-A3

A wide variety of tasty drinks, some of them quite unusual, ensure your mouth will have a good time. The Chameleon is a great way to start or end an evening, and you just might find that the music keeps you there for the whole night. Stylish interior and trendy lighting give the place a pleasing look. The food is reasonable to say the least, with vegetable and seafood snacks as well as sandwiches to satisfy the mean munchies. Happy hour from 18:00 to 21:00.

Food●●●○○ Serv●●●●○ Venue●●●●○ Value●●●●○

Cubar

Location → Hilton Jumeirah · Marsa Dubai   **399 1111**
Hours → 18:00 - 24:00
Web/email → www.hilton.com   Map Ref → 2-D2

Cubar is a sophisticated venue, worth visiting either in preparation for dining at the adjoining Pachanga restaurant or in its own right. The décor is colonial, creating a relaxed atmosphere for evening drinks. Latin-themed snacks are available at the bar, along with the opportunity to sample an aperitif from the extensive cocktail list. Unfortunately, the service can be slow as there doesn't seem to be enough staff to deal with all the drinks requirements for both Pachanga and Cubar at the same time.

> ### DUI
> *Drinking and driving is illegal in Dubai, and although it's tempting to jump in the car after just one beer - don't! You may find yourself locked up for a month. Be responsible when it comes to drinking and driving and always take a taxi - they're cheap, reliable and plentiful.*

Food●●●●○ Serv●●○○○ Venue●●●●○ Value●●●●○

Koubba

Location → Al Qasr Hotel · Umm Suqeim   **366 8888**
Hours → 12:00 - 02:00
Web/email → www.jumeirahinternational.com   Map Ref → 4-A2

A stunning venue, both inside and out, where you can languish in regal luxury with the finest views of the Madinat's sprawling resort. Outside, the dome-topped terrace offers a stunning panorama over the waterways, gardens, pool and beach. Inside, the beautifully decorated rustic stone-walled lounge also encourages lingering. Service is convivial and one of the delicious cocktails from the wide ranging menu is a must. Koubba is quite literally palatial and you just can't help feeling like royalty.

Food●●●●○ Serv●●●●● Venue●●●●● Value●●●●●

Going Out — *General Bars*

La Terrasse

Location → Entr. from Villa Moda · Trade Centre 2 | **050 353 3223**
Hours → Thu 21:00 -03:00
Web/email → www.glamourdubai.com | Map Ref → 9-D2

The new ultra-modern venue may be somewhat pretentious but then would you expect anything less from Emirates Towers. Furthermore, only held on Thursdays you have just a small window of opportunity to enjoy the absolutely fabulous sculptured architecture of the towers and poolside chill out with an eclectic mix of Dubai's funky fashionistas. The music is R'n'B, funky house and oriental beats and the dress code is chic and glamorous.

Food na   Serv na   Venue na   Value na

Left Bank

Location → Souk Madinat Jumeirah · Umm Suqeim | **368 6171**
Hours → 12:00 - 02:00
Web/email → www.mmidubai.com | Map Ref →4-A2

This is a stylish yet informal meeting place perfect for a lingering lunch, after work drink or casual evening meal. You can sample something from the cosmopolitan menu on the lounge-style seating indoors, or enjoy sundowners on the laid back terrace with its spectacular waterfront views. There is also a special 15 minute theatre menu, to ensure you don't miss 'curtains up' at the Madinat Theatre close by. Just be warned; as the evening progresses the seating, and even standing space rapidly disappears.

Food●●●●● Serv●●●●● Venue●●●●● Value●●●●○

Loft, The

Location → Emirates Towers Offices · Trade Centre 2 | **na**
Hours → Fri 21:00 - 03:00
Web/email → www.glamourdubai.com | Map Ref → 9-D2

The new place to be seen - but only by a select few! Located on the 13th floor of Emirates Towers, but only unlucky for those who don't get to experience the exclusivity. The Loft is a New York inspired bar where champagne and caviar are the order of the day and limited capacity seating means the atmosphere is more intimate than abuzz. The music combines electro, disco, funk and classic house and the views over the night lights of Dubai make this a venue for those with lofty illusions of grandeur.

Food na   Serv na   Venue na   Value na

Long's Bar

Location → Towers Rotana · Trade Centre 1 | **343 8000**
Hours → 12:00 - 15:00 17:00 - 23:30
Web/email → www.rotana.com | Map Ref → 9-B2

When size matters it's good to know that you'll be sat at the longest bar in the Middle East. Popular with Dubai residents on weekends and ladies' nights in particular, nights start quiet but pick up quickly as the crowd descends. For a quick escape from revellers' noise and commotion, the dedicated dining area offers a good selection of typical European fare, though limited for vegetarian diners. An ideal place to catch up with friends, join the prowl crowd circling the bar or settle into an intimate dinner.

Food●●●●○ Serv●●●●○ Venue●●●○○ Value●●●●○

Marina Roof Deck

Location → The Jumeirah Beach Hotel · Umm Suqeim | **348 0000**
Hours → 18:00 - 24:00
Web/email → www.jumeirahinternational.com | Map Ref → 4-B2

At the end of the jetty and up a flight of stairs (reminiscent of a cruise ship), you'll find this bar a pleasant place to meet for a few drinks and pass the time. The drinks menu is extensive, and the stunning night time views of the Jumeirah Beach Hotel and the Burj Al Arab make the overall experience truly great.

Food●●●○○ Serv●●●○○ Venue●●●●○ Value●●●○○

Nakhuda Bar

Location → Mina A'Salam · Umm Suqeim | **366 8888**
Hours → 12:00 - 15:00 19:00 - 02:00
Web/email → www.jumeirahinternational.com | Map Ref → 4-A2

The description says 'a rustic, harbour-side retreat' and Nakhuda is indeed that and more. A very extensive drinks list (including over forty wines), comfortable seating (inside or out) and a menu that doubles as a storybook, all add up to an enjoyable place for before or after dinner drinks and light snacks. With so much competition and so many differing personalities at the Madinat, Nakhuda is a good option if you want to please everyone.

Food●●●●○ Serv●●●●○ Venue●●●●● Value●●●●●

General Bars

Going Out

Pub, The

Location ➜ Hotel Inter-Continental · Deira | 205 7333
Hours ➜ 11:00 - 15:30 19:00 - 23:00 Fri 11:00 - 16:00, 19:00 - 23:45
Web/email ➜ www.interconti.com   Map Ref ➜ 8-C4

It's all about pints of lager, fish 'n' chips and footie on the big screen at The Pub. A small friendly bar is situated at the entrance and attracts a regular crowd of punters. The Pub's grub is standard, no-fuss fare, and there is something familiar about the atmosphere that makes you feel instantly at home here.⏺
Food●●○○○Serv●●○○○Venue●●●○○Value●●○○○

Rainbow Room

Location ➜ Aviation Club, The · Al Garhoud | 282 4122
Hours ➜ 19:00 - 02:00
Web/email ➜ www.aviationclubonline.com   Map Ref ➜ 14-C3

Hidden from plain view between its more famous neighbours, the Aviation Club gym and The Cellar Restaurant, the Rainbow Room is a relaxing spot for liquid nourishment or a quick bite after a long day. Sharing a kitchen with The Cellar assures a certain level of quality for the limited menu of salads, sandwiches, chicken, beef and fish entrées. More quiet pub then jumping club, a good choice for a quiet evening with playing cards and a TV to keep you awake.⏺
Food●●●○○Serv●●●○○Venue●●○○○Value●●●●○

Satchmo's

Location ➜ Le Royal Meridien · Marsa Dubai | 399 5555
Hours ➜ 17:30 - 03:00
Web/email ➜ www.leroyalmeridien-dubai.com   Map Ref ➜ 2-E2

This place is hip without the pressure of the club scene. Late night entertainment comes with all the gloss and service of a five star hotel venue, plus live music six nights of the week. An intriguing cocktail menu even extends to fun, low calorie choices. Their signature blends show off the talents of the bar staff, who will be delighted to stir up something unique for you. Ideal for celebrating a special anniversary or event.⏺
Food●●●○○Serv●●●●○Venue●●●●○Value●●●●○

Spectrum on One

Location ➜ Fairmont Dubai, The · Trade Centre 1 | 311 8101
Hours ➜ 17:30 - 19:00
Web/email ➜ www.fairmont.com   Map Ref ➜ 9-E1

This multi-award winning, signature restaurant of the Fairmont provides a culinary treat to the discerning diner, a gourmet retail boutique serving delectable chocolates, as well as a famous Friday Brunch where the champagne is free-flowing. But tucked away to the side is a lesser known bar, offering city views, elegant décor, comfortable seating, and an extensive drinks list. Definitely worth visiting, even if you're just passing the time while you wait for your table. ⏺
Food●●●●○Serv●●●●●Venue●●●●○Value●●●○○

Spikes Bar

Location ➜ Nad Al Sheba Club · Nad Al Sheba | 336 3666
Hours ➜ 07:00 - 24:00
Web/email ➜ www.nadalshebaclub.com   Map Ref ➜ 17-A3

First impressions of this sports bar - working mens' club carpet, a plague of televisions and awkward seating under bright lights - may be somewhat disappointing to the restaurant connoisseur. However the terrace is an undiscovered gem with sparsely spread tables, miniature water fountains, a welcoming spherical bar and a view of the rolling green race track with golfers practising their swing in the distance. As for the food - pizza, pasta, golfer's corner (calamari, potato wedges and the like), international flavours and irresistible desserts mean that Spikes could quite possibly be the jewel in Nad Al Sheba's crown.⏺
Food●●●●○Serv●●●○○Venue●●●○○Value●●●○○

Studio One

Location ➜ Hilton Jumeirah · Marsa Dubai | 399 1111
Hours ➜ 16:00 - 01:00
Web/email ➜ www.hilton.com   Map Ref ➜ 2-D2

When Studio One was reincarnated as a sports bar, they retained the trendy chrome look, and simply added a pool table, foosball table, and big screen TVs. Despite the apparent dichotomy, the place

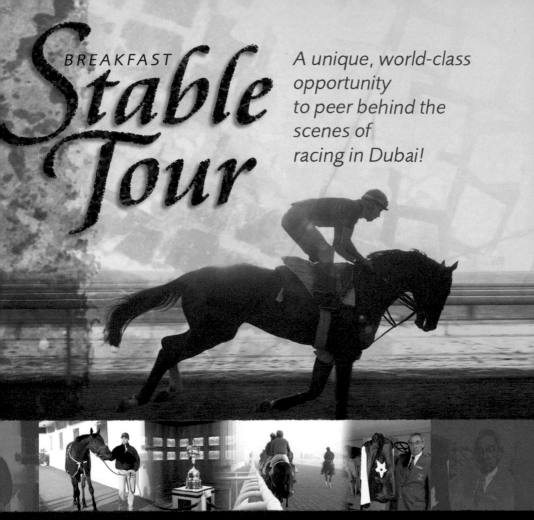

BREAKFAST
Stable Tour

A unique, world-class opportunity to peer behind the scenes of racing in Dubai!

- *A spectacular up-close viewing of the morning gallops!*
- *One-hour tour of the stables.*
- *Full English breakfast in Spikes in the clubhouse over-looking the racecourse.*
- *One-hour behind the scenes tour of the stewards, jockeys and hospitality facilities at Nad Al Sheba, including the Millennium Grandstand.*
- *A visit to the Godolphin gallery.*
- *A personal golf cart.*

Tel: (971) 4 336 3666 • Fax: (971) 4 336 3717
E-mail: info@nadalshebaclub.com
www.nadalshebaclub.com

نادي ند الشبا
NAD AL SHEBA CLUB

offers a cosy and comfortable atmosphere, even if you don't care about the latest footie scores. The usual bar staples – pizza, pasta, wings, sandwiches, and salads – all have sports-related names, and come in generous quantities. Head there during happy hour (20:00 – 22:00) and enjoy the game.

Food●●●●○ Serv●●●●○ Venue●●●●○ Value●●●○○

Uptown

Location → The Jumeirah Beach Hotel · Umm Suqeim | 406 8181
Hours → 18:00 - 02:00
Web/email → www.jumeirahinternational.com   Map Ref → 4-B2

 100

Out on Uptown's terrace you will get one of the best views of the Burj Al Arab in town, as well as the sprawling metropolis of Dubai at sunset. That is not to say that during the hotter months this venue becomes obsolete - far from it, as the interior piano bar is intimate and inviting. The cocktail menu is divine, while the service is first class yet unpretentious and the added touches, such as the complimentary mini canapés put the icing on the cake. There is also a tempting range of 'lite bites'.

Food●●●●○ Serv●●●●○ Venue●●●●● Value●●●○○

VICE

Location → Wafi City · Umm Hurair | 324 4777
Hours → 19:00 - 02:00   Mon closed
Web/email → wwwaficity.com   Map Ref → 13-D2

 50

Dubai has received its very first dedicated vodka and champagne bar, offering – surprise, surprise – an extensive choice of top quality vodkas, the highest standard champagnes and related cocktails. Accessing the bar is a little less straightforward since you have to traipse through Chameleon. Well worth the visit if you like vodka, champagne or both. Don't feel left out if you don't, as the bar is talking up its 'Raw Bar', serving freshly prepared sushi, maki, oysters, smoked salmon and the like.

Food na   Serv na   Venue na   Value na

Vu's Bar

Location → Emirates Towers Hotel · Trade Centre 2 | 319 8088
Hours → 18:00 - 02:00
Web/email → www.jumeirahinternational.com   Map Ref → 9-C2

 100

Towering above all other bars in Dubai (literally), Vu's is a stylish venue with unmatched views of the

city. Popular for a quiet drink before dinner or as a livelier bar later on for the pre-nightclub crowd, drinks are reasonably priced considering its premier location.   Cocktails are expensive but authentically and generously mixed - not as easy on the palate as beach bar, alco-pop style cocktails, but they will definitely satisfy the connoisseur.   Drinks are accompanied by tasty, posh nibbles. Definitely a must do during anyone's time in Dubai. Make sure you take the glass lift on the way up to check out the view.

Food●●●●○ Serv●●●●○ Venue●●●●● Value●●●●○

Jazz Bars

Blue Bar

Location → Novotel World Trade Centre · Trade Centre 2 | 332 0000
Hours → 14:00 - 02:00
Web/email → www.novotel.com   Map Ref → 9-E3

50

A hip and happening place for socialising to foot-tapping blues and jazz, the contemporary chic of the Blue Bar is currently all the rage with the cosmopolitan Dubai clientele. On Thursday nights the bar hosts a live jazz session and a DJ keeps the crowd jumping on Wednesdays. Savour a selection of Belgium's finest draft and bottled beers. Reasonably priced drinks and snacks make a night that's good value for money. Head there early for a quiet drink and a chat or join the bustling crowd later.

Food●●●●○ Serv●●●●○ Venue●●●●○ Value●●●●○

Issimo

Location → Hilton Creek · Deira | 212 7570
Hours → 07:00 - 01:00
Web/email → www.hilton.com   Map Ref → 11-C2

50

All sleek modernism and chic loungers, this place resonates subtle trendiness and understated cool. Settle into fabulous black leather chairs or perch on a stool while the bar staff shake, shimmy and mix up tasty drinks or pour you a slick glass of wine from a healthy sized wine list. A tasty menu caters to the peckish with anything from jumbo prawns to spicy chicken wings. Seized by this town's latest chillout trend, Issimo makes for the perfect layover before, after or even instead of a boisterous night out.

Food●●●●○ Serv●●●○○ Venue●●●○○ Value●●●●○

General Bars | Jazz Bars

Going Out

426

NOVOTEL
ACCOR hotels

World Trade Centre
Dubai

Add a touch of colour
to your evenings

Discover Belgium's finest beverages with a hint of **Jazz** in the
air at the Blue Bar. A subtly lit ambience enhances the sultry
strains of music, award-winning pouring techniques add a
sparkle to the spirits while 7 to 9 pm are the happiest
hours of the night. Now, shouldn't you be thinking Blue?
For more information, call (04) 332 0000

Blue Bar

Jambase

Location ➔ Souk Madinat Jumeirah · Umm Suqeim | 366 8888
Hours ➔ 19:00 - 02:00 Sun closed
Web/email ➔ www.jumeirahinternational.com   Map Ref ➔ 4-A2

  100

Like many of the venues within the Madinat, Jambase is a hedonistic hideaway. Offering nouveau Cajun dining from a limited yet exquisite menu, the crawfish appetiser served with lobster cappuccino sauce and the grilled veal chop are a tasty testament to the creativity of the food. Complemented by a good cocktail selection, attentive service and the subdued sounds of a blues/jazz band in the evening, this hidden gem is worth the find.

Food●●●●○ Serv●●●●○ Venue●●●●○ Value●●●●○

Karaoke Bars

Harry Ghatto's

Location ➔ The Boulevard at Emirates Towers | 319 8088
Hours ➔ 20:00 - 03:00
Web/email ➔ www.jumeirahinternational.com   Map Ref ➔ 9-C2

50

With over a thousand songs to choose from, this small karaoke bar is very popular with wannabe pop stars and Dubai divas. The karaoke starts at 22:00, but the bar is open from 20:00 so you can go early and muster up some courage with a few cocktails before you take to the stage. There is a small menu of bar snacks, but this is a fun way to round off the evening after you've had your dinner in one of the other restaurants in the Emirates Towers.

Food●●●○○ Serv●●●●○ Venue●●●○○ Value●●●●○

Hibiki Karaoke Lounge

Location ➔ Hyatt Regency · Deira | 209 1444
Hours ➔ 19:30 - 03:00
Web/email ➔ www.dubai.regency.hyatt.com   Map Ref ➔ 8-D2

 100

Within the Hyatt Regency and through tassel-strung doors, lies a karaoke lounge that will appeal to the diva deep within every one of us. Though it seems like quite a small room with a fairly expansive bar, stage and seating area, the setting is friendly and private rooms can be hired for special occasions or even just to croon away

from the crowds. Appealing to a mixed clientele of varied nationalities, this friendly bar/nightclub promises a great night out.

Food●●●●○ Serv●●●○○ Venue●●●○○ Value●●○○○

Sports Bars

Aussie Legends

Location ➔ Rydges Plaza Hotel · Al Satwa | 398 2222
Hours ➔ 15:00 - 03:00 Thu 12:00 - 03:00
Web/email ➔ www.rydges.com   Map Ref ➔ 7-A4

     100

This convivial and fun Aussie sports bar is a favourite for its relaxed atmosphere and service. In the style of a friendly chilled out local, Aussie Legends offers numerous sporting events on its big screen TVs, a pool table and some of the best bar music in Dubai. As well as the wide variety of drinks, the menu provides a good range of tasty pub grub.

Family Explorer

Written by Mums and Dads residing in the Emirates, this guidebook is the only essential resource for families with kids, providing you a multitude of indoor and outdoor activity options with your little ones. Make your life easier by following tips on practical topics, such as education and medical care.

Food●●●○○ Serv●●●●○ Venue●●●●○ Value●●●●○

Champions

Location ➔ JW Marriott Hotel · Deira | 262 4444
Hours ➔ 12:30 - 24:00
Web/email ➔ www.marriott.com   Map Ref ➔ 12-A3

  100

One of Dubai's better sports bars, Champions offers large portions of fresh, tasty American cuisine at great value prices. From bar snacks to steaks with all the trimmings, diverse tastes are catered for on the surprisingly comprehensive menu. Lunchtime specials are the biggest bargain at Dhs.27.50 for soup of the day, a main course from the lunch express menu and soft drinks. The atmosphere can be quiet and relaxed (ideal for a nice game of pool) or rowdy, depending on which game is on the screens around the bar.

Food●●●○○ Serv●●●●○ Venue●●●○○ Value●●●●○

Going Out | Jazz Bars | Sports Bars

Tapas Bars

Other options → **Cuban [p.346]**
Spanish [p.392]

Pachanga Terrace

Location → Hilton Jumeirah · Marsa Dubai
Hours → 18:00 - 24:00
Web/email → www.hilton.com | **399 1111**

Map Ref → 2-D2

Please refer to the Pachanga review under Latin American restaurants. [p.379].
Food●●●●○Serv●●●●○Venue●●●●●Value●●●●○

Seville's

Location → Wafi City · Umm Hurair
Hours → 12:00 - 02:00 Thu & Fri 12:00 - 03:00
Web/email → www.waficity.com | **324 7300**

Map Ref → 13-D2

Make a reservation – Seville's has lots of good food, good service and a great crowd. The menu is extensive and both vegetarians and meat lovers are taken care of with a variety of choices. Every palate gets attention at this Dubai stalwart, with spicy, mild, hot and cold dishes. Outside seating in the cooler months is excellent, and if you're inside you can listen to the Spanish guitarist in the evening. Happy hour from 18:00 to 20:00, call for information about salsa and flamenco dancing.
Food●●●○○Serv●●●●○Venue●●●●○Value●●●●○

Wine Bars

Other options → **Cocktail Lounges [p.420]**

Agency, The

Location → The Boulevard at Emirates Towers
Hours → 12:30 - 03:00 Fri 15:00 - 12:30
Web/email → www.jumeirahinternational.com | **319 8088**

Map Ref → 9-C2

Step back from the hustle and bustle of city life with a bottle or two at this stylish wine bar. Whether you sit in the smokers' bar or on the outside terrace, you can enjoy the rather impressive wine list and the small (but adequate) tapas menu as you feel your tensions just floating away. Although the dress code falls on the smarter side of smart casual, and this is definitely one of

the places to be seen, prices won't necessarily burn a hole in your (designer) purse.
Food●●●●○Serv●●●●○Venue●●●●○Value●●●●○

Agency, The

Location → Souk Madinat Jumeirah · Umm Suqeim
Hours → 12:00 - 01:00
Web/email → www.jumeirahinternational.com | **366 8888**

Map Ref → 4-A2

Following on the success of The Agency in the Emirates Towers, this new branch at the Madinat has all the qualities that make the original great – a huge wine list, tasty tapas, a trendy crowd and fairly reasonable prices. However, what makes this particular venue so unique is the setting. You can sit out on the balcony, with the lagoon lapping below you, the stars twinkling above you, and amazing views of the Burj Al Arab blushing in various hues throughout the evening. Highly recommended.
Food●●●●○Serv●●●●○Venue●●●●●Value●●●●○

Chianti's

Location → Ibis World Trade Centre · Trade Centre 2
Hours → 10:00 - 01:00
Web/email → www.accorhotels.com | **332 4444**

Map Ref → 9-E3

Chianti's looks like a bar, a welcome watering hole in the vast aridity of the exhibition space adjoining the Ibis Hotel. Bottles fill almost a quarter of the huge wine racks prominently flanking the bar wall. Consistent in spirit, the servers offer a choice of wines. Oddly no napkins accompany mature nuts and unconventionally mixed drinks, so be prepared to find a home for your olive stones. Though a little off the mark, this place certainly offers an alternative to the 'same-old-same-old' pubs proliferating the city.
Food●●●○○Serv●●○○○Venue●●○○○Value●●●○○

Vinoteca

Location → Grand Hyatt Dubai · Umm Hurair
Hours → 12:00 - 15:00 18:00 - 24:00
Web/email → www.dubai.grand.hyatt.com | **317 2222**

Map Ref → 13-E3

Vinoteca, the Grand Hyatt's wine bar, is a perfect place to stop for an aperitif before dining at one of the hotel's restaurants. The focus of this venue is certainly wine with Vinoteca's collection being a showcase that forms a backdrop to the main bar seating area. If you're not good with decisions, the knowledgeable bartender will offer suggestions and samples. While all of the elements seem cool to the point of cold, Vinoteca gets cosier once you've settled in for a drink, guaranteeing you'll be late for your reservation!

Food●●●●○ Serv●●●●○ Venue●●●○○ Value●●●○○

Vintage

Location → Pyramids · Umm Hurair | 324 4100
Hours → 18:00 - 01:00 Thu 16:00 - 02:00
Web/email → www.waficity.com | Map Ref → 13-D2

   100

At Vintage the gentle lighting, smooth music and Dubai's largest wine menu will help you unwind, relax and forget the world's woes. Choose a couch or perch at the bar and cruise through the impressive menu. Delicious food from traditional fondue, snails, oysters, cheese (more than you knew existed) to surprisingly good desserts. The wine samplers, which change every two weeks, are a great way to experiment. A wonderful place to end the day or week. Call for promotions.

Food●●●●○ Serv●●●●○ Venue●●●●○ Value●●●●○

Pubs

Other options → **Bars [p.417]**

Pubs in Dubai generally look close enough to the real thing to transport you from the brown desert to the green, green grass of home – not most people's vision of the Middle East! Some of these pubs (the English ones especially) are very well established and were among the first modern places for socialising in Dubai. The Irish pubs are some of the favourite and best drinking venues around town. Popular with all nationalities, a good number of pubs manage very successfully to recreate the warm, friendly atmosphere of a typical hostelry. Thousands of miles from their proper location, these places have become genuine locals for many

people, offering just what they've always done – good beer, tasty food and great craic.

Biggles

Location → Millennium Airport Hotel · Al Garhoud | 282 3464
Hours → 12:00 - 01:30
Web/email → www.millenniumhotels.com | Map Ref → 14-D3

   50

Biggles is very much an English style pub with a befitting menu to boot. The décor links its name, theme and location to the airport and the staff are attentive and friendly in their flight crew uniforms. Popular with the middle-aged British expat crowd, it offers good pub food at very reasonable prices. Loyal locals keep the bar busy and give it a genuine British pub feel. The quiz nights are very popular as are the value for money lunch buffets (Dhs.39 a head).

Food●●●○○ Serv●●●●○ Venue●●●○○ Value●●●○○

Chelsea Arms, The

Location → Sheraton Hotel & Towers · Deira | 207 1721
Hours → 12:00 - 16:00 18:00 - 02:00
Web/email → www.starwood.com | Map Ref → 11-C1

  50

Tucked away behind a jewellery shop in the main lobby area, The Chelsea Arms is a hidden gem of a bar. Complete with dartboard and large screen TV for the pub sports enthusiast, the atmosphere is intimate and relaxed - added to by its small size. The food menu is reasonably priced and impressive, both in range and quality. Standing head and shoulders above the normal standard of hotel pubs, The Chelsea Arms won't disappoint.

Food●●●○○ Serv●●●○○ Venue●●●○○ Value●●●○○

Churchill's

Location → Sofitel City Centre · Al Garhoud | 603 8400
Hours → 12:00 - 15:00 18:00 - 02:00
Web/email → www.accorhotels.com | Map Ref → 14-D1

   50

Churchill's is a well-appointed pub styled bar, conveniently located in the Sofitel Hotel for when the City Centre hubbub gets too much. A big TV, pool table and dartboard will keep the most avid of sports enthusiasts happy. A simple but limited food menu complements the wide selection of beverages. Though it doesn't excel in any particular category, Churchill's does succeed in offering a good variety of facilities and central location to attract a mixed clientele.

Food●●○○○ Serv●●●○○ Venue●●●○○ Value●●●○○

Dhow & Anchor

Location → The Jumeirah Beach Hotel · Umm Suqeim | 406 8181
Hours → 12:00 - 24:30
Web/email → www.jumeirahinternational.com   Map Ref → 4-B2

    100

The Dhow & Anchor has the best of both worlds - a traditional pub interior with hearty food and a cosy atmosphere, and the spacious terrace with splendid views of the mesmerising Burj Al Arab and the majestic seas. The menu is as diverse as it is delicious, including salads, curries, seafood, meat, sandwiches and simple, well executed desserts. The wine list is worthy of a fine dining venue while the service is courteous and relaxed. This is a great place to while away a winter afternoon.

Food●●●●○ Serv●●●●○ Venue●●●●○ Value●●●○○

Dubliner's

Location → Le Meridien Dubai · Al Garhoud | 282 4040
Hours → 12:00 - 02:45
Web/email → www.lemeridien.com   Map Ref → 14-E3

   100

Irish bars may be obligatory in any international social scene but Dubliner's doesn't just rest on its laurels. Not only can you get a fine pint of Guinness and a good hearty meal with steaks cooked to perfection, there is also sport on the TV and a busy bar. If you want to avoid the smoke clouds, however, you might be best opting for the outside area. The staff are especially friendly and if you're looking for a real pub atmosphere this is the place.

Food●●●●○ Serv●●●●● Venue●●●●○ Value●●●●●

Fibber Magees

Location → Beh White Swan Bldg · Trade Centre 1 | 332 2400
Hours → 12:00 - 01:00   12:00 - 02:00 Wed - Fri
Web/email → www.fibbersdubai.com   Map Ref → 9-D1

  50

It's back! After three years off the scene, Fibber Magees is once again open for business. The place hasn't changed at all, same location and management - right now there is a little more laid back atmosphere than before - but once they're up to speed, all that remains to be seen is whether the old Fibbers magic can be cranked up again. Some great value happy hours and special nights could be just what's needed to attract back the old regulars and find a whole new crowd to enjoy what it used to be, a quality pub serving great beer and good quality, reasonably priced food.

Food●●●○○ Serv●●●○○ Venue●●●●○ Value●●●○○

Harvesters Pub

Location → Crowne Plaza · Trade Centre 1 | 331 1111
Hours → 12:00 - 01:00
Web/email → www.crowneplaza.com   Map Ref → 9-D2

     100

A popular, after work watering hole serving typical British pub fare, with different cuisines featuring in the monthly promotions. A large screen airs live sporting events and a singing duo adds to the already vibrant atmosphere. Stars of the show are the succulent steaks and fresh, imaginative salads, particularly the avocado and prawn, although starter and dessert choices are somewhat limited. Not the setting for an evening

Hidden Charges

When the bill arrives, subtly check out the dreaded small print (slyly lurking at the bottom of the bill) that says 'INCLUSIVE +15% +5%'. Be careful what you touch, as you may find that even the most innocent eye contact with a nut bowl can result in surplus charges.

of quiet chatting, nonetheless it offers a lively spot to meet with friends for a casual dinner.

Food●●●●○ Serv●●●●○ Venue●●●●○ Value●●●●○

Irish Village

Location → Aviation Club, The · Al Garhoud | 282 4750
Hours → 11:00 - 23:00 Wed & Thu 11:00 - 02:30
Web/email → www.aviationclubonline.com   Map Ref → 14-C3

 100

Deservedly Dubai's most popular pub, the Irish Village is much more than a Dublinland film-set stuck to the side of the tennis courts. With fine low-key live music, chatty service, generous portions of hearty food (including probably the best Fish'n'Chips in Dubai), and an impressive range of foaming ales, the 'Village' guarantees a good 'craic'! It is welcoming, unpretentious and cosmopolitan and its sizeable, yet serene, beer garden attracts a large and friendly crowd, including cats and ducks.

Food●●●●○ Serv●●●●● Venue●●●●○ Value●●●●○

Old Vic

Location → Ramada Hotel · Bur Dubai
Hours → 12:00 - 01:00
Web/email → www.ramadadubai.com
Map Ref → 7-E3

| 351 9999

  100

This Dubai stalwart is still going strong. Boasting live pop music and decent pub grub in authentic surrounds, the Old Vic attracts a dedicated following of resident old boy Brits. Cheerful bar staff keep your drinks and popcorn topped up, and when it's time to nosh, you'll find Bangers and Pies competing with Thai and Indian curries for your attention. Live football matches, a pool table, dartboard, and even chessboards are available for your entertainment. ●

Food●●●○○ Serv●●●●○ Venue●●●●○ Value●●●●○

Red Lion

Location → Metropolitan · Shk Zayed Rd
Hours → 12:00 - 01:00
Web/email → www.methotels.com
Map Ref → 5-C4

| 343 0000

   100

You could almost be forgiven for thinking you'd just set foot in an English country tavern – the Red Lion looks and feels the part, and has a dedicated crowd of regulars that come here for pies, peas, pints and Premier League football in a cosy, relaxed atmosphere. The typical pub grub fare is fair, service is satisfactory, but pints are pricey. Nevertheless, a great stress-busting venue for the overworked, and a good starting point for newcomers to meet some unpretentious, down to earth Britfolk who've been in town a while. ●

Food●●●○○ Serv●●●○○ Venue●●●●○ Value●●●●○

Somerset's

Location → Mövenpick Hotel · Oud Metha
Hours → 12:00 - 16:00 18:00 - 01:00
Web/email → www.movenpick-hotels.com
Map Ref → 10-D4

| 336 6000

  100

Named after the famed novelist and playwright William Somerset Maugham, Somerset's is a sincere effort to create an authentic English pub within a five star hotel – a popular concept in Dubai. Comfy Chesterfields, dark wood and moody lighting make for a relaxed atmosphere, and a diverse crowd gives the place a bit of a buzz, particularly during promotional nights such as 'Boys Night' - half price drinks and complimentary

snack buffet every Monday (strangely for ladies too). Enthusiastic, attentive service, good grub and value drinking make Somerset's a great option for an easy night out. ●

Food●●●●○ Serv●●●●● Venue●●●○○ Value●●●●○

Viceroy, The

Location → Four Points Sheraton · Bur Dubai
Hours → 12:00 - 03:00
Web/email → www.starwood.com
Map Ref → 8-A4

| 397 7444

  50

The Viceroy offers a friendly bar atmosphere, benefiting from a convenient location and great facilities for the sports enthusiast. A wide range of beers and a comprehensive cocktail menu are complemented by an extensive food menu. A large screen television and friendly efficient service makes this the ideal place for watching the match and its location makes it a handy base to move on to the night spots and fleshpots of Bur Dubai. Overall a thoroughly decent pub worthy of a visit. ●

Food●●●●○ Serv●●●○○ Venue●●●○○ Value●●●●○

Waxy O'Conner's

Location → Ascot Hotel · Bur Dubai
Hours → 12:00 - 03:00
Web/email → www.ascothoteldubai.com
Map Ref → 7-E3

| 352 0900

 50

An Irish pub, and a brilliant one at that, Waxy's has gone from strength to strength and is now one of the top party bars in Dubai. Special music nights, sport on TV, drinks competitions and the lavish distribution of free beverage benefits for the lads and lassies creates a buzz that pulls in a joyous crowd. For the peckish, Waxy's Little Restaurant upstairs offers decent food from their menu of regular pub favourites and some Irish specialities in a relaxed atmosphere. Their Friday brunch is particularly worth checking out with a full breakfast, five drinks and Sunday lunch for an amazing Dhs.50. ●

Food●●●○○ Serv●●●○○ Venue●●●●○ Value●●●●○

Nightclubs

Packed with all nationalities, Dubai's nightclubs are very popular from about 23:00 until well into the small hours. Even on weeknights, there's a good scene, and at the weekend, many places are full to overflowing. There are a reasonable number of dedicated nightclubs, as well as numerous other venues with schizophrenic personalities that are bars or restaurants earlier in the evening, and then later turn into the perfect place to cut loose and shake your groove thang. For authentic club nights, look out for the increasingly common visits by international DJs and the special nights held all over Dubai by various event organisers (these are mostly held in winter).

Additionally, since you're in the Middle East, don't forget the option of Arabic nightclubs. Here you can sample a variety of Arabic food and enjoy a night of traditional Arabic entertainment, usually with a belly dancer, a live band and singer. These venues only start getting busy very late in the evening, and can still be empty when most other nightspots are packed, reflecting the Arabic way of starting late and finishing, well... later. For information on door policy and dress code, refer to the introduction to Bars.

Trilogy

Bollywood Café

Location ➜ Regent Palace Hotel · Bur Dubai
Hours ➜ 19:00 - 03:00   **396 3888**
Web/email ➜ www.ramee-group.com   Map Ref ➜ 11-A1

For Hindi movie lovers the popular Bollywood Café's song and dance show is a total immersion experience. Dim lighting, a stage backdrop of the Taj Mahal, frieze of famous actors and actresses and giant screens is enough to make you feel like you're on a film set. Although offering a wide range of Indian starters, tandooris, main dishes, breads and

sweets, the menu also has a selection of snacks if you just want to sit back and enjoy the show.

Food ●●●○○ Serv ●●●●○ Venue ●●●○○ Value ●●●○○

Chameleon

Location ➜ Wafi City · Umm Hurair
Hours ➜ 19:00 - 02:00   Mon closed   **324 0072**
Web/email ➜ www.waficity.com   Map Ref ➜ 13-D2

What used to be Planetarium has morphed, chameleon style, into Dubai's latest hip and trendy nightspot. Offering a fusion of sounds and occasional live music, the ambience of the revamped venue promises to be everything its predecessor was and some. Open nightly from 19:00 (with the exception of Mondays), Chameleon also tempts patrons with a simple yet tempting food menu, mainly meze and so called speciality dishes with distinct Arabic, Latin and African influences.

Food na   Serv na   Venue na   Value na

Cyclone

Location ➜ Nr American Hospital · Oud Metha
Hours ➜ 19:00 - 03:00   **336 9991**
Web/email ➜ cyclone@emirates.net.ae   Map Ref ➜ 10-D4

Cyclone has remained the 'infamous' late night spot due to a mostly male clientele out to meet the many 'international' girls who 'hang' there. Once past the strict doormen (who may relieve you of Dhs.50), the large oval bar anchors the action, although a good sized dance floor does exist. Cyclone is an interesting venue for an adult night out in varied company, and you may find yourself waking up not quite in the circumstances you're accustomed to.

Food ●●●○○ Serv ●●●●○ Venue ●●○○○ Value ●●○○○

Jimmy Dix

Location ➜ Mövenpick Hotel · Oud Metha
Hours ➜ 12:00 - 16:00   18:00 - 03:00   **336 8800**
Web/email ➜ jimmydixdxb@hotmail.com   Map Ref ➜ 10-D4

A friendly, unpretentious bar/nightclub that can always be counted on for a good crowd and a lively buzz. Generally busy, but with a relaxed dress/entry code, the drinks flow, and the live band and DJ always satisfy the crowds, especially on theme nights and their 'Thursday Thump' weekend party. For those wishing to make a night

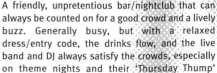

Nightclubs

Going Out

of it, the food is unexpectedly excellent. A real mix of Tex Mex, grills, burgers and home style sausage and mash and crumbles are served, making this a great one stop eating/drinking/partying venue.
Food●●●●○ Serv●●●●○ Venue●●●○○ Value●●●●○

Kasbar

Location ➜ One&Only Palace · Al Sufouh
Hours ➜ 21:00 - 03:00   Sun closed
Web/email ➜ www.oneandonlyroyalmirage.com   Map Ref ➜ 3-A2

| 399 9999

   50

The Arabesque décor, the candle lighting, the expansive cocktail menu and wine list all combine to make Kasbar less of a meat market and more of an unusually sultry and romantic nightclub. A spiral staircase traverses three levels of entertainment; the main floor is predominantly a dance floor with a few tables for the weary, the mezzanine looks out onto the dance floor and the basement is an Arabian lounge style area. Good music, funky mood and a finger clickingly cool ambience all make this a venue not to be missed.
Food●●●●○ Serv●●●●○ Venue●●●●○ Value●●●●○

Lodge, The

Location ➜ Al Nasr Leisureland · Oud Metha
Hours ➜ 11:00 - 15:00 19:30 - 06:00
Web/email ➜ www.alnasrleisureland.ae   Map Ref ➜ 10-E4

| 337 9470

The Lodge is unique for its substantial open air dance floor. Around the edge, you can mingle without the usual smoke or crushed bodies. Split into several bars, restaurants and a nightclub, such as Rockefellas and Tahiti Garden, this is a refreshingly unpretentious late night venue. Getting in (and getting served!) may be tough at times – especially if your face doesn't fit – but the prospect of unbridled revelry under the stars means The Lodge will always attract a boisterous crowd.
Food●●●○○ Serv●●●●○ Venue●●●●○ Value●●○○○

MIX

Location ➜ Grand Hyatt Dubai · Umm Hurair
Hours ➜ 21:00 - 03:00   Sat closed
Web/email ➜ www.dubai.grand.hyatt.com   Map Ref ➜ 13-E3

| 317 1234

50

Lots of flesh shakes and shimmies alongside razor sharp fashion in this town's (supposedly)

only 'superclub'. Three tiers will leave you out of breath and the island bar, sprawling dance floor, seating/lounge area, two VIP rooms, a cigar bar and a sound proofed live music room will have you bowled over. Bartenders are eager to show off their flair and talent for bottle spinning so it's worth choosing your drinks based on entertainment value. With a capacity of 800 guests, this place never gets uncomfortably packed but is always stylishly busy.
Food●●●●○ Serv●●●●○ Venue●●●●○ Value●●●●○

Oxygen

Location ➜ Al Bustan Rotana Hotel · Al Garhoud
Hours ➜ 18:00 - 03:00
Web/email ➜ www.rotana.com   Map Ref ➜ 14-E3

| 282 0000

    100

This beautifully designed nightclub plays a range of music styles, depending on the night, although there seems to be a slight leaning towards R&B, hip-hop and house. There are regular, generous promotions, especially for the ladies who get free champagne all night on Tuesdays and two free drinks on Wednesdays. And there is

Flash Carry!

If you're feeling flash, you can rent a stretch Hummer or Lincoln from Dubai Exotic Limo [p.45] to arrive at your destination in style.

no need to go hungry after dancing the night away, as Oxygen incorporates a rather excellent restaurant, featuring a fusion menu, fine wines, and regular eat/drink special deals.
Food●●●●○ Serv●●●●○ Venue●●●●○ Value●●●●○

Premiere, The

Location ➜ Hyatt Regency · Deira
Hours ➜ 22:00 - 03:00
Web/email ➜ www.dubai.regency.hyatt.com   Map Ref ➜ 8-D2

| 209 1333

 50

Admittedly this bar-cum-club may have seen better days, but there's something to be said about a venue that adamantly sticks to the 80s style décor it acquired more than a decade ago. But superficiality has no value here since the venue remains a popular haunt, particularly with the late night singles crowd, more interested in people watching than dancing. There's definitely a sense of hunt and prey here and groups and couples may be purposely discouraged by the lack of seating.
Food●●○○○ Serv●●○○○ Venue●●○○○ Value●●○○○

Nightclubs

Going Out

Experience Swiss hospitality in Dubai.

he Swiss, renowned for their discretion in usiness and personal affairs are equally well nown for their rich hospitality. This rich ospitality is much in evidence at the 1övenpick Hotel Bur Dubai.

, five-star property located close to the opular shopping malls and business centres f Bur Dubai, the hotel offers 232 well-ppointed rooms and suites with the most nodern facilities, including high speed

wireless Internet access. 7 dining and entertainment venues await our guests, while 6 meeting rooms and a 600-guest capacity ballroom, complete with revolving hydraulic stage, high speed wireless Internet and street-level access, offer ideal conference and banqueting solutions.

So, business or pleasure, step into our foyers for an experience like no other.

Iövenpick Hotel Bur Dubai
?th Street, Oud Metha
O. Box 32733, Dubai, United Arab Emirates
none +971 4 336 60 00
ax +971 4 336 66 26
otel.burdubai@moevenpick-hotels.com
ww.moevenpick-burdubai.com
entral Reservations Office:
all toll free within UAE 800 4934

www.moevenpick-hotels.com
True Excellence in Swiss Hospitality.

MÖVENPICK
Hotel Bur Dubai

Rocky's Café

Location → Regent Palace Hotel · Bur Dubai
Hours → 19:00 - 03:00
Web/email → www.ramee-group.com   Map Ref → 11-A1

396 3897

If you're out for an evening of fun, live entertainment, and cheap and potent drinks then you may have found just the spot. The three roomed venue houses a dining area, a pool room and a staged nightclub area where bands perform throughout the evening. Diners can look forward to a well stocked menu with eclectic Euro/American fare. The bar is a popular late night venue, especially populated by smoking single males and others looking to let loose and enjoy themselves. ●

Food●●●○○Serv●●●○○Venue●●●○○Value●●●○○

Tangerine

Location → Fairmont Dubai, The · Trade Centre 1   **311 8105**
Hours → 20:00 - 03:00
Web/email → www.fairmont.com   Map Ref → 9-E1

This sumptuously decorated Moroccan-inspired club fills guests with pumping tunes and awesome acoustics. Well known international DJs regularly spin here, and attract a diverse crowd of hip wannabes, lounging leerers and older boppers. Dark and cosy booths are serviced by attentive staff delivering quality cocktails, but you'll need to book in advance if you want to enjoy this luxury. Tough door policies mean that not everyone gets in here, especially on busy nights. A place more befitting to funky groovesters, and not so much lager louts looking for action. ●

Food●●●●○Serv●●●●○Venue●●●●○Value●●●●○

Trilogy

Location → Souk Madinat Jumeirah · Umm Suqeim   **366 8888**
Hours → 21:00 - 03:00 Sun closed
Web/email → www.jumeirahinternational.com   Map Ref → 4-A2

Trilogy is the latest edition to Dubai's booming nightclub scene. Taking its name from the number of floors, the club is spacious and open, with a capacity of around a thousand people. There are six bars to choose from, as well as private lounges, which can also be hired for private parties. The crowd is mixed, while the music is typically of the funky house variety. And for a truly decadent

experience, treat yourself and friends to a VIP Glass Cage on the second level and peer down on the action below. ●

Food●●●●○Serv●●●●○Venue●●●●○Value●●●●○

Zinc

Location → Crowne Plaza · Trade Centre 1   **331 1111**
Hours → 19:00 - 03:00
Web/email → www.crowneplaza.com   Map Ref → 9-D2

No more platters of fried scampi elegantly washed down at the side of the dance floor. The latest trend hitting nightspots is a more avant-garde menu, which, although unappealing to young clubbers, is a more refined way for the older contingent to sneak through. The overcomplicated bar system often delays swift service and the prices are customary hotel, but with live 70s music, disco and R&B, and plenty of promotions, this spacious metallic interior is a hot and happening local haunt. ●

Food●●●○○Serv●●●○○Venue●●●●○Value●●●●○

Entertainment

Cinemas

A trip to the cinema is one of the most popular forms of entertainment in the UAE, and movie lovers here are reasonably well catered for, although showings are generally limited to the latest Arabic, Bollywood or Hollywood releases. At present there are five cinemas in Dubai and three in Sharjah showing English language films, with another few showing Indian and Arabic films, including the unique Rex Drive-In cinema at the Mirdif Interchange, Airport Road.

The newer cinemas are generally multi-screen sites, while the older cinemas tend to be larger, with fewer screens and a traditional, crowded cinema atmosphere. Dubai has seen an explosion in the number of screens available over the past couple of years, with the opening of an eleven screen complex near Wafi City and another eleven screen outlet as part of Deira City Centre Mall. These two sites alone have a capacity of 6,000 seats. These will be added to with multi screen cinemas as part of the expansion of both Al Ghurair City and BurJuman Centre.

Cinema timings can be found in the daily newspapers, as well as in an entertainment special in the *Gulf News* every Wednesday.

CENTURY CINEMAS

THE ULTIMATE CINEMA EXPERIENCE

believe...

Release dates vary considerably, with new Western films reaching the UAE anywhere from four weeks to a year after release in the USA and Europe. New movies are released every Wednesday. Films often don't hang around for too long, so if there's something you really want to see, don't delay too much or it will be gone! The cinemas tend to be cold, so make sure you take a sweater. During the weekends, there are extra shows at midnight or 01:00 – check press for details. Tickets can be reserved, but usually have to be collected an hour before the show. With so many screens around now, you will often find cinemas half empty, except for the first couple of days after the release of an eagerly awaited blockbuster.

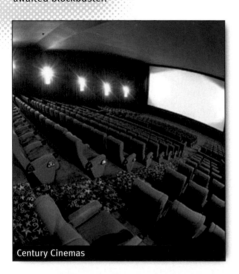
Century Cinemas

Comedy

The regular comedy scene in Dubai is limited. However, there are regular visits from the Laughter Factory, as well as the occasional comical theatre production or one-off event. Comedy shows tend to be aimed at British expats, and other nationalities may not find the sense of humour as funny as the Brits in the audience do. Events are often promoted only a short time before they actually take place, so keep your ears to the ground and your eyes on the daily press and magazines for what's coming up.

Concerts

Throughout the year, Dubai hosts a variety of concerts and festivals, with visits from international artists, bands and musicians. Most events are held in the winter, as well as during the Dubai Shopping Festival and international sporting events. Ticket prices are around the same, or a bit higher, than you would expect to pay elsewhere. There's no regular calendar of events for music lovers, so for details of what's going on, check the daily press, magazines, and listen out for announcements and adverts on the radio. Promoters may be able to supply information on events, but usually no long-term programmes exist, and details are only available about a month in advance. Tickets go on sale at the venues and through other outlets, such as Virgin Megastore. Tickets for some concerts can also be purchased online at www.ibuytickets.com or www.itptickets.com.

Cinemas

Name	Tel No.	Map	Location	No. of Languages	Screens	Prices Normal	Special
Al Nasr	337 4353	10-E3	Oud Metha	M, T	1	15	20
Century Cinemas P.437	349 9773	5-E1	Mercato Mall	A, E, H	7	30	–
CineStar	294 9000	14-D1	Deira City Centre	A, E, H	11	30	40
Deira Cinema	222 3551	11-D1	Deira	M, T	1	15	20
Dubai Cinema	266 0632	12-A3	Deira	H	1	15	20
Galleria	209 6470	8-D2	Hyatt Regency	H, M, T	2	20	–
Grand Cinecity	228 98 98	11-D1	Al Ghurair City	E, A, H	8	25	30
Grand Cineplex	324 2000	13-D3	Umm Hurair 2	A, E	12	30	50
Lamcy	336 8808	10-D4	Lamcy Plaza	H	2	20	–
Metroplex	343 8383	5-C4	Sheikh Zayed Rd	A, E	8	30	55
Plaza	393 9966	8-A2	Bur Dubai	H, M	1	15	20
Rex Drive-In	288 6447	Overview	Madinat Badr	H	1	15	–
Strand	396 1644	11-A2	Al Karama	H	1	15	20

Key: A = Arabic; E = English; H = Hindi; M = Malayalam; T= Tamil

Going Out

Cinemas | Concerts

Classical Concerts

There is only a small number of classical music events held each year in the city. Most notably, the Crowne Plaza Hotel hosts visiting orchestras, musicians and singers from all over the world. Other venues have performances by musical groups or artistes, mainly during special events such as the gala dinners of large trade exhibitions.

Dance Events

Dubai is building itself a surprisingly good club scene, offering some great nights on a fairly regular basis. Different themed nights are organised by international promoters at various clubs around the city, as well as special events like the 'In The Mix' and Ministry of Sound events, which bring in international DJs for epic line-ups and non-stop action. Previous world-class names include Paul Oakenfold, Judge Jules, Sasha, Grooverider, Ian Van Dhal and Roger Sanchez. Like many events in Dubai, dance events are often announced at very short notice, and while the main action is widely publicised, other events can sometimes be promoted in a more underground sort of way.

Pop Concerts

Cynics could say that Dubai, and the Gulf in general, is only honoured by visits from Western bands that are 'on their way down'. However, over the last few years there have been improvements in the standard of performers, and 'big' names have included Elton John, Jamiroquai, Deep Purple, Roger Waters, UB40, Bryan Adams, Rod Stewart, Tom Jones, Sting, Maxi Priest and James Brown. Concerts are usually held at venues such as the Dubai Tennis Stadium, Irish Village, Dubai Creek Golf & Yacht Club, Dubai Media City and the Dubai International Marine Club (DIMC). Smaller venues, notably the Cyclone and Premiere nightclubs, and Rock Bottom Café, have hosted the likes of Bad Manners or Leo Sayer, as well as Abba or Madness tribute bands. Good fun, if not exactly cutting edge stuff. For Asian and Arabic music lovers, there is a range of concerts and musical programmes held in venues like Al Nasr Leisureland and DIMC. These feature some of the biggest names from the Middle East, India, Pakistan and Sri Lanka.

See also: Nightclubs [p.432].

Fashion Shows

Complementing Dubai's reputation as one of the best places to shop for clothes in the Middle East, there are regular fashion shows held in the city. However, very little is arranged on a long-term basis. Keep an eye out in the daily press, monthly entertainment publications, hotels, etc, for what's happening in the month to come. During Dubai Shopping Festival, there are up to 30 fashion shows organised over the month. These are mainly held in hotels and shopping malls; the press during the Festival usually carries information on dates and times.

Theatre

Other options → **Drama Groups [p.310]**

The theatre scene in Dubai is rather limited, with fans relying chiefly on touring companies and the occasional amateur dramatics performance. The amateur theatre scene always welcomes new members, either on stage or behind the scenes. There are also the occasional murder mystery dinners where you're encouraged to display your thespian skills by being part of the performance.

The lack of venues for hosting productions has been a major issue in the past, but should be remedied by the new Madinat Theatre at Madinat Jumeirah and the proposed Dubai Community Theatre and Art Centre at Mall of the Emirates. Facilities will include a theatre, a studio, rehearsal space, art galleries, exhibition space and classrooms, and the centre is due to open in September 2005.

Madinat Theatre

Location → Souk Madinat Jumeirah · Umm Suqeim | 366 8888
Hours → na
Web/email → www.jumeirahinternational.com   Map Ref → 4-A2

With its penchant for make-believe it is no surprise that the Madinat Jumeirah added a theatre to its entertainment menu. Nestled within the myriad of alleyways in the Souk Madinat this 424 seat luxury theatre is a godsend for Dubai's cultural entertainment scene. Designed by professionals with lofty ambitions, from drama to dance, plays to screenings, it is destined for theatrical greatness or at the very least is sure to fill the void in theatrical venues. Check with the venue for up-coming productions.

Maps

User's Guide

To further assist you in locating your destination, we have superimposed additional information, such as main roads, roundabouts and landmarks on the maps. Many places listed throughout the guidebook also have a map reference alongside, so you know precisely where you need to go (or what you need to tell the taxi driver).

To make it easier to find places, and give better visualisation, the maps have all been orientated parallel to Dubai's coastline rather than the customary north orientation. While the overview map on this page is at a scale of approximately 1:200,000 (1 cm = 2 km), all other maps range from 1:12,500 (1 cm = 125 m) to 1:50,000 (1cm = 500 m).

Technical Info – Satellite Images

The maps in this section are based on rectified QuickBird satellite imagery taken in 2003 and 2004.

The QuickBird satellite was launched in October 2001 and is operated by DigitalGlobe™, a private company based in Colorado (USA). Today, DigitalGlobe's QuickBird satellite provides the highest resolution (61 cm), largest swath width and largest onboard storage of any currently available or planned commercial satellite.

MAPS geosystems are the Digital Globe master resellers for the Middle East, West, Central and East Africa. They also provide a wide range of mapping services and systems. For more information, visit www.digitalglobe.com (QuickBird) and www.maps-geosystems.com (mapping services) or contact MAPS geosystems on 06 572 5411.

What's new?

Street Map Explorer

At last! The most accurate and up to date map of Dubai has arrived. The Street Map Explorer (Dubai) provides a concise, comprehensive and cross referenced compendium of street names, with a full A to Z index of businesses and tourist attractions. This handy book will soon become your favourite travel mate and a standard tool for navigating the streets of Dubai.

Map Legend

Activity	Café/Cinema	Shopping/Souk
Area/Roundabout	Embassy/Hospital	Important Landmark
Business	Hotel	Exploring

Online Maps

If you want to surf for maps online, Dubai Municipality's www.exploredubai.ae is an excellent Website for navigating through maps and routes. On www.dubailocator.com, you can actually pin point your location and will be supplied with a Web address for your personal map. Just give out this URL for your next party! For those owning property, the Land Department's Website, www.dubailand.gov.ae is worth a bookmark.

User's Guide

Maps

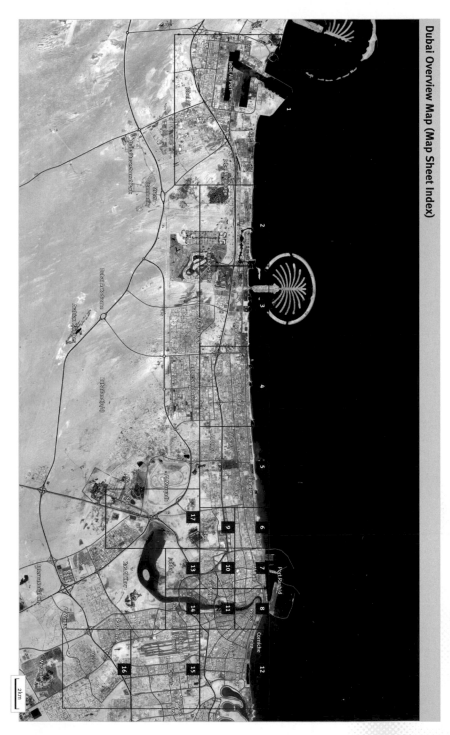

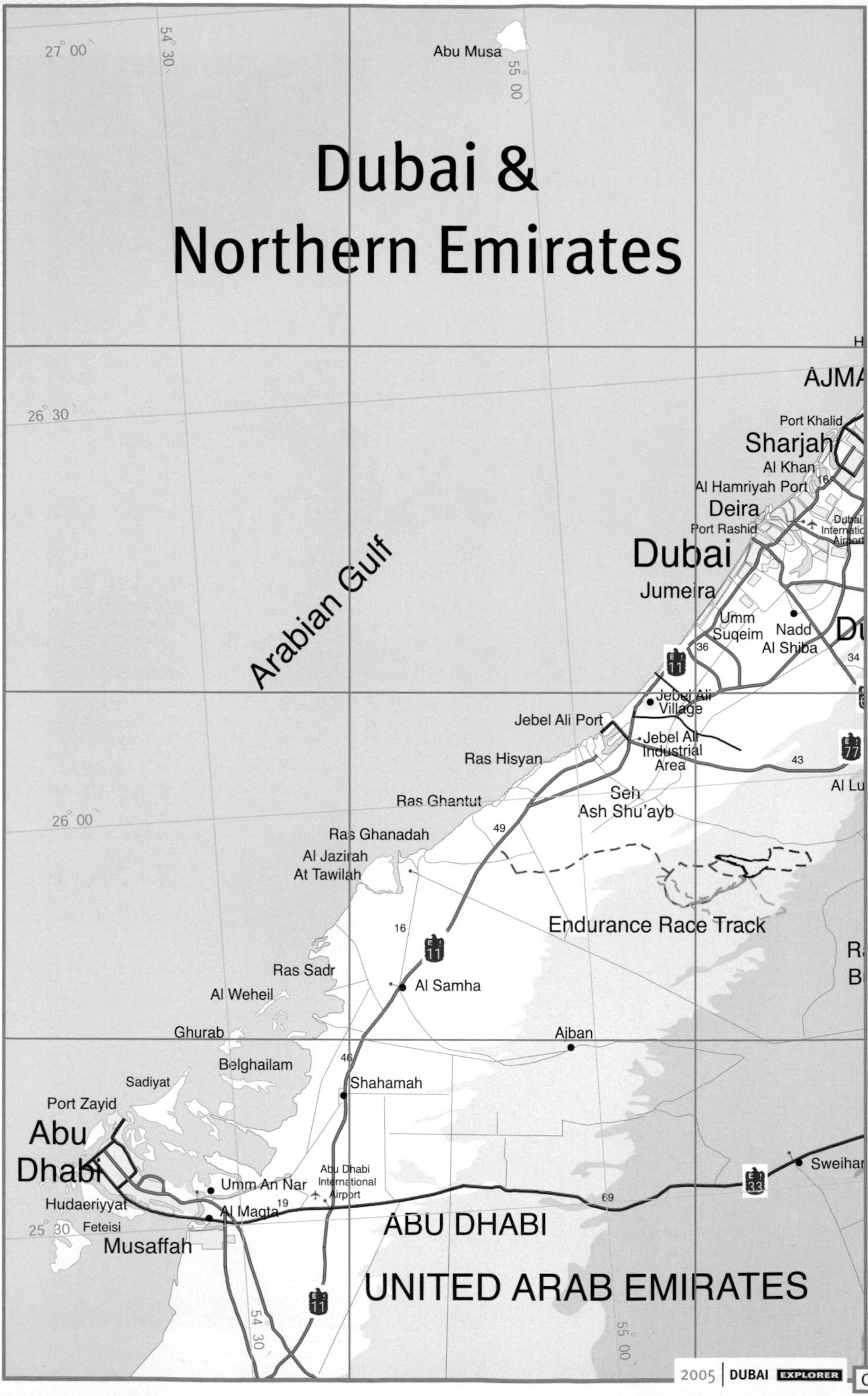

Dubai & Northern Emirates

Abu Musa

27° 00

54° 30

55 00

26° 30

AJMA

Port Khalid

Sharjah

Al Khan

Al Hamriyah Port

Deira

Port Rashid

Dubai International Airport

Arabian Gulf

Dubai

Jumeira

Umm Suqeim

Nadd Al Shiba

D

36

34

Jebel Ali Village

Jebel Ali Port

Jebel Ali Industrial Area

Ras Hisyan

43

77

Al Lu

Ras Ghantut

Seh Ash Shu'ayb

26° 00

Ras Ghanadah

Al Jazirah At Tawilah

49

Endurance Race Track

R B

16

11

Ras Sadr

Al Weheil

Al Samha

Ajban

Ghurab

Belghailam

46

Sadiyat

Shahamah

Port Zayid

Abu Dhabi

Umm An Nar

Abu Dhabi International Airport

19

Sweihar

33

Hudaeriyyat

Al Magta

E9

25° 30 Feteisi

Musaffah

ABU DHABI

11

UNITED ARAB EMIRATES

54 30

55 00

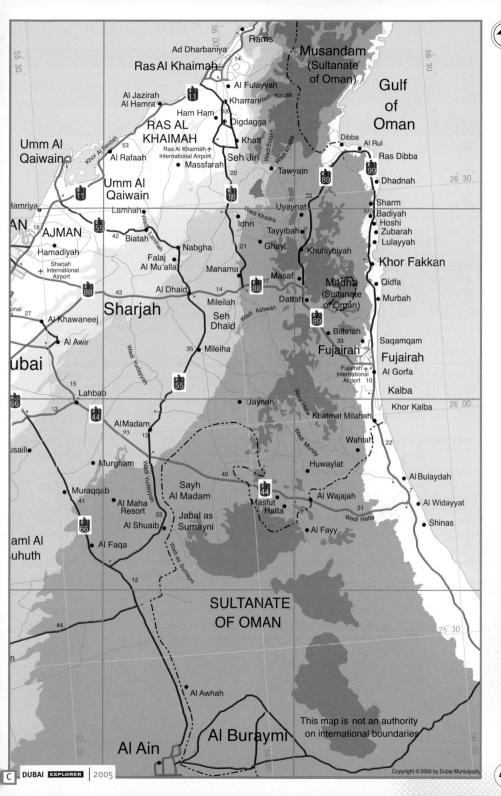

Rams

Ad Dharbaniya

Ras Al Khaimah

14

Al Fulayyah

Musandam
(Sultanate
of Oman)

Gulf
of
Oman

Al Jazirah
Al Hamra

11

Kharran Wadi Naqab

Ham Ham

18

Digdagga

Dibba

Al Rul

Ras Dibba

RAS AL
KHAIMAH

Khatt

89

99

Umm Al
Qaiwain

53

Al Rafaah

Ras Al Khaimah
International Airport

Seh Jiri

Massfarah

20

Dhadnah

26 30

Umm Al
Qaiwain

11

Tawyain

Sharm

Badiyah
Hoshi

AN

Hamriya

18

AJMAN

Lamhah

55

Biatah

42

Nabgha

Idhn

Wadi Khadra

Ulaynat

37

Tayyibah

33

Zubarah
Lulayyah

21

Ghayl

Khulaybiyah

Khor Fakkan

Hamadiyah

Falaj
Al Mu'alla

Manama

Masaf

88

Madha

Qidfa

Sharjah
International
Airport

88

43

Al Dhaid

14

88

17

Masaf

(Sultanate
of Oman)

Murbah

onal

27

Al Khawaneej

Mileilah

Seh
Dhaid

Wadi Ashwan

Dattah

89

Saqamqam

Al Awir

35

Mileiha

Bithnah

33

Fujairah

Fujairah

ubai

15

Lahbab

55

Fujairah
International
Airport 10

Al Gorfa

66

13

Daynah

Kalba

44

Al Madam

23

12

Khatmat Milahah

Khor Kalba

26 00

Murgham

Wahlah

22

Al Bulaydah

Muraqqab

41

Sayh
Al Madam

40

Huwaylat

Al Maha
Resort

33

Jabal as
Sumayni

44

Masfut

Al Wajajah

31

Al Widayyat

66

Al Shuaib

Hatta

Wadi Hatta

Shinas

aml Al
uhuth

Al Faqa

Al Fayy

12

SULTANATE
OF OMAN

44

25 30

Al Awhah

Al Ain

Al Buraymi

This map is not an authority
on international boundaries

UAE

Maps

Copyright © 2000 by Dubai Municipality

The following is a list of the main communities and streets in Dubai, which are referenced on the map pages. Many extend beyond one grid reference, in which case the main grid reference has been given.

Community	Map Ref	Community	Map Ref
Al Barsha	3-D4	Emirates Hills 1	2-E4
Al Garhoud	14-D4	Emirates Hills 2	3-A3
Al Hamriya	12-C3	Hor Al Anz	12-B3
Al Jafilia	7-B4	Jaddaf	13-E4
Al Karama	10-D2	Jebel Ali FZ	1-B2
Al Mamzar	12-E2	Jumeira	6-B3
Al Mankhool	7-C4	Jumeira 2	5-E2
Al Quoz	5-B4	Jumeira 3	5-B2
Al Quoz Ind. 1	4-E4	Marsa Dubai	2-D2
Al Quoz Ind. 3	4-B4	Mirdif	16-B4
Al Qusais	15-D2	Muhaisnah	16-D3
Al Qusais Ind.	15-E3	Oud Metha	10-D4
Al Safa 1	5-B3	Port Rashid	7-C2
Al Safa 2	4-E3	Port Saeed	11-C2
Al Satwa	6-C4	Rashidiya	16-A2
Al Satwa East	10-B1	Shindagha	8-B1
Al Sufouh	3-E3	Trade Centre 1	9-B1
Al Tawar	15-C2	Trade Centre 2	9-C2
Al Wasl	5-D3	Umm Hurair 2	13-E1
Bastakiya	8-B3	Umm Suqeim 1	4-E2
Bur Dubai	8-A3	Umm Suqeim 2	4-C2
Deira	8-C3	Umm Suqeim 3	4-B2
Dubai Int. Airport	15-A2	Za'abeel	10-B3

Street	Map Ref	Street	Map Ref
2nd Za'abeel Rd	17-C1	Al Wasl Rd	4-B3
Abu Hail Rd	12-B4	Algiers Rd	16-D3
Airport Rd	14-E2	Baghdad Rd	15-D3
Al Adhid Rd	7-C4	Beirut Rd	15-B4
Al Diyafah St	7-A3	Beniyas Rd	8-B3
Al Garhoud Rd	14-C2	Casablanca Rd	14-D3
Al Ittihad Rd	12-A4	Damascus Rd	15-E2
Al Jumeira Rd	4-B2	Doha Rd	17-A1
Al Khaleej Rd	8-A1	Dubai - Al Ain Rd	17-A4
Al Khawaneej Rd	15-A4	Dubai - Sharjah	
Al Maktoum Rd	11-D2	Highway	12-D4
Al Manara Rd	4-D2	Khalid Bin Al	
Al Mankhool Rd	7-B3	Waleed Rd	7-E2
Al Mina Rd	7-B2	Muscat Rd	5-C4
Al Muraqqabat Rd	11-E2	Oud Metha Rd	13-B2
Al Musallah Rd	8-A3	Rabat Rd	16-A4
Al Naif Rd	8-D3	Riyadh Rd	13-E3
Al Quds Rd	15-B2	Salah Al Din Rd	12-A4
Al Quta'eyat Rd	13-D3	Sheikh Zayed Rd	2-B3
Al Rasheed Rd	12-B3	Trade Centre Rd	10-B1
Al Rigga Rd	11-D2	Tunis Rd	16-D2
Al Satwa Rd	6-C4	Umm Hurair Rd	10-E3
Al Sufouh Rd	3-B2	Za'abeel Rd	10-D3

Dubai Address System

Dubai is in the process of completing a Comprehensive Addressing System that consists of two complementary number systems – the Route Numbering System and the Community, Street & Building Numbering System. The former helps an individual to develop and follow a simple series of directions for travelling from one area to another in Dubai; the latter helps a visitor to locate a particular building or house in the city.

Routes Numbering System

Various routes connecting Dubai to other emirates of the UAE, or to main cities within an emirate, are classified as 'Emirate-Routes' or 'E-Routes'. They comprise two or three digit numbers on a falcon emblem as shown on the UAE Map. Routes connecting main communities within Dubai are designated as 'Dubai-Routes' or 'D-Routes'. They comprise two digit numbers on a fort emblem. D-Routes parallel to the coast are even numbered, starting from D94 and decreasing as you move away from the coast. D-Routes perpendicular to

the coast are odd numbered, starting from D53 and decreasing as you move away from the Abu Dhabi border.

Community, Street Numbering System

This system helps an individual to locate a particular building or house in Dubai. The emirate is divided into nine sectors:

Sectors 1, 2, 3, 4 and 6 represent urban areas.
Sector 5 represents Jebel Ali.
Sectors 7, 8 and 9 represent rural areas
Sectors are sub-divided into communities, which are bound by main roads. A three digit number identifies each community. The first is the number of the sector, while the following two digits denote the location of the community in relation to neighbouring communities in sequential order.

Buildings on the left hand side of the street have odd numbers, while those on the right hand side take even numbers. Again, building numbers increase as you move away from the city centre. The complete address of a building in Dubai is given as Community Number, Street Number and Building Number.

Community & Street Index

Maps

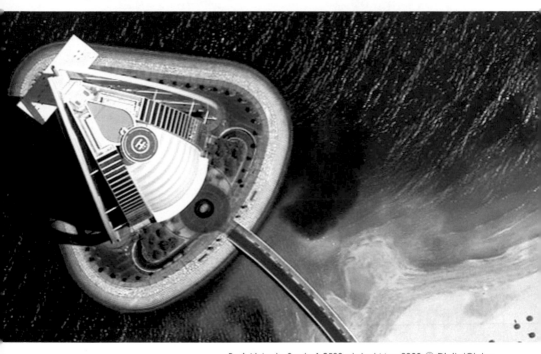

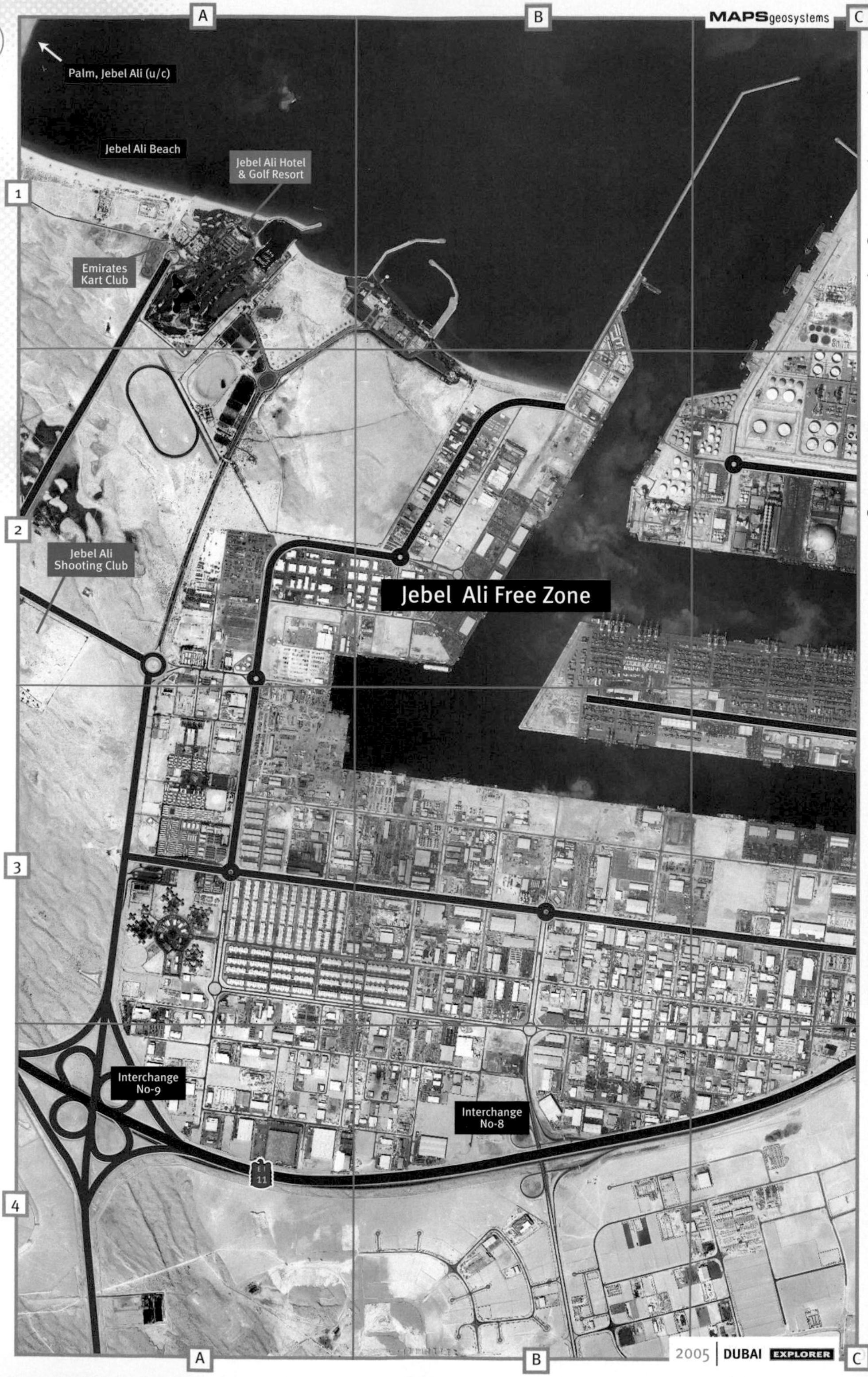
A
B
C
MAPSgeosystems
1
2
3
4
Palm, Jebel Ali (u/c)
Jebel Ali Beach
Jebel Ali Hotel & Golf Resort
Emirates Kart Club
Jebel Ali Shooting Club
Jebel Ali Free Zone
Interchange No-9
Interchange No-8
E11

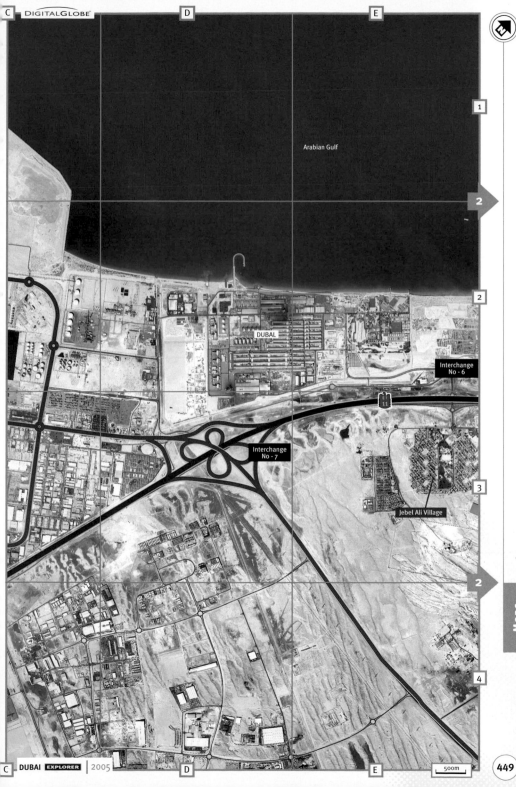

C · DIGITALGLOBE · D · E

Arabian Gulf

DUBAL

Interchange
No - 6

11

Interchange
No - 7

Jebel Ali Village

1
2
2
3
2
4

Maps

1

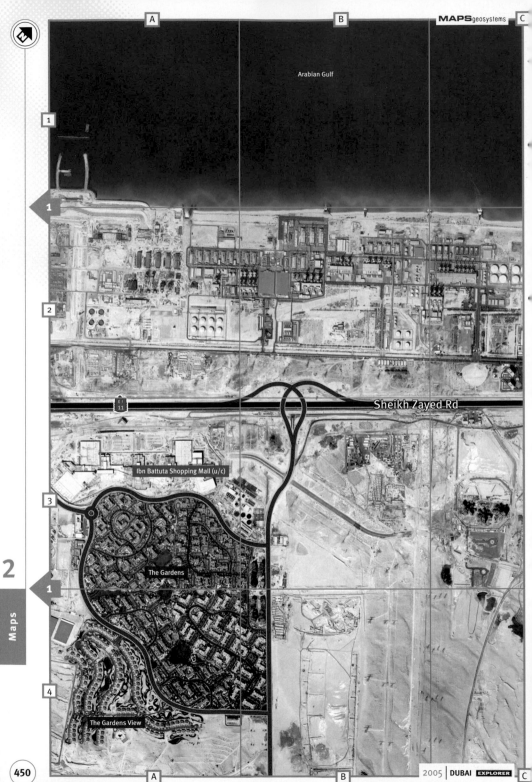

1

1

2

Arabian Gulf

Sheikh Zayed Rd

E 11

Ibn Battuta Shopping Mall (u/c)

3

The Gardens

2

1

Maps

4

The Gardens View

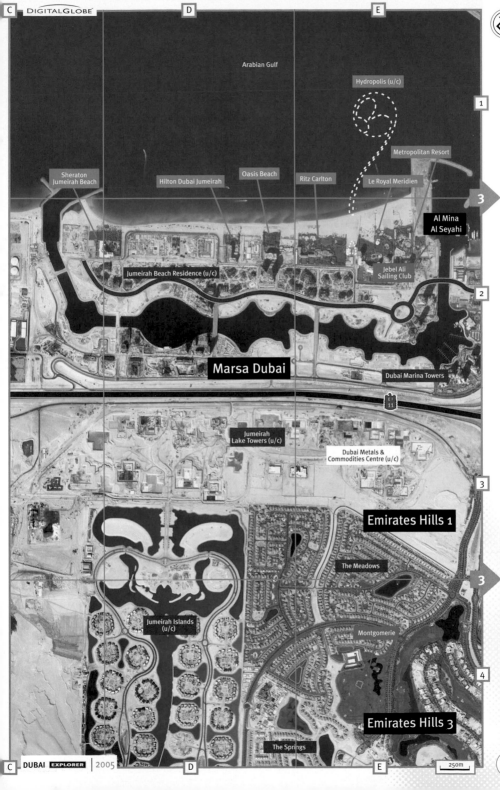

DIGITALGLOBE

1

Arabian Gulf

Hydropolis (u/c)

Metropolitan Resort

Sheraton
Jumeirah Beach

Hilton Dubai Jumeirah

Oasis Beach

Ritz Carlton

Le Royal Meridien

3

Al Mina
Al Seyahi

Jumeirah Beach Residence (u/c)

Jebel Ali
Sailing Club

2

Marsa Dubai

Dubai Marina Towers

11

Jumeirah
Lake Towers (u/c)

Dubai Metals &
Commodities Centre (u/c)

3

Emirates Hills 1

The Meadows

3

2

Maps

Jumeirah Islands
(u/c)

Montgomerie

4

Emirates Hills 3

The Springs

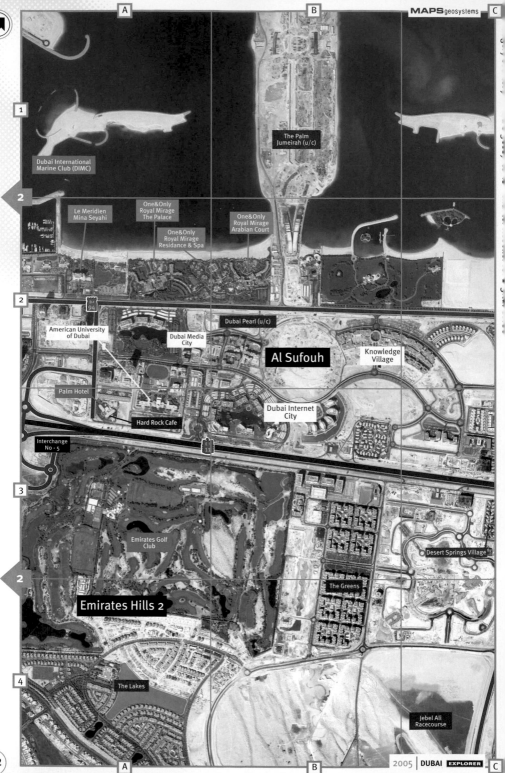

A

B

C

1

Dubai International
Marine Club (DIMC)

The Palm
Jumeirah (u/c)

2

2

Le Meridien
Mina Seyahi

One&Only
Royal Mirage
The Palace

One&Only
Royal Mirage
Residence & Spa

One&Only
Royal Mirage
Arabian Court

94

American University
of Dubai

Dubai Pearl (u/c)

Dubai Media
City

Al Sufouh

Knowledge
Village

Palm Hotel

Dubai Internet
City

Hard Rock Cafe

Interchange
No - 5

11

3

Emirates Golf
Club

Desert Springs Village

2

The Greens

Emirates Hills 2

3

Maps

4

The Lakes

Jebel Ali
Racecourse

A

B

C

1

4

2

Al Sufouh Rd

Dubai College

94

Al Sufouh

3

Sheikh Zayed Rd

4

Al Barsha

11

Mall of the
Emirates (u/c)

4

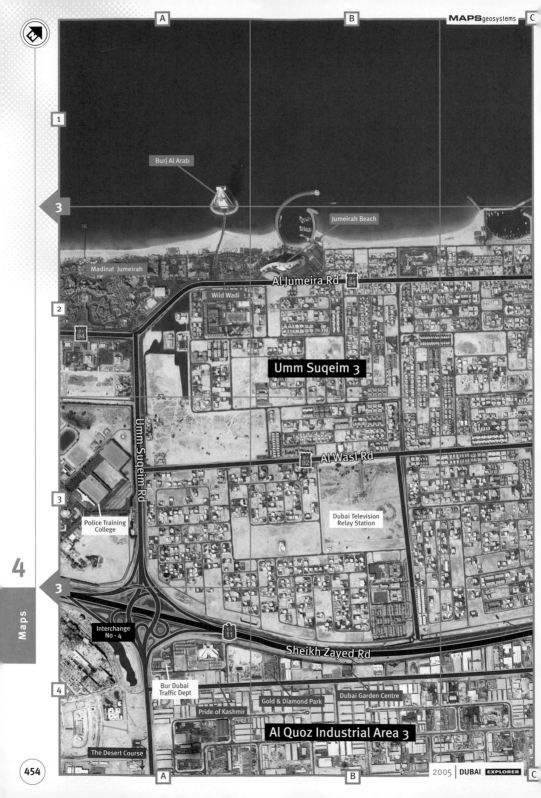

1

Burj Al Arab

3

Jumeirah Beach

Madinat Jumeirah

Al Jumeira Rd [94]

Wild Wadi

2

[94]

Umm Suqeim 3

Umm Suqeim Rd

Al Wasl Rd [92]

3

Police Training College

Dubai Television Relay Station

3

Interchange No - 4

11

Sheikh Zayed Rd

4

Bur Dubai Traffic Dept

Pride of Kashmir

Gold & Diamond Park

Dubai Garden Centre

Al Quoz Industrial Area 3

The Desert Course

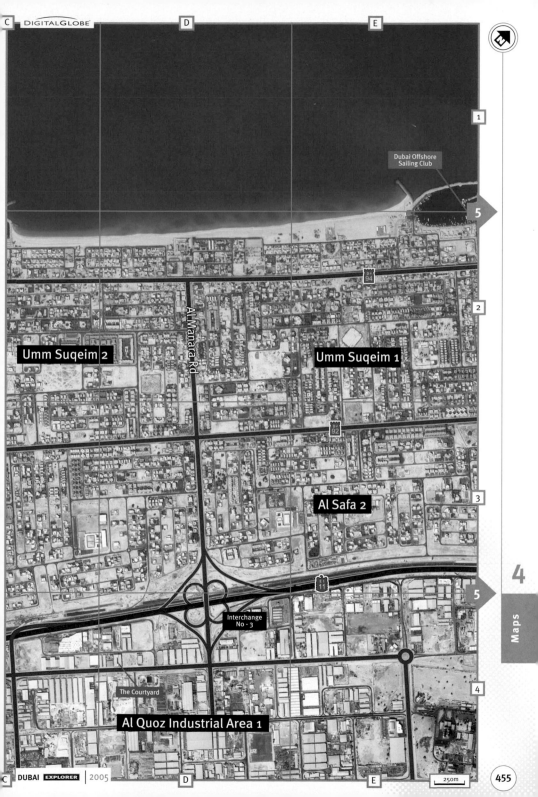

C D E

1

Dubai Offshore
Sailing Club

5

94

2

Al Manara Rd

Umm Suqeim 2

Umm Suqeim 1

92

Al Safa 2

3

5

Interchange
No - 3

4

Maps

The Courtyard

Al Quoz Industrial Area 1

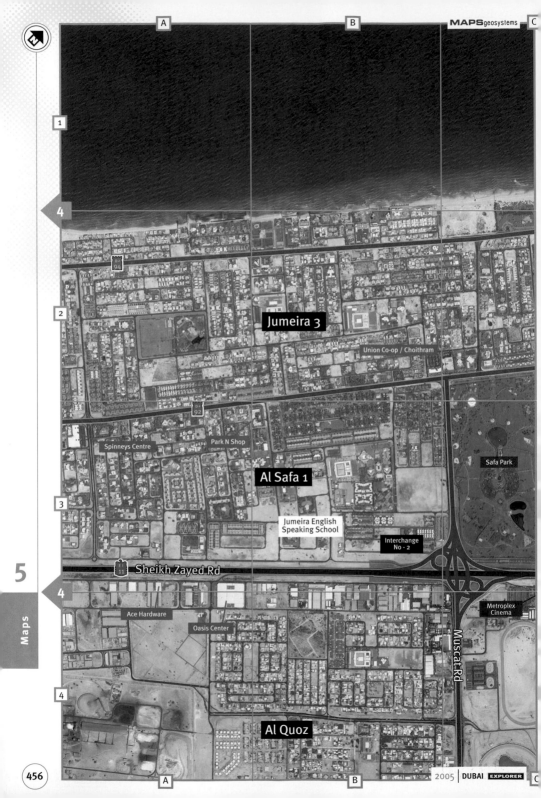

Jumeira 3

Union Co-op / Choithram

Spinneys Centre

Park N Shop

Al Safa 1

Safa Park

Jumeira English
Speaking School

Interchange
No - 2

Sheikh Zayed Rd

Ace Hardware

Oasis Center

Metroplex
Cinema

Muscat Rd

Al Quoz

5

Maps

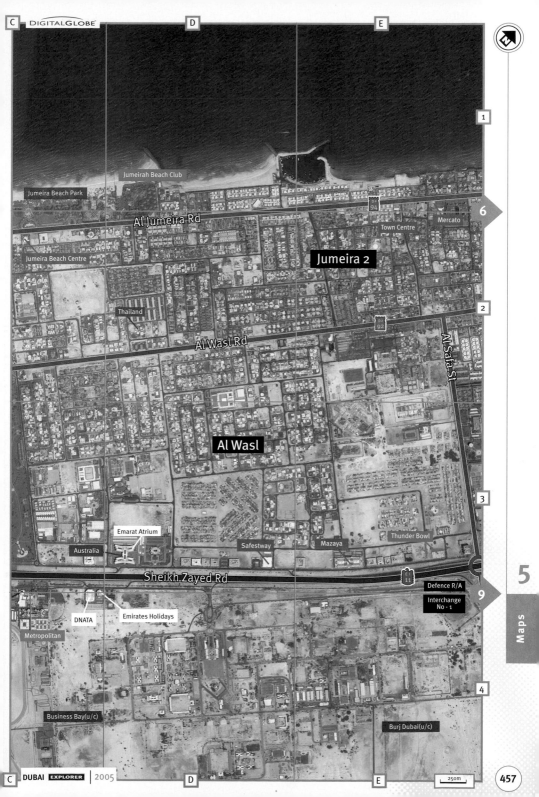

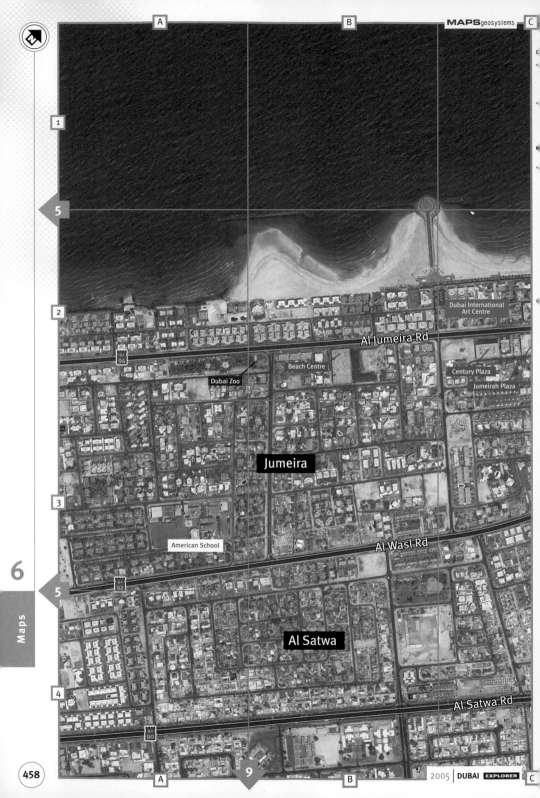

Dubai International
Art Centre

Al Jumeira Rd

Beach Centre

Century Plaza

Jumeirah Plaza

Dubai Zoo

Jumeira

American School

Al Wasl Rd

Al Satwa

Al Satwa Rd

Jumeira Beach Corniche

Dubai Marine

Palm Strip

Union House

The Village

94

Jumeirah Centre

Magrudy's

Jumeira Mosque

THE One

Jumeira Rotana

92

Iran

Iranian Hospital

Dune Centre

'Plant Street'

Al Satwa

90

6

Maps

9

250m

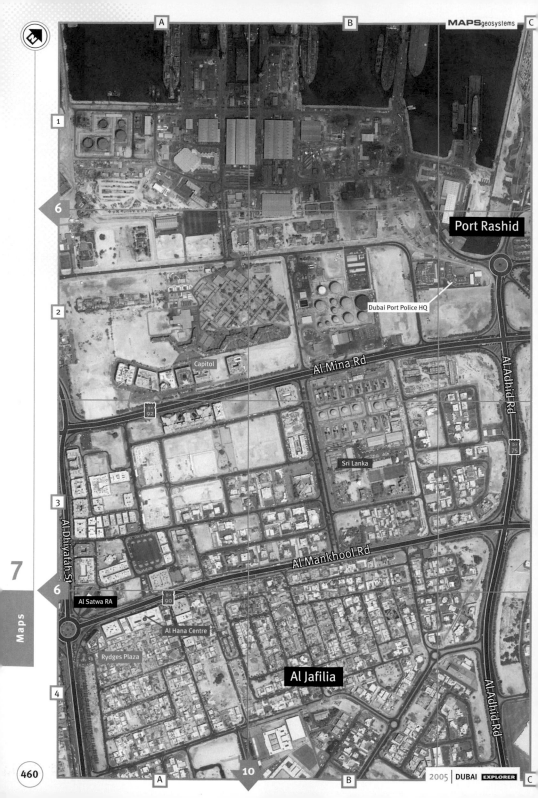

1

6

2

Port Rashid

Dubai Port Police HQ

Capitol

Al Mina Rd

Al-Adhid Rd

92

Sri Lanka

75

3

Al-Dhiyafah St

7

Maps

Al Mankhool Rd

6

Al Satwa RA

90

Al Hana Centre

Al Jafilia

Rydges Plaza

Al-Adhid Rd

4

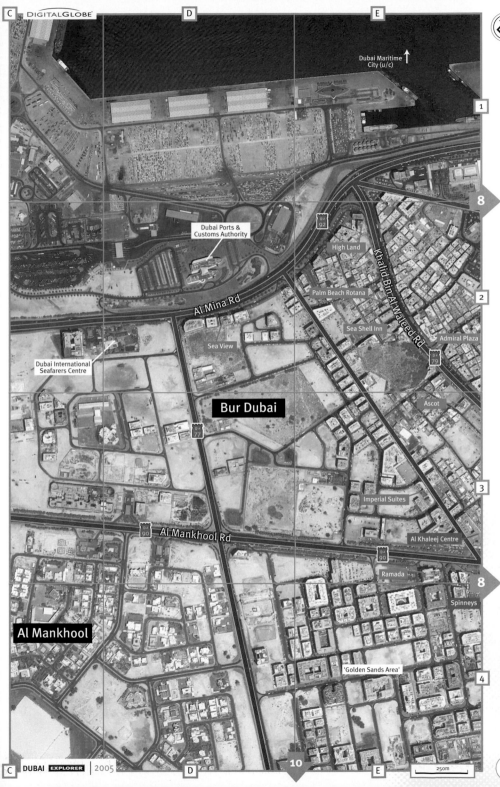

DIGITALGLOBE

C   D   E

Dubai Maritime
City (u/c)

1

8

Dubai Ports &
Customs Authority

High Land

Palm Beach Rotana

Al Mina Rd

Sea Shell Inn

Admiral Plaza

2

Sea View

Dubai International
Seafarers Centre

Bur Dubai

Ascot

3

Imperial Suites

Al Khaleej Centre

Al Mankhool Rd

Ramada

8

Spinneys

Al Mankhool

'Golden Sands Area'

4

7

Maps

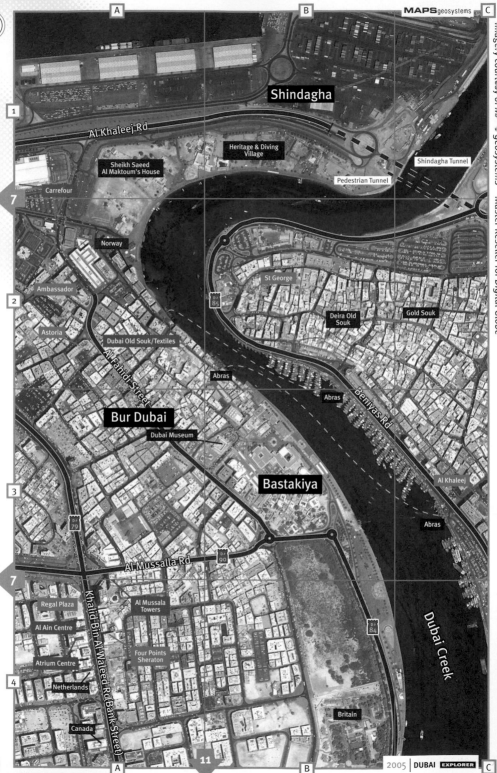

Shindagha

Al Khaleej Rd

Heritage & Diving Village

Shindagha Tunnel

Sheikh Saeed Al Maktoum's House

Pedestrian Tunnel

Carrefour

Norway

St George

Ambassador

2

Deira Old Souk

Gold Souk

Astoria

Dubai Old Souk/Textiles

Al Fahidi Street

Abras

Abras

Benyas Rd

Bur Dubai

Dubai Museum

Al Khaleej

3

Bastakiya

79

Abras

8

90

Al Mussalla Rd

Maps

7

84

Regal Plaza

Al Mussala Towers

Dubai Creek

Khalid Bin Al Waleed Rd (Bank Street)

Al Ain Centre

Atrium Centre

Four Points Sheraton

4

Netherlands

Canada

Britain

11

A | B | 2005 | **DUBAI** EXPLORER | C

C   D   E

1

12

Deira Fish, Meat &
Vegetable Market

Hyatt Regency

2

Hyatt Golf Park

Al Khaleej Rd

Deira

Deira Covered Souk

Naif RA

Naif Park

Al Naif Rd

3

8

Maps

Carlton Tower

12

Riviera

Twin Towers

Al Maktoum
Hospital

4

Inter Continental

Fish RA

Marco Polo

11

Trade Centre 1

Al Safa

Al Moosa 2
Zabeel

Al Moosa

Al Salam   Doha

Sahara

Kalantar   Al Rostamani

Wafa

Towers Rotana

Shk Ahmed   Number One

Oasis

Shangri-La

Sheikh Zayed Rd

E 11

21st Century
Tower   Oasis

Al Attar

Al Ghadier

Capricorn

Al Kawakeb

Ghaya Residence

Sky

Kendah House

Interchange
No 1

Dusit

Jumeira

Dubai International
Financial Centre (u/c)

The Gate

Etisalat

Al Murooj
Complex

C   D   **6**   E

Al Satwa

1

Khalid Al Attaar

City 2   White Swan   API World Tower   Fairmont

Al Wasl   Saeed   White Crowne

City   Al Durrah   France

Crowne Plaza

10

Sheikh Zayed Road

Trade Centre 2

Trade Centre Apartments

Ibis

2

The Tower   Dubai International
Exhibition Centre

Emirates Towers   Dubai International
Conference Centre

Emirates Towers
Office

Novotel

3

9

10

Maps

4

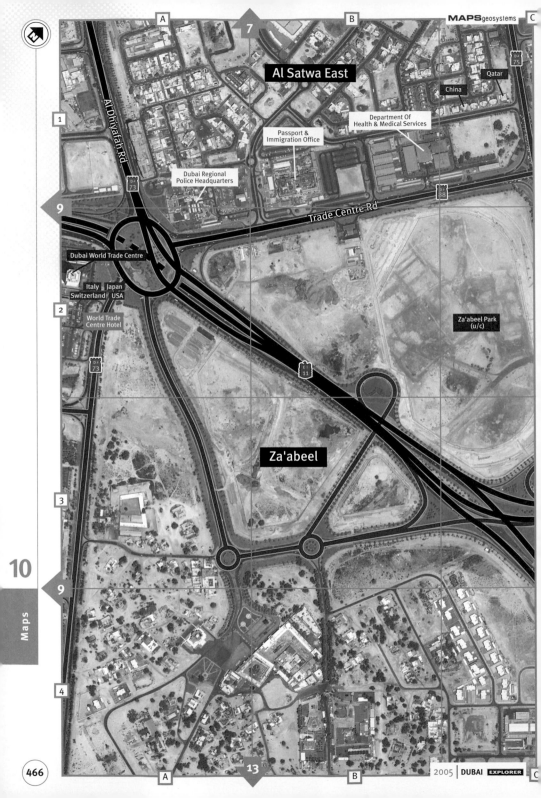

MAPSgeosystems

Al Satwa East

Qatar

China

Department Of
Health & Medical Services

Passport &
Immigration Office

Al Dhiyafah Rd.

Dubai Regional
Police Headquarters

Trade Centre Rd.

Dubai World Trade Centre

Italy | Japan
Switzerland | USA

World Trade
Centre Hotel

Za'abeel Park
(u/c)

Za'abeel

10

Maps

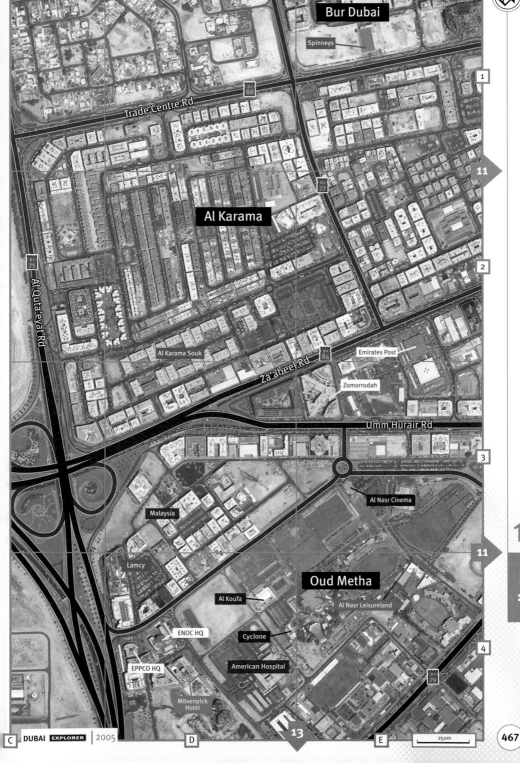

Bur Dubai

Spinneys

Trade Centre Rd

Al Karama

Al Quta'eyat Rd

Al Karama Souk

Za'abeel Rd

Emirates Post

Zomorrodah

Umm Hurair Rd

Al Nasr Cinema

Malaysia

Oud Metha

Lamcy

Al Koufa

Al Nasr Leisureland

ENOC HQ

Cyclone

EPPCO HQ

American Hospital

Mövenpick Hotel

10

Maps

250m

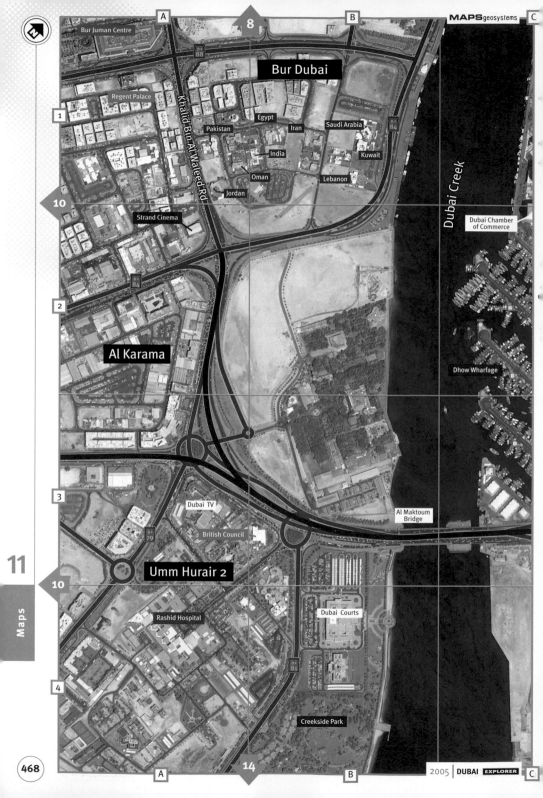

Bur Juman Centre

Bur Dubai

Regent Palace

Egypt

Pakistan

Iran

Saudi Arabia

India

Kuwait

Oman

Lebanon

Jordan

Khalid Bin Al Waleed Rd

Strand Cinema

Dubai Creek

Dubai Chamber of Commerce

Al Karama

Dhow Wharfage

Dubai TV

British Council

Al Maktoum Bridge

Umm Hurair 2

Rashid Hospital

Dubai Courts

Creekside Park

11

Maps

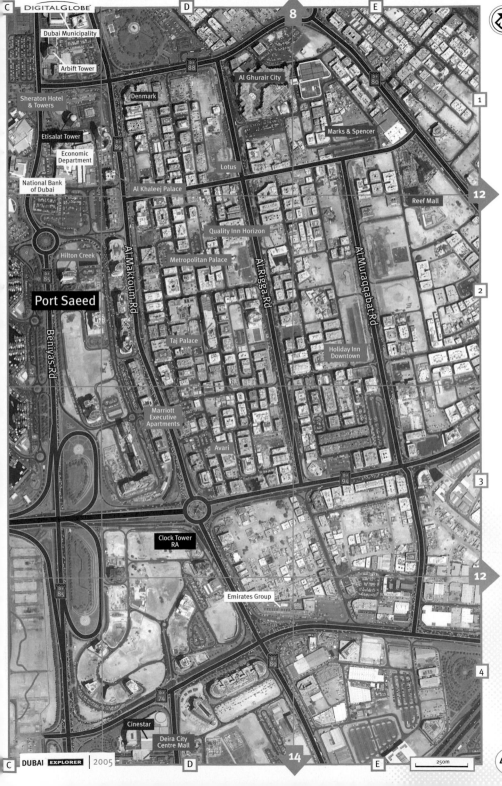

DIGITALGLOBE

Dubai Municipality

Arbift Tower

Sheraton Hotel & Towers

Etisalat Tower

Economic Department

National Bank of Dubai

Denmark

88

Al Ghurair City

80

1

Lotus

Al Khaleej Palace

Marks & Spencer

12

Reef Mall

89

Hilton Creek

85

Port Saeed

Quality Inn Horizon

Metropolitan Palace

Al Maktoum Rd

Al Rigga Rd

Al Muraqqabat Rd

2

Beniyas Rd

Taj Palace

Holiday Inn Downtown

Marriott Executive Apartments

Avari

94

3

Clock Tower RA

85

12

Emirates Group

89

4

74

Cinestar

Deira City Centre Mall

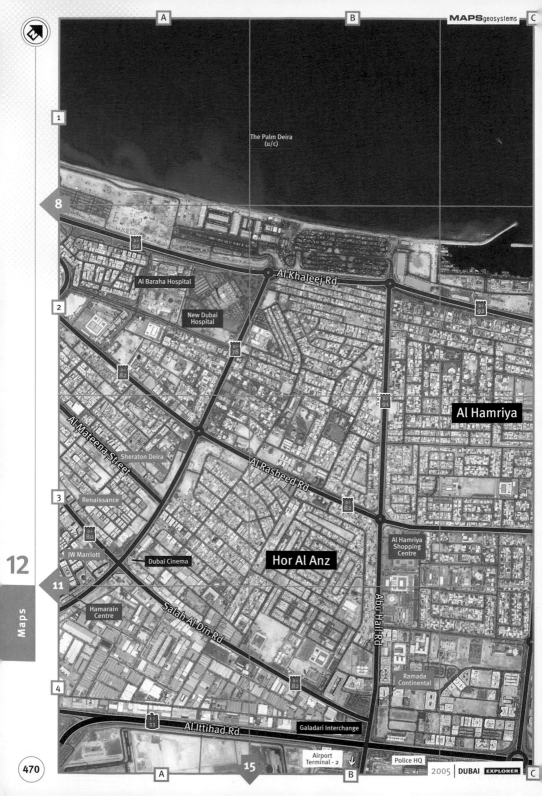

1

The Palm Deira
(u/c)

8

92

Al Baraha Hospital

Al Khaleej Rd

New Dubai
Hospital

2

92

78

82

91

Al Hamriya

Al Mateena Street

Sheraton Deira

Al Rasheed Rd

3

Renaissance

82

80

JW Marriott

Dubai Cinema

Hor Al Anz

Al Hamriya
Shopping
Centre

11

Hamarain
Centre

Salah Al Din Rd

Abu Hail Rd

Ramada
Continental

4

11

Al Ittihad Rd

Galadari Interchange

15

Airport
Terminal - 2

Police HQ

2005 | **DUBAI** EXPLORER

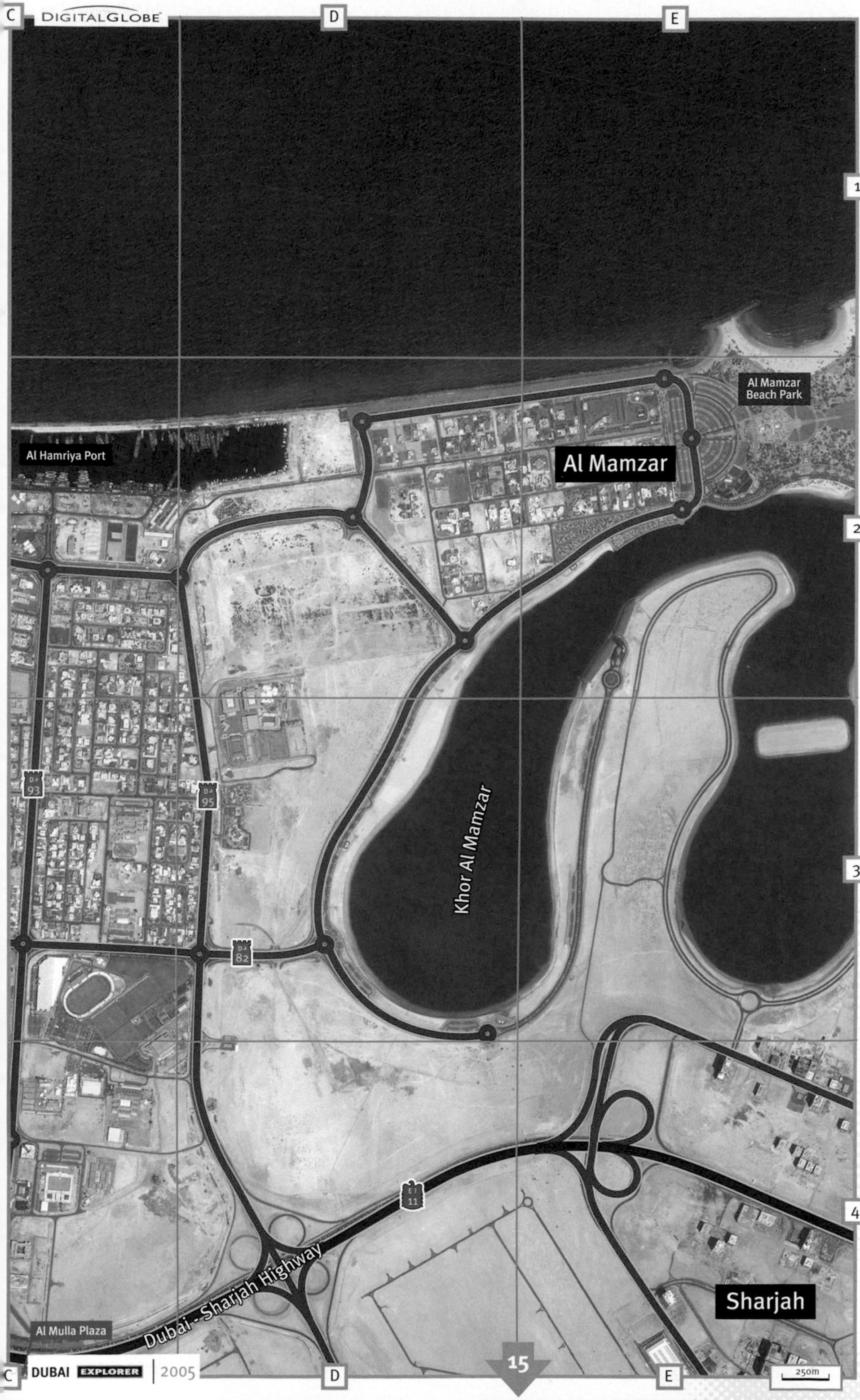
DIGITALGLOBE
C
D
E
1
2
3
4
Al Mamzar Beach Park
Al Hamriya Port
Al Mamzar
Khor Al Mamzar
93
95
82
11
Dubai - Sharjah Highway
Al Mulla Plaza
Sharjah
15
250m

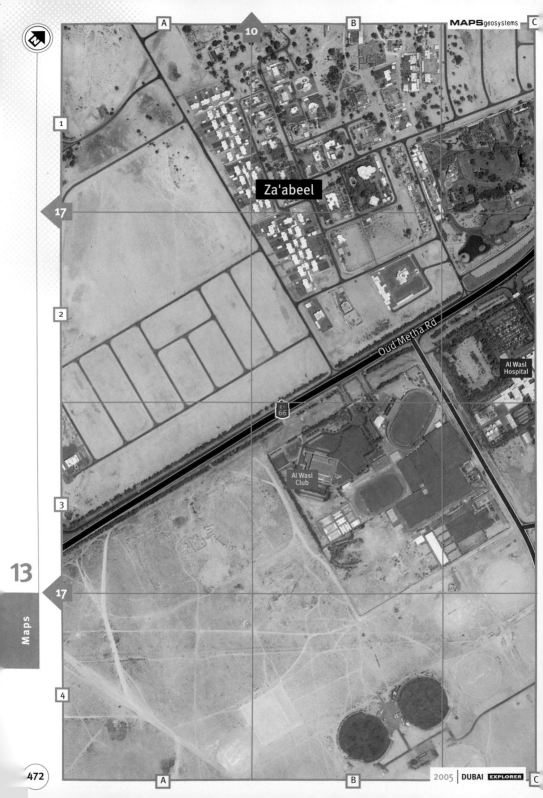

Za'abeel

Oud Metha Rd

Al Wasl Hospital

66

Al Wasl Club

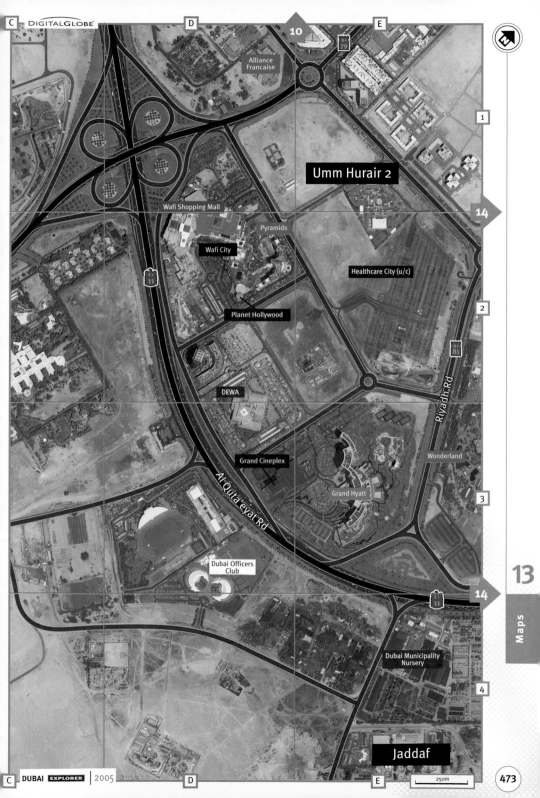

C — D — **10** — E

Alliance Francaise

79

1

Umm Hurair 2

14

Wafi Shopping Mall

Pyramids

Wafi City

Healthcare City (u/c)

E1 11

Planet Hollywood

2

81

DEWA

Riyadh Rd

Grand Cineplex

Wonderland

Al Quta'eyat Rd

Grand Hyatt

3

Dubai Officers Club

13

Maps

11

14

Dubai Municipality Nursery

4

Jaddaf

1

13

Riyadh Rd

81

Creekside Park

Dubai Creek Marina

2

Childrens City

Dubai Creek

Dubai Creek Golf & Yacht Club

WonderLand

3

Al Boom Tourist Village

E 11

13

Jet Ski Area

Al Garhoud Bridge

4

Dhow Building Yard

Festival City (u/c)

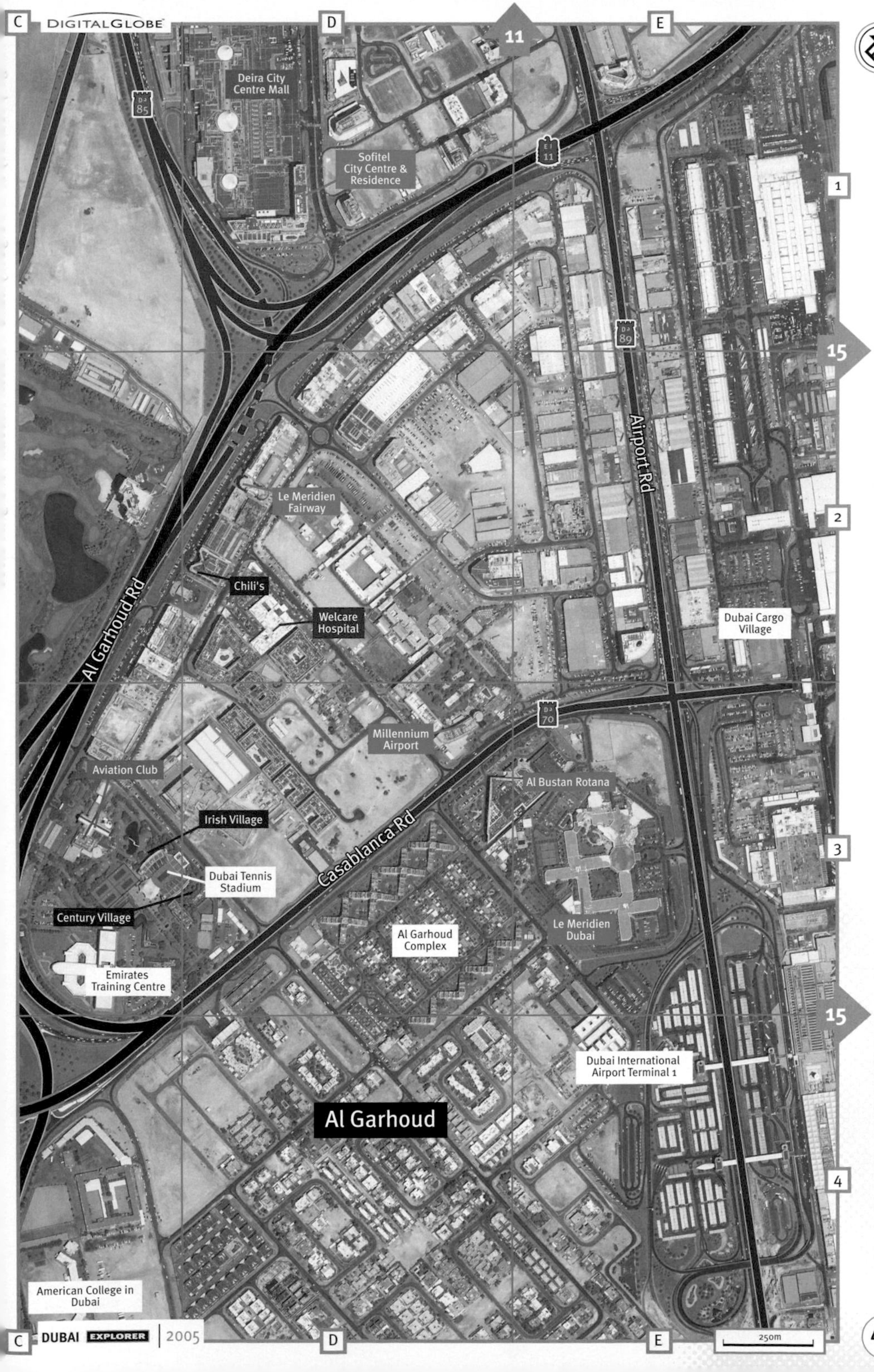

C | D | E

11

Deira City
Centre Mall

Sofitel
City Centre &
Residence

1

89

15

Airport Rd

2

Le Meridien
Fairway

Dubai Cargo
Village

Chili's

Welcare
Hospital

Al Garhoud Rd

Millennium
Airport

70

Al Bustan Rotana

Aviation Club

Casablanca Rd

Irish Village

Dubai Tennis
Stadium

Al Garhoud
Complex

Le Meridien
Dubai

3

Century Village

Emirates
Training Centre

14

15

Al Garhoud

Dubai International
Airport Terminal 1

Maps

4

American College in
Dubai

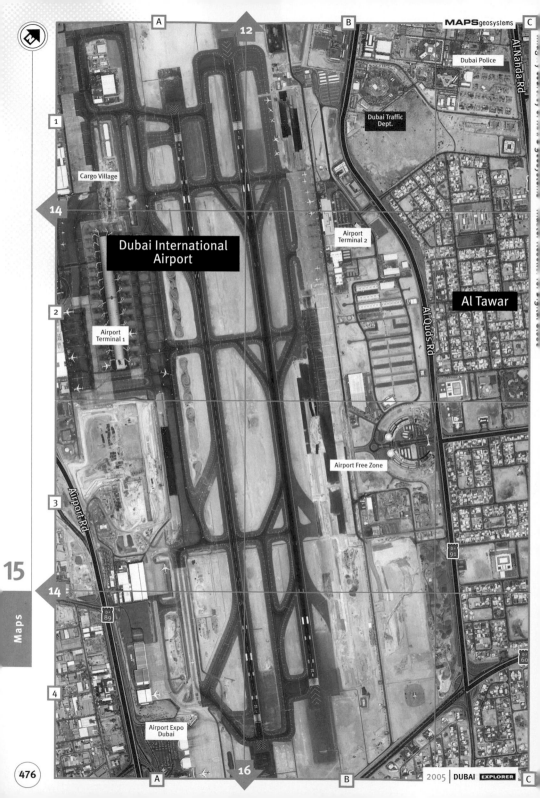

Al Nahda Rd

Dubai Police

Dubai Traffic Dept.

1

Cargo Village

14

Dubai International Airport

Airport Terminal 2

Al Tawar

2

Airport Terminal 1

Al Quds Rd

Airport Free Zone

Airport Rd

3

D4 91

15

Maps

14

D4 89

D4 60

4

Airport Expo Dubai

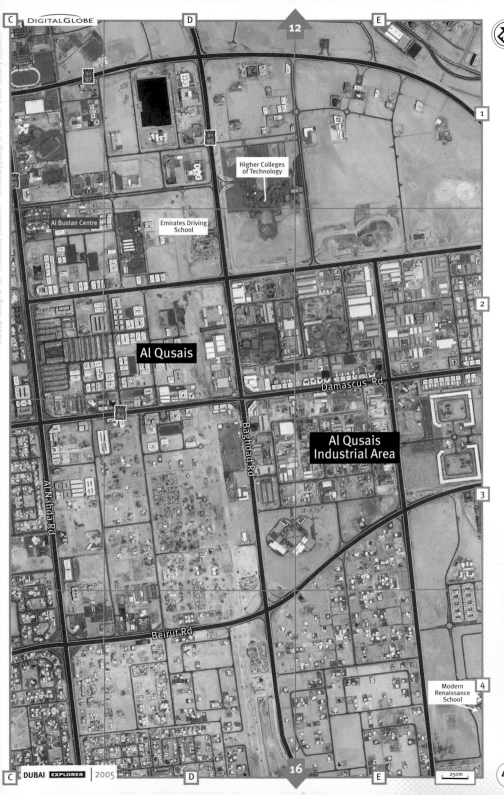

Higher Colleges
of Technology

Al Bustan Centre

Emirates Driving
School

Al Qusais

Damascus Rd

Baghdad Rd

**Al Qusais
Industrial Area**

Al Nahda Rd

Beirut Rd

Modern
Renaissance
School

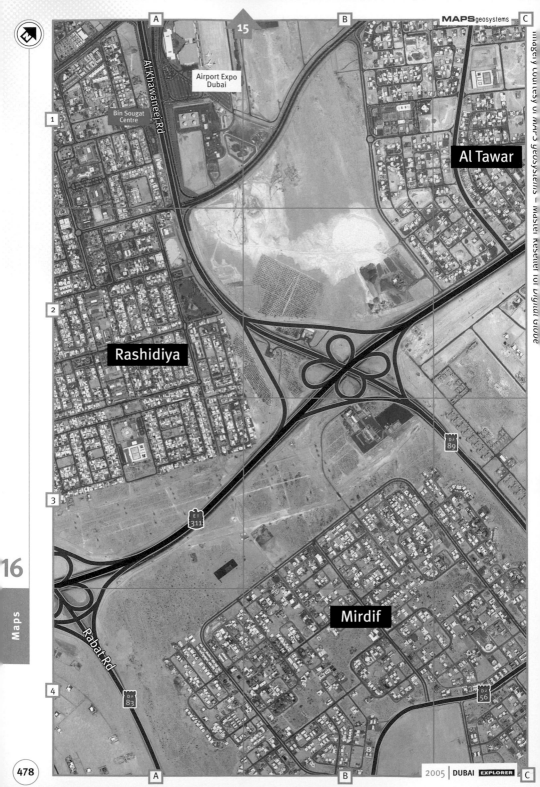

15

Airport Expo
Dubai

Bin Sougat
Centre

Al-Khawaneej Rd

1

Al Tawar

2

Rashidiya

D4
89

3

E
311

16

Maps

Rabat Rd

Mirdif

4

D4
83

D4
56

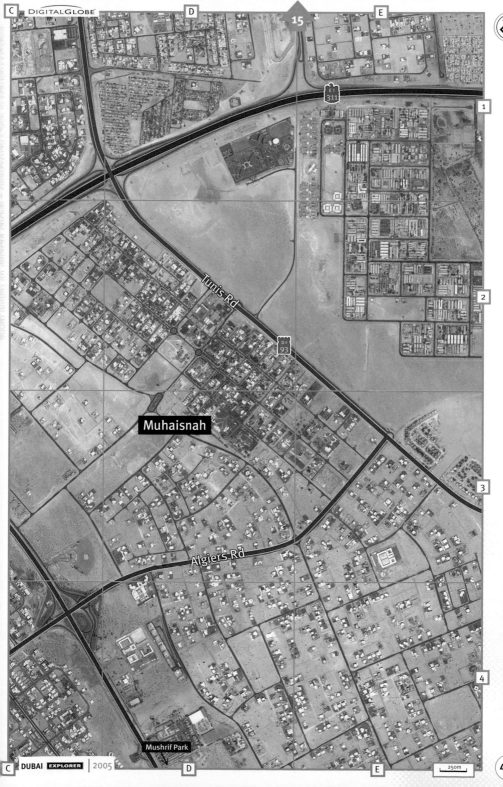

E11
311

1

Tunis Rd

2

D4
93

Muhaisnah

3

Algiers Rd

16

Maps

4

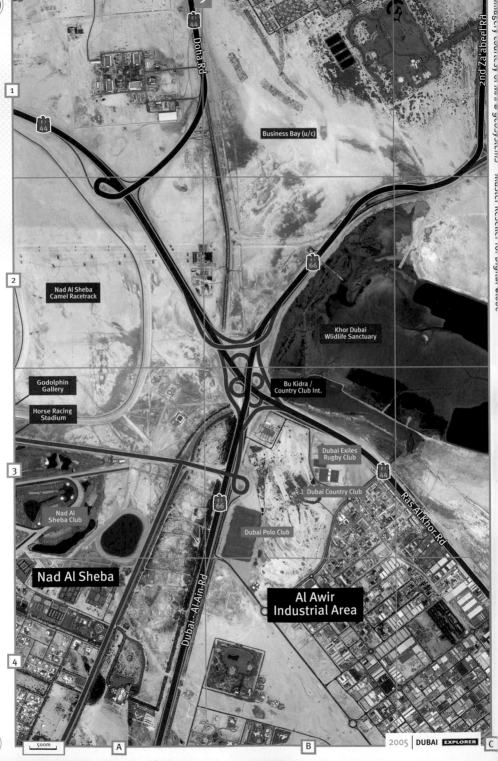

Business Bay (u/c)

44

66

Nad Al Sheba
Camel Racetrack

Khor Dubai
Wlidlife Sanctuary

Godolphin
Gallery

Horse Racing
Stadium

Bu Kidra /
Country Club Int.

Dubai Exiles
Rugby Club

44

Nad Al
Sheba Club

Ras Al Khor Rd

Dubai Country Club

66

Dubai Polo Club

Nad Al Sheba

Dubai - Al-Ain Rd

**Al Awir
Industrial Area**

Index

EXPLORER

Dum Biryani

A Royal delicacy of Nawab's and Maharaja's,

a recipe passed down through generations...

...experience the exotic cuisine in an authentic palatial ambience.

Dine like a Maharaja at India Palace

India Palace

An Authentic Indian Restaurant

A Member of SFC Group

AbuDhabi 02-644 8777, Dubai 04-286 9600

Index

Emergencies

Police	999
Ambulance	998 / 999
Fire	997
DEWA	991
Dubai Police HQ	229 2222
Municipality 24 Hour Hotline	223 2323

Pharmacies/Chemists – 24 hours

Each emirate has at least one pharmacy open 24 hours. The location and telephone numbers are in the daily newspapers. The Municipality has an emergency number (223 2323) which gives the name and location of open chemists.

Cinemas

Al Nasr	337 4353
Century Cinemas	349 9773
Cinestar	294 9000
Deira Cinema	222 3551
Dubai Cinema	266 0632
Galleria	209 6469 / 70
Grand Cinecity	228 98 98
Grand Cineplex	324 2000
Lamcy	336 8808
Metroplex	343 8383
Plaza	393 9966
Rex Drive-In	288 6447
Strand	396 1644

Hospitals

Al Amal Hospital	344 4010
Al Baraha Hospital	271 0000
Al Maktoum Hospital	222 1211
Al Wasl Hospital	324 1111
Al Zahra Hospital	06 561 9999
American Hospital	336 7777
Belhoul European Hospital	345 4000
Dubai Hospital	271 4444
Emirates Hospital	349 6666
International Private Hospital	221 2484
Iranian Hospital	344 0250
Rashid Hospital	337 4000
Welcare Hospital	282 7788

Useful Numbers

Directory Enquiries	181	Fault Reports	171
Operator	100	Billing Information	142
Etisalat Contact Centre	101	Sahm Technologies	390 5555

Airlines

Air Arabia	06 508 8888
Air France	294 5899
Air India	227 6787
Alitalia	224 2256
Austrian Airlines	294 5675
British Airways	307 5777
Cathay Pacific Airways	295 0400
CSA Czech Airlines	295 9502
Cyprus Airways	221 5325
Emirates	214 4444
Etihad	02 505 8000
Gulf Air	271 3111
KLM Royal Dutch Airlines	335 5777
Kuwait Airways	228 1106
Lufthansa	343 2121
Malaysia Airlines	397 0250
Olympic Airways	221 4761
Oman Air	351 8080
PIA	222 2154
Qatar Airways	229 2229
Royal Brunei Airlines	351 4111
Royal Jet	02 575 7000
Royal Jordanian	266 8667
Royal Nepal Airlines	295 5444
Saudi Arabian Airlines	295 7747
Singapore Airlines	223 2300
South African Airways	397 0766
Sri Lankan Airlines	294 9119
Swiss	294 5051
United Airlines	316 6942

Private Centres/Clinics

Al Borj Medical Centre	321 2220
Al Zahra Private Medical Centre	331 5000
Allied Diagnostic Centre	332 8111
Belhoul European Hospital	345 4000
Dr Akel's General Medical Clinic	344 2773
Dubai London Clinic	344 6663
Dubai Medical Village	395 6200
Dubai Physiotherapy Clinic	349 6333
General Medical Centre	349 5959
Health Care Medical Center	344 5550
Jebel Ali Medical Centre	881 4000
Manchester Clinic	344 0300
New Medical Centre	268 3131

Dubai Airport

DNATA	295 1111
Dubai Airport	224 5555
Flight Enquiry	216 6666

Hotels

Five-Star	Phone
Al Bustan Rotana Hotel	282 0000
Al Maha Resort	832 9900
Burj Al Arab	301 7777
Crowne Plaza	331 1111
Dubai Marine Beach Resort & Spa	346 1111
Dusit Dubai	343 3333
Emirates Towers Hotel	330 0000
Fairmont Hotel	332 5555
Grand Hyatt Dubai	317 1234
Hilton Dubai Creek	227 1111
Hilton Dubai Jumeirah	399 1111
Hotel Inter-Continental Dubai	222 /171
Hyatt Regency Hotel	209 1234
Jebel Ali Golf Resort & Spa	883 6000
Jumeirah Beach Club, The	344 5333
Jumeirah Beach Hotel, The	348 0000
JW Marriott Hotel	262 4444
Le Meridien Dubai	282 4040
Le Meridien Mina Seyahi	399 3333
Le Royal Meridien Beach Resort & Spa	399 5555
Metropolitan Palace Hotel	227 0000
Mina A'Salam	366 8888
Mövenpick Hotel Bur Dubai	336 6000
Palace at One&Only Royal Mirage, The	399 9999
Renaissance Hotel	262 5555
Ritz-Carlton Dubai	399 4000
Safir Deira Hotel	224 8587
Shangri-La Hotel	343 8888
Sheraton Deira	268 8888
Sheraton Dubai Creek Hotel & Towers	228 1111
Sheraton Jumeirah Beach Resort	399 5533
Sofitel City Centre Hotel	295 5522
Taj Palace Hotel	223 2222
World Trade Centre Hotel, The	331 4000

Four-Star	Phone
Al Khaleej Palace Hotel	223 1000
Ascot Hotel	352 0900
Avari Dubai International	295 6666
Best Western Dubai Grand	263 2555
Capitol Hotel	346 0111
Carlton Tower, The	222 7111
Four Points Sheraton	397 7444
Golden Tulip Aeroplane Hotel	272 2999
Holiday Inn Downtown	228 8889
Ibis World Trade Centre	332 4444
Jumeira Rotana Hotel	345 5888
Marco Polo Hotel	272 0000
Metropolitan Deira	295 9171
Metropolitan Hotel	343 0000
Metropolitan Resort & Beach Club Hotel	399 5000
Millennium Airport Hotel	282 3464
Novotel World Trade Centre	332 0000
Oasis Beach Hotel	399 4444

Hotels

Four Star	Phone
Ramada Continental Hotel	266 2666
Ramada Hotel	351 9999
Regent Palace Hotel	396 3888
Riviera Hotel	222 2131
Rydges Plaza Hotel	398 2222
Sea View Hotel	355 8080
Towers Rotana Hotel	343 8000

Three Star	Phone
Admiral Plaza, The	393 5333
Al Khaleej Holiday Hotel	22/ 6565
Ambassador Hotel	393 9444
Astoria Hotel	353 4300
Claridge Hotel	271 6666
Comfort Inn	222 7393
Dubai Palm Hotel	271 0021
Gulf Inn Hotel	224 3433
Imperial Suites Hotel	351 5100
Kings Park Hotel	228 9999
Lords Hotel	228 9977
Lotus Hotel	227 8888
Nihal Hotel	295 7666
Palm Beach Rotana Inn	393 1999
Palm Hotel Dubai, The	399 2222
Princess Hotel	263 5500
Quality Inn Horizon	227 1919
Sea Shell Inn	393 4777
Vendome Plaza Hotel	222 2333

Two Star	Phone
Deira Park Hotel	223 9922
New Peninsula Hotel	393 9111
Phoenicia Hotel	222 7191
President Hotel	334 6565
Ramee International Hotel	224 0222
San Marco	272 2333

One Star	Phone
Dallas Hotel	351 1223
Middle East Hotel	222 6688
Vasantam Hotel	393 8006
West Hotel	271 7001

Taxi Companies

Cars Taxis	269 3344
Dubai Transport Company	208 0808
Gulf Radio Taxi	223 6666
Metro Taxis	267 3222
National Taxis	339 0002
Sharjah: Delta Taxis	06 559 8598

Quick Reference

I like to Wafi
on my own
MISS SIX
CHANE
Do you Wafi too?
Over 200 stores & 1000 fashion brands.
24 lively restaurants and cafés.
Luxurious spa for men & ladies.
A-list nightlife.
Health & Leisure club.
WAFI CITY
Experience the magic
Tel: 04 3244426 www.waficity.com